CW01499607

Allegiance and Loyalty in Service

My Life in the Nigerian Navy

Adonis & Abbey Publishers Ltd
Office: United Kingdom:
24 Old Queen Street,
London SW1H 9HP
Tel:0845 873 0262
Website: http://www.adonis-abbey.com
E-mail Address: editor@adonis-abbey.com

Nigeria:
No. 39 Jimmy Carter Street,
Suites C3 – C6 J-Plus Plaza
Asokoro, Abuja, Nigeria
Tel: +234 (0) 7058078841/08052213212

British Library Cataloguing-in-Publication Data
A catalogue record for this book is available from the British Library

ISBN: 9781913976149

Allegiance and Loyalty in Service
My Life in the Nigerian Navy

Anthony O.M.A. Isa

Table of Contents

Acknowledgement

I was first introduced to the idea of writing a book about my experiences in the Nigerian Navy (NN) by Commodore O Oladimeji. I must commend and acknowledge him for his foresight. Others followed suit for about three decades. Several times, I had words of encouragement from Rear Admiral Suleiman Sa'idu, former Chief of the Naval Staff (CNS).

Major General Niyi Oyebade, during his tenure as Commandant, Nigerian Defence Academy (NDA), helped with information from the archives on events and personalities related to my cadet time. Major General CA Jemitola was most helpful in giving me useful guides to managing some of the important presentations I had to make while Professor Emilia Anagbogu-Ezenwa demonstrated outstanding initiatives in rendering assistance at a tough moment in the final stages of the project. I gratefully acknowledge their efforts and commitment.

I acknowledge the guide of Rev Fr George O. Ehusani who linked me up to the Publisher, Professor Jideofor Adibe (Adonis & Abbey Publishers) who generously deployed his intellect to guide me and made available to me his Layout Artist and Graphic Designer, the most patient and skilled Mr Gabriel Ujah. Professor Adibe's partnership with Mr Dan Agbese defined several paths I followed for the project. Dan Agbese's outstanding and rare experiences with the military establishment, Newswatch Magazine, and as the author of the book on Nigeria's former military President, went beyond his schedule to avail me of his wealth of experience. He was the perfect taskmaster I needed to get the job done. I acknowledge his very valuable contributions including his use of what I call iron-brush on my manuscript to keep me in check.

Mr Jimoh Isa, my elder brother and patriarch of the family, my sisters Mrs Rabi Jimoh and Mrs Ayiba Isah, and my cousin Mr Victor Adinoyi patiently educated me on family relationships. I had the rare opportunity of interacting with Fr Peter McCawille who gave me updates on the reverend fathers who were in charge at St John's College, Kaduna. I consider his kind words of encouragement as an essential blessing for this project. I also acknowledge the encouragement from some ambassadors of Nigeria's foreign service and some distinguished members of the Society for International Relations Awareness, SIRA, for their encouragement to write and share my experiences. I treasure the guide and wisdom of Prof Tom Aaze Adaba for his frequent checks on me as I worked on this book. The encouragement he gave reminded me of the inspiring mentor role of his father. His invitations to cultural events improved my understanding of Ebira culture. I acknowledge the contributions made by them all with profound appreciation.

My career run was greatly influenced by education, training and work experiences in selected advanced countries' institutions. This most generously availed me of an unlimited knowledge base and experiences that greatly informed the direction of this book. I owe a debt of gratitude to all those involved in teaching, mentoring and grooming me through the relevant institutions. Among all the distinguished personalities involved, I fondly remembered those good-natured staff at Royal Naval Engineering College mess accommodation who faithfully woke me up every morning with a cup of typical English tea thereby making sure I was ready to commence my daily routines. Their joy and good nature with those of the others reinforced my understanding of service for the common good. I would later in my career experience a most profound and fulfilling time at National Defense University, Washington DC, the USA that set me up for the challenges at the higher direction of national defence and security. I hereby acknowledge and profusely thanked all those involved in my development on both sides of the Atlantic.

My loving wife Linda has always showered me with everything love has to offer and is solidly standing by me, as ever, with prayers. She has held forth the home front with extraordinary endurance. Our children Daniel Enesi, David Ahaorvi who contributed a laptop to this project, Diana Ahaoiza and Augustine Adaeiza who constantly reminded me to keep to my promise to write my memoirs, have been our constant inspiration in the management of our career challenges essential for our parental roles. We share the blessings and joys of five grandchildren, Maria Avosuahi, Joseph Adanavize, Michael Ozavize, Juliana Ometere Wanda, and Philip Adavuruku Charles. I acknowledge them as they contributed to shape my thoughts while I wrote this book constantly reflecting on what their impression of Nigeria would be when they read this book as they grow up.

To the taxpayers of Nigeria, I constantly remember their huge investments in my development and provision of excellent welfare in the form of very sophisticated weapon platforms to the Nigerian Navy that inspired me in the formative years of my career. I acknowledge their immense sacrifices and costs incurred.

I finally acknowledge the wonderful acts of God to whom all powers belong; the source of all inspirations, initiatives, and commitment to good causes, as an act of thanksgiving.

Anthony O.M.A. ISA
Abuja, 2022

Foreword

Military training places great emphasis on core values such as loyalty, discipline, integrity, honour, commitment, service, competence, sacrifice, and duty. These are the qualities with which the performance, and indeed the careers, of officers, should be judged. They are also the qualities which make or mar the militaries of nations across the world.

The history of the Nigerian military is one that creates mixed feelings. While the Nigerian military evokes a sense of pride for its achievements in keeping the nation together and in peace-keeping operations in Africa and beyond particularly in countries such as Congo, Liberia, Sierra Leone, Yugoslavia, Chad, Tanzania, Cambodia, Lebanon, and Guinea among others, it has also created a feeling of disappointment, frustration and even anger due to what can be termed the falling standards of professionalism. Indeed, since the first Nigerian coup d'etat of 1966, the Nigerian military has struggled with multiple problems including the politicization of the military, ethnic and religious bigotry, poor training, corruption, human rights abuses, indiscipline, and conduct to the prejudice of military order and discipline.

The 1966 coup, and subsequent ones, opened a chapter of the Nigerian military's foray into politics at the expense of the military profession. Officers from different arms of the military began occupying political positions in government, ministries, departments, agencies and public corporations. Appointments into these positions became the aspiration of most officers who saw them as financially rewarding. Lobbying for appointments became the order of the day. Scheming and undermining took deep roots among officers. All of these factors created cracks in the military and have unfortunately remained totally unended.

These were the circumstances under which Rear Admiral Anthony Isa joined the Nigerian military in 1972. His book, **Allegiance and Loyalty in Service-My Life in the Nigerian Navy,** is a recount of his life, his contributions to the Nigerian military, as well as his efforts to keep his personal and professional values in a challenging system. The book is an important addition to the literature on the Nigerian military from the perspective of a military officer out of service and I recommend it to anyone with an interest in the Nigerian military.

Chief Olusegun O. Obasanjo GCFR
Former President of Nigeria, Commander-in-Chief of the Armed Forces

Introduction

On Human Nature

"Human nature will not change. In any future great national trial, compared with men of this, we shall have as weak and as strong, as silly and as wise, as bad and as good. Let us, therefore, study the incidents in this war as philosophy to learn wisdom from and none of them as wrongs to be avenged." Abraham Lincoln *(US Civil War President, November 10, 1864).*

On Respect for Country

"The world would never respect Africa until Nigeria earns that respect. The black people of the world are looking up to Nigeria to be a source of pride and confidence. Every Nigerian citizen should be made to understand this truth."
Nelson_Rolihlahla Mandela (*a great moral force and leader).*

Sometime in 1990, some of my close friends suggested I should write a book about my experiences in the Nigerian Navy (NN). I had just been promoted to the rank of a Commander and had been involved in a major transformation process of the NN. I did not give it much thought but the pressure has continued to mount since then. In 2017, more friends pressured me to do so. By this time, out of my duty post in controversial circumstances and with the rank of Rear Admiral, I saw their point and felt I had a duty to write about my experiences, principally to avail the Nigerian military establishment and community the opportunity to have a very profound look at the way military and nation-state affairs are being conducted and the implications for national defence and security. I set to work.

I had a teenage dream in my final year in secondary school to go into the military and serve my country as a marine engineer. I did not have any idea of what the demands were and the bumpy road ahead. However, I was committed as a teenager to serve the country, inspired by those who served during the Nigerian civil war.

I was attracted by the word- SERVE. I believe that telling my life story so far should reveal why serving the country with total submission to authority for the common good attracted and sustained me in my career in the Nigerian Navy. I connected those essential family values, ethics, and examples that guided me with organisational values and ethics as these were constantly brought to bear in the military institutions I was educated, trained, and served in, mostly abroad, and to some extent at home.

Against the background of Nigeria's unique history and a republic, I had to study and experience the nexus between allegiance and loyalty in the course of my career. To serve the country, one had to be in a state of being loyal; that is loyalty. This is essential for the expression of the unity of command in the military command chain with a President, Commander-in-Chief, mandated by the people in an election, acting in the national interest at the apex. Allegiance is loyalty to higher causes, nation-state or ruler. Nigeria's republican status eliminates allegiance to a ruler thereby making the nation-state and its causes higher than any individual to be the focus.

The book weaves through my diverse upbringing, early education with a dose of triple religious influences, and entry into the Nigerian Defence Academy where I saw the reality of a politicized military in Nigeria and which will be the theatre of my experiences throughout my military career. After I graduated from the NDA, I turned down a nomination to proceed to the prestigious Britannia Royal Naval College, Dartmouth, in the UK. This was to focus on my pursuit of marine engineering qualification. I got my chance to start my engineering education at the Royal Naval Engineering College, Manadon, Plymouth.

I qualified as a marine engineer officer after scaling a height that had eluded NN officers at Manadon since the inception of the Nigerian Defence Academy. I had a taste of the general attitude to success and knowledge acquisition in the NN as a very young officer and was advised by a senior colleague to watch out and try not to be like other 'normal' officers.

The engineering education and training I had prepared me to be first and foremost a naval officer who had the opportunity to qualify as a marine engineer officer. This was a guide to acquiring a community of knowledge and experiences to fit in as a sound professional naval officer and also meet the demanding requirements of a specialist naval engineer officer. I had the opportunity to be associated on my first-degree course with an emerging material technology, glass-reinforced plastic plates, that gave me a gratifying naval engineering achievement in Europe with successful application in the design and construction of two warships for the NN that attracted the attention of the United States Navy.

I had the unique opportunity of being selected for courses at two of the finest military education and training institutions on both sides of the Atlantic Ocean; Royal Naval Engineering College, Manadon, UK, and the National Defense University, Washington DC, US. I could not have had better preparations for my career runs as a junior officer and at the later stages for the higher direction of national defence and security. The military commander's task, I was taught, is solely to prepare the human and material resources to states of readiness for commitment to the war effort. It is in the performance of this task that I find the Armed Forces of Nigeria (AFN) most lacking, due principally to the poor leadership being provided. The mental and moral attributes required are not developed in personnel. To prepare others to serve, the commander must first do justice to himself by being ready to be an example to those under command undergoing the relevant routines and must never be part of the problems that the nation-state suffer.

The NN challenges were opportunities to try and give back and justify returns on investment in my education and training. I had a fair share of exposures which I tried to capture and present for a study on the NN and AFN in this book.

In 2005, I emerged and was appointed as the Chief of the Naval Staff after a scrutiny exercise under the direction of the President, Commander-in-Chief of the Armed Forces of the Federal Republic of Nigeria. The incumbent Chief of the Naval Staff was retired and left office but his reliever was not announced. This has never occurred in the history of the Armed Forces of Nigeria and it generated a complex web of intrigues. The implications for the NN and the extraordinary spotlight I was put under had their burdens and eventually, I was denied the appointment and instead named as the Commandant of the National War College which I successfully transformed to National Defence College inspired by the President, Commander-in-Chief. The attempt by the next President, Commander-in-Chief to implement my appointment as the CNS in the second half of 2007 faced the same obstacles.

The decision of the President was later changed and he appointed me as the Chief of Defence Staff and this also suffered the same trap of influences. In 2015, the intention to appoint me as Minister of Defence changed at the last moment when I was declared as not being a politician.

I have given account, in this book, of the bruising battles I had to fight in transforming the National War College to National Defence College among others. I had the unique support of a former Head of

State, Commander-in-Chief, and two sitting Presidents, Commanders-in-Chief. General AA Abubakar, GCFR handed over to Chief Olusegun O. Obasanjo, GCFR and he was succeeded by Alhaji Umaru Musa Yar'Adua, GCFR. They all caused a most perfect good run of support that gave birth and sustained the National Defence College permanent site project as I experienced a most eventful tenure as Commandant at the country's highest military education establishment.

I am currently struggling for justice to be done to me, the country, and its military institution so that it would better manage the human and material resources devoted to national defence and security which are currently being wasted. I believe that when justice is done to the institution by allowing it to function properly under best practices, I would receive justice.

The experiences I have gone through reveal the stark reality that Nigeria is not functioning properly and is not being managed to meet the needs and aspirations of the people. Nigeria is not allowed to participate in the knowledge industry, the largest industry on earth, to release the creative energy of the people to get on with their lives in dignity. I have detailed in this work how Nigeria is being wasted by a power structure that relegates the President, Commander-in-Chief to a subordinate role.

I believe strongly that Nigeria is in dire need of a moral rebirth to reconstitute the mindset of Nigerians as happened during the Renaissance period that took Europe out of the Dark Ages into the modern era. I have struggled to navigate my way through the obstacles of an improper functioning nation-state by holding on to the principles and covenant of allegiance and loyalty and it has been a very lonely and turbulent path for me in my career. I am constrained to reflect on what would inspire Nigerian elites to serve nation-state causes as the agreed system they cherish and uphold is all about undermining authority to waste the country. Normal best practices acts are considered as fighting against their agreed system that does not serve nation-state causes efficiently for the common good.

As I recorded my experiences in this book I was conscious of my human effort that is not perfect. I accept responsibility for any errors. My experiences swung between highly intensive and complex actions that I struggled to capture and narrate and which occurred in difficult and often in very intriguing circumstances. In addition, I constantly remembered our brave troops in harm's way involved in hybrid warfare to bring about a secured Nigerian environment and defend the country. I have not tried to project an image of myself and it is fine with me whatever impression anyone may have after reading through this book.

It is not easy to be fulfilled in a challenging career setting but I have consistently reflected on my life and career run and believe that there is nothing I would have done differently. The shining lights of allegiance to the country that necessitates absolute loyalty to the President, Commander-in-Chief shone brightly as a constant guide as I struggled against formidable odds. This kept me going. I hope this book detailing my struggles, frustrations, and successes would inspire officers and men in the Armed Forces of Nigeria to use my experience as important professional lessons towards rebuilding and repositioning the defence and security community for the greater good of the country. The AFN had been my life. I remain hopeful that it will rise from the despair of its current problems and become the great fighting and security force envisaged by the framers of our national constitution.

CHAPTER ONE

Okene, the Ebira Heartland

The Ebira people historically trace their origin to the defunct Kwararafa Empire, south of the now equally defunct Borno Empire, before the process that brought together the Northern and the Southern protectorates in 1914 to form a new country called Nigeria. When the Kwararafa Empire ceased to be, the various tribes under its umbrella scattered to different parts of the country. Most of them such as the Ebira, Igala, the Idoma, the Alago, the Iyala, etc moved south of the former empire and settled in the North-Central zone of the country. The Iyala moved further south to what became the Eastern Region.

The Ebira people passed through the present Taraba, Benue, Edo, and Nasarawa states before finally founding their settlement called Okene their present major city. Okene was part of Kabba Province, one of the twelve provinces in the Northern Region. In 1991, Kabba Province was carved out into a new state called Kogi State by the General Ibrahim Babangida's military administration. The Ebira is one of the major tribes in that state.

Up to about the end of the last century, the Ebira tribe was called Igbirra, a corruption of their correct, original name. Other Nigerian tribes, such as the Gbagyi, called Gwari, suffered the same burden of the corruption of their names by the British colonialists. Okene was originally called Okorune, the Ebira word for land of antelopes. Okorune too was corrupted and forever lost its original Ebira name. Okene town nestles in the feet of beautiful rocky hills that provided rugged natural defences in the days of tribal wars. The hills provide limited building spaces in the city, forcing the residents to build their homes close to one another.

The hills that surround Okene have rich iron ore deposits worked by blacksmiths to create farming and hunting implements and appliances. The ancient ironworks left their mark that can still be seen on Itakpe Hills.

The main occupations of the Ebira are farming, weaving, hunting, blacksmithing, and fishing. Okene became famous in Nigeria, thanks to its unique traditional woven cloth which is much beloved by other Nigerian tribes.

I was born in Okene, the famous Ebira city that shaped my early childhood, in 1952. My father, Isa Ifache Anda, had four wives. My mother, Avahi Avosuahi Asmau Anikoh, was the first wife. She was popularly called Onyi-Jimoh, meaning the 'mother of Jimoh.' Jimoh is her first son. My father had five children with my mother – three girls and two boys. Jimoh and I were the two boys. I was named Odogba, Ebira for the elephant. The girls were Ozohu, Rabi, and Ayiba.

The second wife, Madam Eyivovo, also had five children for my father. They are Yakubu, Sumonu, Adamu, Garba, and Aminatu, the only daughter. The third wife had Momoh, Karimu, Yaruba, and Idrisu who was the last born of our father. Yaruba is the only female among them. The fourth wife had a son, Salami, and two girls, Barikisu and Marehdo.

In our tradition, children, as a mark of respect, do not call their parents by their names. They call their father, 'Inda' and their mother, 'Inya.' My brothers were attached to older relatives to learn farming and trade. In our tradition, male children are not necessarily trained by their parents; instead, they are entrusted to uncles and cousins to bring up as culturally, we believe that it takes a community to raise a child.

We were a Muslim family but I later converted to the Roman Catholic faith. It may be better to say that I carried out a switch operation and started attending Sunday masses at Christ the King Catholic Church very close by without understanding either the Christian or the Islamic faith. I will dwell on this switch operation later.

At the commencement of my Islamic education, I was given the name Musa and was under the watchful eyes of the family imam, Mallam Enieyiamire Anda, an uncle. I was taken around the koranic schools he ran and at a stage lived with him in the compound of the Chief Imam of Okene at Uruvucheba in central Okene. The Okene Central Mosque is within a strolling distance from my family compound and we easily heard the call to prayers from the minaret just as the church bell on top of the hill - about two hundred metres away - reminded the Roman Catholic church community of the times for various devotions during the day.

I was always proud to carry my uncle's (Inda Ajoku) prayer mat and his colourful umbrella and lead the way to the Central Mosque for the Friday Juma'at prayers. He was consistently in the best of attires and highly regarded by his peers. One of his best friends was Inda Etudaiye who often accompanied him home after the Juma'at prayers for lunch and entertainment. My father followed the Juma'at prayers from the front lobby of his house as he could hear and see the proceedings from there. The mosque could no longer accommodate the population growth and on Fridays, the worshippers spill outside the mosque.

I grew up in an extended polygamous family where enduring values were taught in demonstration of love, trust, competition, and communal sharing. My uncle, Inda Onosachi Ajoku Anda, is the most senior of my three paternal uncles (including Inda Omoyi Yusuf) and he assumed the role of the patriarch of the family when their father died. He took me as his most-loved son while my father also took his second son, Emmanuel Obansa Kekere Ajoku, as his favourite son. Emmanuel Ajoku was the first child in the large extended family set up to have western education. He became a teacher because teaching was the most respected profession then.

My mother's two-room apartment as a senior wife was in my uncle's compound close to that of his first wife, Madam Monica Ajoku, a staunch Catholic. My childhood experiences were happy interactions under the watchful eyes of elders and older relations in the three adjoining compounds of two brothers and their cousin along Idogido Street, located at the foot of the stretch of a hill on which was built the first Roman Catholic Mission Church, Christ the King, in Okene and the nursery and primary schools called Christ the King Nursery and Primary School respectively. Later, they added a secondary school. The area is called Okene North.

The spread of my extended family in Okene gave me the excitement of visits, and most often, in the company of my parents and sisters. As I matured, I was sent on errands which I was always excited to carry out. I would sometimes stray on my own to my favourite relations especially those who gave me money to buy snacks such as groundnut cakes. My maternal grandmother, Inya Eyino Anikoh, stood out as the most generous among them. I also experienced the love of my maternal uncle Inda Chegede Anikoh who lived at Kuroko, Okene. I was equally excited to go on errands for my mother after lunch. Sometimes, I could hardly wait for her to brief me and tried to set out before she was ready. She tried to slow me down by telling me to wait until the food I ate had 'entered into my stomach.'

My closeness to my mother gives me fond memories of my early childhood. I remember her struggles to make ends meet and equally care for the family. She engaged in small-scale trading by buying matches in boxes; she then tied the match sticks in threes or fours and sold them to make a profit. She took me along to buy the matches and would explain to me how she would sell them to make a little profit depending on the brand. On the wall of her sitting-room, she had chalk strokes depicting the progress of the savings contributions she made with her close friends. I got to know when it was her turn to collect her contributions because I always ran errands for her. She had been part of my father's business ventures in her younger years until an accident got her hospitalized while I was still breastfeeding.

I ate breakfast and dinner with my mother and the children of my eldest sister, Ozohu. The breakfast menu could be from the leftover of the dinner which my mother preserved with the overnight soup she warmed up in a small clay pot. This had a very appealing flavour. We also had bean cakes and bread eaten with maize or guinea corn pap.

I ate lunch most times with my father in his sitting room. My mother would always tell me when she was about to take lunch to my father. This was to ensure I ate the food with him. My stepmothers took lunch to my father too. We, his male children, would then gather to have lunch with him. When he was certain that we were all gathered, he would order that the dishes be laid out. We would form a semi-cycle with him at the open end in his reclining low chair. Most of the lunch menu was pounded yam or something similar. After our father had taken his first bite, the oldest of the children followed by taking his seat on the floor; followed by the rest of the boys in descending order of age. The youngest boy was the last to take his turn.

No one dared touch the meat in the soup until our dad had taken his share; we were then allowed to take a piece each. If the pieces of meat or fish could not go round, the eldest shared it among the rest of us. Our father's dignified presence ensured there was order among us. After lunch, whoever was not satisfied went to his mother's room for additional food.

The Roman Catholic Mission School playground was about a hundred metres away and the bigger boys who arrived later would normally displace my age group to the sidelines as we watched them play soccer. We left the playground at sunset and I would join my mother and my sisters for dinner. After dinner, we freshened up and shared family moments before going to sleep on mats for the night. Often, I was with my mother in her bedroom and got her full attention.

There was no electricity network system for public use in Okene then. My mother had a palm kernel oil lamp that used a bundle of cotton wick. The rooms were dimly lit. The few places in Okene that had generators included the residence of the Roman Catholic Reverend Fathers and Sisters all of whom were expatriates. Mr George Uru Ohikere, then a minister in the government of Sir Ahmadu Bello, the Premier of Northern Region, also had a generator in his house. Each time a reverend father went to start the generator at sunset, children hailed the electricity with shouts of 'Oyibo!'

My father took me to Christ the King Primary School one morning in 1958 to start my Western education. I had no birth certificate but relied on an estimate of age based on what adults remembered of events at the time I was born. This was how age was then determined in the country by the white men. My father ensured I was drilled on how to loop my right arm over my head to touch my left ear. We were taken for screening on the raised pavement entrance into the church. When it came to my turn, my father, standing some distance away, made signs to me to ensure that the tips of my right fingers touched my left ear when I stretched and looped my arm over my head. My father paced past the base of the raised pavement entrance and I stretched my arm harder.

I was admitted to the school. Some days later, I was dressed in the school uniform of a white pair of shorts and a shirt. I did not know what it was all about. I thought I was dressed up for a game. I found myself among other children also dressed like me. But I had to be withdrawn because I was considered to be under-age for school. This would later help in establishing December as my birth month. My father, however, took me, some days later, to a shop belonging to the headmaster's wife. I went with my school slate and he bought some chalk for me to get used to some school tools at home without a teacher. That was the only time my father ever took me to any place to buy anything for me. I did not know what to do with the slate and the chalk. I remained at home for the next one year, getting used to the chalk and slate and growing up to increase the length of my arms to touch my ear lobe when looped over my head with ease as needed to determine my right school age to start school. In 1959, I fitted well with the school admission requirements and was admitted to the school.

I became the first child in our family to be sent to school. My other brothers, Karimu and Idrisu, were later sent to school. On leaving school, Karimu worked as a technician with Ajaokuta Steel Company while Idirisu, who earned a diploma in computer science, is now self-employed.

I had been attending koranic lessons with the family imam. He would pick me up on his bicycle after the afternoon prayers. He had about three koranic schools to run and he alternated his presence among them. The senior boys who took charge of the pupils never spared the whips to ensure our recitals.

I compared that mode of learning with the primary school method which I considered more pupil-friendly since I was never flogged except when I committed an offence. I consequently started hiding whenever I knew the Imam was approaching to take me to a koranic school. The imam had no time to waste looking for me and would ride away to his koranic schools.

My uncle's first wife was a devout Catholic. She attended daily morning mass regularly at Christ the King Catholic Church about two hundred metres away on the Catholic Mission hill. I started dressing up on Sundays to follow her to church for mass. For me, it was simply a continuation of going to school but on Sundays. On Fridays, I would dress up and carry my uncle's (Inda Ajoku) prayer mat and umbrella to the central mosque for the Juma'at prayers. After helping to spread his prayer mat, he would ask me to stay away until the end of the Juma'at prayers. No one ever discussed with me or instructed me as regards what my religious intentions were or should be. I experienced the opportunities of harmonious co-existence of Traditional, Islamic, and Catholic (Christian) beliefs. There was a deep respect for Christian and Islamic religions in the neighbourhood sandwiched between the Christ the King Catholic Church and the Okene Central Mosque.

It was a perfect setting for experiencing the two dominant religious faiths in the world without compulsion. This was the switch operation I mentioned earlier. The traditional religion with the day and night masquerades also held sway being the dominant religion of our people before the arrival of the two religions that originated from the Middle East. I have never bothered to think of comparing the two faiths (Islam and Christianity) to determine my preference. I will elaborate on further developments later and how I evolved my attitude to religious matters.

I owe a lot to my father and his brothers (my dear uncles), for their exemplary lives that accommodated a diversity of tribes and religions in perfect harmony. This was the moral foundation of my life. It was considered very shameful to be associated with telling lies, stealing, and other bad character traits. As children, we were constantly reminded to be of good behaviour. Interestingly, if a thatched house went up in flames, it was taken for granted that someone living there had been associated with stealing and was being punished. This was meant to keep us, the children, in check and be of good character. My father told my older relations not to fight with anyone over a plot of land and gave the advice that they should give such up and look for another land in the

precincts of Okene. He led the efforts in this regard by guiding and securing land for my relations that were of age and entitled to own such property.

My father was involved in farming, commodity trading with the regional marketing board, and politics. He liked travelling. He was good at caring for others as he would always go round visiting relations and friends to ask about their well-being. He had a very open mind and was a disciplinarian who was both feared and respected in the extended family. He ensured that selected children of his brothers were appropriately engaged to become farmers or learn trades as commodity traders and artisans. He also ensured that the boys in the family who were selected for western education were adequately supported.

It was then not the tradition that all children in a family should acquire western education. There was no allowance for any female child to go to school and they were married off once they were of age. My father's engagement in business and politics could have contributed to his open-minded approach to issues in addition to family values as he travelled widely within Nigeria. He had a friend whom I grew up to know. His name was Dele and he had a room close to my father's bedroom. Dele could hardly speak Ebira but we got along very well and he only left my father's compound after my father died on 09 April 1992.

After his early morning prayers according to Islamic injunctions, my father would go round to respected family elders and nearby friends in the neighbourhood to greet them and ask about their well-being as well as those he knew were sick. This endeared him to many and later in the day, he was always busy attending to people who called on him. I learnt as part of my upbringing the need to have respect for people of different ethnic or tribal backgrounds. I never heard any adverse comments from my father and my uncles about any one of a different tribe or orientation. I was too young to pay attention anyway. When there were disagreements among relations, efforts were made to get all parties together to state their cases and everyone was given a fair hearing most of the time.

The festivals of Ebiraland are rooted in a very rich cultural heritage that includes the traditional religious belief that was the source of moral instructions. The incursion of Christianity and Islam added variety rather than displacement. This is my family experience. There are two categories of masquerades; day masquerades and night masquerades. The night masquerades were considered as beings from the realm of spirits as their identities were closely guarded secrets. A highly respected night masquerade is *Obversaraki* whose songs and musical performances were the epitome of Ebira philosophy. The other night masquerade in his category was *Okevbere* whose appearance was in the class of a fashion model with fantastic dance routines.

The day masquerades were always fully covered with colourful attires and carried canes that served many purposes including instilling fear in people they chose to run after just for entertainment. The night masquerades have their distinctive modes of dressing and are never allowed to be seen by women. A very important rule is that the men and boys who are allowed to see and follow them must never discuss what they see with the women. The night masquerades' outing is preceded by local displays by young boys basically to warn women to get indoors and little children to be properly taken care of. At this stage, my senior brother Jimoh would take charge of me and ensure I sit on the ground beside his chair among the elders. The songs of the masquerades were expressions of Ebira philosophy and teachings related to morality and reference to *Ohomorihi* which is the same name of the one God referred to by Christians and Moslems.

As a child growing up in Okene, I would sit by and listen to the adults discuss the masquerades performances and recitation of their songs. It was a way of enriching my vocabulary and mastery of the Ebira language. The belief in reincarnation and the seeking of the blessings of our ancestors help to keep track of family lineage and these aspects are also reflected in the outings of the masquerades. I was always reminded that I am the reincarnation of my maternal grandfather and was thus respected.

Christians and Moslems respect the practices that advance the celebration of humanity. The triple heritage of Christianity, Islam, and Traditionalists is united in the belief in one good God. The traditional breaking of kola nuts to start traditional ceremonies in Ebiraland begins with the invocation of *Ohomorihi*. I witnessed the same reference to *Ohomorihi* in the mosque and church. All three religions seem to have one *Ohomorihi* and I wonder what difference in the mode of worship was all about.

I have over the years come to terms with the struggles and clash of religions. I learnt how to relate with others for the common good. Anyone with strong family roots in Ebiraland finds it virtually impossible to ignore the traditional practices mostly carried out by elders on behalf of every member of the household whether they are present or not and whether they believe in the practices or not. My choice of religious belief has been respected as it evolved and this demands my reciprocal respect for members of the extended family regarding their adherence to Islamic and traditional faiths. I was the only Christian in my father's family. We never argued and no one questioned my choice. My father always expressed his submission to '*Ohomorihi ananyi ubanyi*' that is 'almighty God the owner of power or to whom all power belongs.'

My highly respected uncle, Indah Ajoku, on passing away in 1969 was buried according to Islamic injunctions and was celebrated according to traditional rites with night and day masquerade outings and a thanksgiving mass was celebrated for him in Christ the King Catholic Church. This was a rare occurrence and a reflection of the appreciation of his great respect for the beliefs of others and firm belief that all power belongs to one God. What is left for me to learn regarding religious harmony after such experiences are how to expand my understanding and this is a life-long undertaking. I always found it difficult that Nigeria's present elites resort to religious intolerance and divisive cleavages that my father and his brothers never practised. I thank them always for that upbringing and the family values inculcated in me that has always served me extremely well as I travelled around the world and experienced different cultures. It has been an exciting journey into the diversity of human nature that never changes and the challenges inherent in such a nature.

I spent two years at Christ the King Primary School and by December 1960, my cousin, Mr Emmanuel Obansa Ajoku, who would take care of me and have just completed his Grade Two Teachers College education, came home for the Christmas holidays. Some family discussions were going on about my leaving Okene to live with him and continue my education. He put up in my father's compound in a room next to my father's bedroom. I was asked to take my small box which was virtually empty to sleep with him in the same room. This was the first time since I started school that I would leave my mother's living spaces in my uncle's compound to sleep elsewhere in the two compounds.

What were my primary school experiences so far? I spent my first year trying to learn how to look after myself under the care of some expatriate reverend sisters and experienced Ebira teachers, the learning of alphabets and numerals and how to write them on slates with white chalks dominated the activities. At times, the elderly Ebira teachers took us out of our well-equipped classrooms into the open spaces under very cool tree shades to learn songs such as 'John Bull My Son', 'I love to go a Wandering' and the Yoruba song 'Iwe Ki Ko.'

On other occasions, we were taken to the open field and taught how to spell the Ebira names of common objects and living things on sand. I remember vividly being taught how to spell vulture pronouncing the Ebira alphabets as UU KI O (KI O) EL O—UKOKOLO. My second year in primary school was more exciting as I had matured and become less playful. We were then taught to write with pencils and the use of erasers in exercise books with horizontal lines that determined the height and size of characters. We later graduated to the use of ink and J-nibs which needed more care to avoid spills that could mess up uniforms and exercise books. The use of J-nib to write with blue ink gave me the greatest excitement as my class teacher would at times hold my exercise book close to his chest in admiration of my good handwriting. I also had the excitement of marching and waving a green and white flag followed by a meal of rice in a celebration I later learnt was about the independence of Nigeria from Britain.

As I prepared to leave home with my cousin, I went on a visit with him and as we returned home we met with my class teacher who was at his balcony. After exchanging some pleasantries with my cousin, he turned his attention to me and told my cousin how excited he was with my use of J-nib.

My cousin had bought clothes for me for Christmas and these I folded carefully and placed in my small box waiting for the Christmas day when I would follow him for mass. He is the only child of my uncle who is a Catholic. It was his mother that I followed to church.

On Christmas Day, I went to mass with my cousin and proudly showed off my new clothes. In the afternoon after lunch, I followed my cousin to visit relations. I followed wherever he led and looked forward to having my share of Christmas rice wherever he was served. Rice was only served then at Christmas and on other important occasions. I vividly remembered the stop at the late Mr George Ohikere's imposing residence on the Inike Road and later at the residence of one of his close relatives, a middle-aged lady who prepared some rice meal to entertain guests. I waited outside the sitting room while my cousin joined others to be served. My prayers were answered early as I was given my share which I did not waste time cleaning off the plate so that no child of my age would turn up and be asked to share my portion.

The Christmas mood was wearing off some days after the event and one evening I was told to secure my box and standby for departure. It was when my mother gave me a new hand-woven cloth for use at night as a parting gift that it dawned on me that I was leaving home. I had nothing else to fill the box with other than my new set of Christmas clothes and the hand-woven clothes my sisters made for me. My mother would continue to send me new clothes from her loom periodically.

My mother was stoical and hardly showed emotion but I could feel her fear about my future, her last born. She had been close to me for the first seven years of my life. Early in the morning, my mother was awake and my cousin woke me up as we slept in the same room and asked me to get ready to leave for the motor park for our departure from Okene. My cousin went to bid my father bye and receive his blessing and that of his father, my very caring uncle Inda Ajoku. Both of them had been most caring and had planned over the years my education under the supervision of my cousin. The four brothers had agreed that one of their male children will be sent to school to acquire western education while others were apprenticed to respected elders to learn farming, trading, masonry, and carpentry.

At dawn and when we could hardly see, we headed for the motor park. It was at the motor park that I knew we were heading for Ilorin. My life journey of experiencing some diversities of God's creation had begun.

CHAPTER TWO

Leaving Home

We travelled to Ilorin in a passenger lorry with wooden seats. I longed to stretch my legs and have something to eat. The lorry had two compartments. The small compartment had two rows of bench seats and the larger compartment had more bench seats with spaces beneath for luggage. I was in a small compartment with my cousin.

At a point on the road, the driver stopped to pick up a well-dressed passenger with a small bag. He joined us in the relatively comfortable small compartment looking relieved. He told us that he waited for transport the previous day but none came and he had to be up early to look out for one going his way. Toward evening, we arrived Ilorin and I found myself in the Mr Ambrose Otonoku's house whose father's apartment was close to that of my father in Okene. We spent barely two days and one evening we parked and headed for the railway station on the next leg of our journey. I had no idea of our final destination.

Many other passengers were waiting for the train. I heard a rumbling sound that shook the ground. This was the passenger train pulled by a locomotive steam engine. It was my first time seeing a railway passenger train. When it stopped, my cousin took me into one of the coaches with my small box and told me to sit down. The seat was more comfortable than the wooden one in the lorry. We settled in for the journey to the next stop.

I had a good sleep and by early morning, I looked out through the window and saw settlements along the route. My first experience with the Kaduna railway junction was beyond description. Kaduna Township was more sophisticated than Ilorin and Okene. We were taken to a building on a road I would know many years later as Rabah Road. There, my cousin was given a room in an enclosed extension to the main building. I was given essentials like clean water and meals and enjoyed electricity for the first time in my life. There was constant traffic on Rabah Road in and out of the complex which I knew many years later as the official residence of Sir Ahmadu Bello, Sardauna of Sokoto, Premier of Northern Region. I was enjoying the hospitality of Mr George U Ohikere, a minister in the regional government.

The minister's wife was the most motherly to me. She appeared to be at ease with my childish ways and only reacted when I was in danger. I hovered around her just like I did around my mother in Okene to have some taste of the food before the main meal. In her concern for my safety due to the large open fire for cooking, she took out some of the plantains to be cooked and put them in a small tray and asked me to take a back path out of the house and sell them. I was recalled not long after since I could not communicate fluently in English or Hausa. I could not have marketed the plantains. I continued to enjoy her motherly watch over me.

Mr Ohikere was a member of the Igbirra (now Ebira) Tribal Union (ITU), a political party that was dominant in Okene. It was on the platform of this political party that he found accommodation in the Northern Peoples Congress party led by Sir Ahmadu Bello. My father was a political associate of Mr Ohikere to whom he entrusted my cousin. I had followed my father and cousin on visits to the residence of Mr Ohikere and relations near his apartment in Okene. I had enjoyed very warm hospitality at the minister's residence in Kaduna for about two weeks and had to leave for another undisclosed destination.

We left Kaduna by rail for Zonkwa where we spent a few days at the residence of my cousin's friend. Victor Enyisi Adinoyi, a second cousin who had finished his primary education and was waiting for admission into college, later joined us. At last, I had a big brother figure with me. Victor's father was my father's first cousin. His compound was next to my father's in Okene. There exists a network of three compounds of two brothers and a cousin that I roamed as a child. After Inda Ajoku, my father, and their first cousin, Indah Adinoyi decided that my uncle's son, Mr Emmanuel Ajoku, be the first to have western education to be funded by my father; it was later decided that Victor would follow and it would be his responsibility. I was the third beneficiary of this arrangement and we constitute the pioneers of western education in the extended family. More children followed us years later and all children now have equal opportunities and many of them have acquired university education in diverse fields.

My cousin Mr Emmanuel Ajoku while pursuing his grade two teacher's education had Victor staying with his friend Mr Emmanuel Onotu, a railway senior staff and a station master at Guni in Kaduna State. It was from there that he joined us at Zonkwa. Mr Emmanuel

Onotu is the elder brother to Mr Michael Onotu who was my cousin's contemporary at St Enda's Teachers Training College, Zaria, and would be my godfather at my baptism in 1962. Networks of relationships are very characteristic of Ebira people.

The Roman Catholic mission managed some schools and colleges that catered for the rural areas and it was a policy to post fresh graduates from teachers' training colleges to rural areas. My cousin had his college education in the Archdiocese of Kaduna and consequently, his area of service was defined. Kaduna South has a rural area he would start his service. We prepared to leave Zonkwa with a commercial vehicle owned and operated by Ado.

The journey out of Zonkwa took us through Zango Kataf to an outskirt where we were dropped by the bank of a rocky stream that Ado's vehicle could not cross. There was no bridge, so, we crossed the stream carrying our loads on our heads and trekked the remaining distance to Magamiya. There was no settlement insight along the laterite road until we sighted the school buildings made up of two rows of classrooms, a football field, a headmaster's small house, and a row of single-room apartments for three teachers. The only infrastructure was a freshwater well close to the residences and the classrooms. The schools in rural areas were closely monitored through regular visits by the reverend fathers in charge who came either on a motorcycle or a bicycle. I never saw a car in the location for a year.

Initially, we occupied one classroom for accommodation and this was shared between two teachers who had to install cloth dividers secured by strings tied to nails on the walls. We had a corner to put our pressure cooker and a few cooking utensils in and had private corners outside for bathing and toilets. After some experiments, Victor and I settled for night accommodation in one of the classrooms and were joined by other boys who were with the other teachers. We got up very early in the morning to clear the spaces for regular classes before the pupils started streaming in through bush paths into the school compound from different directions. There was no local residence insight and I never sighted any for the one year I was at St Pius Catholic Primary School, Magamiya, in 1961. It was a unique experience.

My cousin was upgraded and left the classroom for a spacious one-room apartment on the teachers' housing row. The kitchen space was shared with others and was more convenient. I still had my night accommodation in the designated classroom with other boys. After dinner, I would have a reading session with my cousin who had a collection of children's storybooks for me. Noticing my struggle with the English language in primary three, he decided to use the English language in communicating with me. During the after-dinner reading sessions with him, he noticed that I could not pronounce the word 'beautiful' I had to go through the drill of getting it right before going on to new pages. The other words I had some difficulty with were given similar attention. As my English language skills improved, he gave me a notebook for short essays and composition on topics that were based on my daily experiences. I was taught to narrate my experiences in simple flowing prose. This greatly helped in developing my observatory and writing skills.

The living routine in Magamiya was boring. I had no room to move around and play with my age mates. I had much older boys with whom I could not discuss and play with as I had to take orders from them. There were occasional football practices and games. I could hardly kick the normal football because of my small size. However, I was content with picking up balls out of play and trying my kicking skills to get it back to the big boys on the field. As the sunset daily, we left whatever we were doing and went to the kitchen to prepare dinner and thereafter settle into preparations for the following day and do school homework, if any. I was very much attracted to cooking from being near my mother in Okene as she prepared meals. I learnt some cooking skills from the senior boys. The various types of soups and dishes were determined by the seasons; that is when the ingredients were available.

There was no electricity and no cold storage facilities. The meat was mainly chicken which had to be killed, skinned, cut into pieces, and cooked immediately. The nearest market was at Zango Kataf and it was too far for me to trek; only the big boys ventured. A bicycle was made available when the foodstuffs to be bought were heavy. My cousin Victor once took the bicycle to ride to Zango Kataf during the rainy season and on his way back there was a rainstorm and he was thoroughly soaked by the rain. The perishable items such as gari were destroyed and had to be thrown away. Victor was to return and cook lunch but because of the rain, he was late.

My cousin, seemingly hungry and busy with his note of lessons, did not know whether to take the risk and ask me to cook. As he checked the available foodstuff, I summoned courage and told him that I would be able to cook rice and beans. He gave me the nod and I cooked delicious rice and beans. When Victor returned, a bowl of hot rice and beans meal awaited him. I passed a very important test and thereafter I was given other responsibilities. Sometimes, I washed my cousin's white shirts and used charcoal-fired iron to iron them without leaving a black charcoal mark on them. This helped me to keep myself clean.

Drawing water from the well was considered risky and I was not allowed to do that for some time. But one day, I tried to fetch water from the well with a small container tied to a long rope. The top was wet. I bent over to look inside and gauge the depth of water and let go of the container secured to the rope. As I was struggling to pull it up, I slipped and the heavy container filled with water started to drag me into the well. I was lying across the entrance into the well and still struggling to hold on to the rope. I managed to wriggle myself to safety. I was badly shaken and wondered who would have rescued me if I had fallen into the well. I walked away with the water in the bucket, happy that I did not attract attention.

I had no age mates to meaningfully interact with after school hours at Magamiya. The little time I had during school break I used it to learn Hausa the language spoken by the people in addition to their Kataf language. I was in the third year of my primary school education. The teachers at Magamiya had small radio sets; my cousin also owned the only turntable in the school. His favourite artists were Congolese musicians. I mimicked the sounds and enjoyed the beats.

Life generally at Magamiya was serene and only occasionally did we see people on the laterite road leading to Zango Kataf. The Fulani herdsmen and their cattle were regular sights. During the rainy season, the big boys took advantage of their free time to plant millet, maize, beans, tomatoes, and local spinach. The farmers nearby brought yams, sweet potatoes, and bush meat to sell and at times gave them out as gifts to the teachers.

The school calendar rolled by very quickly but I had no clue how I performed in class in the examinations. At the year's end in 1961, I found myself at Zonkwa in a new setting. My cousin was posted to St Paul's Catholic Primary School, Zonkwa in 1962 as headmaster and I was going to be in primary four. The school was in a large Catholic mission area that also had the St Louis Girls Convent School with boarding facilities and St Louis Girls Teachers Training College. The Catholic Church and the reverend fathers' and reverend sisters' residences and the residences of the female teachers were in the secure mission area that had a vast expanse of land.

St Paul's Catholic Primary School had three blocks of buildings that accommodated a single stream for seven classes and an office for the headmaster and a common room for the teachers. My class teacher, Miss Anne, was a pleasant fair lady and very well organized. I sat in the front row close to her desk. I was under her close watch. St Louis Teachers' Training College for girls frequently used St Paul's Primary School for practical teaching of the student teachers under the supervision of a mix of Irish reverend sisters and other European tutors. The white reverend sisters with their students on teaching practice taught us how to sing.

Miss Anne taught me to be competitive and I was always anxious to complete assignments and take notes neatly. The first two terms went by and I started to note the trend of class gradings at the end of each term.

My cousin rented a bedroom and a parlour from an Ibo man. A very likeable boy, the son of my cousin's friend who had been of assistance to him in the past when he looked after Victor Adinoyi, later joined me. The boy's name is Anthony Onotu and his father, Mr Emmanuel Onotu, a senior railway staff was in the United Kingdom for training; my cousin was looking after his son in his absence. He was younger than me and I had to look after him. Victor had gained admission to St Enda's Teachers Training College, Samaru, Zaria, and left.

I enjoyed the one year stay in Zonkwa but for an incident that taught me a very good lesson. As we were returning home from school one hot afternoon, there was an argument among the group of boys and girls. A girl named Monica made a comment that I thought was inappropriate. I approached her to make my case and this was followed by brief sparring that made her school box fall onto the dusty road.

I could not stop her from crying but as other pupils in our company did not complain about my behaviour, I thought it was all over. As I got ready to prepare dinner, Monica turned up in our compound with her father. They made their complaint and left. I waited to be called, but I was not called. We had dinner and I did my night preparations and study before going to bed.

The following day I left for school, thinking that the incident had been forgotten. But just before the bell rang for break, the headmaster turned up in my class and Monica was standing beside him in front of the class. He called me out and also called out two of the big boys who held me down and he caned me. I was sent back to my seat and I could not hide my shame. The headmaster warned me and other boys never to beat a girl. Lesson properly learnt and imbibed. There was no advantage of being related to the headmaster.

At St Paul's Catholic Church, Zonkwa, I attended Sunday Mass with my cousin. Catechism lessons were part of our school routines. It was therefore easy to prepare me for baptism. My cousin had noticed the attention I gave to mass and prayers. I was prepared for baptism and I passed the test. On the 8th of December 1962, I was baptized. My godfather was Mr Michael Onotu, a teacher and my cousin's friend. My cousin gave me a careful account of the period I was born. He remembered that it was a day in December because they were looking forward to the Christmas holidays when he returned home from school in the afternoon and was greeted with the news of my birth. He told my father that he would be my guardian and take care of me. From what my cousin said about the period of my birth, I chose December 8, 1952, as my birthday.

As the year 1962 came to an end my cousin was on the move again. I was not told where we were going. I packed my few belongings into my small box that had not been upgraded so far, though the number of my books had increased my cousin packed them in his luggage. It had been two years now since I left Okene. My mother had sent woven cloth to me to use at night while sleeping to keep warm.

The journey by train from Kaduna took us to Jos. I appreciate the names and geography of Northern Nigeria. The journey from Jos to Bauchi was by road on a small bus. It made me appreciate the topography of the plateau and the Bauchi plains. I had no idea where the journey would end until I started hearing Yelwa-Bauchi.

At Yelwa, there was the Rural Education College (REC) where qualified grade two teachers on gaining some teaching experience were admitted to start a two-year programme for teachers' grade one qualification. There was the final one year course at the Rural Education College at Bosso just outside Minna town. Yelwa REC was a serene environment with well laid out living quarters and academic and administrative buildings. There were no settlements close to the college except the Bauchi Teacher's Training College across the main road from Bauchi to Tafawa Balewa, the home town of the late Sir Abubakar Tafawa Balewa, the Prime Minister of Nigeria. The college was served with electricity. Martin Tauna, a Kataf, from Southern Zaria joined us. He was mature and in the final year of his primary education. He could handle farming implements and did all the cooking. He was very protective of me and I was well fed.

It was 1963 and I was expected to be in primary five. The primary school in Bauchi town was considered too far away for me to trek and there was no public transportation. My cousin decided that I should repeat the primary four at the Bauchi Teacher's Training College Practising School (BTTCPS) across the main road. Martin and the other big boys trekked or hitched a ride daily to and from the primary school in Bauchi town. We were constantly warned about snakes. I once saw a long green snake hidden under a concrete washtub in the kitchen when I moved the tub aside to gain access to the drain chamber for cleaning. Just as I moved the tub and exposed the snake, it escaped through the drain exit. I also dashed out of the kitchen.

The BTTCPS was located on the campus of the college near the football field between the dormitories and the lecture classrooms. It was a single row building with four classrooms and the headmaster's office. Provision was made for assembly, playground, and open spaces for lessons when the classrooms were too hot. The school was well equipped. All the pupils were issued with uniforms; caps for boys and scarves for girls.

There was a small first aid box for first aid treatments. Serious cases were referred to appropriate health care centres. I was in charge of the first aid box and taught how to wash and dress wounds. I was selected probably due to my cleanliness. A teacher was assigned to supervise me and would make sure that those who needed treatment were orderly.

While repeating the primary four, my cousin bought some primary five books for me to keep me busy. At school, we were engaged in hand craftwork using species of local grass popularly called tall grass we gathered from nearby streams depending on the season. Such materials were selected and prepared for use to make hats and other items which were assessed as handcraft. My year at Yelwa allowed me to learn more songs than anywhere else in my primary school years. The songs we were taught were inspiring and developed in us the joy of teamwork, appreciating nature, the commemoration of important historical events such as Nigeria becoming a Republic in 1963. We were taught songs praying for our national leaders who were working for us. They were Chief Obafemi Awolowo, Dr Nnamdi Azikiwe, and Alhaji Sir Abubakar Tafawa Balewa whose hometown was nearby. I was part of the celebration of Independence Day in 1963, when Nigeria became a

Republic, with the national flag and along with pupils from ours and other schools, treated to a meal of rice and soft drinks.

My little knowledge of Bauchi town was possible due to the few occasions I followed Martin to Bauchi's main market to buy foodstuff. As we trekked part of the distance, Martin had the skill of attracting motorists to stop and give us lifts, especially when we had to carry the foodstuff we bought from the market. Life at REC Yelwa was exciting and peaceful. There were plenty of fruits available to harvest and eat from the students' farms.

As the year 1963 was drawing to an end, we wrote the end of year promotional examinations. The examination supervisor who came to assess those who would qualify to go to senior primary school starting, with primary five, seemed to be impressed with my performance. He sent a message to my cousin that he would like to have me come over to Bauchi town to stay with him and take advantage of the opportunities there under his supervision. My cousin would not let me out of his sight and I had to leave Yelwa-Bauchi with him for the second year of his course at REC Bosso, Minna. Martin was still preparing for his first school leaving certificate examination and was sad that the letter inviting him to sit for the entrance to Nigerian Army Military School, Zaria arrived late and he missed the opportunity. Martin had to stay behind with a friend in Bauchi town to finish his examination. I would not see Martin again until after he joined the Nigerian Air Force and was serving at Kaduna Air Force Base.

My cousin and I left Yelwa-Bauchi for Zonkwa and on arrival, it was just a few days before the end of the year examinations started. I was left with my godfather, Mr Michael Onotu, a teacher, who had moved into our former accommodation. I was assigned to prepare for the primary five ends of year promotion examination to primary six with my classmates in primary four at St Paul's Primary School in 1962. I borrowed notes and copied and tried to comfort myself. Mr Onotu asked me several times if I would be able to cope and I assured him that I was doing my best.

As the school closed for the 1963 Christmas holidays, the examination results were announced on the last day of the school year. All primary 5-7 pupils were assembled in one classroom. The top pupils' results were announced for each class and given their report cards. The rest were asked to wait and collect their report cards to know how well they had performed. A classmate, Okechukwu, whose result was announced and given his report card as he took the second position, noted that I had not collected my report card. He went to search for my card and brought it to me without opening it. He was curious to know how well I performed and I opened the card in his presence only to find out that I also took the second position. I later got to know that I could not be announced because I was just passing through and had not been a member of the class. Both of us were very happy and Okechukwu was very kind to me as we left the school together following the familiar route I had taken home the previous year. I did not stay long in Zonkwa and when my cousin returned after the Christmas break, he was informed of my performance and he remarked that he was then convinced that I was qualified to go on to primary six. We were joined by Paul Bako, also a Kataf from Southern Kaduna like Martin, and then set off for REC Bosso Minna through Kaduna.

We stayed for about two days in Kaduna at the residence of a friend of my cousin near Ahmadu Bello Stadium close to Kaduna Junction railway station. We left Kaduna for Minna by train. The routines at REC Bossa were similar to what was obtained at Yelwa-Bauchi. The residential building allocated to us had two apartments shared by two students. Our neighbour was a young couple with two children. There was an allocation of small parcels of land to each student for growing vegetables and fruits.

St Malachy's Primary School, Bosso, was located near St Malachy's Teachers' Training College where my cousin graduated as a grade 3 Teacher. I and Paul Bako were admitted into primary six. It was 1964 and I had no idea that this would be my last primary school year. My cousin decided that I should try some entrance examinations into secondary schools in which pupils in primary seven were given priority in their final years.

The first try was the national common entrance examination and the second attempt was to St John's College, Kaduna. It was an adventure for me as I still had a year left to complete my primary school education. The result from St John's came out and I was successful as well as my classmate Michael Okon. We were the only ones that passed the entrance examination from the school. I was worried that Paul Bako was not successful. When we got back home, I did not inform my cousin that I had passed because I was afraid of telling him that Paul did not make it. We had our lunch and later dinner and as we prepared to turn in for the night Paul urged me to inform my cousin of my success. I refused. He pushed me forward to my cousin and told him that I passed the entrance examination to St John's College but he did not make it. How I wished I was able to share this joy with Paul.

I was at home after school playing around near the lawn tennis court one day when I saw an expatriate pull up in a Volkswagen beetle car near my cousin's residence. He was directed to our residence and he asked for my cousin. I rushed into our apartment to inform him that a white man was looking for him. The white man was a reverend father from St Malachy's Teachers' Training College opposite my primary school. After the exchange of pleasantries between them and the reverend father confirmed that my cousin was my guardian, he told him to get me ready for an interview at St Michael's Parish residence in Minna town the following day after school. He said that the principal of St John's College, Kaduna, Reverend Father S. Rafferty, was in Minna to conduct the interview.

My cousin took me to the residence of the reverend fathers at St Malachy's Teachers' Training College the next day after classes. We were then driven to meet the principal at the Catholic Mission parish. The interview was brief; the principal gave me an arithmetic test. The principal observed me struggling with the answer and walked past me to engage my cousin in a discussion. I was worried as we were driven back to St Malachy's to take our bicycle and ride back to our residence. But on our way, my cousin informed me that the principal told him that he was impressed with me and had offered me admission into the college.

The following day at school I got to know that Michael Okon was not successful at the interview. I was the only pupil to gain admission into St John's College Kaduna, from St Malachy's Primary School for the school year beginning in January 1965.

I looked forward to receiving the formal letter of admission to St John's College with a list of what I was required to take to the college. I eventually received the admission letter and was quite excited about it. I was told to bring one pair of sandals, multiple pairs of school uniforms, my non-uniform clothes called house wears, and a mattress. The Rural Education College at Bosso closed for the year before my school sat for the end of the year examination. There was no need for me to wait for the end of year examination because I no longer needed my first school leaving certificate. It was not required for my admission to the college.

My cousin and I travelled home to Okene for the Christmas holidays to inform our parents that I had been admitted into St John's College,

Kaduna, for my secondary school education. I was glad to be home and be with my parents and my relations. I was now four years older and receiving respectful treatment from them.

My parents were informed of my admission and the process of taking permission from my father and his senior brother, the patriarch of the collection of families, was set in motion. I received a bombshell when I learnt that my turn in primary school was all the opportunity they could give me and that my first school leaving certificate was enough for me to be employed as a policeman. They reasoned that I had gone far in education and I needed to stop there and give other children in the family their chance to be taken away from home by my cousin. The final decision lay with my biological father and the patriarch of the entire family, my caring uncle, and highly respected elder Inda Ajoku Onosachi Andah. My father had to sort out the polygamous family politics and my cousin worked on seeking his father's blessing to take responsibility for my secondary school education.

My senior brother Jimoh was directed to take me to the Okene central market and find out the cost of some items such as school sandals, canvas shoes among others. The sandals were out of Jimoh's reach but he was able to buy a few items on the list after Christmas. My cousin and Jimoh discussed their arrangements and I was told that the others would be taken care of later. I knew that as a farmer, Jimoh earned most of his money during the harvest season, which was about eight months away. After the Christmas celebrations, I was informed that I would be allowed to take up my admission into St John's College and that my uncle had agreed for my cousin to take care of my secondary school education. This was a great expression of the rare relationship of love I experienced in the polygamous family I was born into. I was grateful and will always be as I continue to be guided at all times by the family ideals I shared. Indeed, it takes a village or community to bring up a child.

I left Okene with my cousin after the Christmas and New Year 1965 celebrations and headed for Kaduna. In the past four years (1961-1964), I experienced rural diversities in Southern Kaduna, Yelwa near Bauchi, and Bosso near Minna and tried to understand the contrasts in the development strides. I had the opportunity of interacting with all major ethnic groups in Nigeria. The serene rural settings, fresh farm foods, and the diversity of cultures made great impressions on me. I had not had more than a year in one location since I left Okene and my family four years ago. The experiences of moving from one place to another every year enriched my understanding of the diversity of Nigeria and I looked forward to the challenges of life in a secondary school boarding house.

CHAPTER THREE

Stepping into the Unknown

O n my way to St John's College, Kaduna, on a sunny harmattan day in January 1965, I was with the children of Pa Adaba and Pa Ogido - neighbours to my father at Idogido area of Okene. My seniors in the college made most of my arrangements for me without my knowledge as I stayed in Pa Adaba's place at Kaduna on Sardauna Crescent near Ahmadu Bello Stadium. The senior boys took charge of me.

I was allocated St Benedict's dormitory that shared the same building as St Augustine's dormitory. A passage and lobby separated them. I did not come with a mattress but my cousin sent me one through Mr Joseph Ogido, a Higher School Certificate student. My cousin was still in Kaduna awaiting his posting to a primary school on completing his course at REC, Minna.

St John's College, located at Unguwar Rimi area of Kaduna, was established in 1949 by Irish missionary fathers of the order of Society of Missionaries for Africa (SMA). Archbishop John McCarthy of Kaduna Archdiocese had an official residence overlooking the main entrance to the College. He was the pioneer principal. The other dormitories were named after saints Joseph, Augustine, Cyprian, Clement, and Cyril. My dormitory shared facilities such as dining halls, standpipes for freshwater supply with four dormitories.

The toilets and bathrooms were allocated according to classes. The one for form one students was near St Joseph and St Cyril dormitories, quite a distance away. The closest were those for forms three to five. The central football field was nearby as well as the lecture classrooms. There were five standard football fields and an athletics track with football field facilities. There was also a cricket pitch. The only lawn tennis court was for the seniors as the junior students settled for table tennis for which standard tables and bats were provided. There were other games that students invented. The outside walls of classrooms for the first and third-year students were used for the game of fives.

The Church building was close to the Archbishop's residence. The science laboratories (physics, chemistry, and biology) were in the same area as the assembly hall. The Higher School Certificate classes had their separate science laboratories. All the classes were double stream and from the second year, A and B were used to differentiate science and arts disciplines. Latin and French were also taught. Latin was taken off in the second year and after the third year, French was for art students who elected to take it.

St John's College had an excellent mix of tutors. It was certainly one of the best secondary schools in Nigeria at the time and the student population and diversity reflected its impact on education in the country. There were four reverend fathers on the academic staff. The principal who interviewed me in Minna, Fr S. Rafferty, had left and had been replaced by Fr Sean Canty, at about the time I entered the college. We also had tutors from Australia, India, England, Ireland, Poland, and France. The Nigerian tutors were very few. Senior students were selected to take charge of various aspects of college activities as prefects with the tutors in supervisory roles. The Reverend Fathers had more than a fair share of responsibilities as they were multi-tasked. In addition to looking after our religious activities and the general administration of the College, the Reverend Fathers ensured lights were out at 2200 hours daily and maintained surveillance so students did not stray out of the college.

The first-year students were taught how to obey their seniors as a start in a series of actions for their refinement in their first year. The form two students were most active in disciplining the freshers with bullying tactics. The college administration stopped the initiation ceremony because of excesses in the practice before I entered the college. Respect for seniors was always emphasized and was a good aspect of our character formation. In the dining halls, tables were arranged in rows and allocated to dormitories.

Cyril Nwaozo, a prefect, said the grace before and after meals was also responsible for preparing students for receiving the sacraments. He was my godfather at my Confirmation. Mr Gregory Deinde was saddled with teaching us how to serve at mass using Latin; Mr Patrick Adaba was the choirmaster. I was a mass server and also in the choir.

There were athletics and football competitions between the colleges and we were invited to Police College games in Kaduna. The Phillip's Cup competition was for athletics and designated colleges in the zone took part. The Davies cup was for football. The range of recreational activities at St John's College gave the students a chance to discover their potentials. I was active in football, table tennis, and lawn tennis.

St John's College had good facilities for the lower forms and the Higher School Certificate streams for science and art students. In my first year, I enjoyed history, geography, and the English language. I also took Latin, arithmetic, English literature, religious studies, and general science. As the years rolled by, subject changes and introductions found us taking more subjects such as French, physics, chemistry, biology, mathematics and additional mathematics. The College Library had some foreign magazines from the countries of the expatriate tutors and I liked the articles and pictures on their ways of life. Each day at the College had a challenging programme of activities; the reverend fathers who were involved in the classrooms as tutors, football and athletics coaches, and our spiritual upbringing were a constant presence. I have fond memories of Fr John Haverty, my geography tutor in form two, and Fr J Gubbins who was our football coach for some of the years. A level playing field prevailed and the Muslim students had their needs provided for especially during the Ramadan period.

On 15 January 1966, I arrived at the Kaduna Junction railway station from Otukpo to a sombre atmosphere. I travelled from Okene to Otukpo with Pa Ambrose Otonoku, the father of my cousin's wife Janet. I had gone home to Okene for my cousin's wedding and had to return to Kaduna ahead of them through Otukpo where his father-in-law Pa Ambrose Otonoku was working. At the Kaduna railway station, I saw some soldiers and from their look, I thought something must be wrong. I found my way to the College where the news of the coup that day filtered in. I got to know that the Premier of Northern Region, Sir Ahmadu Bello, the Sardauna of Sokoto, had been killed. We also learnt that the Prime Minister, Sir Abubakar Tafawa Balewa the Premier of Western Region, Chief Samuel Ladoke Akintola, and the finance minister, Chief Festus Okotie-Eboh, had been killed too. We did not have the list of the very senior army officers killed in the coup. The leader of the coup was Major Chukwuma Kaduna Nzeogwu, a former student of St John's College.

I was too young to understand what was happening but I kept asking myself why would soldiers trained and armed to defend Nigerians turn out to be killers of their leaders? In the days following the coup, the newspapers reported graphic details of the killings.

With the escalation of the crisis, our safety became a matter of serious concern to the college authorities. We were warned to stop wearing our college badge to town to avoid attracting hostile attacks. I was shaken. I was in form two and formed a close-knit relationship with my classmates from the other regions. It was sad when we started hearing that students from the Eastern and Mid-Western regions would have to leave the College for their respective regions for safety. It was difficult to understand that some of my mates were no longer safe among us.

Transport arrangements were made for them and as each batch of students left us, we gathered around them confused and in tears. Some students started donating whatever they could give to their departing colleagues and brothers. We gave them powdered milk, sugar, gari, plates, cups, spoons, among other things we could lay our hands-on. I gave my favourite cutlery to Raphael Udeh, who was a very good footballer and would have made the College first eleven. I thrust the cutlery into his luggage at his feet and ran away in tears. We were not sure if they would survive the journey from the news of the spate of killings going on.

It is difficult to recall those moments of our young lives today without tears rolling down my cheeks. I have moved about freely enjoying the blessings of the country and this rude shock of separation started defining a new Nigerian reality for me. Some of those who were displaced from the Eastern Region and colleges owned by Ibos in the Northern Region were admitted to fill up some of the vacancies left by the students from the Eastern and the Mid-Western regions. Ibrahim Abdullahi from Stella Maris College, Port Harcourt, became my very good friend. The situation deteriorated and led to another coup in July 1966 and consequently the civil war from July 6th, 1967, to 15th January 1970.

The civil disturbances in Kaduna and some other towns in the Northern Region up to May 1967 led to killings and instilled fears of insecurity in us. There were stories in the media about the possible disintegration of Nigeria. I followed events as closely as I could and developed the habit of reading books and other publications on the country.

I became more aware of the political developments in the country and would get all information I could from newspapers, radio, and word of mouth. I adjusted to new friends among those students displaced from other parts of the country but the memories of the sudden departure of my old friends from the college remained with me. I never saw any of them again. In 1969 when we were in form five, one of them, Charles Ikimi, wrote to inform us that he survived and was also preparing for his final exams. Much later after the civil war, I received information on Innocent Eke whose mother was Fulani. He lost his father during the war and changed his surname to Hassan to survive in the new Nigeria. Alexander Okeke who used me for his football kicks survived and later served in the Nigerian Police as a medical doctor.

In my fourth year, I was selected to take charge of the Oratory in the residence of the reverend fathers. I had to wake up early and be at the Oratory to get it organized for mass. The mass vestments and altar had to be ready and as soon as the first reverend father entered, he headed straight to the laid out vestments and got dressed while I stood by and served at Mass. On Saturdays, I was at the Oratory to get the mass boxes packed with all required for dressing an altar, complete vestments, chalice, and all that go with mass celebration. Early in the morning on Sundays, I would be on standby to depart for out of college locations to celebrate mass. On occasions, we went to Kaduna Prison to celebrate mass with the inmates who were Catholic and we sometimes went to the outskirts of Kaduna to new parishes without parish priests.

On one occasion I missed out on the chasuble that should have been in the mass box and on arrival at the Kaduna Prison Reverend Father J Gubbins was embarrassed but he carried on and said the mass. I could not offer enough apologies for this lapse. I expected to be relieved of my coveted position at the Oratory but I was allowed to continue for some time. One of the functions I was expected to carry out at the outstation parish mass was to translate the sermon delivered by the Irish priests into Hausa. I was fluent enough in the Hausa language to negotiate prices in the markets but I thought it was a different situation for precise translation of sermons at Sunday masses. I still needed to greatly improve my Hausa for use at mass.

Two students from form three who were very fluent in Hausa were selected to understudy me and my classmate Jacob Yakubu, with excellent command of Hausa, was selected to take over from me and the Oratory was better managed with three able translators. One morning, I went for the routines but I was told that there was a message from Fr J Hession for me to leave the Oratory and that my classmate from the same dormitory would replace me. Fr J Hession was in charge of the Oratory and had been very patient with me. I felt relieved as the two third-year students had become used to the routines I put them through but was sad to leave the Oratory that gave me so much time for personal meditation.

My experiences serving at the Oratory allowed me to interact with people in prisons and in rural communities where the Church was not fully established. I also studied the austere life of the Reverend Fathers in their single-room apartments.

The year 1968 rolled by and I had completed my fourth year and was promoted to form five and laden with science subjects for the West African School Certificate Examination. Those who studied science subjects had the option of thinking about engineering and medicine among others. The College offered Higher School Certificate for subjects that would lead to medical studies and art disciplines at the university level. It was, however, popular to think of a combination (pure mathematics, additional mathematics, and physics) for engineering which the College did not offer at Higher School Certificate level (Advanced Level). I was drawn to engineering and would spend time in the College library assessing what was required for the course and the career prospects from available magazines.

My fifth year at College had a sobering effect on me. I tried to be more mature as a finalist and enjoyed all subjects I had taken to study. There was more freedom to plan study times and as I noticed some of my classmates waking up very early in the morning to study in classrooms and some hiding in unusual places beavering away, I decided to join those on early morning runs. I did not know that one has to have some coffee on standby to survive the lectures during the day. I tried one early morning run and really could not concentrate as I felt strange. I returned to my dormitory as the day was breaking and got ready for the daily routines. I never really got myself composed for the lectures. It was a wasted day and night. I never again tried it and took no notice of the very serious students who made me feel as if I was not serious. I stuck to the normal routines and made the best of the times available to me.

I developed an attitude of not having special preparations for examinations. My approach had a lot of shortcomings because I did not feel the urge to push myself harder. I was doing fine and I felt I was not in competition with anyone but myself. I eventually made this my standard approach throughout my academic pursuits and focused on getting things done routinely and avoided the accumulation of work that would demand a lot of time to revise for examinations.

I have formed the habit of praying and making petitions. I remember praying for guidance and leaving things in the hands of God. I went through the challenge of the mock certificate examinations without any major problems. The college released the mock examination results during the summer holidays. My classmates told me that I had done very well and would certainly get a scholarship for the Higher School Certificate Course. The scholarship was expected from my state government and our names in order of merit based on our performance were sent to Ilorin, Kwara State.

I was not given the scholarship despite being on top of the list in order of merit. The principal was disappointed and informed my cousin who was very annoyed. He later informed me that the quota system was used to encourage students from other areas.

This incident reinforced my decision to focus on an engineering career instead of medicine. I have attracted to mechanical engineering and future searches led me to ponder over what next should I succeed in going through a mechanical engineering degree course. I thought of specialization and marine engineering and life at sea appeared fascinating to me. I considered a career with merchant ships. When I visited the Nigerian Defence Academy (NDA) where some of the cadets were former students of St John's College, I got more information about marine engineering in the Nigerian Navy. This path also fitted my desire for where I would best serve my country. The military is one of the best establishments to serve the country. I had no idea how to proceed and get admission into the Nigerian Defence Academy than to keep on doing what I was doing until the opportunity would come knocking.

We completed the West African School Certificate Examinations by about the second week of December 1969. I had turned seventeen years. It was time to start packing and doing departure routines. There were several photographic sessions and a send-off party by the College. It was now our turn to hear the sobering parting words from our Principal Rev Fr Sean Canty: 'My dear passing out students, you are going into the world….'

We were too absorbed with the college party attended by girls from Queen of Apostles College, Kakuri, St Faith's College, and Sacred Heart Teachers Training College to even listen to him. It was fun and at this final farewell supervised by the reverend fathers, all of us tried hard to behave well. I had gradually moved my belongings to my cousin's house along Market Road, Kaduna. I gave some of my belongings to a handful of the students I was leaving behind. Some of the prayer books I had used were the most treasured items I gave away. The College had groomed me to the highest standards that could only be attained in a seminary and I believed that I would be faithful and live up to expectations. I thank all the reverend fathers and tutors/teachers from several countries and the few Nigerians among them who gave me so much to treasure all my life. No seminary was better than my St John's College, Kaduna. It will always be my shining light: Lucerna Lucens -the College motto.

Christopher Bode Odetunde was a year ahead of me at St John's College and had moved to Lagos after leaving St John's College in 1968. He studied art subjects. He lived close to Dele Akpomuje who was a friend of my classmate Mohammed Ahmed who transferred from St Thomas's Secondary School, Kano which was closed down due to the 1966 crisis. I thought I had a circle of friends to draw me to Lagos for further studies. Dele stayed with Mohammed when he came to Kaduna in an attempt to get a visa for studies abroad and I was introduced to him. He was mature and ready to advise me on matters related to further studies abroad and we kept in touch by correspondence when he returned to Lagos.

On completion of my WAEC examinations, I travelled to Lagos to sit for entrance examinations into the Federal School of Science for my Advanced Level certificate in pure mathematics, applied mathematics, and physics. Dele who was staying with an older relative gave me exceptional hospitality. Christopher lived close by and had been his close friend. I was fortunate to have Christopher as a guide as he had done an Ordinary Level course in science subjects and was now on course for his Advanced Level Certificate course to enable him to pursue an engineering career. He eventually became a Professor of Aeronautical Engineering in the US where he studied.

After my examination, I returned to Kaduna and Christopher promised to follow up on my result when it was released. I was glad to receive a letter notifying me of my success and admission into the Federal School of Science, Onikan in Lagos. I showed my admission letter to my cousin. He seemed very reluctant to make any comment. I left it for some days after which I reminded him. I was told bluntly that I was pretty young for him to release me out of his sight and he had no one in Lagos to whom he could entrust me. I was disappointed and informed Dele and Christopher that I would not be taking up my admission.

My cousin later informed me that he had secured admission for me to do secretarial studies at the Staff Development Centre, Kaduna. The WAEC results were not yet out and I faithfully settled into learning how to use the typewriter and write Pitman's shorthand among other subjects. The Pitman shorthand lecturer was Mr M. Icha who was also the Head of Department. My admission was to be confirmed when the WAEC results were released. When they were released and I had passed, Mr Icha was surprised that I was a science student and he asked me what I was doing studying in the department to be a secretary. He advised me that I should look for a place to do my Advanced Level Certificate course and informed me that the College of Science and Technology, Faculty of Kaduna Polytechnic had a course for the London GCE Advanced Level that had started and I should transfer there and catch up.

This was an evening programme that ran between 4-9 pm during the week. I enrolled for pure mathematics taught by a Canadian lecturer; applied mathematics taught by a Nigerian lecturer and physics taught by an Indian lecturer. I found odd jobs to do from morning to early afternoon to earn some money. We had a class of about ten students including one Arvind Sodhani from India whose father worked at one of the textile factories at Kakuri. We all assisted one another to ease our transportation difficulties. Arvind had a car and a driver and as he passed by along Ahmadu Bello Way to Kaduna Polytechnic Campus, he gave us a mustering point near where my cousin had a rented apartment along Market Road. The others had bicycles, a motorcycle, and the rest of us relied on our pair of legs.

The two years 1970 to 1971 rolled by with me working to earn some money during the day and attending lectures for my GCE Advanced Level Certificate in the evenings. Some of my course mates sat for the NDA entrance examination and one succeeded and was admitted. While waiting for the GCE results, I secured a teaching job at Our Lady of Apostles Secondary School beside Sacred Heart Teachers Training College both for girls. I also took advantage of the time there to sit for the Nigerian Defence Academy entrance examination and applied to Ahmadu Bello University for engineering, architecture, or in a single science subject in order of preference.

I almost missed the NDA entrance examination because my cousin refused to sign the form for me as my guardian fearing that my father would object to my joining the military so soon after the civil war ended in 1970. One afternoon, Mr Joseph Adaba, the father of Professor Tom Aaze Adaba and an elder Ebira in Kaduna and relation of my mother stopped over at our Market Road residence. He noticed my countenance and asked me what the problem was. I told him about the problem I was having with my NDA form. He told me not to worry. Upon entering my cousin's apartment he asked why my NDA form had not been signed. My cousin explained that he would not sign as he would not be able to explain why he allowed me to join the military to my father. We had lost a relation, Ovosi Adinoyi and a friend, Paul Bako, during the civil war and the military was a no go area. Mr Adaba told him that he was my father right in front of him and told him to sign the form to allow me to sit for the NDA entrance examination. He said that my cousin should leave him and my father to deal with the issue. My cousin duly signed the form and I sat for the entrance examination and passed and was called for the selection board. My GCE Advanced Level result was released at about the same time but I did not make the grades for engineering or architecture.

I went for the two weeks selection board. Before the individual candidates' final appearance before the members of the selection board, we were put through a series of military drills and exercises. As a civilian mixing with boys from the Nigerian Military School, Zaria, I was in a strange environment. The military schoolboys were already familiar with the military environment and were more relaxed with the drill sergeants as they understood the basic military terms for communications. The selection board procedures covered physical examination as part of a comprehensive medical test, individual and group tasks. The team exercises alerted me to the political influences and individualism that undermine the attainment of objectives among the would-be cadets that can affect any team cohesion.

The final aspect of the proceedings was when the individual appears before the Armed Forces Selection Board after all the results had been collated and presented to them. The final appearance I had before the Selection Board was a drama. I had no idea of the ranks of the officers on the selection board table. I was taken by surprise by the chairman of the selection board, an army officer I thought was an ordinary member. I was asked to take my seat. The chairman looked at the sheets spread before him and took a hard look at me. I had my eyes fixed on him as he asked me abruptly: 'Why do you want to join the Navy and not the Army?'

I said that I wanted to be a marine engineer. He took a hard look at me again for some seconds and then asked other members of the selection board if they had any questions for me. It was then I realized that I had probably been rude to the chairman in the manner I answered his question without hesitation. No other member of the board asked me a question. The Chairman asked me to take my leave.

I left wondering whether I had messed up my chances. I was directed by the staff handling our movements to go and wait for leaving instructions. I cannot remember anything that happened again until we were dismissed to take our leave of the Nigerian Defence Academy.

I visited Lieutenant (later Lieutenant Colonel) Christian A Oche who was serving at the Nigerian Defence Academy and had been part of the NDA administration team organising us for the selection board. I had known him through social interactions in Kaduna. I confessed to him that my encounter with the selection board chairman was not impressive. He told me that I should have confidence in myself and have a rest of my mind. At least I did not get a reprimand from him.

Some weeks later, I received a letter informing me that I was successful and given the period within which to report at the Nigerian Defence Academy to start cadet officer training as a member of the 12th Regular Combatant Course. I entered the NDA on 26 June 1972. About a month later after resuming at the academy, I received a letter of admission to Ahmadu Bello University to take up a single honours science subject. I was only 19 years old. I chose to remain at NDA and pursue a career as an engineer in the Nigerian Navy which had become my only choice.

CHAPTER FOUR

The Making of a Naval Officer

By the time I reported at the Nigerian Defence Academy on 26 June 1972, some of the new cadets had already reported and were being given a taste of military life. On my way to the reception, I noticed some of them in their shorts and singlets being drilled by senior cadets on the tarred road in the hot afternoon.

At the reception, I was put through the established routine and assigned to Dalet Company which was one of the two newly-built companies to be occupied for the first time. The two newly-built companies (Dalet and Burma) were very close to the parade ground and several open-drain gutters provided muddy swimming pools for dealing with very stubborn new cadets. I was assigned to a spacious room that I shared with a senior cadet.

I can hardly remember what happened on my first night in Dalet Company because of so many instructions designed to turn civilians into military men. I was on the alert to adjust and follow the crowd of new cadets. My senior cadet roommate was Cadet A Nyam. He was very observant and took charge of me and rarely spoke to me.

The introduction to academic and military wings was interesting as I wondered how the challenges ahead would play out. The programmes were well structured. The academic staff was a mix of education corps officers mostly from the Nigerian Army and civilians to handle the various combinations of subjects for the Nigerian Defence Academy Certificate of Education (NDACE) of the University of Ibadan. The NDACE is the equivalent of HSC and 'A' levels. I took pure and applied mathematics and physics.

The general military training programme included basic weapon handling, equitation, map reading, field exercises, obstacle courses, and drills. These constituted the common services subjects among others. We had lectures in military subjects given by a combination of Indian and Nigerian military personnel. The common services subjects were taken together with all cadets from the three services. The Commandant of the NDA was Major General RA Adebayo and the Deputy Commandant was an Indian army officer, Brigadier General HS Chandel. He later became the Acting Commandant. The Naval Wing was under the command of an Indian Navy Lieutenant Commander KK Kohli and the second in command was Lieutenant Godwin Ndubuisi Kanu. They covered all naval subjects together with some senior naval ratings. This setup was similar to that of the army and air force wings. The equitation was taken by a British Army officer Major H Filipiak who helped us overcome the fear of horses and introduced us to the polo games.

The drill square was considered the sacred ground and it was here that the drill staff under the Regimental Sergeant Major Bulama Biu held sway. The drill parade ground that was very close to Dalet and Burma companies constrained our movements because it was forbidden to cross the ground. The parade ground was where our discipline was forged and it was also the ground that the most hilarious events we had to observe in silence took place.

Bulama Biu knew how to diffuse tense situations especially when the NDA Adjutant, Lieutenant Colonel IOS Nwachukwu, was imparting his polished English language skills with effortless ease on the parade ground as he corrected our errors. The drill staff had their brand of English language that carried the final words of execution.

The initial drill test was conducted by the NDA Adjutant. The drill staff took us through the group routines with the Adjutant keeping a very watchful eye. The final routine was to march up to the Adjutant individually for his assessment and thereafter turn about and march away.

I took my turn and tried to be as natural as possible and do the swings and digging of the heels as instructed several times by the drill staff. The Adjutant took a close look at me from head to toe and after some jottings on the paper on his notepad, he dismissed me and I was expected to salute and turn about to march away. I failed to salute and did my turn only for the Adjutant to smartly order me to turn and face him again. The Adjutant, Lieutenant Colonel IOS Nwachukwu was a highly respected officer at NDA with exemplary trim stature and very neat turn out. On turning back to face him again, I acknowledged my mistake before he could utter a word and he gave me the dismissal order again. I mustered the courage to give the best salute I could manage to give and turn about to march away. I expected a failure and a repeat another day. I passed the drill test.

The Adjutant spared me and I joined others who passed their drill test on the first attempt. The Adjutant would later be appointed the Cadet Battalion Commander and I continued to admire him at NDA for his turnout, command of the English language, and horsemanship. He used to tell us that he was a fine officer and that was what he wanted all of us to be. He taught us first-class examples. He was posted out of NDA before the end of my 18 months programme. The success at the drill test was the passport for our first outing to have a taste of freedom.

The confidence boost from the drill tests increased as we started rehearsals for the first passing out parade ceremony I would participate in on 9th September 1972 for the 8th Regular Course. The parade was commanded by 8th Regular Course Cadet Academy Senior Under Officer, ML Agwai. The Guest of Honour was represented by the CNS, Vice Admiral JEA Wey, a Marine Engineer Officer.

For naval and air force cadets, the duration of the programme was 18 months at NDA and a further 12 months on passing out at the respective service establishments while the Army cadets remained behind to complete their programme. All cadets were eventually commissioned at the end of 30 months on the completion of all programmes. The interval between courses was then six months. This meant that there were two passing out parades annually. There were camping training exercises starting with Camp Initial and later Camp Ruwan Babban Yaro. Camp Initial was for all cadets in the rural neighbourhood of Kaduna for three days while Camp Ruwan Babban Yaro was in Lagos at the Naval Base onboard ships.

The sporting activities included basketball, field hockey, football, cross country race, athletics, and horse riding among others. I participated in cross country races, field hockey, and athletics (steeplechase and 5,000 metres races). I stayed away from the boxing ring largely because my small stature would have made me a good punching bag. I represented my company in the steeplechase race during the athletics competition in 1973. I was in a position to aim for a prize when a competitor fell. I reached out immediately to help him but my company cheerleader nearby shouted at me to leave him and continue with the race. I instantly gathered myself up to continue the race but I lost momentum in the last final 100 metres of the race and lost.

The prizes were awarded to the winners and I stood alone thinking of the cadet whose fall cost me the prize. After the award ceremony as the crowd dispersed and the cadets headed for their companies, I walked near the table on which all the prizes had been displayed and given out. There was a small trophy remaining on the table. I noticed the senior cadet in charge staring at it. He noticed me drawing near and he quite suddenly beckoned me and presented the trophy to me with the words:

'Take this; you too deserve a trophy.' This I consider worthy as a most treasured sports trophy in my collection. It is a souvenir.

The action of the senior cadet whose name I did not even know, convinced me that it is right to care for others in danger even when you are in a fierce competition for a prize. His action became part of my experiences that have influenced my relationship with people that I come into contact with. I owe a debt of gratitude to the unknown senior cadet.

The academic lectures for me were principally pure and applied mathematics and physics. It meant that I had only one laboratory exercise to deal with. The pure mathematics lectures provided some moments for reflection. The elderly lecturer would sometimes start his lectures by writing a problem on the blackboard and asking the cadets to provide a solution. It was common on occasions that the problems were relatively easy for many cadets to put up their hands even after alternative methods had been used successfully. On one occasion, the lecturer allowed the alternative solution providers to continue the drama and when all the lecture time had been exhausted and there were still hands up to provide alternative ways to solve the problems, he informed the class that we had wasted the lecture period providing alternative methods to solve a problem. He advised us to learn how to complement one another and avoid wasting valuable time to show off.

The final term at NDA was a hectic flow of activities. The final examinations and tests were programmed and cadets shared study experiences. The examinations and tests were broadly categorized into academics and common services subjects for all cadet course groups and the professional subjects for the army, naval, and air force cadets. After the examinations and tests, the final drills were for rehearsals for the passing out parade.

I was taken to task by one of the naval cadets in my group as we met on the road by the parade ground moving in opposite directions. He stopped me and in a jovial manner put it to me that I was making my course mates look as if they did not exist before our instructors. He drew my attention to my performance. It was as if I was tormenting them and I should slow down. I was always seated in front as I was among the smallest in stature and never bothered to look at what others were doing. I was speechless and my coursemate and I parted amicably.

During one of our final examinations that started with a physics practical, I was moving fast ahead as I was conversant with a short-cut procedure to establish a preliminary parameter. I did not know I was being observed as the supervisor took hold of my paper and asked why I was so fast and getting it right. I was accused of seeing the examination question paper before coming to the hall. I was searched and allowed to continue but was noted down for examination malpractices which would have earned me expulsion as punishment.

I went straight to Lieutenant GN Kanu after the physics practical examination and reported the incident. The Indian Naval Officer-in-Charge of the Naval Wing, Lieutenant Commander KK Kohli, was briefed by Lieutenant GN Kanu. I did not know what happened but I was informed that Kohli told the academic community about to investigate me that he had observed that I was always ahead of the others in all assignments including the navigation exercises he conducted for the Naval Cadets and in other courses conducted for the combined course comprising Army, Navy and Air Force Cadets. I never thought of any prize and never felt I was competing with anybody but myself and my weaknesses as a human being.

Dalet Company did not fare well in sports competitions. The company distinguished itself in the drill competition and was the winner. It was judged as the most disciplined company at NDA. At the company level, I was considered and awarded recognition as the most disciplined cadet in the company. It was hard coping with the fact that there were many late nights because of my course mates who misbehaved resulting in all members of the group being called out at awkward times of the night for punishment drills. A problem was caused for our night punishment drill as a cadet claimed he missed a muster because he fell asleep on a toilet seat.

I had enjoyed Dalet Company for two terms being the first occupant of the newly constructed blocks. The third and final term was spent in one of the old blocks near the mess, the academic block, and military training grounds. It was named Cameroon Company. I had a first-term Cadet Robert Iyedor of the 14 Regular Course as my roommate. Sadly, his dreams were shattered when he took ill and was admitted to the Military Hospital, Kaduna, where he died. He was given a full military burial at the Kaduna Military Cemetery.

We were allowed to receive and entertain visitors on visiting days within the prescribed social limits. At the end of every term, there was a company party for the send-off of the passing out cadets. All cadets were allowed to invite their girlfriends to the event. A general function was held for all cadets and the officers of the military and academic training teams to which family members were invited to attend. Kaduna is a very lively large city and it was not unusual to have a few cadets coming late from town on free days. The junior cadets caught coming in late at various times from the start of the muster parade to the next routine sometimes provided entertainment as regards reasons for coming late despite the punishment routines. I was drawn close to senior cadets for various reasons; some for my enthusiasm for sports such as cross country, athletics, and hockey, and others for protection. I was very close to my coursemate Cadet EE Ita whose parents were based in Lagos where he was brought up. We formed a partnership for social outings while in Kaduna and Lagos and I was very welcome at the family house at Falolu Street, Lagos.

Lieutenant Colonel IOS Nwachukwu was posted out of NDA and Major Lawrence A Uwumarogie was appointed as the new Academy Adjutant. His first time on the parade ground for rehearsal was real fun. As he tried to mount the saluting dais, he missed a step up the dais and fell. The RSM, Bulama Biu, smartly marched to the dais and demonstrated how to march up the steps. He turned to the new adjutant, saluted, and remarked that there was nothing wrong with the saluting dais. The RSM marched back to his position behind our formation.

As we approached the final rehearsals, the award winners were named so that they could practice the drill of receiving their awards from the guest of honour. The adjutant let some of the cats out of the bag when he asked a few of us to identify ourselves. Later that day, I overheard that there was a debate as to who would be the overall best cadet for the course, and my company officer was said to be neutral and would not favour any cadet because both of us were from his company. The details of the awards were thereafter closely kept secret.

It was at the final rehearsal that I knew I would be given two awards and Cadet OF Iyanalu an Air Force Cadet from the same company, Dalet, would be given the Best all Round award in addition to the two other awards. Lieutenant Commander KK Kohli commented on the closeness of our scores. We brought all six awards to Dalet Company as Cadet OA Azazi also won an award. It was a clean sweep of all the medals for the 12th Regular Course for Dalet Company. They were perhaps rewards for the discipline in the company. The company commander wore the smile of a conquering general on the few occasions I saw him walk past me and especially at the passing out parade.

On a pleasant sunny day 15th December 1973, the passing out parade took place. The guest of honour, the Head of State, Commander-in-Chief of the Armed Forces of the Federal Republic of Nigeria, General Yakubu Gowon was represented by Major General Hassan Usman Katsina, Chief of Army Staff, Supreme Headquarters. My cousin and some friends were present at the colourful passing out parade. This was the beginning of the end of my days at NDA.

On completion of the Colour Party march in with the escorts presenting their arms the entire Academy Cadets, with the passing out cadets were brought to marching position and marched on to the parade ground. The band had the three services' contributions and provided excellent music that brought out the best in us. After the march past in slow and quick times, the award presentation ceremony took place. The master of ceremony announced loud and clear thus: 'At the end of every term, awards are made to cadets who have shown outstanding performances in various fields. In making these awards, consideration is given to ………. and……..'

The factors considered were summed up and included extracurricular activities. I was on top of my world as I marched to take a position for the awards and made sure I kept to the drill instructions before the distinguished guest of honour who as a Major was the Military Governor of Northern Region while I was in a secondary school in Kaduna. I was the shortest cadet among the award winners and received good public applause for my two awards.

The passing out cadets took positions for filing past the guest of honour. The beautiful music tune was 'Auld Lang Sangyne.' As I marched past, I proudly caught the sight of my cousin who had sacrificed so much to see me through to this stage since 1961 when I left Okene with him. After handing in my rifle, I went straight to my cousin to show him my awards. I had bought some drinks to entertain him and other guests with him. Thereafter, I went for the group photograph sessions with the Acting Commandant Brigadier HS Chandel of the Indian Army. I was lost among senior officers we had dreaded going near. Lieutenant Commander KK Kohli of the Indian Navy was the most protective of me and I felt comfortable. He made sure I got a good seat next to the Commandant. I was lost in the turnout of senior officers and failed to observe the crossing of legs that all officers except the Commandant had to do. The Naval Wing photo session was emotional for me. I had two familiar senior officers, Lieutenant Commander KK Kohli and Lieutenant GN Kanu (later Rear Admiral), and was more composed. The last session was with my course mates and when I look at the series of photographs now I reflect on how small I looked among the big boys.

There was a message directing me and three of my course mates (Cadets EO Ibitolu, A Udofia, and J Kalu) to report to the office of

Lieutenant GN Kanu for briefing. He informed us that based on our performances, we had been selected to proceed to Britannia Royal Naval College (BRNC), Dartmouth, UK for the next phase of our naval training, which is the Midshipman course. The College is a very prestigious one where the British Royal family members have their naval training.

I asked Lieutenant GN Kanu if there was a vacancy for an engineering course at BRNC for me. I was told that there was none. I immediately told Lieutenant Kanu to take me off the list and let my nomination be given to another cadet. There was a stern look at me from Lieutenant Kanu who asked if I had been abroad before and my answer was NO SIR. He did his best to explain to me the prestige attached to doing my Midshipman course at BRNC and added that I would be available for an engineering course thereafter. But I would not change my mind. I had chosen engineering as a career way back in secondary school. I made my choice clear to the Chairman of the NDA Selection Board in 1972 that I was coming in to serve the country in the Nigerian Navy just for that reason. I said that I would do my Midshipman course in Nigeria to make me available early for my engineering course.

I was given twenty four hours to think over my refusal to take up the nomination. I sought the opinions of some of the senior ratings at the Naval Wing who advised me to go to BRNC. The following day I went to Lieutenant Kanu and told him that my mind was firmly made up not to go to BRNC. I felt his mentor's concern for me and this would always endear him to me and there would be more exciting occasions when I needed his critical support in my career and which he readily gave in a very inspiring manner without being asked.

He briefed the officer-in-charge of the Naval Wing, Lieutenant Commander KK Kohli, and told him that I was firm in my decision. I was left off the BRNC nomination. Cadet D Omessa was nominated to replace me. I was relieved to have some respite at home.

I told my cousin at Kaduna that there were prospects for further training at home and abroad but I would now report to Naval Base at Apapa, Lagos, and start the next phase of my training. I did not mention to him that I opted out of the nomination to leave immediately for the UK to attend the prestigious BRNC. This would have put me under further pressure and possibly forcing me to change my mind as I have always deferred to him to take the final decisions in such matters.

At the Naval Base, Apapa, Lagos, the Staff Officer Sea Training (SOST) was Lieutenant Commander FIO Nesiama (later Rear Admiral) in charge of Midshipman training. He was a Navigation and Direction specialist officer with very good handwriting. The Nigerian Naval Ship (NNS) QUORRA was within the choked Naval Base and there was competition for instruction classrooms. This made us move around the Base and understand its history and space constraints. All Midshipmen were taken and accommodated onboard the Flag Ship NNS NIGERIA (later renamed OBUMA). NNS NIGERIA was commissioned into service on 16 September 1965.

The Commanding Officer was Commander DE Okujagu who would later be Rear Admiral and Flag Officer Commanding, Western Naval Command. The First Lieutenant/Executive Officer was Lieutenant Commander Augustus A Aikhomu, a Gunnery Officer who became Vice Admiral and Chief of the Naval Staff. He later became the Chief of General Staff and later still Vice President to President Ibrahim Babangida. He attained the full rank of Admiral; the first in NN.

In March 1974, there was a vacancy for a Midshipman at Britannia Royal Naval College, Dartmouth. The SOST came onboard and took me to the space between the ship's funnels. He made sure we were alone before letting me know that there was a vacancy and I was nominated to go for the course at the College. I did not hesitate to tell him that I would not take it up. He warned me it might be my last opportunity to go for any course in the UK and that if I insisted on engineering, I might have to seek admission at a university in Nigeria, possibly the University of Lagos. I said that I did not mind any university in Nigeria as long as it was a mechanical engineering degree course that I would pursue.

Midshipman Anthony Eboreime was nominated to replace me. A month earlier, the last of the NDA product to go to Royal Naval Engineering College (RNEC), Manadon, UK, returned home because he was unable to continue the course just like all the others from NDA before him. The College had become a dreaded institution as no NDA product had succeeded in going beyond the first term in the college. The latest withdrawal from the course joined us for the midshipman training and told me the problems he faced in the college.

I was determined to stay on course and wait for any mechanical engineering degree course billet except that for RNEC, Manadon. I heard a lot about the casualties of the strict regime of RNEC and how difficult the engineering course was. I was attached to Sub Lieutenant (later Rear Admiral and military Governor of Oyo State) Adetoye Sode, a mechanical engineer, waiting for the Marine Engineering Application Course to qualify him as a marine engineer officer. He was lively and easy-going and soft-spoken and would take me to Lagos in his car when he had free time to attend to personal matters.

The Flag-Ship had a programme for a West African cruise and we were occupied with all aspects of naval training with an emphasis on practical experiences. The midshipmen had a gun room mess and would only be allowed to peep into what the Wardroom Mess looked like with commissioned officers enjoying the perks of their ranks.

The West African cruise took us to Sierra Leone, Ivory Coast, and Ghana. The Navy Band came along and provided entertainment at the cocktails and parties. This was my first time visiting any foreign countries and I had an open mind for new experiences. Sierra Leone was our first stop and I heard the Kreo language for the first time. There were many Nigerian traders owning shops in the city. There was a reception for us at the Nigerian High Commissioner's residence and a cocktail party on board. The evening parties during our stay were opportunities for the midshipmen to rub shoulders with other officers. On an occasion, the midshipmen were too active and confined their seniors to their seats as they engaged the ladies on the dance floor most of the time.

The officers found a solution after a crucial meeting between the First Lieutenant/Executive Officer and the SOST. The Supply Officer came with a master plan by suggesting that we should be kept onboard on ROB, that is Remain On Board and the reason would be a scarcity of funds to pay our allowances. The Supply Officer implemented the plan. The following day, all officers onboard were paid their allowances by the Supply Officer on return from the bank. The Midshipmen were not paid and the explanation given to us was that the Central Bank of Sierra Leone refused to recognize that we were officers under training and therefore did not release the money to cover our allowance. He added that the bank also had a shortage of funds. It was, therefore, decided that all of us be on ROB because we had no allowances to spend ashore.

The next foreign country port of call was Abidjan, the capital of the Ivory Coast. In the approach to a narrow channel of entry, the hydraulic system of one of the controllable pitch propellers developed a problem and there was repeated use of the acronym KaMeWa being the trade name of the manufacturers. The CO aborted the entry approach and headed the ship towards the fairway buoy to allow time for sorting out the problem. The next approach and entry into the harbour were problem-free.

We were in a French-speaking country and all the French language courses at St John's College and NDA did not provide me with enough vocabulary to communicate effectively. We were lucky that the citizens of Abidjan were much better with the English language than we were with the French language. On our tour of the city, my group of adventurous midshipmen who went into shops and entertainment centres attracted the attention of the mostly European audience. We were determined to be free wherever we found ourselves and all we could hear in French was that these were from Nigeria. We loved it and carried on as if we were the owners of the land.

At the cocktail party at the Nigerian ambassador's residence, there was plenty to eat and drink and for the first time, I was introduced to a collection of French wines. I hardly knew what to order and just followed the popular demand. I was high on the cocktail and I took a lady I was discussing with to where I thought was the dance floor. The Navy Band was playing a popular Nigerian tune and we both turned the cocktail party into a dance party as others paired up and joined us. I exhausted there, the Midshipmen allowance for acceptable mischief. She later led me to the table laid out with food. I tried to eat but could not and those officers around me who noticed my state took control. I was helped into the bus and on getting to our ship I was helped up the gangway and up to my bunk. I woke up the following morning and I was told of my behaviour. I resolved that never would I be in that state again. To this day, I have adhered to the principle of moderation.

The final country was Ghana. NNS NIGERIA first called at Tema for Accra and later Sekondi. I was impressed with the Sekondi harbour facility. The CO loved the setting and took us alongside without the aid of a tug. It was the same procedure of receptions, tour of the cities and towns, parties and shopping centres. The orderly layout of Accra impressed me and the bold display of the Black Star national flag popularized by the late Dr Kwame Nkrumah, first premier and later President of Ghana also impressed me.

We arrived home at the Naval Base Apapa to a rousing welcome with Captain Leslie Wright at the jetty. His presence at the jetty kept the commanding officers on their toes. The Midshipmen training made me experience the best of our Commanding Officers onboard NNS NIGERIA, NNS DORINA, and NNS OTOBO. It was tedious work and fun that groomed me regarding the realities in home waters.

The cruise enabled us to get used to various navigation pieces of equipment on board. The various watches we had to keep enabled us to understudy the watchkeeping officers who taught us how to observe ship routines during the day and at night to interpret the Rules of the Road provisions. The training programme was designed to rotate us in groups round the various departments according to specializations. When I was off watch keeping and had spare time, I was fond of going to the stern part of the ship and watching the propellers churn the seawater into the wake stream. I would later at sea in my career repeat this retreat as a marine engineer officer and have the satisfaction of seeing all the efforts of my department in the productive output of moving the ship.

The Midshipmen were split into two groups for the continuation of their training onboard NNS OTOBO and NNS DORINA commanded by Commander PS Koshoni and Lt Commander OP Fingesi respectively. The two ships were Mark 3 Corvettes and were operated as a squadron. They were deployed on coastal patrol duties. This Midshipmen training on theses ships gave us a more intimate and closer professional relationship with the officers as there was no dedicated space for a midshipmen gunroom. We had our grooming on board the Flag Ship and we had no difficulty adjusting to the mess routines onboard. We had comfortable bunk spaces and I was completely at home including weekends spent with Midshipman Ita at his family residence.

I was assigned to the Navigation and Direction officer of NNS DORINA, Lieutenant OO Deinde who would later in his career be Military Governor of Ogun State and CO of NNS ARADU, the Flag Ship before his retirement as a Rear Admiral. The rotation of Midshipmen around the departments onboard was easily facilitated as we were few and in a smaller warship. The ships rarely stayed alongside for more than three weeks before the next deployment. The frequent ports of call were Port Harcourt and Calabar with Lagos as their home port.

Deinde had me close and watched my progress during training and would later take me as his assistant navigation officer. He taught me how to organize his department and would rely on me to take fixes at sea. The commanding officer rarely spoke to us but showed good examples of an excellent CO at ease in a very demanding environment. He was calm in difficult situations. On an occasion when the ship was passing Tom Shot sandbank off Calabar fairway buoy, he had gone down to his cabin for rest and handed over to the XO. The ship was in shallow waters. On coming to the bridge, he heard a report of the echo sounder reading zero. He simply ordered: 'I have the ship.' He took over and calmly took the ship out of the danger of being stuck in the mud and grounded, taking advantage of the wave surges.

He was steady with a combination of engine and conning orders to take advantage of the crest of waves that were coming towards the ship until the ship was fully floating and the echo sounder was giving encouraging readings. The ship safely got away and his exemplary calm in such great danger without blaming anyone was an important experience for me. The lesson I learnt is that as a commander, you do not blame your subordinates but take responsibility and lead with dignity.

The two ships spent days on Eastern patrol and were scheduled to berth at Port Harcourt for some days to replenish. This was June 1974 and our Midshipman course was approaching the concluding phase when we should be ready for the Midshipman board. While we were still in Port Harcourt, a signal was released directing those officers waiting for engineering degree courses (mechanical and electrical) from NDA 11 and 12 courses to proceed to India for their degree course at the Indian Navy Engineering College. I was left out and was a bit disappointed.

I received a letter from the SOST, Lieutenant Commander FIO Nesiama explaining to me why my name was not on the signal for India. I was informed by the letter that I was nominated to go to RNEC, Manadon, Plymouth UK. I will always be grateful to SOST for his almost two-page letter to me in his unique beautiful handwriting. In the letter, he tried to assure me that the Nigerian Navy had confidence in me to make it where all others before me, from NDA, had failed. To allay my fear of being alone, I was informed in the letter that the next junior course that had just passed out of NDA had three cadets that would join me and thus solve the loneliness problem. Only Cadet Daniel Emagu Opuoro showed up and he would be for electrical engineering. I have one companion though both of us would be on different programmes and could no longer turn down going to the famous land of the revered Queen of England. The die was cast.

On our return to Lagos, we continued our Midshipman course which had reached the conclusive phase thereby allowing us to start revisions and preparations for the Midshipman Board. The SOST was taking us through a navigation session at the old NNS QUORRA classroom we had always used for navigation when a Leading Writer from the Nigerian Naval Headquarters came asking for Midshipman AA Isa. On identifying me and in the presence of the SOST, he made me sign for a bulging brown envelope containing several letters attached to the main letter. I was informed to read through the content carefully and bring two passport photographs to the Naval Headquarters to start documentation for the course.

After the navigation session, I opened the bulging envelope and the first letter stated that I had been nominated for the mechanical engineering degree course at RNEC, Manadon, for three years 1974-1977. I was directed to be prepared to depart for the UK by 09 September 1974. Captain Wright took charge of the UK visa after my first Nigerian passport was issued. It was assessed that I had completed my midshipman training and was allowed towards the end of August 1974 to detach and concentrate on my preparations to depart for the UK. I took a train ride to Kaduna to visit my cousin and guardian to brief him and have a family discussion. He was delighted to see me go to the UK and I made arrangements with a bank order for my parents' upkeep with monthly remittance from my salary for the duration of my course in the UK. On 09 September 1974, Daniel E Opuoro and I, together with other NN officers going to the UK for other studies, gathered at the designated departure point at NNS QUORA opposite the mechanical workshop and we were driven in a bus to Lagos International Airport to board a Nigeria Airways flight to London Heathrow.

CHAPTER FIVE

Realising the Big Dream at Manadon

The staff of the Nigerian High Commission London, Defence Adviser's section, received us at Heathrow Airport and took us by bus to Centre Point Hotel, Hammersmith. I was paired up with Dan, my Manadon coursemate, to save money as we had to pay for our hotel bills from our allowance. The Deputy Defence Adviser, Navy was Lieutenant Commander (later Rear Admiral) EO Omotehinwa, He was sensitive to our needs. The more experienced officers who had been in London advised us to use the London underground to move around the city. Our first ride was to Embankment Underground near the Nigerian High Commission.

Dan and I were told that RNEC, Manadon, was on summer holidays and closed. We had to wait in London for about two weeks before going to college. This gave us time to get the essential civil suits and other clothing items to ensure we maintained our officer status with temperate /winter clothing although we were not yet commissioned.

The hotel bills were draining our allowances fast and we were advised to find a cheap Bed and Breakfast hotel nearby. We left for Manadon on 21 September 1974. The High Commission gave us transportation to Paddington station to take a train for Plymouth. We were received at the Plymouth station by the College reception team with a small Royal Navy (RN) bus.

I thought about the college during the drive to Manadon. This famous and strict institution had been a heart breaker for all NDA products so far; no NN officer had earned its degree since its recognition by the UK Council for National Academic Awards (CNAA). The College took its Manadon name from the estate on which it was established. Manadon is interchangeable with RNEC as the name of the College. It commands remarkable respect within the RN establishment and the British engineering community.

Plymouth appeared to me as a sleepy but sprawling city. The reception we had at the college was brief and we were given our accommodation in the main College Mess building on the first floor after documentation.

We were all considered and treated as naval officers at the College including the few constructor branch personnel some of whom would remain as civilians throughout their careers. Civilian clothes in the mess for meals were a suit or jacket and tie. I had bought two suits in London and taken photographs at Trafalgar Square near the Nigerian High Commission on Northumberland Avenue. These complimented my multi-coloured suit whose material I had bought in Abidjan and sewn for me by a tailor on Ojuelegba Street in Lagos. This would cause some stir each time I wore the unusually bright multi-coloured suit. The specified naval uniforms were strictly RN, except for the cap badges which were those of the NN that would be worn at all times for lectures and mess functions.

I had finally arrived at an institution where I would be allowed to study and earn a mechanical engineering degree to get my naval career underway. The teenage thoughts and dreams during my secondary school days were about to be given real expression. As I got acquainted with the college surroundings and routines, I constantly prayed and thanked God for this opportunity. The stage was set for life and career-changing experiences.

The first day at the instructional block was a simple introduction to our divisional officers who took charge of us. The course had been divided into three divisions as indicated in our joining instructions. I was grouped in 74 BM. The system was AM, BM, and CM Divisions for the mechanical engineering students for the year of entry which was 1974 for my course.

The electrical engineering students were in AL, BL, and CL divisions. The RN uses M ad L to identify mechanical and electrical/electronic engineers. The Divisional Officer for 74 BM was Lieutenant Peter Hadden, a distinguished naval diver, and lecturer in metallurgy. Hadden was a quiet and thoroughly efficient officer who showed a good understanding of our needs. He would take extra care to reach out to us and ensured we did get into the College routines. He sewed for me a divers vest to wear underneath my uniform on the parade ground during winter. I was given all initial texts, notebooks, and stationery from the College bookstore. We were advised to call back for the replenishment of our exhausted items. The College Library was well stocked and the staff gave us all information we needed to get us started. All new students were registered and given library cards for borrowing books.

The morning routine started in the accommodation wings with a steward offering a cup of tea to each student to wake us up. There was hardly enough time to have a bath or shower in the morning; this had to be done the previous evening. A washbasin with a tap was in each room for us to freshen up and get dressed. The breakfast routine in the mess was brief and then the lectures. The first three weeks of lectures were quite challenging for me as the English language I had been used to was now being spoken with traditional British or Cockney accents. I was the only foreigner in my Division. I resisted forcing myself to report to my Divisional Officer that I found it very difficult to understand the lecturers.

In the first lecture session, I arrived early and took a front seat, and placed my Nigerian traditional leather bag on the long desk shared by about five students. A curious student came and sat near me and asked me if the skin of the animal I killed was used to make the leather bag without processing. I thought he should have admired the traditional craftsmanship that made me proudly use the bag for my lecture materials. I replied that since I lived on trees, I simply grabbed a choice animal at the foot of the tree and skinned it to make the bag. The speed with which he moved away from me kept others away from the long desk. I was isolated and this made it difficult for me to understand some of the jokes by the lecturers.

The drawing and design office instructor I first met thought that I was as knowledgeable as most students in my division who had some basic technical drawing experiences before coming for the first-degree course. The drawing sets and other materials issued were supposed to be familiar to us and we were all expected to set up the drawing paper with clips and start some basic instructions on the use of the drawing instruments. I was in a strange environment and when the instructor observed that I was doing nothing of value and could not follow instructions, he passed beside as he walked around the row of drawing boards. He was having discussions with other students who were tasking him with questions. I wondered how I would become an engineer without understanding engineering drawing and design office procedures.

I remembered the late Professor Ayodele Awojobi of the University of Lagos who observed that Nigerian engineering students naturally had difficulty coping with engineering drawings. This was due to their early childhood backgrounds without toys that children in developed countries had access to and which helped them to develop their appreciation of different shapes.

I noticed that engineering drawing did not require much spoken English grammar as in other lectures. It was the appreciation of shapes and the use of drawing instruments to communicate and express engineering ideas. I needed to spend more time on this important subject at the heart of engineering communication. I enquired and the instructor told me that I could come into the drawing office at any time and sign for the keys and practice.

I met my Divisional Officer and told him that the first three weeks of lectures had been useless to me due to difficulty in understanding the lecturers. He looked worried and promised to look into it. He invited me to a meeting with the Head of the Complementary Studies Department, a grey-haired Commander at a time that did not interfere with the lectures.

Both of us were relaxed and we had general discussions. I did not know what to expect. Some students were asking me how long I hoped to hang on before dropping out of the course because they knew that I had reported that I was not able to follow the lectures in the strange English accent. But in the end, I was happy when the Commander authoritatively told me that I had an excellent command of the English language and that I spoke well with clarity. I told him that my problems were with short expressions and new phrases such as 'articulated lorry.' I wanted to know what an articulated lorry looked like.

He paused for a few seconds and told me that the solution to my problem was very simple and would require a few minutes of my free period. I had to go into the English language laboratory and listen to a selection of recorded tapes. I used the laboratory thrice and my problem was solved substantially. I dropped my beautifully crafted leather bag and bought a brown tarpaulin RN bag which blended with others. Besides, I started changing my seating positions to mix with other students.

The lectures became more intense and I was beginning to enjoy them. Thermodynamics had a dedicated lecturer, Lieutenant Commander R Taylor while the Dean of the College, Captain Henry E Morgan took us in small group (3-4) tutorials. My division was divided into smaller groups of threes and fours to face the Dean for tutorials of a difficult subject. At the Naval Base in Lagos, the sight of a Lieutenant Commander sent us Midshipmen running to hide from view. And now Midshipman Isa had to face a grey-haired stern-looking but caring RN Captain for tutorials. He was patient and methodical. The Dean patiently tested our grasp of the fundamentals in turns. He assessed first hand those who would make it.

The first term of the first year had quite a lot of interesting moments and important decisions were made about registration with the Council for National Academic Awards (CNAA) and progressing with the degree course. I could not be registered along with other first-year students for the mechanical engineering degree course with CNAA. I did not have my NDA Certificate of Education (NDACE) which was to complement my London GCE A-Level results and the basis for accepting me on the course.

The NDACE was no longer acceptable as all graduates of NDA had not been able to successfully earn an engineering degree from Manadon. I was allowed complementary use of the NDACE in which I had high grades in the three subjects required for the engineering degree course. Towards the last week of November 1974, my Divisional Officer called me and told me to go and see the Dean, Captain Henry E Morgan. I was not briefed on why I was going to see the Dean. The Dean informed me calmly but firmly that my NDACE had not arrived from Nigeria and that I was the only student who had not been registered with CNAA. He made it clear that I had been illegally attending lectures and the College was well past halfway into the first term. He then informed me that I had to pack my belongings and leave the College. I had been withdrawn. I was speechless. He told me to take my leave from his office.

As I turned towards the exit door, I heard him say that I was doing well but my system, which is the Nigerian system, had failed me. I froze at the exit door as I heard that I was good and Nigeria was bad. He added that he had been having problems with the bad Nigerian system. Instantly, I lost control of whatever was preventing me from talking. I turned to face the Dean again as if in a rage. I could not bear to hear that I was good and my country was bad. Almost in tears, I said: "Sir, just tell me that I have not measured up to the standards and that I have failed. It is I who is bad and failed my country. I will be more comforted with such an assessment sir."

The Dean was visibly shaken but composed. He paused for a few seconds as he fixed his gaze on me, a miserable Midshipman blotting out nonsense. The good man, Captain Henry E Morgan, the Dean, and my thermodynamics tutorial master, calmly told me to leave my belongings at the College but leave the College and report to the Nigerian Defence Adviser at 9 Northumberland Avenue, London, to see what could be done.

I gathered myself and was grateful that he, a man who commanded with much authority, was not annoyed with me and respectfully left his office. I went and told my Divisional Officer that I had been asked to leave my belongings behind and report to the Defence Adviser. I also briefed Midshipman Daniel E Opuoro of my journey to London and made my way to Plymouth British Rail station the following morning.

I reported to the Deputy Defence Adviser (Navy), Lieutenant Commander E O Omotehinwa who had been briefed by the College authorities. He directed that I should be accommodated at a hotel in St John's Wood area of London while he made efforts to get the required documents including the certificates from the authorities in Nigeria. I reported daily at the Defence Adviser's office and monitored his efforts to get a response from Nigeria. I had spent just over two weeks in London and it was towards the second week of December 1974 that response came from NDA. The Deputy Defence Adviser decided to phone the Dean and brief him of the efforts made so far. The Dean directed that I should return to the College with the statement of result taken from the University of Ibadan statement of result sheet available at NDA. I reported back to continue with the degree programme while moves to get the required documents related to the syllabi for the three subjects for NDACE went on. The certificate was also expected.

I returned to the College on 06 December 1974. I had missed two weeks of lectures and course work. The general mood was simply that of getting away for the Christmas break to resume the first Monday of the New Year 1975. The social programme was the College Christmas Ball that I was detailed to keep sentry duties as I did not register to take part. This applied to other students who did not register. The academic programme was geared to the progress examination which would start immediately after the College resumed after the Christmas break.

Sub Lieutenant Adetoye Sode attending a marine engineering specialisation course and Midshipman Dan Opuoro informed me of the serious concern expressed by Midshipman John Coulthard, Royal Navy, who pestered them for information about what was happening to me. They were surprised at his concern for me. He seemed to have faith that I would be back. When he saw that I had returned, he was relieved and told me that he would help me to catch up on the lectures and notes and other programmes I had missed for over two weeks. I submitted the essential laboratory work reports and updated my lecture notes files, and collected all tutorial handouts.

Midshipman Coulthard was inspiring and available to assist me. He was a great asset and our friendship deepened with mutual respect. The next four weeks were critical as I tried to catch up. I submitted the assignments I missed before the break. There were barely any lectures during the week that ended with the Christmas Ball. My thoughts were fixed on the Progress Examination in less than three weeks. I decided not to travel to have the first Christmas holiday in England; a dream. But I would remain at the College to catch up and prepare for the examinations. St Peter's Catholic Church was just about a hundred meters away from the College entrance gate facing Crownhill residential area. I updated myself with the season's Mass routines for Christmas. I submitted my name on a register for those staying around for the Christmas break at the College Mess reception. It was a lonely list. Indeed there was hardly anyone in sight for most of the days.

The meals provided during the holidays were for the lonely ones as they were mainly cold buffet. The Wardroom Mess Great Hall for dining was not opened. Meals were prepared and arranged on a table at the lobby for self-service. I entertained myself with my books, lecture notes, tutorial handouts, and the Radio Diffusion system that provided news and music to relax.

I attended the Christmas Vigil Mass at St Peter's Catholic Church and also went for the Nativity Mass on the morning of 25 December 1974. As I exited the church after the Nativity Mass, I noticed an elderly man beckoning me from an elevated ground in front of the church exit doors. I reciprocated by walking towards him through the crowd. He stepped down from the heights and greeted me warmly, wishing me a merry Christmas. He informed me that he looked for me after the Vigil Mass and could not locate me and was determined not to miss me this time. It was dark outside after the Vigil Mass and it was very easy for any typical dark African to blend and vanish into the night. He asked me if anyone had invited me for Christmas and I told him that I was being catered for at the College. He invited me to spend Christmas day with his family. He gave me time to come over to the College gate from where he would pick me for the drive to his residence at 168 Fort Austin Avenue, Crownhill, Plymouth. Mr Walter Wedlake was a Second World War veteran who served in the Royal Air Force.

He picked me up at the College gate at the appointed time and drove me to his residence where his wife, a tall lovely beautiful elderly lady, welcomed me as if I was her child. Her name is Nan. She was the second wife of Walter and they had a son named Peter. John is the first son by the first wife who was late. Nan made me feel at home. I had joined Walter and Nan for a typical English Christmas day celebration. I was put through the ritual for the special Christmas cake, its liquor content and the roasted turkey and the stuffing. I surrendered myself to my gracious hosts and enjoyed the day together with some of their relations. John and

Peter were not around for Christmas. Both were married and called to wish their parents a Merry Christmas. I was treated with special recognition in their telephone conversations. The foundation for a very special and close family relationship was thus laid. The family introduced me to the idea of visiting historic sites such as the residence of Sir Francis Drake near Tavistock near Plymouth and Cotehele Castle.

The College resumed from the Christmas break on the first Monday after the New Year. The Progress Examinations were held to start the new term. I had tried to use the Christmas break to prepare. The examination results were collated and lectures resumed. Few lecturers returned our examinations scripts they marked. I was in the drawing office preparing to start a session about two weeks after the progress examination when my Divisional Officer came in wearing a smile. He looked at a small notebook in his hands and told me that I had done well in the examinations and went on to congratulate me with a broader smile. He told me that based on my performance, the College had registered me for the mechanical engineering degree programme with the CNAA. This lifted my spirit greatly. Lieutenant Peter Hadden told me to settle down and concentrate on my studies as I had been fully and legally accepted as a student for the degree programme. I was instantly relieved of the anxiety of waiting for documents from Nigeria. The threat of being expelled from the College vanished and instantly I could proudly feel that I was a student at RNEC.

I phoned the Deputy Defence Adviser in London to thank him for his efforts in getting me on the degree course. He congratulated me profusely, stating that my impressive performance in the progress examinations was conveyed to him by the College authority and I had done Nigeria proud. He urged me to stay focused. I will always remember this period as a defining moment of the finest impression RNEC, Manadon, made on me. I will continue to value and respect the United Kingdom and the Royal Navy for the high-quality personnel in their institutions and the manner my issue had been expertly managed.

It was not long after that I was informed by the Deputy Defence Adviser that I had been commissioned and promoted to Acting Sub Lieutenant with effect from 12 December 1974. I had happy news to share with my Divisional Officer. Some days later, there was a Divisional-Run-Ashore attended also by our Divisional Officer at a pub where I performed the tradition of buying drinks for all members of my Division. I wore my traditional kaftan and a hand embroidery cap which was admired by my mates for its many colours. This was the most important month of January for me; January 1975.

I continued to settle into the College routines and attend to matters that had been on hold as my future in the College was subjected to uncertainties as narrated. Gieves and Hawkes of Savile Row supplied me with the necessary outfits for normal and ceremonial outings including the mess dresses. I had a minor challenge of learning how to tie bow ties and it was considered inappropriate to use the ties with clips. The stiff collars and stiff fronted shirts for mess guest nights and other ceremonials proved difficult. After I succeeded in putting it all together, I found myself stiff and conscious of attachments. At the mess dinners for special guests when stiff fronted shirts were worn with stiff neck collars, it was difficult for me to enjoy the sumptuous meals. The outfits made me eat at attention as if I was on a parade ground.

An arrangement was made for me to go in a car from the College to collect some items of clothing from the Naval Stores at HMS DRAKE Naval Base. I was at the main entrance into the Administration Block at the appointed time when I saw a staff car with the Captain of the College, Captain William Thomas Pillar, in the back seat. The staff car came to the spot for the Captain to get out of the car. He came out and I saluted him. He smiled at me and acknowledged my fidgety efforts and walked into the building. I was still waiting for the car to take me to appear when the driver of the vehicle that brought the Captain came to me and asked if I was Isa. I confirmed that I was. He asked me to get into the same car that brought the Captain of the College. He said he was detailed to take me to HMS DRAKE. I got into the front passenger seat perplexed and wondering what type of military set up would allow me to use the same car as the Captain of the College.

At HMS DRAKE, all my items were available and I signed for them. I was driven back to the College. The Captain would later in his illustrious career be promoted to four-star Admiral and appointed Commandant of the Royal College of Defence Studies and Third Sea Lord. He was the first engineer officer in the Royal Navy to achieve these feats. He was an icon of the old specialization which spearheaded revolutionary changes in the Royal Navy that overcame branch divisive tendencies which adversely affected naval developments. He encouraged generations of engineering officers to believe and remember that they were first and foremost essentially naval officers who had specialized and not the other way round. This was what he imparted and what I learnt about him and took note of. It was a rare opportunity to serve under his command as an engineering student at RNEC, Manadon. He gave me a lot of career headwinds.

Midshipman Coulthard had his room on the ground floor of the West Wing. I changed accommodation to the West Wing Block ground floor basement with more comfortable rooms and we became very close and worked out our evening studies routines. After dinner, we devoted about 30 minutes to watching BBC TV and Independent TV programmes of our choice and thereafter go to our rooms for studies till 2300 hours. At exactly 2300 hours, he would walk into my room and fill my electric kettle with water and switch it on to boil water for tea. It was over our cups of tea that we discussed the day and any problems related to our studies before retiring to bed.

Coulthard was a soft-spoken, serious, and reserved person. If he did not see me at weekends, he would knock on my door to find out how I was doing. He was very intelligent and focused. John set the standard of academic performance for us. It was speculated that some lecturers would like to score him 110 over 100 if they were allowed to do so. Some of our course mates had to resit some subjects because John set so high a standard that the cut off marks had to be raised. It was difficult to distract him from his studies. He was only interested in playing cricket during the summer months. Some of our course mates approached me to encourage him to devote more time to sports and socials to wear him down. I spoke with John and advised him but he was not the sportsman but promised to do some socials. I promised him assistance and companionship.

I was more into sports such as table tennis, field hockey, cross country racing, and athletics in which I was in the College teams. The College had excellent facilities for sports and recreation in addition to the excellent academic facilities. We were often told to define our involvement in sports and academics for a balanced development of naval officers first and foremost and then a naval engineer. This was the ultimate challenge for the naval engineering students on the first-degree programme at Manadon. Lecturers were involved in all College activities, including sports and we were well monitored.

Students whose studies were suffering because of their involvement in sports and other recreational activities were advised to scale down and devote more time to meet their academic objectives. I remember that the Captain of the College 1st XI Hockey Team was asked to hand over to a Midshipman a year behind him to enable him to devote more time to his studies. His captainship duty, in his second year, was affecting his studies. I went on a two days weekend camping exercise on the Dartmoor with some members of my Division under the guidance of our Divisional Officer. Our camping gears were prepacked and delivered to us to get acquainted. I was loaned the sweater of the wife of my coursemate Sub Lieutenant Paul Cariss as he noticed that I did not have appropriate warm clothing for the cold on the moors. We had a pleasant camping exercise and ended up with a pub run before returning to the College.

I had not learnt how to drive a car by the time I arrived at RNEC. I could only ride motorcycles while in Nigeria before joining NDA. My coursemate Sub Lieutenant Steve George had a small two-door Austin car and he offered to give some driving lessons. My first and only attempt was not impressive. I could hardly move the car but I was excited that I was at the wheels for the first time.

Steve advised me to enrol with a driving school as their cars had dual controls installed for safety. I decided to enrol in a driving school after the first year examinations and the commencement of the second year in the autumn of 1975. I made time to go for driving lessons and was scheduled for a test in early spring 1976. The test went on smoothly during the drive through traffic and as we returned to the test centre I met a crowd of instructors and their students for test watching my approach. I was asked to pack inline between two cars. As I reversed into space the engine stalled. That was all I needed to fail my first attempt.

I was rescheduled for another test some weeks later. Nan was annoyed when she heard that I failed my first test. She told me to get rid of my driving instructor so that she would take over the responsibility to prepare me for the second test. This she did and on my second attempt, as I was pulling out of the test centre, the examiner asked me to turn right on to Mannamead Road but I executed a left turn. He was quiet and observed me struggling with my blunder. He let me continue driving and when I noticed that he was not giving me further instructions, I apologized for executing a wrong turn. He then started giving me instructions again for the duration of the test until we returned to the test centre. The parking lot was not congested and I could pack the car following his instructions without stalling. I was pleasantly surprised when on completing the assessment form, he turned to me and said, 'Congratulations. You have passed.'

The Royal Naval Engineering College, Manadon, has been described as "...a place of learning but much more than that alone. It required so much from its students in so many diverse ways that none could meet all of its standards all of the time." (The Royal Naval Engineering College, A Commemoration, Manadon edited by Stephen Haines and Richard Clarke, page 26).

In the words of Admiral William Thomas Pillar, "RNEC provided the mortar which bound the whole Navy together." (Same page 26). In life, there is no bond equal to that formed between people who share a common learning experience. This bond was well understood by Admiral Fisher who sought for all officers of the Navy "…to a certain extent community of knowledge and lifelong community of sentiment. The only machinery which can produce this result is early companionship and community of instruction." As a centre for learning, it was considered that no university was better. I was lucky to experience the tough routines. In addition, I was in a very good company of RN officers as course mates looking after me as their brother.

I had to define my strategy for the next three years to earn the mechanical engineering degree and also experience the development of other faculties for a complete naval officer development. The strategy was simply to take part in as many diverse activities as the academic programme would allow and at the same time not be carried away by the huge demands of the academic programmes. In the same vein, I would not be carried away by extreme indulgence in sports and social activities. I ensured that whatever activity I undertook would be given adequate attention. I was introduced to The International Institute for Strategic Studies, London. The publications I subscribed to included Adelphi Papers, Strategic Survey, and Military Balance. The Journal of Naval Engineering, a Royal Navy publication was also easily available among other publications.

The academic programmes were hectic and very interesting. The major problem I had was with engineering drawing and this needed extra time to enable me to pass the subject at a first attempt in the first year. This was a major headache for several students. Students were allowed to carry it over into the second year. But I succeeded in passing the subject at my first attempt. John and I had good studies ethics and on all joint projects, we paired up for assignments for the first two years. It was only in the third and final year that we did individual research projects. We strictly adhered to not working late into the night beyond 1100 hours even during revisions for examinations.

As I progressed in my studies, I received letters from some officers of NN in Lagos and on courses in India. Lieutenant Ibrahim J Ogohi (later Admiral and Chief of Defence Staff) and Sub Lieutenant Shaibu

Amodu (later Rear Admiral) wanted to know how I was progressing with my programme. They advised me to withdraw from the course if I found it too tough and could not cope and go for a course that would set me on a path to specialize as a seaman officer (executive branch officer). They must have known about the problem that led to my brief withdrawal from the College. I coined a phrase thus in my replies to the letters 'The battle of Manadon rages and it is fierce.' I refused to entertain any idea about not being able to make it and could not bear to think of withdrawing because of any challenges.

The first year Part I examination was held between 16 June-02 July 1975. My nightmare subject was engineering drawing and I devised a way to ensure I did enough in the examination to pass. The lecturers in charge had advised us to avoid repeating a form established and which would be used repeatedly to have a complete drawing once the essential sequence was correctly established so that more time would be spent on the main drawing. This approach helped me and I was assured I had done enough to pass.

The mechanics of machines was a tough call and I had a reference. I pitied the lecturer who thought he gave us very simple questions but the unusually high number of students who did not pass suggested there was something wrong. Other subjects did not give us as much challenge. I passed Part 1 and I was notified to proceed to the second year or Part II. It was a relief.

Daniel and I went on a cruise on a Nigerian Merchant Navy vessel from Bristol Avon-mouth to Liverpool Docks. We spent more time alongside Liverpool Harbour and had a good tour of the city. We visited the Nigerian National Shipping Line office in Liverpool and we were impressed with the worldwide spread of Nigerian merchant ships.

In the second year, Daniel and I bought an old car that had gone well past the second user. I had driven the car into the college workshop bay to do some repairs when a light grey Austin car was driven in. The driver, wearing a white overall came out and started checking the nearby ramp to take his car. His grey hair drew my attention and I realized that he was the Captain of the College, Captain William T Pillar. I rushed to help him but he stopped me and told me that he was on his own and needed no help. The few students who were around and were used to minding their business only saluted him and carried on with their work. The Captain finished his work, cleaned the bay, and drove his car away.

What other lessons did I need in leadership on how to make things work for the common good? Leadership by example? Absolutely yes.

These were ingrained in my young mind as a Midshipman and Acting Sub Lieutenant. I had arrived at Manadon with an open mind to learn lessons and grow by continuous education and training, unbroken so far since my primary school days.

The years 1974 to 1976 were trying times for the UK government defence and security agencies because of the Irish Republican Army (IRA) bombings on the mainland. After the famous Birmingham pub bombing of 21st November 1974, the South-Western part of the UK was threatened and put on alert. Plymouth had a major Naval Base and other military establishments. The RNEC had prepared to react to the IRA threats of attacks and bombings. Threat level warning signs were conspicuously displayed and we were constantly briefed on what to do.

Students were placed on sentry duty watch at the gates and other selected key points and locations after lecture hours and up to late-night hours. At the highest threat level warning, all designated areas were manned by students after lecture hours and throughout the night. There were assigned security operatives that were effectively in charge but hardly seen when students manned their posts. In the Winter of 1974/1975 when the IRA attack was considered imminent, I was assigned to keep watch at one of the remote gate locations in the early hours of the morning. I was well kitted to survive the night cold. The weapon fit was grossly inadequate because we had been used to a police baton and whistle for protection and raising alarm for support. I reasoned that if an attack was imminent I should not be 'armed' with a police baton and whistle.

I went to the Officer of the Day (OOD) and demanded to know from him the weapons the IRA were expected to use for the attack. He gave me a good professional response. I replied that I was inadequately armed to respond to an attack by the IRA. I requested for an appropriate weapon(s) to be issued to me from the College armoury.

The OOD was taken by surprise. He stared at me for a few seconds and gave me an answer that was left to my imagination to interpret. I took leave of him and went to wait for further instructions. It was not long before I was informed that I had been relieved of my sentry duty watch. The following morning as I signed off duty just before lectures, I saw members of a ready force with intimidating combat gear and appropriate weapons patrolling the College grounds. All students were taken off duty and the experts were in charge. I went to lectures feeling secure that the system was functioning and we were all in very safe hands. I was very impressed and this greatly endeared me to the system.

I was doing quite well in academics and sporting activities and made friendships. I was a regular member of the College 1ˢᵗ XI Hockey team and represented the College in Cross Country races. I was a member of the College team that played in the Plymouth Table Tennis league. In the summer months, I played lawn tennis with my friends. A senior course colleague Sub Lieutenant Richard A Harrison who was pursuing a degree in electrical engineering would always invite me to have a game with him. His coursemate Sub Lieutenant Dave J Iron was into cross country races and would also invite me to have some evening runs during autumn and winter months.

I had a German Naval officer, Lieutenant Friedhelm L Stappen, who engaged me in table tennis during winter and would always come around to fix a match and have fun. He introduced me to a squash racquets game and I learnt and loved to play it. Friedhelm was in the electrical engineering 1974 stream. I would later discover that the circle of friends I was attracted to were very serious with their academic pursuits. I used this circle of close friends to moderate my involvement in sports and recreational activities as we casually compared notes regarding how our courses were progressing. I had friends across mechanical and electrical engineering disciplines as well as my seniors. Sub Lieutenants Ku Yuen Mun and Ong Nee Hock were my course mates from Malaysia. Both had Malaysian girlfriends studying in the neighbouring county of Cornwall and on occasions, we organized social activities and sight-seeing at weekends at Lands End, Truro, and Falmouth. Ong later married his girlfriend on their return to Malaysia.

In the autumn of 1975, I was part of the College Hockey 1ˢᵗ XI team that visited the Royal Netherlands Naval College at Den Helder, near Amsterdam, from 29 October to 02 November 1975. I thought I was covered by the NATO group travel document and College RN Service identity card and therefore did not need a visa. But at Hoek, the immigration officer asked for my passport and decided to stop me from entry for having no visa. Others were allowed to proceed to Amsterdam. Lieutenant Commander J R Smith, a staff member of the Hockey Team, remained with me while contacts were made to seek authorization for my entry. After I was cleared to enter the country, we were able to meet the bus to the relief of the team members.

At Den Helder, we were accommodated at Willemsoord Naval Barracks. After lunch, we had team training and had three matches during our tour with the Naval College, Netherlands Navy Team, and Watagenzen Hockey Club team. I can hardly remember the scores but we had our fun. The other attractions at the Naval Base were my first close contact with a submarine and the use of a bicycle by the guest of honour, a senior naval officer in uniform. It was a break from the hectic routines at Manadon and it was well worth it because we carried away good memories with jokes about our conduct in the dressing rooms. We departed Den Helder at 0730 hours on 02 November and arrived in Plymouth by the same route at 0700hours on 03 November.

In the spring of 1976, Friedhelm took me by surprise when he informed me that his parents in Germany at Castrop-Rauxel near Dusseldorf had agreed to have me over for the three weeks of Easter break. He sorted out my visa application with the German Embassy in London and I flew from Heathrow to Dusseldorf from where we drove to Castrop-Rauxel and arrived at a very warm family reception. The parents vacated their master bedroom for both of us to share. I was overwhelmed.

Friedhelm made me feel at home by explaining the German food culture and his mother's special cuisine. In the evenings Friedhelm and I would play chess. It was fun and when we were tired, we went to bed. His mother released her car to us to drive down to Mayen to visit Friedhelm's elder brother and his family and thence to the Alpine Ski resort of Oberstoff and Zinthofen where the family had their holidays. At the holiday resort of Oberstoff, we stayed at a family guest inn. I was introduced to two daughters of the owner. The older daughter was very close to Friedhelm. He had planned to marry her but she was not keen to leave the southern part of Germany and family for the North where most naval facilities are located and where Friedhelm's naval career would play out. We had an evening out with the two sisters and had a very good dinner tasting the local foods.

On resumption from the Easter holiday break in 1976, the weather was warm and the prospects for a good summer were bright. There were many outdoor activities. There was a boat show in Plymouth which Friedhelm and I attended and we got an invitation to another one in Portsmouth on a weekend. We continued our German safari together and we set out for Portsmouth for the weekend. On our return leg, we decided to break our journey and spend the night in Bread and Breakfast Inn. We shared a double bed.

After the end of the second-year examinations, we had a week of industrial visits to selected areas in the UK. Friedhelm and I managed to get on the same list to visit Glasgow between 5-9 July 1976. The visiting teams were accommodated at Hamilton Teacher Training College,

Bothwell Road, Hamilton, Lanarks. The industries we visited were Philips, National Engineering Laboratory, British Steel, Honeywell, and General Motors Scotland Limited. The industrial visit featured in our overall degree programmes covering many parts of the UK.

I had very interesting information during industrial visits about the impressive procurement of military hardware for the Nigerian Armed Forces and especially the Nigerian Navy in the UK and Europe. There was intense competition among industries to be part of the acquisition programs. I was frequently asked questions by the executives of industries about the impressive range of equipment covered and was proud that the leadership of the country under the Head of State General Olusegun O Obasanjo GCFR was giving me very bright career prospects. It was inspiring to note that the rare experiences of the Nigerian civil war were brought to bear in the impressive acquisition programs.

I also got to know the efforts NN was making regarding the procurement of warships and how several defence industries were competing to be part of the procurement processes. I was taken to task on some occasions to explain what was driving Nigeria's procurements. I was really surprised at the scope of the procurement activities in Europe and the diversity of defence industries involved. The Complementary Studies programmes offered guidance and I subscribed to publications of The International Institute for Strategic Studies, Adams Street, London. I had access to Adelphi Papers, Strategic Survey, and Military Balance among others. These enabled me to understand some of the related issues, the international politics of arms sales, and strategic thinking. In later years I was able to relate with the Defence Policy post-civil war which was concise in summing up Nigeria's military strategic thinking that captured the experiences of the civil war, threats and aspirations that shaped the most profound military hardware procurement the Armed Forces of Nigeria has ever embarked upon. This defined the Wey-Soroh-Adelanwa era I will elaborate upon later. It was inspiring though acquisition targets were never met.

The College had lecturers from the University of Exeter for the Complementary Studies programme in addition to the resource persons within. These covered Industrial Archaeology, Law and Engineer, English Literature, Britain and British Institutions, Politics and International Affairs, Technology and Society. These lecture series studies broadened our world view and military affairs for the balanced development of a military officer. These lectures guided my investment in books such as 'Low-Intensity Operations' and the 'Bunch of Five' by Brigadier Frank Kitson of the British Army covering various aspects of irregular warfare. These books, among several others, have remained a source of reference on irregular warfare to date.

The mechanical engineering first-degree course programme had heavy doses of electrical and electronic engineering in line with current trends in equipment and machinery designs and the relevant transformation envisaged by the RN Engineering Branch re-organisation that transferred responsibilities for High Electric Power Generation and Distribution to the Marine Engineering branch. Also, automation, remote control, and surveillance demanded a good grasp of electrical and electronic systems by marine engineers. It was exciting to be among the generation of naval engineers that were educated and trained to spearhead this transformation.

I was put on notice by the leader of the study group during a dinner with the group regarding the challenges ahead on my return to NN. I sat next to him during the dinner and he explained to me the need to take note of the requirements for this transformation as NN had been informed and would need drivers of the process in Nigeria for efficient management of modern sophisticated warships.

I successfully scaled through the second year Part II examinations in June 1976 and I began to look ahead to a very exciting summer and to prepare for the final year Part III. John and I had a joint second-year project which we did not manage properly but what we presented was enough to get us through. I learnt some lessons regarding planning and expectations to meet time targets. We were notified of research project topics and proposals for the final year on the noticeboard. I was attracted to a vibration topic titled "Transverse Vibration of Free-Free Glass Reinforced Plastic Plates."

The research proposal involved understanding and integrating a new computer software programme with the College system. The Glass Reinforced Plastic (GRP) plates were an emerging technology for the construction of a class of warship but there was no analytical tool to study its characteristics like the metal plates that were widely used. I was aware of the experience of a senior student who was very good at computing and had a project that required a similar demand for integration and the use of a new software programme. He spent all the time on the software integration and eventually did not have time to use it to do the project. Indeed, he was unable to integrate the programme into the College system. Eventually, he was assessed on the efforts made with the software integration.

I got to know about this during one of our hockey bus rides for a game with a club in the Plymouth area. I tinkered with the idea of plans A and B and set a time limit for the switch to get the project done. I started my degree course in 1974 using a slide rule that could be used for all relevant calculations. Later, simple electronic calculators were allowed just as the use of computers was introduced and generated tremendous activities in the College. Computers enabling more sophisticated calculations have become an integral part of engineering studies. The impact was phenomenal that at a stage I was doing an assignment and when I was challenged with a 2+2 problem, I reached for a calculator to make sure that the answer would be 4. I had to be careful with very attractive computer applications that completely take over my mental capacity to solve problems.

The summer of 1976 was very warm and drought was reported in some places in the UK. On completing our second-year examinations in early July, I still had not decided how to spend the summer. I was walking back to the West Wing block when I met Sub Lieutenant Ku Yuen Mun. He asked me where I would be spending the summer holidays. I told him that I had not decided. He informed me that he spent the 1975 summer travelling in Europe with Sub Lieutenant Ong Nee Hock and made use of campsites to save the cost of hotel bills. The camping kits were from the College. I showed interest and got to know that the College Expedition store was very well stocked with a variety of gears for diverse outdoor activities including camping and I could draw a complete set of campsite survival gears and also map reading items for my leisure.

Ku and Ong had decided on a date to leave but I could not join them immediately because Daniel lost his father back home in Nigeria and I had to drive him to Heathrow Airport, London, on his way home. I later joined them at Dinar Farm campsite in Bangor, North Wales. Sub Lieutenant Andrew O Momodu who was on the Weapon Engineering Application course made a late entry and joined us as we completed the Welsh and Midlands legs covering campsites outside Bangor, Carmarthen, Swansea, Cardiff, and Cotswold Hills. We spent two days in the Cotswold Hills in the English Midlands and headed for the Lake District and Carlisle. The Lake District was at its best with the very warm summer and we had a lot of outdoor activities in the countrysides and tourist areas. Hexham near the coastal town of Newcastle-upon-Tyne was our next stop. The campsite was the largest we had used so far and it was congested. We spent about three days there. We became familiar with the Cook family, our campsite neighbour, and their two grown-up daughters Joana and her elder sister who was an undergraduate at the University of Newcastle. The two sisters asked to join us on a short cross country run with Andrew and me. We had a warm family evening.

Andrew had to detach and return to Plymouth to prepare and resume at HMS COLLINGWOOD, Portsmouth where he would continue his Weapon Engineering Application Course on completion of the Manadon phase of the course. He left Inverness with Ong Nee Hock and I had to take Ku Yuen Mun with me in my car for the rest of the tour. Ku and I decided to push further up North to the northernmost town of Wick. We stopped at Dornock and decided that there was no prize for reaching Wick because we were exhausted.

The Edinburgh annual festival was in full swing and in the last week of August 1976. We spent two days at a campsite outside Edinburgh and attended the Military Tattoo at the Edinburgh castle that was part of the festival. The display of the Gurkhas impressed me and their history of performances in battles was inspiring for a military professional. Ku had contacted a relation of his at Telford who ran a restaurant business to host us for a night. This would be the first time in three weeks that we would stay and sleep in a house. We had a good night's rest and after breakfast the following day, we called off our camp life and returned to Plymouth.

Back in Plymouth, I had some days to spare before resuming for the Part III academic year. I had information that NNS DORINA had completed a refit programme with Vosper Thornycroft Shipyard at Portsmouth and was at Portland for a work-up routine with the RN. The Commanding Officer (CO) was Commander (later Commodore) AA Ajanaku. He was the most senior Ebira naval officer followed by Lieutenant Commander (later Rear Admiral) HM Sani. As a Midshipman on board NNS NIGERIA, I knew there was no junior officer from Ebiraland that I could relate with and I would have to make an effort to get close to the two senior officers and introduce myself.

I managed to attend the naming ceremony of Lieutenant Commander Sani's child in Lagos in 1974 before my departure for Manadon without getting close to him for an introduction. I felt that as a Sub Lieutenant I should travel to Portland and introduce myself to the CO. At the Naval Base at Portland, I went on board NNS DORINA and went to greet the officers in the Wardroom and find out how I can see the CO. I was asked to approach the steward who told me that the best time to see him was after lunch when he was busy reading the newspapers and relaxed. The steward came to the Wardroom later and signalled me that the CO had finished his lunch. I knocked on his open door to draw his attention and he took a glance at me. I introduced myself and added in Ebira language that I was an Ebira man. I then told him that I was leaving for Plymouth and I took my leave. I was so glad that I was able to see him. I had achieved my aim.

I was close to the family of the new Deputy Dean of the College, Captain (later Rear Admiral) John Franklin. I attended the College Catholic Chapel where I served mass on Sundays. His four children, two girls, and two boys were close to me and I would invite the boys to the College sports halls especially the squash racquets. Sarah and Michael were undergraduates at the University of London and Nottingham studying social sciences and architecture respectively. The other two were still in high school. In my interactions with the family, I learnt some aspects of the discipline of frugal management of resources.

On 8th December 1976, RNEC 1st XI Hockey Team was in Portsmouth for the final of the RN Hockey championship match with HMS NELSON, the Royal Naval Marine Engineering School, Gosport, Portsmouth. I was used to celebrating my birthday quietly and I did not inform members of our team. The match was keenly contested. I played in the outside left position and just ensured I got the crosses through to our strikers, Ong Nee Hock and Allan York. They were the most skilled players in the team in addition to Phil Carr in defence. Both York and Carr were RN Commanders by rank and Heads of Department at the College.

We had a very good team spirit and it was scoreless at full time. The first half of the extra time allowed us to win the championship when we were awarded a penalty flick. It was taken by Allan York who missed it. Our opponents scored a goal and won the championship. We received our runner's up prize with a commendation for our team effort. I did not let the team know that the day we lost the RN championship was my birthday. It took me several days to get over the loss. It was painful for us to have so narrowly lost the match. Allan York was full of apology and never agreed to take any penalty flick for the team again.

The Cook family invited me over for Christmas 1976 at Barton-Under-Needwood in Staffordshire. I asked Daniel to come along with me as the two sisters would leave for Inverness to camp and work on a farm after Boxing Day to earn some money to supplement their allowances. Dan and I had taken delivery of our Lancia cars and as we had to carry extra camping loads for the two girls, we drove the two cars to Staffordshire. We arrived in the afternoon of Christmas eve and had a pub run in the evening with other youths. We were with local youths who drove us round in their cars. Christmas day was marked with the traditional family meals. On Boxing day, I was invited to join a hockey team for a match. The match was a draw. Joana and her elder sister felt disappointed because they had boasted that I would make a difference.

The two teams had a pub run and a good boxing day atmosphere. We set out on the morning of 27 December 1976 for Inverness and stopped over at Newcastle. The drive the following day to Inverness was long but my camping experience in the summer in the area made parts of the route familiar and I was able to show Dan some of the places we visited during the summer with Andrew and my two Malaysian friends. We spent the night at Inverness after dropping the two sisters at a farm camp and the following day we set off for Edinburgh to visit Captain (later Lieutenant Colonel) Gabriel A Nyam, and Nottingham to visit Captain (later Major General) Patrick A Akpa and his young family. Both of them, of the Nigerian Army, were our seniors of the 9th Regular Course at NDA, Kaduna.

In the evening at Nottingham, Akpa took us to visit Mr Joseph Makoju who graduated from the University of Nottingham with an engineering degree and was in industrial training. Though we did not meet him at home, years later I told him of our visit when I visited him at Ewekoro Portland Cement factory in Ogun State in 1992 where he was the Managing Director. I was a Commander then and was looking for allocation of cement to build my country home in Okene.

The final year was in full swing. My choice of a research project had been approved. I had done some preliminary searches on related topics to understand the nature of glass-reinforced plastic (GRP) plates (woven roven and chopped strand forms) and the relevant theories and practices related to past works on vibration of steel plates that were well established. There was nothing on GRPs and I had to rely on works on metallic plates. I decided on a method used by Mary Warburton in the late 1800s. I thought it was out of place to rely on a method used about 100 years ago but went into the details and related theories. I used this as my plan A and familiarized myself with the computer-based method for plan B.

Lieutenant Commander Mike North was my project supervisor. I kept to the schedule of the brief on the direction of the project and when it came to the stage of the final meeting for my supervisor to approve to proceed with my course of action, I was convinced that the old method was better and would be the better tool to get results for analysis. I sought the assistance of the mechanics' laboratory supervisors and assembled the necessary materials, equipment, and test rig. I had a supply of the GRP plates and studied their characteristics. I prepared to meet my supervisor and convince him to give me the approval to proceed.

The meeting with my project supervisor was a difficult one for both of us. When I thought I had won him over, he would raise a point and draw my attention to the advantages of the new software and the computer-based analytical tool. I did not dare mention my fear of being trapped by the uncertainties of new software and the College computer network system that I found cumbersome though the latest at the time. It was almost time for my supervisor to go for his next lecture and we had to round off. I told my supervisor to allow me to proceed with my first choice and if within two weeks I could not make progress, I would switch to the computer approach. He told me that in his career so far, he had never come across the use of this ancient method and that since it was my project I should feel free to proceed as I had planned.

I rushed to the mechanics laboratory where I had assembled all I needed to start. The test rig and the frequency analyser were set up. I had to drill a slot on the woven roven GRP plate to attach a vibration sensor using Mary Warbutton's theory and related nodal patterns as a guide. The aeroplane rubbers for suspension and means for securing had been readied. The drill I was using was noisy and distracting to other students in their allocated project bays. I used the walkway by the laboratory which was near my project supervisor's office.

I was drilling the slot on a nodal path marked when I saw my project supervisor stopping abruptly as he was rushing to take his lecture. He looked at the nodal pattern drawn on the plate for a guide and the point on a node I was drilling and indicating the set up of my rig and said: "Remember your second-year vibration lectures on this subject and know that you cannot excite the plate where you expect the nodal path to form."

He rushed off and I drilled the right spot nearby. I attached the vibrator accessory and took the subassembly to attach to the vibrator (shaker) with the plate supported on the rig at the four corners with aeroplane rubber. I called the laboratory supervisor to help me check the entire set up with the plate in a free-free mode of suspension as I was going to switch on the equipment and start exciting the plate after spreading the fine grains of pattern indicators. He gave me the go-ahead with some safety instructions and I started cautiously. I generated the first nodal pattern successfully and thereafter I proceeded to generate a few more. In excitement, I rushed into the office of Lieutenant Commander M North and found him relaxing to get some rest before his next session. I told him that I was already generating some nodes.

North sprang to his feet and rushed into the mechanics laboratory and took over the controls generating the same nodal patterns I had generated and I told him the frequencies. He asked me what next. I told him that Mary Warburton had established an array of patterns for a steel plate and if I could replicate them for the GRP plate, then I would be in a good position to determine if the methods for the analysis of metallic plates could be used for GRP plates and this was what the project was all about.

He smiled at me and assured me that he had given approval for me to proceed and I should forget my plan B. What a man! North could have walked past me as he was rushing to meet a lecture schedule and leave me to suffer my lack of understanding of the application of a knowledge he had imparted in my second year. He could have walked past a student who stubbornly stuck to an archaic method. He had many reasons to leave me to suffer and possibly fail. I learnt great lessons from a good man and would always admire him. He genuinely was for progress. Thank you, Mike North.

There was a change of project supervisor when Lieutenant Graham T Reader (later Commander and on retiring, Professor in Canada) was posted to the College and was assigned to me. He was involved in the Stirling engine research effort with other international scholars. He was well briefed and told me to keep to my schedule and brief him on my progress in stages. I was determined to have a draft of the project report ready well ahead of the submission date to make room for corrections and additions. I was surprised when my project supervisor told me that I had done more than enough for a first degree and that what I had achieved would be enough for a master's degree.

He advised me to get a metallic plate of the same dimension as the GRP plates I used and reproduce the nodal patterns I had achieved and note the frequencies at which they were achieved and thereafter conclude and submit my final report as scheduled. I got an aluminium plate from the Materials Department laboratory and concluded my laboratory work and subsequent analysis. I made the final submission and I then started preparing for the final Part III examinations in June 1977. About two weeks into the examinations I started getting feelers that my project was being considered for an award. I still had to prepare for the defence before a panel of examiners. The defence was successful. A few days later, I was informed that I would be meeting with the Deputy Dean, Captain John Franklin.

At the meeting with the Deputy Dean, he profusely praised the work and informed me that my project had won a prize to be presented during the graduation ceremony. He observed that I was not excited about the achievement. I did not even appreciate the importance of the project for warships design and construction though GRP was an emerging material technology at the time. I was doing the project to succeed and be awarded a degree from Manadon, a first for the NN.

What was going on in my mind? It was like letting off pressure from several years of frustrations NN officers have had at the institution and the high attrition rate in the programmes. I narrated how I swam against the unnecessary tide of not being expected to last long before throwing in the towel and withdrawing like all other NN officers before me. This did not create the necessary level playing field. I thought this needed urgent attention for the sake of the incoming students and the ones preparing for their part one examinations. He got up from his seat and paced across the room very worried.

He returned to his seat and asked me what could be done for me to address the situation that had adversely affected me. I told him that the final examinations were a few days away and important decisions had been made early in the course. I explained that I did not want any opportunity for my benefit but pleaded for the NN officers that were behind me starting with those preparing for their Part I examinations. I pleaded that some of the strict procedures that did not allow Nigerian students to successfully go through the degree courses be relaxed. They were psychological issues and not about lowering academic and military standards. Of the thirteen students left in my 74BM Division (group) by the Spring of 1975, seven did not make it to earn a degree. Six of us earned our first degree out of which four won prizes. The attrition in my Division was about 50%.

The Deputy Dean congratulated me again warmly and promised that the College would address the issues I raised regarding a level playing field and high attrition rate. I was not surprised when some changes were introduced immediately, making the three Nigerian officers going through their Part I examinations in June 1977 beneficiaries of the level playing field that Daniel and I never had and which inspired confidence in those that had just done their Part I examinations. According to Nicholas Rescher, morality is geared to the real interest of others in our deliberations and actions. I would later know from Daniel's fiancée in Portsmouth that Daniel thought of withdrawing from the electrical engineering degree course but was encouraged to remain and face the challenges drawing inspiration from the way I handled the serious problems I encountered.

Throughout the course, I had very close relationships with Fred Stappen from the German Navy, Dave Iron of RN, and my closest academic confidant John Coulthard of RN, the best graduating student, all of whom made first-class degrees. I was happy to be recognized for the award of a prize and about the reform I had suggested. Manadon would continue the path of reforms that all great institutions timely undertake and still maintain its extremely high standards. I will always remember the great minds such as the Dean Captain HE Morgan, Deputy Dean Captain J Franklin, and many more that managed RNEC, Manadon. They will always be my inspiration on how to respond to institutional demands for reforms.

I passed my Part III examinations but I did not think I had done my best. It was like a marathon race in which one was determined to complete by crossing the finishing line without any concern about the position. A most important part of the three years degree programme was the continuous assessment in which I was never found wanting. I would be receiving a prize at my graduation on 28th July 1977. I had shifted my focus to the task ahead regarding the marine engineering specialization course. I followed through with the application I had made to Naval Headquarters in autumn 1976 to allow me to proceed with the Marine Engineering Application Course (MEAC) starting September 1977. I received the approval and Daniel also received approval to proceed with the Weapon Engineering Application Course (WEAC). I was happy to get this approval before graduation and this helped to lift my morale and made me better appreciate being the first NDA graduate to earn a mechanical engineering degree from Manadon with a prize as the icing on the cake.

Sub Lieutenant John Coulthard won the Queen's Gold Medal for the best results among student officers at RNEC, Manadon, and Cambridge University (Naval College Entry Officers) on completion of the three years BSc degree course. He also won the prize for the best final year student. Sub Lieutenant Paul Cariss, whose wife gave me her sweater for the spring camping exercise on the moors, and Sub

Lieutenant Steve A George who gave me the first feel of driving a car, were joint project prize winners for the best project in the Department of Mechanical Engineering. Sub Lieutenant DJ Issitt, Royal Navy, and I shared the RNEC Project Prize for the best interdisciplinary BSc degree course project. In the citation, it was stated that the projects of the year 1977 were of 'unusually high standard' and that 'It has been decided to make an exceptional award from RNEC Funds for the best projects in 1977.'

This was the first time at the College that such a prize would be awarded for the best interdisciplinary project. When I was called to receive my prize from Dr E McEwen again after receiving a historic first degree for the NN I fought back tears when I gazed briefly at the Nigerian national flag draped beautifully on a pole on the stage. I was almost singing aloud the Nigerian National Anthem when I realized that 'God Save the Queen' rules in the UK.

After leaving the graduation hall, I took a lonely walk past the Administrative Block, Mechanical Laboratory, and Workshop to reflect briefly on the journey so far and to come to terms that I was holding in my hands a UK CNAA BSc Mechanical Engineering degree certificate from the dreaded RNEC, Manadon, and a historic RNEC Project Prize I never dreamt of winning. The lonely walk continued and I could not utter a word when I walked past Lieutenant Peter Hadden and his wife. He gave me his usual smile. I wished I could hug him and thank him for managing my November 1974 crisis. He had always been a very quiet and reserved officer and I respected him for that.

I had received approval to start the marine engineering course and training by September 1977. I had gotten approval to travel home to Nigeria for the summer holidays following the regulations that allow those on long courses to make such journeys home. Almost all of my RN colleagues would proceed to sea before returning for the application courses. I would be starting the application course with the class ahead of me returning from their sea experiences.

Daniel drove me in our jointly owned old Austin car to London Heathrow Airport early in the morning for my Nigeria Airways flight home. I had informed Sub Lieutenant Ekpenyong E Ita of my arrival details and he promised to receive me at the Lagos International Airport. I arrived on 30 July 1977 and to my surprise, Sub Lieutenant Joseph Ekeng Ewa (NDA Regular Course 10) was also at the airport. Both officers were in uniform to receive me. It was a wonderful gesture from them. Joseph's residence was near the airport and after dropping him off at home, Ekpenyong and I drove to our familiar No 2 Falolu Street, Surulere. Ekpenyong's mother had looked after the items I left behind when I headed for Manadon on 9th September 1974.

I spent a few days in Lagos and took a flight to Kaduna. My cousin was delighted to receive me and was full of prayers for my safe arrival. He reminded me that I was the first in the entire family to travel outside the country and also to earn a degree. He told me we would travel to Okene to be with our family. I was happy to be with him, his wife, and his children. We visited close family friends in Kaduna and prepared for the journey to Okene. There was no prior information regarding my arrival at home and it was a pleasant surprise when we arrived. There was spontaneous rejoicing and singing with praises to Almighty God. My father was full of joy. He ordered his saluting gun, only used in celebrating rare events be brought out. He refused to be persuaded not to fire the gun and had his way. The loud booms rented the air for some minutes. He thereafter went into the sitting room to receive visitors who came to felicitate with him.

My mother was the quiet one but was full of joy which she expressed silently. She repeatedly welcomed me home with 'Nyia'ase,' which is the Ebira word for welcome. She was joined by two of my aunties, Inya Metuhuor and Inya Ayisetu, the mother of Professor Nuhu Omeiza Yaqub. The stream of well-wishers was overwhelming. Their joy was that I had been to England, the first in the family, and was back home safely. We spent the weekend at home and attended Sunday Mass at Christ the King Catholic Church. The memories of the beginning of my primary school flooded my mind. It was nice to be at home.

We left Okene very early in the morning for the drive back to Kaduna and it was still dark. I could not tell them at home that I would be returning to England to continue my engineering education and training to specialize as a marine engineer. It was difficult to explain what it all meant. My father still did not ask why I had joined the military. Throughout my years at NDA, I did not go home. My cousin and I had trusted Mr Joseph Adaba to discuss the matter with my father as he promised to do when he directed my cousin to sign my NDA form in 1972. It was proper to believe that the elders had discussed and agreed. It was when I got to Manadon that I wrote directly to my father stating that I was at a college studying engineering.

I was about to enter the car when I saw my mother standing alone behind the car. I went to her and bade her farewell again. I wanted to capture the special moment by taking a photograph of her with my camera but hesitated as I thought it would draw unnecessary attention. It was the last moment I had with my mother. She passed away on 16 September 1978 while I was at sea on HMS TORQUAY off the coast of Scotland. She was dearly loved and respected.

Back in Kaduna, we visited Kafanchan to see Mr Onotu's family. Anthony Onotu, the first son, and I lived with my cousin at Zonkwa. The trip was to introduce me to Mr Onotu's daughter Theresa who had just finished her secondary school education. We were well received and my cousin must have done a lot of preliminary discussion with the family. I had some private chats with her. She showed me her album and I took two of her photographs away. I promised to keep in touch when I returned to the UK and I kept my word. On our way back my cousin asked for my impression and I informed him that I was keeping an open mind and would make no commitment other than to communicate with her for now as I hardly knew her. It was time to return to Lagos and take the return flight back to the UK.

CHAPTER SIX

The Return to Manadon

I arrived at Heathrow Airport on Friday 2nd September 1977 and took the train to Plymouth because I did not inform Daniel of my exact date of return. He had his summer holiday plans and I did not want to interrupt him.

I started the Marine Engineering Application Course (MEAC) specialisation on the 5th September 1977 in the No 3 Hangar Building. There were three hangar buildings at Manadon dedicated to Air Engineering, Weapon Engineering, and Marine Engineering specializations. The No 3 Hangar is the largest and has an impressive array of model equipment such as steam turbines, boilers, gas turbines, diesel engines, and auxiliaries installed for instructions. There were dedicated rooms and spaces in which real machinery are set up to instruct students on starting, operation, and stopping procedures. We spent the most time on practical work. It was time to face the reality of marine engineering.

Those RN students who had graduated from Manadon a year earlier had already spent one year at sea before coming for this course. Three of us who were foreign students did not have that opportunity and had a hard time learning new terms and systems functioning logic circuits. The routines and high standards at Manadon remained the same. This phase of the course was based on continuous assessments with routine tests on completion of modules and lasted for seven months followed by five months (determined by Nigerian Deputy Defence Adviser) for me on the training ship, HMS TORQUAY, for the acquisition of certificates of competency on various machinery in the Boiler and Main Engine Rooms and Auxiliary Machinery.

The training ship was steam-driven and the only two diesel engines onboard were for electric power generation in addition to the steam-driven ones in the main machinery rooms. I had limited time onboard based on the duration given by the Defence Adviser (Navy) at the Nigerian High Commission. I acquired Auxiliary Machinery and Boiler Room Watch Keeping Certificates and had completed all tasks and passed the written examination for the Steam Engine Room Watch

Keeping Certificate. I had left the ship and could not meet the requirements for the Unit Watch Keeping Certificate despite passing the written examinations. I had to forgo some of the onboard training which were mainly on steam turbines and administration which would largely not apply to the NN. Also, I had been programmed for the Internal Combustion Engines Course at HMS SULTAN, the Marine Engineering School at Gosport as well as the High Electric Power Generation and Distribution Course at HMS COLLINGWOOD, the Weapon Engineering School. There were short courses on Nuclear, Biological, Chemical, and Damage Control (NBCD) at Whale Island that I had to go through. These were more relevant to the NN. I had excellent exposure to grasp foundational principles for skills acquisition and application as a Marine Engineer Officer is expected to make routine judgements on states of the ship related to performances of men and machinery and as in war.

I attended the 1978 New Year party at the residence of Peter and Jane Wedlake at Bradenstoke near Wiltshire and returned to Plymouth on the 1st of January. This was followed by an engagement party a few weeks later at Shoreditch, London for Daniel who was now based in Portsmouth for the final phase of his WEAC. As I ushered in the New Year 1978 with the Wedlakes, the issue of marriage flashed by and I told myself to take care not to break a heart in the UK and leave for Nigeria. On arrival at the venue of the party, I carried the carton of assorted drinks on my head for cover into Daniel's house for the engagement party. I dropped the carton and settled into a corner away from the girls and engaged some of the men in a conversation. A very attractive, shy and beautiful young Asian girl came to sit by my side holding a camera with the flash detached. I was thinking of my New Year resolution and tried very hard not to take notice of her for some time. She felt uncomfortable and went away but she came back a few minutes later still struggling with her camera. Daniel's fiancée, Tola, had asked her to give me the camera to fix. She told me that she was having a problem with her camera and was directed by Daniel's fiancee to me so I can fix it for her. I took the camera and the flash and worked on them. I gave the camera back to her thinking I had managed to solve the problem only to see that my repair job was not very successful. She returned to me with the camera. I got it fixed and more followed.

I knew that my New Year resolution had been broken when we started chatting and getting acquainted with each other. Her name is Linda Goh Siew Kee and she was a mathematics-statistics student at Portsmouth Polytechnic (now University of Portsmouth) where Daniel's fiancee was studying and had come in the company of her other colleagues. She was in the second year of her BSc honours degree course. She told me of her bias for statistics and her plan for actuarial specialization. I became involved with my future wife and spent most of the evening with her charting and dancing.

The morning after the engagement party I went to tell Daniel's fiancée that I was leaving for Plymouth and she said that was rather early because Linda was just waking up from sleep and had told her during the night that she was impressed with my handling of her camera problem and she might be interested in knowing more about me. I was advised to be a gentleman and take her for a drive before leaving for Plymouth. I invited Linda to come with me for a drive after breakfast. The drive did not last long but we had established a bond and agreed on a date.

I visited Linda in Portsmouth as agreed. She had accommodation at the YMCA hostel within walking distance of the Polytechnic. YMCA had a section for women. I had a good tour of Portsmouth and got acquainted with some of her friends.

I invited her to the Lady's Night at Manadon which was a very formal military occasion on a weekend in February. She arrived in Plymouth and I put her up in a Bed and Breakfast facility not far from the College. She told me it was lonely but when I offered to spend the night with her, she exploded in rage and told me that she would return to Portsmouth the following morning. I pleaded with her to at least attend the Lady's Night and she reluctantly agreed.

She asked me to come over and have breakfast with her in the morning. I drove her around Plymouth and we had lunch at a restaurant. I returned to the College and prepared for the Lady's Night in the College Great Hall and went to pick her up. I looked smart in my mess dress and bow tie. The Great Hall of the Wardroom Mess is intimidating for its stately grandeur. Linda was not comfortable at all and she told me several times during the dinner that she would not come this way again. After dinner, I took her to my room to change and take her to her hotel. I was in my casual wear. She smiled at me and I gave her a long kiss. I took her to her hotel and returned the following morning to have breakfast with her and take her to the railway station to return to Portsmouth. Our frequent telephone calls started and have not stopped till today when I travel.

I completed the RNEC Manadon phase of MEAC by April 1978 and received a briefing for the sea training phase on HMS TORQUAY, the RN sea training ship for marine engineering and navigation officers. It was time to say goodbye to RNEC Manadon that had been home to me for three years and eight months. I had completed a phase that all NN officers who came for MEAC completed and returned to Nigeria. I would be the first to go aboard HMS TORQUAY for the practical consolidation of what had been imparted to me since September 1974.

All my friends had left Manadon. I had achieved what I set out to achieve to my entire satisfaction and I walked around the College with great respect and admiration for the set-up at RNEC Manadon and thanked God for the opportunity. The report on me issued from RNEC Manadon concluded thus '…a popular character who has made his mark at the College and will be greatly missed.' Character is very important in the military and it was constantly assessed at the College for a balanced development of an officer expected to provide leadership to troops in wars.

The six months at sea with HMS TORQUAY were the most exciting time I had with the RN. At the HMS NELSON Naval Base in Portsmouth in April 1978, I was directed to the training frigate berth. We were assembled and received on the jetty by the Marine Engineer Officer, Lieutenant Commander Michael Craig. He handed us over to the Fleet Chief Petty Officer (FCPO) who would be in charge. We were warned to drop our engineering degrees and qualifications ashore as we climbed up the gangway into the ship to get our hands dirty. All lectures will be given by the FCPO and the ratings onboard. We were issued task books detailing all the tasks that had to be accomplished onboard and the routine tests which were all conducted by the ratings in charge of sections and machinery. The ratings signed off only on successful execution.

We had to understudy all categories of ratings from the most junior to the most senior and each would sign off on completing their practical tests. I was absorbed and learnt the tasks starting with making tea for all ratings on watch and cleaning the decks. The next in the hierarchy were assigned on the successful completion of tasks and signing off by the ratings in charge. The middle categories of ratings handled the auxiliary machinery and each took their turn to ensure we learnt how to carry out pre-start checks, starting procedures, safe operation, and stopping procedures. The maintenance routines were also taught. There were special readings of machinery and equipment performances taken from gauges and other displays located outside main machinery spaces. We were drilled on safety to avoid accidents and ensure we carried the right tools for the readings. On completion of this routine of going through all the categories of ratings, the machinery under their charge, and passing their tests, we were then allowed to start under-studying the Assistant

Marine Engineer Officer and finally the Marine Engineer Officer of the frigate.

This most important phase of my education and training taught me to appreciate and understand the challenges ratings who work so hard to operate and maintain the various equipment and machinery face in their duties. It is important to have a feel of the sweat, the risks, and dangers, the level of skills and expertise to be developed and applied for the successful management of diverse equipment and machinery. There is a special type of leadership required of marine engineers to effectively and successfully manage men, machinery, and material together in a most demanding environment in war and while preparing for war; this is characterised by the fortitude to withstand challenges that will inspire the men.

The tracing of major systems onboard was very interesting for me. This enabled the identification of components and sequence of arrangements to function. The understanding of the use of engineering symbols was enhanced. I used the periods off watch and when in a harbour to do system tracing and draw them neatly in the sketch notebook. This was periodically submitted to MEO for assessment. Any student lagging was denied going ashore.

HMS TORQUAY was mostly at sea except when allocated for self and assisted maintenance periods. The ship sailed around the British Isles and made approaches in and out of major bases. We had brief stops at Faslane submarine base in Scotland and visited Funchal (Madeira), La Rochelle (France), Haugesund (Norway), and Gibraltar. The ship was about to sail for Amsterdam when I had to detach from the programme on board to do the short courses considered more relevant to NN. I missed the final stages of the phase of steam turbine engines and administration. I had obtained the Auxiliary Machinery Certificate, Boiler Room Watchkeeping Certificate and preparing for the written phase of the Engine Room Watchkeeping Certificate which I later sat for and passed while at HMS SULTAN.

A most memorable moment onboard HMS TORQUAY was our encounter with very harsh North Sea weather as the ship transited to Haugesund, Norway. The weather deck was declared out of bounds and all external access doors were secured. HMS TORQUAY was tossed about riding the crest of the huge waves and hurricane-force winds. The condition on board was frightening at times and most challenging but we all went about our routines. The accommodation areas were messed up with vomits. It was impossible to sleep on the bunks for fear of being thrown off on to the deck. Many lost their appetite.

There were casualties with other ships in our vicinity losing propulsion power and risking grounding. They sent out distress calls. HMS TORQUAY had to carry out a salvage operation to save a merchant ship that was drifting and in danger of hitting rocks and grounding. HMS TORQUAY had to spend an extra day in the harsh weather and this delayed our arrival at Haugesund. There were several damages to various machinery that needed urgent attention to enable the ship to catch up with its programme. There was no rest for the engineering department staff. We worked for about twenty hours to complete assigned repairs and was linked to local volunteers to take us around Haugesund for socials to unwind.

HMS TORQUAY won a salvage award for the effort in the harsh North Sea and all the crew shared this award as is the practice. I received my award at the British High Commission in Lagos. The most outstanding man during the North Sea experience was the chef who prepared the most delightful meals that improved the appetite of the crew and helped to maintain morale. He and his men were given special mention in the dispatch from the ship.

I left HMS TORQUAY towards the end of September 1978 to complete the other short courses as mentioned in the preceding paragraph and was accommodated in the Wardroom Mess at HMS SULTAN, the RN Marine Engineering School at Gosport. I started the Internal Combustion Engines Additional Qualification Course at HMS SULTAN and followed up with the High Power Generation and Distribution Course at HMS COLLINGWOOD, RN Weapon Engineering School, Fareham, near Gosport. I also had to tidy up some assignments to meet certain watchkeeping requirements on HMS TORQUAY as I was still in touch. This helped me to sit for the final written examination which I passed.

I collected my letters from my mailbox in the Wardroom Mess after working hours one afternoon and headed to my room to rest. One of the letters was from my cousin Mr Emmanuel O Ajoku. I expected to get updates on the family in Kaduna and Okene but I opened his letter only to read the sad news of the death of the love of my life, my mother, on 16 September 1978. I recollected that around when she died, I was on board HMS TORQUAY off the coast of East Scotland and dreamed of losing someone who loved me dearly. My mind went first to my mother and then to Linda and wondered then what was going on in my life. I was devastated and collapsed on the floor and wept. I was advised in the letter not to come home as she was buried immediately according to Muslim rites. I read the letter many times over to come to terms that I would not see my mother again. Linda and her parents were on holiday in Europe and it was on their return to Portsmouth that I had some company as I mourned my mother.

I was focused on rounding up and flying back to Nigeria. The HMS SULTAN Wardroom Mess accommodation was in Gosport and the YMCA hostel was in Portsmouth. I had to shuttle and take a connecting ferry to cross over to Portsmouth to visit Linda and return by the last ferry schedule. I was linked up with some NN officers standing by for the Mark 9 Corvettes (NNS ERINOMI and NNS ENYIMIRI). I visited their office where I met Captain MAH Nyako (later Vice Admiral and Chief of the Naval Staff), Lieutenant GA Shiyanbade (later Rear Admiral and Commandant, National War College). I have heard of both officers but this was my first contact with them.

Captain Nyako, NNS ERINOMI Commanding Officer designate, on hearing that I had graduated from Manadon and was rounding up my marine engineering specialization course programme, engaged me immediately to know more about me. He was delighted to hear of my progress and asked me to visit him and his family at his residence. Lieutenant Shiyanbade also invited me to visit him and his family at his residence. Captain Nyako's wife, Mrs Zainab Nyako, was in the final stages of pregnancy, and on my second visit, I went with Linda who struck a lasting friendship with her.

I had concluded all courses by the first week of November 1978 and was issued a flight ticket by the Deputy Defence Adviser (Navy) to depart the UK on 17 November 1978. I travelled to RNEC Manadon where most of my luggage had earlier been packed since April 1978 and kept safely in a store in the basement of the West Wing. Linda was around to assist with labelling and documentation for handing over to a freighting agent. I noticed that she was feeling lonely; she became pensive. I tried to cheer her up by reminding her of the invitation given to her to visit Captain Nyako's family. After collecting my luggage from the College, I drove around the College and paid a farewell visit to the Wedlakes at 168 Fort Austin Avenue.

I left Manadon and Plymouth with a most pleasant memory of a beautiful quiet sprawling city and the iconic Manadon Estate. I left Plymouth for Portsmouth with Linda and stopped over in Bournemouth to attend a concert by a South African theatre group (Ipi Tombi) on tour. I spent the next two days in Portsmouth to pack and do my leaving routine from HMS NELSON after which I drove my Lancia Beta saloon car to the shippers at London East End for shipping along with my additional luggage. I was given an additional shipping charge. I had exhausted my account allowance doing last-minute unexpected shopping for a coursemate at NDA. Linda noticed my predicament and to my surprise, she helped me with the additional shipping charge of £300. She had bought a Jerusalem Bible and presented it to me some months earlier to show her commitment to me.

I paid the shipping agent and paid a farewell visit to Captain Nyako and his family. On the day of my departure from Portsmouth, I was informed that his wife, Mrs Zainab Nyako, had given birth to a baby. Captain Nyako asked me to contact a senior police officer living in Ikoyi on my arrival in Lagos so the officer could contact the Nyako family in Yola to name the child. The child, a boy, was named Mahmoud.

Linda and I took a train from Portsmouth for London Heathrow. The flight was at night and Linda waited until I completed the boarding procedure before returning to Portsmouth. I was lucky that staff from the Defence Adviser's office was around to see me off and agreed to my request to see her to the bus station at Heathrow.

The Nigeria Airways flight into Lagos from London Heathrow arrived in the morning of Sunday 19 November and I was met by the Naval reception team. I was cleared through immigration, collected my luggage, cleared customs, and was driven to the Naval Base, NNS BEECROFT. There was no vacant room at the Base Flats. NNS RUWAN YARO, the training ship was alongside and I requested the Officer Of the Day (OOD) for accommodation and he granted my request.

It had been an adventure since my departure from NNS QUORRA on 9 September 1974 to 17 November 1978, a period of four years, two months, and a day over a week. I had successfully gone through the RNEC, Manadon mechanical engineering first-degree programme as well as specializing as a marine engineer through a post-graduate programme with a rare opportunity for practical consolidation at sea on HMS TORQUAY. The sea practical experiences constitute one of the finest experiences of my life. In the process, I also went through a series of short courses in specialized areas required to carry out a broad range of tasks as a marine engineer officer on board a warship. These gave me an in-depth idea of the range and enormity of the responsibilities of the marine engineer on a warship and how operational experiences acquired are brought to bear in relationship with industry and relevant design processes to meet requirements.

I went through the process of defining a career path as a teenager in secondary school to have a mechanical engineering degree and specialize as a marine engineer so that I could be positioned to best serve my country. I precisely achieved that in the very best engineering establishment in the world. The enabling environment shaped my belief that Nigeria deserves nothing but the best that the world can offer. I realised that I was beginning to understand that I bear true allegiance to Nigeria with faith and was proud.

The RN was the empire and the empire was the RN in popular British thinking. Naval engineering was the mortar that held all together. An island nation with a population less than that of Nigeria created an empire spanning the globe. I learnt how individuals took ownership of their country and acted to serve the common good so that the blessings of the land and the best the world can offer in terms of opportunities can be secured for all British citizens. I thank the Nigerian taxpayer that never failed to support and sustain me at a great expense. I was back home to justify returns on investment and nothing else.

I formally reported at NHQ and was told that I would be appointed to NNS NIGERIA, the Flag Ship, for watchkeeping duties. I was granted disembarkation leave. I returned to the Naval Base and contacted the Base Administration Officer for accommodation at the Base Flats. I was happy to have secure accommodation. My first visitor was Lieutenant Ibrahim IJ Ogohi (later Admiral and CDS). He reminded me that I was his junior at St John's College, Kaduna and he was entitled to inspect my luggage and make his choice. I obeyed my senior at St John's College and I opened my two boxes. He took my satellite radio and I gladly packed it with the other items he selected for him.

I got a Nigeria Air Force (NAF) flight to Kaduna and found my way to 34 Kadanya Road, Costain. It was a very happy reunion with my cousin and his family. I presented the family with the gifts I bought (including a suit my cousin always treasured) for them from the UK and settled to prepare for the journey to Okene.

We travelled to Okene on public transport because my cousin's car had problems. My mother's passing away generated a lot of sympathy for me from the family members and other relations. My father led a celebration last year and this time it was a very sombre time for me and well-wishers. My aunties were now filling the vacuum left by my mother. Alhaji Seidu Yaqub, the elder brother of Professor Nuhu O Yaqub took charge of the maintenance of my mother's grave and he was the one that took me and my elder brother Jimoh to visit the grave. It is a simple grave and on a concrete slab was written "Avahi Avosuahi Asmau Died 16/9/78."

Jimoh and I fell on our knees as if we both were begging her to forgive us. My sisters told me that the night she went into a coma, they were with her and as they bade her good night, she prayed for me and asked them to make sure they looked after me. They did not understand why she did that until they were awakened in the early hours of the morning and told of the sad news. My role model and mother and the most genuine love of my life were gone forever. I can never pay enough tribute to her. I feel she is alive looking after me because the connection between us is too special. She was my constant source of inspiration. She is at peace with God. Thank you for the precious gift of being my mother.

Jimoh and I left her graveside and the cemetery with Alhaji Seidu Yaqub and visited our aunties who lived in the same neighbourhood not far from the cemetery. My father was relieved that I was home and had paid tribute to my mother.

I left Okene for Kaduna with my cousin by public transport through Uruvucheba. I was seated beside my cousin and was lost in my thoughts. It was still dark. I suddenly felt as if my mother was sitting next to me with her arms around me and telling me to ensure I marry Linda. I was not dreaming. This encounter with my mother was repeated.

I returned to Lagos and prepared to resume duty onboard NNS NIGERIA as a marine engineer watchkeeping officer. This was a good starting appointment to gain some experience before taking responsibility as a Marine Engineer Officer.

CHAPTER SEVEN

Junior Naval Marine Engineer Officer

I looked forward to reporting onboard the NN Flag Ship, a combined diesel engine driven frigate commissioned into service in 1965. The Commanding Officer was Captain PS Koshoni. My immediate concern was to know the Marine Engineer Officer (MEO) of the ship, Lieutenant Commander Felix S Ebohon, and other technical staff of the Marine Engineering Department. The Assistant Marine Engineer Officer (AMEO) was Lieutenant Valentine Egwuatu whom I had to work closely with. He was a member of the 10th Regular Course of NDA and did his engineering course in India with the Indian Navy. I went on board the ship in the evenings to get some information.

I reported onboard NNS NIGERIA in time for the morning muster routines. The AMEO took charge of me and arranged my meeting with the MEO in his cabin. It was a brief welcome onboard and introduction to the Marine Engineering Department. I followed the AMEO for the departmental muster routine in the Machinery Control Room (MCR) situated between the forward and aft engine rooms. I was introduced to the senior rates and sections they were in charge of.

After the departmental muster routine, everyone left to carry out their assigned tasks for the day and the planned maintenance schedule assignments. The AMEO and I changed into our overalls and he took me around the main, auxiliary, and outside spaces machinery rooms. I was asked to take note of the location of the tight space housing the hydraulic power system for the control of the pitch of the propellers. The AMEO and I ended up in the engineering workshop where he was working to service a component part from the hydraulic power system (Oil Distribution Box).

I was also keen on understanding the major systems onboard. Using my task book on board HMS TORQUAY as a guide, I compiled a list relevant to NNS NIGERIA and collected the relevant drawings from the documentation room. The task book has a format based on general principles for the correct and safe management of machinery onboard a frigate. It does not matter whether the propulsion machinery is a diesel engine, steam, or gas turbine engine. I was set to get acquainted with the ship.

The morning tea break was observed in the Wardroom. I took the opportunity to interact with officers from the other departments and catch up with news from the collection of newspapers and magazines available. My allocated cabin was near the Wardroom Mess. I was now a full member of the mess. The Executive Officer (XO) of the ship was Commander S Akano who succeeded Commander EO Omotehinwa as DDA (Navy) at the Nigerian High Commission, London. I did not have much interaction with him in London. The XO who was also the Mess President was quite approachable and made the mess lively.

He told me that the new frigate NNS ARADU being constructed in Germany would carry helicopters and there was the need to train Aircraft Engineer Officers (AEO). He felt that having just qualified as a Marine Engineer Officer while still a Sub Lieutenant, I should be considered to start the training while the new construction was in progress so that I could join the pre-commissioning and other training programmes. He gave me information and asked me to apply through the ship. The policy was to have the MEO/AEO specializations combination for an appointment rather than having a single specialization as AEO that would not have much to do onboard as the NN had no air wing department in its organization then. I applied early in the first quarter of 1979 and a few weeks later, I was promoted to the rank of Lieutenant with effect from 01 April 1979.

I settled into a routine that combined officially assigned tasks and my programme to trace systems and understand the ship. The ship spent the most time on Self Maintenance Periods and Assisted Maintenance Periods when base support was required. There were no programmed sea trips. The ship was put to sea for day runs on two occasions and remained at sea overnight once while I was onboard between December 1978 and January 1980.

There were many maintenance tasks behind schedule in addition to several breakdowns requiring various levels of intervention up to the factory level. The Nigerian Ports Authority floating dock was the only dockyard facility that could take the ship for routine docking and essential defects repair procedures. This facility could not satisfy the NN requirements and so dockyards in Ghana and Senegal were considered for urgent requirements. Much time was spent on maintenance on board and we worked late hours on some occasions. The first outing was an adventure for me. I went through the procedures for preparing the ship for sea. I was assigned the Controllable Pitch Propeller hydraulic oil distribution box compartment which just had enough headroom for me to squat as my station for leaving and entering harbour routines. This was to ensure I quickly reset manually an erring mechanism on the oil distribution box that failed to return to the correct position due to the degraded state. The only ventilation was through the only hatch for entrance and exit from the small space.

The day run at sea was not very demanding as I did not stay too long in the confined compartment. The third sea trip was for annual sea inspection and staff from the Naval Headquarters (NHQ) were onboard. On getting to sea, I stayed there for some time to ensure quick reset actions. I went to the MCR as I was relieved to have some fresh air because I was drenched in sweat. At the MCR, I met a senior officer from NHQ seated there. He looked at me and asked who I was. I introduced myself and he asked me if it was raining outside. I told him that I could not confirm that. He then asked how I became so drenched as if I had been standing in torrential rain. I told him of my leaving and entering the harbour duty station that is confined and without provision for ventilation. He was the Director of Weapon Engineering, Commander E Archibong, at NHQ. Commander SB Atukum the Director of Marine Engineering (DME) at NHQ was also onboard as I later met him on the Quarter Deck with the MEO on our return to harbour.

There was a gathering of officers on the quarter deck as the ship returned to harbour. I happened to be standing near the MEO and DME who were discussing the problems of the ship. I noticed that both officers were unhappy about the maintenance of the ship. There were divergent views and I considered it inappropriate to eavesdrop on them. I left immediately for my cabin and stayed away until all the officers from NHQ had left the ship.

The frustration that I observed in the MEO as he discussed the problems of the NN with DME made me think about possible solutions. It was a complex mix of various levels of authority for operation and maintenance of warships that had not been in harmony or synergy. This was a glimpse into the nature of the challenges that would be faced. The MEO did not last long in the NN before he retired. The advice he gave to me before my promotion to the rank of Lieutenant would be a constant guide as I served in the years ahead. This would be elaborated upon later.

The programme I defined for myself regarding understanding the ship involved tracing systems and studying the drawings and manuals available on board. I went around the ship routinely doing system tracing and learning about the main features and organization of the various departments and documented my findings using the HMS TORQUAY task book as a guide. These, I would develop further to reflect the set up on most NN capital warships that were all diesel engine driven until NNS ARADU came into service with gas turbine engines. I made sure that I kept to the work ethics I had been taken through during my education and training so far.

I have had the very best exposure regarding the marine engineering profession so far. The AMEO was very approachable and hard working. I was happy to be a watchkeeping officer under him and quickly learnt a lot about the ship and the challenges of maintenance. He observed that I was always on board and doing a lot of system tracing in addition to the tasks he assigned me. The senior rates were well trained and took effective charge of their sections. I was aware of how jealously they took charge of their sections and would normally not want the AMEO and MEO to interfere with the routines they were in charge of. I made them feel that they were my superiors that I had to learn from and I learnt a lot from them.

I would always remember WCPOs Odumeru, Gansallo, and Oni, at various times, whose expert handling of maintenance tasks and operation of machinery was very good. I would later in 1983 be taken care of by WCPO Odumeru when he was appointed for technical duty with DDA(Navy) in London, as he took charge of ensuring my personal effects were safely shipped to Lagos.

In the latter half of 1979, I was given an internal appointment as AMEO1 to assist the AMEO. This gave me a feeling of responsibility. I noticed that personnel of the marine engineering department onboard were not given refreshments that were freely available to those keeping watch on the bridge and Combat Information Centre (CIC) which were air-conditioned. I was informed that the department's requests were never approved. The heat in the machinery spaces easily makes personnel sweat excessively and they were usually forced to leave duty posts to get some cool fresh air. I tried to convince the Supply Officer to take into consideration the harsh conditions in the machinery areas and provide us with refreshments to no avail.

During the second sea outing when the ship remained at sea overnight I found the Supply Officer, a Lieutenant Commander, alone outside the senior rates mess on the open deck relaxing. I approached him and in the course of our very relaxed discussion, I invited him for a conducted tour of the aft main engine room. He took the bait and I led him down below into the engine room. I took the longest route walking through the engine room to ensure he had a good dose of the heat and the noise in the main engine room. I noticed he was sweating profusely about mid-way through the engine room and I slowed down to explain the functions of the machinery. Both of us were wearing our tropical mess dress as required for dinner which was the white uniform shirt and black trousers with a cummerbund.

The Supply Officer's white shirt was in a mess drenched with his sweat and I led him out of the aft main engine room and led him towards the quarter deck. I apologized to him for the sweat that had messed up his shirt within the short time that we walked through the main engine room. I told him that the men on watch in the main engine room stay there for several hours enduring the heat and noise without refreshment. I did not have to request as he promptly told me to fill the demand form for refreshments and bring it to him directly for approval. I filled the form promptly and got all our requirements and thereafter there was a regular supply for the Marine Engineering Department personnel onboard.

The MEO sometimes gave me tasks to accomplish for him to have a first-hand assessment. He once gave me a research project paper to review for his assessment. I was given a deadline and I met the deadline. The following day after reading through my submission he called me and told me that he was satisfied with what I had done. He then became personal and told me that he was advising me to be very, very careful if I wanted to go far in my career. I was puzzled, shaken, and waited for his elaboration to clarify the situation. He told me that many officers were not happy with my achievements at such an early stage of my career (young and just a Sub Lieutenant) and the reason was my going through RNEC Manadon successfully and with an award. Also, I had qualified as a Marine Engineer Officer having completed courses other NN officers completed in the rank of Lieutenant. It is also the rank officers of other branches qualified in their specializations.

He added that he had observed me for several months since I came on board and found me very quiet and focused on what I was assigned to do and could not find any reasons to fault my conduct and had wondered why they had such feelings until he found out that it was hatred as a result of the envy of my achievements. He warned me that I could be prematurely retired to get me out of their sight.

I thanked him for his advice. I had unknowingly incurred the hatred of colleagues known and unknown and this would be my burden at all times throughout my career. I had become a major threat. This hatred and envy would always come to play in my career and be aggravated as I continued to be focused on dutifully serving the country by achieving more. It was the most important advice that was given to me as a Sub Lieutenant as a 27- year old officer. I felt very lonely. How can such a wasting orientation and attitude be freely accommodated in an environment of engineering that categorically demands with stringency routine adaptation to technological innovations to prepare for war a top-quality organisation expected of a modern Navy? I must have gone to the wrong institution for my engineering education and training, I thought, considering the reality been experienced.

As I progressed in my career some junior officers would be part of this intrigue that enthrones mediocrity as a result of the repeated acts of betrayal and preferences by most of my course mates and seniors that created a very dangerous and lonely road despite the best of my efforts to reach out and endure. I would endure all of their hate and ill-treatments, even humiliation without respite.

Lieutenant Commander FS Ebohon was one of the few officers to identify and draw my attention to the issues of hate, jealousy, and envy until the Minister of State for Defence Mrs O Obada asked me the question directly in 2013 in her office with Navy Captain IA Idewu, her Naval Assistant present. She asked me as she tried to solve the problem I was going through: "Why do they all hate you?" I had to put in writing and convey to the HMOD that they hate the NN/AFN institution and the development of the country and not me by their dirty attitudes wasting assets.

The civil servants at the Ministry of Defence by then had joined the hate train because of the permanent site project money I fought for and on which they were feasting. I will elaborate on this later as I proceed with this story in this book. Vice Admiral DJ Ezeoba had become CNS at this time and was showing his true character and feeling towards me because of my lukewarm attitude to his overtures to me to lobby for my appointment as CNS in 2005 and 2007 in which he wanted to play a role.

My time as watchkeeping officer on board the Flag Ship came to an end when I was appointed in January 1980 as the MEO NNS OTOBO, a Mark III Corvette, built by Vosper Thornycroft Shipyard of Portsmouth. I put finishing touches to the documentation of the tasks I had carried out onboard the Flag Ship and virtually had a draft of a task book that is dedicated to the ship. I was set to take up my first responsibility as MEO of a warship. I had served as a Midshipman on NNS DORINA which was also a Mark III Corvette and this helped me to prepare and take up my appointment on the sister ship. The Commanding Officer of the ship was Lieutenant Commander Monde

Umoh who was on the Staff Officer Sea Training Team when I was a Midshipman.

The challenges before me as MEO onboard NNS OTOBO were two-fold. The first was the defective three main generators onboard for which there were no sufficient spare parts. The emergency generator was serviceable. The maintenance schedules for machinery and equipment had not been observed for long.

The second challenge was the lack of experienced technical rates for the demanding repair and maintenance tasks needing urgent attention. The numerous warships being constructed for the NN in Europe had drawn virtually all the experienced hands and new intakes passing out of training schools were being drafted onboard ships to replace them. The machinery control problems tasked me greatly and having exhausted the options available to me on board and with none available in the base maintenance organisations, a retired Special Duty officer, Lieutenant Commander Ernest O Eyetan was on a visit when he was spotted by the CO who asked him to come onboard and render assistance. He was a senior rate onboard the ship while it was being built in Portsmouth in the early 1970s and had a good experience of service onboard.

I explained the problem with the control system and all the steps taken to solve the problems for him. All manuals and drawings, as well as the maintenance and operational history, I could gather were presented to him. I showed him the tools and the personnel available to enable him to take effective charge. He was with us for a few days and the problems were solved. I noticed his smile as we tested the controls and he explained to me that he was apprehensive initially as most engineer officers would not allow such intervention and appreciated the freehand I gave him. We established mutual respect thereafter.

The problems with the three main diesel generators presented an interesting challenge. One of the generators had a defective diesel engine as well as a defective alternator; the other two had either a defective diesel engine or a defective alternator. I searched the onboard stores and the base technical stores depot and assembled as many spares as were available. I saw that what was available could not solve any of the problems.

I decided to interchange alternators so that I could transfer the good one to the operational diesel engine to have one operational generator. This would involve heavy-lift gears and a dedicated team. I identified the strong lifting points that could be used and provided strong wooden platforms for the transfers. The generator room was in a mess for several days and the CO wondered if the desired results would be achieved. The dearth of experienced senior rates was felt and I decided to take my time and pay attention to details of the procedures and also took the opportunity to train the newly drafted young ratings onboard. The draft of the task book from the Flag Ship was modified and photocopied for the ratings for the onboard training as the work in the generator room progressed.

The team dedicated to the alternators succeeded in the swap and the coupling of the operational diesel engine and alternator being interchanged was achieved. On getting one generator operational I assessed the remaining two generators and was able to transfer parts to get one additional generator going with very questionable reliability. I surveyed the emergency cables for the power supply from the emergency generator and how the switchboard could be supplied and managed. The Weapon Enginee Officer was Lieutenant AE Effiong. He rose to the task and we determined what essentials could be supplied should there be a failure of the two main generators. The combined departments' drill exercise enabled us to identify all cables for emergency runs and the accessories for their connection and storage points.

The CO had been briefing the Flotilla Technical Officer (FTO), Commander (later Rear Admiral) IN Katagum, of the efforts being made. I did not know until he came on board and inspected the work we were doing. It was from the questions that he asked that I got to know that he had been kept abreast of the problems and our efforts. I now had direct access to him as he told me to come straight to him should I need his attention. I was pleased with his encouragement and the team was inspired to keep on trying and improve on what had been achieved.

The CO was encouraged to prepare for trials and a possible sea day run. The basin trials were programmed and successfully executed. The next trial was to cast off and manoeuvre within the harbour. The generators went off and the emergency generator could not be brought in to provide emergency power. I advised the CO to request tug assistance to secure alongside the allocated berth. There was a review of all that happened and we learnt some lessons and were able to take the ship to the sea up to Lagos fairway buoy on our next attempt. I kept a tab on the progress with the onboard training using the modified task book.

The Chief of the Naval Staff was Vice-Admiral MA Adelanwa. His annual inspection came on stream and the Flotilla Command should be able to send some capital ships to sea. This did not happen. It was within the same period that cadets from NDA were around and had to be taken to sea as part of the Camp Ruwan Baban Yaro exercise. NNS OTOBO was assigned the task and had to remain at sea overnight. I did not have enough complement for the normal watchkeeping duties and had to adapt since it was an overnight trip. There was no sleep for me but I made sure key senior rates were well briefed and rested for the priority tasks.

There was no use taking unnecessary risks going too far out to sea. The CO decided to go to anchorage and this was successfully executed and the following morning after breakfast the ship left the anchorage and returned to harbour successfully. The following day the CNS was at the base for inspection and was happy that NNS OTOBO was able to satisfy the training requirements for the cadets from NDA. He gave the ship special recognition and decided to come on board and go down the machinery spaces to see the efforts being made to keep the ship going despite the challenges. He saw the old parts being recycled and paused for a moment to reflect. I could see the weight of responsibility weigh him down as he silently and slowly walked away.

The CNS was right to come around and encourage us but I felt we deserved to do far more to meet the standard befitting the CNS. I had observed that the Wardroom Mess at the Naval Base, Apapa, was where COs and ship's staff came to unwind after coming back from the sea on daily runs. They usually celebrated their achievements and I wondered what was there to celebrate.

I never saw Commander PS Koshoni and Commander OP Fingesi do that after several days at sea on exercises when both commanded the ships of Mark III Squadron. More so I noticed while with RN that HMS TORQUAY had no time to spare alongside, except for maintenance periods that were strictly timed, during the time I spent on board. The sea is the ultimate school and the sailor's career domain that has to be mastered by long sea voyages to be fulfilled. There was an emerging trend I was noticing from 1980 and it was sadly the less emphasis on sea time experiences in the NN.

I was given an additional appointment as Staff Officer Engineering at Flotilla Naval Command, Apapa. This marked the beginning of one of my most fulfilling professional relationships because I came under the official scrutiny of Commander IN Katagum. It was not long before Sub Lieutenant EC Abiagom, a recent graduate of RNEC, Manadon, was appointed for watchkeeping duties on board. I made available to him the draft copy of the Task Book updated for officers under training to assist him to grasp the essentials of the Marine Engineering Department responsibilities onboard. The additional appointment given to me enabled me to attract more resources to the NNS OTOBO. I also took some interest in the problems of NNS DORINA that was virtually abandoned. I had the opportunity to come to terms with the challenges being faced by other ships most of which had similar machinery fitted as onboard NNS OTOBO.

The CNS addressed all officers in the Western Naval Command area onboard the Landing Ship Tank (LST) NNS AMBE on the troop deck. He spoke of his concern for the future of the NN Fleet and remarked that the challenges of leadership for the expanding NN Fleet weighed him down. It appeared that he was not happy with the prevailing situation, especially as regards the availability of qualified personnel to meet the challenges of modern warships entering into service. I saw some of the challenges while I was in the UK. The concern of the CNS, Vice Admiral MA Adelanwa would appear justified.

There was a transition from military to civil rule on 1st October 1979. The new President, Commander-in-Chief of the Armed Forces was Alhaji Shehu Shagari. In the second quarter of 1980, not long after the CNS address onboard NNS AMBE, there were top leadership changes in the Armed Forces. Vice Admiral AA Aduwo became the new CNS. There were organizational changes in the NN that necessitated new appointments. Commodore AA Aikhomu emerged as the Flag Officer Commanding Flotilla Command (FOC FLOT).

I was involved in solving other ships' problems and these necessitated tasking some base maintenance facilities such as the workshops and stores depot. I had to close from work late. I was notified of the programme for Presidential Steam Past (PSP) for 1st October 1980. This was the first Independence Day celebration for the President, Commander-in-Chief. The preparations went into full gear immediately. I went about the routines I had already established and got the ships' technical staff organized for Assisted Maintenance Periods. These necessitated the availability of full base maintenance facilities. Targets were set and progress monitored with routine briefs to FTO whose office used to be that of RN Captain Leslie Wright from where he had the most vantage view of the ships when I was a Midshipman.

There was progress also onboard NNS DORINA and this encouraged the appointment of Lieutenant Commander (later Vice Admiral and CNS) J Ayinla as the CO for the Presidential Steam Past. The President was on Marina Pier for the PSP. Eight ships participated including NN DORINA that had been in reserve and not moved for over two years. The exercise earned the NN Presidential Commendation and the CNS was most gracious in conveying the message and his gratitude to FOC FLOT by signal, Date-Time-Group-Month 021420 OCT informing FOC WEST, NOC EAST, and FLOTILLA thus:

> "//Personal from CNS. 011150 OCT-011250 OCT was my happiest hour so far since assuming office.
> Eight NN ships participated in Presidential Steam Past as part of the 20th National Day Ceremony.
> It made me proud as they gave the Navy a brand new image of an effective Defence Force to be reckoned with.
> Mr President and C-in-C expressed gracious pleasure while his accompanying party and other Service Chiefs showered their praises.
> Have also received congratulatory tel messages from two former CNS and one former Army Chief who watched it on television. It was the Navy's greatest hour.
> 2// I was particularly happy to see DORINA arrive from over two years in mothballs to fully take part in that proud hour.
> 3//Bravo-Zulu and repeat well done.
> We must however realise that we can not avoid henceforth to lower this high impression and expectation. We must maintain and improve upon it at all cost.
> 4//Onward Together."

The FOC FLOT shared his joy at a meeting with his principal staff officers and singled out FTO for his commendation for the efforts put in to make the ships available for the Presidential Steam Past. The FTO, Commander IN Katagum in his response told the meeting that he would pass on this recognition to a quiet Lieutenant AAM Isa who took up additional responsibilities as Flotilla Staff Officer Engineering to get tasks accomplished on all the ships including NNS DORINA.

I was surprised at the FTO's humility in such a gathering of senior officers at a meeting with the FOC. This also revealed the simplicity of this principled great officer. I must state that without knowing it I had earned a mentor. The FOC FLOT took notice and future associations with him later in my career development would reveal his fatherly care for me.

I had been left behind as regards appointments for the new ships undergoing construction in Europe as all junior engineer officers had been appointed. The NNS ARADU construction programme was on course. I had earlier been informed officially that the next Air Engineering Application Course would be in August 1980. There was no one appointed as the year passed. I focused on the enormous challenges I was privileged to face. I was the secretary of a committee that was winding up proceedings in late February 1981 when I was informed that there was a signal nominating me for a course in the UK. I thought it was for the Air Engineering Application Course and did not bother to check the signal for details as I decided to focus on the assignment at hand and submit the committee's report as scheduled.

It was about a week later after handing in the report of the committee that I saw the signal. I was not given the Air Engineering Course slot but the Advanced Marine Engineering Course both at RNEC Manadon. I was taken by surprise. I immediately disqualified myself from the Advanced Marine Engineering Course which was an MSc degree programme. I had an idea of the demand for this course and the few RN officers that succeeded in going through the course. It was a course that prepared officers for the challenges of warship projects and design management. This involves leading defence industries with operational experiences to meet warships acquisition project requirements.

I had been wondering if NN was prepared for such challenges as there were no structures and policies as a guide to meeting the challenges. These thoughts flooded my mind and wondered why I was not allowed to start the Air Engineering Application Course by 1980 as I was officially informed.

I went to the office of my boss, Commander IN Katagum. I told him that I had been nominated to go on a course for which I was neither recommended nor qualified to take up. I wanted him to help me contact the NHQ and get me off the hook. He was surprised at the way I ran down myself and was wondering how to handle the situation when Commander (later Rear Admiral and CNS) Suleiman Sa'idu walked into the office and met a tense situation.

Commander Sa'idu was informed by my boss that I was nominated for a course in the UK but I wanted to turn it down. I wanted him to say I had turned it down but how could I interrupt senior officers. They discussed the issue and reasoned that if I turned it down I would be disobeying an order of the CNS since it was by a signal from NHQ. They phoned the Staff Officer in charge of course nominations and he explained the decision to them. I was asked to leave the office while they deliberated. When I was called back in they both reminded me of their earlier observation as regards obedience to CNS order and told me to go and give it a shot. I thanked them and came to terms with reality.

The Advanced Marine Engineering Course at RNEC was for the elite of the RN and those programmed for more demanding tasks related to warship design and acquisition project management processes. There has been no NN officer nominated for this course even though for a long time there had been billets. If I was being targeted for premature retirement for succeeding in the first-degree programme and the marine engineering specialisation courses why should I give myself an additional burden? I have just been denied an opportunity for an appointment on the new ship through the Air Engineering Course and I was battling with old ships and their maintenance demands in Lagos.

I would later appreciate the wisdom of the FTO and Commander Suleiman Sa'idu. I was later informed by NHQ that I would go for the next course starting 1982 and would be departing for the UK by December 1981 instead of March 1981 as stated in the nomination signal. There were lots of jobs to keep me busy at the WNC and I did not ask why the delay.

The NN had to be reorganized given the large number of ships being built and due to come into service within the next year. NNS ERINOMI and NNS ENYIMIRI, Mark 9 Corvettes, had joined the Fleet. The NN opted for two Fleet organizations. The Western Fleet and Eastern Fleet would each be organic to Western and Eastern Naval Commands with a Fleet Commander in charge of each. The Flotilla Command was thus split and ceased to exist by 30 April 1981. I was posted to Western Naval Command as Staff Officer Engineering with responsibilities for ship maintenance in the Western Naval Command and Western Fleet by implication. Also as part of the schedule of duty, I was the Officer-in-Charge of the NN Technical Training School which was at the Naval Base, Apapa. Indeed the Naval Base, NNS BEECROFT was home to the entire NN. It needed decongestion.

I assumed duties at the Western Naval Command Headquarters on 1st May 1981. The Command Technical Officer (CTO) Commander A Ademoroti was the head of the department reporting to the FOC for technical matters. I was coming from Flotilla Command to face the challenge of merging ship upkeep duties with Naval Base duties which included depot stores management, jetties and berthing facilities, victualling, and accommodation including barracks maintenance. I was kept abreast of the delivery plans for boats and ships from Europe and the nightmare was where to allocate to them and administer them. There were no new facilities and the Naval Dockyard at Victoria Island was not yet commissioned. The boats and ships expected were: 15x water-jet propulsion Inshore Patrol Craft (IPC), 3x Fast Attack Craft (FAC) from Fr Lurssen, Germany with Otomat Missiles, 2x Landing Ship Tanks (LST) from HDW Germany, 3x Fast Attack Craft from France with

Exocet missiles and 1xMEKO Frigate from Blohm and Voss, Germany with Otomat and Aspide Missiles.

The ships had sophisticated weapons and propulsion systems. The MEKO Frigate was the first of its type in the world. There were visits from the relevant shipyards to assess the available jetty and berthing facilities. It was my lot after their meetings at NHQ and Command Headquarters with principal staff officers to inspect the facilities with the various visiting teams. It was obvious that what was available did not meet the standards.

I had the experience of requirements at Portsmouth HMS NELSON Naval Base that was the home port for HMS TORQUAY. Nigeria was not the UK. There was an immediate need to adapt and improve. The MEKO Frigate NNS ARADU would not be able to berth at the Naval Base. The Marina jetty and the Naval Dockyard pool jetty were inspected and it was decided that the Dockyard jetty was the most appropriate and the installation of appropriate bollards and other facilities should be undertaken to safely berth NNS ARADU. The Inshore Patrol Craft Squadrons were shared between the Naval Base and the Naval Dockyard mini basin opposite the main basin. The other ships would be crowded up at the Naval Base, Apapa.

The Command took delivery of the inshore patrol craft and the three German Fast Attack Crafts. I was responsible for receiving base support documentation and spare parts. Their immediate requirements for Petroleum Oils and Lubricants (POLs) as well as freshwater, air, and shore electric power supplies were my direct responsibility. There were varying requirements and specifications that I had to quickly harmonise and establish local equivalents that met the ship's standards. There were several testing of POL samples at the major oil companies' facilities. The arrival of the two LSTs crowded the base and stretched the limits of what the command could cope with in terms of supplies of POL and water.

After a few weeks of settling down and rest from the long voyages from Europe, the ships had to be deployed in the Gulf of Guinea and coastal waters. The FACs consumption of diesel fuel was high in addition to the demands of other ships. I had to draw the attention of the FOC West to adhere to the operational deployment patterns of the ships. The ships of the FAC Squadron were not for patrol but maritime interdiction and if they had to be used for patrols they should be limited.

The CTO was nominated for the Senior Executive Course at National Institute for Policy and Strategic Studies, Kuru-Jos, Plateau State. Captain E Archibong was appointed as the new CTO. He failed to take up the appointment on the departure of Commander AA Ademoroti. I was a Lieutenant and though not the most senior in rank among technical officers at WNC the FOC approved my appointment to carry out the duties of CTO in addition to my substantive appointment as Staff Officer Engineering. The technical officers of the rank of Lieutenant Commanders at WNC were of the Special Duty commission and by NN regulations they could not hold the appointment of CTO. I was asked to move in and operate from the office of the CTO given the demand of the office. The Chief Staff Officer was Captain HM Sanni and he supervised financial aspects of my new office but on all other matters, I was in direct contact with the FOC. This arrangement served me very well as I operated undercover and focused on technical matters. I was most impressed with the support of the FOC WEST Rear Admiral DE Okujagu who had so much confidence in me and expressed his happiness with the way I was handling the office.

I had to assist the COs of the new ships in presenting their demands to FOC WEST when they could not be met to enable the ships to sail. The COs came to rely on my judgement and the FOC WEST Rear Admiral DE Okujagu never went against my judgement and recommendation. He would always remember me in later years as his CTO.

In 2004 when I was the Admiral Superintendent Naval Dockyard, the Admiral then retired was admitted at the Dockyard Medical Centre. I went to visit him and on hearing, I was entering his admission room he sat upright on his bed and exclaimed: 'My CTO, how are you? Please come in.' The Admiral told his physician, who was surprised at his sudden burst of energy, of the special affection he had for me while serving under him and how happy he was to see me again.

The need to decongest the Naval Base was uppermost in my mind and I had the support of FOC to move out the Barracks Maintenance Unit from the Naval Base to the newly commissioned Naval Barracks at Ojo. I met with very stiff resistance from the civilian workers used to the Naval Base. I studied their reactions and fears. I made sure I replicated the facilities they were used to at the Naval Barracks at Ojo which included a workshop and stores. When they saw they had better facilities and administrative arrangements at Ojo they moved without any incident and this marked the beginning of the elaborate establishment at Ojo, called NNS WEY.

I devolved responsibilities for the issuance of store items to avoid shuttles to Naval Base for approval. I made sure that bulk purchases of items like air conditioners and refrigerators meant for houses at Ojo were delivered directly to the stores there and administered accordingly. The Technical Stores depot at the Naval Base was choked with the arrival of new ships and this made it very difficult to operate and identify the items in stock. I remember vividly the problem encountered when HMS MERMAID and HMS LLANDAFF visited Lagos and there was a demand for a cylinder head for the Paxman diesel generator on one of the ships. This demand was made as the needed part was on the way from the UK and by the time it arrived the ships would be behind schedule. The British Defence Adviser assured us that the spare part from our store would be replaced within 24 hours.

The Stores Officer at the Naval Base reported to me that there was no spare Paxman diesel engine cylinder head as specified in our stores. This was relayed to the UK authorities which replied that no matter the usage rate of what the UK sold to Nigeria there would be one left to spare. When I got the message I went to the store for a search. At the entrance to the store, I discovered a raised platform that was being used as a passageway. I stepped on it and felt a solid metal structure beneath my feet and on noticing the special preservative wrap that had suffered from trampling I ordered an inspection and it was discovered that the items being used as a raised platform were the Paxman diesel engine cylinder heads.

I instructed the store assistants to remove one close to the shelves that had not been stepped on. It was cleaned and repacked with neat preservative wrap and delivered. The following day as the ships departed on schedule the UK Defence Adviser handed over the one sent from the UK that had just been collected from the airport. This incident would influence some decisions I took years later for the reorganization of the Technical Stores Depot at the Naval Dockyard and the subsequent computerization which greatly assisted in a robust response to the crisis in Liberia and Sierra Leone as from 1990.

NNS ENYIMIRI of the Mark 9 Squadron suffered damage in the Eastern Naval Command area and needed immediate docking. The Nigeria Ports Authority Floating Dock was the only available facility in Nigeria that could take the ship and it was fully booked for merchant ships. The Chief of Materials (COM) Rear Admiral Olufemi Olumide, a soft-spoken and highly respected Marine Engineer Officer concluded arrangements for docking the ship at Tema, Ghana. There had been speculations as regards the cause of the damage. There was no evidence apart from hearsay.

The COM went to Ghana for an on-the-spot assessment when the ship was docked. The visual inspection revealed that one of the propeller blades was missing but the root of the propeller was still in place. There was no damage to the other propeller blades and the A-bracket. The COM ordered the removal of the damaged propeller blade root and the other parts that were carefully packed and freighted to Lagos. I was directed to take the damaged propeller blade root into my custody and I took it to my office for safekeeping and my study of the nature of failure and reported on it. The manufacturer's representative had arrived from Europe and after his meeting with the COM and other NHQ staff he was directed to meet me in my office.

He arrived in my office late afternoon on a Friday. It had been a very busy day for me and it was not possible to have an uninterrupted discussion with him. He agreed and I asked him to come the following day being a Saturday. I had observed the classic beach marks of progressive fatigue failure. At our meeting, I showed him the propeller blade root and asked his opinion regarding how such a failure could occur. He tried to fall back on a typical best alternative to have an advantageous footing to evade a precise description of what he was seeing. I listened for quite a while and I then took him through the issue of material inconsistency that showed clearly and referred to the practice of refilling defective parts of old propellers and polishing them to look new. He agreed with me. The point at which the beach mark started the progressive failure was then shown to him. I explained the different time-based progressions leading to the failure. The propeller was an old recycled propeller and a filling imperfection at the root created a critical crack size that initiated the fatigue failure while the propeller was in use. We both agreed and there was no doubt in his mind what my report that would be forwarded to COM was going to be. I thanked him for his time and we parted amicably.

I reported our findings to COM and he told me that I should take note of the procedures taken so far in ensuring the ship got into the dock for inspection of underwater failures as a standard marine engineering practice. I heard no further comment from the great mind and a man of few words. This I believe was the path to follow rather than relying only on wild speculations and hearsay which most of the time were misleading and damaged careers. Rear Admiral Olumide had a stint as a Federal Commissioner in charge of the Ministry of Works when General Yakubu Gowon was the Head of State between 1966-1975.

I cannot but continue to respect the professionalism and integrity of my ultimate engineering professional boss and draw inspiration from him. He never guided me or gave me leads to suit any preconceived ideas or biases. He simply told me in very few words to study and report and made available the shipyard representative and damaged materials without a committee that would report to another committee which would end up distorting facts with many parochial interests interplay. My boss was an Admiral and I was a Lieutenant; what an act of confidence he had in me and the humility to rely on and trust my judgement. The CO who was to be punished for whatever reason had no case to answer. This experience would serve me well some years later when I had to deal with NNS ARADU's loss of five propeller blades from the starboard shaft hub.

As I sat daily in the office of the Command Technical Officer at Western Naval Command as a Lieutenant my attention was frequently drawn to a large framed RN publication hanging on the wall titled "Icons of the Royal Navy." I reflected many times on what it takes to serve the country as I read the actions recorded in the publication hanging. I read the exploits of sixteen-year-old Boy Seaman First Class John Travers Cornwell VC (Boy Cornwell), Commander Louis Mountbatten and the legendary HMS KELLY cited as firing defiantly at the enemy as it sank at sea, and King Alfred for his defeat of the Viking ships and credited as the father of RN among others and reflected on the contributions of the boy, men, and material as they served their country. Cornwell suffering severe wound he would eventually die from and with all his gun crew dead around him stood at his duty post awaiting orders; the very best of honourable conduct. I had experienced the expression of the dedication to the duty of RN officers at Manadon to serve and know their sources of inspiration. I seek no less for Nigeria.

I requested the Director of Marine Engineering (DME) Commander SB Atukum (later Rear Admiral and Admiral Superintendent Naval Dockyard) to assist with the printing and publication of task books for Marine Engineer Officers Under Training (MEOUT) and for two categories of the rating cadre based on the extensive tracing and experiences onboard NNS NIGERIA, NNS OTOBO and other ships I worked on during the preparations for the Presidential Steam Past. I had noticed this deficiency in terms of guides for personnel under training who consequently go onboard ships and idle away until they are given responsibilities they are not properly prepared for. The poor performance of personnel on board ships can be attributed to a very poor foundation at critical stages of their training due to lack of supervision and performance of practical tasks.

I was able to present and defend the relevant facts before the DME. He took copies of the final draft manuscripts from me and some days later he sent a printer to me to discuss further details before the award of the contract. I was pleased to have this official backing. I had tried to process the printing and publication through the WNC set up but it was considered a personal matter. I was not writing task books to print, publish, and make money. After meetings with the contractor, I reported back to DME that the contractor would meet all the requirements and was ready to accommodate some adjustments and corrections during proofreading before final printing and publication. I was able to produce the final edition of the manuscripts for final printing by the first week of December 1981 and the contractor was awarded the contract. Copies of the books were delivered to NN while I was at RNEC for the Advanced Marine Engineering Course. I was glad they were put to good use. The books did not feature me as the author to avoid controversies.

CHAPTER EIGHT

My Ultimate Prize from Manadon

In November 1981 I received the final movement orders for my departure to RNEC Manadon for the Advanced Marine Engineering Course. I did not have details of the course duration but I was directed to report in early January 1982. I left Lagos on 21 December 1981 for the UK and spent Christmas with Linda.

I reported at RNEC, Manadon, immediately after the Christmas and New Year 1982 celebrations during which Linda and I visited the Wedlakes at their Someries home at Stogumber in the county of Somerset. At RNEC, I was given temporary accommodation at the West Wing of the Wardroom Mess. I had to secure accommodation outside the College which I would pay for as most officers on the Advanced Marine Engineering Course who were married officers with requirements for privacy do. I secured accommodation just outside the College gate at 25 Manadon Close and within walking distance of the College. I had no car and Linda was winding up from her job in London to join me in Plymouth.

I had to conclude arrangements and have our wedding solemnization on 17 April 1982 as there would be no time to fit this in as from June 1982. The Wedlake family provided me with more than family support. They secured the date at their parish Sacred Heart Catholic Church, Townsend Road, Minehead, and identified local events organisers. The neighbour of the Wedlakes, Mr Arthur, gave his farmhouse Bed and Breakfast accommodation free to my guests. Peter and Jane accommodated Linda and her bridesmaid Caroline Chiang at their Cottage residence just outside Stogumber. John Wedlake, the first son of Walter Wedlake from his first marriage, volunteered to clean up his car and drive the bride and her father to the church but decided to cause me a little anxiety by arriving slightly behind schedule.

The parish priest, Father J Stonestreet, was most generous with the use of the parish choir for the Church service and facilities for the reception. The communities at Stogumber and the parish at Minehead were most helpful. Peter volunteered to take the wedding photographs at the church and the reception. Minehead is a holiday resort and the parks are really lovely. The photographer Andrew Priddy knew the best of the parks. The beautiful park photographs captured the lively spirit of the local support we had.

There was an incident in February 1982 involving the Nigerian Navy squadron of the German built FAC heading to Fr Lurssen shipyard for guarantee refit. The ships were caught up in a terrible Bay of Biscay storm that had been predicted. One of the ships was damaged in the storm and was taking in water that put her at risk of sinking. I faced a barrage of questions from my course mates who wanted to know why they failed to heed the storm warning. The exact nature of the damage was not known and I had to fall back on my little knowledge of the ships as I received them in Lagos in 1981 and knew that the ships had to be at the shipyard within an agreed time calculated from the time of delivery for the guarantee refit terms to apply. This scrutiny was part of the normal sharing of knowledge during the course.

The pre-course study programme was progressing fine and I had enough information on the course programme. The period between January and May 1982 was devoted to pre-course preparations and most importantly an assessment of our academic preparedness to commence the course in June 1982. There were selected lectures and tutorials including self-study periods. At various times within the same period other students from India, Canada, Brazil, and RN joined the pre-course preparations and by the end of May the result of the assessment carried out was published and all of us were set to go.

Argentina invaded the Falkland Islands on 2 April 1982. This had been expected by the UK Government. The government under Prime Minister Margaret Thatcher did not waste time in constituting a task force group commanded by Rear-Admiral Sandy Woodward. The Prime Minister stated that the people of the Falkland Islands were British and wished to remain so. She promised that the Island would be recovered.

This meant war. The unfolding events leading to the war were excellent opportunities for me to experience what it takes for a nation-state to mobilize for war. The speed with which the Task Force Group was assembled and sailed 8,000 miles to fight and win the war had many lessons for developing nation-states. Plymouth is home to the UK major Naval Base that also accommodates a major submarine base. I lived in an area occupied mostly by naval officers. It was easy for me to watch the preparations and I was impressed by how a serious nation-state prepares for and commits forces for war. I knew it takes years of training and material preparations to have the military capabilities for deployment when the time of reckoning is upon the nation-state.

A cruise ship taken from trade sailed into Plymouth Naval Base (Her Majesty Naval Base, Devonport) and it was in the news as it arrived. Frigates and destroyers at Her Majesty Naval Base, Portsmouth was shown on television being loaded with materials of war and readied for the scheduled departure. Rear Admiral Sandy Woodward would use Ascension Island as a forward operational base and he set off from the Mediterranean with another group of ships.

The RAF deployed long-range bombers that refuelled in flight to carry out the bombing of the runways in the Falklands. The logistic train was set up for deployment of about 25,000 men. Some of my RN course mates of appropriate specializations were assigned tasks to prepare and be ready for deployment should the need arise. We feared that the course would be cancelled should the war require such deployments. We followed with keen interest the conduct of the war.

The first blow for the RN was the sinking of HMS SHEFFIELD, a guided-missile destroyer on picket duties. This was the first of such losses since after the Second World War. The news of our colleagues whose ships were sunk touched us. Britain was at war indeed and the home front showed it. The sinking of the Argentinian battle cruiser leading to heavy loss of lives drew mixed international reactions. There was speculation that one of the warplanes was lost while on exercise. But a reporter on the aircraft carrier, Brian Hanrahan, reported that he "counted them all out and counted them all in" and stated the exact number of warplanes involved. There was no loss. I was disappointed with the press after the successful Carlos Waters amphibious landing when the press reported the operational plans giving away the position of the parachute battalion preparing to engage the enemy. There were so much of the Falkland war inputs into our preparations for the course proper and its conduct.

The Advanced Marine Engineering Course at RNEC had a nuclear equivalent run for nuclear engineers at Royal Naval College, London. Lieutenant John Coulthard was on the Nuclear Dagger course and we kept in touch. The course programme was pitched at a level much higher than what obtains in the universities. The two options at RNEC, Manadon, were steam and gas turbines. The gas turbine engines for warship propulsion had eclipsed steam and diesel engines. The gas turbine option was the core of ours and other course programmes involved in warship design, project management, and industrial relations regarding how naval operational experiences are brought to bear to direct industrial efforts. In broad terms, the academic lectures phase culminated at the end of year examinations. Those who passed proceeded to the final phase.

The second phase was devoted to research projects, project management, and more industrial studies. It was a struggle to catch up with academics and new technologies related to digital control systems and materials. I could no longer engage in any sports. My superiors thought I could participate in some sports and represent the college; consequently, I received invitations from various team captains. It was painful to turn down the hockey team invitation because there was no time to participate as I had done in the past.

The end of the year examinations almost created a major problem for me due to a thoroughly disappointing performance in an open book early examination on vibrations which was essential to gain maximum marks. There was a very simple equation involving defining acceleration that I had to state in a differential form that had indications for two-stage differentiations. I indicated one stage differentiation and was going around filling pages without the desired result. By the time I discovered my mistake, I had wasted more than half of the time allocated to the entire examination period for the subject. This was the easiest question in the examination and I had wanted to finish it quickly to give me time to deal with the more difficult questions later. I had to quickly close the books, abandon the question, and try to attempt the others to gain marks.

I did not achieve much. I left the examination hall devastated and wondered what I was doing on an MSc degree course if I could miss the second dot in the differential equation to indicate acceleration. How could I face the lecturer and explain that I could not define a simple equation that I had played with for many years in many forms? I tried to pick myself up and concentrate on the other examinations ahead but it seemed like I had made a very strategic mistake I would never recover from. I had a standard and I had fallen short.

The examinations ended and my course group embarked immediately on an industrial visit near London. My wife was in the later stages of her first pregnancy and expected to deliver at the end of January. The thoughts of being withdrawn from the course occupied my mind.

In keeping with the schedule, we began industrial visits immediately while the scripts were being marked and the results collated so that the results would be released before we returned to the college within the one week allocated to the industrial visits. I avoided the course officer as much as I could. It was about mid-week that news filtered in that there were no failures; that is no one performed badly enough to be withdrawn from the course. On my return to the College, I ran into the senior officer in charge of the course Commander S Stone, Head of Marine Engineering, and he asked me: 'Tony, what happened to you during the examinations? This is not you that we know.'

When he saw that I had some difficulty answering his question, he advised me to put this behind me and concentrate on the hurdles ahead. He wished me well. This was like a huge load lifted off my shoulders. Commander Stone was noted for asking the killer questions during the research project defence that attracted an array of experts from outside the College in addition to College faculty. No student escaped his scrutiny without scars. I have given this narrative to support a caption I noticed in the College Design Office as I spent extra time on engineering drawing to make sure I passed the subject on the first attempt during my first-degree course. The caption read: 'Small things make perfection, but perfection is not a small thing.' The one small dot I missed in a differential equation almost caused me the total happy picture of an MSc degree that would turn out to be very significant in my career.

I had chosen a corrosion topic for my research project. The project was titled 'Cathodic Protection in Pipes and Annuli.' This had implications for submarine piping systems protection. The Materials Department had been very helpful to me during my first-degree project work and on getting the approval to proceed with the project I looked forward to the staff of the department. I did not know that there was a tussle going on between the staff as regards a piece of new equipment that had been projected to be bought for the materials laboratory to help advance the study of aspects of corrosion for which the College had established a reputation as a leader. I wanted to move forward beyond performing experiments and using existing corrosion theories to explain the trends and derive a predictive formula. I had used such an approach extensively for the first-degree project with a lot of success. I discussed my proposals with the technicians in charge of the laboratories as regards sourcing for equipment and materials such as fresh seawater that had to be taken from HMS DRAKE, Plymouth Naval Base, and delivered to the College on the days required.

One of the technicians at the forefront of the drive to buy the new equipment for the laboratory convinced me of the huge benefits of getting the equipment to use as he described to me how this would facilitate the work I intended to undertake. He told me that this would help the department to get the equipment in time so that I could solve the problems of setting it up and use it. I had two project supervisors; the Head of the Department, an RN Captain, and a civilian senior lecturer. In discussing the set-up of my laboratory during one of my briefs, I mentioned the important role the new equipment would play and prayed that it be provided.

The senior lecturer did not like this idea and dismissed it immediately. He told me to get my hands dirty in seawater and proceed. I decided to avoid the departmental tussle and focus on my project to no avail. Though I never mentioned it again and never had the equipment, I was under pressure to proceed and forget about the new equipment each time I highlighted the complex nature of the investigation I had to carry out and the pipe and annuli configuration which was equally very complicated. I decided to remove the annuli to have a simpler shape to facilitate the new approach that I was developing. It was agreed.

An appointment was booked for me to visit a professor, a leading expert, on corrosion at the University of Manchester Institute of Science and Technology (UMIST). I could not have a staff to accompany me as was done for other students. I went alone and keep the appointment as scheduled. It was getting to the last two weeks of January 1983 and time was important as regards getting my project on a soundtrack. The day before my departure Linda developed complications with her pregnancy and I took her to Plymouth General Hospital. She was admitted and I opted to cancel the appointment at UMIST and stay with her. After going through some tests and observations she was kept in the hospital for further observation. I was assured that there was nothing serious. A Malaysian midwife undergoing training at the Hospital was most helpful and assured me that Linda was in good hands.

With the assurances and seeing that Linda was in good condition, we decided that I should keep the appointment at UMIST. I spent the night in Manchester. I requested an early appointment from Professor the following day so that I can return to Plymouth and be at the hospital with Linda. The Professor was scheduled to fly out of the UK that day and his luggage was already with him in his small office. In that small office setting, the Professor gave me a thorough brief using various presentation aids and made references relevant to students on PhD programmes he was supervising. After our discussions, he asked me to see two PhD students because their research was relevant to my topic. I had achieved my objective and even gathered useful reference materials. He assured me of his availability on my return to RNEC. It was Friday 21 January 1983. I was relieved to be on my way to Plymouth to witness the birth of our first child.

I called the hospital in Plymouth and I was informed that Linda was in labour. I arrived in Plymouth late afternoon and went straight to the hospital and she was relieved to see me. The labour extended to midnight and she was getting exhausted. It was just past midnight when the consultant was called and she was moved into the operating theatre. The name of the Consultant was Mr Blood and it was very difficult for me to witness what Linda had to endure during the procedures. I was allowed to watch the procedure. The Consultant took out the baby and held him upside down and gave him a tap on the back; the first cry of our baby assured us that all was well with him. He was placed in my waiting arms. I kissed and cuddled him before the nurse took him away to be cleaned.

Linda was moved into a room and was comfortable. It was the early hours of Saturday 22 January 1983 and we had our first child, a baby boy. I never left her side till she slept. The Malaysian midwife was around to support her.

I phoned to brief the course officer, Lieutenant SPC Westwood and he informed the Captain of the College, Captain RV Holley (later Rear Admiral). The Wedlakes were informed and they contacted the parents of Jane, the wife of their son Peter. Jane Wedlake's parents were based in Plymouth and were put on standby to take care of the house and receive Linda and our baby boy when they were discharged and returned home. I went to the hospital on Monday after lectures to receive the happy news of Captain & Mrs RV Holley's visit. They presented beautiful flowers to Linda, expressing their enduring love for us. My first son, Daniel, as an undergraduate at the University of Portsmouth, visited Rear Admiral & Mrs RV Holley in 2008. The support given by Nan and Vera was superb. They both took turns to look after Linda and the child at our 25 Manadon Close residence until Linda's parents arrived from Kuala Lumpur to take charge. I was relieved to face my studies by the magnificent support we had. There were regular visits to the house by the National Health Service doctor covering the area and we had good reports of progress as regards the child and the healing of the mother's surgical wounds.

I briefed my project supervisors and the course officer of the outcome of my visit to UMIST and proceeded with my research work. I was now better armed to determine the direction of my efforts and I tried to evade the issue of the departmental equipment purchase. I decided to defend a modification to the project title if I was going to achieve something that would be satisfactory and considered appropriate for the award of an MSc degree. I intended to explore some theories that would explain the trends observed and documented so far. I had to simplify the topic and jettison the complexity of annuli to focus on a simple pipe. I used the series of results established to test appropriate theories and requested a presentation to my supervisors. I had a long drilling and rough time which convinced them that I was bringing in something new. I scaled their thorough scrutiny and was approved to proceed. The experimentation phase was labour intensive and it was evident that dropping the annuli was right. I had to be careful in managing the situation.

The other course programmes were based on gas turbines and involved design evaluations using some of the latest software programs and warship acquisition processes exercises. These were complemented by visits to and interaction with the Staff of Ship Department at Bath and project staff at Rolls Royce (Gas Turbines) establishment at Ansty near Coventry among several others. These interactions helped us understand the limitations of technological developments and the risks that had to be managed. It was in March that news filtered in that Her Majesty, Queen Elizabeth II, The Lord High Admiral, would be at the College graduation. This was an incentive to work harder to ensure graduation.

On submission of our research project reports, we began to prepare for their defence. It was a difficult waiting period as we tried to get information regarding preliminary assessments by our supervisors. We needed the support of our supervisors especially in resolving contentious issues. My project defence was towards the end of the presentation schedule. I was encouraged and ready to explain why I dropped the annuli component to have a simple pipe for my project. On my presentation day, I passed by the room where we collected aids for the event and the attendant graciously gave me a telescopic pointer to use and remarked, 'Good luck to you.'

I needed to be prepared and focused for good luck to occur. I reminded myself of the contentious areas of my research project and how to respond to questions. On my way to the lobby entrance into the hall, I noticed an RN Commodore from one of the establishments who had come as an external examiner. I saw a copy of my project among the pack of publications with him. When I was called to get ready and start my defence, I remembered that Linda promised to light a candle and pray for me at home and this calmed my nerves. I faced the question and answer phase in a packed hall after my presentation.

Commodore's intervention was a complimentary remark. He said that he came to the proceedings as my research subject was important for submarine project studies being undertaken. I had so far managed to scale through some questions and the scare-giving Head of Marine Engineering, Commander S Stone, was given the opportunity as was done for all students. I noticed that he had a standard structure to his questions for all students to probe the originality of the work being presented and defended.

He asked me what was new that I contributed to knowledge and why the annuli were not considered. I stated the reasons I had earlier defended before my supervisors and added that that pipe alone was very complicated because the very complex phenomena being investigated had to have a practical predictive analytical tool to be established in my work. As regards contribution to knowledge, I emphatically stated that the diffusion theory applied to derive the prediction formula was unique. I then explained the results and how I established a method to predict the development of cathodic protection in pipes on warships highlighting the fact that it was also unique and from research, I did not come across similar previous work by any author and will like to know from the distinguished audience if there was any.

I stopped and waited to be bombarded only to find pin drop silence. I looked around the packed hall and there was no response from our scare-giver, Commander Stone. The moderator called the proceeding to an end. In the tea room, my course mates were jubilant that one of us had been able to silence our internal tormentor. He was a good man and I will always remember him for the encouragement he gave me after the December examinations. He had a job to do and as students, we had to do our best to meet the very high standards associated with the College.

At the end of our project defence, the internal and external examiners met to conclude their deliberations and we were immediately informed of the outcome: 'You have all made it. Congratulations' was the terse message from our course officer. This was a relief and I felt very light-headed as I walked the corridors of the academic block and met Lieutenant Commander Peter Whelan, a gas turbine lecturer. He gave me a broad smile and a very warm congratulatory greeting. He went to tell me that the way was now clear for me to go for a PhD. I told him that I would not spoil the joy of having the Advanced Marine Engineering Course MSc degree with the RNEC Dagger awards from Her Majesty, The Lord High Admiral for any PhD in the world. I would not pursue more degrees. We had a good laugh.

The next major task was to receive our Master of Science degree award from the Lord High Admiral, Her Majesty the Queen. There were invitations to high commissioners/Ambassadors of the countries of the graduating foreign students for the BSc and MSc degrees. The Nigerian High Commissioner arrived in his official Rolls Royce and was received by the designated College staff, Head of Control Engineering, who had briefed me of the opportunity I would have after the graduation and the departure of Her Majesty to meet him with other Nigerian students.

At the graduation lunch, I was surprised to be seated very close to Her Majesty, The Lord High Admiral, and Prince Philip at the high table facing us directly. I advised Linda to pay attention to the cutlery setting and follow the high table manners and avoid looking straight into the eyes of Her Majesty the Queen. Her Majesty's dress was not the latest from the designer's stable. It was elegant and showed signs of being on duty several times. Prince Philip's Admiral of the Fleet service outfit was not new and the gold laces had changed colour showing signs of ageing. This royal couple commands enormous respect and influence worldwide. There are wealth and pomp always around them. What definition of classic simplicity am I witnessing? My admiration for the royal couple soared. It was as if I was touching them and feeling at ease. Linda and I were in the most-watched position close to royalty and had to make sure we were prim and proper. We had a good lunch and the Great Hall was cleared and readied for the graduation ceremony.

The graduation procession began with the students filing in and taking their allocated seats. The academic staff filed in and took their seats. The Dean, Captain of the College, and the Heads of Departments were all given their due respect. The Dean of the College was the host for the Graduation ceremony proper though the Captain of the College was in overall command of the College. Her Majesty the Queen took her position with the Dean and Captain of the College on her flanks seated and the graduation ceremony went into full swing. Her Majesty was on her feet throughout to receive and award degrees to each graduate. It was my turn and I was called to receive a historic MSc. I climbed the steps on to the stage to shake Her Majesty's hand and receive my degree award with a respectful bow. She caught my attention with a measured royal smile, asked me: "How long have you been at the College?" I was struck dumb. What would I say to Her Majesty, The Lord High Admiral, after about six years on three courses at the College and capping it up with this ultimate MSc(+); + for Dagger? Her Majesty on noticing my difficulty with finding the words graciously gave me a smile that signalled my dismissal. Silence came to my rescue as a safe answer. I was relieved to turn right and walked away to exit the stage from the side row of steps.

I walked back to my seat following the designated route. The group photograph with Her Majesty and Prince Philip and all the graduating students and academic staff led by the Dean and the Captain of the College took place at the main entrance into the Great Hall. The MSc students were arranged to stand directly behind the row of seats arranged for the dignitaries. I found myself again standing directly behind the seat reserved for Her Majesty the Queen. As she sat, I noticed other students had abandoned their allocated positions and were crowding away from the Queen. I adjusted accordingly slightly towards the students. With the photo session over, the Queen and Prince Philip departed immediately.

I was introduced to the Nigerian High Commissioner to the UK, His Excellency Alhaji Shehu Awak, and I took him to meet other Nigerian students. I was not used to these high-level diplomatic contacts but I did my best by allowing the students to freely talk to him. When I noticed he had heard enough, I thanked him and led him to the officer designated to handle his departure protocols.

I had some time with Mr Walter Wedlake and John Honeywell who were excited to be present at my graduation and were very curious to know what I was discussing with her Majesty. It was then that I knew that my audience with Her Majesty was newsworthy that a Nigerian naval officer had a brief discussion with the Queen. I have admired her since my early years in primary school when I first saw a photograph of her sitting on a lawn with her children. My audience with Her Majesty remains a very special event in my life.

In 2008, my first son Daniel visited Rear Admiral RV Holley (Captain of the College during the graduation) in his Portsmouth retirement home and he was very happy to show Daniel the albums of the Queen at RNEC, Manadon Graduation on 22 July 1983. He told Daniel something I did not know and that was that in the very long reign of Her Majesty, RNEC Manadon was the only degree-awarding institution at which she ever attended the graduation ceremony.

I have a bundle of history in my possession. I have the only MSc degree certificate ever given to an African by Her Majesty, Queen Elizabeth II, The Lord High Admiral. This was a royal seal on all my struggles and modest achievements at RNEC Manadon. I believe the choice of RNEC Manadon for this unique graduation presence by Her Majesty was to show her gratitude to the British Armed Forces and the RN in particular for Britain's victory in the Falkland War of the previous year. The RN is the senior service in the UK Armed Forces and led the war efforts. I was in a very special institution that provided officers with very unique leadership qualities required in war. The naval engineer officers, according to Admiral WT Pillar, constituted the mortar that bound all efforts that built and sustained one of the most impressive empires in world history. I was lucky to experience the pains of a great nation-state at war that set the scene for the dagger course I had just completed and also started a family. This was a trinity of blessings.

I slowly wound down and gave my young family time to settle in and get used to me after patiently enduring my long struggles with a very hectic course. I began to pack our belongings, preparatory for their shipment to Lagos. Nuhu O Yaqub (later Professor and Vice-Chancellor of University of Abuja and Sokoto State University), my cousin, who had just completed his MSc degree programme at the University of Toronto, Canada, and his wife stopped over to visit us on their way back to Nigeria. It was exciting for Lieutenant John Coulthard who had just concluded his Nuclear Engineering Dagger Course (MSc +) at Royal Naval College, London to visit me. I invited him over to spend some time with my family at 25 Manadon Close. It was a fantastic reunion.

Nuhu and his young wife arrived the day after John left and we visited some historic places in Plymouth including Plymouth Hoe where we walked down the steps to the beach. We also visited the Plymouth Hoe lawn on which Sir Francis Drake was reputed to have finished his game of bowls before boarding his ship to defeat the Spanish Armada in 1588. After the departure of my cousin, I concluded plans for leaving Manadon-Plymouth for the final time.

The Nigerian High Commission, Defence Section had concluded plans for shipping my personal effects home. They were collected from our 25 Manadon Close residence. I drove our car, a red Honda Accord saloon, to the shipping agent just outside London and then concluded our flight arrangements with the Defence Section. I was greatly assisted by WCPO Odumeru who I served with onboard NNS NIGERIA.

I returned to Plymouth by train and prepared our residence for inspection by the owner Lieutenant Commander RG Kenworthy who had been represented by Lieutenant Commander Peter Whelan, the ever sailing enthusiast and lecturer in gas turbines at RNEC. On 3 August 1983, I took Linda and our little boy Daniel for a stroll on the College grounds. As we pushed the pram with Daniel in it sweet memories flooded my mind. A teenage dream realized beyond all expectations. I started a family and now a baby boy was unknowingly sharing the joy of my success. Nigeria had done its duty and the investment in my development had been enormous. I would have no reason not to do my best for my country at any time.

This family stroll in the College grounds took us to the Wardroom Mess reception at the entrance to the grand Great Hall. Suddenly an officer in mufti appeared and said: "Hello Tony, what are you still doing here; are you not tired of this place? There is nothing here for you anymore to accomplish!" This location where I was welcomed in 1974 was most appropriate for the summary by the officer.

I smiled at him. We climbed down the steps and faced the College mast flying the ensign with the distinctive bust of Royal Adelaide beside it. It was appropriate to say goodbye, with the summary by an officer, to RNEC Manadon at the same point where I was received in September 1974 when I arrived as a Midshipman to start my engineering education and training.

After the inspection and the handing over of our residence to the owner, we left for Plymouth railway station. Lieutenant Commander RG Kenworthy was most gracious and drove us to Plymouth Railway Station and helped with our departure by rail. In London, we stayed with Linda's friends and former housemates Ms Agatha Kong and Ms Mei Lee from Malaysia at 66B Rowley Way, not far from the famous Abbey Road Recording Studio used by the Beatles and the Seekers pop groups. We departed London for Lagos on the evening of 4 August 1983.

I arrived in Lagos with my family in the early hours of 5 August 1983. In our flat at 13 Liverpool Road, I was confronted with the realities of the loss of many valuables to thieves who burgled our flat. Lieutenant Valentine Egwuatu had written to me and explained what happened and I understood his predicament. I was grateful that I still had accommodation. I cleaned up the flat and we waited for our personal effects to arrive.

My first task was to report to NHQ and request for disembarkation leave. I was informed that there were two options for my deployment. These were an appointment to Eastern Naval Command on the staff of FOC under the CTO and the other was Engineering Watch Keeping Duties onboard NNS ARADU. The preference of the appointing officer was for me to go to Eastern Naval Command because, according to him, I had not served in the East and needed to take my turn to experience family separation. I was disappointed that such thoughts should cross the mind of a senior officer but that is the reality experienced by many officers. NNS ARADU is the only ship in the NN Fleet with gas turbine propulsion engines and my MSc (+) was based on gas turbines.

I used the disembarkation leave to clear my car and other personal effects from the ports at Tin Can Island and Apapa. It was very important to see to the needs of the family to settle down and having access to medical facilities was most important. I had help from my neighbours and colleagues in the Apapa area. The issue of erratic power supply was already known and it was the challenge of adjusting to the situation. I needed to learn quickly how to balance family responsibilities and the demands of my job. I needed to have some of my brothers and sisters' children around with us to forge close ties and allow my son to learn the Ebira language which Linda was very keen to learn also. As for my career, the blueprint had already been firmly laid for professional expression as a military officer and a marine engineer. I have to manage the work and home to ensure that none suffered.

After my disembarkation holiday leave, I was given a letter of appointment directing me to report onboard NNS ARADU and appointed as Engineering Watch Keeping Officer. The Assistant Marine Engineer Officer was Lieutenant Commander Peter O Ijebu and the Marine Engineer Officer was Commander Mohammed A Lawal (later Rear Admiral and military governor of Ogun State and later a civilian governor of Kwara State after retirement).

NNS ARADU was commissioned into service in 1982 and it was the first of its type in the world that a novel modular construction technique was adopted by the shipyard Blom+Voss of Germany. It is a heavily armed warship with an impressive fit of Otomat and Aspide missiles and a range of automated guns. The ship had six launchers for anti-submarine smart torpedoes. The propulsion machinery controls and surveillance systems were highly automated. The main marine engineering pieces of machinery were the two Rolls Royce gas turbine engines and two diesel engines for propulsion in a Combined Diesel or Gas Turbine (CODOG) combination. The modular construction technique introduced some compact packages of main and auxiliary machinery that made their maintenance very difficult. The sophisticated technology pack onboard demands modification to the onboard technical departments' organization so that the Marine Engineering Department has effective control of electronic and electrical systems integrated into marine engineering systems in line with the training I had at RNEC.

The Marine Engineering Department onboard NNS ARADU could not embark on the needed re-organization because the NN had no policy to drive the process despite being kept abreast of the developments by RN. The old entrenched ways, therefore, continued to thrive. In the performance of my Watch Keeping duties, I did some systems tracings and had the MEOUT Task Book that had been published while I was away on the Advanced Marine Engineering Course as a guide. This also helped assess relevance and additions to be made to subsequent editions which would be used onboard NNS ARADU.

I submitted my course report to NHQ. On an official visit there some days later, I checked with the Personnel Branch to know if they had received and studied the report. I was told that the Advanced Marine Engineering Course was quite expensive and no officer would be sent again for the course. I was surprised and tried to convince the staff officer in charge of the benefits of the course. He reminded me that I had done the course and I had no business lobbying passionately as if I was asking to go back and do it all over again.

The use of the word 'lobbying' stung me because I never sought to use it for personal gain. I do not mind lobbying for what will benefit the organization. I argued that although the course was expensive, more officers should be sent there to create a critical mass of officers to make the desired impact in the management of the complex warships coming into service.

I went to see some of the Engineering Department officers at NHQ and met the Weapon Engineering Staff Officer, Lieutenant Andrew O Momodu in his office. I briefed him on the benefits of the course and expressed my fear about the thinking that the NN would no longer send officers for the course. I asked him to sensitize the relevant officers in the Personnel and Engineering Departments at NHQ to ensure the course was not stopped for NN personnel. This was a major issue for me as regards broadening the knowledge base and because I did want to be the only favoured officer given the special treatment as most of my colleagues thought. The sensitization I embarked upon was successful and more officers were sent about two years after I had graduated. Lieutenant Andrew O Momodu was a successful nominee and others followed.

NNS ARADU was new and expected to be available for deployments. I was assigned duty daily and tasked to sort out the ship's Planned Maintenance System that was already showing signs of being disorganized due to non-availability of spare parts, relevant tools, and in some cases, expertise as many of the highly trained personnel had been appointed out of the ship. The base facilities for the more complex tasks such as calibration of precision equipment on board were not available. The defects were piling up and this made Planned Maintenance routines difficult to carry out. It was less than two years since the ship came into service but it was now encountering more repair routines beyond the scope of the ship's staff.

In the performance of my duties, I had to visit some of the workshops at the Nigerian Naval Dockyard that provides berthing facilities for NNS ARADU. The construction of the Naval Dockyard was behind schedule but some workshops had reached advanced stages of equipment installation that could be put into use. However, the specialized workshops that could be used for the calibration of precision equipment on NNS ARADU and maintenance of some of the modular equipment were still not ready. Although it was evident that NN, aware of the challenges ahead, had plans in various stages of implementation, there was no continuity, and various stages of implementation activities were abandoned in many places abroad and Nigeria. There were many pieces of machinery and equipment in storage facilities and many in containers at the seaports. Onboard, the ship, the stores were not properly organized and many items expected to be in stock were missing. I was saddened by the negligence in the management of very sophisticated products of technology onboard.

A modern warship requires absolute attention to details and NN personnel was just not prepared and trained to the requisite standards. The preferred approach was for everyone to define their standards and impose on subordinates what they thought fit. This was a chaotic approach to the management of technology. The Western world had opened up to NN and allowed the possession of sophisticated cutting edge technologies. The NN had simply failed to rise to the challenges and instead opted for mediocre efforts. Most NN personnel felt they could only do better with what they had been introduced to provided they had money. I was very disappointed at a stage at the huge waste onboard NNS ARADU and the Naval Dockyard.

I had to quickly adjust to the realities of deficiencies in the management of sophisticated technology, the poor attitude and orientation. Onboard, it was taken as normal to bypass surveillance sensors that were considered frequent indicators of problems to be solved. The damaged sensors were simply neglected and the protective measures were ignored. It was difficult to advise your superiors to follow what the relevant manuals detailed for the safe and efficient operation and maintenance of machinery and equipment onboard.

There was a piece of equipment called the Electro-Pneumatic Converter for the control of the propulsion diesel engine in a capsule. This equipment was built in a box mounted outside of the capsule and classified as a piece of precision equipment that requires calibration. There was nothing in the box that could be repaired on board. Also, if a defective component is replaced, the entire box has to be taken to the test bench in the specialized workshop and calibrated. A defective box would have to be replaced by a calibrated one that should be part of the ship's technical store holding. It was impossible to start the starboard (right side) diesel engine and this entailed many checks to identify the problem.

I was tasked with the control system aspect and discovered that some of the components in the box were corroded. I reported that I needed a new box with a certificate of calibration for replacement. I was branded as a theoretical Marine Engineer Officer who did not want to get his hands dirty. I was overruled and asked to remove the corroded components for repair. I removed them and carefully labelled all connecting lines. I was directed to clean them and fit them back. I complied. The engine could not be started after these efforts. The list of the defective components was taken from me and submitted for ordering from the manufacturers in the UK.

The response from the UK manufacturers was very embarrassing. The manufacturers replied that the box assembly was a piece of precision equipment and there was nothing in the box that could be repaired or adjusted. Any intervention in the box would require calibration. The manufacturers also pointed out that a calibrated box was available onboard NNS ARADU and should be installed and the defective one should be returned to them for necessary interventions and calibration.

The MEO and WEO called for a meeting of the ship's technical officers and all technical stores on board, both Marine and Weapon Engineering Departments stores, were searched and the box was found well-preserved in a fine furniture-grade wooden box with internal padding of velvet material that would be the envy of a jeweller. It was in the Weapon Engineering Department store and formalities were concluded to transfer the item to the Marine Engineering Departments stock. I took the box and went through the installation instructions and successfully installed it. The diesel engine was started without further problems. I took the opportunity to highlight that many similar types of equipment onboard required replacement with a calibrated one. Repair by the replacement for many equipment and systems onboard became the practice.

The situation in the NN is that despite the information available and the advice of RN and experts in the industry in Europe regarding the challenges of managing sophisticated technology, there was no policy to guide implementation. The appreciation of the engineering requirements of the NN had been pathetically poor and even the engineer officers could not lead the way when they had the opportunities.

The problems only multiplied. It was amid of these challenges that I was appointed Assistant Marine Engineer Officer (AMEO) of NNS ARADU and moved to the relevant designated onboard accommodation close to the entrance to the Machinery Control Room. I took a careful tour of the ship and appreciated the enormity of the responsibilities and investment of the taxpayers' money in the sophisticated array of machinery and equipment on NNS ARADU. I decided to keep on adhering to relevant reference publications and also cope with the realities of unprofessional engineering practices and highlight what must be done to remedy the situation and achieve the required standards.

Sometime in November 1983, a staff officer from NHQ came onboard NNS ARADU with others after working hours to have some refreshments in the Wardroom Mess onboard. This is a routine practice to unwind before going home. The staff officer of NDA Course 10 engaged me in conversation as we were familiar with each other and he often teased me. He said "congratulations" to me and I wondered what he was up to. I told him that I returned four months ago from my course at Manadon and that he was congratulating me four months late. He realised that I was not aware of the latest developments at NHQ.

He broke the news to me by telling me that COM Rear Admiral SJ Uguna had nominated me for appointment as Federal Government Delegate to Intermarine Shipyard in Italy and it had been approved by the Chief of the Naval Staff (CNS). Once again he said "congratulations." I told him that I should be allowed to settle in and see through my present appointment as AMEO of the Flag Ship NNS ARADU. He said I might have to leave the country again before the end of the year.

I cannot remember how we ended this conversation because I was worried about the unsettled life I had been living. I was admitted at NDA in June 1972, a little over eleven years ago by November 1983. I had so far spent five years and nine months with RN undergoing engineering education and training. The thought of heading back to Europe did not excite me because I felt that I needed some home working experience. Manadon had unknown to me set me up with its ultimate prize.

The problems onboard NNS ARADU kept me on board with little time to spare. I had more overalls than the normal work rig in my collection of uniforms. The locker for clothes in my cabin was converted to an emergency spare parts locker for a series of generator fuel pipes of different configurations that were frequently breaking and no spares for replacement. I had to detail an experienced shipwright senior rate with excellent welding and repair skills to be on standby for repairs when at sea. The diesel generators and alternator couplings had started deteriorating and needed spares that were not available. I checked out Dunlop and Michelin factories in the Lagos area to see if they could be relied upon to produce one for trial as the coupling was mainly rubber-based material. This effort yielded no result and was abandoned.

The generators deteriorated rapidly and needed factory level interventions which were not going to be available for a long period. I had to embark on some of the work that I could reasonably manage onboard and, on occasions, many doubted if any tangible results would be achieved. I had a very good working relationship with the MEO Commander MA Lawal. He understood the challenges and would always consider my inputs in projecting the ship's requirements to the higher authorities. He could count on me to hold the department and respond to emerging situations in his absence as he followed up actions with the higher authorities. He never queried my judgements. I earned his trust and it was my responsibility not to betray such trust earned from a senior officer and head of my department. The Commanding Officer of the ship was Captain Suleiman Sa'idu whose quiet carriage conveyed his passion for professionalism.

As a Lieutenant on board, I had to keep Officer of the Day (OOD) duties based on a roster supervised by the Executive Officer (XO) of the ship, then Commander IJ Ogohi (later Admiral and Chief of Defence Staff). I set off for work early on the morning of 31 December 1983. I got to the Ijora area and took the feeder road onto the Apongbon second mainland (Eko bridge). The road was free until I got to the point where the road joins the main highway onto the bridge. I saw an armed soldier sitting on the sidewalk looking tired. I stopped and called him; he came closer and reluctantly saluted me. Given the traffic situation, I told him to be smart on duty and not appear sluggish in the public glare. He saluted and turned to man his duty post.

As I drove further onto the bridge, there was a traffic jam and the queue moved very slowly. I thought it was caused by a routine check by the police. I was already getting late to take over duty from my course mate at NDA, Lieutenant Ekeopre Beredugo. When I drove to the point where all vehicles were being checked I saw a senior Army Non-Commissioned Officer in charge. I had a feeling that something must be wrong but I did not think of anything serious such as a military coup. The officer waved me on and I sped off to catch up on time. I met other checkpoints along the way past Marina and Bonny Camp; the approach to the Nigeria Television Authority (NTA) was heavily guarded. My mind was on getting to the ship. I turned into the Naval Dockyard beside NTA and drove to the car park lot by NNS ARADU. I raced up the gangway and I asked for the whereabouts of the OOD I was to relieve. I was told he had just left for the Wardroom. I dashed in and saw him seated and went straight into a profuse apology for keeping him waiting. I noticed the television was on but took no notice of what was being broadcast.

He said he was surprised that I braved it to report for work while a coup was going on and there was no clue who the head of state was going to be yet. He told me he had some rough time handling senior military officers coming to seek refuge or passage by boat from NNS ARADU. Besides, he informed me of the nature of the contacts or no contact from the CO and the XO and it was clear to me that the OOD had to take full charge of the ship and would be responsible for whatever transpired. I was shown the keys to the small arms locker and ammunition storage facilities onboard. I was briefed in very few words and I told Beredugo that I was ready to take over. It was not a time for asking probing questions but focus on what must be done and see how the situation unfolded. I took over. Be prepared and watchful, I told myself.

I mustered the ratings on duty and asked that others on board should also be accounted for and taken on strength if they were not leaving the ship because of the serious security situation. I was worried about the proximity of the NTA as regards control of the station having sighted heavily armed soldiers on guard there as I entered the Naval Dockyard. I focused on the ship's routine for Saturday and did not attempt to phone anyone. I took two of the most senior rates on board to inspect the magazines and assess the stock of small arms and ammunition including grenades. I only told them that it was necessary to know what was in stock because of the tense situation and the need to take charge of the ship.

There was still no announcement of the new Head of State. I avoided contact with any officers and ordered that no officers should be allowed on board and the gangway staff should be on full alert and report any vehicles or persons approaching the ship. The safety of the ship was a priority. It was after the evening muster for the fire fighting drill that I started thinking of what to do if there was no announcement of the head of state by nightfall. It would be dark and difficult to manage emergencies that could result based on the briefs and my assessment of the situation.

I allowed the duty watch and others onboard to have dinner and some rest before I called them out after 2100 hours when there was still no announcement regarding the incoming head of state. I had a plan. I informed the ratings to be very conscious of movements on board and around the ship including canoes that normally strayed from the ship. All sightings must be appropriately dealt with because I would not allow the ship to be a battleground. I assigned the key ratings to look-out points and had the two that went for the magazine rounds standby and be ready to take orders should there be the need to draw arms and ammunition including grenades. I had drilled them on the use, only outside the ship, should there be a problem from the dockyard gate to the twin docks that also were boundaries to NTA. I sent a senior rate to survey the Naval Dockyard surroundings and the main entrance gate near NTA. The lighting on the route to the ship was good except for a blind spot near the twin dock area.

I issued verbal orders and directives regarding surveillance and actions to take to prevent the ship from being endangered during the night. At 2200 hours, the lights out onboard were observed. I called for muster and told the ratings that I would be calling them for muster at irregular intervals and no one should go to sleep. We had practice sessions and I was able to identify the good hands that could be relied upon to effectively and decisively carry out orders. It was past midnight when the Head of State, Major General Muhammadu Buhari, was announced.

I watched the follow-up news on the television in the wardroom after which I relaxed the men to return to normal ship routine. It was not long before Commodore AA Aikhomu came on board and asked for the OOD. I met him standing some metres away from the gangway staff. He was calm and relaxed as I paid him compliments. He asked me to give him a good team to provide him with security to take him to his house at FESTAC town on the Lagos-Badagry expressway. I already knew the best among the men I had and the calm composure of the Commodore under whom I had served in the Flotilla Command was very reassuring. I called out the best I had identified and armed them to take him home. Those ratings were not returned to the ship. They earned the admiration of the Commodore who was announced hours later as the new Chief of the Naval Staff.

Not long after Commodore Aikhomu left the ship, Captain Ebitu O Ukiwe came around and asked for armed escorts. I obliged and he was safely escorted home. It had been a long night. I was satisfied with the precautionary steps I took to be ready to defend the NN Flag Ship should it be necessary. I handed over duty to the next officer with a depleted crew and briefed him on the steps I took, including the provision of the two armed escorts for Aikhomu and Ukiwe. I got home and informed my wife that there had been a coup and the military was now in charge. It was as if I had gone and participated in a successful coup and returned home. I had only a few hours of sleep. Later in the day, I went for evening Sunday Mass at the nearby Catholic Church.

I expected comments and criticism of my actions on the previous duty as I reported for work the following Monday. No officer discussed anything with me. A senior rate later in the day smiled at me and told me that he heard about all the tough decisions I took. The new CNS was a beneficiary of our drills and preparations. Captain Ebitu O Ukiwe was appointed a member of the Supreme Military Council. Case closed.

I returned to my marine engineering duty routines and a few days later my name was out as a member of a team to go to the Niger Delta region to monitor Nigerian National Petroleum Corporation (NNPC) handling of oil lifting facilities. This was strange to me as I had never gone near the oil industry installations. The new administration was not happy with oil theft and was determined to stamp out the practice. I was lucky to be dropped from the list based on the intervention of the MEO who reasoned that both the AMEO and AWEO Lieutenant Commander JNJ Aneke (later Commodore and Military Governor of a South Eastern State) were being taken from the ship. Ironically, I was happy about the change of government for a rather selfish reason. The administration promised to review all contracts. I took it that this would delay my appointment as a Federal Government Delegate to Italy and there was even the possibility that the project would be cancelled and I would remain at home and serve.

NNS ARADU had a Change of Command. The new CO was Captain SO Aloko (later Rear Admiral and Commandant National War College). The XO left the ship, and for some time, the ship had no second in command. The reason for this was not tenable but I would not go into it. The ship sailed for duties off Bonny Island and after some days patrolling let go anchor at a strategic point that helped us to arrest some vessels used for oil bunkering. The ship organized some social activities with the local communities to assure them of their protection by the NN and thus foster cordial relationships while the navy policed the waters to check illegal bunkering.

The CO had an interesting approach to command and one had to be on his toes to cope. He had interactive sessions with officers and was very inquisitive regarding equipment performances and how problems were solved. He came on board at odd hours to check on OODs. In one of his interactive sessions with officers, he brought up the problem of pollution in the Lagos lagoon and especially in the Dockyard pool that was blocking sea inlet passages and causing machinery failures. There were many suggestions and he seemed impressed. He then asked those who had made suggestions to put them in writing and be ready to defend them at the next interactive session. No officer was able to present any solution in writing at the next session. The CO then told us that it was very easy to spin off answers during discussions and advised that when we were confronted with problems we should cultivate the habit of going through problem statements or descriptions and proceed to define solutions. He then said that if he had to make a choice between intelligent officers and those who readily obeyed orders he would choose to work with those who readily obeyed orders for they would be more useful during operations or in battles. This was his guiding principle and I tried to understand him.

NNS ARADU had been at sea several times and usually, when machinery failure occurred, he was on the bridge and contacted the Machinery Control Room (MCR). He was always told that I was around and taking charge. He hardly contacted the MCR thereafter. He called me to the Captain's Cabin one day and asked me how I managed to be in the MCR any time there were machinery failures at any hour especially at night. I could not even attempt an answer and he changed the topic to the fluid coupling that transmits power from the diesel main engines to the propeller shafts. He asked me how a fluid transmitted such enormous power. I brought the manuals and drawings and explained how it was done.

NNS ARADU was at an anchorage near Bonny Camp and had to remain there over the weekend. I was the OOD and the ship had a boat routine for liberty men. When I was to keep the duty, I woke up at home to a rude shock of burglary. The main entrance door was damaged and we lost some valuable property in the store close to the living room. But I had to hurry and report for duty without repairing the damage to the door. At work, I observed the tidal variations and when I thought all was calm and would remain so for about two hours I asked the Assistant OOD to stand in for me to enable me to dash home and secure the damaged door and return. As the liberty boat was approaching the jetty at the Army Mess near Bonny Camp, the CO appeared from nowhere and asked why I had left the ship. I told him that there was a security problem in my flat I needed to quickly solve to secure my family because our flat was on the ground floor along a very busy road. He asked if I was aware of the gravity of the offence I was committing. I told him that my mind was not at ease and that there was no phone I could use to seek assistance. I immediately returned to the ship and prayed that nothing happened to my family.

When the ship returned to the Naval Dockyard berth, he saw me as he left the ship and told me: "Yes, I have been trying to find a fault in you for a long time and could find none. Now I have something to add to your report. There is no one without a deficiency."

I was speechless but he was right. I accepted his observations. No military personnel should leave his or her duty post. A ship at anchor was most vulnerable and it was poor judgement on my part to have left the ship. I did not hear any comments from the MEO and I went about my duty as AMEO as usual.

NNS ADRADU's situation as regards operational availability gave me some pains. A large number of officers and ratings making up the ship's complement had requirements for training and operational experiences. This is to ensure a high standard of operational availability. The real danger was spending time on board alongside and seeing the progressive deterioration of the ship. This had implications for the manpower development and perception of the NN by the shipyard that pioneered the novel modular construction method.

The capability of the NN to manage modern products of technology was often called to question. I had some proud moments of interacting with the management of industries in Europe and welcomed the procurements the NN was undertaking. But the quality manpower required was never developed and this allowed everyone to decide their mediocre standards. The NN had no clue as regards the serious efforts that ought to be made for naval preparedness and readiness of the fleet for war. Discussion amid these daunting challenges was usually about competitions for access to personal comfort and promotion.

The problems of maintenance and operational availability of the ships in the NN Fleet was a major cause for concern. The CNS came onboard the ship in July 1983 with some principal staff officers from NHQ. It was not a programmed or notified event. I had no clue what was happening as I went about, dressed in my overalls, managing the enormous maintenance and repair tasks in the machinery areas.

I was moving to a compartment below in the vicinity of the Wardroom when I was brought into direct contact with the CNS and the accompanying team. I was about to descend the ladder to the alleyway below when the CNS suddenly engaged me in a brief chat. He seemed to have noticed my dirty hands and overalls and the sweat on my face. He asked why I was not concerned with getting over to Italy but feeling very comfortable onboard by my composure as he observed. He asked if I was not interested in going to Italy. I kept quiet. He understood my silence and allowed me to continue my movement to the compartment I was in a hurry to get to.

I later found out that the Federal Government had scaled down the procurement contracts and the Mine Counter Measure Vessels (MCMV) project had survived. There was an ongoing intense lobby to replace me by over-turning the earlier approval by the immediate past CNS, Vice Admiral Akin Aduwo, appointing me the Federal Government Delegate for the project. I had no idea what to do and I could not think of leaving the warship during working hours to find out what was happening. I usually returned home late from work because of the traffic bottleneck. I got up early in the morning to be ready to beat the heavy traffic to get to NNS ARADU early enough to attend the muster parade. This was my strict routine.

Commander Peter Jerome was appointed to NNS ARADU as the MEO and became my boss. I was in the web of intrigues and my only strategy was to continue doing my best days and not lose focus. It was not easy for me as excuses were being sought to use against me to prevent me from taking up the appointment in Italy. The MCMV project suffered a lack of supervisory inspections due. Commander Peter Jerome who was the recognized signatory at Central Bank of Nigeria (CBN) had to travel to Italy for the inspection and issuance of the inspection certificate due. As the new Federal Government Chief Delegate, I had to travel with him in August 1984.

Commander Peter Jerome and I passed through London and I grabbed the chance to visit some shops and bought a series of repair kits for use onboard NNS ARADU on return. These were mostly various types of adhesives and thread seals to help in managing minor leakages.

The construction of the lead ship of the MCMV squadron had started and reached a stage for inspection and raising certificate for processing stage payment with the CBN. This was a tedious process that needed the timely generation of the necessary inspection certificates for payments using letters of credit. The CNS was given the impression that I had gone and assumed duty at the Shipyard, not knowing that I had returned and continued to serve as AMEO onboard NNS ARADU.

The Superintendent Naval Dockyard was Captain IN Katagum. He set up a naval court-martial in 1984 and appointed me the prosecutor. The case involved a Marine Engineer Officer, Lieutenant M Onwusa, charged with professional misconduct and theft. The President of the court-martial was Lieutenant Commander Joseph Badeji, a naval architect, DME at NHQ. The court-martial proceedings went well and I successfully did my job as a prosecutor. I was at home on a Saturday morning when an officer Sub Lieutenant EG Ofik who just got off duty on NNS ARADU turned up and broke the news that I had been promoted, Lieutenant Commander.

The CNS and Commodore PS Koshoni were promoted at the same time in November 1984 to the rank of Rear Admiral and had a joint reception in the Lagoon Bar at Naval Base, Apapa. I was with a group of Lieutenants when the CNS saw me and exploded and asked me what I was doing in Nigeria as he was told that I had taken up my appointment in Italy. I told him that I had no orders from NHQ. He called the attention of the Principal Staff Officers who were supposed to have acted at NHQ. Their answers were evasive. The CNS ordered the Chief of Operations (COOPs) Captain D Oshunmakinde to take charge and ensure I got out of Nigeria to take up the appointment in Italy as approved and reconfirmed by him. The CNS ordered me to see the Chief of Operations the next day for the processing of my documents. The Chief of Operations directed me to report at NHQ early in the morning to sort things out.

He was right to be angry when he saw me at the promotion reception for him and Rear Admiral PS Koshoni in November 1984 as he had been told that I was already in Italy. The NN project at the shipyard was being undermined. The earlier plan by November 1983 was to have a senior officer, Commander Peter Jerome, to head a much broader project team that involved a logistics ship in another country in Europe and I would be responsible to him but based in Italy in charge of the MCMV project.

Early the next morning, I went to see the DME in charge of processing my departure to Italy but was acting to undermine my appointment by the CNS. I told him that the CNS gave orders that I should report to the COOPs. The DME immediately started clearing his desk and told me that the court-martial would resume sitting at Naval Dockyard within an hour and that he was going to inform other members to report there immediately and get ready to commence proceedings. He told me to leave the NHQ and ensure he did not get to the court-martial venue before me.

I reported to the COOPs as ordered by CNS. I spent a long time in his office because he could not locate the file that had the CNS approval. This file was never found. The Director of Weapon Engineering (DWE), Commander (later Rear Admiral) O Dada was directed to open a new file and since it was common knowledge that the CNS had approved, the processing for my departure could commence. I was with DWE when he made his minutes in the new file and forwarded it to COOPs. The

COOPs made his minutes in the file and forwarded it to Chief of Personnel (COP) Commodore GN Kanu (later Rear Admiral). I told COOPs that I was a prosecutor at a court-martial about to commence sitting and he told me that I could leave NHQ as my presence was no longer required until later as the processing was underway.

The Naval Dockyard was not far away and I wasted no time getting to the court-martial venue. As I entered the room, everyone was seated and the President of the Court Martial ordered the commencement of proceedings. I was late. There was urgency in the actions of the President of the Court Martial. He asked me to stand up and I did. In an instant, I was in the dock as an accused. He called me lieutenant but I told the panel that I had been promoted Lieutenant Commander in case that information was needed for the proceedings I was about to go through.

The President of the Court Martial asked me to explain why I disobeyed his orders by failing to leave the NHQ and be present at the venue at the time he gave me. I explained that I was obeying the CNS order to report to the COOPs and the DWE but the issue of the missing file delayed them because they had to raise a new file to start processing my departure to Italy as the Federal Government Delegate.

The President of the Court Martial became more furious and said that I had disobeyed him and that I was in contempt of the court. He found me guilty and passed a judgement awarding me the punishment of confinement for some days long enough, as he reasoned, to cancel my appointment. The officer being court-martialed had his judgement proceeding and was found guilty. The President of the Court Martial immediately told the secretary to transcribe the portion of the proceedings related to me and type it out for members of the court-martial panel to sign. This was done and he dissolved the court-martial and dismissed the panel.

Lieutenant Commander Badeji's actions against me were part of the intrigues to stop me from taking up my appointment as Federal Government Delegate in Italy. He was one of those opposed to my appointment and advanced several reasons to replace me with a more senior officer to undermine the CNS. He argued that I was too junior as a Lieutenant at the time of my appointment in 1983 to lead the project team in Italy. The important considerations by CNS for my appointment did not matter to him.

The convening authority was also informed that evening of the unfolding drama. I went home and had a good sleep and resumed duties the following day onboard NNS ARADU. There was a reception onboard the ship and there were many officers from NHQ in attendance. I was a lonely figure until one officer found me in a lonely corner and told me that Lieutenant Commander J Badeji had taken my file at NHQ and inserted the court-martial proceedings and the judgement passed on me and my punishment. He told me that my career had been damaged and I needed the urgent intervention of senior officers to save my career. I thanked the officer and told him that I did not know anyone who would tolerate my lobbying and as such let the case go through the normal official process.

The Director of Personnel (DOP) was Commander OM Akhigbe (later Vice Admiral and CNS). He was furious when the file got to him. He sent for me to appear before him to tell him what happened. I told him all that happened with evidence; he dismissed me and told me to wait for the outcome. I left NHQ a bit worried. I was called to the NHQ about a week later by DOP. He sat me down and warned me that I must speak the truth about what happened. I told him that I had spoken the truth and was ready to repeat it before anyone all that I earlier had told him.

The DOP then told me that COP, Commodore GN Kanu would be calling me to appear before him together with Lieutenant Commander J Badeji. On the day of the meeting in COP's office, I arrived at NHQ and reported to DOP. He took me to COP's office lobby and went in to brief the COP that I had arrived. Lieutenant Commander J Badeji was sent for to appear before COP. We waited for over two hours but attempts to reach him failed even though he was a staff at NHQ as DME. The COP called for me. He asked me to tell him what happened. He had an open file in front of him. I repeated what I told the DOP. When I finished my narrative, the COP looked sternly at me and I thought hell would be let loose. But he calmly told me: "Isa, I was your training officer when you were a cadet at NDA. I am happy that you have not changed. Case dismissed. Go and complete your departure routine to take up your appointment in Italy."

What was I experiencing if not divine intervention? What a moment in my life. Commodore N Kanu did the NN proud. He has been an inspiration to me till today. He belongs to a special breed of leaders who are ever ready to mentor younger people.

I briefed the DOP in his office nearby and he asked me to see him the following day. On reporting back as directed, I met him and saw that he had given directives to fasten the processing of my papers. He advised me to ensure I maintained my professional standards and not soil my hands with any financial scandal. He told me that I still had a very long way to go due to my junior rank although he was aware of my recent promotion. The DOP had been on the NN Inspection Commission for new ships in Germany and France and was speaking from his experiences. He told me that each time any matter affecting me came before him, he was always under self-imposed pressure to act quickly. I thanked him for fighting the causes of junior officers for which he was well-known and he stared at me. This was the beginning of the very close professional relationships I had with him until he passed away after retirement from active service in 1999 having served as Chief of General Staff to the Head of State General Abdulsalami A Abubakar.

I reported at NHQ daily to keep track of development. Sub Lieutenant Emeraku Ijioma, a naval architect, who was a staff officer to DME was appointed inspector for naval architecture. He was to serve on my staff at the Nigerian Navy Inspection Commission at Intermarine Shipyard, Sarzana, La Spezia, Italy. The DME had played prominent roles in the negotiations with the shipyard and was expected to brief me on the technical and contractual challenges of the project in Italy. This, he failed to do. And to avoid any further incidents, I told Ijioma to collect all important drawings, specifications, and contract documents if he could access them and take them along to Italy.

I was asked to report at NHQ to meet the owner of Sennforce Limited, representing Intermarine Shipyard. He was Dr GIM Otubu who was also the spiritual leader of Cherubim and Seraphim Church and popularly called Baba Aladura. He was a retired civil service director and a financial expert. He was a soft-spoken man and his son Dere Otubu was always in the background understudying his father. The meeting was brief and to the point. He would be responsible for the liaison with the Italian embassy for our visas and make other travel arrangements. He told me, to my surprise, that he knows my wife was pregnant and would have to join me immediately. I had to tread softly and know who told him of my family situation. I found out that it was Commodore MAH Nyako (later Vice Admiral and CNS) who had been very close to my family through his wife, Madam Zainab Nyako, at Portsmouth.

The second meeting with Dr GIM Otubu was within the last week before Christmas and he informed me that construction had started and progressed during the year. He said I was expected to be at the shipyard, and according to the construction and contractual schedule, some inspection had to be done before the end of 1984 to avoid the complications of roll over payment schedules into the new year, 1985. The NHQ had cleared me to leave before Christmas.

I assured Dr GIM Otubu that I would be in Italy with the Shipyard before Christmas and that I would travel with Sub Lieutenant E Ijioma, my assistant. We secured our visas from the Italian embassy and booked our flight to London which was to be our temporary base because of the Christmas holiday period.

The Managing Director of Intermarine, Engr Michael Trimming, a British citizen, could not meet us because his son had an accident with a Christmas cracker that exploded on his face and he needed urgent medical attention. The owner of the shipyard was Mr Rocco Canelli. We completed the inspection procedure by 24 December and flew back to London to spend the Christmas and the New Year holidays because there was no accommodation for us in Italy We bought some Italian language books to learn the language.

During our stay in London, I got in touch with Lieutenant John Coulthard at RN Ship Department at Bath. He agreed to host me. I travelled over and spent a day with him at his residence. We had a good reunion. He told me that his nuclear submarine project work was progressing fine. I briefed him on my assignment at Intermarine Shipyard, Italy, and he asked me how I managed to get such a job at that stage of my career. We spent more time remembering our days together at RNEC Manadon.

I returned to London and visited the Institute of Marine Engineering then located at Mark Lane to get some publications on how to set up an inspection commission at a shipyard. I had a treasure of reference publications some of which I bought and others that were given to me. I also told Ijioma to visit the Institute of Naval Architects and get as many publications as would be relevant to our assignment. We returned to Italy on 10th January 1985. As we departed the UK for Italy it hit me that my experiences at Manadon were setting me up for a unique and exciting professional challenge. The project achievement turned out to be the product of my ultimate prize from Manadon and I was adequately prepared.

CHAPTER NINE

The Intrigues and Professional Challenges

O n our return to Italy, we checked into a hotel, Rhondine, near the Shipyard close to a famous restaurant, Paracucchi Locanda D'Angelo, whose chef reputedly travelled around exotic restaurants in Europe, the USA, and Japan. Rondine was most convenient for commuting between locations for work and meeting our immediate needs until suitable accommodation was secured for us as our families waited to join us.

I had a meeting with Engr Michael Trimming, Managing Director of Intermarine Spa to discuss how to get my team started. I was given a conducted tour of the shipyard. The shipyard was simple, compact, and adequately equipped for the hull, and other structural constructions as well as programmed major equipment installations. The shipyard relies on the INMA shipyard for detailed outfitting works. The ground floor of the administrative block accommodated the Research and Development Department and the Design and Drawing Offices. At the entrance to the Design and Drawing Offices, I was shown a small office undergoing repainting after renovation. I was told that the office was one of the two being considered as our office. The alternative office was on the top floor of the restaurant building. It was spacious but would require much work to be ready. I chose the small office to start immediately.

The shipyard staff told me they would search for an appropriate office table to buy to make the office fit for use. I saw an abandoned typewriter in a corner in the nearby Design and Drawing Office. The shipyard staff told me that it would take some days to get the office tables for me and Ijioma but I did not want to wait for that; instead, I took the dirty table being used by the painters and had it cleaned for use as my office table. The typewriter was operational and we sourced typing sheets from a nearby office.

The following morning, the office had a good table with a functioning telephone set, a seat for me, and a typewriter on the floor. I phoned the COP at NHQ and informed him that the Nigeria Navy Inspection Commission (NNIC) at Intermarine Shipyard had been successfully set up and a letter would follow giving him details of our office address. I gave him the office telephone number. I repeated the call to Commodore SJ Uguna and gave him our telephone number also.

I gave Ijioma the first task to type a draft of a letter informing the NHQ that NNIC had been set up. I then directed him to move the 'visitor's' chair to the opposite side of the table facing me. I sat down. When I asked him to do so and let us get going, he refused and stated that he could not share a table with his boss. I told him it was an order and we would share the table until the shipyard provided a table for him.

I instructed Ijioma to inform DME that we had established NNIC at the Shipyard as I did for other selected senior officers at NHQ. Lieutenant Commander J Badeji was the most senior naval architect in NN and was heavily involved in the negotiations for the MVMVs, and as DME, he must be involved. I decided not to be in direct contact with him and allowed Ijioma to give him regular briefings. This arrangement worked well.

As the Chief Delegate, I was the representative of the Federal Government of Nigeria at Intermarine Shipyard in Italy. I was directly responsible to the Minister of Defence and the Permanent Secretary in the ministry. The CNS was my ultimate professional boss and the professionals I had to first satisfy were at NHQ and they were my vital link to MOD. I ensured all staff branches at NHQ were adequately briefed.

The Managing Director of the Shipyard, Engr Michael Trimming pioneered the Glass Reinforced Plastic (GRP) monocoque single skin hull construction technique which removed the complication of GRP in sandwich material combination for hull construction. The monocoque did not find favour with the British Defence establishment and industry and with most European shipbuilders. Mr Rocco Canelli was an Italian financier who teamed up with Engr Michael Trimming to utilize the monocoque hull for the Lerici Class MCMVs for the Italian Navy and Malaysian Navy. They were the largest warship hull of 50-metre length wholly GRP and of monocoque design. The NN had an extended hull length of 51 metres.

I was excited to be involved again with GRP material that was an emerging technology when I established in my prize-winning first-degree project at RNEC in 1977 that the analytical tools for the study and analysis of the characteristics of metallic plates could also be used for GRP. The monocoque hull design was the exploitation of the strength of the material for MCMVs with the added advantage of its nonmagnetic properties. I was determined to keep the shipyard design and construction staff busy to meet the high standards required and they were kept busy throughout with impressive results that will be elaborated upon later.

We started with mutual respect but knew that we had differences as regards the interests of the NN and the Shipyard. The Shipyard had to make a profit but my task was to demand the best for the NN ships at all times. I was to make them spend to achieve engineering objectives to meet exact military and NATO standards as specified in the contract. We established the modalities for raising stage inspection documents and it was my responsibility to ensure that NNIC had a procedure for routine monitoring of several activities.

The Managing Director was invited to NHQ in early January 1985 to follow up on outstanding issues related to the signing of the contract for the second ship of the squadron. I accompanied him to Nigeria and took advantage of my visit to conclude arrangements to move my family to London. My wife was pregnant with our second child and was having problems. Sub Lieutenant E Ijioma's wife was expecting their first child. Ijioma requested me to also bring his wife to join him. I got the support of the NHQ and on completion of our consultations, I travelled to London with our wives and put them up with friends we had individually made arrangements with. The pressure was on the shipyard to get us accommodation. As the flat meant for Ijioma was being secured, my wife gave birth to our second son at St Mary's Hospital, London. I had to take up the flat and move my family to Italy. But a house was secured for me at Via Canaletto, Molliciara, near Castelnuovo Magra. When Ijioma's wife arrived in Italy, we had our families with us.

I had started with the assessments of the drawings received from the shipyard and the general arrangement drawings we brought from NHQ. I demanded other drawings and technical specifications related to major systems and equipment. The various standards to be met and how to verify and ensure compliance was a major challenge. Ijioma brought me up to speed regarding the discussions during negotiations between the Shipyard and NHQ. The proximity of our office to the Design and Drawing Office facilitated interactions with the various categories of staff including the draughtsmen and those using the computer-assisted design applications.

We needed to quickly catch up with the pace of construction because we were very late in arriving at the Shipyard to set up NNIC. We should have arrived and set up NNIC as the cradle for the lamination of the hull of the first ship was being prepared to familiarize ourselves with the GRP lamination and laying schedule and how the varying thickness of the hull varied from the keel upward. The internal partitions also had different types of GRP materials and laying methods. This was essential and we established a monitoring chart in our office regarding the progress of the hull construction. I had experienced the various forms of GRP materials during my first-degree course project at RNEC and it was a delight seeing the confidence with which they were being applied to warship construction.

We had to bring naval operational experiences to bear in our interaction with the industry so that they understood NN exact requirements. After several days of analyzing the general arrangement design drawings of the major systems and equipment, we established that a third generator was needed. The shipyard staff were apprehensive of such a major addition that would require major alterations to the design now at advanced stages of implementation. I directed that we first do a comprehensive study of the stages of design achieved and the systems that would be affected. The most important consideration we established was to find space and the naval architect at NNIC led the way.

There was no time to waste due to the need to convince the Shipyard design staff and subsequently the management of the feasibility of the addition and alterations at this stage of the design and construction. We had several brainstorming sessions on the options for implementation. We needed NHQ to be solidly behind us. I targeted key staff at NHQ and we started preliminary consultations on having a third generator.

At the same time, we engaged the Shipyard staff to convince them of the operational requirement and the feasibility of implementation. We answered most of their questions to convince them that we had given serious thoughts to the issue and the pressure was on them to be on the same page with us. I appreciated their concerns and I spent some time with them on the design tables with the draughtsmen. I approached the Managing Director whose staff had been briefing him. I assessed his comments and concluded that he had no major reason to convince NHQ to turn down our proposal.

I started the draft of our paper to NHQ on the issue articulating the well-known operational experiences of NN and the maintenance aspects. The paper also addressed the concerns of the shipyard and I had to convince NHQ that we were leading the efforts for solutions and not just making wild suggestions. The paper was modified as we engaged the shipyard staff as I was not ready to experience defeat in this first major battle. I put up a cover letter after getting assurance from COM Commodore SJ Uguna that he would consider our proposals. This, I considered to be a positive indicator and I kept up the momentum.

The challenge of verifying compliance with classification society and military standards specified in the contract document had to be resolved. The shipyard engaged the services of RINA the Italian equivalent of Lloyds Register responsible for the maritime classification of ships related to the safety of life, property, and the environment thereby helping clients to ensure the quality of construction and operation of ships. The Italian Navy would be the authority for the verification of compliance with all military standards.

I could not relate with the Italian Navy yet because the Federal Government of Nigeria had not signed a Memorandum of Understanding (MOU) with the Italian government on the issue. The Malaysian Navy team at the shipyard had a Marine Engineer Officer who was two years ahead of me at RNEC Manadon. He gave me some advice. I received the clear from the Principal Staff Officers at NHQ to initiate the process of relating with the Italian Navy staff attached to the shipyard for the Lerici Class of the MCMVs that were the first to enter service before the Malaysian Navy squadron being constructed. I secured an appointment for a meeting with the Italian Ministry of Defence in Rome. I flew to Rome and met with the relevant staff responsible for the MOU negotiation. I was given some conditions to fulfil beginning with a formal letter from the Nigerian Government requesting an MOU that would cover the specific requirements.

I advised the NHQ to follow through with the process and I was directed to cause the draft MOU to be forwarded to the Ministry of Defence, Lagos, as this was a government to government agreement. I got a positive response from the Italian Navy authorities that the process had effectively commenced and was progressing well. I kept the NHQ and Nigerian MOD on track. Commander Giancarlo Gambacciani was appointed as the Italian liaison officer to NNIC at Intermarine Shipyard. He was a most valuable resource and I forged a good relationship with him and Commander Carpani of the Italian Navy Research and Development establishment.

It was evident as soon as the NNIC office was set up that we needed more staff at NNIC. I needed a Weapon Engineer Officer and a naval writer for the secretariat to organize the massive flow of technical drawings and specifications and routine correspondences. I also needed a complement of technical ratings. The ships' complement would be programmed to arrive as the progress on the construction milestones dictated.

The NHQ was against the presence of the full complement in Italy and I was directed not to request for them. I still pressed for the NNIC staff appointments and received a favourable response. The first to be appointed was Leading Writer Alexander Egharevba. He was a writer by NN standards but had very little typing skills. I appreciated his commitment as he took extra lessons to improve his typing skills learning from us. He took the initiative and worked extra hours without prompting to complete all typing assignments. He was very dedicated and organized and provided an effective link with the shipyard bureaucracy.

The next to arrive were two technical senior rates: Marine Engineering Artificer Second Class, B Nwokoro, and Mechanician Second Class, B Saifa from Weapon Engineering Department. I was accused of demanding what was considered excessive but I could see the difficulties ahead and did not relent.

I sent my family back to Nigeria in March 1985 because my wife's maternity leave from the Federal Office of Statistics had ended and she had to resume work. I drove my family to Rome and put them on the flight to Lagos. On my return journey, I had an accident when a foreign diplomat's car rammed into mine from the rear. There was not much damage to my car and I let the diplomat who was struggling to speak English, go.

In April, we were informed that the CNS, Rear Admiral A Aikhomu, would be on a state visit to Italy. I tried to get information on the programme of the visit from the Italian authorities in La Spezia but because the MOU was not yet signed, I had no access; the flag officer in charge of La Spezia which covered Sarzana, the location of the Shipyard, did not recognize my presence in his area of authority. I had to rely on NHQ for any information I could get and try to fill in the gaps as much as I could from local sources in Italy. I knew his arrival date and the hotel where he would be staying. I checked into a hotel nearby. I had a written brief and arranged a small reception for him in Sarzana and La Spezia should there be the opportunity.

I waited at the hotel lobby/reception area until the CNS arrived. The CNS was checked in and taken to his room. The Flag Lieutenant came down to the reception to get details of the accommodation for other senior officers on the entourage still being checked in. I made my move and we were happy to see each other. The Flag Lieutenant to CNS was Lieutenant A Bello who kindly brought some foodstuff for me from my wife in Lagos. The most senior NN officer on the entourage was Captain SO Aloko (later Rear Admiral and Commandant National War College), my former CO when I served onboard NNS ARADU. I collected details of the room numbers of the members of the CNS entourage.

I later contacted the Flag Lieutenant and went into his room. He opened his bag to give me the foodstuff from my wife; lo and behold some of the foodstuffs had messed up his personal effects inside his box. I took the opportunity to go through the official programme for the duration of the visit.

The CNS was told I was around and he granted me an audience. I welcomed him and told him that I could not be at the airport on his arrival because I was not officially recognized in Italy as the MOU was yet to be signed between the two governments. I handed him the full copy of my brief. My mission in Rome was accomplished.

I went to Captain SO Aloko's room to brief him and also gave him a copy of my brief to the CNS. I told him of the difficulties I was facing as there was no MOU and I would have to go back to my station and wait for them. He was impressed and told me so. He told me that I had acted appropriately by briefing the CNS and recognizing that he was the most senior officer on the entourage and that I had given him due respect. He then jokingly remarked that I had come to recognize my former CO on the Flag Ship. He then asked me if I had done the Command, Appointment, and Promotion Examination (CAPEX) as a Lieutenant Commander. I told him that I had not but would like to come home and do the next one when I know the date. He told me that he was the Chairman of the CAPEX Board and that it would be nice if I could make it so that it would not prevent me from progressing in my career on completion of my assignment in Italy.

In the early hours of the day the CNS was to arrive at Sarzana airstrip, I got an urgent message from the Flag Officer La Spezia telling me that I had to be at the airstrip for the reception of the CNS. I left for La Spezia. The CNS and his entourage were already there. The staff detailed to brief me told me that clearance had been received from Rome MOD and naval authorities for me to join the official proceedings. I was detailed to be in the same car with the Italian Rear Admiral who was the Aide de Camp to CNS for the visit. The CNS was in the same car as the Flag Officer.

During the short drive to the mess, the Rear Admiral told me that he was highly impressed with what the CNS told him about me about my contributions to the development of NN; he told me to remain focused and keep it up. My inclusion in the CNS entourage and recognition was essential to advance the process of the signing of the MOU. We visited the Italian Navy Mine Warfare Centre and I was pleased that the CNS emphasised the need for the centre to render all necessary assistance to NNIC. This would be covered by the MOU. I was introduced to the commander, a Rear Admiral, who was most helpful throughout the project.

The CNS programme included visits to Italian industries such as Selenia, Fincantieri Navale, Crestitalia, and Oto Melara. These industries were heavily involved in the NN procurements in Europe from the late 1970s to late 1980s except Fincantieri Navale near Sarzana that had submitted proposals to NN for Landing Ship Dock which was being seriously considered to replace the Landing Ships Tank (NNS AMBE and NNS OFIOM) whose shortcomings had been identified during exercises. Selenia and Oto Melara were involved in the supply of Otomat and Aspide missiles and main guns to NNS ARADU and the German-built FACs and other related services.

Oto Melara's main facilities were in La Spezia. The equipment ordered for the outfitting of the Monomono missiles depot project at Kirikiri Armament Depot had been ready and packed in containers for delivery and installation. The Nigerian contractors handling the basic infrastructure they claimed they could handle never met the project milestones and specifications. The containers packed for several years awaiting delivery were shown to CNS. It was evident that the NN was unserious and/ or could not handle the missiles ordered and paid for and they remained with the suppliers in Europe in their storage facilities.

My hope and aspirations while at RNEC for a demanding and fulfilling career were being dashed because I could not see how the NN could cope with the huge unfinished acquisition tasks. The NN acquired hard wares and never really mastered them. These unfortunate experiences tallied perfectly with my experiences onboard NNS ARADU as AMEO. It was a depressing waste of taxpayers' funds which NN personnel, given their orientation and attitude, did not seem to bother about. I learnt some good lessons from these interactions to bring to bear on the MCMV project. Will the NN personnel orientation and attitude change?

The third day was a visit to the Shipyard and departure for Rome. The CNS arrived at the Shipyard and was received by the management and given a briefing in the conference room. There were no major issues.

I made a mini arrangement to brief the CNS on our activities in our small office. He met the three ratings at NNIC in the shipbuilding main workshop including the enclosed dock where the first ship was still in the cradle on the dock rails. The CNS was conducted around the Design and Drawing Offices sections handling various stages of the design and construction. I then led him to the NNIC office. The construction progress of the programme was displayed on the walls and it clearly showed the current situation and also the lamination schedules that result in the hull form of varying thickness. The CNS was satisfied with our briefing. He called for the shipyard management team standing outside and told them that he was not happy with the small office allocated to NNIC. He asked the shipyard management to provide an appropriate office for NNIC.

The CNS thereafter met the ratings mustered nearby. He had been briefed on the controversy regarding the Leading Writer after interacting with them, he asked me about his performance so far. I told the CNS that I was very pleased with his performance. The Marine Engineering Department wanted the Leading Writer to be selected from the engineering branch and not from the Supply and Secretariat Branch.

The CNS was satisfied with my answer and as we walked away from the ratings towards a secluded area, he surprised me by suddenly venting his rage. He said loudly: "I will not do it. These people do not seem to understand how complex this project is by asking me to change you. You will remain here and complete the project. Just focus on what you are doing."

It was apparent that the lobby group of senior officers had not given up on removing me as the Chief Delegate. Failing that, they wanted me to spend a year and let the position be rotated yearly. The CNS must have been under intense pressure but he recognized the complexity of the project as this was not the normal steel hull construction. He praised our efforts at NNIC and asked me if there was anything he could do for NNIC.

I asked for a second officer for the weapon engineering aspects of the project and made a case for us to be independent of the shipyard in meeting our administrative requirements. The interests of the shipyard and those of NN were bound to conflict and I should be free at NNIC to permanently pursue NN interests. The CNS promised to look into the issues on his return to Lagos.

The visit to Brescia where the MISAR mine factory was located was cancelled and the CNS had a free evening so I hosted him at a restaurant in Lerici on the coast. We had two vehicles at NNIC and could only take a few people. The CNS graciously trimmed down his entourage to just what the two vehicles could comfortably contain. Security considerations were a priority. He enjoyed the dinner and the choice of Italian wines. After dinner, I drove him back to his hotel.

The CNS concluded his official engagement with the Italian authorities in Rome and was checked into another hotel in the city more befitting for him. The programme was more relaxed and visits were arranged for sightseeing in Rome. It gave the members of the delegation time to wind down and prepare for departure to Lagos. I stayed in Rome and followed through with the remaining programme until the CNS's departure. It was during this short stay that I was introduced to his close friend, architect Tom Ikimi (later a traditional chief and Minister of Foreign Affairs). . The night before CNS' departure, he directed that I would be contacted to come to Lagos for consultation as he was going to approve an imprest to enable me to run the NNIC office independently of the Shipyard. His visit was a morale boost for the NNIC staff. I was delighted.

When the CNS returned to Lagos, I was directed to come home and report to NHQ for consultation. I also used this opportunity to review the situation regarding my wife holding on to her new job at the Federal Office of Statistics (now National Bureau of Statistics). At NHQ, I was directed to report to the Chief of Accounts and Budget (CAB), Rear Admiral E Okpo, who was most receptive. He told me that the CNS had approved thirty thousand British pounds for me as imprest. I thought this was a dream. He advised me to go and attend to other matters and return in about two hours to collect the letter conveying the CNS approval and the cheque.

I used the chance to check on the issue of a second inspector for the NNIC with the DWE and was assured that one would soon be appointed. On my return to his office, the CAB allowed me to read the letter after signing it. I noticed that there was no indication regarding how I would account for the money. How can I ask a Rear Admiral to alter a letter or convey to him that something was missing in the letter? He noticed my change of mood and asked me if everything was okay. I said, "Sir, how do I account for the money and get replenishment on exhaustion? To whom do I render an account?" He asked me to whom did I want to account for the money? I told him that I wanted to account for the money to the Defence Adviser in London who should also be asked to replenish on satisfactory rendering of account. He went out of his office with the letter and asked me to wait for him.

He returned moments later and informed me that he went to discuss it with the CNS and he agreed to my request. The CAB remarked that the CNS was trying to make things easy for me and I was inviting problems for myself. He altered the letter and copied the Defence Adviser, London. I thanked the CAB for his kind attention and collected all documents and left his office. I called on the COM, COP, and other officers that I had been sending briefs to at NHQ. I would very much later know that the CNS was impressed with my handling of the imprest as he mentioned it on many occasions to the gathering of officers stressing what I stood for. I would later reap the benefit of opting to account to the Defence Adviser when there was a change of CNS a few months later due to the 01 October 1985 military power tussle.

I looked into the situation with my family in Lagos and decided that since I would be in Italy until the completion of the project, it would be better for my wife to sacrifice her job and join me in Italy with the children. I concluded the arrangement and my family joined me in Italy.

Commodore Albert A Ajanaku, who had retired early 1984, was posted as Nigeria's Ambassador to Italy later that year. I took the opportunity to call on him in Rome. I did not have a formal appointment with the Ambassador but the protocol officer squeezed me into his schedule for the day. After a long wait, I finally met with the Ambassador and briefed him on my job in Italy. He was happy that he was kept abreast of the NN MCMV project in Italy. We chatted for some time and I then signed the visitor's book. I could hardly contain my joy at this honour. I returned to my station happy that I had established contact with the Nigerian Embassy at the highest level.

The activities at the NNIC office were getting more intense and working into the late hours of the evening became a routine. I followed up on the gains of the CNS visit. The Shipyard showed us the upper floor of a large building that had a dining hall on the ground floor for the entire shipyard workforce including the management. It had ample space. A section of the large hall was partitioned into offices. I and Sub Lieutenant E Ijioma had separate offices. Two spacious additional offices were carved out and we had a total of five offices. The conference room was converted into the secretariat and I demanded from the Shipyard that it should be fitted with document and book racks. It soon became a library. Lieutenant Samuel O Odusola, a Weapon Engineer Officer, joined us at NNIC. I was relieved because matters related to weapons and related systems and electric power generation and distribution would be fully taken care of by him.

I considered the complement of three officers and three ratings at NNIC adequate but I expected that more personnel would arrive in phases in due course to start training to man the ships. I was advised not to request for the complement of ships' staff as their presence in Italy would cause diversionary problems. I considered this sound advice based on unpleasant experiences of indiscipline during past NN construction programmes in Europe but this being a complex project with many novel features, I argued against the advice and recommended the presence of the ships complement in Italy. I used the programmes agreed with the

Italian Navy Warfare Training centre for the development of mine warfare capabilities and the agreement to allow the NN MCMV Squadron to participate in the NATO Exercise scheduled for the summer of 1987 in Italy in support of my recommendation.

I was glad I made the recommendation because I was convinced that by the time the majority of the crew arrived, there would be enough work to keep them busy and minimize incidences of indiscipline. I had timed their arrival to coincide with training and inspection of construction activities to familiarize them with the sophisticated technology on board. Also, the NN was developing the Underwater Warfare School and NNIC was tasked to make contributions related to mine warfare and diving. The NN had no quality personnel to commit and that was the problem.

The NNIC team worked hard to organize the documentation and procedures for monitoring the design processes, construction activities at factories and in the shipyards, and acceptance trials at various locations within and outside Italy. The adherence to specified military and classification society standards were reflected in various stages of documentation. The assessment of design drawings took several days and sometimes weeks. Some of these drawings and related specifications had to have inputs from the Italian Navy Research and Development and the Classification Society. The documentation for acceptance trials at the factory, harbour, and sea trials was defined and each checked for compliance with standards and established procedures. These were to ensure we had a functioning system for orderly conduct in a very complex undertaking.

At NNIC, there was a meeting on the final definitions and the shipyard was requested to print the required number of copies after the Chief Delegate had appended his signature and stamp on all pages of the agreed document. All approved drawings were also duly signed and stamped for distribution to various construction sites. This elaborate procedure for handling documentation ensured that correct documents and accurate information as agreed and in compliance with standards were used at all times. The ship's technical crew were the first to arrive with some key seamen personnel. This improved our monitoring efforts.

The construction stage for the lead ship that was achieved before our late arrival at the Shipyard meant that some of the inspections and oversights could not be carried out. Those equipment delivered to the shipyard without vital factory inspection and acceptance trials being witnessed by the NN inspection team had been installed onboard. They had been installed onboard following construction schedules.

I took note of such equipment and ensured that the factory inspection and trials for the second ship were carried out so that any observed shortcomings or faults were resolved before installation. Such solutions were then implemented on the first ship. The lead ship was being readied for launching and outfitting. I ensured the NNIC was open to all personnel for access to information. The well-organized secretariat that was more of a library facilitated access. Leading Writer Alexander Egharevba was impressive in organization and record keeping and I knew he could be relied upon to retrieve any documents needed.

I got to know of the boats, tugs and other auxiliary craft being contracted to foreign builders at MOD and NHQ for inshore operations while I was being documented to leave for Italy in 1984. The various classes of vessels were being built in the USA (Savannah Boatyard), Netherlands (Damen Shipyard, Van Mill Shipyard, and Verhoff Boatyard), UK (Water Craft), France (Simoneaux of Fontenay Le Comte/La Rochelle), and Italy (Crestitalia). There was an initial delegation that came to Europe from MOD/NHQ for inspection before I was told to take over the responsibility, together with the Deputy Defence Adviser (Navy), London, for the various stages of inspection, construction, trials, and delivery. This added to my already hectic schedule.

I ensured all officers adhered to their official schedules following their appointments. All NN personnel were in Italy at NNIC for the only objective defined by NHQ for the successful design, construction, and delivery of two warships-MCMVs. Some officers appointed to serve on board the ship wanted to take over the functions of the inspectors at NNIC because they were senior officers. I told them that I would not go against the orders given by NHQ and do internal re-appointments just to massage their egos. Sub Lieutenant E Ijioma was mainly the target; he had an MSc in naval architecture and had been playing very important roles. It would be unwise to allow his expertise to be stifled by imposing senior officers who were not naval architects to supervise him. I knew his operational limitations and I had so far managed them well to get the best out of him. I told all officers that I respected seniority but I had a job to do.

There were areas of differing technical opinions with the shipyard technical staff at Intermarine Spa, Italy. These were largely resolved at management meetings; those that could not be satisfactorily resolved were referred to consultants. Three such consultants were engaged in the Netherlands, USA, and Germany where facilities existed for specific designs evaluation. The Italian Navy establishments were also handy in this regard as NNIC took advantage of the MOU provisions.

I had some difficulty in convincing the Shipyard to carry out the factory acceptance trial at Termomeccanica factory in La Spezia for the two water jet (hydro-jet) propulsion modules. The two for the lead ship had already been installed without the trials as earlier narrated. I was determined that this important trial would not be skipped again because it was easier to resolve identified problems at the factory where the components could be easily dismantled for interventions and corrective actions than when the equipment had been installed onboard the ships.

The shipyard was adamant and I ordered NNIC inspectors not to allow the installation of the two propulsion modules on board the second ship NNS BARAMA. I was told that there was no test facility at the factory for the trial and that I was stupid to be insisting on the trial. It appeared I was alone as all sources of information I had relied upon for this stage of equipment trials supported the shipyard position.

I heard of the vibration problems on the Mark 9 Corvettes during construction in the UK and the eventual problems caused by the failure, a few years later in service, of a propeller blade that Rear Admiral Olufemi Olumide had so professionally involved me in the investigation and failure analysis. I was almost alone and it dawned on me that leadership can be a very lonely undertaking. I had to make the hard decisions and needed information.

Commander Carpani with whom I had grown into friends came to the shipyard and called on me. I took the opportunity to validate my stupidity label. I told him the problems I was having convincing the shipyard to carry out the factory trials. I then asked him how the Italian Navy managed similar water jets propulsion systems for the Italian Navy small craft project and specifically asked him about the availability or otherwise of the test facility at the factory in La Spezia.

He told me that a facility existed but was dedicated to Italian Navy projects. I had the MOU and official access to the Italian Navy Research and Development establishment. This was now a navy to the navy relationship being put to the test. I had what I wanted and maintained my stupid posture. No one at NNIC knew I had information on the existence of the test facility at the factory. I was warned by the Shipyard management about the delays being caused by my stupidity.

The shipyard informed NHQ through their representative in Lagos and the matter was taken up at NHQ. Some of the key staff at NHQ contacted me. I told them that I considered this a mandatory test and advanced the technical reasons backed up by experiences of NN with vibration problems during new constructions. I was ordered to report to NHQ and MOD for consultation. I prepared the necessary brief and recommended conveying that the factory trial must be carried out. Before I departed for Lagos, I briefed my staff and told them to maintain surveillance and ensured the hydro-jet modules were not taken on board and installed.

I arrived in Lagos in the evening. I reported early in the morning the following day at NHQ for an audience with the CNS. I had several copies of my brief. This was an initial meeting with CNS and it was very brief. He told me that I was directly responsible to the Honourable Minister of Defence, General Domkat Bali. He directed that I should go, brief, and submit the original of my brief to the offices of the Minister and give a copy to the Permanent Secretary before briefing him.

The MA to the Minister told me that the Minister was not yet in the office. He directed me to go and brief the Permanent Secretary and give him a copy of my brief. I was lucky to have quick access to the Permanent Secretary. I was alone actor being watched by very important personalities at MOD and NHQ. I gave a copy of my brief to the Permanent Secretary and verbally highlighted the main points. The Permanent Secretary did not ask for any clarifications and simply asked how I was faring in Italy. I told him I was fine and he dismissed me.

I went back to the MA to the Honourable Minister and gave him the original copy of my brief for the Minister. I rushed back to the office of the CNS. He asked for his copy of the brief. He glanced through the first page and went straight to the brief recommendation. The CNS thundered the Gunnery Officer's orders: "They will carry out the factory trial."

He immediately phoned the Shipyard Representative in Nigeria and informed him that the trial must be carried out. Dr GIM Otubu told the CNS that the shipyard would carry out the test the next day. What a happy turn of events! The great man, the CNS, saw my pensive military mood and dismissed me. I was speechless. He simply told me to carry on. I told him instantly that I am leaving Nigeria immediately to witness the test the following day. How? I did not know but simply felt it was doable as my ultimate professional boss had uttered: 'Carry on.'

I rushed out of NHQ and got into the personal vehicle Major LKK Are had given me to use while in Lagos and drove straight to the travel agent's office nearby and requested the next flight schedule that would take me to Italy and specifically to Pisa or Genoa or Milan. I was ready to move at immediate notice starting from that day. The travel agent got me a flight to Rome and with a connection to Pisa. I relayed the message to

Lieutenant Samuel Odusola and told him to convey to the shipyard my arrival schedule and that I would be witnessing the trial. I flew to Pisa airport and was picked up by Samuel because Ijioma had to be at the factory in La Spezia to ensure adherence to the trial protocols.

I arrived at the factory and it was already dark. I was told that all was set and was taken to the section of the factory building securely separated from other facilities. I knew why and played along. The test had just commenced and the loud noise from the module made hearing extremely difficult. I did not utter a word to the senior shipyard management and technical staff present who were trying to speak to me. I covered my ears with my index fingers and gestured that I could not hear them because of the loud noise from the water jet propulsion module on the test rig. There was a look of embarrassment on their faces. I told the NNIC staff to leave and return to the factory in the morning.

I left the factory and went home to the warm welcome of my family. The NNIC team was at the factory at the stipulated time the next day and we were taken into a laboratory where the water jet grid responsible for the noise was rigged with a massive array of sensors, wirings, and display consoles indicating a component in an excellent intensive care unit for investigation. The team wore a weary look. It indicated that they worked overnight to dismantle the waterjet module and remove the offending water jet grid and guide vane assembly designed for thrust vectoring that was identified as causing the loud noise. I inspected the vane assembly and all sensors attached for the investigation and had a brief discussion with the technical team managing the investigation. I was confident that a solution would be found.

The following day the shipyard informed me that the design of the vanes profile was faulty and the assembly would have to be re-designed and a new one manufactured. This was done and a new date was set for the factory trial and this time it was a very quiet run. It was a relief. I called NHQ and briefed them as events unfolded. The construction programme was back on course. I visited the other major equipment manufacturers in France and Germany for the weapon system and ship control system respectively.

I visited the Thomson CSF factory located outside Paris. I inspected the sonar assembly and the Combat Information Centre equipment at various stages of design and construction. I discussed the problems of fouling the sonar assembly housing in the polluted waters of Lagos with them and they promised to make modifications to it. We also discussed the nature of the factory acceptance tests before delivery to the shipyard and identified the special equipment we had to use. Lieutenant Samuel

Odusola was the Weapon Engineer and he led the discussions. The visit to the MTU factory at Friedrichshafen in Germany covered the main propulsion diesel engines, generator engines, and alternators, and the ship control system including the machinery control sub-system fit.

There was a problem and delay in the control system design and this was highlighted to the project manager. The control problem for which solution would be found in the design for implementation had not been defined to guide the design process. A second visit was planned to enable presentation and investigation into the problem identified. The second visit confirmed the problem and the delay. The project manager allowed the control system team leader to defend the state of affairs and he confirmed the problems.

There were no further discussions and it was some weeks later that the control system design team leader visited the shipyard and had a lunch meeting with NNIC officers and shipyard representatives. I was surprised to learn later that the team leader lost his job at MTU because of the lapses. I sincerely felt for him losing his job. This action reflects the high standard for which MTU is known and it also showed that no organization is perfect.

As the manuals were delivered, experienced senior rates were tasked to use them for the operational and maintenance tasks; where the information contained was inadequate, the observations were discussed and forwarded to the manufacturers for updating the manuals. Such manuals were only accepted after validation by experienced NN personnel on the ships.

The lead ship was launched in November 1985 by the wife of the CNS, Mrs Rebecca Aikhomu, at a well-attended ceremony. The ship was named NNS OHUE. The Nigerian Ambassador to Italy, Commodore AA Ajanaku, attended the ceremony. The NN delegation was led by Commodore MAH Nyako and the Deputy Defence Adviser (Navy) from London was in attendance.

The chaperone to the guest of honour was a lady Sub Lieutenant. We expected her to be in uniform. The Italians were looking forward to seeing a female naval officer in uniform as there were no women in the Italian Armed Forces then. But the uniform she came with did not fit her; it belonged to another officer. It was a disappointment. The leader of the NN delegation was informed and approved her being dressed in mufti.

The second ship, NNS BARAMA, was launched in June 1986, a few weeks after the birth of my daughter, Ahaoiza Diana. The Defence Minister's wife, Mrs Esther Bali, was the guest of honour. The NN delegation was led by Commodore OP Fingesi, the Chief of Operations at NHQ. The Nigeria Ambassador to Italy was again present accompanied this time by his wife and I had the honour to host them in my residence at Moliciara near Castelnuovo Magra. They wanted to meet my family and see our baby daughter. They brought presents for Ahaoiza Diana who was born on 20 May 1986. They invited my family to visit them in Rome and we accepted.

Mrs Esther Bali and Mrs Rebecca Aikhomu wowed the crowd with their simplicity and humility at the respective launching ceremonies. They were excellent ambassadors of Nigeria and made us proud with their grace and composure.

Lieutenant Commander Andrew O Momodu, a Weapon Engineer Officer, had earned his MSc degree in Advanced Marine Engineering and was to be formally awarded his degree certificate at the RNEC graduation ceremony of July 1986. The Deputy Defence Adviser was invited to the ceremony and he asked me to join him in London and we drove to Plymouth. We had been having a joint inspection of the boats being built in some countries in Europe and the USA and I had been regular at the Nigerian High Commission. I was glad to be back at the College and equally glad that an officer from the NN had successfully gone through the course after me. With this, I believed more officers would be encouraged to take up the challenge. My lobby efforts to have more officers nominated for the course was working. I would be back the following year for the graduation ceremony of my coursemate at NDA who left the seaman branch at the time I was graduating in 1977 from RNEC.

I had the chance to see Commander GT Reader who was my research project supervisor, that is, the project on GRP plates that won a prize in 1977. After the 1986 graduation ceremony, we stood on the front lawn of the Great Hall and enjoyed the lovely sunny summer day. He teased me and asked me what I was doing in the UK again as if he was tired of seeing me at the College.

I told him my experience at the shipyard in Italy involving GRP and the boats that were being constructed in several boatyards which were taking me around some countries in Europe and the USA. He found my experience fascinating. He congratulated me and told me that the job I was doing in Italy was the dream of engineers worldwide but only very few have the chance to go through my experiences and achievements so far with GRP and the range of constructions I was involved with. I sensed he was proud of his product.

He asked me if I was related to the Institute of Marine Engineers in

London. I told him that I was a Member. He said that that was not appropriate and that I should be a Fellow. He told me that he was a Council Member of the Institute of Marine Engineers and that the responsibilities I was saddled with in Italy qualified me as a Fellow of the Institute of Marine Engineers. He told me to fill the membership form for election as a Fellow. He directed me to properly fill the portion requesting information on the job I was doing in Italy and my data and give it to the Managing Director at Intermarine Shipyard to authenticate and sign and thereafter send the form to him. At the next Council meeting, I was elected Fellow of the Institute of Marine Engineers. I treasure this recognition so much as it marks the height of my professional achievements rarely achieved. It was absolutely special for me to have Commander GT Reader associated with this recognition.

This recognition means a lot to me and made me aware of the journey with GRP plates since the RNEC Manadon research project findings. It is rare to win a prize on emerging material technology and seven years later to be involved in using that material for the design and construction of a warship the size of the NN MCMVs. Commander GT Reader retired from the RN and became a professor of mechanical engineering at the University of Calgary and later Windsor both in Canada.

At the beginning of 1986, I argued again for the release of key technical personnel to start training preparatory to manning the ships upon delivery. I had drawn up a programme and convinced the NHQ to allow the ship's crew to come over, work up the ships after delivery and prepare to take part in the NATO Mine Warfare exercise in 1987 and then prepare to sail the squadron to Lagos. I felt this was a fantastic opportunity for capacity building that would facilitate the development of credible mine warfare capabilities. The remaining members of the crew were programmed to arrive in 1987 in keeping with their training programmes. The divers sent for their course were mostly sick or old men despite the stringent medical requirements made known. In their medical test conducted by the Italian Navy only one diver, a Marine Engineering Artificer (MEA Ofili), passed the test and was considered fit for the course. He was safe to go the depth required for mine warfare. This was a serious setback as NN missed the opportunity of training at the Italian Navy special facility. That would have introduced NN to aspects of special forces training.

Commander Gambacciani felt devastated when he came to my office to discuss the matter with me and told me that the Italian Navy Diving School would not conduct a course for a class of one. He wondered whether the NN conducted basic medical checks at all. I discovered that all of them except the Artificer were selected on welfare and other parochial grounds. I dared not send them back to Nigeria and request for qualified divers.

The arrival programme of the crew from the middle of 1986 was no longer adhered to and a rating decided to buy his ticket and fly into Italy from Kano whereas all departures were from Lagos. On arrival in Rome, he was stranded, and when I was alerted I cleared him for entry. On his arrival at the shipyard, I had a meeting with the two relevant heads of department present namely Lieutenant Commanders S Amodu and Ekeopre Beredugo. They were appointed Executive Officers for the two ships and were my course mates at NDA. It was decided that I should inform NHQ and send the rating back to return through the proper official channel to avoid the chaos of others seeking their routes when not officially approved.

The rating was returned to Lagos and there was a protest at NHQ by the family representative accusing me of refusing their brother to come to Europe. He was cleared and sent back to Italy through Lagos airport with the next batch. I now had a taste of the experiences that informed the advice that I should not request for the crew to be in Italy.

This experience was just the tip of the iceberg in embarrassments in the international arena.

The project programmes were on course and the orderly documentation for trials, handling of drawings and technical specifications helped the ship's crew to get acquainted with the activities they were to be engaged in when not attending courses and in preparations for their courses. Some of the officers had opportunities to attend factory acceptance trials which involved travels out of the station. All crew members attended all harbour and sea acceptance trials to build on the training courses conducted for them by specialist training establishments and equipment suppliers.

The Shipyard Design and Drawing Office staff were kept very busy for the best part of the project duration and the NNIC team closed late on many days to maintain the pressure and focus. There were technologies that the NN would be experiencing, for the first time, such as monocoque GRP hull, reverse osmosis freshwater plant, water jet propulsors capable of 360-degree thrust vectoring, and the integration of the propulsion and weapon control system that makes it possible for the CO to manoeuver the ship from a portable console with a joystick and more. The sea trials were exciting opportunities for me to experience all that has been put together in design and construction sites in the past years.

I received a request from the Shipyard that a USA team would like to visit NNS OHUE. I had been hearing of how the USA Navy had shortlisted Intermarine Spa for their Mine Counter Measure Vessels project but teamed up with another European shipyard for a hull material design very different from that used for the LERICI class for the Italian Navy and Malaysian Navy and also used for the NN project. The NN ships were the first to have a waterjet propulsion system and the design modifications the NNIC team had introduced for which credit must be given to the shipyard design team, had greatly improved upon the previous constructions. The trial results as regards the signatures for mine countermeasures had been very impressive and confirmed with the Italian Navy Research and Development Centre staff at various stages. The trial results and performances were the best around. The US Navy efforts with the selected European Shipyard had failed to meet the standards. I could understand the interest in NN Squadron achievements by the US Navy.

I gave them permission and assigned NNIC staff to monitor the visit. The US Navy team was highly impressed with the ship. It was not long after this visit that I learnt that the US Navy had cancelled their going contract and would be adopting the monocoque glass-reinforced plastic hull design and construction. The US Navy project team had its project office set up opposite NNIC on the same floor. This was the US Navy OSPREY class minehunters project attracted to Intermarine Spa. The Italian and Malaysian Navies ships did not convince the Americans until they were wowed by NNS OHUE design. The USN took note of the impressive trial results complemented by the good ergonomics of internal arrangements and excellent use of space despite the increased installation due to NNIC efforts.

The presence of the US Navy project team at the shipyard with offices close to NNIC made us appreciate the steps we had been taking such as the long time we took to study drawings, technical specifications, and compliance with various specified standards were proper. The US Navy team was supported by a lot of reference documents on various aspects of their job at the shipyard. Despite the long history in the procurement of warships from very reputable shipyards with equipment manufacturers from diverse industries in Europe, NN failed to acquire detailed design, construction, and trial documentation with comprehensive documentation to produce a set of publications to guide inspectors at shipyards.

The NNIC never received any input and feedback. The NNIC set up reached out from the start in Europe and built an impressive library at the shipyard with identification coding related to onboard installations. The support facilities such as the geodetic points for the location of beacons for precision positioning during mine warfare operations in Nigeria's coastal waters were never addressed despite the volume of documents containing relevant information that was never used or attended to seriously by NHQ. There were many more areas that NNIC provided copious information for NHQ actions that were never followed through for relevant results. It was a very sad situation and I was not surprised. I drew attention to the negligence of NN before the arrival of the US Navy team and the failure for decades to get its act together and benefit from exposure to the best the defence industry in Europe afforded and which Brazil at the same time took advantage of to develop its impressive defence industry.

The arrival, in Europe, of the COs of the two ships, NNS BARAMA and NNS OHUE in the last quarter of 1986 signalled the presence of the full complement for the squadron. I had arranged for the most senior officer in each group departing Lagos for Italy to collect the letter authorizing payment of allowances called estacode for members of the group from MOD for administration by DA London. It was my decision.

I had turned down the arrangement for me to manage their allowance(s) in Italy to enable me to focus on the project challenges in Italy and beyond. It was also most appropriate for the Defence Adviser to handle the crew allowance(s) as they had good standing with banks in London and could cope with exchange rate fluctuations Nigeria started experiencing as from 1985 so that the exact amount designated in British pounds was paid at all times. This was the arrangement at NNIC that catered nicely for the crew as they arrived in batches.

The Shipyard helped NNIC to secure central accommodation for the crew at rates negotiated with the crew representatives. The NNIC invoked articles of the MOU to provide medical assistance in cases of emergency that needed hospitalisation. The arrangement on the ground worked well and we all focused on the project objectives despite minor personnel problems.

But the arrival of the two COs created immense problems because the arrangements on the ground were not strictly followed. The allowances for the last group of the crew that arrived were collected but not processed with the Defence Adviser in London. The Squadron CO remained in London and sent the Supply Officer to me in Italy without a fund for the last batch that had arrived. It was autumn and winter was approaching. Those affected by this interference had no money to buy warm clothes. The message from the COs through the Supply Officer to the crew was that I was in charge and whatever they were suffering was my fault. I held the fort and would not join issues. I was seen as the cause of the problems rather than the solution provider.

The Squadron CO after an extended stay in London holding on to the money for the group already in Italy without paying them, arrived believing that my efforts had diverted attention from his actions. I welcomed him and provided befitting accommodation for him. He had a car to himself and the second car I managed to get from the shipyard for the second CO, he also took and gave it to his wife who arrived in Italy with a medical condition. I had to make arrangements for her treatment.

I briefed the COs about the project and the NNIC set up. I appealed to them not to disrupt the arrangement made for the crew accommodation and upkeep. The shipyard was reluctant to provide office accommodation for the COs and I told them that my office and the NNIC offices were available for their use until offices were provided for them. On one of the days I was not at Sarzana, they went to my office very early and went through all lockers and drawers to find any documents they could use against me. They also had access to payment vouchers that were used for the imprest fund expenditures.

One day, the senior (Squadron) CO came to my office and told me that I could not run an office where things were done without fault, especially as regards finances. He had a mission and I was not surprised. The Supply Officer had been around and done many rounds of the NNIC and Shipyard to find out financial links they thought I had established with the shipyard that was not common knowledge and found none. The money the CO and his Supply Officer were to use to pay the allowances of some of the personnel in Italy were not available. Reports filtered into NHQ about the problems of delayed payment and the consequences being suffered by the crew.

There was a change of CNS in October 1986 when Admiral AA Aikhomu was appointed Chief of General Staff (CGS), the number two man to President IB Babangida. He replaced Commodore Ebitu Ukiwe who had lost out in a power tussle in the ruling hierarchy. Vice Admiral PS Koshoni succeeded Admiral Aikhomu as CNS. The programme for the arrival of the ships' crew continued uninterrupted despite the leadership change at NHQ. I did not make any efforts to get in touch with the new CNS to congratulate him on his new appointment. I also did not reach out to the new CGS who had supported me greatly and inspired leadership. I felt I was too low in rank to be involved in such a high-level political undertaking.

I was informed that the new CNS, Vice Admiral PS Koshoni, would visit Italy on completion of his tour of NN establishments at home. The visit was scheduled for February 1987. I received the details of his visit from the arrival date to departure. The officers and men whose allowances were with the CO had problems with getting warm clothing and some fell sick. I sought assistance from the Italian Navy medical facilities for emergencies and also pacified the landlords of the crew members who had not paid their rent.

I set in motion the plans for the CNS visit and planned for all NN personnel at the shipyard to interact with him and discuss their problems. I vowed not to complain and warned all personnel that if they failed to bring their problems to the CNS, I would not do so as their COs would be present during the visit.

The senior CO travelled back to Lagos while preparations for the CNS visit was going on without informing me of the reasons for his return to Lagos after a few weeks in London and Italy. I was informed that he was seen at NHQ and MOD pursuing the next round of release of funds meant for payment of the crew in Italy.

I received the CNS at Pisa airport and we drove into town in a convoy of vehicles provided by the shipyard. I was in the same car with the CNS and took the time to act as an amateur tourist guide. The CNS was accompanied by his wife, Margaret; his entourage included Commodore EO Omotenhinwa. The Nigeria Ambassador to Italy, Commodore AA Ajanaku, the Defence Adviser, Colonel D Dyeris, and the Deputy Defence Adviser (Navy) Commander PI Eluma were all there with us during the visit. In his hotel room, I briefed the CNS on the programme of his visit and told him that he would be meeting all the officers and ratings separately to enable him to discuss their problems with them.

The separate programme of the visit for Mrs Margaret Koshoni was handled by my wife and a female representative of the shipyard. As I took leave of the CNS in his hotel, he suddenly told me to retire my imprest account and stop running the account. I indicated my immediate compliance and went about implementing the visit programme which was the most important task of the moment.

The CNS and his entourage were conducted round the shipyard and the two ships at their locations. Thereafter, the shipyard staff detached and I took the CNS and the entourage to meet with the officers and men in the rooms prepared for the meetings. When the CNS heard the complaints from the ships' officers regarding the non-payment of their allowances and the problems arising therefrom, he dropped his head on his visibly shaken hands. He turned to the Defence Adviser, Col D Dyeris, and pleaded with him to lend him money which he directed should be released to me to pay the crew. The CNS turned to me and ordered me to travel to London immediately after his departure and collect the money he was borrowing from the DA for the payments.

The CNS was very embarrassed because he was not properly briefed in Lagos because of the politics that had created divisions at NHQ in the management of the funds by Commander K Olukotun, the senior CO, for the payment of the crew. The interaction with the ratings addressed similar problems. It was evident how the problems were caused and why the senior CO was not in Italy for the CNS visit.

The visit went well and the final lunch took place at Paracuchi Restaurant that had an international celebrity chef near the shipyard. I prepared to leave for Rome with the CNS. When I met him in his hotel at Viareggio for the departure from Pisa, the CNS told me that he had restored my imprest account and told the Defence Adviser to continue funding it. He informed me that the Defence Adviser briefed him on how well I had been rendering the account.

I handed the money the CNS gave me as a gift to my wife. We decided to invest the money in a piano, as she was a music teacher, to earn some money on our return to Lagos. The piano has been a proud piece of very treasured furniture in our home.

The night before the CNS left Rome for Lagos, he had a quiet walk after dinner not far from the hotel. I followed him to provide security assistance. But when he insisted that he wanted to be alone, I went back and waited for him at the hotel lobby. On his return, he walked towards the bar and I followed him. He sat on one of the bar stools where he took his drink. I went to sit some distance away within view.

He called me and asked me to sit on the barstool facing him and order a drink. I told him that I did not want to be seen having a drink at the bar with the CNS. I was too low in rank to do that. He looked at me for a while and ordered me to ask for my drink and have my seat facing him. As I sipped my drink, he saw that I was uncomfortable. He then told me that he could not believe that I was a coursemate at NDA with some influential army Majors who looked down on him even as CNS because of their political appointments and connections. He told me that he noticed I was very focused professionally and had no political inclinations. He remarked that hard times awaited me as I progressed with my career. His remarks reminded me of what Lieutenant

Commander FS Ebohon told me years back to be careful if I wanted to go far in my career. I was full of pity for the CNS that he had to suffer such humiliation from army Majors who looked down on him. This, I believed, was a trend resulting from military involvement in politics that was destroying the Armed Forces of Nigeria (AFN).

The CNS flew out of Rome from the Leonardo Da Vinci International Airport, Fiumicino. I bade him farewell. I returned to Sarzana and went to London to collect the money to pay the crew. On my return to Sarzana, I called the Executive Officers of the two ships and gave them the payment vouchers and the money to pay their crew and return the vouchers to the DA's office at the Nigerian High Commission in London. The sea trials programmes of NNS OHUE and NNS BARAMA were our main focus after the CNS visit.

The lead ship NNS OHUE that was accepted on 28 April 1987 was programmed for delivery by the shipyard on 28 May 1987. The programme was published to guide the ship's staff on all necessary preparations to get the ship ready for the officers and men to start manning it. The ship had been transferred to the final outfitting yard INMA at La Spezia where the shipyard could provide office accommodation for the COs and the crew. I had to do daily shuttling and the Italian Liaison Officer did his best concerning the necessary short courses and onboard preparations for the crew to take over the ship on delivery.

The first outfit of stores procurements defined by the shipyard was handed over to the CO to manage and the fund released by MOD for the victualling onboard. The fund was not utilized for the purpose and this created problems for me. The NATO Exercise the NN squadron would be taking part in by September 1987 was a major reason the crew was in Italy as it was considered a rare opportunity for the ships' staff to learn how to conduct mine warfare operations. The first steps to get the ships ready were not being taken seriously, thanks to the actions of the CO.

I had attended most of the sea trials. On an occasion, we were going through the trial protocol for the external communications system at sea and after placing calls to some shore establishments in the locality, I put a call to the Chief of Operations (COOPS), Rear Admiral GN Kanu who had been promoted and moved from personnel. I told him that we were at sea carrying out trials and wanted to test the external communication system by putting this call to him as COOPs. He asked me about a defect on an engine onboard NNS OHUE and wanted to know what I was doing about it. The ship's technical staff had advised the CO that the water leakage into the engine sump from the engine housing (block) due to porosity resulting from casting imperfection was a problem that demanded a new propulsion engine. The shipyard contacted the German manufacturer, MTU, to trace the cause of the problem and solve it satisfactorily.

There was much dismantling of components for tests and examinations which made some of the ship's technical staff think that the engine would no longer be in use. The shipyard's staff conducting the sea trail were shocked that the issue would generate such reactions within NN but I told COOPs that it was a problem of casting imperfection and there was no finding yet to justify the change of the engine. I was directed to forward a report to NHQ for the final decision to be made. I assured the COOPs that the report would be forwarded as directed.

The location of the casting imperfection was identified and confirmed to be due to porosity and though difficult to locate the repair was easily carried out. I studied the nature of the defect and the location and had a meeting with the Shipyard technical staff and the engine manufacturer in Germany. I got what I wanted. The engine manufacturer gave a guarantee for the life of the engine and committed it in writing. I had enough technical information to describe the casting defect, the location in the engine block, the repair method, and its effectiveness and recommended to NHQ to accept the repaired engine as new with the documented guarantee for the life of the engine.

I forwarded the report to NHQ and the CNS took charge. He got the services of a consultant to study my report and recommendations. The consultant agreed with my report and its recommendations. The issue was put to rest and NNIC continued with the Sea Acceptance Trials for NNS BARAMA. There were issues to be resolved at NHQ that needed my attention and that of the COs. A meeting was fixed for us with COOPs.

We travelled to Lagos. The meeting was chaired by COOPs, Rear Admiral GN Kanu. He asked me, as the Chief Delegate, to give a brief on the situation in Italy. I focused on the project milestones achieved and the progress with crew training to meet the schedule for the delivery of NNS BARAMA and further training with the Italian Navy Mine Warfare School to enable the Squadron to participate in the planned NATO exercise. The senior CO gave a very evasive response to questions raised about the delayed payments to the crew. I was asked if there was any problem affecting the crew and I concurred with the senior CO that there was none as the CO stated that he was going to pursue the allowances for crew payments.

I had no more dealing with the payment of allowances to the crew since the Squadron CO intervened and I would not want to appear to be speculative about or exposing what was happening as I had no concrete evidence to present being alone without any NNIC team member with me. The meeting ended with COOP's closing remarks that since the Chief Delegate had assured him that there was no problem there was nothing to discuss further regarding the matter. I later learnt, and as I envisaged, that if I had reported the non-payment there would have been serious consequences for the COs. I was sure there was adequate information from other sources already at NHQ that I was expected to confirm.

There was also the need to prepare for the sailing of the ships to Lagos and I had to help the COs to produce the cost estimates for consideration by NHQ. On presenting the estimate covering all the essential requirements, the costs were defended and approved. I was asked for an account to remit the amount to NNIC for me to take charge of the disbursement to the ships. I suggested that the money should be transferred to the Defence Adviser, London. I was not ready to handle such a large amount of money in a very charged situation in addition to the problems of foreign exchange fluctuations. I was emphatic about having nothing to do with the money and COOPs/NHQ took notice. The advice I gave was agreed to and we left Lagos for Sarzana.

The acceptance of NNS OHUE was attended by a delegation led by Captain MA Davies. Commander G Oladejo (later Rear Admiral) a Marine Engineer Officer was the senior technical officer on the team. There were minefields for me as the ship's technical staff had their hidden lists of matters they wanted to be attended to. I explained the steps taken by NNIC and the Shipyard representatives had the responsibility to satisfy the delegation. I was taken by surprise with the pipe marking scheme for identification of services that I had given to the ships' Marine Engineer Officers and Lieutenant E Ijioma to jointly study and supervise the Shipyard staff for implementation. It was wrongly done for the freshwater pipes and no one informed me of any observations to that effect. The ships' technical staff waited for their moment and used it as an example of the failure of NNIC to allow them to supervise Ijioma.

I took responsibility. Commander G Oladejo had experienced similar situations in Germany with the construction of the Landing Ship Tanks and the Fast Attack Craft Squadrons. He explained the error to me and I told him that it would be rectified in conformity with NN standard scheme. He generously sent a scheme to me on return to Lagos which I then tasked the ships' technical staff to supervise the implementation. In their concluding remarks after a series of joint meetings, the delegation commended the efforts and stated that when the German ships were accepted the state of NNS OHUE was much better as the shipyard would normally still have some minor tasks to accomplish before delivery. There was a procedure for handling all observations and related documentation that was shown to the delegation. This was also commended and showed that all NN personnel at the Shipyard had the opportunity to make contributions. There was, however, a desperate attempt to derail the programmes simply to prolong their stay in Italy.

I was requested to represent the Defence Adviser again at the RNEC graduation ceremony of July 1987 as two NN officers Lieutenant Commander E Ibitolu and Lieutenant Commander P Okpe were graduating from the Advanced Marine Engineering Course. I had a break from the hectic schedule at Sarzana, Italy. The graduation ceremony was the usual grand affair and I had the appropriate academic gown for the procession into the Great Hall where the graduation ceremony was held. The evening before graduation, I called my wife and she told me that Mr John Wedlake had called to inform us that his father Mr Walter Wedlake had died. He had been sick for some time. This was indeed very sad news for us to lose such a great, caring, and close family friend. I informed the Deputy Defence Adviser that I would be branching off to pay my respect at Stogumber, near Taunton, Somerset on my way back to London. I was dejected to see Nan struggling to cope. The body was in the mortuary and Nan wanted to arrange for me to go and see him. I told her not to worry and promised to be back for the burial which was two days away. I returned to Stogumber two days later and joined the family for the funeral Mass and ceremony at the crematorium.

At the Crematorium, Rev Fr Stonestreet told me he was very surprised to see me again and glad that I was around to pay my respect to my dear friend. He asked me to take the only reading at the ceremony at the Crematorium. I took it as family duty and Nan was pleased that I performed it. It was goodbye to my dear friend.

The outfitting of NNS OHUE at INMA Shipyard was completed after the acceptance and NN had to take delivery. The programme for the delivery was discussed and finalized. The CO of the ship, Commander K Olukotun, whom I had been referring to as the senior CO, travelled out of Italy as the day of delivery approached and I had no idea why he left the station at the height of the final preparations for the delivery of the ship. I was in contact with the Executive Officer, that is the second in command and briefed him on the need to keep the crew informed and prepared to move onboard as part of the delivery programme. The day before the delivery, I could not contact the CO but prevailed on the Executive Officer to try and keep him informed.

I contacted the NHQ and informed COOPs of the situation and the problem caused by the absence of the CO. I was ordered to ensure the delivery took place and directed to inform the Executive Officer to take charge and make sure the crew moved onboard on delivery. The rehearsal of the delivery programme with the crew took place and all was set for the delivery ceremony. The crew was dressed in their ceremonial uniform and I had an Italian Navy team on board to assist with all the checks for the safety of the crew onboard. Also, other checks to ensure that the shipyard met the standard for the delivery following the standard check-off lists were carried out.

The ceremony was brief and for the first time, the Nigerian flag was flying on the ship's mast. The ship was programmed to move from INMA shipyard to the Italian Navy Mine Warfare Centre berthing basin, all within La Spezia, and commence the preparations to start the mine warfare training programme that would also prepare the NN Squadron to participate in the NATO exercise some months later. The CO turned up suddenly after the delivery of the ship. The ship was moved to the Italian Navy Mine Warfare Centre and allocated a berth at the entrance to the basin.

The tactical data link was the final equipment scheduled to be installed and tested at the same time as the ones for NNS BARAMA due for delivery some months later in 1987. This would be used as an excuse by the CO NNS OHUE (Squadron CO) and the ship's staff to claim that the ship was not ready for delivery even though the ship had since completed Sea Acceptance Trials and a team was onboard assisting the crew to get used to the ship. The tactical data link was identified as essential equipment when we arrived and steps were taken over time for implementation as agreed so that the major project milestones were not distorted.

The remaining sea trials for NNS BARAMA were carried out as scheduled but the COs were not serious about the training programme at the Italian Navy Mine Warfare Centre. Commander Gambacciani came to my office on a day I was expecting feedback from him regarding the progress of the NN crew that had started the training at the centre. He was almost in tears as he wondered why I went through such a rigorous schedule over the years and official preparation to secure slots on the NATO programme only for the COs to tell him that the crew would not participate in the NATO exercise and had requested for an alteration of the training programme. I told him that it was not based on any directives from NHQ. He told me that the ships' crew had decided what they wanted and it was just introductory basic training.

The NN had approved the cost estimates for the sea time required for the NATO exercise and this was included in the approved fund sent to the Defence Adviser in London for the ships. I was devastated that all efforts to develop credible mine warfare capabilities were being sabotaged and there was no one to order compliance as NHQ was polarized for various reasons. I told the Italian Navy authorities that I had no order from NHQ cancelling the comprehensive Mine Warfare training up to the practical consolidation with the NATO exercise. The COs were on running their navy with the taxpayer's resources being wasted and no one to check them. I kept vigil.

The money for sailing the ships to Lagos was sent to the Defence Adviser in London and on receipt, the Deputy Defence Adviser, (Navy) Commander PI Eluma, informed me that my imprest account would no longer be funded despite the provision for it in the approved estimates. The COs now had direct dealings with the Defence Adviser on their financial requirements. I handed over the list of items classified as the first outfit of stores that the shipyard had to provide and the contractors had direct access to the COs to execute their contracts. I was apprehensive that the high-quality wristwatches for divers and other attractive items might be converted to personal use and no one would ask questions.

The sea trial of NNS BARAMA was completed but the ship could not be moved to the Italian Navy Mine Warfare Centre because the COs had their hidden agenda. I kept watch over what remained to be done and kept the team at NNIC busy with preparations to wind up the project. The COs and the Defence Adviser in London were in direct contact and I detached NNIC personnel from the ongoing financial relationships to focus on meeting the needs of the ships.

I was kept abreast of the invitations sent to the COs for the availability of the crew for training at the Mine Warfare Centre which they refused to honour. The NATO ships arrived at the Centre and the invitation sent for the officers to attend a reception for the participating countries was turned down. There was no NN officer at the reception who was to get acquainted before the commencement of the lectures, planning exercises, and subsequently the sea exercise.

I informed the NHQ of the development. In the intervening period, there was the complaint that the first outfit of stores had not been delivered and the crew was having difficulty feeding onboard despite the earlier efforts I had made before the release of the money to the Defence Adviser for the ships. I had to plead with the Shipyard administration to help me and provide for the ship what the Nigerian Government had adequately provided for. I knew money was being released to the ship and was not ready to be involved in asking for anything from the funds with the Defence Adviser which the ships' COs were accessing.

The CNS was on an annual inspection in the Eastern Naval Command area in December 1987 when he received a telegram from the CO NNS OHUE complaining about the disbursement of funds from the Defence Adviser in London. The CNS was furious and ordered drastic action to be taken against the COs for the embarrassment. I kept away from the fray. I had concluded plans to send my family back to Nigeria and wait out the drama unfolding. I flew to Frankfurt with my family from Milan and put them on a flight to Lagos and returned immediately to the station in Italy the same day.

I went onboard NNS OHUE to inspect the tactical data link equipment being installed. This was an alteration to the original design to which it was agreed that its installation would not delay the ships' programme. I went to the CO's cabin to meet him and inform him of my presence on board and he refused to see me. I went about my routine on board and I was winding up when the CO told the Executive Officer, Lieutenant Commander S Amodu, to tell me to leave his ship and not to come on board again. I told him that I had a job to do onboard as the Chief Delegate in Italy.

I was prevailed upon to leave the ship to avoid an ugly scene that could be witnessed by the Italian naval personnel. I left so as not to put my coursemate at NDA in a difficult situation. I called the ship's technical officers to follow through with the work being done and ensure satisfactory completion as documented. I had involved them in trials at factories, harbour and sea and were very familiar with the procedures and documentation.

After the 1988 New Year break, I got information from the Deputy Defence Adviser (Navy) that the CNS had ordered the evacuation of the COs and the crew of the ships from Italy and that tickets had already been bought for all of them to depart Italy from Rome. I was directed to arrange buses to convey the crew from Sarzana to Fiumicino International Airport at short notice. The crew also had short notice to pack their belongings and, consequently, there was leftover luggage I had to deal with. I was directed to retain only the NNIC team, conclude the project, and freight the two ships to Lagos. This was the original NHQ plan I got approval to change.

I was never consulted as regards how to look after two ships in two different locations. The very day the COs received the evacuation order NNS OHUE and NNS BARAMA were abandoned at the Italian Navy Mine Warfare Centre and INMA shipyard respectively. I was getting the buses ready to take them to Rome when I got an order that the Flag Officer in La Spezia Vice Admiral Vinci Guerra wanted to see me in his office. I was not told why but was asked to leave to see him immediately as he was waiting for me. He received me and wasted no time in asking if I knew that NNS OHUE was without any NN crew or personnel on board as all the crew had abandoned the ship with the Nigerian Flag flying on the mast. He informed me that the ship must leave the location immediately as it was in danger and also constituting a danger to other ships. The turbulent weather in the area was a major concern and the ship could be easily parted from its berthing hawsers and lost. I immediately asked for a safer berth and the Italian Navy crew.

The Admiral asked me if I was ready to bring down the Nigerian Flag. I told him that I could not lower my national flag and he then told me to provide NN crew and ensure the safety of the ship before he would allow movement to a safer berth. He told me that he had heard of my background and that I should have no difficulty taking over command of the ship. I told him that I would get organized and move the ship to a safer berth before sunset and requested for tug and berthing party ashore. He assured me that all I requested would be provided but I must provide the crew to run essential services for the safety of the ship.

I dashed back to Sarzana and rang the Deputy Defence Adviser for assistance and advice and he told me that he would be arriving the following morning and the bus convoy to Rome must be on the move. I phoned COOPs and told him of the situation and what I discussed with the Flag Officer. He ordered me to take over command of the ships and move NNS OHUE to the allocated berth before sunset and ensure the safety of the ships. I did take command and quickly relayed the information from NHQ to the Flag Officer and I told him of the limitation in terms of the number of personnel available to me. The money meant for the sailing of the ships home had been spent and I was brought in to take over command for the safety of the ships and make all preparations to get them back to Nigeria. I had no time to think of the daunting challenges other than to start taking charge and start doing what needed to be done.

I tried to ask the Deputy Defence Adviser to allow me to retain some of the crew to manage the enormous challenges ahead. I was told that the CNS order was for the crew to return to Lagos and that order must be implemented fully. I did not try to ask NHQ for a review due to the disposition of the Defence Adviser who should have taken the lead. The CNS order was final.

I called the six members of the NNIC team and briefed them on the challenges ahead and what the plans were. It would be many days of sleepless nights and more responsibilities. I mustered all NNIC team on NNS OHUE and got the ship moved to the safe berth with the tug assistance and berthing party provided by the Italian Navy Base and berthed with the stern to the jetty secured close to the training block buildings. This was the safest part of the base.

I was grateful to the Flag Officer for securing the safest berth space in the basin for NNS OHUE. The following day and very early in the morning, I was following up on the convoy of buses with the crew by flight to Rome. I was with the Deputy Defence Adviser (Navy) as directed by NHQ. I had to see through the departure procedures. The officers departing were very pensive and some of the ratings complained of some of their luggage that did not get to the shipping agent warehouse before departure and would be abandoned.

The Executive Officer of NNS OHUE, Lieutenant Commander S Amodu managed to say goodbye and remarked that I had a very difficult task ahead as I was now responsible for the two ships and their safe arrival in Lagos. I returned immediately to the base and went to assess the situation onboard NNS OHUE and had to give extra instructions to the Officer of the Day (OOD), Lieutenant E Ijioma. He was overstretched and there was an outburst from him. I only warned him to get composed. He apologised to me the next day. I now had responsibilities as Squadron Commanding Officer for the ships.

I will always be grateful to the officers and men at NNIC for their dedication and hard work till the very end. Lieutenant SO Odusola and Leading Writer Alexander Egharevba were outstanding in this respect. The NNIC had achieved all set objectives for the project with the great support of the Italian Navy and was never found wanting. The departure of the ships' crew for Nigeria was heartbreaking for me. The Malaysians proudly sailed their squadron home. I looked forward to the NN Squadron training with the Italian Navy Mine Warfare Centre and successfully participating in the NATO exercise as planned for the development of credible mine warfare capabilities.

All these evaporated as NNS OHUE was abandoned at the Italian Naval Base with the Nigeria National Flag flying and not a single crew onboard. This was a defining moment showing the lack of commitment to the nation-state by personnel and poor leadership being provided by officers of the NN and by implication the Armed Forces of the Federal Republic of Nigeria. The sight of the beautiful national flag proudly and defiantly fluttering on the warship abandoned in a foreign naval base by those entrusted with its defence devastated me; Nigeria abandoned in the international arena. The ultimate symbol of the allegiance all citizens should bear truly with faith and which military personnel would sacrifice their lives for is so poorly treated and yet fluttered so beautifully.

I witnessed order, discipline, and commitment to excellence in the European and USA defence industries involved in the NN projects. The down part of this experience was the impression that Nigeria is not serious about complex undertakings for its development. The preference is for a way of doing things characterised by disorder, mediocrity, indiscipline, and lack of commitment to excellence leading to reckless and casual approaches. This is called the 'Nigerian way' of getting things done which is derogatory. Nigeria was exposed to cutting edge technologies and NNIC took advantage to ensure the NN had the best MCMV of the era in terms of performance characteristics which swayed the US Navy to the design.

I deeply reflected on Nigerian military personnel without commitment to the nation-state causes. They mostly do not want to know what allegiance is all about and what inspires loyalty. The Nigerian experience since 1914 peaceful formation of the state is that most military personnel joined Royal military institutions pledging allegiance to the King or Queen of United Kingdom, their successors and heirs just as the British citizens who joined the UK military institutions but know that they serve their country. Nigerians were conditioned to join Royal military institutions in Nigeria and West Africa to serve another country they hardly knew or experienced. Their home country, Nigeria, and its defence and security meant nothing to them as they marched to wars to play in battlefields where bullets fly about. This orientation has never been corrected and the schedule of oaths for Nigerian military personnel still reflects bearing allegiance to the President, Commander-in-Chief. What is wrong with this posture is that there is no sense of country and its sovereignty and if allegiance is to the President, Commander-in-Chief, then loyalty can be pledged to service commanders under the Commander-in-Chief thereby creating conditions for undermining authority as I experienced with the NN MCMV crew in Italy.

The UK nation-state setup has vested sovereignty in the monarchy and those in charge of government are respected for the mandate given to them by the electorates to run the government-owned by the monarchy. In the USA, the method of bearing allegiance to serve the democratic republic is expressed using the flag of the country and its constitution. It was the flag that inspired the Star-Spangled Banner, the USA national anthem. The citizens of the Federal Republic of Nigeria do not have an idea of the method of bearing allegiance and pledging loyalty in a modern nation-state based on the principles of the Westphalia Treaty of 1648 which gave prominence to the principle of sovereignty vested in a country or state, not on an individual.

The Constitution and the Flag of the Federal Republic of Nigeria define Nigeria, no matter the imperfections of the Constitution, and these should always guide how to bear true allegiance faithfully. Absolutely loyalty must be pledged to the President, Commander-in-Chief of the Federal Republic of Nigeria only because he or she is the only one that has been so mandated by the electorates in a general election to be the only legal executive or CEO of the state. This is essential for commitment and unity of command. There must be no other authority to undermine this vital set up if Nigeria is to be properly run as a modern nation-state. The problem with the Constitution is that it is a compendium and mix-up of all of the issues (culture, religion, and ethnicity) that do not conform to the principles guiding the conduct of the affairs of a modern nation-state for decisive actions in the international arena. It is why internal contradictions take centre stage to waste Nigeria as the people reap crises and insecurity with impotent state institutions. State power is abused to weaken state institutions so that strong individuals prevail. There are no tangible outputs from weak state institutions for nation-building by citizens.

Nigerians have to give meaning to a modern nation-state being called the Federal Republic of Nigeria which connotes allegiance to an entity with sovereignty and loyalty to the elected President, Commander-in-Chief for the education of its citizens and the members of the Armed Forces to inspire commitment to the nation-state causes. Education is essential to avoid the diffusion of power and responsibilities. These are required for the commitment of military personnel to serve the country and generate in popular minds that patriotic fervour as in the UK and US whose citizens truly bear allegiance and pledge loyalty to country and mandated authority respectively. The Nigerian flag is an important symbol of the expression of sovereignty and it should not have been abandoned as I witnessed at the Italian Navy Base. It reflected a military whose personnel have not been properly oriented to acquire the correct attitude towards the nation-state they should wholeheartedly serve.

The abandoning of a modern nation-state's warship with the national flag flying in a foreign base by a crew whose officers swore an oath to

God on commission must be noted for a thorough study so that lessons and wisdom would be learnt and gained. I have very deep feelings about this incident solely because of the negative implications for the nation-state and its institutions and how it draws attention to how casual and reckless the country's affairs are conducted. These considerations constituted my take-off point and a reflection of my state of mind to face the challenges of getting the warships to Nigeria.

CHAPTER TEN

My Major Feat: Freighting Two Warships Home on a Floating Dock

The shipyard had delivered NNS OHUE after successful sea trials that ended with the speed trials. The second ship NNS BARAMA was still at INMA shipyard, La Spezia where she was outfitted and was awaiting delivery before joining NNS OHUE at the Italian Navy Mine Warfare base as planned. This was scuttled by the problems caused by the ships' staff as earlier narrated. NNS BARAMA was delivered at INMA at a secure berth where the ship remained.

There was no NN crew out of 110 officers and men that had been in Italy who were recalled to Lagos. I had to plan with the Shipyard for NNS BARAMA to remain at INMA, La Spezia for safety. I provided a skeletal presence on board. The few personnel at NNIC were stretched at three locations, Intermarine, Sarzana where the NNIC office was based, INMA Shipyard at La Spezia (NNS BARAMA location), and the Italian Naval Base where NNS OHUE was berthed. There was much movement daily and I had to ensure that I did not exhaust the little money left in my imprest account at the time it was abruptly stopped.

When the crew was ordered to be evacuated to Lagos, I was directed to start the process of getting a floating dock ship to take the ships home. I made inquiries and got information on 'Happy Mammoet' owned by a Dutch shipowner. I needed an agent. I contacted the Deputy Defence Adviser (London) for some assistance in getting an agent. I knew it would not be a simple operation. The Deputy Defence Adviser (Navy) secured one for me. I was tasked with coordinating the availability of the floating dock ship and insurance and these were the main challenges. I was in a deeper crisis due to the inexperience of the shipping agent I was stuck with.

I contacted NHQ to arrange for an insurance policy and it was decided that a Nigerian insurance company would be used but with a UK London office. The NHQ sent a representative of the insurance company to me. He arrived with no funds for accommodation. As my family had left for Lagos, I invited him to stay with me at my house. I was expected to pay for his hotel accommodation yet I had no access to funds and could not approach the shipyard for funding as I had never done so.

I requested for the necessary insurance papers from my guest to cover the two ships transit operations to Lagos. He informed me that he only came to Italy on fact-finding. I requested the UK London office address from him and I was given a letter headed paper giving different insurance company details. My guest told me that the insurance company in London was a partner to the Nigerian insurance company that was relied on for international operations. He left the following day after I took him to see both ships.

I could not get through the London phone number on the letter headed paper given to me and I decided to go to London to locate the address before discussing it with the Deputy Defence Adviser (Navy). I managed to get to the grid area as indicated in the letter headed paper given to me. I spent considerable time searching for a non-existent address with an experienced London taxi driver. I sadly found that there was no such address.

I went to the DDA's office and told him of my findings and he was mute. The message was clear. There would be no insurance cover and I had already told the shipping company that the NN had an insurance cover for the two ships. I dared not raise alarm as there were other related matters of getting the floating dock ship date of availability confirmed and I was managing an inexperienced agent. Furthermore, I had no idea what the Italian authorities might do should they know about the problem. I feared they might take steps to prevent the ships from leaving the country.

The shipyard had assured me that they were following through the official export procedures with relevant Italian establishments for getting the warships to Nigeria. I had to coordinate several activities in London, Lagos, and Sarzana/La Spezia. The La Spezia port would take the floating dock ship on arrival about the middle of February 1988. There were visits from several sub-contractors to bid us farewell and offered assistance to NNIC. I informed Lieutenants SO Odusola and E Ijioma to liaise with them and focus on the items such as sports equipment for the ships. The project was completed and I was never in a compromised position despite the temptations and challenges I faced.

Commodore AA Ajanaku had completed his tenure as Ambassador to Italy and was replaced by Ambassador James Kolo. I paid the new ambassador a courtesy visit towards the end of 1987 and briefed him on the project and the excellent support the Embassy gave me in many matters related to NNIC and the crew in Italy. He attended the delivery ceremony of NNS BARAMA at INMA.

I was invited by the Managing Director of the Shipyard at Sarzana to an urgent meeting with the Board of Directors at their headquarters in Rome. I did not know the purpose of the meeting but I later understood why they found it necessary to keep me in the dark. I flew to Rome early in the morning from Pisa airport and went to the headquarters of the shipyard. I was well-received, accorded all courtesies, and ushered into the meeting room where all members or team gathered were seated with Mr Rocco Canelli, the chairman. I was informed that there was a serious problem that would prevent the ships, NNS OHUE, and NNS BARAMA, from leaving Italy as scheduled. I told them that all arrangements for the arrival of the floating dock was on track and gave them the date the ship was to be in La Spezia. I was then informed that the Italian customs had stopped processing the papers for the export and were preparing to seize the ships because of an incident in the Arabian Gulf where there was a major NATO effort to clear mines that threatened shipping through the Strait of Hormuz.

I had a new crisis on my hands. I wanted to know specifically why or what happened or was happening in the Arabian Gulf that would lead to the seizure of the two ships. I asked if they had difficulties with their customs department or infringed any law. I was told there was a serious debate in the Italian parliament where it was reported that some of the mines being cleared by the NATO mine countermeasures force in the Arabian Gulf was manufactured in Italy and exported to Iran using a Nigerian Ministry of Defence issued end-user certificate. There was a feeling of terrible bangs stumping my ears as the implications were reeled out to me.

The parliament demanded explanations and threatened sanctions. The NN ships would be seized to start with. There was a quick flash across my mind of the Iraqi Navy warships that were seized and not allowed to leave Italy as I arrived in Italy in late 1984 and were on open display at La Spezia port for all to see. I asked what stage they had reached with the customs and other departments processing before the uproar in parliament and I was told they were at the final stages.

I immediately asked to use their phone to call the Nigerian Ambassador James Kolo. A phone was made available and I told the Ambassador that I was at a meeting with the Board of Directors and had been told of the actions being taken to seize NNS OHUE and NNS BARAMA by the Italian authorities based on the outcome of a debate in the Italian parliament regarding Italian mines that got to the Arabian

Gulf with Nigerian connection. I requested him to grant me audience immediately together with a team to be put together by the Shipyard directors. I had to be timely decisive to be convincing.

He granted immediate audience and permission to come together with the team representing the Board of Directors. I asked the board for the composition of their team to follow me and one was immediately put together without objection. It was rare to have such a fruitful meeting with the Italians followed up with appropriate actions and no argument. I was impressed.

I arrived with the team at the Nigeria Embassy and we were taken straight to the Ambassador who was waiting. I introduced the members of the team and we went straight into the meeting. I told the meeting that the NNIC MCMV project team members had nothing to do with the mines manufacturer in Italy and as such the Italian parliament and customs should be prevailed upon not to seize NN warships due to leave Italy in a few weeks. I then stressed that the shipyard should muster their political clout and ensure the processes at advanced stages to enable the NN ships to leave Italy were not derailed.

The Board of Directors team gave the Ambassador more information to make him appreciate the complicated nature of the matter including some court cases that were being initiated. Ambassador James Kolo prevailed on the shipyard to make sure the programme for the departure of the ships was not derailed. He promised to brief the Nigerian government on the serious problem that had caused an uproar in the Italian parliament and assured that the issue of the end-user certificate that caused the embarrassment would be decisively dealt with. The Board of Directors team left the Nigerian Embassy and I escorted them out and thanked them for their understanding as they promised to do all in their power to ensure the ships were not seized and that all official documentation with Italian authorities would be pursued and secured.

I returned to the office of the Ambassador and met a team with him. The Minister Counsellor at the Embassy was Mr Uche Okeke (later Ambassador and Director General of Nigeria Intelligence Agency). The Ambassador shared tasks between me and the Minister Counsellor and directed that court activities related to the matter in the Rome area and in the area where the shipyard and the mine weapon manufacturer in Brescia were located should be closely monitored. The Ambassador told me that a member of the Armed Forces Ruling Council was passing through Rome returning to Lagos and he would give him a brief for the urgent attention of the President, Commander-in-Chief.

I was fortunate to have the full force of the Nigeria Embassy deployed so effectively. I would later have a wonderful official relationship with Ambassador Uche Okeke when he was Director-General, Nigeria Intelligence Agency and I was Commandant, National War College, Abuja. As I was about to leave Rome, I got a call from the DDA (Navy) that he was arriving at Pisa airport and would be heading for Sarzana. I made arrangements for his reception as he would arrive before me later in the evening.

I returned to base in Sarzana and called the two officers with me and told them briefly of the complicated situation on the ground and the actions being taken. Their task was to monitor developments and report any news about the court cases and actions of the mine weapon manufacturer at Brescia. Though we had very little or no capacity, I advised we should be on the lookout and avoid the careless talk as we focus also on winding up and keep to our schedules.

I had dinner at a restaurant with the DDA (Navy) and briefed him. I gave him accommodation at the Hotel Rondine near the shipyard as he wanted to join me to travel to Germany to meet with a team from NHQ led by Commodore S Akano that was visiting Dornier in Munich. I had been invited for long by Dornier because of the inputs NNIC had to make in the development of NN Underwater Warfare School at Ojo, Lagos, and could not honour the invitation. I was now informed that I would be part of a larger NN delegation. It was a two-day visit and I would have the opportunity of having the NHQ team and DDA (Navy) around to understand the challenges in Italy. I considered it appropriate to attend. I discussed the challenges in Italy with Commodore S Akano and also highlighted to DDA (Navy) the difficulties with the shipping and insurance agents. I have had cups full of crises and challenges.

Back in Italy, I kept in touch with the Nigerian Ambassador in Rome and also the Minister-Counselor Mr Uche Okeke. There were no further eruptions in the Italian parliament and the shipyard was progressing with processing the export papers. The shipping programme was also on the course and the date for the arrival of the ship was set. I had to safely get the ships out of Italy, across the seas, and deliver them in Lagos.

The docking operation was also a challenge as I had the additional responsibility as the Squadron Commanding Officer. No NN seaman officer volunteered to be in Italy at the moment the floating dock ship arrived to take on the challenges. The Italian Navy was also watching a complex operation unfolding. I had very few hands to man the ships. I needed help and made the necessary calls without hesitation. It was decided to have the ships by their side at an angle to the centre line of the floating dock ship as it was not long enough to take both ships in line. The non-magnetic steel cradles for the shipping had been fabricated under the direction of the shipyard to assure the safety of the ships in transit and they were jointly inspected to ensure they were adequate. The shipping agent from London had a representative around to attend the meetings and carry out inspections. I had to cover all aspects the NN was responsible for and ensure the ships departed Italy as scheduled. The date and time for the docking weres set and I had to move the ships from two different locations within the tight schedule of the favourable tide.

The ships were taken from the Italian Navy Mine Warfare Centre and INMA shipyard both in La Spezia within four hours and successfully docked without incident. The shipyard had prepared to do some cleaning and painting of the underwater hull areas. This was speedily accomplished. I appointed Lieutenant S Odusola and two technical ratings to sail with the ships. Lieutenant E Ijioma and Leading Writer Alexander Egharevba would tidy up the NNIC office with me and seal up the containers for shipping after which I would close up and stay in London to monitor proceedings.

The day after the departure of the ships from La Spezia, I was asked to dress up in my ceremonial uniform for an audience with the Flag Officer La Spezia Admiral Vinci Guerra. I was taken unawares by his very warm reception. The Admiral had a pleasant discussion with me and seemed relieved that the challenges and crises had been well managed and the ships were safely on board the Floating Dock bound for Lagos. He had been very supportive at the most trying period. He gave me his crest as a parting gift. I had to arrange a reciprocal gesture and it was later delivered to him. I took my leave of the Admiral and returned to Sarzana. It was now evident that my mission in Italy was accomplished. The focus was now on getting the floating dock ship to arrive in Lagos safely with its cargo on schedule.

I gave Lieutenant Odusola a security briefing about how to get the ships to Lagos safely and keep to the determined or planned route plan I got from the floating dock ship Captain. The Unmanned Remotely Piloted Vehicle, Pluto, for mine warfare operations had a dedicated compartment on the main deck. This had been carefully secured for each ship and I bought appropriate keys and securing devices for the two compartments on both ships. I briefed Odusola that he should not open any of the compartments until the ships arrived Lagos and should do security rounds with the keys secured to his waist as Officer Of the Day (OOD) throughout the passage. He should not discuss details with the

Captain and the crew onboard including the NN personnel on passage with him.

This arrangement was my insurance for getting the ships safely to Lagos without proper insurance coverage. I had been impressed with Odusola's dedication and trustworthiness. He understood the challenges we faced and was once instigated that as someone from a dominant ethnic group, he should undermine me being from a minority ethnic group. He resisted and suffered for it. In a rare gesture, as we departed Italy, he noticed that I did not have time to shop for my children. He bought some children bicycles and other toys and brought them to my residence. I was glad he took the initiative but when I asked for the cost to repay him, he walked away stating that it was in appreciation of the leadership that I had provided at NNIC. I was lucky to have him on my staff.

The shipyard had a farewell reception for NNIC and it was Ijioma and me at the beginning of the project who were still there. Leading Writer A Egharevba also attended. The reception was held at Paraccuci Restaurant and was well attended. I was invited by the Group Managing Director, Mr Arcangelo Ferrari, for a final meeting in his office. During the parley, we discussed the programme of disengagement of NNIC from the shipyard. I asked him to ensure all documents that I needed to sign were presented for due diligence. The final stage for the NNIC was to secure all official documents into containers at the shipyard and in which no personal effects would be allowed. The various cartons were labelled with details of classification and description of the contents. I was proud of the work and diligence of Leading Writer Alexander Egharevba. All office file cabinets were locked and loaded into the containers each with its locks and keys. These would be part of the library in Lagos. All payment vouchers for salaries as administered from London and the impress account I managed were carefully packed. A day was set to inspect all containers with the relevant Italian authority and shipyard staff before finally sealing the cartons and locking the containers for shipment.

We arranged our departure so that Lieutenant E Ijioma and Alexander Egharevba would leave for Lagos from Rome. I would fly to London and monitor, for a few days, the passage of the floating dock ship with the NN MCMV Squadron. The last report I received was that the ship had cleared Gibraltar straits and was heading southwards in the Atlantic Ocean. I envisaged that within three days the ship should be clear off the coast of North Africa heading towards Senegal. I departed for London from Pisa airport and the following day the last of the NNIC staff departed. I was satisfied that NNIC had accomplished its task and the final phase of safe delivery of the products, ships and design as in the contract between the Federal Government of Nigeria and the Shipyard had been achieved and secured and much more. It had been a lot of work and sacrifices. The impressive performances of the ships were acknowledged and were of a high standard for reference.

I stayed with the Deputy Defence Adviser (Navy) at his residence in London and followed him to the Nigerian High Commission office daily. On the first day at the office. I ensured the shipping agent briefed us on the progress of the passage to Lagos. I was informed that the ship would call at Las Palmas. This was not the planned programme and I raised my objection. There was no operational reason for this change as regards the port of call.

I was then told that Lieutenant Samuel Odusola refused to open the Pluto Compartments for inspection and it was thought to be carrying ammunition that was not covered by the contract. I told the Deputy Defence Adviser to inform the shipping agent to tell the ship that the NN MCMVs were warships and with a complement of NN personnel accompanying the ships. It should be expected that an appropriate scale of arm and ammunition would be carried and properly secured for protection while on transit.

I was unaware of any law that prevents the protection of military assets in a civilian setting. The compartments locked were only to be accessed by NN personnel onboard. Lieutenant Odusola had a lanyard around his waist with the keys. The Captain of the Floating Dock Ship had overall responsibility for the safe passage of the ship, cargo and NN personnel. The NN had a responsibility to respond to any contingency that may manifest during the passage. I advised the DDA (Navy) to tell the shipping agent to inform the Captain that the original passage plan should be strictly adhered to and the date and time of arrival in Lagos should be met. There was no room for indiscriminate port calls and excuses as the principal cargo had a purely military status.

This was my insurance cover for the ships and Lieutenant Odusola had enough information as regards the limited but very important role he and the two men so ably carried out. The NNIC crew that carried out a rare feat of very complex docking routines for two warships in less than four hours under my command in an unstable floating dock ship remained dedicated to the very end. I am sure a seaman commanding officer carrying out such a feat would have been given wide publicity that would earn him a national honour and the crew duly recognised. Instead,

I was being trailed for punishment by petty minds that continuously fail the NN.

The following day I got a report that the port call at Las Palmas had been shelved and there would be no alteration to the voyage plan and ETA (Expected Time of Arrival) Lagos. I requested the location of the ship and I was given a satisfactory report indicating all was going on well. The NN personnel onboard were being given their due respect as military personnel with their defined role that would not interfere with the Captain's management of the voyage to Lagos as long as the Captain kept to the schedule. I left London the following day for Lagos to prepare for the safe berthing of the ship and discharge of the MCMVs for my delivery to NN and it would then be a truly accomplished mission.

On arrival in Lagos, I briefed NHQ staff on the arrival date and requirements for the undocking of the MCMVs. The crew for the ships would have to man the ships immediately as they were floating. They insisted that they wanted to inspect the ship to certify there were no damages caused under my command. A committee was set up to determine if there were damages among other terms of reference. I was on my guard. It is normal to inspect what was being received. On the ship's arrival day, I went to the Naval Dockyard and took a position to welcome the ship as scheduled. I had information from the Nigerian Ports Authority office that handled the shipping manifest.

As I sighted the floating dock ship passing the East and West moles towards Atlas Cove jetty towards the Naval Dockyard, I started waving and gave a silent thanksgiving. I waved the ship past the Naval Dockyard and then drove to Tin Can Island to meet the ship already docked. I congratulated Lieutenant Samuel Odusola and the men for their achievement and walked around the ships with them. I told Lieutenant Odusola and the men to take time off and reunite with their families and wait till the ships were taken to the Naval Dockyard pool jetty and the crew settled with their inspection.

I gave Lieutenant Odusola the allowances for the NNIC personnel and the payment vouchers I collected from the Nigerian High Commission to pay them and returned the vouchers to London. The planned inspection was the next item and I left the ships' COs and their crew to do whatever they pleased. I was present alongside Lieutenant Ijioma. There was no damage due to the 'poor' seamanship skill of a marine engineer officer and his technical team. The other very complex issues that we had to pull through in Italy and get the ships to Lagos did not matter. I was being haunted for punishment. No one was questioned for leaving NNS OHUE unmanned with the national flag flying at the Italian Naval Base.

The Pluto Compartments were kept under lock until the ships were safely in the Naval Dockyard and out of view of the Captain of the Floating Dock ship. I kept it to myself that there was no insurance cover for the ships and I had to improvise military insurance and ensured there was no delay or change of route. The contents of the locked compartments were items for the ships, Pluto vehicles and some personal effects.

The next major task was to have meetings with the various departments that would handle several aspects of the MCMVs operation and maintenance. I visited the Underwater Warfare Training School at Ojo where a dedicated jetty and store complex for handling non-magnetic spare parts were being developed. The jetty and the buildings for storage were far from being ready. The Underwater Warfare Training School had installed some training equipment similar to those on the MCMVs based on the inputs provided by NNIC to DORNIER in Germany for that purpose. At the NHQ, there was no progress with the location of geodetic points for the positioning system for the MCMVs. There was virtually no progress on the documents forwarded to NHQ for over three years to sensitize the staff on the special requirements for the development of relevant mine countermeasures capabilities. I was disappointed with this neglect and I could not complain because no one would listen. The focus was access to what would bring money.

I had concluded my tenure as the Chief Delegate for the NN MCMVs. I had successfully handed over the ships and addressed all matters at various meetings. I still wonder how God took charge despite my human failings and there was no setback at NNIC in Italy. I remember the very frequent journeys by air and road especially during winter months when accidents on the roads were common on ice and snow-covered roads and airport runways. It was the special dedicated commitment to the performance of tasks by all members of the NNIC team to succeed that helped. I owe them all eternal gratitude for their service and duty to the country.

I was appointed as the Fleet Support Group Executive Officer with effect from April 1988 at Western Naval Command, Apapa, Lagos. I was already due for the Command and Staff College course at Jaji, near Kaduna. My new appointment would have a short tenure as the next course would start in August 1988. I used the opportunity to get myself acquainted with the current challenges of NN as the major warships of NN was based in Lagos.

I had handed over the MCMVs and was still being called to NHQ to attend to matters needing my attention. I had a feeling that it would be preferable if I was out of the NN environment for some time and in this regard would prefer doing my Command and Staff College Course abroad. As the appointment signal was released, I knew it was not going to be considered. There were attempts in this regard from other quarters which would delay me from doing the course by a year. However, I eventually prepared to leave for the course at Jaji and get it through with. I took my annual leave and started preparations for the course. I had very good reviews from the CNS and senior officers about my excellent career prospects and the statement that the sky was the limit was quite encouraging as I was also hinted about being a candidate for CNS from among my peers to end my career. I considered such a rating as extra pressure and exposure to further intrigues and had to be very careful.

Samuel Odusola was a Lieutenant Commander attending his senior staff course at Armed Forces Command and Staff College when sadly he died in a C130 Nigerian Air Force plane crash that wiped away a generation of officers on 26 September 1992. I can never thank him enough for his dedication and contributions towards the internationally recognized success of the NN MCMV project. I looked forward to having him around on further appointments as our career progressed but it was not to be. I rated him highly as the most trustworthy officer that served under me. Lieutenant E Ijioma would later rise to the rank of Rear Admiral and Head of Engineering Branch before retiring from active service. I had expected more from him but I knew his limitations. I tried to encourage him but there were other influences he deferred to. The Engineering Branch in NN has suffered the cumulative effects of such influences that make engineering officers focus on personal survival strategies and related intrigues at the expense of the pressing need to pay attention to growing the NN institution on sound engineering foundations.

The Engineering Branch in NN has been progressively run down and its personnel, though expected to play leading roles, are being denied opportunities. They were made to believe that they cannot hold some high profile appointments that seamen officers occupy whereas it has never been an official policy. I never felt any limitation as regards what I could aspire to be and considered myself as the architect of my limitations and no one else. This has been my belief. The NN did not take note of the international recognition for the outstanding performance characteristics achieved on the MCMVs and the library of documentation on all stages of the design, construction and trials that have never been so achieved in the past NN foreign acquisitions. The routine waste of opportunity goes on effortlessly.

CHAPTER ELEVEN

My Experience at the Command and Staff College, Jaji

I took my annual leave and had the opportunity to take my family to visit my cousin at Kaduna. This was a time to catch up on family matters and get the children to pay respect to my cousin and also for me to inform him I was going to the Command and Staff College, Jaji. We returned to Lagos and I began to prepare for the Senior Division course at Command and Staff College, Jaji.

I had the check-off list of items required from the College for the course and upkeep. It was easy for me to get together the course reading materials required but I had some difficulty adjusting to the reality of the requirements for my upkeep. I had to get a kerosene hurricane lantern and cooking stove and other items that indicated the basic facilities would not be readily available. I went to Alaba Market and picked up the items I could find.

The hurricane lamp reminded me of the same kind of lamp we used at Okene, Magamiya, and Zonkwa until I was about ten years old. I reflected deeply on the throwback to my childhood and was sad that having extensively trained and practised the profession of arms and engineering in Europe and been exposed to cutting edge technologies in the international arena, I was back to Nigeria and retrogressing into primitive existence as I prepared to attend a course at a military institution without efficient basic facilities such as public electric power supply despite all the opportunities to do better and be a developed country.

The thoughts of what could become of the MCMVs flooded my mind and I had no hope that the very high standards attained would be appreciated and maintained. The realities at Command and Staff College would further rub it in that the NN was not prepared or ready to adapt to technological innovations despite the impressive inventory of cutting edge technologies from the advanced countries. I hit the road for the Command and Staff College.

I gave a lift to Lieutenant Commander Shola Egunjobi, a Weapon Engineer Officer, who was also nominated for the course. I picked him up from his residence at FESTAC Town off Lagos-Badagry Expressway. I was driving a new Mercedes Benz car and had been warned about security on the road. I was advised that it would be better for me to use an old car to Jaji. I did not have the choice of a car. I was hoping that there would be no night driving through the danger zones. We got to Kaduna while it was getting dark.

On arrival at the College, we located the reception team and got our accommodation allocations. Three officers would occupy the three-bedroom house and I was allocated the main bedroom with an ensuite bathroom and toilet. I was comfortable and had no problem settling in. I was ready with candles and a kerosene lantern. I set up the cooking stove because the electric cooker in the kitchen shared by the officers was barely functional. I relied on my stove throughout the course. We arrived on Friday night and spent the weekend settling down and getting acquainted with the vast College grounds. The facilities looked rather unkempt and fittings in kitchens and bathrooms needed attention.

The layout of the College was simple but very much spread out. The accommodation for the Directing Staff was similar to the students' houses. The Senior Division Directing Staff were Commanders while the Junior Division Directing Staffs were Lieutenant Commanders and some of them paired up in the houses. The Chief Instructor and Directors of the Faculties had their institutional houses separated from the Directing Staff and Students cluster accommodations. The Commandant and Deputy Commandant had their houses well located as if to monitor all that goes in and out of the roads that lead to the two main gates out of the establishment by their residences. It was easy to move around and have access to the Directing Staff.

The first day at the instructional block was spent receiving briefings and course materials. We were assigned to syndicates and each had a Directing Staff and Student Leader to manage the administration. Though it was meant to be a Command and Staff Course, the focus was mainly on staff duties. The Naval Faculty had its central lecture hall and three syndicate rooms. The Army and Air Force Faculties had similar arrangements and each had sections for the Junior Division Courses. There was the Joint Faculty Division. The main College Auditorium was located near the Army and Joint Faculties. The main Administrative block was located near the Naval Faculty. It was easy moving for lectures and syndicate sessions in designated rooms and auditoriums.

There were lectures on Naval subjects given in the Department Auditorium. There followed syndicate discussions moderated by the syndicate Directing Staff. Lectures on geostrategic studies and others common to the three services were delivered in the main College Auditorium. Written assignments were assessed by the Directing Staff and moderated by the Chief Instructor. Most of these were assessed and graded. There was a faculty research paper based on a selected topic to which a project supervisor was allocated. The geo-strategic study module comprised selected lectures by external resource persons and tour of selected states in Nigeria based on a theme and a tour of selected foreign countries to which a mixed team of the three services visited. There was a programme visit to military installations. These sum up the course content.

The Directing Staff at the College had a mix of British Armed Forces Training team members and some Ghanaian officers. The British Training team members were winding up and they departed before the completion of my course. It was left to an all Nigerian training team with one Ghanaian naval officer, a Commander, to handle the affairs of the Naval Faculty. I had a good start and had to make some minor adjustments as regards the use of the English language and getting familiar with the staff writing manual.

There were various grades of assessment during the course. The major one for grading was called "Red Ink Correction" (RIC) and each exercise so designated had what was called the "Green Solution" which the students were not allowed to see. The "Green Solutions" were in the custody of the Directing Staff concerned with the exercises to guide the gradings. There were operational exercises conducted in the Naval Faculty Auditorium. The electives were assessed but not weighted as the RIC exercises, which included a research project that was the most important assessment exercise and attracted a prize.

I was getting on well and improving on my scores with each exercise. I was always early in arriving at the Naval Faculty to update myself on the programmes and notifications. As I approached my syndicate room one morning, I met a Directing Staff standing at the entrance to his office. All other Directing Staff offices were not open as it was still early. As I greeted and passed by him, he called me into his office. He showed me my exercise for RIC which he had assessed but left out the B grading he told me he was going to give.

I was shocked when he asked me to give him something in the form of gratification for the grading to be inserted. He considered the B grading as something rare to get and it was up for sale. I was speechless and could not look him in the face. I was ashamed. He was embarrassed by my silence and composure. He then asked me to make a promise to fulfil later. As I was not talking and students and other Directing Staff would soon be trooping in, he dismissed me asking me to think about it and get back to him before his submission to the Chief Instructor.

I left and never wanted to see him again but he was a Directing Staff with more roles to play during the course. I wanted to make a report to the Chief Instructor or confide in a senior Directing Staff on how to handle the matter. I also considered seeking the opinion of other students on the course in the Naval Faculty. But I decided to keep it all to myself because I could not trust them to protect me if the matter blew up.

At a reception at the residence of one of the Directing Staff for all members of the faculty and the students of the faculty, I noticed that members of the Directing Staff gave me the cold shoulders. I managed to engage the Ghanaian Directing Staff and in our discussion, he told me that it was the opinion of most of the Directing Staff that I was too confident on the course. He advised me not to be. I thanked him for the advice because I knew why. I maintained my silence on the issue throughout the course. Still, I suffered the consequences. I was eventually given C+ for that course work but I did not complain. The next Directing Staff that handled my syndicate started giving me low marks; still, I did not complain despite the harassment. But my decision not to complain was considered as over-confidence and used against me.

It was difficult to continue with the tense situation with the Directing Staff with the impression they had that I was too confident. I was very careful about making contributions which were very essential for many assessments. I had to read widely and prepare well so that my contributions were up to standard and relevant. As the syndicate Directing Staff were changed periodically and some were assigned different course programmes to conduct, I was able to cope and minimise the effects of the harassment.

I chose a mine warfare topic for the Naval Faculty paper and military logistics topic for the Joint Faculty paper. I had a supervisor for each paper that was submitted in the last term for assessment. The two papers had guidelines issued at joint briefings and documents were issued as reference. These guidelines focussed on structure, length or number of words and character sizes among other requirements. I had the close attention of my supervisors and kept to schedules, corrections and advice.

The study tour package was jointly organised. The first covered state study tours by syndicates formed by the students and staff of the three services. Similar syndicate groups were formed for the Africa tours to selected countries. I was a member of the syndicates that toured Ogun State and the Republic of Togo.

The state tour revealed the serious problems of the international border areas that were neglected and easily infiltrated. My syndicate was informed that a house had a toilet divided between Nigeria and the Republic of Benin. There were no concerns for threats to national security.

Besides, the common language of the border areas in both countries makes border demarcation difficult. I considered this situation a security risk but others thought it was not a problem as people of the same language were free to move about unchecked.

The visit to Togo was during the tenure of the late President Gynassingbe Eyadema. The team from the College was led by the Commandant Major General Mohammed B. Mamman, a fine orator. His presence ensured we had a state visit rather than a study tour alone. I was in charge of gifts for presentation and was briefed on the occasions that gifts would be given and their categories. I had to sit close enough to the Commandant for the management of the gifts and this gave me the advantage of being served well with food and refreshments. The team had an audience with the President in his office conference room and he elaborated on how he miraculously survived a plane crash. According to him, it was an assassination attempt on his life. We visited the wreckage of the plane which was then a national monument. We visited some military formations and the town of Atakpame where we went to the market that had many Nigerian traders selling mainly yams and other farm produce. We rounded off the visit with a state dinner.

I had the opportunity to interact with a European guest at the hotel bar on our last evening in Porto Novo. He had travelled extensively to many West African countries and had very good knowledge of developments in Nigeria. I was not surprised when he started discussing the economic situation in Nigeria and he zeroed in on the Ajaokuta Steel project. He was on point as at 1989 that there was no need for Nigeria to have a steel plant as the world major steel producers had enough stock for the West Africa market that would make it impossible for Ajaokuta Steel Company to compete for market share. He opined that Nigeria should scuttle the Ajaokuta Steel project and sell it off as scrap because Nigeria cannot manage the company and market its products.

I listened attentively and urged him on. He then elaborated on the international politics related to the development and how the developed countries could satisfy the needs of African countries. He never knew that I had attended military education and training institutions in Europe and worked extensively on a warship design and construction project that involved several industries in some European countries and the USA. I was well educated and introduced to an economic hitman in Africa. This experience would serve me well when I was a member of the National Committee on Science and Engineering Infrastructure set up by the then Minister of Science and Technology, Professor Gordian Ezekwe in 1990. I will elaborate on this later.

There were external lecturers from outside the country sourced from the UN and India. The Indian Army General who was in command during the Indian Peace Keeping Force intervention in 1987 in the Sri Lanka civil war gave a very impressive lecture on the operations and the massive logistics component. During the interactive session, a student asked how much money was involved. The Indian General was confused and struggled to understand the question. He was helped when someone from the audience repeated the question thus: "How many Rupees were you given for the operation?" The General said that he did not see or handle Rupee because he was too busy planning and conducting operations.

This question and the answer given by the General showed how rotten the Nigerian Armed Forces had become as of 1989 when the question was asked. We could see why Nigeria cannot make tangible progress and its military establishment has no developed capabilities for the defence of the country. Money in the hands of operational commanders to conduct military operations simply shows a lack of preparedness and readiness.

A lecturer from Ahmadu Bello University, Zaria who gave a lecture on technology development was asked whether Nigeria could develop a nuclear capability. He responded by drawing attention to the rear row of steps down to the front stage and observed that the dirty and worn carpet on the steps of the main auditorium of the then apex military institution in Nigeria lacks the discipline to develop nuclear capability which requires a very clean environment. The hall was silent and no more questions were asked.

I had a particularly difficult second term as I noticed that my assessments were dropping and at a stage, I was given C minus grading. I took the time to read the submissions of some students with better grading and I noticed the differences. I kept my observation to myself and kept on doing my best as I earned more low scores.

In the third and final term, I had a change of Directing Staff and more group exercises and presentations during which individual contributions were easily noted and scored. I made up for the second term set back. This term was also devoted to finishing the two research papers: the Naval Faculty and Joint Warfare Department papers.

The submission of the two papers virtually marked the beginning of the end of the course as Directing Staff had to read and score the papers and submit them to the Chief Instructors for final assessment. There was a final exercise on joint operations called EXERCISE JAGUN. Jagun is a Yoruba name for war. I had an Army officer, Lieutenant Colonel E Coker as the Directing Staff. I was the only Naval representative in my syndicate and it was an amphibious operation setting for the exercise for which there was a staff green solution. The Army, Navy and Air Force list of platforms and order of battle was provided and the area of intended operation was between the coastlines of Sierra Leone and Liberian at a time the rebel forces of Charles Taylor were threatening to overthrow the government of President Samuel Doe in Monrovia.

There were Directing Staff assessments of our progress to ensure we followed the classical planning and conduct of amphibious operations. There were discussions across syndicates and I noticed that all the syndicates had the same standard solution which was expected if the guidelines were followed. The landing area to establish a beachhead would require forces to engage in further battles to secure Monrovia which was the main objective. This would stretch the supply line.

I convinced my syndicate to be realistic as the naval platforms listed for the amphibious operation were of the Royal Navy standard which was not realistic for the wargaming exercise because of the developments in Liberia. I suggested that, instead, we would rely on the two Landing Ship Tank (LST), NNS AMBE and NNS OFIOM and take over a landing area around the capital, Monrovia, and fight through into the urban area. The enemy would be expecting something much different. This was the only odd solution among all the syndicates.

There was concern by the Army Directing Staff who contacted the most experienced Naval Directing Staff Commander John Adoko, Ghanaian Navy. Commander Adoko came to the room where my syndicate was meeting and observed that we had gone far. He called me out of the room and asked if I was involved in the out of the box solution my syndicate was implementing. I told him that I took time to convince the syndicate and I summarised how we arrived at our decision. He confided in me that my syndicate solution was different from all others. I told him that we wanted something different and realistic. I was cautioned to be ready to answer a lot of questions. I did not discuss this interaction with other members of the syndicate and only assured them that our position had been explained and we could proceed as planned.

As we concluded our exercise and were preparing for a presentation, I was called for an interview with the Naval Faculty Chief Instructor regarding my overall assessment. The Chief Instructor started by informing me that the members of the Directing Staff observed that I was very confident and that I was going to top the class in performance and did not take the course seriously. My mind went back to the incident that led to this contrived observation and I wrestled within myself not to report what happened between me and Directing Staff referred to much earlier in the first term that made demand from me for the grading earned.

The Chief Instructor then went on to refer to my dip in performance in the second term. I had to tell the Chief Instructor that I always gave my best and hardly had time to rest and besides took a very active part in team sports and other activities. I also drew attention to several group exercises that I had done more than a fair share of the assignments to ensure group success. He insisted that the supposed confidence was because I refused to interact with the Directing Staff properly and this affected my second term performance. I had to request that all my second term written submissions for assessment be reassessed along with others in my second term syndicate by a neutral Directing Staff. This was accepted and the Chief Instructor for the Junior Division at the Naval Faculty Lieutenant Commander Anthony K Amauchechukwu was nominated to head the panel for the reassessment.

There was no Directing Staff from the Senior Division as all of them were Commanders. The panel set up was disbanded and I was told that there was no need for reassessment. It was in the evening some days later that the Chief Instructor drove to the students' accommodation block and asked a student to call me. I approached his car virtually in motion, he gestured to me that I should not worry and he drove off asking me to see him in the office the following day.

I went across to Major (later Lieutenant Colonel and Military Governor of Edo State) Mohammed A.S. Onuka's room in a nearby block and discussed the issue with him. We agreed that I should take precautions and still be prepared for reassessment. I went to see the Chief Instructor hoping that he would shed more light on the situation but he kept me guessing their intentions. I then told him that I would prefer the reassessment to put the records straight because I was not prepared to be labelled as a student that did not take the course seriously. He asked me to take my leave. I left.

The following day as we settled into our syndicate routine to rehearse for our EXERCISE JAGUN presentation, Commander John

Adoko called me to his office to hand over to me my Naval Faculty research paper that I had unofficially been informed was assessed B and selected for an award. This paper should have been handed over to me by the supervisor and so I was prepared for another round of intrigue. When I entered his office, I noticed an uneasy look on his face. He was the most senior and experienced among the Directing Staff at the Naval Faculty. He asked me to sit down and then started rambling incoherently trying to find excuses to down-grade my paper. I had seen the B grading tip-exed with C+ (C plus) grading written beside it. The reasons for the down-grading did not add up and when he asked me if I had any questions, I told him I had none and politely left.

I went to my syndicate and collected my bag and materials and informed members of the syndicate that I was not feeling fine and needed some time to myself and have some rest. I went to my room. The tri-service syndicate members knew more about the intrigues I was going through and briefed the Army Directing Staff who could have ordered my return to the syndicate but he did not. The members of the syndicate after the day's session sent a representative to me, offering their sympathy for what I was going through; I appreciated their understanding and gesture.

I had some rest and after dinner, I went to see Commander John Adoko at his official residence nearby without invitation. He was surprised to see me and welcomed me to his living room. He asked his wife who had come from Ghana for the graduation to excuse us. He offered me drinks which I politely declined and requested that we use the veranda where there was some fresh air as he had started sweating. I did not want his wife to hear our discussion.

I told him I was disappointed that he allowed himself to be used to down-grade my Naval Faculty paper which was to be awarded a prize. I asked him why he did such a shameful thing when his usual wise counsel should have prevailed. I reminded him that in the first term at a reception, he was kind enough to hint to me about being described as too confident and advised me to improve on my approach in my relations with the DS group after which I related very well with him and the others.

Commander Adoko was speechless and was now sweating profusely with his singlet drenched. I pitied his state and told him that I just wanted to tell him that I was fully aware of what was happening and it was a shame that he had to damage his reputation. I wished him well and politely took my leave. He could not utter a word.

The following evening, a Wednesday, was the regimental mess dinner night for the graduating students. The sitting plan had already been finalised and the names of the top students from Army, Navy and Air Force faculties were on the high table with the guest of honour Major General (later Lieutenant General) Rufus Kupolati. Though I had been downgraded I was still allowed the honour of the high table for the best naval graduating student for reasons best known to them.

The evening was very tense for me. It was supposed to be a moment of celebration but it seemed everyone knew of my agony. The following day, I was informed that the finalised results were being amended two days to graduation and the two prizes I had won would be taken away and my overall course B grading would be brought down to C+ and would be the sixth in order of merit. 'A' grading is hardly ever awarded even in exercises at the College.

I went through my Naval Faculty paper again and observed all the fresh marks and lines scribbled without explanation. I went to the Chief Instructor and requested to see the Director of the Naval Faculty Commodore FIO Nesiama. I was called at the appointed time into the office of the Director and he was fully prepared with all the assessment sheets related to the Naval Faculty paper for all the students. I told him what I had been experiencing and that recently my research paper was downgraded. He opened his desk drawer and brought out the assessment sheets and located mine. He said that I did not put in a section in the paper as the assessment sheet indicated and this attracted a big allocation of marks. I made two observations instantly. The first was that the section was considered not required and the assessment sheet sample given to us as a guide did not contain that section. Secondly, the assessment sheets were freshly printed and did not carry the correct shade; the removed section was re-inserted and allocated marks and this was only on my assessment sheet.

The Director was shocked and asked how I knew as he hurriedly packed the assessment sheets to hideaway. I looked across his window and saw a group of the Naval Faculty students returning from the College Auditorium and I requested that they be called in to testify. The Director obliged and I went out and called them to the Director's office. He asked the students about the brief to leave out the mentioned section and they all confirmed that we were all asked to leave it out and that they all did not include it in their papers. The students were instantly dismissed.

I summed up the Director's reactions and concluded that he had sanctioned what was happening. I then requested that the case be taken up for me to see the Commandant. The Director was most disturbed and I left to prepare and see the Commandant. The torment I was suffering had become common knowledge in the College. I learnt that the Commandant got to know and was waiting. The outcome would be terrible for the Naval Faculty should the matter go before the Commandant.

I thought over the issue and later in the evening I went to see the Director at his residence and informed him that as the most senior officer in the Naval Faulty I would not go beyond him and would leave everything in his hands and accept whatever was the outcome. The Director asked me to see him the week after graduation as he was travelling out for a few days immediately after graduation. I met him and assured him that I bore him no grudge for what happened and would not take up the case. I had been denied the first position I earned and the College Tie prize and research paper prize and in addition to being downgraded to C+ grading overall and reduced to the 6th position in the class.

I refused to bribe a faculty member to be awarded a B grade for a first-term exercise and thereafter I was falsely accused of being too confident throughout the course no matter how hard I tried. There was a post-graduation exercise that we went through and I focused on getting out of the Armed Forces Command and Staff College, Jaji. In my course report, there was an attempt to discredit me and a recommendation was made that I was not recommended to return to the College as a Directing Staff and should not be given a diplomatic posting. I had just completed a very important diplomatic posting as Federal Government Chief Delegate in Italy and it had become part of my career record. The same Faculty would later request me to return as a Directing Staff at the Senior Division but the report that was written would not be changed.

My wife flew to Kaduna for the graduation ceremony. I ensure she enjoyed the graduation ceremony and left the following day. I continued what I considered was damage control to avoid the situation deteriorating further and needed to keep up with the intrigues. I believed that it would not be good for the Navy Faculty if the matter got to the Commandant. I would still have to work with the officers back in the Nigerian Navy. They were my superiors. I knew that my course mates who were the beneficiaries of my down gradings and denial of prizes needed to be fulfilled that they truly deserved what they got. I met two of them separately and assured them that they truly deserved the awards and explained to them that I would not want the matter to go outside the Naval Faculty and cause further anxiety. I sincerely congratulated them.

I kept to myself the real reason for all I had to endure. I had earned a humiliation in a tri-service establishment and this would be the only military institution I attended within and outside Nigeria that I experienced such impunity from the academic staff and did not pass out with a prize. I have imbibed the family value of perseverance and the avoidance of seeking revenge. I enlisted in the military to serve my country and had been taught the value of honesty and teamwork. I am not very religious but regularly remember my father's short prayer extolling the greatness of God; many officers and sailors hardly knew my religious belief and tribe because I tried to relate with all who come my way. I always want to be trusted and relate with my colleagues in a manner that will inspire confidence.

I was in Italy and did not compromise these principles and values. I couldn't bribe for marks or good grading. I have never and will never ask for a bribe to serve my country. These weighed on my mind and determined the decisions I made. I also remembered the crisis I had at the Nigerian Defence Academy where I was considered too young to top the class and win medals on passing out. The Command and Staff College Naval Faculty were oozing with corruption in a most ferocious manner targeted against me.

The Directing Staff at the Naval Faculty after the humiliating show of denial during graduation started making overtures that I should forget and not take it too seriously. The same group had already crafted and documented phrases in my report to create problems for me in my career. They started organising students farewell reception sessions during break time and I attended them but refused to discuss the matter with any Directing Staff. I steered clear and at a stage walked away. I ensured what transpired between me and the faculty member who asked me for a bribe remained between us. I kept the faith.

There was a shift of the final farewell party that was to hold in a senior Directing Staff residence for the students by the Naval Faculty. I was also invited to attend a private party at the residence of Major(later Major General) AS Abdulrahman who was the best Army graduating student and with whom I shared the high table as the best Naval graduating student during the regimental dinner night two days before. I drove past the residence of the Deputy Commandant, a Naval Officer, to where the reception was shifted to avoid them and have my peace of mind. Their shifting of the venue of the reception was probably to force me to attend and make me smile with my tormentors. I went for the reception celebrating Major Abdulrahman's achievements and returned late at night to a hail of complaints from some people that I stayed away from the Naval Faculty reception. I focused on winding up and returning to Lagos to recover.

I completed the leaving routine and took my leave of the College with very sad memories, not only of what happened to me but of the pervasive corruption and the level of immaturity displayed by my superior officers at the Naval Faculty between 1988-1989. I began a serious search for why AFN personnel lack commitment to serve the country they claim to bear allegiance but fiercely believe that the institution must always be compromised to satisfy them.

I have reflected on my experiences so far and noticed a trend that is destroying the nation-state of Nigeria. There is a poor political direction that drives excessive greed and makes Nigerians seek power for the accumulation of personal wealth. This mentality or mindset is used to allocate appointments to people who are not qualified to head national institutions. After they destroy such institutions through incompetence, those who are qualified but initially denied the positions are reluctantly smuggled in and given an impossible task to rescue the institutions while those who destroyed them are accorded the status of accomplished public officers.

In the AFN, it is established that you must show evidence of loyalty to individuals and the capacity to destroy the system the institution should rely upon for growth in the national interest. This is also observed in civil institutions. The military as a professional institution should never allow such trend to become pervasive because it destroys quality manpower and material assets, and makes the institution unattractive to qualified and competent people who want to serve their country as officers and gentlemen in the armed forces. It takes a top-quality organization to attract and retain the best quality manpower available essential for the credibility of a modern military establishment.

I was appointed as the Fleet Marine Engineer Officer at the Western Naval Command Fleet Support Group. I had served as Command Technical Officer at the Command when Rear Admiral DE Okujagu was FOC. I reported for duty on 31 July 1989 and was given additional responsibility as the Executive Officer to the Commander of the Fleet Support Group, Commander M E Okwesa. I was settling into routines when I was appointed to Naval Training Command three months later. I used the brief period to look into how the MCMV Squadron was faring at the Command and tried to explain the requirements for upkeep to ensure the unique performance characteristics that make the ships perform their mine warfare roles were maintained. It was a difficult task due to inadequate facilities which should have been provided before the arrival of the ships from Italy.

CHAPTER TWELVE

Transforming the Nigerian Navy

I was appointed Command Technical Training Officer at the Naval Training Command (NAVTRAC) Headquarters at Apapa, Lagos on 2 November 1989. The Flag Officer Commanding (FOC) was Rear Admiral Murtala AH Nyako. I have been close to the FOC and was happy to be appointed as a principal staff officer to him. I was privileged to know some of his thoughts and passion for the transformation of the NN. I took this as an opportunity to focus on contributing to getting the NN transformed to cope with the huge and diverse modern products of technology spread among the various classes of warships, the latest being the MCMVs that was commissioned into service in 1988.

There were growing concerns about the inadequacies in terms of training, operations, and upkeep. Admiral Nyako having commanded NNS ENYIMIRI and being the first Commanding Officer of the ship from the shipyard in Portsmouth where I first met him as I was concluding my Marine Engineering specialization course, was abreast of the challenges. This appointment made me quickly forget the incident at Command and Staff College. Admiral Nyako had become my mentor and close family friend whom I treasured. He had followed my career progress as closely as he did for so many other officers in the NN in particular and the Armed Forces in general. I was determined to give our professional relationship my best and avoid a mix up with our close relationship.

On assuming duty, I went through the protocol of being formally introduced to the FOC by the Chief Staff Officer (CSO) Commodore (later Rear Admiral) D Osunmakinde. The formalities were brief and to the point. The FOC stressed the challenges facing NN that had to be urgently addressed. I went through the schedules of duty and the scope of responsibilities with emphasis on naval training. The scope was wide and included the spread of training establishments and the warships of the NN Fleet. NAVTRAC had the responsibility for formulating tactical doctrine and with the current developments in technologies applied to warships, there was much to do starting with the awareness of the technical complexities to be managed for war.

I attended the first meeting with the FOC NAVTRAC with his principal staff officers. It was a weekly routine. At the meeting, the FOC NAVTRAC emphasised the logistics needs of the NN and the training requirements in the service. This emphasis reflected his clear understanding of the challenges facing NN. His address summarised that the NN needed to be urgently transformed by domesticating the roots of its logistics. He said that dinosaurs became extinct because they refused to adapt to changes and expressed the hope that NN would not suffer the same fate.

I went through the Nigerian Navy Order (NNO) establishing the Naval Training Command and the schedule of duty for all staff officers. The responsibility for the formulation of tactical doctrine got my attention. The NN had to face the realities of sophisticated ships with an array of modern weapons comprising various modern missiles, torpedoes, guns, weapons control systems, sensors, communication equipment, and propulsion plants.

The Combat Information Centres of the capital warships were equipped with sophisticated computers and display consoles. Although the need for Principal Warfare Officers (PWOs) and Advanced Principal Warfare Officers (APWO) had been established, there had been resistance to change as the Gunnery Officers held on to their tradition; the same trend held sway in the Weapon and Marine Engineering Departments. The NN had not been able to restructure the onboard warship organisation to reflect the impact of sophisticated technologies and take advantage of them for operational efficiency.

At a meeting with the FOC NAVTRAC and the principal staff officers at the Command Headquarters, I made a presentation drawing attention to one of the principal tasks assigned to the Command which was the formulation of tactical doctrines for the NN. This required dedicated simulation facilities and team training that would draw officers from the Weapon Engineering and other relevant departments for the operation of weapons and associated systems in the Combat Information Centres of the ships were not defined and implemented for operational effectiveness.

The FOC NAVTRAC immediately grasped the ideas and asked for inputs. The meeting agreed that the NN needed a computerised Action-Speed-Tactical-Trainer (ASTT) that would be established at the Naval College at Onne, Port Harcourt. The FOC NAVTRAC phoned the Chief of the Naval Staff, Vice Admiral Patrick Seubo Koshoni, and convinced him that the NN needed to adopt the recommendation of the meeting. The Chief of the Naval Staff directed that the idea should be developed and the proposals forwarded to him.

I had bought myself a task. I had a pool of officers I could rely on to draw up the specifications with inputs from other relevant departments. We duly produced the proposal and the specifications. These were forwarded to Naval Headquarters. It was approved immediately.

A new building was constructed and a German logistics company, DORNIER, was contracted for the supply, installation, and commissioning of the ASTT facility. The company sourced the relevant expertise for the operation and maintenance of the facility and the training of the Principal Warfare Officer was embarked upon. This was the basic training for the Advanced Warfare Officers qualification course required for ships such as NNS ARADU and the Mark 9 Corvettes.

The Command had responsibilities for training schools in various locations in Lagos (NNS QUORRA), Onne (Port Harcourt), Sapele (Naval Engineering College), and Owerrinta (Logistics) among others. The NNS QUORRA had many schools for the Seaman Branch specialisations and there was a lot of work being done by DORNIER in curriculum design and development, installation of training equipment, and logistics. The maintenance requirement of the Headquarters and the schools located at NNS QUORRA were additional responsibilities beyond the Commanding Officer's schedule. I did not carry out any familiarisation tours of the schools outside the Lagos area. It would be time-consuming and exorbitant. NNS QUORRA had many professional schools within its complex and a parade ground located with the NAVTRAC Headquarters.

NNS QUORRA had a Wardroom Mess facility and a good auditorium used for activities by Western Naval Command and the Naval Headquarters, especially for conferences. The parade ground of NNS QUORRA was also used for all major ceremonial naval parades in the Lagos area. The Naval Training Command Headquarters was very busy as its location attracted several activities. I was Command Technical Officer Western Naval Command in 1981 when the main complex that was to be the Headquarters of the Western Naval Command was completed and gave rise to a debate about which of the NN needs should be given priority.

The pressing need for accommodation for various training schools due to Fleet expansion and the demand to decongest Western Naval Command led to priority being given to training schools. The decision was taken to decongest the Western Naval Command by moving out NNS QUORRA to the present newly completed site; the Barracks

Maintenance Unit was also moved to Navy Town, Ojo. I was happy to have participated actively in decongesting Naval Base, Apapa.

NNS ARADU was in the news towards the end of 1989. The ship was having serious vibration problems as it limped into the harbour from the sea. This limited her participation in the annual CNS sea exercise. The CNS was unhappy with the development and he set up a Board of Inquiry to investigate what led to the ship's problem and make recommendations. Rear Admiral SB Atukum was appointed chairman of the board; I was appointed its secretary. Commander J Badeji was a member among others. I was assigned to a subcommittee with Commander Badeji. I noticed he was not feeling at ease and I knew why. I focused on our assigned task. The Board of Inquiry was going to last into the new year 1990. The FOC WEST Rear Admiral OP Fingesi was under much pressure. I later gathered he had a very rough time at sea with the CNS on the Mark 9 Corvette that replaced NNS ARADU.

There had been some anticipation of an impending change in the leadership of NN at Naval Headquarters. A new Chief of the Naval Staff (CNS) was expected to be appointed towards the end of the year. Rear Admiral MAH Nyako, FOC NAVTRAC was in the running among those being considered. He had prepared himself for the high command and it was a matter of time. The announcement in January 1990 of his eventual appointment was not a surprise. I had closely watched his contributions to many important programmes of the NN and how he improved himself to understand the complexities of the NN. He fought hard to get the NN MCMV project started and developed the various training schools including the Underwater Warfare School at Navy Town, Ojo, Lagos. He had a good grasp of the NN logistics requirements and he had a passion for modernisation. He was very keen on transforming NN and would state most often that the NN must adapt and change to survive and grow. Rear Admiral MAH Nyako was appointed CNS in January 1990.

I knew I had to be at my professional best at all times so that I would not take things for granted and possibly let him down. Several receptions were held for the new CNS which I was expected to attend being close to him. But I was careful not to be seen gate crashing into the receptions to which I had not been invited. Some officers who had been attending the receptions asked me why I missed some of the receptions. I told them that I was not invited and they were surprised. I felt that this might be misconstrued as my being too important by waiting to be invited. My wife was close to the CNS second wife, Mrs Zainab Nyako. This helped us to keep up with the tempo of some of the activities.

At a reception in a restaurant near our residence at Victoria Island, my wife and I had arrived early. I noticed that the CNS was sitting all by himself and in a reflective mood. I approached him to pay my respect. In my stiff formal greeting, he must have felt I was stage acting and in his usual jovial manner, he grabbed and held me to sit by his side. I knew the CNS felt I was not comfortable and he did his best as if to reassure me that nothing would change in our relationship. The reception went very well and ended in time to let the CNS catch up on other matters, I assumed.

The new FOC NAVTRAC was Rear Admiral Edward S Buba. I had known him as he had a family residence close to mine in Victoria Island and we occasionally met. The change of command ceremony was brief. The new CNS told me to remain at the command, commended me, and asked that I keep up the good work.

The new CNS had an excellent grasp of the problems of the NN and in an important address to the NHQ staff, he told them that naval engineering was at the heart of naval operations, and as such, he would give priority to making the NN engineering branch more effective. He ordered the naval engineers to come up with a reorganization plan and other suggestions for effectiveness. Due to the poor maintenance state of NN Fleet, he promised to set up immediately a maintenance command to commence his transformation agenda.

The use of the word 'command' did not go down well with the officers of the Seaman Branch who were not prepared to have a senior engineering branch officer as Flag Officer Commanding. According to them, only Seaman Officers were entitled to being Flag Officers Commanding or Commanding Officers. This is a tribal cult mentality and a sense of entitlement being displayed. Unfortunately, some engineer officers sided with seamen officers to spite their colleagues that could be appointed as Flag Officer Commanding.

There were suggestions of names such as Maintenance Division and Maintenance Corps. It was again considered not appropriate to use Division so that the status would not be mistaken for an Army Division. It was finally decided to settle for Fleet Maintenance Corps and a signal was released creating the establishment. It is note worthy that Nigerian political elites are used to FOC, GOC and AOC for political appointment and have no use for Corps Commanders.

The first Commander, Fleet Maintenance Corps, (CFMC) was Commodore IN Katagum. He was tasked with establishing a functioning organisation. The CNS mandated some officers to prepare drafts of appropriate NNO; the Engineering Branch had the primary responsibility to lead the effort. Many opinions had to be harmonised. I was given some of the drafts the CNS considered reflected his vision of the setup and wanted a coherent NNO draft.

I was progressing with my job at the Naval Training Command and on one of my routine visits to Commodore IN Katagum, we discussed the challenges ahead and the poor state of NN warships. I gave him a very short paper addressing the salient points with suggested solutions. When he read my paper, he said nothing. He asked me how long I had been at the Naval Training Command. I had spent less than six months there. I resisted the temptation to ask him to allow me to serve under him at the Corps. We had light-hearted discussions to get our minds off the pressing urgent tasks regarding getting the Corps established. I was convinced that the Corps was where I should be to influence actions in readiness for Nigeria's possible intervention in the Liberian political crisis. The war game exercise at Command and Staff College gave me appropriate directions.

About two days after my meeting with Commodore Katagum, I saw him at the FOC NAVTRAC premises in the company of FOC about leaving the Command Headquarters. I saluted them as I passed by. The FOC NAVTRAC later told me that he had been requested to release me to be appointed to the Corps. The FOC told me that he was impressed that the pioneer Commander, Fleet Maintenance Corps had to come to him and discuss the matter in a very formal and open manner and that he was willing to release me. I soon received a signal from NHQ appointing me as Captain, Research, and Development.

My new office was a former Base Flat for the Naval Dockyard and had been used for several purposes over the years. I arranged for some temporary work to clean up the office and make it useable but I did not ask for money to make it functional. I had time to study the drafts of the NNO for the Fleet Maintenance Corps. I dug deep into my experience so far at the RN Ship Maintenance Authority at Portsmouth Naval Base.

I had several drafts that got me worried as I wrestled with convincing myself what would work well for the NN and would not be a problem for the Corps. This was an assignment given to me by CNS and I had to submit my final draft directly to him. The draft I submitted directly to CNS was further circulated and finally went through the scrutiny of NHQ principal staff officers. The final document reflected minor adjustments to my submission and was promulgated as NNO 1/1990 establishing the NN Fleet Maintenance Corps.

The CNS had ideas for a comprehensive logistics set-up for the NN and his satisfaction with my handling of the first NNO for the Fleet Maintenance Corps attracted more assignments from him. There were drafts for Naval Material Supply Corps and Naval Ordnance Corps NNOs. I enjoyed researching and writing a faculty of Joint Warfare paper on the Military Logistics system in which I emphasised the science and art of preparation for war. This, alongside my experiences on the MCMV project and RN set up, gave me a good background to attempt these NNOs. I believe I would do a better job on these NNOs if the CNS passed the order to work on them to the Commander, Fleet Maintenance Corps so that he could ask other officers to make inputs into whatever I might come up with. The CNS passed the order accordingly to my immediate boss to enable other officers at FMC to also make contributions and very good drafts emerged and the NNOs were promulgated with almost no amendments.

Commander FMC held several meetings to determine the state of ships and priorities. I suggested that all ships of Western and Eastern Fleets be brought together in Lagos that had more facilities for the various levels of maintenance up to depot/dockyard level. Also, the Landing Ships Tank (LSTs), NNS AMBE, and NNS OFIOM, the three German Fast Attack Craft, NNS ERINOMI, and NNS ENYIMIRI were to be given priority. I was mandated to determine maintenance requirements and this engaged my department to the fullest.

The priority from NHQ was to get the NNS ARADU major refit specifications submitted by Blom+Voss the shipbuilders studied for proposals on the options that the NN could meet to get the ship operational. The state of the ship was pathetic and it could not sail to Germany for the major refit required. I was asked to determine the requirements for a refit in Nigeria to make the ship operational. I recommended that the major equipment manufacturers be contacted to determine the availability of their personnel in Lagos in phases. The limited refit specifications to be carried out in Nigeria was approved and this would be one of the major undertakings of FMC.

I was rudely woken up on one Sunday morning in April 1990 by a neighbour's wife who came to inform my wife that there had been a military coup and wanted to know if I was aware. I got up and went to the living room to meet her and ask her for more information. She told me that there was an announcement and also the order restricting movement. Her husband was a Rear Admiral. We were all close to the CNS and his family. I told my wife to get ready for the Sunday Mass at the Papal Nunciature along Anifowoshe Street, Victoria Island. I used the drive to test the imposed movement restrictions by the coup plotters.

After mass, we drove to Obalende the location of a private hospital where Mrs Zainab Nyako, the wife of CNS had given birth to a baby the previous day. I wanted to evacuate mother and child from the hospital to a safe location and leave my wife with them.

On approaching the Radio Station at Obalende, the fight for control of the station was on and sporadic gunshots sent people in the vicinity into panic as they ran for safety. I slowed down and assessed the situation and on noticing that people were running towards us, I turned back primarily for the safety of my wife who called me a coward. Her priority was the evacuation of the newborn child and mother from the danger zone. We drove to Mr Dalhatu Nyako's house, a cousin to the CNS, on Kofo Abayomi Street. There, we met Mrs Zainab Nyako and the baby and we were relieved even though we were all worried about the fate of the CNS. I was contemplating on what to do when Commodore IN Katagum, my boss, walked in and comforted the family assuring all present that the CNS was safe but was involved in the efforts to crush the coup. I saw him off to his car and he drove off.

I returned to my house but decided to go to the residence of CNS on Temple Road, Ikoyi, and assess the situation there. I met some members of his family. The main living and smaller inner living rooms were empty. I considered the security arrangement at the gate most unsatisfactory and unsafe for the family. I sat in the large living room from where I could assess situations and I informed the family that I would be around for some time.

Rear Admiral GN Kanu drove into the residence and asked if I had seen the CNS. I told him that I had not seen him but that some members of his family were upstairs. He went and greeted them and left. When I saw that the family was not in danger, I went back to meet my wife with Mrs Zainab Nyako. The news of the arrest of the coup plotters filtered in. The coup had failed and normality was being restored by late afternoon. My wife and I returned to our residence. The leader of the failed coup, Major Gideon Orkar, was my course mate at NDA and Lieutenant Colonel Gabriel Nyam, our senior, was my roommate and we were all in DALET Company. Since leaving NDA I had not met Major Orkar; I met Lieutenant Colonel Nyam once in Edinburgh alongside Dan Opuoro as we stopped over when we drove from Inverness to Nottingham to see Nyam's coursemate at NDA, then Captain PA Akpa (later Major General), who was at the university and was with his wife Rose and very young children.

Many stories were flying around. The most disturbing for me was the coup plotter's alleged choices for appointments. The NDA course mates of Major Gideon Orkar and Lieutenant Colonel Gabriel Nyam in the Army, Navy, and Air Force came under intense scrutiny. Lieutenant Commander Anthony Isa would have been made a CNS had the coup succeeded was one story. I kept my cool. I was seen at some locations by my superior officers and in the residences, I had earlier mentioned. I was never called for questioning. I visited the CNS mid-week and in a private discussion, I told him that the residence at Temple Road was not secure based on my observations while he was involved in operations to foil the coup. I advised him to move immediately to the official residence of the CNS on Queen's Drive which was on the lagoon waterfront and more secure. He took my advice and moved into the residence on Queen's Drive which was still undergoing renovation.

My new job and the CNS agenda for NN pre-occupied me and I did not bother about the rumours flying around. The need for more office space for the Fleet Maintenance Corps came to the fore as the NNO was promulgated and became operative. The scope of activities and staff strength gave compelling reasons for the demand for more office spaces. The Ministry of Foreign Affairs had moved to Abuja towards the end of 1991 and the vast office complex at 23 Marina, Lagos was virtually available. There was the option of constructing a new office complex for FMC near the Army Garrison Mess along Marina close to the Lagos sailing club. This was going to take a toll on NN meagre resources and the waiting time would be a long one.

I was asked to inspect 23 Marina complex and I reported that we could use the furniture left behind by the Ministry of Foreign Affairs and start moving in immediately in phases as the Army and Air Force were also thinking of taking over some floors. The National War College had already taken up three floors and the rotunda conference room to start its operation with the British Assistance Training Team already in Lagos. I was allowed to move in and take over two floors for FMC. I took over a wing for my department and had spaces for a spacious library and rooms for computer facilities and a drawing office. I secured the two floors with a lot of office spaces for the Corps Headquarters. My responsibilities increased as I was asked to take up additional duties as Captain, Marine Engineering, and Naval Construction with the posting out of the Head of Department.

My assignments were related to drawing up scaled-down refit of NNS ARADU and a plan for the involvement of competent Nigerian contractors with the capacity to cope with warships systems such as refrigeration and air conditioning, communication and hull repairs; monitoring of the refit of the French Fast Attack Craft at CMN

Shipyard, Cherbourg, France, and depot-level maintenance, including docking for essential defects, for other ships in the merged Fleet.

There was also the spare parts management challenge; it was found that there were many containers at the ports in Lagos piled up over the years that remained uncleared. There had been selective sanctions on Nigeria because of the prolonged military involvement in the political governance of Nigeria. These, I believe, were also to put pressure on the military government to complete the transition to democratic government. The CNS was sensitised to this situation as we had problems getting spare parts from shipbuilders and equipment suppliers. Also, the CNS was very focused on designing and implementing a logistics system for the NN for which the services of the German Logistics firm DORNIER were secured. The responsibility for Research and Development was an innovation in NN and it was difficult for others to understand what it was all about. I started by focusing on data acquisition related to the design and construction of warships and identifying Nigerian industries able to develop relevant capabilities for warship maintenance and repairs. The research and development establishments within Nigeria and NN facilities that could be used for tests and trials were to be identified and put to use in solving problems and studies. These constituted the road map for the multiple tasks assigned to me as Captain Research and Development.

The refit specifications for NNS ARADU were defined and the major equipment manufacturers would send their skilled personnel to carry out relevant jobs and knew where they would work with Nigerian contractors for proper coordination. The schedules for the arrival and departure of the skilled foreign personnel would have to be carefully planned to reduce costs. The NN teams that would work with the contractors had to be organised at ship and base maintenance levels. The monitoring and trial protocols were the responsibility of the Research and Development Department. The monitoring was done mostly by the ship's staff.

The Nigerian industry involved in refrigeration and air conditioning systems was Debo Industries. This was the only industry that had the capacity and was engaged on several ships in home waters and Liberia during the civil war. The refit of NNS ARADU was an opportunity to expose NN personnel to gain experiences in the refit of warships and also to expose Nigerian industries. The refit was concluded by January 1993 and on the conclusion of the sea trial, the ship joined the Fleet.

The crises in Liberia worsened by mid-1990. The USA and other countries that were considering the evacuation of their citizens from

Liberia had sent evacuation task forces to the region. A conference was held in the Rotunda Conference Room at 23 Marina with scholars from the Nigerian Institute for International Affairs and the military to brainstorm on Nigeria's response to the deteriorating crises. The issue of ECOWAS protocol and lack of provision for armed forces involvement in the internal affairs of member countries was discussed. The need to take other countries in the sub-region along with Nigeria leading the efforts was considered the most appropriate as the crisis could destabilise the West African sub-region.

Nigeria also started thinking of setting up a task force to standby to evacuate Nigerian citizens. NNS AMBE had undergone priority docking for essential underwater repairs and was seaworthy after a series of trials and could be deployed. NNS DAMISA and NNS AGU were available too for deployment as escorts. The first Task Force in the series of ECOMOG Task Forces set sail. It became evident that NNS AMBE and the escorts could not handle the evacuation of a large number of Nigerians in Liberia.

Captain F Biambo, the Command and Staff College Joint Warfare Exercise Director for EXERCISE JAGUN in 1989 was appointed the Naval Component Commander. I believe my syndicate solution during EXERCISE JAGUN came in handy as he collected all syndicate solutions and promised to use them as references should the need arise.

The birth of the ECOWAS Monitoring Group (ECOMOG) brought about the periodic deployment of Task Forces based on troops rotation. The NN had very few warships and limited personnel to man them. This was a serious problem compounded by the sanctions that shut off sources of spare parts. The three French-built Fast Attack Craft fitted with Exocet missiles had been in France for what was termed guarantee refit that was to last for about nine months. They were trapped in an extended refit programme that was not planned and budgeted for.

I suggested getting the ships back to Lagos on completing work on the propulsion plants and auxiliary machinery as the guns were in operational states but needed some maintenance checks. There was an assessment of the state of the three ships and it was established that they could provide effective naval gunfire support to troops on the ground. The demand for ships became pressing with the escalation of the fighting in Liberia and the breakdown of the available few ships. The NHQ was advised to get the ships in France back to Lagos and they had to be freighted to preserve their operational state which would have deteriorated if they had sailed to Lagos. The ships had no crew with them in France. And it would take more time and resources to get them ready in France.

When they were brought back to Lagos, the problem of getting the crew trained to man the ships surfaced and the Sea Training Command was not ready to take on the task. I informed the CFMC that I would take on the responsibility of organising pre-joining and harbour training for the crew and carry out basic trials. I set to work with my team and drew up the programmes and handouts for the crew. The crew was very reluctant to go through the programme and I had to seek the cooperation of the three Commanding Officers and their officers and men. The pre-joining training was conducted onboard and made the transition to onboard harbour training and trials easier. There was a remarkable improvement in the morale of the crew and this made the harbour trials successful.

The progress made was monitored up to NHQ with feedback from Western Naval Command and Sea Training Command. I requested a day run sea trip for each ship over three days. I went to sea with each ship with my team and got the crew more acquainted with the systems onboard. On successful completion of this phase and with good crew confidence, I requested for the three ships to sail and Remain at Sea Over Night (RASON) operating as a squadron. I got the approval and the sailing order was issued. I was at sea and had a great outing. The feeding arrangement was not up to standard, I requested that it should be given urgent attention to maintain and improve the morale of the crew.

The NHQ was informed of the progress made on successful completion of the RASON and the ships were handed over to Western Naval Command to prepare them for deployment. The urgent demand for the services of the ships to provide naval gunfire support to the Nigerian Army troops under enemy pressure in Liberia fast-tracked the preparations and departure of the ships for Liberia. I was involved with getting more ships ready for deployment to ECOMOG and had three of my course mates from NDA as Commanding Officers of NNS DAMISA, NNS AMBE, and NNS EKPE. They were Commander GT Adekeye, Commander G Onah, and Commander EE Ita at various times between 1990 and 1993. They gave an excellent account of the investment in their training over the years. I was proud of my close friend Commander Ita from whom I demanded two spent shells of the 76mm ammunition he ordered to be fired in providing naval gunfire support from the main gun of NNS EKPE in Liberia. He gave me the shells which I treasure as my souvenirs from the Liberian civil war. I would also remember the brave exploits of Commander GT Adekeye.

I was appointed a member of the National Committee on Science and Engineering Infrastructure between January 1990 and July 1990 set up by the Federal Ministry of Science and Technology with Professor Gordian Ezekwe as the Minister. This was a committee of over 150 members. I was in the Mechanical Engineering Tools subcommittee. The issue of Ajaokuta Steel Company featured prominently as the Federal Government was about accepting the recommendation to scrap the project. I suggested for an engineer from the Steel Company to address the entire committee and it was accepted. Engineer M Ogirima was sent and after his detailed brief on the concept, design and construction of the complex, he was co-opted into the subcommittee that handled similar industries. A strong recommendation was made to continue with the Ajaokuta Steel project and it was accepted by the Federal Government. The overall committee work leads to the formation of the National Agency for Science and Engineering Infrastructure (NASENI) with the President, Commander-in-Chief as the Chairman and the Director General of NASENI as the Executive Vice Chairman to accelerate the industrial development of Nigeria. This has facilitated the establishment of many complexes across the country.

I took up an appointment as Captain Research and Development as a Lieutenant Commander and I have so far referred to my course mates as Commanders. What happened to me? I was promoted at the same time in 1990 with my course mates from NDA but had a worrying moment during the promotion board. The Board discovered that I had no performance evaluation report for my time as a Lieutenant Commander covering 1984-1990. The last report was to been written by my last boss or commanding officer before my present appointment. The Board members in their wisdom decided that due to my performances, I was well-known and fit for promotion. The board said they would approach the CNS and ask him to write my performance evaluation report for them to use as a cover for the years I was a Lieutenant Commander. After the Board concluded proceedings and submitted the report, the Secretary of the Board Commander C Ehanmo phoned me and told me what happened and calmed my nerves. He informed me that they secured a report for me and I was recommended. He, however, said I had to contact the Personnel Branch and sign my performance evaluation report as required so that it can be properly filed for reference. The years 1984 -1989 had been very busy and turbulent for me and the issue of a file related to me getting missing at the NHQ in 1984 after the court-martial incident to prevent my appointment in Italy created problems for me. I greatly appreciated the wisdom of the members of the Promotion Board.

When the signal releasing the promotion came out, I was too busy with the Corps, ECOMOG Task Forces, refit programmes, research and development, NASENI committee and transformation of NN. I received a phone call at home after work many hours after the signal was released. I cannot remember much of the transition to Commander but as I had the Commander's brass hat and rank on my uniform hanging in my bedroom, I reflected that I had put in eighteen years of active service since 1972 and I would not have another eighteen years of service. I started the count down to my retirement.

The large number of containers accumulated over many years at the seaports in Lagos needed to be identified with their contents. I proposed the computerization of the NN Technical Stores Depot and reorganisation of the entire NN technical store system. Lieutenant Commander E Ijioma was excellent with computer software programming and was a staff officer at the Technical Stores Depot at Naval Dockyard, Victoria Island, Lagos. I requested the definition of the problem of spare parts management from him to develop a computer software programme solution. I went through his paper and was satisfied with his excellent grasp of the problem. More work was done on the suggested solution with inputs from other technical store managers and users. Ijioma harmonised all inputs and wrote a software programme that was validated.

DORNIER was contracted by NHQ to provide the computers and installation and the Research and Development Department was asked to implement the contract. The software developed was given to DORNIER for their validation. This was improved upon and became the basis for their design.

The technical stores' depots at Naval Base, Apapa, and Naval Dockyard were reorganised and given a new look with reception, issuing and computer facilities areas demarcated and equipped. The containers from the ports started arriving and as each was received and opened the spare parts and other contents were identified and the coding system developed was used for the shelf arrangements for storage and computerisation. It was then easy to know the stockholding and cross- referencing increased efficiency. It was discovered that NN had plenty of spare parts to support ECOMOG operations and this would not have been known if the computerisation and re-organisation had not taken place.

I was to go to Germany for the inspection of the computer facilities and do test runs at DORNIER facility. At the last moment, my department was shut off and another group was set up. As the new team tried to evade me, I approached their leader and told him that I would provide them with the details of the inspection protocol that had been developed and even volunteered my warm clothing as a gesture of goodwill. I had the computers delivered and installed and we put them to good use.

The next assignment I focused on was developing a logistics system for the NN. The CNS had been thinking about this project. I had several meetings with DORNIER staff on their resource base for developing the relevant logistics system for NN. I was assured of their experiences with the German Armed Forces and NATO, and the extensive database at DORNIER's disposal. I relied on the NNOs promulgated for the three Corps covering Fleet Maintenance, Naval Material Supply, and Naval Ordnance to develop a plan and a reference index of systems for NN.

I had the complete documentation for the design, construction, factory acceptance trials, harbour acceptance trials, and sea acceptance trials for the MCMVs. This was a huge set of documents that were used to start the library at FMC Headquarters and would be integrated with the logistics system sets of documents being developed. These formed the basis for developing a unique logistics system to meet the specific needs of NN. A final copy of each document was promulgated and with the approval of NHQ, it was signed by the Commander, FMC. This would engage me in one of the most intensive developments of documentations I would ever be involved with. The procedure was simple and effective.

I would lead a team to meet with DORNIER staff to determine the structure of the publication and its purpose. The DORNIER team would rely on their database and produce the first draft. This would be studied and edited to meet NN requirements. The first translation from the German language to the English language had its challenges and my team had a lot of work to do re-writing and checking the facts. The draft considered meeting NN requirements was produced and circulated for inputs which would result in our further editing and NHQ approval before a final copy was submitted to Commander FMC for signature and subsequent production of copies for distribution. I had to organise workshops to introduce the publications in subject batches and this necessitated movements to various NN establishments.

After the rounds of conducting the workshops, I made a case for establishing the NN Logistics School to train NN officers of all branches and specialisations of the rank of Lieutenant Commanders. The proposal was approved alongside the curriculum drawn up based on the over 15 Logistics systems documentation developed and promulgated. DORNIER provided the instructors and the school was established at NNS QUORRA.

But the school and the course programme were not sustained and the Nigerian Army bought the idea and established a Logistic School at 23 Marina which NN later sent officers to attend. The reason for running out of the NN Logistics School was due to resistance to the eventual setting up of the Logistics Command which would have an engineer officer as the Flag Officer Commanding. This was opposed for very parochial reasons that have badly affected the development and transformation of the NN.

On 17 May 1991, Linda gave birth to our last child and Son Augustine Adaeiza Ibrahim, at Gold Cross Hospital, Keffi Road, Obalande-Lagos. The traditional 8th day was marked with prayers and naming. It was a combined Muslim-Christian gathering conducted by my boss Rear Admiral IN Katagum with recitals from the Bible and Quran. The CNS, Vice-Admiral MAH NYAKO named the child Ibrahim and all the given names were revealed to the gathering by Admiral Katagum. Back at the office, he was pleased as he told me with a smile, that I had almost cause a religious war in my residence. The following week, our son received the Sacrament of Baptism at the Church of the Assumption Falomo-Lagos with the names Ibrahim, Augustine and Adaeiza. The celebration at Okene by my father was with a ram in an act of thanksgiving to God and blessing for the child. It was my father's unique act of blessing as he was very happy that one of our children was born in Nigeria. He was of the opinion that my other children born abroad were born in the bush as it took long for him to receive information about their birth. He had a special connection with each of his grand children and was very fond of my wife and her parents.

Fierce competition for resource allocation among the Commands put the FMC under a very unfavourable spotlight. There was an impression that FMC sought to get a lot done because of the favourable allocation of funds while other Commands were starved of funds. The Chief of the Naval Staff Annual Conference at Akure in 1991 was the setting for the showdown over the alleged favourable treatment the FMC was enjoying. The CFMC was naturally worried about the rumours and allegations. He asked me to coordinate the paper he was to present because I had been very much involved in the activities of the Corps. I did an analysis of the jobs undertaken and the results achieved especially as related to making operational ships available for ECOMOG Task Forces. I concluded that the Corps had achieved much and considering the volume of funds released, it was grossly under-funded. The computerisa8tion and re-organisation of the Technical Stores which enabled spares parts accumulated over the years at the Ports to be delivered and taken under charge released a lot of resources for the ship's maintenance and repairs.

I approached the CFMC at a right time in his office and made an odd request. I wanted his approval to have access to all the financial records to determine the amount of money released to the Corps since January 1990 when the Corps was established. I emphasised the need to order the Corps Finance Office to cooperate. I told him that I needed to have facts related to the Corps finances to enable him to present authentic financial facts at the Conference.

He took a hard look at me for some seconds and called the Corps Finance Officer, Commander Umaru Gadu directing him to grant me access to the Corps financial records. I told the Commander FMC that I would feed him back with my findings. In summary, I had the list of the work done by the Corps as I was the secretary of the Corps Tenders Board and the financial releases since January 1990. I noticed that there was so much achieved that the funds released could never justify.

The Corps was grossly under-funded and the question would be how CFMC achieved so much with such pittance. I went to the CFMC and briefed him on my findings. He called the Finance Officer and told him that he should add the take-off grant to raise the total funds to be presented. This was done and yet it did not improve the total funds received to the Corps disadvantage. I proceeded to write the paper and had enough facts to justify the demand for more funding. The other Commands would then be forced to disclose the fund released to them and what they did with it.

At the Conference, the CFMC presentation drew much attention and when the facts were displayed, there was a deliberate pause for the audience to fully digest them. There was silence and the CFMC made a joke that he was reading his paper without reading glasses and wished to confirm that he had not lost his sight as was being speculated. The emphasis was now on other Commands to disclose how much they received and what they did with it. There was uneasiness but the CFMC confidently stated that so much was achieved not because of any huge amount of money received but through prudent management of resources that had always been available over the years but neglected; the spare parts in large numbers of containers abandoned. At the interactive sessions after the presentation of other Commands, no one considered the Corps as being favoured any more and there was no commendation for the impressive achievement even related to ECOMOG Task Forces.

Back in Lagos and at a meeting with CNS at NHQ, the FOC WEST complained again of inadequate funding and the CNS revealed that more funds were released to him than CFMC and yet not much was achieved by his command. This put an end to the blackmail as all NHQ Branch Chiefs, FOCs and CFMC were present in closed-door sessions with CNS that I attended.

The economic sanction against Nigeria made it difficult to buy critically needed spare parts for NNS AMBE underwater fittings repairs and the ship had to be undocked while efforts were made to convince the shipbuilders to respond as funds came. The shipyard in Germany was not responding despite fund availability.

The CNS and NHQ staff were worried and called a meeting to consider what to do as there was pressure for the ship to return to Liberia. The delays and the urgent demands for the ship to return to Liberia weighed us down. It was while we were preparing to enter the CNS office that I alerted CFMC of the sanctioning effect on the German shipbuilders. I advised him that NN should look for an alternative route to the shipyard. The CNS was informed about this and he took over the responsibility. The spare parts were eventually sourced and delivered. NNS AMBE was docked and repaired and available for ECOMOG deployment.

I had established the Research and Development Department with a fully functioning library, a drawing office with a very experienced draughtsman under a very brilliant and quiet Naval Architect, Lieutenant Commander S Akinbola. The Naval Shipyard, a former Witt and Busch facility at Port Harcourt that NN bought was under the command of Captain (later Rear Admiral) G Oladejo. The shipyard had designed a flat-bottom boat for inshore operations. The design specifications were documented and forwarded to the Department for further evaluation. I had discussions with the Chief of Naval Operations at NHQ, Rear Admiral E Okpo who made valuable inputs. The team at FMC did a design evaluation and made some improvements to the design and started the process of getting NHQ approval for the shipyard to start the construction.

I was impressed with the work done by Lieutenant Commander Akinbola and the draughtsman. They followed other ships' drawings needing reproduction. The computer facilities for the management of

NN spare parts had the main server at the Research and Development Department. The Research and Development Department at FMC Headquarters was well established with good facilities in addition to identified facilities for testing and evaluation within NN and Federal Government Research and Development centres. The Ajaokuta Steel Company had an excellent metallurgy centre with facilities for material testing and analysis which was used on occasions that demanded their services. The Research and Development Department was now attracting attention and the DHQ Chief of Research and Development had his offices operating from 23 Marina and on inspection concluded that the FMC Department set up would be taken as a reference for other services.

There was a change of CNS on February 7, 1992. Vice Admiral MAH Nyako was removed as CNS and was succeeded by Vice Admiral Dan P. Omatsola. Nyako was appointed Deputy Chief of Defence Staff. General S Abacha was the Chief of Defence Staff and Minister of Defence.

The appointment in February 1992 of a new CNS, Vice Admiral Dan P. Omatsola, brought about some retirements of senior officers that included Rear Admiral IN Katagum. There were demands for a probe of the FMC under Admiral Katagum and re-organization aimed at crippling the establishment. I was made a member of the committee to re-organise the Corps. The probe of FMC was dropped. I was the secretary of the Tenders Board and had faithfully recorded the proceedings.

The Chairman of the Committee set up for the reorganisation or dismantling of FMC was Vice Admiral Chijoke O. Kaja. There were many senior engineer officers on the committee and I was the junior as a Commander, while the seamen officers were few and led by Commodore OM Akhigbe who was Director of Plans at NHQ. I could hear some of the engineers on the committee loudly complaining about how FMC denied them opportunities to travel abroad and award contracts.

I was very disappointed with the betrayal and pettiness by engineers I was experiencing. The comment that even Rear Admiral IN Katagum was about being called FOC was most insulting to the engineering branch officers. I fumed. I focused on presenting the correct picture of why the FMC was created, its activities, and its achievements. The FMC had to continue to exist to serve NN in the national interest.

I was given much latitude to explain why the Corps was established and the important role it played in ECOMOG and submitted that what was required was to transform the Corps into a Logistics Command to consolidate on its impressive achievements. I was alone as the senior engineers kept quiet. I reminded the committee of the demand for engineering training and education and how officers who failed engineering courses moved on to be seamen. Commodore Akhighbe exploded with emotion and demanded that I should be called to order otherwise he would walk out of the committee. He stood up and picked his beret to leave when the chairman calmed frayed nerves and asked the members of the committee to go on break while he consulted the CNS.

As I rushed out of the conference room, Commodore Akhigbe came from behind and gently tapped my shoulder. I turned and he said to me: "Tony, you are the most junior among the engineers present and they all left you alone. They will regret their actions in the future. You have done enough." I then realised how jealousy, envy, greed, and ambition have created petty mindsets in officers expected to provide leadership. Such petty mindsets easily spread hate and cannot be relied upon to take on the challenges of strategic force planning, force generation, and employment. The NN, I observed, has become a colossal wasteland of abandoned naval capabilities projects including warships. Nigeria had access to the same opportunities in Europe as Brazil and wasted it.

When the committee reconvened after consultation with CNS, a position paper on making the FMC less effective was faxed to the committee from FOC EAST. I was disappointed. Commodore Akhigbe read through and handed over the paper to the Chairman. The meeting ended and I was co-opted into the Secretariat sub-committee to write the report. There would be a need for a Logistics Command but crippled the Corps in the interim. I signed the final report as a member.

Not long after this, Commodore OM Akhigbe rose to the rank of Rear Admiral and was appointed CNS during the tenure of General Sani Abacha, the Head of State in 1994. He made me a member of the CONSAC committee throughout his tenure (1994-1998) as CNS and always had me around to work on keynote addresses for special guests of honour. While we were waiting for the approval of his draft speech one day, he told me that the same engineers who were sabotaging the FMC came to him to strengthen the organisation and appoint them into command. He told them that he would not and did not trust them.

The presidential election, the last in the series of elections under the transition to civil rule programme, was held on 12 June 1993. It featured two presidential candidates: Chief MKO Abiola, Social Democratic Party (SDP) and Alhaji Bashir Tofa, National Republican Convention (NRC). The election was peaceful and raised hopes of a successful transition. But an intriguing mix of political interests came to the fore and the election was annulled. The country was engulfed in crises. The image of the military government was badly dented. There was a reign of uncertainty about the future of the country.

The Military President, General IB Babangida, was under intense pressure to de-annul the election and announce the winner between Chief MKO Abiola and Bashir Tofa. He chose instead to step aside and left office on 27 August 1993 after instituting the Interim National Government headed by Chief Ernest Shonekan. Its enabling law was Decree 61 of 1993. The Armed Forces Defence and Security Council had decided that all service chiefs and the CDS and his Deputy, should retire from service with the President. The service chiefs were Lt General Salihu Ibrahim (Army), Vice Admiral Dan P. Omatsola (Navy) and Air Marshal Nureini Yusuf (Air Force) as well as Vice Admiral Murtala AH Nyako, Deputy CDS. They refused to retire with the president. They retired on September 18 instead.

The new service chiefs appointed were Lieutenant General Aliyu Mohammed Gusau (Army), Rear Admiral Suleiman Sa'idu (Navy), and Air Vice Marshal Femi J. Femi (Air Force). Lieutenant General Joshua Dogonyaro was appointed as CDS.

The President changed the decision of the Council and decided that General Abacha should remain in office as Secretary of Defence, ostensibly, to protect the ING from military adventurers. He also inserted a clause in the Decree stipulating that in the event the ING faced any challenges, the most senior military officer in the government should take over. General Abacha was the most senior uniformed man in the government.

Barely three months, later, Abacha made his move. He and Lieutenant General Oladipo Diya went to Chief Shonekan's office and forced him to resign. However, General Abacha claimed that the Head of State resigned voluntarily. He stepped in as Head of State on November 17, 1993, to the surprise of a few people. He fired the service chiefs and the CDS and replaced them with his appointees. Major General AA Abubakar was appointed CDS; Major General MC Alli was appointed COAS and Rear Admiral Allison Madueke became the new CNS. The Chief of Air Staff Air Marshal FJ Femi survived the change. This turnover of appointments and the instability it created in the system reflected a military institution in need of redemption from itself.

I began to seriously reflect on what allegiance to country and loyalty to Commander-in-Chief mean in the minds of the personnel of AFN and their reflection in the principle and practice of unity of command which dictates an orderly and unified approach in the conduct of military affairs always. Military politicians are dictating deliberate chaotic disorder. It appeared everyone wanted to do things the way they liked and disregard articles of war for proper functioning. This would generate many visions for a mission or objective. Why would the President, Commander-in-Chief sign two documents and issue them to officers when they are commissioned demanding adherence to faith, truth, and service with trust? The requirement is to bear allegiance to causes higher than any individual.

The two documents are the First Schedule Armed Force Oath and the Parchment of Commission. No group in Nigeria is given such documents. It is arguable if officers understand why they are commissioned into the AFN and the attendant obligations to observe the unity of command for the stability and growth of the institution. The June 12 general election crises raised many questions about the foundation of the AFN and the impact of the colonial heritage of allegiance and loyalty being thought of as due to foreign entities and not Nigeria. Indeed military involvement in the political governance of a country is an aberration and it has jeopardised efforts geared towards professional development and growth of AFN institutions. Allegiance and loyalty do not seem to matter and do not attract attention for study and understanding.

On 01 October 1993, the National Day Golf Tournament took place at Ikoyi Club Golf Section. I had a good run and after completing my round, I went home and was having my rest when I got a phone call informing me that I had won the competition and should quickly show up for the prize presentation. I went with my first son Daniel. The June 12 crisis had dampened the celebrations and the interaction with those present showed how devastating the effects of the crisis have been. I reflected that my winning the tournament was a good omen for the country despite fears about the future. I would win another major club tournament at the IBB Golf and Country Club at Abuja in 2003, ten years later at the annual CMCL Open (Professional-Amateur) competition. The two trophies for 1993 and 2003 continue to remind me to strengthen the faith that Nigeria for which I bear allegiance to serve would always prevail. It is a beautiful country and what we do with it should be the expression of a grateful people.

I went to play golf at Ikoyi Golf Club as the service chiefs were retired and joined a group of naval officers who were my seniors. They expressed happiness that the group of the Chief of Army Staff Lieutenant General Salihu Ibrahim and Deputy Chief of Defence, Vice Admiral Murtala AH Nyako among others were retired. All of them were still young; perhaps the oldest was just above 50 years. The reason for their happiness at the retirement of these officers was that it would soon be their turn to have a shot at the top job in the services. I disagreed with them and pointed out that those very seasoned officers were being eased out due to military involvement in politics. I warned that the Armed Forces of the Federal Republic of Nigeria would be worse for it. The discussion ended on this observation and I knew I was alone.

It would have been better if Vice Admiral Patrick S. Koshoni had been allowed more time to consolidate his efforts to lay the foundation for strategic planning before Vice-Admiral Nyako took over the mantle from him to consolidate those plans and programmes, given his vast knowledge of the logistic needs of NN and strong connections for getting things done. This would have served the NN cause of building a strong institution. The complementary efforts of Wey-Soroh-Adelanwa set a standard.

The huge complex at 23 Marina provided accommodation for the Naval Material Supply Corps, Directorate of Naval Education, and Directorate of Naval Information. The FMC was the largest setup and the Corps Research and Development Department attracted visits from many officers looking forward to finding some excitement and comment on the developments there. It had excellent facilities and some considered it an island of order and a conducive environment that a senior officer said could only be found in Europe. I had spent more than three years (1990-1993) at the Corps Headquarters.

I was eventually appointed as Commander, Fleet Support Group (FSG) at Western Naval Command Headquarters in the last quarter of 1993 as NNS ARADU concluded refit and started sea acceptance trials. The situation in Liberia had stabilized and the civil war in Sierra Leone had been an additional burden on NN resources. The plans put together by FMC for NN warships had yielded good results and contributed immensely to the resolution of the civil wars in Liberia and Sierra Leone.

The NN transformation following the CNS (Vice Admiral Nyako) vision had succeeded with the establishment of relevant Corps and the development of a logistics system for the NN. These would eventually evolve and lead to the establishment of Logistics Command with a Flag Officer Commanding which was the original intention in 1990 but delayed due to unhealthy NN branch rivalry. I took leave of FMC fully satisfied with the achievements that improved operational efficiency of NN warships proven in ECOMOG operation and better-organised logistics system.

CHAPTER THIRTEEN

From Fleet Support Group Command to NNS ARADU

I took over command of Fleet Support Group (FSG) at the Naval Base, Apapa, in November 1993. The office space was the same as occupied by Captain Leslie Wright RN in 1974 when he was the Naval Officer Commanding, Flotilla. Rear Admiral (then Commander) IN Katagum occupied the same office as Commander, Fleet Support Group 1980-1981.

The creation of the Fleet Maintenance Corps led to the Fleet Support Groups formerly under the Western and Eastern Naval Commands being part of the Corps. This was one of the reasons CFMC had some opposition from the FOCs Western and Eastern Naval Commands. I had initiated a lot of jobs being carried out on ships in Western Naval Command and had no problem settling down as Commander Fleet Support Group. NNS AMBE had been back from ECOMOG deployment and was undergoing some major works. I gave the warship priority and controlled the scope and pace of work should there be a need for an immediate return to ECOMOG duties.

The routine at FSG started with a brief meeting with staff officers on the progress of jobs and assignments of new ones. This was a short meeting to allow officers to return to work on the various ships. NNS AMBE was in dock at Naval Dockyard Victoria Island. I had insisted on strictly following standards in the execution of jobs and the procedures had been part of the work I had done at FMC. The availability of spare parts was still a problem because of international sanctions on Nigeria. I had to emphasise adaptations and documentation of alterations and additions and crew training to handle the changes.

The NN Flagship, NNS ARADU, had completed sea acceptance trials and was back in service for operational deployment. The first deployment was to the Eastern Naval Command areas. In January 1994, the ship was passing through Bonny channel to Port Harcourt when an incident occurred. It was attributed to hitting or riding over a wreck. The ship lost all five propeller blades on the starboard (right-hand side) shaft and because of the very loud noise and vibration, it was feared that the ship hit a wreck. There was no failure investigation but speculations were rife and no officer wanted to be appointed or remain onboard as Marine Engineer Officer to lead efforts to get the ship back into operation.

The Commanding Officer, Commodore Victor K Ombu, took responsibility for the accident and reported by a signal that due to navigation error (went into shallow water), the ship hit a wreck and lost the five propeller blades. There was no precise and convincing incident report and I thought there was a need for a professional investigation. Several efforts made to locate the missing blades failed and the ship sailed back to Lagos on one shaft. No one thought seriously of technical investigation that would require NNS ARADU immediate docking when the ship arrived at the Naval Dockyard pool berth. Some of the officers and men started looking for an escape route to leave the ship.

I was about rounding off an early morning meeting with officers when Lieutenant Commander S Oguntade interrupted the meeting to say that it appeared I was not aware that I had been appointed as the Marine Engineer Officer of NNS ARADU. I confirmed that I was not aware that a signal was released by NHQ the previous day to that effect. The signal board was brought to me. I informed the officers that I was no longer the Commander FSG. I told them to continue with the schedule of work on all ships. I requested the financial vote book from the Finance Officer who did not know why. I showed the vote book to the officers and drew a line and signed off to avoid any further commitment. I wrote my handing over notes before leaving my table. I felt relieved and looked forward to NNS ARADU once more. I would serve on board the Flag Ship between 1994-1996.

I went home relaxed and reflected on all the work being done on NN warships. NNS AMBE was required for deployment to ECOMOG and I knew I would be needed. I contacted Commander FMC who gave me an order to go onboard and see to the conclusion of the job being done. NNS AMBE was in dock at the Naval Dockyard, Victoria Island.

At a dockside meeting with NHQ Chief of Operations and FSG technical staff, I assessed the urgent operational requirements. I went on board with the technical staff after the departure of the Chief of Operations and explained to them that the urgency expressed by NHQ did not allow time for the planned repairs on the remote controls. I was convinced that the manual controls if mastered would serve. The FSG and ship's technical staff were taken through the routines. All preparations went well and the ship's staff acquired the confidence required. NNS AMBE was ready and successfully deployed. In the haste to get me out of FSG, I left immediately. I had no office as it took about two weeks before I reported onboard NNS ARADU. I had two weeks with the staff of FSG and got NNS AMBE ready for ECOMOG deployment.

I reported to NNS ARADU and took over as MEO from Commander E Ibitolu, my NDA course mate, who took the ship through the refit programme. I noticed many of the ships' technical staff were being taken off the ship and a video clip was circulating showing the starboard hub without the five blades. There were many speculations about what and how it happened. I inspected the ship and assessed her state. I prepared a report on my findings on the state of shafting systems and fluids. The ship's air conditioning system was not working and this made conditions onboard very unbearable. I had to set up a lecture space in the large helicopter hangar that had natural ventilation. The sorting out of the documentation revealed the need to train the officers and men on how to read technical drawings. There were lectures on the shafting systems and more information was gathered on the state of the ship and the accident. Discussions were going on about the board of inquiry and possible court-martial. There was no serious consideration for docking to start a technical investigation and I considered this very odd but not surprising. I avoided the intrigues.

I had some Midshipmen who graduated from NDA with engineering first degrees. They had decided not to specialise as marine engineers and weapon engineers. They wanted to be seamen officers with appropriate qualifications so that they would be allowed appointments being denied, engineers. They reasoned that they did not decide to study engineering as they were chosen based on the order of merit while the rest of their class were for the seaman branch. The best were selected to study engineering and told that their career prospects were not as bright as the others that could not qualify to study engineering. I had to convince them to go for their specialisation courses. I worried about the bleak future of engineering in NN.

I went to the 1938 Ikoyi Golf Club for a game after working hours and met the new Commanding Officer, Captain OO Deinde, who asked me to join him so that we could play nine holes before sunset. As we were closing up on the holes, he asked me if I had seen the video clip showing the underwater damages on NNS ARADU. I told him that I had not seen the video clip and added that I did not intend to see it. Some moments later, he asked me what we should do. I told him that the standard naval practice after such a serious accident is to get the ship docked immediately and have a good underwater inspection to find clues on how the incident occurred, determine the problems, and what should be done about them. I explained to him the limitations of relying on the video clips and the dangers of drawing wrong conclusions.

He ordered me to give him a brief based on our discussions and stated that he would see the Chief of the Naval Staff the following morning and give an oral brief. The following morning, after briefing the CNS, I had the brief prepared and took it to him with my recommendations. I had recommended that NNS ARADU should be docked immediately and the manufacturers of major shafting equipment and systems informed of the accident and invited to send representatives for inspection. I was later informed that the CNS had approved our plan.

The Admiral Superintendent Naval Dockyard would not be very happy with the sudden interruption of his docking programmes. I went to see some of his staff officers to establish cordial relationships. I told them that I would walk around their workshops to familiarise myself with the facilities I could rely on for routine maintenance of NNS ARADU. The controversial manner of my appointment onboard NNS ARADU was now common knowledge and it was important not to allow it to affect my dedication to duty. The CNS approved the recommendation for immediate docking of NNS ARADU and preparations got into full gear. In the course of the lectures onboard, I identified the relevant competencies available on board. I told the CO to take steps to stop the ship's crew from being posted out of the ship because there were no replacements for those who had left.

I had meetings with the Dock Master and other relevant staff of the Naval Dockyard and I convinced them to arrange the blocks to accept the ship with stern entry so that there would be enough space for withdrawal of the shaft and fitting of the heavy propeller shafts, hub, and blades. The idea of withdrawing the shaft was a nightmare but I assured them that NHQ was making arrangements to have the manufacturers around. I was ready to dismantle the entire shafting up to the Controllable Pitch Propeller Oil Distribution Box assembly and the gearbox but I had to get ready to defend my plans.

There were differing opinions on the extent of the failure inspection jobs and I maintained my stand that we should go as far as possible to establish the extent of damages. I was warned that I would incur the displeasure of senior technical officers at NHQ if no damage was identified beyond the hub. It is common in the NN to be warned simply for doing what is correct if your name sounds like mine.

The ship was successfully docked and I immediately went round with my staff to do an underwater hull and fittings inspection. It was noticed that there were no scratches on the hull areas around the hub and the supporting structures such as the A-bracket and yet about five propeller blades each weighing about one ton were ripped off. It was observed that female threadings holding the blade roots were worn out. Did NNS ARADU hit anything at all? I remember the experience Rear Admiral Olufemi Olumide put me through regarding the NNS ENYIMIRI incident in 1981. I intensified the lectures on the shafting systems to prepare the technical staff for knowledge-based interaction with the equipment manufacturers.

The first manufacturer's representative to arrive was from the KaMeWa, the propeller manufacturer. I detailed some of my staff to accompany him on inspection of the damaged shaft and after his inspection, he told me that it would be a very odd occurrence to lose five blades on a hub at the same time. He also observed that there was no scratch indicating damage at the hull area near the propellers and the hub. It was decided that the hub would have to be changed as the threads for screwing the propeller blade roots were badly damaged. The technical staff at NHQ had concluded that all that was required was to replace the propeller blades and did not take into consideration the state of the five threaded recesses on the hub with damaged internal female threads.

Commander Daniel E. Opuoro was appointed as the Weapon Engineer Officer and was later replaced by Commander Caleb Olubolade. In 1994, the 12 June 1993 Presidential election crisis took a nasty turn. I was quite sad that the military institution had been so damaged by its involvement in politics that officers were asking one another when they would detach and go back to their regions or enclaves being carved out along tribal/ethnic lines. I was having some fresh air standing near the gangway one day when Opuoro joined me. As we strayed into discussing the 12 June 1993 crisis, he asked me when I would leave Lagos for my region or ethnic enclave. I have never known or asked where he was from in Nigeria since we met at NDA in 1973 and later at RNEC, Manadon for over three years. I asked him for the first time where he was from in Nigeria and he told me, Sapele, Delta State. The AFN has lost control; it can no longer perform its integrative function to forge a cohesive force.

Commander DE Opuoro told me that Commodore VK Ombu had been recalled from his course at National Institute for Policy and Strategic Studies (NIPSS) at Vom-Kuru, Jos, and was looking for a pair of white gloves to wear with his ceremonial uniform for a court-martial convened to try him for the NNS ARADU accident. I promised that I would make a pair available the next day. I had a new pair of gloves that had not been used. I brought it on board and handed it over for delivery to Commodore Ombu. I sent a message to Commodore VK Ombu that he would not wear the gloves for any Court Martial because the inspection in the dock so far showed that NNS ARADU did not hit a wreck or hard object due to grounding. Despite his acceptance of responsibility and admission of navigation error that caused a grounding, there was no need to proceed with a Court Martial and interrupt an important strategic course. My pair of white gloves was returned to me some days later. I was informed that Commodore VK Ombu had gone back to NIPSS to continue with his course.

There were moves by NHQ to involve some local contractors in the dismantling and repairs of the shafting components and I was expected to have meetings with them and provide any information and drawings they might need. I took this opportunity to find out if they had experience working on warships complex propulsion shafting systems. In one of such meetings, the contractor got annoyed. He thought being an expatriate, I was incompetent to ask him questions.

I explained to him that it was the normal procedure for the award of contracts that I was following because I was tasked to supervise their work as the MEO of NN Flag Ship who was enjoying a most prestigious job in the NN. I was reported to NHQ technical staff for being difficult as I did not allow shortcuts to future disasters. I had done my duty and I made reports to the Commanding Officer (CO) regarding the difficulties I was facing. The recommendation from the ship was to have the manufacturers do critical jobs. I explained to the CO the need to maintain standards as regards materials, procedures, and repair actions which the contractors must be made to adhere to.

The NHQ engaged one of the contractors I had interviewed with my technical staff despite our findings that they were incompetent. It was an order from above and I had to take steps to avoid disaster. I engaged the contractor's staff and provided a very conducive atmosphere which included providing technical information and equipment to them and detailing my very experienced technical staff to be attached to them. There were routine meetings to assess progress and determine requirements for the dismantling of components. The contractor's staff were monitored on reporting for duty throughout all activities and see off the ship after work hours. I instructed the ship's technical staff to closely monitor the staff of the contractor and report any observed shortcomings that might result in material damages which would be very costly in terms of replacement and time. I harmonised the availability of the manufacturers representative to supervise the dismantling but took precautions to avoid taking responsibility for damages that might occur due to the contractor's lack of experience.

I went to NHQ on some occasions to brief some technical staff officers and explain to them as much as I could, the need to adhere to standards as required by the books of reference. I also had to attend committee meetings for the Chief of the Naval Staff Annual Conference (CONSAC) of which I was a member selected on yearly basis between 1990-1996. After one of the meetings I attended, I was in a discussion near the exit gate of the Moloney Street Ministry of Defence when Rear Admiral FBI Porbeni, Chief of Naval Personnel saw me and we got talking about my appointment as MEO NNS ARADU. He asked me to see him in his office. The following day, I kept the appointment. He asked me if I liked the appointment onboard NNS ARADU. I replied that the signal appointing me conveyed the appointment from NHQ as an order of the CNS. Consequently, there is no question of whether I liked the appointment or not. He said that I should not hesitate to contact him if I needed help. I got to know that an officer, junior to me, was given a letter of appointment to report as MEO NNS ARADU but rejected the appointment. NNS ARADU was in danger of being abandoned alongside to waste away as had happened to other ships. I felt I had a challenge to overcome and a duty to perform.

I was returning to the ship one day after collecting my mail from the Victoria Island post office and on entering the Naval Dockyard, I stopped at a quiet spot near the twin docks to read a letter from Mr John Wedlake, the first son of my friend Mr Walter Wedlake. He gave me the news of the passing away of Mrs Nan Wedlake, his stepmother. He described her last moments because he was with her all through. John was kind enough to note how close I was to his parents and felt I deserved to be informed by him of his step-mother's death. Another letter was from Nan's only son and second son of Mr Walter Wedlake, Peter, who also informed me of his mother's death. The lovely memories of Walter and Nan linger on forever in my life. They gave me a family home in the UK.

The damaged hub was successfully removed and I decided to drain the oil in the very long stern tube which housed some bearings and sensors. The oil had turned sluggish and on checking the shaft and bearing at the outer end, I noticed the shaft had been scored. I was again warned to confine myself to the limited inspection and underwater video that was relied upon to make decisions at NHQ. The damaged shaft indicated bearing damage and I convinced the NHQ technical staff to allow the dismantling of the tail and intermediate shafts for inspection. The shafts were dismantled and it was discovered that the outer cylindrical bearing of about one metre in length was badly damaged.

Since NNS ARADU came into service in 1981, this oil in the stern tube had never been changed for both shafts. The ship went aground on a visit to the Democratic Republic of Congo and some of the propeller blades were damaged. Back in Lagos, the blades were replaced without detailed technical inspection. The ship had been experiencing vibrations at sea since then and the cause was never established. During the refit that ended December 1993, the refit team did not consider the provisions in the trials and inspection protocol issued by FMC necessary and it specified mandatory interventions.

The dismantled shafts and cylindrical shell bearing were taken to the NND Mechanical workshop for further inspection. It was necessary to repair the shaft first to establish the new dimension that would be used as a guide for repairing the bearing. I advised the CO on what should be done and a meeting was called at the NHQ for me to make a presentation on the way forward. The CNS chaired the meeting. I had enough drawings to show to the audience and I succeeded in drawing attention to the urgent requirements. The bearing was packed in a crate and freighted to the manufacturers in Europe and a machining expert was sent to NND to use the largest lathe machine in NN to repair the damaged shaft and take new dimensions for the bearing repairs.

The shaft was properly machined and repaired and the measurements were taken as required for the bearing repairs. I had a respite from very unprofessional diversionary suggestions and I focused on the segment of the shaft from the Oil Distribution Box (ODB) to the GearBox. I had earlier noticed the metal chips in the ODB hydraulic oil metal detector necessitating a check on the bearings in the assembly. I discussed my observations with the KaMeWa representative regarding taking clearance readings to compare with the values stated in the drawings. It took me several days to convince him to inform his establishment in Europe of a possible dismantling of the ODB to inspect the internal components to identify damages if any. The clearance readings as indicated in the drawings were taken and they indicated a major problem. The manufacturer's representative told me that I should not bother informing NHQ to decide what to do as that would be done by his company from Europe.

I detailed some of my very experienced staff to work under the supervision of the KaMeWa representative. It was December 1994 and the manufacturer's representative had gone for the Christmas holidays, leaving behind the dismantling instructions and the tools required. In his absence, the ship's technical staff did a good job of successfully dismantling the oil distribution system to reveal all damaged components.

The spare parts arrived with the manufacturer's representative from the Christmas holidays. The re-assembly of the ODB with the replacement of the damaged parts was undertaken with all concerned now focused on getting the entire shaft system properly repaired. The work on the ODB re-assembly proceeded smoothly under the supervision of the manufacturer's staff both onboard and in Europe. There was no damage between the ODB and the gearbox and the testing of the system was carried out. The ship had been long in the dock and I noticed a tall plant growing in a gap between two concrete blocks that eventually became taller than me. I posed for a photograph with the plant. The shaft tunnel was blanked off and the ship was undocked to wait for the repairs and delivery of the other components.

The senior officers' promotion board for 1995 was reviewed under the chairmanship of Rear Admiral A Arokodare, the Chief of Plans at NHQ. I was the only Commander on the Board for the review. There, I was exposed to the politics of promotions and retirements. Surgeon Commodore Augusta Ofili was unhappy with the limited promotion slots for the Medical Branch and as Director of Medical Services, she was under pressure to get a fair deal. The FOC WEST was Commodore Ibrahim J Ogohi. He was recommended to be promoted to Rear Admiral. There was competition for the limited slots. The Engineering Department had to deal with retiring Commodore MA Lawal who was the Admiral Superintendent, Naval Dockyard though he was due for promotion. I argued that he should be promoted and retained to continue in service. I made a strong case to ensure he was not denied the promotion. There were other considerations and it was decided that he should be promoted and retired.

I was asked to visit Commodore Lawal and inform him of the Board's decision. The issue of the Medical Branch was still not resolved and Commodore Ofili was very worried. I called her aside during one of the breaks and advised her to avoid comparison with the career progression of NDA cadets but should use the normal General Hospital administrative setup ranks and equate them to naval ranks for their promotions. She agreed. The following day, she presented a different proposal based on our previous discussion. She got all her officers except one promoted.

With the arrival of the shell bearing, we fixed a date for docking; this was carried out as scheduled and work commenced on re-assembling the shaft. It was good news that a new set of five propeller blades and hub had arrived with all fittings. The entire shaft system components were in place and tests were carried out in stages. The ODB hydraulic system was tested and the propeller pitch systems settings were calibrated. It was time for the harbour trials after docking and the idea of going to sea again for trials came up. The ship had a new CO, Commodore Boniface O.N. Amusu who never spared good tough decisions. On a day run at sea with CNS, he politely decongested the bridge of the CNS and his entourage to enable us to concentrate. The CNS was Vice-Admiral OM Akhigbe who had also earned his tough reputation.

The preparations to get NNS ARADU ready for trials had progressed to my satisfaction and the Marine Engineering Department staff training had yielded satisfactory results. I reported to the CO the readiness of my department for harbour trials. A programme was drawn up for the entire ship and a date was set. It was December 1995 and the CNS Annual Inspection would terminate at Eastern Naval Command. It was planned that the ships of the Western and the Eastern Fleets would have a joint exercise and converge at Calabar, the Eastern Naval Command Headquarters for the end of the year ceremonial sunset and socials.

It was decided that the FOC West should fly his flag on NNS ARADU and ensure the ship arrived at Calabar for the ceremonial sunset. NNS ARADU had not had time to carry out harbour trials; it was being programmed for sea exercise and entry into Calabar for the ceremonial sunset. The pressure mounted on the CO and meetings were held onboard with the senior technical officers from NHQ. The FOC WEST was in attendance. Some former Marine and Weapon Engineer Officers who had served onboard NNS ARADU were ordered to come on board and bring their experiences to bear. I had my plans scuttled. There would be no harbour trials and I was told that there were four main engines and all, including the two gas turbines, must be available. I told the meeting in the presence of the CO that only the two diesel main engines had been prepared and there were no experienced operators onboard for the gas turbine engines. I also pointed out that the gas turbines had not been serviced and operated for the past four years and were not operationally available.

This advice was not what they wanted to hear. I was told to get the gas turbine ready in addition to the two diesel engines. I lost control as I was ordered to get the ship ready to sail for the sea exercise with other ships and the FOC WEST would be onboard with his staff. I had to prepare the Marine Engineering Department for various emergency runs at sea. This was the first time in four years that NNS ARADU would be going to sea and the ship was not allowed to test the repaired shaft and adequately train and prepare. My superiors had taken a decision. I had to comply.

The FOC WEST and his team boarded NNS ARADU. It left the harbour for the sea with only the port shaft engaged because the control system for the starboard shaft developed a fault that was still being investigated. The ship should never have left. I considered this as a reflection of the prevailing pathetic standard of professionalism in NN. There were tugs in attendance and the ship had no difficulty getting out of the confined harbour to the open sea.

The diesel engine driving the port shaft had a fire incident and the capsule was engulfed in heavy smoke. This would have necessitated an immediate shut down of the engine if there was an alternative. The fire was caused by a damaged and leaking duplex filter mounted near the exhaust bellows that were all red hot. There were problems all lined up for the ship. The diesel engine fire was put out and was kept running while the relevant fuel filter fittings were dismantled with the aid of wet rags as spanners easily became too hot to handle. Being duplex filters, it was possible to keep the engine running by isolating the defective one and repairing it.

There was no further incident after the fire and the diesel engine was operated steadily all night. I was in contact with the CO and we both assessed the state of the ship and adjusted routines. The FOC Team became more active onboard making their reports to FOC WEST. I was taken to task on why I had to introduce water rationing with the FOC onboard. I explained the risks of having no fresh water for the main engine and diesel generator engines while at sea without an operational freshwater distillation plant.

In the early morning of the third day, as we approached the Calabar entry channel, the CO was under intense pressure by the FOC to enter the channel which would take about two hours to transit to arrive at the berth allocated. The CO informed me, as NNS ARADU approached the fair-way buoy which would mark the turn to commence the entry into the channel for Calabar, that he had officially informed the FOC that the ship was not in a good condition to navigate the channel and would turn back for Lagos.

The CO ordered the ship to turn and head on the return journey to Lagos. I had my share of the blame for not taking the ship to Calabar despite the risks. I was fully awake all night and shuttled between the bridge and the machinery control room. As NNS ARADU approached Lagos, I advised the CO against the standard manoeuvres to test responses before entry into the channel and also to ask for the tugs to be ready to assist the ship. On getting near the Naval Dockyard pool entrance, the CO gave manoeuvring orders and everything collapsed as NNS ARADU lost control of the port shaft. The tugs took over and took the ship into the pool and successfully berthed without incident. The CO heaved a sigh of relief.

The FOC and the crew missed the parties at Calabar. It is unimaginable what would have happened if NNS ARADU had lost control of the port shaft in the Calabar channel with mangroves and no tug assistance. I was satisfied that in challenging circumstances, the NNS ARADU took manageable risks and stayed within operating limits of the degraded capabilities of pieces of machinery and control systems. The CO's decision not to enter the Calabar channel where the remote control systems would not respond and there would have been no tug in attendance was most courageous.

The six days at sea made me know more about the men in my department and also the CO's team manning the bridge. The CO and I developed a working relationship and he told me that he would always want me with him on the bridge. The CO called me to the open deck space near the ship's twin funnels one afternoon and asked me to sit down and have a drink with him. He thanked me for the way I had handled the ship's affairs and remarked that actually, the MEO had the command of the ship and wished me to continue doing what I had been doing. This was encouraging. He then asked me if I knew what was happening as regards my promotion to Captain. He advised me to watch out as there were intriguing developments that might result in my name being dropped from the list. I was told that I was first in order of merit and that it was provoking unhealthy reactions. I thanked him for his sincerity.

At the end of the year 1995, the promotion signal was released and I was among those successful. I was elated to earn the rank of Captain. I was excited to earn it on board the NN Flag Ship, NNS ARADU. This was my second promotion onboard the Flag Ship, the other being my promotion to the rank of Lieutenant Commander. I shared the joy with my family. ARADU means thunder in Hausa and the ship name for RNEC Manadon was HMS THUNDERER with a motto: Beat the iron while it is hot. NNS ARADU became a historic home for me serving the country considering all that we went through together. I could feel the pains of the ultimate great work of human creativity demanding absolute attention the NN never knew how to give.

I had to continue the process of improving the material state of the ship based on the observations at sea. The request to have the machinery control systems manufacturers carry out inspection and repairs was refused. I was told that a Nigerian contractor versed in the system had been engaged. The contractor came on board and was identified as a retired technical rating. I established that he was incompetent and made my report to the CO who advised me not to attract the wrath of my senior technical officers at NHQ who had engaged the contractor without consultation.

The first intervention of the contractor failed as some electronic modules suffered damages and emitted smoke. I could not stop the work as I did several times during the shaft systems repairs to ensure the contractor followed the correct procedures to avoid damages. The port shaft repaired could not be tried at sea and the remote control system being damaged was most unfortunate. I advised CO that we should programme harbour and sea trials bypassing the remote control systems for both shafts. The gas turbine engines were brought into service and the two diesel engines were in good condition. The communication system for the manual control was rigged and tested and the sequences for the manual control of the shafts were mastered and tested. A harbour trial was carried out and both shafts were successfully engaged. A sea trial was programmed and the ship sailed to remain at sea overnight.

The CO sent for me to join him on the bridge immediately. He told me the ship was not obeying any orders for movement forward and was constantly engaged going astern. He told me to take over the ship and I did but he remained on the Captain's chair observing my actions to identify the problems and solve them on the spot. I identified the problems after about six hours of several trials during which various readings were taken. The CO left the bridge for his cabin because he became confident that I was handling the ship well and making progress in sequentially solving the problems. I was relying on the Navigation and Direction (ND) Officer, a Lieutenant Commander, to take chart fixes and make the plots on the navigation chart and the processes were progressing fine. The ND Officer left his duty post without informing me. He was not ready to take orders from a Marine Engineer Officer who was senior to him. I had to rely on GPS and later sent for the ND officer after establishing safe operating limits for machinery to take fixes to confirm my plots before handing over command of the ship to CO.

The ship returned to the harbour and safely berthed at Marina jetty as the Navy Week celebration would involve the ship being open to visitors. The CO and I were satisfied that the crew had become familiar with their parts of the ship and worked effectively in teams as reflected in the watch and station bill. The Navy Day celebrations for 1996 started in the last week of May and ended in the first week of June. NNS ARADU was programmed to take some visitors for a day sea trip. The CNS and NHQ principal staff officers were embarked. The CO informed me that he would not like any senior officers including the CNS in the enclosed bridge. The CNS was politely informed that his presence in the enclosed bridge would be brief so that the crew, and especially the team manning the bridge, were not distracted. The CNS was pleased that the evolutions went well without reports of a breakdown.

As Captain, I was the most senior engineer officer afloat. I should have been posted out of the ship. The CO, Commodore BON Amusu was posted out of the ship but I was retained on board to assist the new CO, Commodore AE Oguguo.

The first sea outing with the new CO had proceeded smoothly until the return passage after the breakwaters towards Atlas Cove where a large tanker was discharging petrol with a cargo merchant ship at anchorage nearby. The CO decided to go through the gap between the tanker and the merchant ship. NNS ARADU was moving slowly ahead and had no room to manoeuvre safely through the narrow gap. I advised the CO to immediately request for one of the tugs on standby to come in through the gap and take NNS ARADU on tow. The berthing party at the forward section (foxcle) of the ship was ordered to get ready the towing rope. The tug succeeded temporarily in getting NNS ARADU clear of ramming into either of the two ships. The tow rope suddenly snapped and set NNS ARADU into a swing towards the petrol tanker.

The CO lost control of himself and screamed "Board of Inquiry" repeatedly. I got the message and I took over command of the ship without second thoughts. I ordered the coxswain on the wheel to maintain a steady hold and I put the engine orders to go astern. The engine order astern slowed down the NNS ARADU and by the time the tug took control of the tow, the ship was just a few centimetres from ramming the petrol tanker. The resulting tear could have easily caused a spark with catastrophic consequences. NNS ARADU was taken clear of danger and engine orders returned to ahead mode.

There were moves to get me posted out of the ship as there had never been a Captain as MEO of the Flag Ship in NN history. I was retained to assist COs and provide continuity and successfully led efforts for the shaft repairs after the accident in Bonny channel in January 1994. I had no idea what my next posting would be. Not long after the incident at Atlas Cove, I received a signal that I had been appointed to Naval Dockyard as General Manager Production. This was another pressure cooker appointment. My departure from the NNS ARADU marked the last of the sea-going appointments of my career and I was happy it had been a very good run despite the challenges.

My experiences between 14 February 1994 and 01 September 1996, a period of two years and six months, onboard NNS ARADU offered me a worrying glimpse of the state of NN. It was fast deteriorating due to reckless and casual approach to professional matters. There are no career reviews and planning for commissioned officers. It has been established by experts that the warship demands absolute attention to all details as it is the most sophisticated and complicated engineering creation by man. The NN developed a wasting culture that was adversely affecting personnel and materials of war. It became the culture that those with destructive intentions that undermine the institutions are considered as belonging to the system. The impressive range of modern warships was wasting away at a fast rate and I wondered if NN cared about the international dimensions of such waste. The latest additions, the MCMVs in 1988, were already reduced to ordinary patrol vessels. I wondered whether the NN could appreciate that it had the very best performing warships of their class that attracted the US Navy.

Father

Isa Ifache Anda

Mother

Avahi Avosuahi Asmau

Brother and Sisters

Jimoh

Ozohu

Rabi

Ayiba

Bond of Extended Family in Kaduna 1974: Front row from left to right, Victor Adinoyi, Emmanuel Ajoku, Anthony Isa, Mrs Helen Ajoku with her third child Martin; Second row from left to right, Emmanuel Ajoku Jnr, Theresa Ajoku and third row from left to right, Nasiru Musa, Sefinatu Ajoku, Haruna Ajoku.

Anthony Isa, first row from the right seated, with his 1961 Primary Three pupils at St Pius Primary School, Magamiya.

Anthony Odogba Musa Ajoku Isa, 1964 final year in Primary School.

Main gate into St John's College, Kaduna

With College Final Year Students of St Benedict's Dormitory: From left to right Patrick Abdullahi, Anthony Isa, Friday Herrington, Ibrahim Lutu, House Master, Stephen Ikyator, Theophilus Gana, Jacob Yakubu and Rafiu Ashafa.

Cadet Anthony Isa

Left to right: Cadet Isa Bala, Cadet Anthony Isa and Cadet Sakiru Disu

Guest of Honour, Vice Admiral JEA Wey, Chief of the Naval Staff with Commandant Major General RA Adebayo and Deputy Commandant Brigadier HS Chandel at the first Ceremonial Parade I participated in, September 1972. Parade Commander was Academy Cadet Senior Under Officer Martin Luther Agwai receiving a gold medal award on passing out.

Cadet Anthony Isa receiving awards from Guest of Honour, Major General HU Katsina at his passing out parade on 15 December 1973 with the Deputy Commandant Brigadier HS Chandel looking on.

8th from left Cadet Anthony Isa seated between Lieutenant Commander KK Kohli and Deputy Commandant, Brigedier HS Chandel, Academy Staff Officers(Lieutenant GN Kanu seated fifth from left) with the Naval and Air Force Cadets that passed out on 15 December 1973.

Left to right Sub Lieutenant Ong Nee Hock, Midshipman Anthony Isa and Sub Lieutenant Ku Yuen Mun, at RNEC, Manadon 1974.

25th December 1974, Lunch with Walter and Nan Wedlake at 168 Fort Austin Ave, Plymouth.

Left to right, Midshipman Anthony Isa, Midshipman John Coulthard and Midshipman Daniel Opuoro.

Spring 1975 Camping on Dartmoor, sharing experience with Chris Prior Jones and other coursemates.

On Industrial Visit to Glasgow 1976. Front row second from the right; Anthony Isa. Friedhelm Stappen is second from right of middle row.

Member of College 1st XI Hockey Team

Degree Award to Sub Lieutenant Anthony Isa from Dr E McEwen with Deputy Dean Captain John Franklin on a historic graduation day for the Nigerian Navy, July 1977.

Anthony Isa receiving the RNEC Project Prize for the most outstanding interdisciplinary BSc degree project from Dr E McEwen; partially hidden with a broad smile is the Dean, Captain Henry Morgan

Sub lieutenant Anthony Isa with Lieutenant Kevin Black of New Zealand Navy on board HMS TORQUAY 1978.

Back row third from right, Lieutenant Anthony Isa with members of the class of Advanced Marine Engineering Course 18 (MSc) and Staff 1983.

Lieutenant Anthony Isa receiving MSc Degree Award from Her Majesty, Queen Elizabeth II, The Lord High Admiral.A bundle of history and rare graduation degree award in the long reign of Her Majesty.

Her Majesty the Queen with His Royal Highness, the Duke of Edinburgh seated with Captain RV Holley to the right of Her Majesty and Captain AO Holding, Dean, to her left. Lieutenant Anthony Isa is standing behind

Lieutenant Anthony Isa and Mrs Linda Isa pose with the MSc Degree from Her Majesty, 22 July 1983.

Nigeria's Ambassador to Italy His Excellency Commodore Albert Ajanaku followed by Commodore MAH Nyako and Lieutenant Commander Anthony Isa arriving for the Launching of NNS OHUE at Intermarine Shipyard, Italy.

Mrs. Rebecca Aikhomu wife of the Chief of the Naval Staff set to perform the Launching of NNS OHUE

Mrs. Esther Bali wife of the Minister of Defense arriving with the Nigeria Ambassador to Italy His Excellency Commodore Albert Ajanaku for the Launching of NNS BARAMA.

Left to right, Major General Harold Mashburn, Commandant; Ambassador Jibril Aminu, Nigeria's Ambassador to USA, and Vice Admiral Paul G Gaffney II, President of the National Defense University, with Captain Anthony Isa on receiving the President's Strategic Vision Award, the highest Award given by the University and Distinguished Graduate award.

Captain Anthony Isa with Colonel Brian Duffy, Commander of Space Shuttle Mission STS-92 at Houston Mission Control Centre.

Captain Anthony Isa standing fifth from right with other International fellows of the National Defense University Class of 2001 at Cape Canaveral Launch Site. Space Shuttle in the background being wheeled to launch position.

Lieutenant Commander Anthony Isa, first from right, member of the delegation to Germany led by Commodore Ibrahim Katagum, third from left, Captain Peter Jerome, third from right, and Commander John Aneke,first from left meeting with Dr Klaus Bauer leading the Dornier Team on assessment of logistic facilities required for Nigerian Navy

A tall plant growing between concrete blocks near the main dock gate when NNS ARADU was in dock for major repairs. The plant eventually grew taller giving sign of time due to leave dock.

271

On the Enclosed Bridge of NNS ARADU on training exercise at sea after extensive repairs 1995.

Reconstruction of the Naval Dockyard Administration Block, January to May 2004.

Meeting with a Brazilian technical collaboration team on Warship Design and Construction at Nigerian Naval Dockyard.

Wedding day 17th April 1982 at the Church of the
Sacred Heart, Minehead, Somerset.

Mrs. Linda Isa

Family: Front sitting right to left: Augustine
Adaeiza, Diana Ahooiza, Rear left to right: David
Aharvi, Anthony, Linda and Daniel Enesi.

Ivy Goh, Isa Ifache Anda and Joseph Goh,
Linda's Parents at Okene 1989.

Stappen Family 2020, Germany: Left to right Christopher, Mair,
Friedhelm and Martin.

CHAPTER FOURTEEN

My Bundle of Nigerian Navy Challenges

I reported for duty on 02 September 1996 as General Manager in charge of production at the Nigerian Naval Dockyard (NND) located at Victoria Island, Lagos. The facility formerly belonged to Elder Dempster company and had been modernised and completely rebuilt except for the administrative block that was retained as it was. It is a very integrated facility that involved several European industries and is the pride of the NN but had only reached a stage of implementation when the project execution came to a standstill until it was partially commissioned on 27 August 1990 with the help of the Brazilian Navy Emgepron of Rio de Janeiro, Brazil.

Commodore G Oladejo was the Admiral Superintendent of the Naval Dockyard (ASND) and Chief Executive Officer and had managed the Naval Shipyard, the much smaller and old facility bought from Witt and Busch at Port Harcourt. He was experienced in running a commercial undertaking at the Naval Shipyard where small boats were designed and constructed for the NN and oil companies in addition to carrying out maintenance jobs that were the main activity.

The ASND and the other two General Managers, Captain LOB Agbaje for Planning and Captain AD Odejimi for Yard Services briefed me on the tasks at hand. I had all the workshops, three docks, and a huge number of NND personnel under my charge but I was the junior Captain among the General Managers. I relied on the other two General Managers for materials availability and yard services but all operations related to Production at NND were my responsibility. I had worked closely with some staff of NND while I was onboard NNS ARADU and was already familiar with the available facilities.

I held meetings with the officers and the various categories of staff before having a general rowdy session with all staff of the Production Department. These interactions gave me a clue to the challenges ahead.

The morale of the workforce was sunken and many had no money to commute to work. Those living in the neighbouring state of Ogun in places like Ota preferred to sleep in any available space within the NND and officers took advantage of the soft cushion chairs in the mess.

I noticed a trend whereby the personnel arranged among themselves to come to work three or two days out of the official five working days and cover up for one another.

The ASND had several meetings with the Heads of Department and informed the NHQ to allow commercial activities. The CNS was the Chairman of the Governing Board of the NND with the ASND as a member. The Branch Chiefs at NHQ were also members. I advised the ASND to meet CNS to request approval for the immediate commencement of commercial operations at the NND because the low pay of personnel could not meet their transportation cost for two weeks, and with low morale and nothing coming from the NHQ to improve the situation, it would be impossible to manage NND. The ASND received the approval of the NHQ to do commercial jobs and bring the twin docks into operation immediately to complement the main dock.

I sensitised the personnel of my department on the tasks ahead and told them that based on productivity and earnings from commercial activities, incentives would be paid solely on their contributions. I informed them that I had secured the approval of the ASND to service and commission the twin docks and put them to commercial use. I said that all staff of the NND were marketing officers and whoever could bring a merchant ship in would be paid some incentives based on the total value of the contract.

The twin docks were successfully serviced and commissioned. The NND secured a fishing trawler in the fleet run by some Indians. They were used to getting their trawlers lifted out of the water by a boatyard in Lagos onto a cradle for underwater repairs. I arranged a team of my versed officers and senior rates to meet with the technical staff of the fishing trawler company and convince them that NND had better facilities and would do a better job at a lower cost.

The initial meetings were tough but I urged my staff to keep all potential customers engaged until we got the job or jobs. I was surprised to see that most of the commercial vessel owners did not have docking plan documents. I requested the services of divers that the ASND approved. The visit of the divers to the location of the trawlers to inspect the underwater structure and fittings gave me useful information. As a confidence-building strategy, we invited the technical team representing the trawler owners to inspect and appreciate all steps we took to safely dock their trawlers and do the jobs they wanted. We also showed off some of our sophisticated equipment that other shipyards did not have.

The first fishing trawler contract was secured on paper but I noticed the Indians were still cautious and I felt they could disappoint us at any moment. I targeted some of my staff to visit them daily to work out the date of arrival of the trawler and they were invited and shown all the precautions we would take to avoid any underwater damages as they had no docking plan documents.

I had planned to take the trawler before the Easter week of March 1997. This did not happen as there were deliberate delays by the Indians who were being cautious. The Indian negotiator sent a message that the trawler would be available for docking on Good Friday which was a public holiday. I immediately accepted and told the ASND to declare that day a full working day for the Production Department. Provisions were made for the feeding and transportation of the personnel. I sent a team to the company to board the trawler and ensure the ship arrived at the NND pool.

At about 1345 hours, I had the first challenge from an officer who came to take permission to go for Juma'at prayers at about the same time, I was informed that the trawler was approaching. The officer, a Commander, was the Head of Section and Workshop Manager responsible for sandblasting of structure and was on standby to put the sandblasting equipment into action to signal the commencement of work on the trawler on arrival alongside an assigned jetty. I told the officer that the trawler was approaching and no one would leave their assigned duty post. This was openly resisted.

I ordered the Provost Officer to arrest him and lock him up in one of the containers being used as an office nearby. This action put other personnel on maximum alert. The trawler arrived about thirty minutes later and I ordered the release of the officer to take charge of his men to receive and secure the trawler alongside the pool jetty and commence the sandblasting. The efficiency with which the Commander's team started the first job was very impressive.

I told the Indian team that my staff would start flooding the dock to take the trawler based on the next high tide which was approaching. Commander Peter I Ikre was the Dock Master and was busy getting the dock ready. The twin docks area became a beehive of heightened activities and I was happy with my staff and their patience. By coincidence, Peter was rushing past me when I looked at my watch and it was exactly 1500 hours when all Christians on their most holy day of Good Friday were expected to be in churches for service.

I asked Peter, "What is the time?" He stopped and looked at his watch and said, "It is three o'clock sir." We looked at each other and paused for barely two seconds and he told me one of the most memorable lines I have ever heard in the heat of action. Peter, a Catholic by faith said to me: "Do not worry sir, God is looking at us and can see where we are and will appreciate that we are busy." "To work is to pray" is a Benedictine Monastery motto.

The preparations for the docking went on well and with the help of the divers, the Indians watched as we took their trawler into the dock and safely docked the boat without incident. The NND had secured its first commercial job in the dock and also for the first, time, put to use one of the twin docks that had never been used since the commissioning of the NND in 1990. These were very significant achievements though we had no time to celebrate. God is good!

There were joint market surveys with the Planning Department staff to establish costs and avoid time-wasting bureaucracy. I introduced the concept of single-manager responsibility whereby jobs that required other managers' inputs came under the supervision of the manager with the major part of the overall job so that the jobs were properly coordinated and time targets were met. I reduced the number of departmental meetings so that I had more time to walk around and engage the workers and call in the managers where their attention was required. The jobs on the fishing trawler were satisfactorily completed and the painting scheme gave the ship a very new look. The owners were pleased after inspection and the trawler was undocked and handed over to them.

The Planning Department and the ASND did the follow up on the contracts and payments. I assessed the Production Department requirements and costing and established the savings regarding materials and money collected based on my recommendations to the ASND. I never collected any approved funds and directed the managers responsible to do so and buy materials that were taken into the inventory at the central store and issued on demand for the jobs.

I was approached by my managers regarding what to do with the materials and money saved after the completion of jobs. I directed that the materials should be documented and saved with the various sections in the workshops where the jobs were undertaken so that they had some materials to start new jobs immediately they were assigned to save time. I asked for their suggestion regarding the money left and I was advised to take whatever I wanted and give them the rest to share. I agreed that the money should not be returned to the Finance Department but I refused to have a share. I preferred that it should be used for the Production Department incentive payments. I directed the managers to report their savings and draw up the list of those who carried out the jobs and based on the extent of individual participation, the supervising managers should allocate a share starting with the manager to the least.

The lists and the recommended amounts were forwarded to me for scrutiny and approval and all those on the list signed and collected their incentives. I also followed up on the ASND's incentive for my Department and again I had no share. The focus was on the personnel whose morale had to be quickly raised. I ensured I did not benefit from these incentive schemes so that I would be free to attend promptly and fairly to complaints and problems that might arise.

The job done on the fishing trawler was our best advertisement. The news went round that we could dock merchant ships without docking plans (not recommended practice please!) and had the capabilities for doing an excellent job to the satisfaction of customers. The Indian operators and owners of the trawler gave us good reviews and proposed to the NND to permanently dedicate one of our twin docks for their fleet. This proposal was turned down because of the NN commitments and also due to the increased demands for our services.

The oil industry operators were also attracted to the NND and we had many customers on our waiting list. The sleepy NND became a beehive of activities. The hitherto demoralised workforce surprised me because they took the initiative to work extra hours to meet time targets. They even worked on weekends. I drove to the NND medical centre on a Saturday and noticed most of the workshops were open and men were moving around as if it was a normal workday. I was greeted by their happy faces.

The three docks at the NND were put into operation and each had ships being docked and worked upon including NN warships that had priority. The Dock Master was busy preparing docking plans and dock blocks and wedges for cradles. The damaged equipment and machinery were repaired by NND personnel and this saved the NND many resources.

The dock gate pumps, machinery and other pieces of equipment were routinely serviced and tested to keep up with scheduled docking operations and save cost. One of the twin dock gates was removed and secured alongside to repair a damaged structure that needed welding. But on returning the repaired gate to get it into its slot position, further difficulties arose. The flooding tide was at its highest and the NND pool was quite turbulent. The turbulent nature of the pool did not allow the option of securing the gate alongside as the ropes could part and allow the dock gate float away to open sea just like it happened to the main graving dock gate in 1990 (that cost the career of a senior naval officer).

At a stage, the gate was almost submerged by the turbulent surges and I had to encourage the two ratings onboard to secure themselves properly as they were our only hope of saving the dock gate. I decided to use the centre capstan for a tow using a rope secured to a strong point at the centre of the dock gate in line with the capstan. A senior seaman rating who had been part of the seaman berthing party was selected to jump onboard and secure the rope to a strong point. I gave him a life jacket and arranged the rope with a heaving line attached waiting for the next favourable surge to bring the gate near the dock concrete dockside platform on which we were standing.

When we achieved a safe distance with a favourable surge to jump on the dock gate walkway, I turned to order the rating to jump onboard and he was nowhere to be found. In a flash, I had to jump on board without a life jacket and asked whoever was around to pass the rope to me. There was no time to brief another senior rating on what to do. The two ratings who had been enduring the rough turbulent surges were relieved because I had joined them and enduring the same challenge. I told them to hold on to the support structures and be close to one another as I received the rope using a heaving line and passed it on to them to hold. I climbed down a manhole to select the strong point structure to attach the rope. The rope was passed to me and I secured it to the strong point on the dock gate flooding compartment hull. The capstan motor took control and the team worked hard to secure the gate into the seal slots, and immediately, the dock pumps were started to create a differential depth in the dock that firmly held the gate in a steady position.

I climbed up to the gate walk-way and got to the dockside and saw the ASND approaching. Someone had informed him that we were in danger of having a dock gate sunk in appalling rough pool water conditions. It was getting to midnight and the struggles to save the dock gate started around 1600 hours. It was a close shave and misfortune was averted. This same dock gate sank six years later in 2003 and was in that state for months until January 2004. It was my honour and privilege to salvage the wreck, repair it and put it to use when I took command of the NND as the ASND on promotion to Rear Admiral. Some jobs were cut out to wait for me in NN.

There were several dockings in 1997 and the commercialisation of the operations of the NND was not regretted. The NND earned enough money and part of the profit was ploughed into the NN warships so that the docks would not be tied down waiting for government releases.

There was always a merchant ship waiting to be docked in any of the three docks. There was once a clash of priorities between a merchant ship waiting to be docked at the same time that NN warships also needed some attention.

The NHQ wanted two Fast Attack Crafts to be docked immediately because they were reported to be having serious underwater leakages and the merchant shipowner had paid a deposit to commit NND to a schedule. We were caught between contractual obligations and the NN order. The NN had no money to pay us; the merchant ship contract would give us plenty of money. I had a meeting with my staff and explained to them the difficulties the NND faced. There were moves to have the NN vessels docked just to occupy dock space and prevent commercial jobs from being done. I told my departmental section heads and managers that the Production Department would have to take in all five ships (three NN warships and two merchant ships) and the three docks would be flooded at the same time. Additional ships were added.

I tried to convince them that we should take the two Fast Attack Crafts abreast and the merchant ship behind them so that as soon as the work on the merchant ship was completed it would be taken out of dock without pulling out the two NN warships. One of my officers was not convinced that all the ships could be taken at the same time. I gave him enough time to explain the dangers he envisaged. I noticed that other officers neither criticised nor commented on the dangers he highlighted nor commented on my plan and explanations. I had to be cautious. I asked the officers to think about it and get back to me at our meeting the following day.

One of my officers had informed the ASND of the proceedings and I got to know. At the meeting the following day, I told them that I had considered the plan and the dangers or risks highlighted. I took all points and they were exhaustively discussed. There was consensus that it could be done and that was what I wanted. The officer who opposed the plan and highlighted the risks was adamant.

I informed the ASND after the meeting with my departmental officers and he was a bit worried. I was familiar with his concerns and I knew who had briefed him from my department. The ASND had not doubted my docking plans so far. I was convinced we should give the plan a chance. The ASND reluctantly approved and I started preparations and drills to master how to flood and manage the three docks simultaneously for the first time. The docking order was issued for the five ships to go into the three docks and complied with.

The five ships entered the three docks as planned and the dock gates were closed. The Dock Master and I found ourselves sprinting between docks attending to issues and making sure orders were properly carried out. The merchant ship in the main dock with the two warships had a problem as the cradle shape was not correctly profiled. As the main dock was being pumped down, the huge merchant ship shifted violently and almost everyone ran for shelter. I immediately ordered a stoppage of the pumping down and observed the tilt or list on the huge ship. The diver was sent down and reported his findings.

The Dock Master prepared new sets of wedges as the main dock was flooded again to fully float the merchant ship. The flooding was controlled to observe the ship and it floated upright without incident. The doubting officer in my department was busy taking notes as the incident on the merchant ship occurred and he never volunteered a solution or help. He was waiting to be proved right should there be a disaster.

The following day, there was a stream of officers from outside the NND visiting the docks to see the five ships docked at the same time for the first time in the NN. I visited one of the Fast Attack Crafts to inspect the much-hyped underwater section leakage. I asked the CO of one of the ships to show me the leaking spot(s) on his ship. He reluctantly admitted his mischief. The warships were quickly repaired and undocked at the same time as the merchant ship. The ASND was relieved and to his credit, he never refused to act on any of my decisions on dockings and jobs throughout my tenure under him.

The ASND called me into his office and told me that he received reports that the Production Department was paying incentives leaving out some people who participated in the jobs and some complained that they were not well paid at all. I told the ASND what he already knew that I was paying incentives from the savings made on the approvals he gave and added that I supervised the scheme with documentation. I also told him that as the Head of Department, I never benefited from the scheme. I told him to let me get him the documents so that he could take his time to check what happened to the complainants.

The target was the Dock Master who controlled much of the workforce for cleaning the docks after docking ships before the commencement of works. I walked to the office of the Dock Master and he was not at his seat. I checked the few files on his table and located the one used for the administration of the incentive scheme. I took it straight to the ASND without checking its contents. He checked the name of the staff who complained that he was not paid and saw where he signed for his incentive. He checked other names and was satisfied. He kept the file for some days after which he called me and returned it to me without comment. He was satisfied with the excellent record keeping.

The next report ASND got was that the amount being received by the officers was huge and that some personnel were paid higher. The ASND alerted me and told me to look into their complaints. I assembled the workers by sections in their workshops together with their officers and managers. I got to know that those complaining were from other departments who felt they were not in the mainstream of the Production Department.

I received a report that there were plans to push the Dock Master into the sea during docking to get rid of him. I advised the ASND to assemble the NND workforce in the central dining hall space for his address. On displaying the notice for the ASND address, the narrative changed that the Dock Master took the money for payment of incentives home and exchanged them with dirty notes used to pay them.

In his address, the ASND praised the entire workers for their dedication to duty which had led to record docking and successful execution of jobs. He mentioned the complaints and asked me to address the workforce. I also praised them for their dedication and told them that the incentives being paid were based on the level of participation and that I scrutinized all payments. I stated that I had received information about the threat to push the Dock Master into the sea to get rid of him. I told them that I would always be with the Dock Master henceforth for docking and undocking operations and they should get ready to push me into the sea first before they could succeed in doing that to the Dock Master. I informed them that all reports received had been investigated by the ASND and that they were false.

One of my sad moments at the NND was the death of one of the machine operators in the Steel Workshop. I told the Workshop Manager to get his home address for me to pay a condolence visit to his family. I was told that he had no home in the Lagos area and that he was sleeping in the workshop using a space beside his machine. When he fell sick, he was given sick leave to travel home to Port Harcourt to receive medical attention. I inspected the Workshop and saw that it was being used as accommodation by some of the workers. The hostel for the trainees of the Dockyard Apprentice Training School was available because the school had not been in session for several years. The Ministry of Defence could not work out a career path for the graduates of the school. I took permission from the ASND to use the empty rooms in the hostel as temporary accommodation for personnel who could not afford their residential accommodation. I would some years later as ASND between 2004 -2005 start the construction of two hostels for workers at NND.

The FOC NAVTRAC, Commodore TA Odedina, contacted the ASND and requested him to release me to handle the court-martial cases involving Captain JOP Ogbonna and Lieutenant Commander B George, and Lieutenant Commander EA Adeuti. The FOC said his request was based on his confidence in me to handle the three cases because it had been challenging to get an acceptable officer as president of the court-martial.

The ASND released me for the assignment. I reported to FOC NAVTRAC and asked for a free hand to conduct the proceeding. He readily assured me I had a free hand.

The special court-martial was duly constituted. I was the President. The members were Captain AB Agbaje, Captin MO Fagbote, Captain E Nanna, and Sub Lieutenant CN Anushiem, a lawyer as the Judge Advocate. The prosecution lawyers were all military lawyers. The defence lawyers were civilians with one retired officer.

Captain J Ogbonna was charged with four offences, related to disobedience to particular orders of the DHQ, NHQ, and FOC NAVTRAC to return a DHQ vehicle attached to his former office. Captain Ogbonna had served under me at FMC as a Lieutenant Commander and I had warned him in his annual Performance Evaluation Report that he needed to change his attitude towards respect for authority. He was not happy with me and he had to be told by the Chief Staff Officer at FMC that my report was thoroughly objective before he signed it. I expected him to object to my being the President of the Court Martial but he did not. Lieutenant Commander George was charged with stealing and misapplication of service fund, and Lieutenant Commander Adeuti was charged with forgery related to oil bunkering papers.

At the first sitting, the President and Members of the Special Court-Martial panel and the Defence and Prosecution teams were introduced. Captain J Ogbonna was asked if he had any objections to the composition of the Court Martial panel. He had no objections and the proceedings got underway. At one of the sittings, I noticed that the Prosecution had taken advantage of a lack of knowledge of military law and proceedings by the defence. I consulted the Judge Advocate who also took note of my observation and it was agreed with members that we switch off the recording device and let the exchange proceed as an academic exercise.

The Defence team asked for an adjournment and it was granted by the court. At the next sitting, the defence team introduced a military lawyer and the proceedings were on a level playing field for both parties. The Prosecution had done its job and asked the court to render a guilty verdict on the defendant on the charges. The defence, however, had provided details of earlier actions taken by FOC NAVTRAC against the defendant which was a trial that resulted in a warning being given to the officer to desist from the offending acts. The law is that you cannot try someone twice for the same offence. The first charge was, therefore, dismissed because it would amount to trying the officer twice. The officer was accordingly discharged and acquitted on the first and follow up charges but found guilty on the fourth charge and was sentenced to a loss of seniority for six months. Lieutenant Commander George was found guilty on all five charges and received a prison sentence on each count to run concurrently; Lieutenant Adeuti was discharged on the third count but was found guilty of the first two and was reduced in rank and dismissed.

As the cases went on, threatening telephone calls were made to my family that I was in danger and would be dealt with if one of the officers was convicted. I told my family not to answer any telephone calls and alerted the NHQ Director of Naval Intelligence. Appropriate security measures were put in place to secure my residential neighbourhood. I did not inform the members of the Court Martial panel of the threats until after the court delivered judgements and arrangements were made for the security of the venue and safe passage of the members to their residences. The court concluded its proceedings and was dissolved. We left the premises in a convoy and dispersed in a safe zone.

I had been on the CNS Annual Conference (CONSAC) committee for some years and the conference of 1997 was planned to take place in Abuja. The NHQ and other services headquarters were still at Moloney Street, Lagos. I was always on the team writing several draft papers and speeches for the guests of honour. The Head of State, Commander-in-Chief of the Armed Forces was usually the special guest of honour and in the final stages, I would spend late hours alone with the CNS waiting for comments on the draft speech from the Presidential Villa, Abuja. This went back and forth until the draft was finally approved. I left Lagos with the advance party for Abuja to prepare for the secretariat and programmes. I informed the ASND of this a week ahead of the CONSAC and he objected, reminding me of the pressure on the NND on the three warships programmed for docking in the main dock.

I had already held meetings with my staff on the dockings and I told them that I would not be around because of the CONSAC. The responsibility for the successful docking of the three ships was theirs and I told them that I had confidence in them and that my efforts would be in vain if they could not carry on without me after all we had been through together. I had a meeting with the ASND and informed him that I had always carried my staff officers and workforce along and they were fully ready and competent to carry out the dockings without me. I told him that if they failed I would take it that I had failed and that my success should be measured by my department functioning more efficiently without me. I had signed and released the Docking Operations Orders. The ASND released me to leave for Abuja. A week later, I went to brief him on his arrival at Abuja for the CONSAC and he was full of smiles and confidence that he had good news for the CNS. The docking operation for the three ships was successful.

The CONSAC 1997 was held at Sheraton Hotel, Ladi Kwali Conference Centre, with stunning facilities. I had accommodation at the Niger Barracks where the advance party stayed and moved to a room in the Sheraton Hotel allocated to me a day to the commencement of the conference. I was under pressure in Lagos regarding the court-martials and I was pressured again in Abuja. It was felt that as the President of the Court Martials I was in a position to alter the decisions of the court. I couldn't revisit the court-martial verdicts. I was at peace that the proceedings were fair and the decisions taken were not influenced by any superior authority.

I was asked to deliver a paper on "Combat Engineering Functions and the Future of the Nigerian Navy" due to the obstacles being placed on the career progression of engineers in the NN which was seriously affecting the effective management of sophisticated warships in the NN inventory. In my paper, I spoke of the dangers ahead and pointed out that the decisions naval officers made relating to warships were engineering decisions. The feeling was that marine engineers were about to take over the NN.

The security issue in the oil-producing areas and the militancy of the youths were very worrisome. The NN military governors at the conference responded to questions relevant to their states. Commander C Olubolade, the military governor of Bayelsa State, gave an interesting narrative of his close shaves with the militants.

The conclusion of the CONSAC proceedings at Abuja saddled me with the responsibility to produce an executive summary and compile the papers presented including the keynote address. I had been on the writing team for CONSAC for six years and I concluded that the conference had become a forum for unnecessary diversionary comparisons and competition for resources. I felt this should be my last involvement in the planning and execution of the CONSAC and it turned out that way as I was not included in the CONSAC 1998 held at Ijebu Ode in Ogun State after Vice Admiral J Ayinla took over as the CNS from Vice- Admiral OM Akhigbe. I attended the CONSAC as part of the delegation of the ASND and for once in about six years, I had a view of the proceedings as part of the audience.

I attended the Speech Day activities at King's College as my son was passing out. The Guest Speaker gave a narrative about the unfolding political situation in the country using the condition of a Peugeot car General Olusegun O Obasanjo handed over as the military Head of State in 1979. The journeys and the deteriorating conditions of the car through the various succeeding administrations were described. As of 1998, the state of the Peugeot car was quite bad that an old engine and used tires were bought and fitted in the rickety body and managed to Ota in Ogun State to the residence of the former Head of State with a plea to him to come back on a rescue mission. I drew many lessons from this narrative regarding the poor state of the NN Fleet that the same military Head of State inspired the impressive procurements. My experiences since 1983 when I returned from Manadon is a testimony of the agonies of the wastage of assets taking place in Nigeria. It has become a habit and I have been studying the trend to establish why there is a preference for destruction rather than building and maintaining for progress.

The docking operations at the NND were great and everywhere I turned during my routine inspections showed personnel busy trying to meet schedules. It appeared that the Yard Services Department and the CO, NND, Department at NND felt I was pushing too hard. The GM, Yard Services, Captain AD Odejimi, was my senior at the NDA and the CO was my junior. It is essential to note that an officer below the ASND was designated CO, NND and this was part of the arrogance of the Executive (Seaman) Branch officers of the NN who feel that they should not serve under the command of an Engineer Officer no matter how senior or his special status might be.

The CO was reluctant to carry out my instruction and surprisingly was being supported by the GM, Yard Services. I was disappointed and had to keep up with the arrogance until the GM left for his office. I noticed that the XO also left with his men and there was a shortage of personnel. I sent a message to the XO to report to his assigned duty post as the CO was not around. He sent a message back that he did not take orders from an engineer and refused to turn up. I left instructions at the gate that the XO should not be allowed to pass through the gate at the official closing hour. The XO reported being sick at the NND Medical Centre and was given a bed rest at a place referred to as being Sick-in-Quarters (SIQ) and escaped to go home. I called the doctor who issued him the SIQ and he explained to me that he was unaware of my orders at the gate. I immediately asked him to get the XO to come and do his SIQ at the Medical Centre. There was resistance and I told the doctor that in the military such act of undermining a superior's order by subordinates was never tolerated.

I told him that even if the XO was under drips, an ambulance with escorts should be sent to bring him to the Medical Centre. I had the Military Police ready with hand-cuffs to escort the ambulance. The XO got the message, rallied to get support but no senior officer phoned me to intervene. When the XO reported at the Medical Centre, I told the doctor to cancel the SIQ and let him report for duty. The SIQ was cancelled and the incident cost the XO his job at the NND. He lost control of his executive privilege as I detained him. He was posted out of the NND. I solved a major problem of institutionalised insubordination. There is no room for disobedience of the correct orders of a superior officer to perform an official duty.

In June 1998, the Head of State, General Sani Abacha, died suddenly. General A Abdulsalam Abubakar took over as the new Head of State. Vice-Admiral OM Akighbe was appointed Chief of General Staff, the number two man to him in the administration. Admiral Akhigbe called a meeting of some senior officers at the NHQ to discuss general matters about the new government's programme. The issue of a short duration of the new government was thrown open for discussion after the CNS brief. I raised the issue of the long-term damage that would be done to the country if the transition to civil rule was rushed. I asked if there was any agenda or programme to determine the duration of such a programme. It was suggested that the new administration should not be in haste thereby creating avoidable problems for the country. The administration eventually decided to hand over power on 29 May 1999.

General A Abdulsalami Abubakar GCFR, set about selecting officers of the Armed Forces in the rank bracket of Commander-Captain (Lieutenant Colonel-Colonel/Wing Commander-Group Captain) to be appointed state military administrators. On a Friday afternoon, I was asked to see the ASND in his office. In the office, I met him with Rear Admiral Peter Ebhaleme, the Chief of Personnel (COP) at the

NHQ. The ASND informed me that I had been nominated by the NHQ for an appointment as a Military Administrator. The COP took over and informed me that the announcement would be made on confirmation by the office of the Head of State by the weekend. He told me that I should come to his office next Monday and discuss the nomination of my staff to facilitate their timely release.

I felt uneasy and told him that I would wait until the announcement was made before deciding on the personal staff. I thanked him and the ASND for the information. It was meant to put me on standby. I went to my office and briefly reflected on the information I had received and reviewed the jobs in progress before closing for the day. I went for inspection rounds and met a retired Admiral who told me that he learnt that I would likely be posted to Delta State as the Military Administrator. When I got home at about 2000 hours, I said this very short prayer before the crucifix hanging in my living room: "Lord, I thank you for all that you have done for me; do not let any sudden misfortune happen to me. Your will, be done."

While I was at the dining table having dinner, my wife told me that unusual callers were asking to see me. I got a message from a senior officer living down the road and I went across to see him. He also told me that I would most likely be posted to his state (Delta) as a Military Administrator. I had some discussions with him and told him that I would wait for the announcement and I returned to my residence.

I was worried due to the information from my wife about the stream of callers in my absence. I drove out to visit a friend nearby. The Nigerian Television Authority news at 2100 hours was in progress and the news of the appointments of Military Administrators was released. My name was not mentioned. My coursemate at NDA Captain J Kalu-Igboamah was announced as Military Administrator of Adamawa State. Some years later while I was a Directing Staff at National War College, I was chanced to know why I was abruptly dropped. This would be highlighted later.

General AA Abubakar stuck to his short transition program of about 11 months. It was still a rushed transition that did not allow for proper scrutiny of the background of politicians. The Head of State appreciated the damage done by prolonged military involvement in political governance. He had commanded the ceremonial parade on 01 October 1979 when General Olusegun O Obasanjo handed over to Alhaji Shehu Shagari as President, Commander-in-Chief. I was at Tafawa Balewa Square, Lagos, and an elated spectator of history unfolding with the new National Anthem adding its inspiration. He was destined as Head of State to hand over to a democratically elected Chief Olusegun O Obasanjo GCFR on 29 May 1999 at Eagle Square, Abuja. General AA Abubakar had been the Commandant, National War College. His purely military appointments throughout his career till he became a Head of State in June 1998 served Nigeria well as he inspired trust with the short transition. I looked forward to the AFN returning to professional duties only.

The ASND asked me to determine specifications for the refit of NNS AMBE and give the cost estimate. I told him that I would rely on the quotations from the various manufacturers in Europe to avoid unnecessary inflation of costs. The job was carried out with my staff with enough information at the FMC and NHQ regarding quotations from the various equipment manufacturers. The cost was high for the jobs specified. I submitted the report to the ASND and the cost was outrightly rejected because he expected a much lower cost. I gave him a detailed specification of the jobs to be done considering the state of the ship. I advised the ASND to take his time and determine which job could be taken off and still achieve the objectives of the refit to make the ship operational.

This scrutiny took some days and I was called and informed that nothing could be taken off the job specifications. I advised the ASND that the costs should be denominated in US Dollars, British Pounds, and Naira as reflected in the quotation sources. The estimates were denominated based on the manufacturers' quotations and local content of the jobs to be done. I emphasised the need to allow the NHQ to place orders directly with the manufacturers while the Naira component was released to the NND. The estimates became very attractive and easily defended. It scaled through the NHQ and got the Head of State's approval.

Rear Admiral J Ayinla was appointed as the new CNS and promoted to the rank of Vice-Admiral. On 08 September 1998, I was appointed to the NHQ as Director of Marine Engineering. This was my first appointment at the NHQ and I reported the same day after handing over to my successor at the NND. The Chief of Fleet Support, the Head of Engineering in NN was Rear Admiral Peter Jerome who had been my Head of Department onboard NNS ARADU when I was the Assistant Marine Engineer Officer in 1984, the time I had difficulties taking up my appointment in Italy as Federal Government Chief Delegate at Intermarine Shipyard, Sarzana.

I settled down quickly in a tight office for the Director, Marine Engineering (DME) at the NHQ. The Chief of Logistics office was next door to my office and the opposite wing of the same floor was occupied by the Chief of Personnel while the Chief of Fleet Support my boss was opposite my office. The Directors and staff officers of the three branches shared tight office spaces. The NHQ offices at Moloney Street, Ministry of Defence building were small. I settled down to work and had a summary of the upkeep requirements of the warships in the NN Fleet. This was circulated at the NHQ for information and comments to improve on the information contained. I also gave priority to the issue of onboard technical department reorganization to reflect the demands of modern technology which the NN had neglected for about two decades.

I was assigned to appoint technical officers and liaison with the Chief of Personnel for implementation after clearing with the Chief of Fleet Support at a departmental meeting with the other directors of the Branch. I was the most senior Director of the Engineering Branch at NHQ. The watchkeeping training programme for officers under training was defined and a Nigerian Navy Order was promulgated.

Rear Admiral VK Ombu was the Chief of Plans (CPLANS) and I hardly had interaction with him at NHQ though we had always had a very cordial relationship. I was busy attending to a matter when I noticed that an officer was standing at the door and I thought a departmental officer was deciding whether to come in or not. I did not look up to identify the officer as I was occupied with what I was doing. The CPLANS gave a familiar interruptive gesture with an authoritative demand for my attention. I raised my head to see the CPLANS standing at the door. I sprang to my feet and greeted him respectfully. The Admiral had come to a Captain and I asked him what I could do for him. He informed me that since he had been at the NHQ he had not seen a comprehensive yet so compact a summary of the state of the NN warships in the Fleet and containing the actions to be taken to solve their major problems. He commended my efforts and told me that those two pages were the only planning documents he had laid his hands on as the CPLANS and he would rely on me to do updating of the document for his attention. I was delighted with the Rear Admiral and CPLANS's visit. I updated it and handed it over to him the following day.

I had discussions with the COP, Rear Admiral OO Joseph regarding the training of Principal Warfare Officers at NNS ONURA at Onne, Port Harcourt. I had pushed through the idea to establish the Action Speed Tactical Trainer (ASTT) while at NAVTRAC and the plan was to have some Weapon Engineering Officers train with the other officers nominated for the course.

I nominated Lieutenant Commander MI Danladi and Lieutenant Commander IN Lekwauwa both Weapon Engineer Officers and a signal was released listing the members of the class to report for training. I received a report that the Seamen officers on the course protested that the course was for them only and would not allow the Weapon Engineer Officers to be with them. I took it up with the COP and I never knew why he could not order the CO, NNS ONURA as of 1998 to leave the officers to attend the course as ordered in the signal from the NHQ.

I kept in touch with the officers and as they were being harassed and not allowed on the course, I told the COP that the officers should be ordered to return to their units. This was the last time I had anything to do with the facility at NNS ONURA. Interestingly, officers who understood the computerised facilities for the training were not allowed into the exclusive kingdom of the Seaman or Executive branch officers. Did they know the origin and application of the names they allocated to themselves and used as cult symbols? The plans for Advanced Warfare Officers training were never implemented. The NN was never prepared to make the much needed changes to its organisation for efficient management of modern warships in its inventory despite all the information from RN at its disposal.

I undertook a pending visit to ECOMOG to carry out some interventions on NN warships in Liberia and Sierra Leone. The ships in the two countries needed urgent maintenance and deployment. My predecessor had already done all groundwork. I was briefed by COFS. Staff Officer Weapon Engineering, Commander TJ Lokoson travelled with me. We flew to Monrovia in C130 aircraft from Nigeria Air Force (NAF) Base, Ikeja. As the most senior officer on the flight, I was allowed a space that was part of the cockpit. The reception party at the airport was up to the task; all the items were offloaded and vehicles were lined up to move them to locations. The drive to Monrovia city showed the scars of the ongoing war.

At Monrovia harbour where the NN warships were berthed, I was received and introduced to the setup and had a meeting with the ECOMOG Force Commander, Major General T Shelpidi. The relationship between the ECOMOG Force Commander and Mr Charles Taylor, the leader of the anti-government forces now in control, was not cordial. The Naval Component Commander was Captain SA Timson with Colonel GO Eburu, my coursemate at the NDA, as the Staff Officer in charge of logistics at ECOMOG HQ. After the brief meetings with the hierarchy, I started work immediately in an office space on the upper troop deck of NNS AMBE. I worked out a plan for interventions with Commander TJ Lokoson and the ships' staff. We worked until quite late into the night. I was informed that the situation in the city had deteriorated and the accommodation arranged for us was in a guest house in a relatively safe zone. I was told that I could either sleep on board or risk fighting our way through the city to the guest house. I decided to go to the guest house as a combat-ready escort was on standby. The drive through the city was via all checkpoints and the dangerous spots to the guest house. The situation was still quite tense and sleep was the least of my worries. It was the early hours of the morning.

After breakfast the next morning, we set off for the ships and received reports of the deployment of the two FAC to sea for naval gunfire support and security operation not long after our departure. The Force Commander was awake throughout the night taking charge. I was briefed on the situation and we had to alter our plan as we had to wait for the ships deployed to return to base. The journey to Sierra Leone had to be cancelled given the heightened tension and insecurity. The ships in Sierra Leone sent in their operational states and had a telephone conference with the COs. There were arrangements to ensure that the same allocation of resources was made to them and those requiring attention from NHQ were compiled for a follow-up. The ships had suffered a poor supply of lubricating oils and I ordered changes after flushing the sludge that looked more like coal tar. I wondered why some states in Nigeria were complaining of a shortage of coal tar for road construction when NN warships produced the commodity.

The embarrassing general state of NNS AMBE needed urgent attention in Lagos and I told the Naval Component Commander that on return to Lagos, approval would be sought to get the ship back to Lagos. There had been some international organisations in Monrovia offering some assistance for the stabilization of Liberia and it was simply a pathetic show to have such a battle-weary warship on display.

The journey back to Lagos was tortuous. There was no C130 for a direct flight to Lagos. We took a commercial flight to Accra, Ghana, for a connecting flight to Lagos. On return to the NHQ, I briefed the COFS and his principal staff officers and focused on the critical state of the warships and the need to immediately order the recall of NNS AMBE and subsequent rotation of the other ships. I also highlighted the damages I noticed as a result of the state of lubricating oils in the machinery onboard.

NNS AMBE was recalled home for a refit programme. The ship had served well in all stages of ECOMOG operation from a very difficult beginning till now and I had been involved in all of her deployments. I was glad to be part of the decision to get NNS AMBE back home for well-deserved attention. The actions for other ships were followed up in addition to the routine support that was being given.

The setup at the NHQ changed from May 29, 1999, with the swearing-in of a new President, Commander-in-Chief of the Armed Forces, Chief Olusegun O Obasanjo. Rear Admiral VK Ombu was promoted to Vice-Admiral on appointment as the new CNS. The Armed Forces received a shock with the retirement of all officers who had held political appointments in the previous military administrations.

The appointment of the new CNS also meant some officers senior to him at NHQ would have to retire. The technical department at NHQ had Rear Admiral O Dada replacing Rear Admiral P Jerome as COFS and I had to hold the fort as Acting COFS to the new CNS before the appointment of the new COFS took effect. The new CNS had interacted with me on several occasions in the past and there was no problem getting used to him. I had to brief him on the department as he took office and had routine briefs and advice that made my appearance frequent in his office.

I was due for the next National War College course but when the signal nominating officers for the course was released, I was not on the list. Some officers junior to me and not yet due for promotion were nominated for the course and one was nominated for a similar course abroad. I had settled into the routine of acting COFS and went to brief the CNS on an issue he called me over to his office to discuss. The discussion was a bit tense as I noticed he was unusually uneasy and I thought it was some matters of office weighing on him and I was glad to complete the discussion and leave on a good note. I was heading for the exit door when he called me back and told me that he removed my name from the list for the National War College course because he wanted me to hold on as acting COFS to assist him at the NHQ. I told him that I had no objection and was happy to be of use at the NHQ at the critical moment of transition and his settling in as CNS. Thank you, sir, CNS, for the recognition, I thought.

The new government wanted more platforms for inshore operations to check illegal oil bunkering in the Niger Delta area. A deadline was given for the presentation of a proposal to the President, Commander-in-Chief of the Armed Forces who directed that the NN should be in direct contact with equipment manufacturers for a fair deal. This was a strong and decisive strategic leadership direction and I was inspired by this policy. I established a direct link to all the operational bases where the inshore patrol boats were based for updates on the information I got from documents at NHQ as regards their defects status. Thereafter, I established with my staff the scope of the works that had to be carried out.

There would be a need for new engines for propulsion and electric power generation and major hull repairs. The weapons and other installations onboard had minor intervention requirements. The requirements were determined including the availability of some specialist personnel from the engine manufacturers for major installations works. Total requirements and costing were based on directly dealing with the equipment manufacturers that I had access to under existing policy and directives. The compilations were finalised and after going through the NHQ scrutiny it was submitted to the President, Commander-in-Chief who did not waste much time in approving it. The total cost was in US Dollars denomination as the major equipment manufacturers were foreign and had been directly involved. The next step was to pursue the release of the approved fund of well over fifty million dollars.

I was later tasked with the preparation of the Operations Branch Budget and it was a rare opportunity. I had a great relationship with the Chief of Operations, Rear Admiral E Okpo and he directed his staff officers to be members of my committee for the budget proposals. It was a very rewarding and refreshing exercise. All aspects of naval operations were to be covered and this led to the invitation of officers from various departments for professional inputs. The output from this committee work attracted more responsibility and I was sucked into the NN 2000 fiscal year budget preparation. The summary of NN warships upkeep requirements I had compiled and which the CNS as the CPLANS had commended was the main focus for NN budgeting.

I had a chance to break the cautious approach to budgeting that allowed detailed projections without fear of it being considered outrageous. I reached out to Deputy Defence Adviser in London Commander (later Rear Admiral) BA Raji for information on costs related to new warships and major equipment for comparative analysis. There was a lot of data collected and which were used to defend the proposals. The requirements were well articulated and easy to appreciate the state of NN warships. There was the issue of poor budget releases but the NN presentation was focused on the President's priority for naval presence to checkmate illegal bunkering and crude oil theft. I was absorbed into the NN team for the various stages of budget defence. I had much work to do which exposed me to the intrigues of budget preparations and defence. I was initially confronted with a lack of details in the determination of requirements which made a defence of proposals difficult. Funding appropriation and inadequate release issues tended to make budgeting unrealistic as most essential requirements were not properly determined. This cycle is repeated yearly.

When I was through with the budget defence at the Ministry of Defence, I was appointed a member of the Ministry of Defence Committee including other representatives of the Armed Forces to visit all major military establishments within the country with the members of the Senate and House of Representative Committees on Defence. The visits were to acquaint the members of the National Assembly with the state of the Armed Forces and most importantly to foster cordial relationships with the civilian authority after long years of military rule. The whole of November 1999 was devoted to the exercise and I attended several NN briefings to prepare for the task ahead.

I was invited to deliver a paper on warship project management at the First International Conference on Engineering Design at Sheraton Hotel, Abuja. There was a good turn out and my paper was well received. The discussion session focused on my submission that despite their acquiring good certificates, there had been no quality competencies reflected and applied in solving Nigeria's problems by Nigerian engineers. I argued that engineers dominated certain key government institutions that had failed to deliver on their mandates. The audience was stunned at being forced to come to terms with reality. I was co-opted into the secretariat committee to draft the communique and the final report.

The committee work revealed a member who showed reluctance to support the promotion of Nigerian industries. The issue of Nigerian industries manufacturing hand pumps for water supply in the rural areas was discussed and the preference for importation from countries of Asia came to the fore. The Nigeria Foundries Limited at Ilupeju in Lagos was certified as meeting international standards but was not supported by government policies. The committee member who was against the patronage of the Nigerian industries confessed that he was part of the decision-making process while serving in the Presidency and could not explain the reasons for the decision. I completed the communique with the team and left the committee because I did not want to go into unnecessary discussions about how Nigerian industries were being sabotaged by Nigerians in the Presidency to favour foreign industries despite the superiority of products as in the case of the industry at Ilupeju.

The CNS came to Abuja on the evening of the day the conference ended. I received on his behalf a present from the conference organisers and wanted his aide to give it to him. But I was advised to see the CNS and give him the present as well as brief him on the conference. I saw him and gave him the present and also briefed him. As I was about to leave, he told me that he had approved my appointment to Eastern Naval Command (ENC) as Command Technical Officer. This was the same appointment I had held at Western Naval Command and Naval Training Command.

The CNS insisted that he wanted my opinion about my appointment to Eastern Naval Command. I said that I would not like to comment on my new appointment as it had become his order by a signal in the public domain. I further explained that as I was the one involved it was not proper for me to make any comments.

He told me that he had always relied on my opinions because I was always very objective in my discussions with him and he trusted my judgement. I gave him a rundown on my appointments. The CNS said that he had been wrongly advised with the wrong information to post me out of the NHQ. I asked him not to change or reverse the appointment to avoid setting a precedent that could become a problem for him. I assured him that in the past three and half months I had done enough to stabilize the Engineering Branch at NHQ.

Back at the NHQ, the CPLANS, Rear Admiral P Ebhaleme, briefed me on the meetings at MOD. He told me that the assignment would extend beyond November and I was tempted by him to ask for a reversal of the appointment to Eastern Naval Command to enable me to do a thorough job. I told the CPLANS that I would complete the assignment to his satisfaction after which I would immediately report as CTO at Calabar, the location of ENC HQ. I requested that the FOC ENC should be informed that I would report as soon as I completed the assignment to avoid any controversy.

The new COFS had forwarded my nomination in pencil (really insulting for me) as it had not gone through the normal departmental scrutiny, as I was responsible for forwarding the final list to the Personnel Branch, a meeting was held and I had to do the corrective staff work and normalise my appointment. It was rushed in my twenty-four hours absence for reasons I would not like to subject to speculative discussions and it was related to the impending release of millions of dollars that I had worked to secure the approval of the President, Commander-in-Chief. It was not normal and the Personnel Branch was told I was not wanted at the NHQ by the new Engineering Branch head.

NNS AMBE refit proposal which I initiated while I was GM Production at the NND had been approved by the President, Commander-in-Chief for implementation and the money for the refit of the inshore patrol craft for the operational bases was on the verge of being released. The NNO for the re-organizations of the onboard technical branch was promulgated and the monitoring of implementation was essential. This, I had to leave for my reliever. I concentrated on preparations for the National Assembly assignment after handing over to Captain A Ademoluti on 25 October 1999 and used my residence as an office for the preparation of the draft briefing papers. I used the CPLANS Secretariat to produce all documents and briefs I needed for the National Assembly assignment.

The MOD briefing was well attended by members of the team. There were military officers senior to me and the MOD personnel. It was revealed that the team would first take all the Members of the House Committee on Defence for the first week between 02-07 November 1999 and thereafter the Members of the Senate Committee on Defence also for the period 11-16 November 1999. The General Officers Commanding (GOCs), FOCs, and Air Officers Commanding (AOCs) were informed to provide some aspects of logistics and reception for the guided tours.

The means of transport between locations was by NAF C130. The motor vehicles to be used for the inspections within commands would be the responsibility of the commanders on the spot. The use of C130 did not go down well with most of the officers and at the subsequent meetings, all senior officers opted out and I became the most senior Armed Forces officer that followed the two committees of the National Assembly on Defence. I had to coordinate all the inspections and inputs of the Army, Navy, and Air Force and present their cases as best as I could. I had to answer many of the questions concerning the neglect of the military despite the long years of the institution's involvement in governance.

The Chairman of the House Committee of Defence was Senator Adolf Wabara and Vice-Chairman was Senator Ali Modu Sherif. Some of the Senators who were members were Senator A T Ahmed, Senator

Arthur Nzeribe, and Senator Bello Maitama Yusuf, and ten others. The House of Representative Committee on Defence Chairman was Hon Hassan K Yabo and the Vice-Chairman was Hon Major D Ngadda and twenty-six members. The tour revealed the pathetic state of major military platforms and infrastructure including barracks. The military was abandoned by the military governments and needed urgent attention. It was unbelievable. It was observed that over the years of prolonged military rule extensive damage was done to the assets of the Nigeria Army, Navy, and Air Force. The members of the National Assembly Committees were disappointed and surprised that the military could visit such devastation on itself. The inadequate accommodation, obsolete and unserviceable military hardware and failed or abandoned projects littered the military landscape. It was observed that the military institution has no regard for transparency and accountability despite the huge military expenditures over the years as there was nothing on the ground to justify the expenditures.

The role of the Nigerian Navy was given emphasis based on the mandate I was handed and the relevance of the service to the economy was etched in the minds of the members of the Committees. The committees visited facilities and projects of the three services in Jos, Bauchi, Kano, Kaduna, Kainji, Makurdi, Lagos, Calabar, IBAKA, Port Harcourt, Bonny, and Enugu. The way forward articulated in the final press release highlighted a framework of policies and practices for effective monitoring of defence budget and expenditures.

I submitted my final report to the NHQ and tidied up all related administrative matters and by the first week of December 1999, I reported for duty as the CTO ENC. I had coordinated and contributed to the formulation and defence of the NN budget for the fiscal year 2000 and done a satisfactory job establishing a good working relationship between the National Assembly and the NN.

The FOC ENC was Commodore FE Agbiti who was known to me when he was the Principal Warfare Officer onboard the NNS ARADU when I was appointed on board in 1983 on return from my course at RNEC. He had an excellent work ethic and it was easy for me to settle into routine under his command. It was hard, for me to come to terms with being given the same type of appointment for the third time and serving in all three commands that are WNC, ENC, and NAVTRAC. The FOC ENC had the annual end of year sea exercise at advanced stages of planning and I keyed into the process. The FOC was at sea with the ships of the Eastern Fleet and I was happy to be at sea with him for two days during the highly successful exercise. The end of the year ceremonial sunset was held after the sea exercise and I was released to go to Lagos and pursue some logistics items for the Command. I was allowed enough time to spend the Christmas and New Year holidays with my family in Lagos.

I got many spare parts for the ships of Eastern Fleet and arranged transportation to Calabar and on my return to base after the New Year holidays, I was refreshed to embark on ship maintenance tasks. There were other priorities such as the construction of a link road between the Ibaka Naval Base and the Barrack under construction. I had no staff car or any personal transport and had to rely on officers for my movement.

Calabar had a young civilian Governor, Donald Duke. As I trekked the streets of Calabar, I noticed the Governor's emphasis on the water supply system for Calabar. The execution of the works related to pipe laying was impressive as well as other constructions for housing and road maintenance. This was one of the state capitals in Nigeria in which I had witnessed within five months an impressive execution of infrastructural projects.

I received the sad news of the death of Dr David Saravanamuthu, my mother-in-law's brother, and the patriarch of the Saravanamuthu family. My second son was named after him. We linked up with the family and shared the moment of grief with them. His widow Ms Rosalind Oh (Mrs Rosalind Saravanamuthu) would continue to show her love and affection to my family in the years ahead together with her children Mr Soorya, Dr Suditi, and Dr Sujana.

The USA Deputy Force Commander Europe Rear Admiral Michael Harris was scheduled to visit ENC. The FOC appointed me to handle the programme for the visit. The US Embassy in Lagos sent in a team led by the Air Attache Lieutenant Colonel Patricia K. Coomber to discuss the programme of the visit.

The Admiral arrived in Calabar in his dedicated command aircraft. The FOC led the reception team. The brief airport ceremony was memorable and we drove Admiral Michael Harris, accompanied by FOC, on a tour of the command. My boss FOC ENC was pleased with my handling of all matters related to the visit.

CHAPTER FIFTEEN

On Duty Post as a Student in Washington DC

In the second week of May 2000, I was informed of my nomination for a course at National Defense University, Washington DC that I initially thought was strange. I was nominated to attend the Industrial College of the Armed Forces (ICAF), renamed Eisenhower School (ES), and I was told that the NN was trying to find out from the Deputy Defence Adviser (Navy) in Washington whether the course was equivalent to a War College standard.

I was later told the following week that the course was equivalent to a War College and Brigadier General (later General and Chief of Defence Staff) Martin Luther Agwai was doing the same course for his comparative War College course experience. He had completed the National War College course in Nigeria. I would be the first NN officer to be nominated to go to the National Defense University. I was in for another round of Manadon hate treatment by NN officers both seniors and juniors for being a pioneer again.

I was late going for my War College course but there were indications that some officers felt that I should not be promoted while on the course. The NN assigned me a duty post at the university and my job description was 'Student' and the duration was one year. I was asked to report to the NHQ Lagos on 15 May 200 and start my preparations to travel by early June 2000; the course would start in late June 2000. I received a fat brown envelope addressed to me from the NHQ. The contents were comprehensive documentation on National Defense University and its Industrial College of the Armed Forces, Fort McNair, Washington DC. The NHQ had gone through the brown envelope information pack sent to me and was satisfied that the course at Industrial College of the Armed Forces (ICAF) I had been nominated to attend was of the same standard as the War College.

The College had its name changed to Eisenhower School for National Security and Resource Strategy in 2012. This would have solved the initial misconceptions. I prepared and left the ENC HQ to return to Lagos.

I briefed my wife with the scanty details I had and visited my son Daniel in a hostel near the University of Lagos where he was in his first year as a mechanical engineering undergraduate. I also visited David and Diana at the King's College and Queen's College respectively and told them that I would be away for one year. I promised them that I would arrange for them to visit me in the US. They came home for the weekend to have family photographs for an introduction at the University/College. This would be the first time that I would be posted out of the country and would not be with my family. My wife, David, Diana, and Augustine would visit in August during the official family introductory programme. Daniel was programmed for October when the University of Lagos calendar allowed.

I prepared to give a presentation on Nigeria and the scope given involved economic, social, and political developments in the country. Nigeria had just transited from a prolonged period of military rule to democracy. I bought some books on the recommended reading lists and more for the country presentation. I found that most Nigerian authors wrote from their tribal/ethnic and other perspectives. To have a balanced view, I made a wide selection of titles one of which was a book titled 'We Are All Guilty-The Nigerian Crisis' by G.Oka Orewa. I was impressed by the compressive coverage based on the various interest groups in charge of national institutions/establishments and how, despite their varied tribal/ethnic and religious compositions, they had all been involved in causing the problems Nigeria was suffering. I returned the rest as the 215-page book was comprehensive enough in dealing with the Nigerian crisis and those responsible: we are all guilty. I sourced some publications from the National Bureau of Statistics. A visit to the National Museum near Tafawa Balewa Square provided additional material and I was satisfied that I had more than enough materials for a presentation on Nigeria before an international audience. Lieutenant Colonel Patricia K. Coomber who easily recognised me as the officer who organised the programme for the visit of the USA Admiral to Calabar, received me at the USA Embassy when I went for my visa. I was told that I would be given a visa but a slight modification would be made for my family to get their visa at a later date. I understood why and accepted the inconveniences.

I concluded my arrangements and left Lagos by British Airways night flight on 10 June 2000 for London where I did the essential runs with the assistance of the office of Defence Adviser. I got the two NN outfitters, Marvelfairs of North West area and, Gieves and Hawkes of Savile Row in the Mayfair area of London for some specified uniform items. I visited my favourite bookshop, Foyles, and bought some publications.

I left London on 13 June 2000 for Dulles Airport and was received on arrival by the Deputy Defence Adviser (Navy) Commander George Alily. I was booked into the Holiday Inn near the Catholic Cathedral in central Washington DC. I was received by the Defence Adviser, Group Captain Jon Odey (later Air Vice Marshall). Both the Defence Adviser and the Deputy Defence Adviser briefed me about the College and the University set up.

Brigadier General ML Agwai (promoted Major General but not yet decorated) had passed out of the course in 2000 a few days before my arrival and he had performed excellently. I met him at his residence with Commander Alily at Marina View Towers near the University. I got an introductory brief on what to expect. He advised me to focus on being myself and keep up with the hectic pace. Gen Agwai was packing and would be leaving in the next few days.

I reported on 20 June 2000 at the National Defense College, Room 124 of Eisenhower Building. I had a driver and vehicle for a few days while waiting for the one the NN provided. It would be passed on to me by the NN officer who had just graduated from Naval War College at Rhode Island.

The Naval Attache, Commander G Alily had to travel to Rhode Island for the graduation of Captain N Bakare at the Naval War College. My friend Captain Fred Stappen of the German Navy was also graduating and I had been in touch with him before I left Lagos. I sent contact details to him through the Naval Attache as I was not yet connected by telephone. He would be getting in touch through the Naval Attache. During my courtesy call on General ML Agwai, I expressed interest in having a flat in the same complex as it was very close to the National Defense University. I rented a spacious one-bedroom corner unit.

I was busy assembling the bookshelves in my flat a few days after I had a telephone connection when Fred and Mair rang to tell me they were in the vicinity of the Marina View Towers. It was an exciting reunion; they were my first guests in the flat. Fred joined me on the floor to assemble the two bookshelves. It was like our RNEC Manadon days and here we were, together in Washington, setting up my furniture. We had lunch at their favourite restaurant. Fred had served for three years at Norfolk on a joint missile project with the US Navy and lived in the Washington area. They showed me the old Washington area and other nice places I could find good restaurants. Friedhelm had always taken me as his little brother he must care for. Mair was full of her usual sweet Welsh charms and smiles. It was a great day and it was sad we had to part again as they returned to Rhode Island to prepare for their final departure from the US.

The International Fellows Programme of the National Defense University was for foreign students only drawn mainly from the Industrial College of the Armed Forces (ICAF) and National War College. There were thirty-two students for this programme that would involve tours and studies of the US government at all levels and selected institutions. The ICAF programme had two streams for a Master of Science Degree and Diploma in National Security and Resource Strategy. The Research Fellow programme was an option for eight electives. A handful of students were admitted to the Research Fellows programme. The first week of reporting was devoted to administration and familiarisation with the University and the College routines.

General ML Agwai had left a sterling record at ICAF and there was a demand from the National War College for me to switch over and do my course there. I was informed that General ML Agwai had left too big a shoe that could not be filled. I reminded myself that I was not in competition with anyone but myself. I had nothing to worry about filling any big shoes someone left behind. I was adamant and made it clear that I would not switch to National War College.

A police constable lectured us and demonstrated how to behave on being stopped by the police. There was an introductory session with the other International Fellows at which we showed our family photographs. A team from West Point Military Academy conducted a refresher course on the use of the English language. An essay topic was given to test skills and this was used to assess our capabilities as might be required to fit us in for the various programmes. Having an MSc degree already from RNEC did not exempt me from going through all assessments required to judge if I qualified for the ICAF MSc program. The test for all those who passed the initial screening of the West Point Team was conducted at George Mason University, Washington DC.

I was glad I made the cut-off mark but I was not impressed with my overall performance. As we returned to the NDU, we compared notes regarding our chances and I told my colleagues that I nearly missed the cut-off mark; they could not believe me. I had to improve on my computer interactive skills, my draw back at the test, and each IF was issued a laptop for the course and assisted to get acquainted with the facilities available. The US students joined us after the introductory course programme.

The Industrial College of the Armed Forces (Eisenhower School) was established in 1924. According to Bernard Baruch, Chairman of War Industries Board WW1: "I want to establish a little school….to preserve experience and keep in touch with the industry." This quote is displayed in the College auditorium. It was established for effective coordination or focus on procurement for war and procedures for a nation-state mobilization for war. Major Dwight D Eisenhower graduated from the College in 1933 and later served on the faculty. It was an Army Industrial College and in 1946 the school was named Industrial College of the Armed Forces (ICAF) and moved to Fort McNair near the National War College founded about the same time as the movement.

In 1948, the College (ICAF) was removed from the Army and designated a joint College under the Joint Chiefs of Staff. The College moved in 1960 to the present Eisenhower Hall that was newly constructed. The College evolved with time to focus on educating leaders on managing logistics resources. In 1976, the National Defense University was established. In furtherance of the call in the Goldwater-Nichols Defense Reorganization Act of 1986 for increased attention to joint military education. In 1993, the College was authorized by Congress through legislation to award MSc degree in national security and resource strategy. In 2012, the College was renamed Dwight D. Eisenhower School for National Security and Resource Strategy and is now commonly known as The Eisenhower School.

The official mission is to "Prepare selected military officers and civilians for strategic leadership and success in developing our security strategy and in evaluating, marshalling, and managing resources in the execution of that strategy." The academic departments at the School are Defense Strategy and Resourcing, National Security and Economic Policy, National Security and Industrial Base, and Strategic Leadership. (School sources and Wikipedia). The curriculum focuses on the resource components of national security necessitating a thorough understanding of national security strategy development. I had to understand this background to appreciate the unique institution I was attending and the rare opportunities I had for the benefit of Nigeria.

I was assigned to Seminar 16 group and the members reflected a diversity of military arms and civilians from agencies. The Seminar Leader was Ms Earnestine Ballard, an African-American lady who effectively kept the Seminar together with the motto: "We are not animals." Indeed, we were quite thoughtful and had a wonderful seminar spirit.

I was the only International Fellow in Seminar 16. I made my country presentation to this group and the Faculty team handling the seminar. The presentation was well received and generated questions on the impact of corruption on the economy, politics (1999 general election), and Nigeria's military readiness. I did not address the question of military readiness to the satisfaction of the Professor of Regional Security Studies and obviously, the audience noticed this shortcoming and I was not left off the hook.

The Professor sent me an email directing me to visit a website which I did immediately and there was more information on the pathetic state of Nigerian Armed Forces assets. The NNS ARADU, the NN Flag Ship was presented in very real terms with up-to-date information including that it has not gone to sea for a very long time and was being used as a brothel by the NN personnel. The next moment I saw the Professor, he asked me if had visited the website and I told him I had. I was then cautioned in very friendly terms that there was hardly any information that could be hidden in any situation worldwide. I was advised to always tell it as it was as the means exists to check all facts. It reminded me of a statement a Nigerian President made on handing over to his successor. He said that the only secret that could be kept in modern times is what is retained in the head and which has not been uttered or written. This was a very important and useful experience for me.

I met the requirements for the MSc programme and was confirmed and accepted after appearing before a board which comprised of staff from other Colleges at the university and the National Institute for Policy and Strategic Studies. I had decided to look into military planning which had been a major problem for the NN. The selection of electives and the two-term papers to be presented one for each term would not allow me to satisfactorily treat the problem. I had the option of being admitted to the Research Fellow programme which would allow me to concentrate on the topic of planning and the future of the NN. I had some discussions with the University Director of Research Professor Joseph Goldberg. He put up a team of supervisors led by Colonel James E. Toth USMC (Ret). The members of the team were Professor Joseph Goldberg, Professor Gerry Abbot, and Captain Ralph Janikowsky, USN. Colonel James E Toth was the Chair of Military Logistics and Mobilization. I was accepted as a Research Fellow after defending my proposals before them.

The courses set up for me consisted of the IF, Research Fellow, and the MSc programmes. The IF programme involved travels to many places around the USA during which we were shown how the US system of government works. The Research Fellow programme was a study project alternative to a group of electives and involved some interviews and data collection from British, Israeli, Indian, and Nigerian embassies. I had access to the German and Japanese sources from the officers on the IF programme: Colonel Freers Werner (later General and Chief of Defence Staff) and Captain Shinichi Tokumaru (later Rear Admiral) respectively.

Mr Robert Kohn, State Department Chair at NDU, was my Faculty Advisor who kept a tab on my overall performance. He was a fine diplomat. The first semester courses were to enable us to craft a national security strategy while the second term had a different Seminar composition for the resource aspects termed resourcing the national security strategy.

The interactions at the University revealed a diversity of experts in various fields that one could easily engage in formal and informal sessions. The formal sessions were seminar lectures. There were central lectures in Eisenhower's main hall for ICAF external lecturers and common internal lectures. Information dissemination was superb. I felt I was in a world where nothing failed.

We had social programmes for interactions with the administrative and faculty staff. There were also links to organisations that facilitated interactions with communities outside the NDU. The IFs each had a prominent US citizen attached to him for mentoring and guidance. I was invited to some African-American events and one of them profoundly impressed me. It was a huge social event that showed how the community was struggling to be relevant with the assistance of those who had succeeded and were offering scholarships and mentoring to young people. It was also to celebrate successful African-Americans who told stories of their struggles to inspire others to realise their dreams.

The introductory IF family events were programmed for August 2000. This suited me because my children were on holiday during the period. The important role of the family in the balanced development of military personnel is recognised in the entire programme and provisions were adequately integrated. David and Diana arrived while I was on an IF visit programme out of Washington DC. They were received and accommodated by the Defence Adviser at his official residence for two days. On my arrival back in Washington, my wife and Augustine arrived.

I took them on a family group tour of historic sites in Washington which ended with a group photograph of the IFs and their families on the Washington Mall. My wife and the children returned home in the first week of September 2000. Daniel arrived a few weeks later and stayed with me for a month. He followed me on IFs' visit to the Luray Caverns in Virginia Shenandoah Valley which is an active cave with beautiful scenic formations.

The visits to military establishments and other government departments took us to Silicon Valley in California, Strategic Command (Cheyenne Mountain Range Command facility), Space Command, Sikorsky Helicopter factory, Lockheed Martin, New Mexico Nuclear facility, Cape Canaveral, Johnson, and Kennedy Space Centers. These showed us the very complex structures and the quality personnel committed to defence and security of the USA and its allies. We learnt much about how the USA was formed through visits to selected cities and states such as Chicago, St Louis, Atlanta (home of CNN), Las Vegas, New Mexico, Kalispel in Montana, California, Tennessee, Virginia, Maine, Yale, Stanford, Boston, and others.

The facilities at Johnson and Kennedy Space Center, which is the NASA, at Houston and Florida showed the astonishing American commitment to the development and preparation of human beings and systems to accomplish very dangerous and complex missions for the benefit of mankind. We met and had a warm handshake with the Commander of Space Shuttle Mission STS-92, Colonel Brian Duffy of (USAF) at the Mission Control Center that was sealed with a group photograph. I saw the interior of the Mission Control Centre and it reinforced my belief that the human spirit imbued with zeal for adventure and risk into the unknown surely succeeds beyond expectations. The Cheyenne Mountain Range facility in Colorado gave us a glimpse into the US preparedness and readiness during the Cold War for nuclear warfare.

There were moments for an adventure such as following the trail to the bottom of the Grand Canyon and climbing back and the White Water Rafting in Montana. The White Water Rafting trip was dramatic for me as the raft I was in was tossed up into the air by the huge wave generated by the rapids. The raft was turned upside down in the air and I held on to lashing in a curled up position as we were advised. It landed on the turbulent waters and covered me. I remained inside, trapped but comfortable, and waited for rescue. I was declared missing and a search party focused on the area around the raft. A swimmer in the search party attempted a look under and asked for the occupant. I told him I was okay and I swam out and followed the kayak to the boat where the IF team had gathered.

The scope and depth of the IF programme were varied as it exposed us to various aspects of ways of life, governance at various levels, and an impressive range of industrial power of the USA. The Fall Semester lectures focused on comprehensive national security strategy studies and the Spring Semester lectures on national resourcing of the strategy and exercises. There were a series of external lectures and interactive sessions.

It was when President Chief Olusegun O. Obasanjo was travelling around the world pleading for debt forgiveness that an external lecturer said that African leaders had no strategic focus. I had to explain to the audience of over 500 students that Nigeria had for long viewed the debt trap as a hindrance to economic development. I said that the oil glut that affected the price of crude oil was beyond the control of the country.

The Research Fellow programme covered the two semesters. The Spring Semester covered Information Systems for Strategic Leaders, Economics of National Resource Allocation Strategy, Elements of National Power, Acquisition, Strategic Logistics, Strategic Mobilization, and Industry Study-Shipbuilding. I had a thrilling time with an elective course titled Economic Diplomacy and Economic Warfare. I thus understood how Nigeria's borrowing in the 1970s ballooned into the debt burden on the country for which Obasanjo sought debt relief.

The issue of prominent Nigerians running away from their country into exile was cited by the course officer in a one-on-one discussion. This discussion was related to the sanctions imposed on Nigeria. It was pointed out that the Nigerians in exile pressed for the sanctions. Some of the examples cited showed very biased reasons advanced by some Nigerians in exile and this made me remark that the US should repatriate such persons especially those who had held government appointments.

The IFs visited Memphis, Tennessee, on 4 August 2000. Elvis Presley's home in Memphis and his private aircraft have been turned into a museum which we toured. I was particularly emotional at Lorraine Motel Room 306 baloney where Martin Luther King Jnr was shot dead on 4 April 1968. The Hotel has been incarnated as The National Civil Rights Museum. Judge D'Army Bailey a Yale Law School graduate lawyer and a civil rights activist who contributed immensely to the incarnation followed us as we were conducted around the museum. I shed some tears as we saw the condition of the African-Americans since 1619 and how a lady in 1963 on the Washington Mall prompted King to "tell them we have a dream."

Bailey gave me his book titled- Mine Eyes Have Seen, which chronicles Dr Martin Luther King Jr's final journey that led to the fatal shooting. D'Army was a young man from Memphis and the Director of a Civil Rights organisation in New York that organised a team of lawyers to defend the African-American sanitation workers protesting in Memphis. This protest was responsible for Dr Martin Luther King's visit to Memphis. D'Army summed up the influence of the assassination of Dr Martin Luther King thus in his book: "I have come a long way, but Dr King's death was, in a very real sense, my own beginning."

On 07 November 2000, we departed Andrews Air Force Base for San Francisco, California. The 2000 Presidential Election results were being released and it was expected that as we settled on the Pacific coast, the last set of election results would come in and the winner would emerge. After dinner, we settled in the prepared viewing lounge for the final results of the Presidential Election. California and other West Coast states' results were announced and Al Gore put a call through to George Bush and later withdrew the gesture citing a problem in Florida State results that had issues.

It became evident that Florida results would not be ready for some time as crisis teams were dispatched by both the Democratic and Republican parties. I found out later that Chad was not only the name of a country in Africa. Indeed, hanging chads on voter papers was so much in Florida that a recount had to be undertaken to account for the chads that were still hanging. The drama would last for some weeks until the Supreme Court in Washington DC waded into the issue and ruled in favour of George Bush who was declared the winner of the election. The lesson learnt was that the US could also have problems with its presidential elections.

I was lucky to have a Republican party mentor from the People-to-People organisation throughout the course. I was invited to some exciting functions including the Presidential Inauguration party in January 2001. I was in my ceremonial mess dress with medals for the party. The Americans respect their military and I got a share of the honour. The political science lecturer at ICAF had interesting sessions with us throughout the election process and this enlightened me on political parties, primaries, strong institutions, and processes that ensure the stability of the country.

Our visit to the State of California showed us why the state is among the six leading economies in the world. The IFs visited Silicon Graphics Inc (SGI) considered the world's leader in high-performance computing technology and also dedicated to unleashing the power of human creativity. SGI is a major Defence/Intelligence industry. We appreciated the diversity of the California economy with visits to INTEL. We also visited San Francisco, the famous Alcatraz Island prison, and the Golden Gate Bridge.The visit to Stanford University enabled us to watch a football game between Stanford University Cardinal and Arizona State Sun Devils after a tailgate party hosted by Mr Bill Smythe, NDU Foundation Board Member. Why would a National Defense University need a foundation? I could see at NDU how efforts were made to attract resources from outside government and which are transparently utilized and efficiently accounted for. I saw government and private sector united in common goals of doing their best for the common good related to national defence and security.

I was having a good run and as the Fall Semester was coming to an end, there was some end of the year activities planned at the University. I contacted the Defence Attache at the Nigeria Embassy and I got to know that the promotion boards for the Armed Forces were in full swing. I was informed that I was being left out of the promotions in the NN because I was considered as a candidate on course and was not qualified to be promoted. I was advised to get a mid-term report and forward it to the NHQ so that I could be considered for promotion. I was aware of officers who felt that I have been having a good career run and tried to create problems for me. I recalled vividly that when Vice-Admiral JA Ayinla attended the National War College Course at Rhode Island, USA, as a Captain, he was promoted before leaving Nigeria and told that he would be decorated as Commodore on completion of the course.

I informed the Defence Attache that I would not ask the University to issue an interim report for the sake of promotion and if the promotion Board or the NHQ considered it necessary, the action should be more appropriately initiated without my knowledge. There were candidates of the Chief of Defence Staff from my home state including my junior who were a priority. I knew the intrigues involved. The promotion Board concluded its sitting and I was not promoted but my juniors were promoted to Commodore. The Nigeria Army promoted a Colonel at the US Army War College to Brigadier General while still at the College. This is the Nigerian Armed Forces standard I understand but would not be applied to me.

A Ministry of Defence team led by the Permanent Secretary visited Washington. Commodore AB Alabi of NDA Course 11 was on the team and reached out to me. I promised to see him for a possible tour of

Washington. He informed me that Air Vice-Marshal (AVM) J Wuyep was occupying the room opposite his at the hotel. I visited the AVM. I told him that I came to visit Commodore Alabi but that he was not in his room. He invited me into his room and we had a good chat. I told him that I wanted to take him and the Commodore out to see Washington. He dressed up and we left. I took him around the NDU and Eisenhower Hall housing ICAF. I later took him to my flat for a drink. I returned him to his hotel when I saw that it was getting late in the evening.

Two days after my meeting with AVM J Wuyep, I heard of his appointment as Chief of Air Staff of the Nigerian Air Force. I phoned to congratulate him and he told me to leave whatever I was doing and come over to be with him. I was highly honoured. We shared a bottle of special champagne. He told me that the Chief of Defence Staff Admiral Ibrahim Ogohi wanted him to return to Abuja immediately and prepare to take over. But he said he was on an important assignment in Washington DC and saw no reason to abandon the team and return to Abuja. Abuja should be patient for him to complete his assignment. As I left him, he told me that they would be winding up and he might not see me before returning to Abuja. He wished me well and gave me a gift in an envelope.

I received an unexpected visitor, - Lieutenant Commander AO Memuduaghan, a Weapon Engineer Officer - that baffled me. The Defence Attache informed him on his arrival in Washington on a private visit that I was too busy and it would not be right to disturb me by visiting me. He was desperate to see me. When he got to my flat, he said that he came purposely to Washington to see me and confirm that I had not been given a holiday abroad. He also wanted to know why other engineer officers of the NN were not considered for this "Industrial College" course. I had nothing to discuss with him. What was the business of a Lieutenant Commander with a Naval Captain's career development? I cannot remember how he left my flat after this audacious encounter. The Industrial College is not for engineers only. This act is a reflection of the indiscipline prevailing and how wrong perceptions are freely spread.

The Spring Semester subjected us to more travels as the Industrial Studies programme included visits to shipbuilding yards on the Pacific (San Diego) and Atlantic/ Gulf coasts (New Orleans, Savannah, and Maine). I had the opportunity to discuss propeller failures and it was considered unheard of that all the five blades on the hub of a major ship could come off and disappear in an incident. I also met some of the design and project staff that were sent to the Intermarine shipyard in

1987 for the US Osprey Class Minhunters project as the US cancelled its project with a European shipyard.

The shipbuilding industrial studies also enabled me to identify warship design and construction capabilities that could be utilized by the NN. My industrial paper was written on this issue and I recommended that NN should tap on the identified capabilities to develop its shipbuilding capacity. I considered this option to be better than buying very old ships from the US that was about 60 years old and considered too old and expensive to maintain. The process for the purchase was then in progress and was considered generally unfavourable in naval circles.

I was disappointed that the NN had degenerated from being a favoured customer of leading shipyards and defence industries in Europe and the USA to scavenging for old warships in reserve for scrapping. My course mates asked me why Nigeria was going for such old ships. I could not explain.

Deadlines for submissions were set for the Research Fellow project. I was swimming in about 170-page documents and still struggling to define what the finding was. The planning process had not been that easy to define. I had a session with Colonel Toth and he advised me to reduce the number of pages by merging two chapters which were causing me problems; this enabled me to understand that the most important aspect of the planning process was not a perfect plan but developing and applying quality manpower capable of taking an imperfect plan and improving on it to make it a perfect workable plan in execution.

The date for submitting my Research Fellow paper for assessment was set and I had been working on the final format for the past three weeks till disaster struck. I was putting finishing touches over the weekend starting from Friday evening as I was expected to hand it in to Colonel James E. Toth at 1400 hours the following Monday. I set to work after dinner and some rest.

By early Saturday morning, I had made good progress and was deciding on the requirements for the numbers of hard and soft copies to submit when I came across an item I had to cross-check in a heavy reference book for details. As I was searching for the relevant page, I did not realise that the book rested on the delete key. Unknown to me, it started deleting my paper which was over 150 pages. By the time I moved the heavy book aside, I saw a blank screen. I had lost three weeks of effort. I went into panic mode. I loaded the last disc content I had saved and luckily I had carefully arranged all the reference materials around my study table and could easily remember what I needed from each pack spread neatly around. I took a walk to the nearby Potomac River to clear my head. On return to my flat, I felt encouraged that I could make some order out of the chaos in my flat. I decided to work all through Saturday and Sunday to enable me to meet the deadline by noon on Monday with the hard and soft copies for submission on schedule.

I made appreciable progress working all through Saturday and paced myself to get some other assignments through as a form of relaxation. I went for Sunday Mass at the Basilica. I returned to my flat after Mass and set to work for the final push on the recovery of my research work. I made good progress and was happy that at least I had something to present and was now making improvements rather than ending the show.

The following day, I went for the morning lecture session, and immediately after that, I was in my study cubicle to put the finishing touches and produce copies. At 1400 hours I was still trying out some improvements and was worried that Col Toth would be waiting for me. I knew the closing time was approaching and I would like to print out a hard copy for him and submit the soft copies and other hard copies at designated points as directed.

Colonel Toth found me alone in the study room and asked me if I knew he had been waiting for me since 1400 hours. I apologised for keeping him waiting and explained to him the problems I had and the steps I had taken throughout the weekend to rectify the situation. I told him that I had almost completed the assignment and was getting ready to round up and get a hard copy to present to him. I told him that I was confident that I now had something better than what I lost. Colonel Toth comforted me and told me that I had never disappointed him. He left and I went on with meeting my target of getting all copies submitted before going home. Colonel James E. Toth was an inspiration and great mentor.

The submission of my Research Fellow paper marked a turning point for the final run to finish the course. I had a serious issue with my retention at NDU on the Faculty after graduation and I was not sure of what to expect. On realising the good professors involved in the scheme included Prof Col James E Toth, I told them to get permission from the Chief of Defence Staff. I was told that they wanted me on the faculty. I was informed by the middle of May that I would likely be posted to Defence Industries Corporation of Nigeria (DICON). I then told Col Toth that I would agree to remain with the NDU faculty for one month only as I did not want to create the impression that I was evading the DICON appointment. Approval was given for me to remain with the

NDU Faculty for a month after graduation. But a few days later I was informed that I had been posted to National War College, Abuja as a Directing Staff. It was about the time we were embarking on our last IF tour.

At the beginning of this last leg of IFs Field Study tour of the USA, I was impressed with the humour and dedication of Mr Harry the owner of Top Notch Travel who organised and drove coaches across the length and breadth of the expanse of the USA and never failed us. He was one of us throughout and an embodiment of commitment and humility. He was responsible for the coach drives through the states of Nevada (Las Vegas), Arizona (Grand Canyon), and New Mexico (Santa Fe) as he had always done. On Friday 11 May 2001, we departed Andrews Air Force Base for Nellis Air Force Base, Las Vegas, the home of the American fighter pilots. Nellis is the largest fighter base in the world and is considered a crown jewel with a complex larger than many countries. We checked into the MGM Grand Hotel in Las Vegas and had an idea of the gambling industry. The IFs had a good tour of the Nellis Air Force Base which was a whole day series of events.

The following day, we departed for Grand Canyon and lodged at Yavapai Lodge at the Grand Canyon Village. The Grand Canyon is 446 kilometres long with a gorge of 1.6 kilometres deep and 29 kilometres wide in some places whose layers of rock reveal nearly two billion years of earth's history. We were briefed on survival actions during hiking down and up that would last the whole day. The next visit stop was the Sandia National Labs at Patty Zamora which is a national security laboratory operated by the US Department of Energy where I saw nanotechnology and robotic manufacturing facilities. The complex designs all non-nuclear components for the country's nuclear weapons and performs a wide variety of energy research and development projects that respond to national security threats, be it economic or military. The visit was capped by a tour of the National Atomic Museum and School of American Research dedicated to advanced scholarship in anthropology and humanities worldwide including the promotion of the study, preservation, and creation of Southwest Indian art.

By the time we returned to Washington DC on Sunday 20 May, the graduation day was about three weeks away and the countdown to the end of the course had begun. There were receptions with various groups. I received a letter dated 5 June 2001 from the Commandant, ICAF informing me that I had been selected to receive the NDU President's Strategic Vision Award for my Research Fellow work and other efforts.

This was followed by a letter from the NDU Director of Research explaining the nature of the award and the arrangements for the award ceremony and recognition on 11 June 2001.

The President's Strategic Vision award is the highest award given at the NDU and I was the first foreign student to win it. I was also recognised for a second award as a Distinguished Graduate for being among the top 10% of the class of ICAF 2001. General ML Agwai had won the Ambassador's Award in 2000, the third-highest award at the NDU, and the first foreign student so honoured. The report I received was a compilation of all that was conducted in our programmes. I had one report from Colonel Jim Toth which was a form of warning. He remarked that I would need special care and management of my career within the Nigerian military set up to avoid a waste of potential. The President of NDU was also very optimistic about my bright career prospects. I had been prepared for higher responsibilities having done my duty as a student at National Defense University, Washington DC.

My ICAF course was the Class of 2001, the first course of the 21st Century. My wife had arrived for the weeklong activities of graduation. The Nigerian Ambassador to the USA, Professor Jubril Aminu, and DDA (Navy) attended the award and recognition ceremony. The Ambassador was given the rare honour of having a group photograph with the President of the NDU, Vice Admiral Paul G Gaffney II, USN, Commandant ICAF, and myself on stage at the ceremony on 11 June 2001. At the graduation ceremony on 13 June 2001, the feast day of my patron Saint Anthony of Padua, I was awarded the ICAF MSc degree and IF Diploma certificates. The Chairman of Joint Chiefs of Staff, General Henry H. Shelton, was the guest of honour. The awards and graduation ceremonies were for both NWC and ICAF with about 600 graduands. The Nigeria Embassy Defence Section staff attended the ceremony but the Defence Attache was out of Washington.

A Graduation Banquet for the IFs at The Willard Inter-Continental Hotel, 1401 Pennsylvania Avenue NW, close to the White House and Capitol Hill, was hosted by the President of the NDU. My wife was among the dignitaries in attendance. We had a relaxed evening.

I have given some highlights of IF extensive visits which were solid experiences I relied upon to come to terms with the heavy doses of excellent academic deliveries of the MSc programme focused on the study of how national security strategy is formulated and how national resources are sourced and applied for the realisation of set objectives. The Research Fellow programme enabled me to study in-depth the problems of NN planning within the context of best practices of the planning process. I strongly believed that the lack of an entrenched planning process is the major problem that the NN has to solve for a credible secure future and I found out that quality manpower with ideas is the critical requirement.

My choice of Shipbuilding for Industrial Study programme was to enable a follow up on my experiences in Italy on the MCMV project and the problems associated with ships propulsion propellers on NN major platforms. The absolute attention required by warships demanding continuity of efforts is the practice that the NN does not follow thereby weakening the institution and allowing all manner of indiscipline in approach to matters related to warship acquisition processes. I had heard much of the progress of the Asian Tigers as regards their economic and social developments and decided that my regional security studies would be on South East Asia and for this, there were knowledgeable resource persons from State Department and other agencies that were utilized. The choice of Economic Diplomacy and Economic Warfare also offered me the opportunity to study why Nigeria has been getting poor report cards on the economic front as the country was then begging for debt forgiveness. This sums up my focus throughout the course and I was glad I did not switch to the National War College but remained to do the ICAF stuff.

It is essential, to sum up, my experiences as regards the struggle of the African-Americans and relate to their expectations for a better Nigeria that would give them hope and a sense of pride. I attended several events and was struck by an event during the Black History event on the Washington Mall in 2001. I noticed, going through the exhibitions, the extraordinary resilience of African-Americans since their unfortunate mode of arrival in the Americas stacked all the odds against them. The good news is that they are focused and had survived deprivations and were economically empowering themselves. I saw an elderly African-American seated at an exhibition stand wearing a typical Nigerian popular textile print of the 1960s and I became curious. I approached him and greeted him. He raised his head off his crossed palms resting on his walking stick but did not respond to my greeting. After some time, he again raised his head and said: "You are from Nigeria?" He went on to ask me why Nigeria disappointed them as they (African-Americans) were looking forward to Nigeria as a great source of inspiration after independence in 1960. He went on to tell me that he visited Nigeria just after independence in 1960 and travelled to Kano,

Kaduna, Ibadan, Enugu, and Lagos and came back to the USA full of hope. He asked me again: 'Why did you disappoint us?''

I was cold and unable to utter a word. I left him. It was at the same location Dr Martin Luther King Jr gave his "I Have a Dream" speech during the march on Washington on 28 August 1963.

I had an additional one month to stay at the NDU. The next course had resumed by 18 June 2001. They wanted to retain me for much longer and get me more involved. The option was tempting but I had to consider my pending appointment as a Directing Staff at National War College, Abuja. I prepared to complete my one month programme and leave Washington DC by 12 July 2001.

It was lonely for me walking through the familiar hallways and empty seminar rooms. I was now meeting more of the faculty staff and Colonel J Toth was ever ready to spend more time with me. We had lunch at his favourite restaurant. He offered to drive me to the airport. I informed him a week before my departure that I would be happy to have him take me to the airport.

I left my flat by 30 June 2001 as my contract expired on that day and it would be too expensive for me to extend it for a month only. I was thinking of alternative accommodation when Dr Joseph E Goldberg got to know of my difficulty. He invited me to take over his family house as he would be away on holiday from 1 July 2001 and return on 10 July 2001. This was perfect as I was confirmed to fly out on 12 July 2001. The master bedroom was prepared for me. I would always remember the assistance rendered to me by Commander (later Rear Admiral) Bala Msehiela at the Nigeria Permanent Mission at the UN in New York. He got in touch with me on hearing of my packing out of my flat and assisted me with the fund to settle my bills.

I agreed with Dr Goldberg that I would leave his residence on the outskirts of Washington DC the very day he returns and check into a hotel for an overnight stay near the Nigerian Embassy and later pick him and his wife from the airport. This allowed me to conclude my leaving routine with the Embassy where I would drop the car allocated to me for the course and make it easy for Col Toth to take to Dulles airport.

I had my last day at the NDU/ICAF on 11 June 2001. I wished the IF staff goodbye and I headed to the main entrance into Eisenhower Hall to exit for the final time. My drive out of NDU was slow and deliberate as a mark of respect for the great institution.

The following morning 12 June 2001, I went to the Nigeria Embassy nearby and handed over the car allocated to me. I returned to the hotel and checked out and waited for Col James E Toth. He was on time and I was happy to have him around. We arrived at Dulles Airport and after I had checked in I got a fatherly hug from him. Col Jim E Toth transited from the official status as a Professor and Head of a department to my dear friend. He was one of the finest human beings I have been lucky to meet.

I had planned a stopover in London and had Commander (later Rear Admiral) BA Raji who was the Deputy Defence Adviser to get me a suitable hotel accommodation. I was received at Heathrow Airport and taken to the hotel. The Defence Adviser was Major General (later Lieutenant General) AK Akale who was most receptive at the Defence Section he headed and we had some lively chat. He jokingly warned me to stop accumulating certificates and awards on hearing of my performance. I briefed him of my travel plans to Kuala Lumpur to visit my in-laws and return to London before leaving for Lagos on 28 July 2001. My mother-in-law had a heart problem and I had to visit her and also, explore the possibility of my second son David Ahaorvi continuing his higher education there.

I arrived in Kuala Lumpur on 17 July 2001. My parents-in-law were pleased to have me around. I committed my son Ahaorvi David to see if it would be possible for him to start his medical studies at the International Medical University (IMU). He had finished the final year at King's College, Lagos. My father-in-law took me to the IMU to find out about admission requirements. The entry requirement is an Advanced Level School Certificate in three relevant subjects with A-grades. I requested their preference and Taylor's College, Kuala Lumpur A-level programme was prefered. I was assured of admission if the path of Taylor's College was followed. The following day, we drove to Taylor's College and got their admission requirements which were good O-Level results from King's College, Lagos.

Taylor's College was far; the College had buses for students at different collections and drop off points. I was more interested in the buses rather than a daily run by my in-laws. I was encouraged by the enthusiasm of my in-laws who were already making efforts to prepare a study room with a desktop computer facilities. I was happy they were ready to have David. I was hosted by Mrs Rosalind Oh and family and Mrs Ruby Jesudason and family for dinners and visits. The late Dr David Saravanamuthu was the husband of Mrs Rosalind and the brother of my mother-in-law while Mrs Ruby was the sister. My mother-in-law's health condition was under control; she was receiving sound medical attention.

I left Kuala Lumpur for London on 26 July and departed for Lagos on 28 July 2001. I was glad to be reunited with my family and prepare for the challenges of my new appointment as a Directing Staff at National War College, Abuja. I went to report at the NHQ on Moloney Street and some officers were shocked to see me with my Captain's rank because my mates and my juniors had been promoted eight months earlier. I had a good collection of course materials and books I gathered preparatory to my next job and eagerly waited to clear my luggage to have access.

I had a meeting with the former CNS, Vice-Admiral VK Ombu, at his residence in Ikoyi. I briefed him on my course and thanked him for nominating and supporting me while at ICAF. I showed him the preliminary report given to me at ICAF; after reading through it, he congratulated me and told me that the most important word in the entire two-page report was TRUST. This is part of what the report said about me: "He is an excellent leader, follower, briefer, writer, coordinator, and advocate, as circumstances require; he possesses superior 'people' skills and a well-developed sense of humour, which complements exceptional organisational and analytical skills--everyone wants to be on Tony's team. He is perceived by all as a professional and man of honour who inspires trust across service and national lines." I will continue to remember the keyword TRUST.

REPLY TO
ATTENTION OF:

Office of the President

Chief of the Naval Staff
Nigerian Naval Headquarters
Ministry of Defense
Area 7, Garki
Abuja Nigeria

Dear Sir:

Let me take this opportunity to apprise you of the truly outstanding performance of Captain Anthony Isa during his year as an International Fellow at the National Defense University. Capt Isa's program enabled him to study and conduct research in close association with the faculty of both the National War College and the Industrial College of the Armed Forces, as well as the staff of the Institute for National Strategic Studies. In addition to a diploma from the National Defense University, he also received a Master of Science degree in National Resource Strategy from the Industrial College of the Armed Forces. I assure you no International Fellow learned and contributed more during his year at the National Defense University than Capt Isa.

Capt Isa completed a core curriculum, which provided an understanding of the development and implementation of national security policy and military strategy. His courses addressed the domestic and international contexts within which national security policy and strategy are developed, examined the national security decision-making process, and focused on the formulation of national security and military strategy from every relevant approach. Capt Isa's performance as a student at the Industrial College of the Armed Forces was truly extraordinary. Upon graduation he was given full recognition as a "Distinguished Graduate;" this places him among the top 10% of his class, which exceeded 300 students. He received solid A's and A-'s in each and every one of his classes. He took more credit hours (42 hours) than any other student at ICAF and still greatly exceeded all expectations. Moreover, he received the President's Strategic Vision Award, the highest award given by the National Defense University for research and writing.

For his advanced elective studies, he chose:

- Economic Diplomacy and Economic Warfare
- Industrial Analysis
- Research Fellow

Additionally, he selected Southeast Asia as his Regional Security Study area. In both core and elective studies, he contributed immensely to the open forum seminar discussions. He was among the most highly regarded students in his classes. When Tony spoke, everybody—students and faculty—listened. His discussion contributions were always studied, balanced, and incisive. He could be counted upon to see the ambiguities and complexities of strategic level issues and offer sophisticated interpretations and applications. He was instrumental in helping his seminar perform at a high conceptual level.

321

One of the special aspects of the International Fellows program is the non-American view we want our US students to experience. Capt Isa was outstanding in this area. He showed his US counterparts that other valid viewpoints must be considered in the decision-making process.

Capt Isa was always well prepared throughout the academic year. He understood the complex issues presented in the curriculum and coherently and convincingly articulated his views in both large and small group seminars. He displayed the ability to make logical assumptions and construct and present solid recommendations. In support of the curriculum, he wrote several papers of varying length; all his written work was superb.

Capt Isa did extensive interviews and research on Nigerian naval planning in connection with the President's Strategic Vision Award. Dr. Goldberg, in charge of all research, described Tony as "one of the most diligent research fellows ever to have been in the program." This is quite an accolade. Dr. Gropman echoed the sentiments of the entire faculty when he described Tony as "one of the finest International Fellows we've ever had! He is exceptionally intelligent, highly diligent, articulate, and most importantly for a War College student, completely open to new ideas. He has an exceptional grasp of the strategy-logistics-mobilization connection; which he can relate both to U.S. and Nigerian circumstances. He made singular contributions to the course." Dr. Gropman ended with a plea to "promote Tony and bring him back to Washington as Nigeria's naval attaché!"

Similarly, Tony's Logistics professor observed that he is "an extraordinary officer who possesses infectious enthusiasm, a boundless capacity for work, exceptional powers of reason, and strategic scope together with a mature capacity to evaluate and exploit what ICAF presents in light of the strategic and logistics needs of Nigeria. He is an excellent leader, follower, briefer, writer, coordinator, and advocate, as circumstances require; he possesses superior 'people' skills and a well-developed sense of humor, which complements exceptional organizational and analytic skills—everyone wants to be on Tony's team. He is perceived by all as a professional and man of honor who inspires trust across service and national lines." Additional glowing observations on Captain Isa's performance came from Dr. Crew who oversaw Industry Studies: "Tony's demonstrated ability to understand exceedingly complex multi-dimensional issues and explain them in a concise easily understandable manner clearly distinguishes him as one of the top student in the Shipbuilding Industry Study class. Tony wrote a terrific paper examining the shipbuilding services market in West Africa. His paper was well researched and he did a great job supporting his final recommendations that US shipyards join in partnership with West African shipbuilding professionals to enhance both of their efforts. Tony took an active role in the class and was considered the technical expert by his classmates. He often used his vast experience as a naval engineer to help his classmates understand the implications of esoteric policy issues. Tony is well poised to work at the strategic international level and demonstrated his deep understanding of the interaction between the government and industry at the national and global level."

We were extremely fortunate to have borrowed Capt Isa from you for a year. More than any other student of the Class of 2001, Tony made the fullest out of his academic year at ICAF. He was clearly an extraordinary member of the class and one of the brightest ever to attend this institution of higher learning. He has learned, and taught, a great deal. We are confident that he will continue to serve Nigeria well.

Sincerely,

Paul G. Gaffney II
Vice Admiral, US Navy
President

CHAPTER SIXTEEN

Experiences at National War College, Abuja

I had no problem preparing for my next duty post at Abuja. I flew to the Nnamdi Azikiwe International Airport just before noon and took a taxi to the College along Herbert Macaulay Way in the Central Business District. I met Commodore Shaibu Amodu in his office and he gave me very useful information regarding my residential and office accommodation. He volunteered to take me to my residential accommodation along Thames Street, Maitama. I had a two-bedroom apartment at the Directing Staff Quarters there.

I reported at the National War College within the last week of August 2001. I was almost the last Directing Staff to report and met a situation whereby residential accommodation and offices had been shared out and occupied. The officers recently promoted to the ranks of Brigadier General, Commodore and Air Commodore including my juniors were all over the College, and as a Captain, I was saluting all of them to avoid being called to order. I took whatever was left or reserved for me as considered due to a Captain and settled down to duty. I had no vehicle. I had to rely on other officers for assistance and in this regard, Commodore Shuaibu Amodu was very helpful. Some officers from the Nigerian Air Force and the Nigerian Army who were my course mates also occasionally assisted me by giving me a lift to and from the office.

The Commandant was Rear Admiral HL Okpannachi, a Marine Engineer Officer and the Deputy Commandant was Major General A Owonibi while the College Secretary was Commodore Abel Omonaiye, my coursemate at the NDA and my junior at St John's College, Kaduna. I reported to the Deputy Commandant who welcomed me to the College. He doubled as the Director of Studies. I was later taken to the Commandant for his formalities. Thereafter, I acquainted myself with the administrative and academic staff.

I was assigned, for the first term for the course starting September 2001, as an Augmentee Directing Staff to work with Colonel (later Brigadier General) Nicholas Agbogun NDA 9 Regular Course who had spent a year as Directing Staff at the College. I did not know why he was still a Colonel. He attended the Royal College of Defence Studies,

London between 1999-2000. I was issued the College handbook for Directing Staffs and allocated an office that had a collection of disused and broken office furniture. The office was secured and I set to work. I learnt from the Syndicate Directing Staff how to handle the syndicate and moderate discussions in the first term.

The Ibrahim Badamasi Babangida (IBB) Golf and Country Club offered me avenues for relaxation. Commodore Amodu plays golf and it was easy for me to follow his routines. I understood that some officers on the academic faculty did not think that playing golf would allow enough time for the work of a Directing Staff. But later in the year, when those of us who had time for golf were asked to help those who did not have time for golf, more officers took up golfing and the College had the status of a Corporate Member of the Club and eventually facilitated individual membership.

The NWC curriculum, I noticed, did not reflect that of a War College. I found out that over the years some additions and alterations were not properly studied. The British Assistance Team that helped to set up the College abruptly left the country due to political developments in the country in 1993. This must-have affected the development of the curriculum. A hybrid course was being run with more emphasis on a higher direction of national defence and not enough on war studies. The College programme study blocs are spread over three terms with the final term emphasizing Higher Management of Defence and geo-strategic study tour to selected countries. This emphasis on Higher Management of Defence led to discussions to change the name of the College to National Defence College, among other reasons.

The College programme was conducted through a series of external and internal lectures in the central lecture hall and followed by syndicate discussions moderated by the Directing Staff. Group works were resulting in presentations either in syndicates or central lecture hall and the individual research project. The field study tours within covered military establishments, strategic installation, state and local governments, and countries representing all regions of the world. The range of external lecturers included foreign Heads of State and foreign experts and selected Ministers of the Federal Government of Nigeria and heads of selected departments and agencies. This approach allows a very wide range of studies that could be broadly described as preparing selected senior military officers and their counterparts from the civilian departments and agencies for strategic leadership. The mission of the College dictates this approach. Why is the institution named War College with such a diverse programme of studies without the depth of operational art related to war? There were not enough war studies and the Nigerian Armed Forces had no dedicated institution for the training of officers in warfare and joint effort.

The syndicate sessions were based on sharing knowledge and experiences. There was no structured lecture series based on subject matters to improve on the knowledge base related to joint war studies and higher direction of defence which are mixed in the programme without defined objectives. This means that the participants do not improve much on their knowledge base beyond the pool of what participants possessed before coming for the course. There was a need to redesign the curriculum.

The Directing Staff are simply those who have been recommended by the College during their course at the College or who went to equivalent institutions abroad no matter their performance. There was no other standard and this situation did not allow for improvements in the quality of knowledge imparted. I noticed that Nigerian participants as of 2001 were still using a projector and foils handwritten while most of the foreign participants from other African countries were very knowledgeable about computer Power Point presentations. The College had a computer training centre that has not been properly utilized. There were no reliable functioning internet facilities though some efforts were being made to provide limited services.

The Chief of the Naval Staff as from April 2001, was Vice Admiral SO Afolayan, who as FOC WEST was the Chairman of the senior officer's promotion Board for 2000 while I was at ICAF, Washington DC. He came to the College to give a lecture towards the end of the year, 2001. I joined other officers to greet him as he was preparing to leave. I saluted a particular Commodore who also came to greet him. The CNS knew that had I been promoted as due, I would be senior to the Commodore I saluted. The CNS asked why I was saluting my junior who is a Commodore? I told him that I was a Captain and the officer I saluted was a Commodore and it was normal that I salute him. He was silent for a moment and managed to tell me not to worry as the next promotion was on the cards.

The presentation by the Director of Higher Military Organisation on higher management of defence in Nigeria brought about the issue of Rules of Engagement (ROE). I was pleasantly surprised when Brigadier General Iketunbosun in handling questions related to the use of minimum force within the context of ROE, stated that since he joined the Nigerian Army and till that moment, he had not come across an ROE. I was highly impressed with his humility and sincerity. He asked the audience if anyone had seen one and wanted assistance with an improvement of the lecture delivery.

After the lecture, I went to his office and promised to bring the US Armed Forces publication on peace support operations that had a Standard ROE as an appendix. I also contacted Col James E Toth and asked for ROE covering recent operations. I was generously supplied with information about the management of ROE. I studied the available publications on ROE and indeed the Nigerian Armed Forces had no clue of what constitutes ROE and how it is managed for specific conflicts.

I was tasked to write a brief highlighting the situation and provide information on how ROE could be developed for the Nigerian Armed Forces. The brief was studied and improved upon to assist the Services Headquarters. Thereafter, I was tasked to get the NHQ sensitized and the Army and Air Force Headquarters were similarly sensitized by their officers from the College. This was the origin of the ROE publication to educate officers and men of the Armed Forces and the National Command Authority. The Army had suffered bad publicity and loss of personnel in internal security operations as a result of a lack of knowledge of ROE and its management by the National Command Authority. I would later be tasked to write on military campaigns for use by the participants.

Lieutenant General ML Agwai as COAS in 2005 elaborated on the ROE and had publications distributed including a summarised version on a plastic card that fits into a breast pocket. I had one issued to me.

The first state study tour was to Sokoto and the journey was by road through Gusau, Zamfara State capital. The problem of boundary areas of Nigeria and the general problems of the state was the focus of the study tour. The education of children and the challenge posed by the "almajiri" also drew the attention of the course participants to state government efforts to build schools and convince the parents that the schools would promote Islamic education.

I noticed as we dove out of Gusau and as our convoy of buses reached a long road that disappeared into the horizon, the sparse vegetation and the lonely road that we were on for several minutes before seeing another vehicle. These bothered me that it would be near impossible to defend the territory should there be enemy infiltration from our neighbouring countries. Capabilities for surveillance, targets acquisitions, and rapid deployment of troops by the Armed Forces did not exist. It was in the same zone that a fighter pilot was lost while on a solo flight to qualify him. The training officer at the Kainji training facility then was Group Captain (later Air Marshal and Chief of Defence Staff) O Petinrin. He expressed his grief at the loss of the pilot in November 1999 when I was with the National Assembly Committees on a tour of military establishments. He explained how he had to rely on a handheld device as the only means of communicating with the pilots.

The next state study tour was to Akwa Ibom State in early December 2002. The subject of the study tour was the local government system in the state. The group first met with the state executive governor after which the team had its first session with the State's Council of Chiefs. The Chairman of the Council of Chiefs briefed us and said that there were no results to show for the efforts the State and Local Governments were making. He stated that all projects executed were announced on the radio while there was nothing to show. All they heard, he said, were 'radio roads,' 'radio water' and so on. It was when we interacted with a Local Government Chairman in Uyo that we knew what happened at the local government level. The Chairman had briefed the team on the provision of water for the local government area and was asked to show us the facility. The team was taken to a place with a borehole and two three hundred-litre plastic tanks on a raised concrete platform structure. When the tap was turned on, no water flowed from the tank or the borehole. The Chairman became embarrassed when a participant stated that he had six of such tanks providing water from a borehole at his residence and wondered how two tanks and a borehole would serve an entire local government area.

Back in his office, the chairman explained that the money allocated to the local council was shared amongst themselves to cater to their upkeep as most of the councillors on being elected hardly had good shoes, clothes, and vehicles befitting their status. Also, provisions were made for their wives as "first ladies" of wards. After that, there was almost nothing left for the provision of basic amenities.

The state government had a similar sharing arrangement going on and both governments confirmed the statement of the Chairman of the Council of Chiefs of "air" infrastructure that they could not see or experience. A lot of money simply disappears through government offices at all levels and the culture that supports the wastage gets more sophisticated. It is sad to see so much suffering in the areas visited and yet so many available resources were deliberately wasted with reckless and casual attitudes.

I was promoted to the rank of Commodore towards the end of the year 2001 and my seniority was restored. I had lost nothing except saluting my juniors and being last in the pecking order for dues. The decoration with the new rank by the Commandant took place after the College resumed from a break in January 2002.

The College closed for Christmas break after the study tour of Sokoto State and after presentations on the study, the tour had been made. I travelled to Lagos to be with my family for Christmas. I went to the Mobile petrol station along Malu Road near Navy Barracks to buy petrol and as I was leaving, I saw a young man running towards me. I thought I was about to be attacked. He came to my attention and saluted me. He introduced himself as a Lieutenant. He congratulated me on my performance at ICAF. He told me that he saw the report on me from ICAF and that those junior officers who saw the report had made copies for themselves to keep to motivate them. I was speechless. I gathered myself and thanked him and drove off.

What was going on in my mind? I pitied the young officer and his counterparts or contemporaries who were so impressed with my performance. I had been suffering for performances and this particular report from ICAF was already heightening intrigues for my retirement from service rather than putting me to good use. I had told a senior officer at the NHQ who also appreciated my performance that he should wait and see the trials ahead for me because of the report from ICAF. I was reliably informed that my name was removed from the national honours list the NN committee had recommended based on my performance at National Defense University, Warshington DC. I had a good Christmas and New Year holidays with my family and returned to Abuja.

I was assigned participants to supervise their research projects during my tenure as a Directing Staff. One of them was Captain J Unufe, a Weapon Engineer Officer who had worked closely with me on CONSAC Committees. I noticed from the second term that he was not measuring up despite the constant reminders I sent to him to meet up. He was evasive and when eventually he decided to submit his work for scrutiny, it was embarrassing. I encouraged him, as I did to all participants that I supervised, to consult resource persons within and outside the College that he was comfortable with in addition to my supervision.

Captain J Unufe sadly submitted his research project work without submitting it for my scrutiny. When this was detected by the Director of Academic Research and Studies, I was contacted and I told him that I did not see what was submitted, and the fact that I did not sign confirmed this fact. During the project defence panel chaired by Rear Admiral S Kolawole, it was pointed out that I had not signed the project certifying that I was the supervisor. The Chairman said that when he saw that I did not sign it to certify that I had supervised the work, he was not surprised at the poor quality of work submitted. This put an end to his career.

The supervision of Colonel (later Lieutenant General and Chief of Army Staff) OA Ihejirika's research project was tasking. He was a good listener and worked very hard. He wanted to be with his supervisor at every opportunity and I encouraged him along. I also encouraged him to reach out to other resource persons within and outside the College to give him a wider perspective and options. Besides, I told him that I looked forward to learning from him as a yardstick for measuring the quality of his research work.

The research project was on Military-Industrial Complex and he made good use of his experiences as he is of the Nigerian Army Engineers. I met Colonel Ihejirika waiting to see the Director-General of Defence Industries Corporation of Nigeria (DICON) at his office in Kaduna. I had gone there for a meeting of the Governing Board of DICON on which I represented the NN/CNS. My membership of the Board was the additional duties I performed while I was a Directing Staff at the College.

Colonel Ihejirika told me he had an appointment regarding his research project and I gave him gestures of support. I was happy with Colonel Ihejirika's efforts and the quality of his final submissions. I was not surprised when I learnt that his research project won a prize. It was well deserved. He was the most diligent participant I handled while I was a DS at the College between August 2001 and December 2003.

The staff car allocated to me was like an old horse being forced to sprint. There were several breakdowns on the road. I had travelled to the home town of Admiral Ibrahim Ogohi, the Chief of Defence Staff, for the wedding of his daughter in Kogi State when my staff car gave me another problem while returning to Abuja. I noticed an engine noise that was progressively getting louder. My driver, Army Corporal Mohammed Alfa, felt he could manage the car to Abuja. But I told him to stop at the next petrol station. I told him that we should not manage the car towards Abuja. I would not want to damage the engine beyond repairs. I told him that I would arrange for the car to be towed to Abuja.

The Army Records Command was in Lokoja. I got a taxi to take us to the residence of the Commander for assistance. I met Brigadier

General B Ogundele, my coursemate, at the NDA whom I had not seen since December 1973. It was a pleasant surprise and we settled down to have some drinks. I told him of my problem and the immediate requirement to get the vehicle towed from the petrol station to the safety of his establishment and then to Abuja. He promised to take care of my driver and the car and organise the towing. He arranged a taxi to take me to Abuja.

As we were trying to catch up on the past over our drinks, a retired Nigerian Army officer walked in. He had worked as a staff officer to Brigadier General Leo Ajiborisa who was a principal staff officer to General AA Abubakar, the Head of State between June 1998 and May 1999. I noticed that the retired officer was very uncomfortable and I urged him to have a drink which he reluctantly accepted. He then adjusted his sitting position and took me by surprise by apologising to me about an incident he had not let out yet. He said he felt bad about how, at the last minute, he removed my name from the list of military administrators. He told me that it was the turn of Kogi West since Lieutenant Colonel MAS Onuka from Kogi Central and Colonel Ahmed Usman from Kogi East had taken turns as military governors of Edo and Osun states respectively. He nominated a Nigerian Army officer, Colonel Owoniyi, to take my slot and thereby denied the NN its allotted slot and added to the Army.

I told him not to worry as my prayer was answered by God through his action. I would have served for about nine months as a military administrator of a state and be retired by June 1999 when the new civilian administration retired all politically exposed officers. I had prayed that God should not allow sudden misfortune to come my way after I was told to get ready to travel to Abuja for the swearing-in ceremony on getting confirmation from the Presidential Villa.

I left for Abuja with the taxi cab arranged for me by Brigadier General Ogundele, leaving my driver under his care. Brigadier General Ogundele organised the towing of my staff car to Abuja for repairs.

Sometime later, I would be stuck on the Kaduna-Abuja highway in the night as I was returning from Kaduna after a DICON Board meeting towards the end of 2003. On that occasion, I remained with my driver who trekked some distance to get a motorcycle ride to get a new fan belt from the nearest town while I took cover in the bush waiting for him. I turned down his advice to get a taxi for me to continue to Abuja while he stayed with the car to manage the situation. It was risky to leave him alone. We managed to fix the new belt and returned safely to Abuja.

I experienced a very interesting encounter at a police checkpoint after crossing the Niger Bridge at Koton Karfe. I was in uniform returning from another DICON Board meeting at Kaduna and decided to bypass Abuja and head for Okene where I had pending issues to resolve. On sighting my car with all the indications of a military vehicle, the police constable moved to the centre of the road and waved for the car to stop. As the car slowed down towards him, the constable fired a shot into the air. As we stopped close enough for him to observe the car, my driver and I both in uniform, the constable waved us by.

I told my driver Corporal Alfa that I would like to find out why the constable fired into the air since we had not done anything threatening. He advised me that the constable might be high on substances. I alighted from the vehicle slowly and took some slow deliberate steps towards the constable observing his reactions. On getting close to him, I asked why he fired a shot into the air. He told me that he was testing his weapon. I told him the implication of his action and the waste of live ammunition that constituted an offence. I asked for the constable in charge and he told me that the constable had gone to have a meal. I warned him to avoid such threatening actions and should be conscious that he must account for ammunition at all times.

One evening at our staff quarters in Maitama, Brigadier General OA Azazi phoned me and asked me if he could introduce to me a friend he knew when he was serving at Training and Doctrine Command, Minna. The friend was a real estate manager with a registered company. He was introduced as very capable of seeing through real estate transactions. I was not very experienced in these matters. I held a meeting with him and he convinced me that he was capable. I asked him to buy lands in areas that were not yet developed based on his advice.

I sold off a plot of land I was developing at Satellite Town in Lagos and invested in Abuja. It was from the proceeds of this sale that I paid for two plots on the outskirts of Asokoro that were not yet accessible by road and were affordable. I later bought another two plots at Lugbe on the way to the airport and which would take some years before developments reached the area. These four plots were purchased below two million Naira. I considered them good investments given the pace of development in Abuja. I had trusted a fellow officer and a coursemate from the NDA to use this estate manager friend of his. I had walked into a trap and would lose the four plots later when development caught up with the areas as from 2013.

The international study tours, while I was a DS, took me to Kenya, Equatorial Guinea, and Brazil. The Kenyan study tour was in 2002 and was an interesting exposure to developments taking place in the country. At the National Defence College in Nairobi, we had a joint discussion with the staff and participants moderated by a Kenyan Major General who was a DS at the College. We were told Nigeria was disappointing Africa by failing to provide credible leadership on the continent. In specific terms, our Kenyan counterparts highlighted the fact that the language of discussion of Nigeria's internal problems shows that we could not be taken seriously because they did not understand what Nigerians meant by marginalisation in a country as vibrant as ours.

The study tour to Equatorial Guinea was a terrible embarrassment. There was no direct flight between Malabo the capital and Nigeria despite their proximity. Nigeria had no national airline and none of the private airlines operated the route. A Cameroonian airline took us from Lagos to Douala where we spent an unscheduled night at a hotel. The following day a small aircraft took us to Malabo. The officer expected to receive us on arrival was not at the airport and the Nigerian Embassy staff had to run around to alert the authorities before a Lieutenant Colonel reluctantly showed up and escorted us to the hotel reserved for the team. That was the only real contact we had with the military in that country.

The following morning we were taken to the Nigerian Embassy and briefed. Thereafter, the shuttle to meet with the authorities began. It was past midday and there was no hope of contacting anyone as the liaison officer could no longer be reached. It was decided that a team be sent to the military headquarters to gate crash into offices for a response. I was on the team. At the military headquarters, we saw a naval officer having a meal at his desk. He was identified as the Chief of the Naval Staff or Head of the Navy. We were taken to a waiting room and after experiencing their absentee hospitality, we returned to the Nigerian Embassy and concluded that we were not welcome.

A Nigerian Embassy staff took us around an abandoned construction project expected to provide integrated facilities for the entire Embassy. All accommodation being used by the Embassy was rented and some problems faced by the mission showed that Nigeria was not conducting itself well. I remembered that the NN donated some small patrol boats to the Equatorial Guinea Navy with a promise to maintain them at the Nigerian Naval Shipyard at Port Harcourt. But the boats were abandoned at the shipyard to waste away.

After the face-saving tour of the Nigerian Embassy, we returned to our hotel and decided that we would call off the visit and return to Nigeria. Air Gabon flew us to Douala and handed us over to Cameroonian Airlines. There was no direct flight into Nigeria for another two days and we were running short of temper and cash as we doubled up in hotel rooms in Douala. We took the next available flight over Nigeria to Cotonou, Republic of Benin. We arrived just before dawn the following day and were received by the Defence Adviser who gave us a very early breakfast and arranged for vehicles to take us to Nigeria through the Seme-Badagry-Lagos route.

The study tour to Brazil was a lucky escape as my syndicate was not accepted by the country we were originally programmed to visit. The Brazilian Ambassador to Nigeria was kind enough to accept my team to join the team already approved to visit Brazil. The combined team took flights from Abuja through Amsterdam to Sao Paulo. The other two cities visited were Rio de Janeiro and the capital, Brasilia. The Ambassador, His Excellency Josef Egbuson was most receptive and we had a great outing in Brazil.

In Brasilia, the Defence Ministry briefed us. We toured the new capital with unique features. In the briefings, I was particularly drawn to the programme for the development of the Amazon remote region to the North-West and bordering Columbia. The development of the region was intended to solve two problems of opening up the area to avoid drift of rural population to urban centres and curtailing or stopping drug trade across the border with Columbia.

The Army officer in charge of the programme was a Colonel. There were air and naval components with a very good organisation in which responsibilities were devolved to commanders. The current budget allocation was in the millions in US Dollars. We asked if there were interferences from the authorities and how the money was disbursed. The Colonel explained the transparent way the released funds were disbursed to the commanders on the spot or tied to specific related projects. The success of the programme was attested to by the Nigerian Ambassador who informed us that a team of Nigerian governors from the Niger Delta visited Brazil to study the programme but only ended up in the bright red light areas of the cities and returned to Nigeria.

The study tour programme at the College was facing funding problems with two international travels planned yearly. We tinkered with suggestions to reduce the tours to only one a year. The relevance of the foreign study tours was even questioned and I could see why there was no official input regarding Federal Government policy design and implementation. The College decided the theme for the geostrategic study tours and the findings were merely documented for presentations.

My last state study tour was the visit to Kaduna State in early December 2003. The promotion Board to Rear Admiral had sat and a signal was being expected as we set out for Kaduna State for the state tour. We were received by the Deputy Governor His Excellency Patrick Yakowa, an ex-student of St John's College. The problems of the state were typical of the general collapse of infrastructures and weak governance all over the country. The leader of my group had just been appointed General Officer Commanding, Third Division, Nigeria Army, Jos. He left immediately to take over and I had to take over as the team leader and conclude the tour.

I was informed before departure from Abuja for Kaduna, that the CNS had approved my appointment as Admiral Superintendent (ASND), Naval Dockyard, Victoria Island, Lagos, and I was expected to take over immediately. The incumbent had been asked to hand over to the next most senior officer to act as the ASND.

I received several calls from some officers warning me that efforts were being made for the officer asked to act to take over command of the establishment. Many wondered why I had not shown keen interest in the job. But I could not leave the participants in the middle of the programme when the end of term reports on the participants was to be concluded before closing for Christmas and New Year break.

On my return from the study tour, I received a letter from the NHQ informing me of my promotion to Rear Admiral, and a signal followed appointing me the ASND, Naval Dockyard but the date for my take over of the appointment was not given. This gave me a clear clue of the intense lobbying going on to give the job to the officer acting and who was a Commodore. I was happy that I had been promoted and would be leaving the College where I had been a Directing Staff as Captain, Commodore, and now Rear Admiral. I had an awesome tenure at the National War College. I made the desired impact regarding the proper treatment of participants, the introduction of Rule of Engagement in the Armed Forces, the contribution of papers on campaign studies and development of curriculum, and contributed at the DICON board meetings. I had a good idea of why DICON had been failing. Nigeria has not been serious and there is a dearth of committed expertise and programmes. The composition of the board was highly politically poised to waste resources.

I reported to Naval Secretary, Rear Admiral AR Adesokan, at the NHQ to find out when I would take over as the ASND and saw that consultations were still going on. I waited patiently at the NHQ for the outcome of the consultations before travelling to Lagos for the holidays. The set date for me to take over was 24 December 2003. I sensed that something was going on because of the reluctance to give me a convenient date. I ensured a signal was released confirming the date set.

As I was waiting to collect a copy of the signal, the issue of Rear Admiral TA Sanni who had left the Naval Dockyard for a Commodore to act came up. I noticed he was being branded as difficult, unapproachable, and uncompromising. I saw that the problem arose because the procedures were not being properly and fairly followed, thereby creating avoidable communication gaps. A meeting with the Naval Secretary and possibly the CNS could have sorted out the issues and avoided the unnecessary tension and accusations.

The Naval Secretary said that Rear Admiral TA Sanni had refused to collect the letter of his retirement and no officer could approach him. I told him to give me the letter and I would meet him in Lagos on my arrival and deliver it to him. I collected the letter and also a copy of the signal for my appointment and thanked the Naval Secretary for his services and left his office to meet the Branch Chiefs and thereafter proceed to tidy up and leave National War College, Abuja.

I had meetings with the Branch Chiefs at the Naval Headquarters and with the CNS to have an idea of the priorities of the NN. I was informed of the invitations received by NN from other navies such as the Indian Navy and the Royal Navy to send ships to participate in international events but that the   NN had not been able to honour any of the invitations. NNS ARADU and NNS AMBE were considered as having the best prospects to honour such invitations. I had relevant ideas of NN priorities to help me get focused at NND and keep in line with the thinking at a higher level of command.

CHAPTER SEVENTEEN

Naval Dockyard Command

I reported at the Naval Dockyard on the morning of 24 December to assume command. And because the Acting ASND, Commodore E Kpokpogri, had not arrived at the office, I waited in the officers' mess on the ground floor of the Administrative building. I had expected Rear Admiral TA Sanni to have prepared the handing over notes. I had told him when we met the day I arrived in Lagos that I would be counting on his support for a successful take over of Command as the ASND.

The Acting ASND came to the mess to welcome me and we had a brief chat. It appeared he was not expecting me. I had not phoned him given the tense situation involving the substantive ASND who was still on the premises and had not retired in addition, it was Christmas Eve and the holiday mood had set in. The Acting ASND told me that there was no handing over notes prepared for me. I told him that the NHQ would be informed that I had taken over. I suggested to him what I wanted to be done for the day as it was Christmas eve so that the first working day for me after the Christmas break would be Monday 29 December 2003. I demanded a handing over note.

I resumed duties on 29 December and took effective control of the office of the ASND and sent a signal to the NHQ that I had assumed Command. I still did not have any handing over notes either from Rear Admiral TA Sanni or Commodore E Kpokpogri. I asked Commodore E Kpokpogri to concentrate fully on his appointment as General Manager, Planning, and report to me also as the next most senior officer at the NND. I demanded an oral briefing on the state of affairs since he started Acting as the ASND. I then told him to put in writing a proper handing over note based on the oral briefing. I addressed the senior rates and later the entire NND workforce and continued my piecemeal gathering of information on the state of affairs. The handing over note would be reluctantly submitted to me months after I had settled in as the ASND. I kept it in my drawer but my office would be later ransacked and the hand-over note disappeared. It was a warning on the nature of intrigues in the NN at play on the NND premises.

I travelled to Abuja for the decorating ceremony of the newly-promoted senior officers. The ceremony was conducted in the NHQ conference room. The seating arrangement showed how trivial issues got emotional attention. I noticed that among the Admirals to be decorated, all seamen officers had priority, followed by the engineering branch officers. There was so much time spent adjusting seats and moving us around to ensure the superiors for being seamen, no matter their seniority, were satisfied. I was relieved after the CNS decorated me, and soon, the ceremony was over and the next ritual of small group celebrations ensued.

I wrote a letter for the CNS giving him an assessment of the challenges regarding the state of the Fleet and underlined the need to have major equipment manufacturers on the ground at the NND to work closely with the refit teams whose efforts had been limited due to dearth of expertise and special equipment. I had seen enough in Europe and the USA while on the MCMV project and also took part in the refit of the NNS ARADU that involved the availability of the major equipment manufacturers at the NND. I emphasised that international best practice was what would work. My submissions defined what I set out to achieve at the NND.

I returned to Lagos the following day as the state of the NN Fleet and the poor attitude of officers gave me worries. I was informed that the NND had been contracted to a private company to manage and I received a call from a friend at The Nigerian Society of Engineers asking whether I had a role to play due to the new management team put in place. Some days later as I walked around the premises on inspection, I met a team of expatriates in front of the Steel Workshop having a discussion. It was true that the NND had been given away and I had no document nor official brief on it.

I did not make any official inquiry until I had more details. I received an invitation to report at the office of the Chairman of the company now called the owners of the NND. I did not play the military card and I submitted it to my other 'boss.' I was kept waiting and when I was eventually ushered into the office of the Chairman outside NND premises, I was given some intimidating information that was calculated to draw me into submission. I told the Chairman that I had heard him and had nothing to say to him. The game was on to get the NND back under full NN command in the national interest.

I received a message that an Israeli citizen was flying into Lagos and wanted to have a meeting with me. During my discussion with him, I noted a development that suggested other motives. I knew more about the challenges ahead. On getting an official hint, I demanded the full contract the NHQ had with the company so that I would know how to conduct myself. I was sent a draft copy. I took command and control of the NN property for the defence of Nigeria. I also told the company to leave the premises and go to the NHQ and regularise the contract papers. That was the last I saw or heard of them. I consolidated command of NND firmly under the NN.

The Dorman Long fabrication company had been operating at the NND premises and their contract was about to expire. The company had a foreign partner that wanted to take over the NND contract and bypass the Nigerian partners. I sought directives from the NHQ and I was advised that some powerful national figures were involved and I should be careful. The two sides to the dispute within Dorman Long submitted their proposals for the renewal of the contract to continue with the use of NND facilities. I noticed it was beginning to polarise my staff officers. I passed the proposals round for their study and comments and met with them to forge a common NND position. It was agreed that the NND would be neutral and both parties should amicably settle their dispute and report to the NND for information and action as appropriate. I was still getting reports suggesting a worsening of the situation between the parties. I briefed CNS and took permission to call both parties for a meeting with me alone to broker peace. The CNS agreed and warned me not to be caught up in their dispute. The contract with Dorman Long was beneficial to the NND as the company paid for use of services and their expertise was deployed for some jobs being carried out by the NND. I did not want the dispute to lead to its withdrawal from the NND.

We held the meeting in the NND Board room. I had the tables and chairs arranged for a typical conflict resolution in a single line formation. I was seated at the centre of the long stretch of the table and had the opposing teams to my left and right. I informed them that I was neutral and only present to provide them with the opportunity to sort out their differences. I had printed the NND terms highlighting the requirements they had to meet. I asked for a volunteer to start the discussions. The proceedings got off to a good start.

There was the initial cautious phase that each side used to explore the situation and the firework was sparked. The language went crude at some points and I had to calm frayed nerves and allow them to focus on the salient issues. I kept reminding them to think about meeting the NND terms. There was a tea break and we all agreed to remain in the room.

On resumption, the discussions were more subdued and I sensed that we had reached a point of diminishing returns. I suggested that the meeting should end and gave them two options: either submit a joint bid or separate bids based on NND terms to be forwarded to the NHQ for the final decision. They agreed to end the meeting and submit their bids based on their decisions.

The two sides could not reconcile their differences and submitted separate bids. The NND management analysed the bids and made recommendations regarding which side met NND terms better. I briefed the CNS on the outcome of the meeting and forwarded all relevant documents to NHQ. The side that lost out had the support of a former Minister of Defence and I was satisfied that Dorman Long would remain with renewed terms in favour of the NND. The follow-up issues were swiftly resolved and the fabrication expertise available in the company was readily available to the NND. After an extensive tour of the company's facilities in Lagos, I was particularly impressed with the quality control set-up that met international standards. The company fabricated many pressure vessels of various capacities for the oil industry some of which were exported. The NND would later tap on the design expertise of the company. The resolution of this conflict in favour of the NND consolidated the direction and resolve that the NND was a strategic establishment for the defence and security of Nigeria.

There was a problem with the sunken twin dock gate which had been submerged for several months. There was the lack of progress of the NN local refit team on NNS AMBE and other ships. I needed all docks to be operational and decided to organise some heavy lift cranes and divers to recover the sunk twin dock gate. This was achieved with the help of Dorman Long heavy lift cranes that were being deployed for fabricating pressure vessels for the oil industry. The dock gate was repaired and put back into service thereby giving the NND full docking capacity.

The Commander Fleet Maintenance Corps, Rear Admiral LOB Agbaje, at 23 Marina was in contact with me as my appointment was still being decided. I paid him a courtesy call to find out his ideas regarding how we would work together. He was my main customer as regards the NN warships and jobs. The waterjet inshore patrol boat refit whose programme I had defined as Director of Marine Engineering at NHQ and had been approved by the new President, Commander-in-Chief in 1999 was under Commodore F Osho within the NND as his base for operations. The boats were still not operational as of 2003. This was not in keeping with the speed the President, Commander-in-Chief wanted when I was at the NHQ and worked on the proposals which were approved. I assessed the situation and determined my priorities.

There was a major problem with the 33KVA high tension electric power supply. The power station serving the NND had a problem and the Power Holding Company refused to repair it because the NND was owing to it a huge amount of money. I got information that the NHQ had released funds to clear the bills but it was not paid and there were some administrative issues to clear. I read through the files and observed that Rear Admiral TA Sanni did a good job and wrote a very detailed letter to the Power Holding Company in which he confirmed payment of all outstanding debts.

I had many visitors at the NND from NN establishments in Lagos. One of my guests informed me that the CNS would be in Lagos and I should try to see him. I met the CNS in his official residence with Rear Admiral LOB Agbaje, Commodore Osho, and Commander FSG (W). I could sense that I was being awaited. The electricity bill and power supply problem at NND was brought up. The CNS asked me to set up a Board of Inquiry for Rear Admiral TA Sanni for not paying the bills with the fund released and that his tenure as the ASND would also be investigated. I told the CNS that Admiral TA Sanni did a good job and had paid the bills. I showed him the evidence. He calmed down.

The NN Flagship NNS ARADU was in the main graving dock in a pathetic condition and the NNS AMBE was undergoing a refit at NND. The workshops were in a state of low capacity utilization as there were no major jobs to engage the workers. I had insight into the challenges that would come from the general fleet refit programme. I had done the planning and got approval for the funding while I was on the beat as the General Manager Production and Director of Marine Engineering and later as the Acting Chief of Fleet Support (Head of Engineering Branch).

I had done a similar comprehensive job for the inshore patrol craft squadrons for all operational bases. I was moved as soon as I succeeded in getting financing aspects approved as those who were considered good at sharing the funds were brought in and the excuse usually was that I was principled and only too busy working to get tangible results. It was against this background that I assessed the huge challenges that I would face as the ASND. There would be many ships demanding unprogrammed docking for various reasons among which will be a deception to avoid going to sea and earn a command-at-sea badge. The NN had become used to having ships alongside in harbour making it impossible for officers to acquire sea experience. They are still awarded badges for sea time enabling them to be favourably positioned for higher appointments.

There was a downpour of the typical tropical rainfall in Lagos in early January 2004. I had been in my office for several hours and did not appreciate the flooding of the offices on the ground floor and the Mess. I closed late from work and the officers had gone home. When I went down the stairs to the car porch, I was confronted with heavy flooding. The Officer of the Day told me that this had been the experience for some years. I resolved that a solution should be found and implemented.

The following day, I observed that there would have to be a drainage channel to go under the main drainage channel to a lower level to drain the water to the sea. I started work immediately after setting up a relevant team. We had to construct a drainage channel around the building to take the flood water under the main drainage channel to the lowest point for drainage to the sea. I called the Finance Officer, Commodore Iorta Afeah, and told him of my decision. I informed him that I knew I had not consulted him regarding the source of funding and explained to him that this was a state of emergency to save the building. He assured me of his support and I told him to set up a financial monitoring procedure to control costs.

I started work on the drainage and it was within my spending limits. I informed the CNS during his visit to the NND of the terrible state of the building and the need to take urgent steps to save it. The CNS did not seem to take note and I decided not to press it further. The inspection of the roofing sheets showed terrible deterioration as most had corroded and parts were easily blown away by the wind. It was the same roof the Elder Dempster, the original owner of the old Dockyard, had installed. The roofing sheets would have to be replaced and parts of the building rebuilt and strengthened. I was nicknamed "Hurricane" because of the pace of dismantling or breaking down of damaged structures.

I had drawn up the schedule of work at the NND following the plans derived from the priorities of the NHQ. I made some compromises regarding the use of manufacturer's representatives as the Commander Fleet Maintenance Corps was in favour of a particular Nigerian contractor. I was asked to interview two of them and make a recommendation. I recommended both based on their respective backgrounds. I, however, stressed that they should be closely monitored given our experiences during the NNS ARADU refit. I was in the forefront of involving Nigerian contractors but their proliferation and the belief that they could carry out all jobs including those for which they did not have the expertise led to my request for manufacturer's representatives so that they could handle the more complicated jobs and impart knowledge to the local contractors and the NN refit team.

The CNS on a visit to the NND was pleased with the general progress of work at NND. I told him that we met the cost of the work done on the administrative building so far and the issue of the badly corroded roofing sheets would have to be investigated and necessary action taken. I quickly gave him an impromptu oral briefing and stressed that I would need the NHQ funding to complete the work. The CNS appreciated the enormous problem and was impressed with the drainage constructed to pass under the main drainage system. He gave me the approval to forward to him the estimate of the cost of completing the work. We prepared an estimate and forwarded it to the NHQ without delay. It was approved. I proceeded with the work, aiming to finish it by the end of May 2004.

I saw Rear Admiral SJ Uguna standing by the dismantled heaps of the building materials. He told me that he appreciated the enormous reconstruction work I was undertaking and wished he had done what was being done while he was the ASND. He told me that he wanted to contribute to the reconstruction work. I showed him the internal work going on. The Mess Bar remodelling was ongoing and I told him that I would use marble for the finishing. He promised to fund the cost of the marble works but I told him I would receive no funds from him because his goodwill and appreciation were enough. I completed the marble works and engraved his name on them to honour him. He greatly supported the NNIC team in Italy.

At the beginning of May 2004, the planning of Navy Week celebration activities was being finalised and the President, Commander-in-Chief of the Armed Forces was expected to review the Fleet. It was decided that the NND Mess facilities would be used to host a reception for the President on concluding the review. He was to be taken by helicopter from the NNS ARADU to NND. I had much work to do before painting. The final painting work was completed early in the morning on the day of the Fleet Review.

The early arrivals at the NND were Rear Admiral O Oni and Rear Admiral LOB Agbaje. When I knew of their arrival at the helicopter landing area, I went and received them. Admiral Oni was dazzled with the new look of the Administrative building and while admiring it, he wondered how so much construction could be achieved within five months I took command. Admiral Agbaje cut him off by asking if the seamen would allow me to take over as the CNS to succeed the incumbent.

The President eventually did not do the Fleet Review despite the ships from the Royal Navy and other foreign navies present. I would later know that he was disappointed with the state of the NN Fleet despite the huge expenditure he had made since 1999. I sadly shared his agony as my hopes for the bright future of the NN were being dashed. He left after the ceremonial parade at the NNS QUORA, Apapa. The Minister of Defence, Engr Rabiu Musa Kwankwaso, represented the President at the fleet review. He was received by the CNS; after he inspected the Quarter Guard mounted by the pool jetty, I led the distinguished guests to the reception centre. The CNS was visibly impressed with what he saw and drew the attention of the Minister to what was accomplished. The reception activities were completed.

The NNS AMBE was being programmed for the Defence Headquarters exercise code-named TAKUTE EKPE. The Chief of Defence Staff (CDS) was General A Ogomudia, a coursemate of the CNS at NDA. The CDS had visited the NND to inspect the progress of work on the NNS AMBE and I assured him that every effort would be made to make the ship available for the exercise.

The ship had not gone to sea for a long time and I had the Captain, Naval Dockyard ready to take the ship to sea and train the crew. I knew the Captain also had never taken the NNS AMBE to sea but the job description at the NND involved such undertaking. I knew the enormous risks I was taking and had to secure the services of an experienced tug master on a Nigeria National Petroleum Corporation (NNPC) tug for the trials. The CO of the ship was Commander OC Medani. The first attempt to go to sea after successful harbour trials only got the ship drifting towards the East Mole rocks opposite Atlas Cove. I called off the sea trial and the ship returned to harbour. I had a debriefing session with the CO and Captain of the NND. The issues raised were addressed. The brief to the tug master for the next trial was to accompany the ship to sea and return to harbour. This improved the confidence of the crew and the ship had a good outing and returned safely to harbour.

It was based on the series of further sea trials that I decided to keep the ship at sea and anchorage near the NND basin three days at a stretch. This involved an overnight sea outing followed by an overnight stay at the anchorage while I monitored their progress and the performance of the crew. I had briefed the CO to take the ship to the exercise area about 30 nautical miles from Lagos on Lekki beach and practise landing approaches and test the landing gear as would be required by the NA amphibious troops. The CO did more in the exercise area to inspire confidence.

I had an NND team onboard at sea and while at anchorage overnight, I was at the NND jetty and spent some time in contact with the CO and NND team. All had gone well and I ordered the ship to return to berth at the NND pool jetty designated as convenient and prepare for the embarkation of the amphibious troops of battalion strength. On return to the jetty, the CO came for debriefing and I asked him if he had any worries. He told me that his only fear was facing a board of inquiry and possible court-martial should anything go wrong during the landing operation in the presence of the President, Commander-in-Chief, and all the guests.

I told him that I would take full responsibility and accept the blame at any board of inquiry and court-martial. The CO's task was to land the troops on the beach and the Nigerian Army (NA) had already sent a team to test the waters at the landing area and had a short swim ashore. I had a contingency plan to muster tugs for any recovery plan and the ship being designed with a flat bottom for beaching or shallow waters operations I got the CO's assurance of a successful landing. It was after this that I informed the Chief of Operations at the NHQ that the NNS AMBE was prepared and ready with an NNPC tug for the exercise.

There was a huge relief as the whole exercise depended on the NNS AMBE successfully landing the amphibious component on the beach before the President, Commander-in-Chief. The NNS AMBE was scheduled to embark troops and leave the NND jetty by midnight and sail to take up position for the landing operation at 1000 hours. It was late in the afternoon when I got information from the NHQ that a new tug had been contracted for the operation and paid for in US dollars. I stood down the NNPC Tug and put it on standby to assist in the harbour only on request.

The NA amphibious battalion arrived before sunset and had some rest while their embarkation order was finalised. The embarkation was completed on schedule with an hour or two to spare before midnight. It was midnight when the tug contracted by the NHQ departed the NND pool to take fuel on the Mariner jetty. The FOC WEST, Rear Admiral I. Bob Manuel, and the Exercise Force Commander, Major General Mselbwala were by the jetty monitoring the proceedings. All checks had proceeded well and were monitored and reported to me by my team onboard.

As the ship was about to be cast off on schedule, a steering gear system fault was reported. The CO indicated that he could proceed in emergency mode while the problem was sorted out with my team on board. This caused some delay after which the NNPC tug attended to the NNS AMBE to cast off. It was while the NNS AMBE was getting past the East and West Moles towards the sea that the NHQ contracted tug sailed past the NND to catch up. The NNS AMBE was off my area of responsibility. The Commodore borne onboard the NNS AMBE for the landing operations was Commodore PS Adeniyi. I got home about 0400 hours and was back to my office at 0700 hours to monitor the proceedings. I could not link up with my team and the CO onboard the NNS AMBE at 0600 hours. The landing was scheduled for 1000 hours.

At about 1300hours, I received a call from the CNS at the Lekki Beach reception area. He asked me about the whereabouts of the NNS AMBE. I told him that the ship departed the NND pool with all embarked and I had not received any message about its whereabouts. The ship was no longer my responsibility. I could hear the President, Commander-in-Chief delivering his speech through the CNS handset. It was then I knew that the landing did not take place. I told the CNS that I would keep on waiting to connect with the ship should there be any problem that needed my attention. I remained in my office till I sighted the NNS AMBE and the escorts entering the harbour at about 1730 hours. I immediately contacted the CNS and told him that I had sighted the NNS AMBE entering the harbour. The CNS asked me if the ship was being towed and I told him that from my observations, as I was speaking with him, the ship was entering on her own without any tug assistance. I confirmed to him on request that the ship was sailing into the harbour without tug assistance and getting past Atlas cove and nearer to my observation spot in my office. He was relieved that the ship was safe.

The NNPC tug was available to assist the NNS AMBE berth at the NND pool while the escorts proceeded to the Naval Base at Apapa. I went on board and had a quick assessment of the situation. I had a briefing from my team onboard the ship after which I left the office to reflect on all that had happened so far. The steering gear problem was well managed and as the ship set course for the staging post area as planned, one of the two propulsion diesel main engines overheated due to debris sucked into the seawater cooling system. It was while the technical crew and my team on board were trying to clear the debris that the ship altered out of course to the sea. The contracted tug in attendance never attempted to assist the NNS AMBE. All towing efforts by the Cat Class ships led by Captain G Alily resulted in the parting of towing ropes. The NNS AMBE was too far away. How did the ship get so far out of course, and why was the Joint Force Headquarters not in touch with the Commodore and Commanding Officer of NNS AMBE that I had to be called at 1300 hours to account for the whereabouts of the ship? The blame game and excuses, as always, were about to begin to cover up the real causes.

The following day, I was in the exercise area where the troops were moved to an overnight phase of the exercise. The troops disembarked at the NND pool jetty and were transported by land to the exercise area. I was with the Chief of Air Staff, Air Marshal J Wuyep, discussing the development. He told me that he was informed that the NNS AMBE was not operationally available for the exercise. I told him that the overheating was a routine problem the NN warships encountered in the dirty waters of Lagos harbour and not why the ship could not show up for the exercise. I explained further that the NNS AMBE operational state was the best among the NN warships and the ship had spent three days at sea and anchorage without problems. The exercise was concluded with a debriefing with the CDS in attendance. The arrival of the President, Commander-in-Chief at the beach had to be delayed. He had to be taken to see some other locations while waiting for information on the arrival of the NNS AMBE.

It was at the NN debriefing at the Western Naval Command that the CO, NNS AMBE gave further details with timings of the conflicting orders he was receiving. The CO mentioned that at 1300 hours, he was ordered to alter course and return to the harbour and it was exactly at the same time the CNS was asking for the whereabouts of the ship.

I took up the issue immediately with Rear Admiral F Agbiti who moderated the debriefing session as Chief of Operations and Training at the NHQ. I told him that an investigation must be carried out regarding who gave the order to the NNS AMBE to return to the harbour while the ship was still being expected at the exercise area and the CNS, in the same area with the CDS and the President, were not informed. There was never an investigation and if the fault was mine, I knew the disciplinary measures that would have been advertised with dire consequences for me. There were several incidents since a tug was lately imposed barely eight hours to the expected time of departure of NNS AMBE and the same tug left the NND pool to refuel when it was expected to be on standby for leaving harbour routines. The role of the Commodore onboard the NNS AMBE and the intrigues of inter-services rivalry that needed to be addressed by an investigation were never addressed. I took note of the deafening silence that covered up the issues and moved on.

Commodore PS Adeniyi had some years ago denied the NN the opportunity of acquiring a German training ship Stortebecker because the ship was a single screw; that is a propeller-driven by one propulsion shaft. The NN was having a squadron of Cat Class ships over 50 years old from the US Coast Guard stock of junkyards that were single screw in the escort of the NNS AMBE for the exercise.

I was doing my routine round of the NND one day in June to keep abreast of the progress of various jobs being carried out when a civilian worker walked up to me and started congratulating me. I was surprised and told him that I had already celebrated my promotion to the rank of Rear Admiral with them since January and it was six months now since the promotion was released. He told me that when I assumed command, they were told that I would not be allowed to last beyond March 2004 as I was going to be retired to make way for the officer that the system favoured to be the ASND and who was still a Commodore. The officer was Commodore E Kpokogri, the General Manager Plans at the NND who was very reluctant to give me a handing over note until I forced him to put down something in writing for me to hold on to. I was considered just holding fort at the NND so that excuses would be found to prematurely retire me.

I remembered the advice and observation of Lieutenant Commander FS Ebohon in 1979 which had been a constant reminder. I would also be congratulated by a senior officer on my staff at the end of the year for surviving the intrigues to remain as the ASND. At a stage, the senior civilian staff at the NND told me that I was in grave danger and had to take measures to ensure my safety.

June 2004 saw heavy rainfalls in Lagos and resulted in unusual flooding that badly affected my residence. I had to organise all hands including the sentries on duty at my residence to bail out the flood water and started the drying process. I left for the office and met the worst conditions on Ahmadu Bello Way at the entrance to the NND main entrance gate and that of our neighbour, the Nigerian Television Authority (NTA). I noticed that the chaos outside did not affect the NND and the Administrative building because the drainage channel newly constructed had worked very well as there was no flood in the premises. I inspected other facilities and was satisfied that none was affected.

I was attending to some matters in the office when I received the information that the Governor of Lagos State was at the NND gate and was told to wait for my permission to enter the premises. I ordered the security to let him in. I rushed down the steps to receive His Excellency Bola Ahmed Tinubu and his Deputy Femi Pedro.

I took them with two other aides to my office. I need not ask why they were barefooted. The Governor narrated his ordeal with the flood at his residence in Ikoyi that forced him to wade through the flood barefooted with their trousers rolled up to their knees. They declined my offer of refreshments. The Governor then informed me that NTA told him that the NND was obstructing the flow of stormwater draining to sea through their premises. I took the Governor and his entourage for inspection of the area where a concrete chamber was built to prevent rubbish from being washed into the NND dock water channels.

I explained the complex channels around the NND main dock and the evidence of the debris we had been collecting from the chamber as water drained from the road through NTA. NTA was not making efforts to clear the rubbish collecting at their end. Also, the NTA building was built over the drain channel. The Governor informed me that a team would be set up to interface with the NND to solve the problem of flooding caused by the blockages through NTA. I assured him of full NND cooperation.

As we walked back to the Administrative building, the Governor was impressed with the rebuilt Administrative Block's clean environment and he said to me: "Thank you for beautifying Lagos." He went on to inform me of his plans for the Eko Atlantic City nearby and that he would want the cooperation of the NND to clear the Bar Beach. I assured him of our full cooperation.

The jobs being done on the NNS ARADU and the NNS AMBE continued to receive attention. The local contractor GUS-TEK approved, instead of manufacturers' representatives, did not impress me. Work on the diesel main engines was daunting; a new main engine ordered for the NNS OFIOM while I was at FMC had to be installed. The spare parts also ordered within the same period for major works on the two LST had to be utilized.

The quality of the technicians deployed to work on the main engines was poor but they were the experts the NN gave to me. I could not standby and watch the destruction of sophisticated and very expensive diesel engines and spare parts. The reasons given by the local contractor for failing to complete jobs on the schedule were diversionary. The local contractor management had direct access to CNS through Commander FMC. The local contractor started finding other jobs in the NND to use as a diversion by advising the CNS to allow them to take on the jobs. I noticed that the new engine installed on the NNS AMBE was being damaged due to inexperience and the new spare parts for the old engine was also being wasted. I was really upset that workers without requisite qualifications and expertise were being used and I referred to my letter to the CNS demanding the availability of the manufacturers' representatives to solve the enormous problems being caused. I was branded a saboteur for insisting on basic standards.

Rear Admiral LOB Agbaje, Commodore F Osho, and the local contractor were virtually having a field day at the NND undermining my efforts by their advice and report to the CNS regarding what they thought would make him get annoyed with me. I was no longer wanted on active service by their reckoning as I was accused of high standards and not allowing waste of funds or what they popularly called "eating money." It was that crude and accepted as the system norm.

The other major jobs onboard the NNS ARADU under my supervision and control were progressing well and the ship was beginning to wear a new look. There was an incident of drums of diesel oil being taken from the ship in a civilian truck. The truck and driver were stopped at the gate and I was informed. I ordered that the driver be detained and the truck with its drums of diesel oil be confiscated as an exhibit. Not long after, I started receiving phone calls from senior officers. I was told that the CO NNS ARADU approved that the oil should be taken out and sold to generate funds to run the ship. I was disgusted by this episode. It was not strange for officers and men to ask for small quantities of diesel oil and in some cases lubricating oil for use on their private generators and cars. But this had become big business such that a civil vehicle would be driven into a military establishment after working hours to load drums of oil for sale. The CO eventually phoned me and I told him that the fuel should be returned to the ship's tanks under the supervision of the NND duty personnel and the truck and driver should never be seen on the NND premises again. The CO was shortly replaced by Commodore PS Adeniyi.

I had satisfactorily carried out the major hull repair works onboard the NNS ARADU and started preparing the ship for undocking and continuation of the repair jobs onboard alongside. The painting scheme for the underwater hull had been completed and a date fixed for the undocking. The CO was briefed on the undocking programme and the Undocking Operation Orders was issued. The CO was very reluctant to follow the orders issued and did not prepare his crew as he contested the authority of the ASND, an Admiral, to issue the undocking orders. He thought, perhaps, that being a seaman CO and a Commodore, he was qualified to tell me when to undock the ship.

The ship was to undock on a Monday and the preceding Sunday was declared a working day for the dockworkers detailed for the final checks. I was in a blue rig (action rig) and by the dock after early morning Sunday church service. The CO came onboard in the afternoon nicely dressed in a suit and kept to himself. As he left the ship, he walked past me hardly uttering a word. The MEO onboard reported leakage as the dock was being flooded the following day. This was a false report and when I decided to go down and inspect the leakage, the MEO disappeared. It was when the flooding of the dock continued after I left the ship that the CO realised that he must obey the orders issued by the ASND. I told the CO, NND, Commander AO Joel-Taiwo that as there were enough tugs mustered to get the ship out of the dock and into the pool berth, he should be ready to take charge of the operations and link up with the ship's staff. The high tide timings had to be adhered to but the CO refused to organise his crew to leave the dock.

On missing the target high tide timing, I ordered that the gangway be removed and should remain on the jetty while the CO and his crew would have to remain on board as the NND team started preparations for undocking the following day. The tugs from Nigeria Ports Authority (NPA) were returned and told to be on standby for the next day's timing that would be communicated. I returned to my office to sort out the administrative issues related to the changes to the undocking orders.

I received a message that the FOC WEST, Rear Admiral I Bob Manuel, was by the NNS ARADU and wanted me to see him there with a large number of naval and civilian personnel gathered and watching the acts of indiscipline. I wondered why he could not come to my office first. I wanted to send a message to him to come to my office but changed my mind because I did not want to be seen to be rude to the FOC. I left my office and went to meet him by the jetty close to the NNS ARADU with the CO NNS ARADU watching from above trapped onboard the ship. I saluted the FOC and his immediate response was to order me to mandate my staff to position the gangway and free the CO and the ship's crew.

An order to issue an order in this manner does not work and it is an improper act. I requested the FOC to please follow me to my office as the gangway would not be positioned as he wanted. The FOC followed me to my office and I explained to him that the CO, a Commodore, disobeyed my orders despite being briefed several times about the undocking operations and it was improper that he, FOC WEST, should enter my area of authority and could not come to my office to let me know he was around to intervene. I told him that the CO's acts of indiscipline should never be tolerated and the public order he issued to me to position the gangway was in total disregard for the ASND and the undermining of my authority. I requested the FOC to tell the CO to obey my orders and get ready to undock by the first high tide in the morning of the following day. The FOC agreed and I escorted him out of my office as he headed for the NNS ARADU and left NND. NNS ARADU in the main dock was under my command and not that of the FOC WEST. On completion of repairs, the ship returns to FOC WEST.

I called a meeting of my principal staff officers and had the undocking orders re-issued followed by a signal to the ship giving the time for the undocking. The CO, NND was authorised to position the gangway and go on board to give the CO a copy of my signal and the undocking orders re-issued. On acknowledging receipt of the documents, I authorised the free gangway well after 2200 hours. The following morning I left the vicinity of the operations and asked the CO, NND, and Dock Master to handle any issues that would arise. I was walking towards the pool jetty when the CNS called me on my mobile number and asked what happened the previous day. I told him it was an act of indiscipline as the CO refused to obey the ASND's orders. I told him that the undocking operation was in progress and I would send him a report of the incident. I wrote the report and sent it to the CNS. It was sent to FOC WEST for whatever reason and there was no feedback thereafter.

The focus on the NNS ARADU shifted to the repairs of diesel engines for propulsion, electric power generation, and auxiliary machinery and equipment. It would be impossible to make progress on this range of types of machinery and other equipment to make the ship operationally available if it was still in the dock. I had experienced as MEO of the NNS ARADU how weeds started growing in the dock as we waited for the availability of essential spare parts that were delayed because of obstacles that could have been avoided. One of the weeds was eventually taller than me and I posed for a photograph with it to remind me of the time wasted.

I had done my duty by ensuring the NNS ARADU was undocked to free space for other jobs. I was having the main dock free for other ships at last. The MCMVs had to be docked for essential defects rectification that included the hydro-jets. A contractor was sourced from an East European country for the job and all arrangements were made without informing me. I was only asked to quickly dock the ships as the leakages were getting worse. I detailed my staff to follow and monitor the progress of work and I had my frequent inspections. The main hydro-jet section housing was removed to a workshop in Lagos and on getting information about the procedures that would be used for the repair of the section housing made of stainless steel, I visited the workshop and had discussions with the technical staff. The stainless steel housing would have been damaged had it been treated as an ordinary steel structure. I availed the workshop staff of the special requirements and was with them to see through the repairs and safe return of the section housing for installation on the ship.

I had been isolated from the MCMVs since June 1988 after handing over and debriefing to conclude my assignment as Chief Delegate and the ships were treated as normal patrol vessels without regards to the MCMV characteristics that had to be managed. I suffered in silence as I wondered why so much effort would be put to achieve desired military and safety standards only to be recklessly scorned. The NN never developed mine warfare capabilities despite the huge expenditure of public funds. I was perhaps alone thinking or worrying this way.

There were other major problems and crises to follow. The main dock gate had major damage some years ago that was not repaired; it was no more usable as the seals were badly damaged and it was impossible to pump down the seawater in the dock. I had divers down for investigation and the report indicated major damage and the gate would have to be taken out for repairs. The weight of the dock gate was about 360 tonnes.

I called the Managing Director of Niger Docks on Snake Island, Mr GFE Ravelli, a Swiss national, and told him I had an emergency. He immediately took his boat and was at the NND within thirty minutes. I showed him the damaged dock gate now secured alongside the jetty. He told me that an ocean-going floating crane was around for repairs at his facility. He promised me that he would speak to the owner in Dubai, United Arab Emirates, to allow the crane to be around till the NND dock gate repairs were completed.

This entailed a tight schedule of works execution and approval for the contract. He secured the release to remain in Lagos for the operations and gave me a quotation of nine million Nairas. I sent the quotation for the crane availability to the NHQ as I had kept the CNS fully briefed. I was kept in the dark for several days and Mr Ravelli had expected immediate response as the crane was required for offshore oil rig jobs. I phoned Mr Ravelli to plead with him to be patient when he expressed his displeasure that it seemed I did not trust him nor appreciate his efforts as Commodore F Osho from FMC had gone to him to renegotiate the price.

The Commander FMC and Commodore Osho thought that an alternative land crane could be sourced at a lower cost. I was furious but kept my cool. I told Mr Ravelli that the NHQ was only carrying out a due process that would require some time. I promised to follow up and save time. The turbulent waters in the dockyard pools were making the securing ropes part and I had to muster all available ropes to the jetty beside the dock gate for replacement of any berthing ropes that might part and kept 24-hour watch to avoid a repeat of the disaster when the same gate was lost and floated out of the harbour due to turbulence in the pool in 1990 and led to the termination of the career of Captain J Badeji who faced a court-martial and was found guilty.

I took every opportunity to brief the CNS on the need to approve the floating crane as the dock gate was experiencing more damage due to the turbulence in the pool. Commodore Osho was sent to me to discuss the alternative of hiring a land crane. I called my principal staff officers and we had a meeting with the Commodore who was taken to task as regards how a 360-tonne land crane would be brought to the NND and space and supporting structures to take the weight as the structures around the main dock would be damaged under the weights. I concluded the meeting by telling Commodore Osho to ensure the crane was made available within three days as so much time had been wasted and the danger of the pool turbulence was well known.

I was attracted to the dock gate jetty as I arrived at the NND early one morning and was shown a large anaconda killed by a watchkeeper at night. The snake was lurking to attack when it was noticed, trailed, and killed. I briefed the CNS and demanded that the risks were mounting and it was time to make a decision and approve the floating crane quotation. The Commander FMC was forced to recommend about seven million Naira and the CNS approved. The NND Finance Officer assured me that from our commercial earnings it would be possible to make up the balance. I informed Mr Ravelli that the full contract sum was available and gave him two days to complete all procedures and get the crane into location to commence operations that would involve instructions from NPA to close the channel into Lagos ports.

The money approved by CNS was sent to Commander FMC and I got the information from the NHQ. I contacted Rear Admiral LOB

Agbaje, Commander FMC (CFMC), who told me that he had since given a directive to get the money to the NND, General Manager, Finance. I was informed by GM Finance that the money was reduced at FMC. I contacted the CFMC who graciously sent the balance to make up the amount approved by CNS and from NND sources the amount was brought up to nine million Naira to pay for the floating crane. The full payment was made and preparations started to get the floating crane to the premises of the NND.

The arrival of the floating crane showed the enormousness of the task ahead. I wanted the dock gate lifted out of the water and properly supported to commence repair works. It was a very complex operation carried out without any major incident. The following day, the CNS came to see the dock gate. He could not believe the massive structure and I told him that the next stage of intervention would require funding releases whose estimates would be forwarded to him. I told the CNS that I would engage the services of Dorman Long technical staff working on the pressure vessels fabrication and whose competence I was assured of seeing them at work at the NND. I told him that standards would not be compromised because the structure was not what could be easily lifted out of water for repairs. I secured his approval. I was happy to be free of contractors being sponsored to carry out shoddy jobs for which I would be blamed and called a saboteur.

I met the CNS on my way home in his official residence on Queen's Drive, Ikoyi, not far from my residence. This was to allow me to brief him that I would be asking for the balance of about two million Naira taken from the NND funds to meet the contract sum for the floating crane. The NND was earning from commercial jobs and ploughing the earnings into NN warships and maintenance of NND infrastructure. I met the CNS with Commodore Osho having some refreshments or desserts after a meal and I was offered a seat near the CNS. I waited for a relaxed moment to have the CNS full attention. I thanked him for the approval and release of the seven million Naira and told him that I had to take money from the NND commercial earnings to pay the nine million Naira before the crane was released as that was the amount the owners in Dubai approved.

The CNS turned to Commodore Osho and asked him why he did not inform him correctly. He was evasive and had nothing to say. I informed the CNS that I would be forwarding a letter to the NHQ for his consideration to give the NND the balance. The CNS had seen the impressive crane and massive dock gate and was pleased and surprised with the job done. The CNS agreed to my proposal for a refund and I was grateful. I left having set records straight. My finance officer would do the follow up at the NHQ for the release of the money directly to NND.

I would have another encounter with Commodore Osho when he would come into NND premises and incite some civilian workers to go on strike over fire fighting equipment maintenance. He reported to the CNS that there was low morale at NND and a strike was imminent by the civilian workers. I ordered him out of the NND premises and told him to stay away. I issued an order banning him and as it was being implemented by the security details at the gate, the CNS was immediately alerted. I told the CNS that the report to him about civilian workers threatening to go on strike was contrived by the officer as he had lately developed the habit of parking his car near the fire station hidden from general view and was inciting the workers to go on strike while there were no complaints from them. I told the CNS that the Commodore had no job or appointment at the NND but was always on the premises causing disaffection. The CNS told me that the Commodore should be allowed access to the NND. I had made my point that I would not tolerate the nonsense.

I hosted a delegation from EMGEPRON of Rio de Janeiro, Brazil, led by a Rear Admiral. The visit aimed to explore and determine the scope of supplies for the maintenance of three docks. The commissioning of the NND in 1990 was facilitated by EMGEPRON that trained the NN personnel in Brazil and Lagos and supplied expertise and a lot of equipment and materials for the docks. This was about fourteen years ago and a lot of the supplies needed replenishment.

The composition of the team was mainly naval personnel as EMGEPRON is a Brazilian Navy shipyard managed on a commercial basis under Vice Admiral Napoleao Bonaparte Gomes. I had been briefed by the NHQ regarding MOD involvement and the area of interest. I had the NND Staff detailed to participate in the discussions and inspection of the facilities. The Rear Admiral and myself were left alone in my office as the teams jointly went round for inspection. As we had some refreshments, I asked the Brazilian Admiral what should be taking place in the NND with the range and diversity of installations if it was located in Brazil. He had appreciated the impressive range of facilities at the NND and he knew why I asked. He replied that he was not with the appropriate technical team and would have to send one back to the NND on his return to Brazil to discuss warship design and construction. The joint inspection gave an idea of the state of NND facilities and the scope of supplies. The additional and more important take away was shipbuilding. In this regard, I set in motion steps to revive the design offices in the Steel Workshop. There was decongestion and I invited Dorman Long to assist with the installation of computer-assisted facilities and drawing boards.

The Brazilian Admiral followed up on our discussion and a technical team was sent to the NND for discussion on warship design and construction. The Brazilian team was impressed with the quality of welding on the pressure vessels being fabricated by Dorman Long at the NND and also the major refit of Tugs MIRA and RIMA occupying the two twin docks. There was a consensus that there were high-quality welders available to the NND and emphasis would be on other areas of warship systems design and construction. It was decided that a warship of the NN Town Class be the subject of efforts as it would easily fit in the twin docks. The first ship would be built in Rio De Janeiro at EMGEPRON where the NN staff would be involved at all levels and the second one would be started at the NND after the lead ship was launched in Brazil. This arrangement would allow movement of expertise and the NND staff working with them so that subsequent constructions would take place at NND facilities with the Brazilians fully on the ground. This was to gradually acquire and domesticate the technology for warship design and construction. The report of the proposals was sent to the NHQ after briefing the CNS and it was considered the right way to proceed.

A delegation led by Rear Admiral A Amauchechukwu was sent to EMGEPRON to inspect their facilities and discuss the proposals further. I was a member of the Delegation which was joined by the Nigerian Defence Adviser in Washington. The Nigeria Ambassador to Brazil, His Excellency Josef Egbuson was an exceptional host.

The journey to Rio de Janeiro was through Johannesburg with South African Airways. I had a copy of the autobiography of Rear Admiral NB Soroh, a former Chief of the Naval Staff whom I had been visiting because of his health challenges. He encouraged me to call at any time and I found out that it was most convenient in the evenings between 1900-2100 hours when he was always downstairs watching television programmes. It was during one of the very engaging discussions that he gave me a copy of his autobiography which he graciously autographed for me. This book engaged me on the journey and I had a fantastic idea of the efforts of Vice Admiral JEA Wey, Rear Admiral NB Soroh, and Vice Admiral MA Adelanwa in planning the NN Fleet and the NND well into the future. Admiral NB Soroh chaired the NN Fleet planning committee after the civil war under the guidance of Vice Admiral JEA Wey. Vice Admiral MA Adelanwa went far with implementation.

The delegation had a good appreciation of the scope and spread of the Brazilian defence industry. We had an excellent programme that gave us more than what EMGEPRON had as we visited other defence establishments including the research and development centre. I struck a cordial relationship with the Chief Executive of EMGEPRON Vice Admiral B Napoleao Gomes. He was impressed with the Nigerian handcrafted cap I wore for dinner and demanded one which I sent to him on my return to Lagos through a delegation he sent to follow up on our visit.

On my return, I had an audience with Admiral NB Soroh and asked him what crystal ball he was looking into that gave us the impressive NN Fleet after the civil war. He gave the question some thoughts and told me that there was no crystal ball because the Navy was international and the RN provided a solid background for the planning of the NN Fleet. They sought to meet international standards.

I then asked him why the seamen allowed a Marine Engineer Officer to be the first Nigerian Head of the NN and later Chief of the Naval Staff. He was reflective for a few seconds and told me that there was nothing to stop the most experienced naval officer at the time from being the Chief of the Naval Staff. In a remarkable show of appreciation, he praised Vice Admiral MA Adelanwa for the decision to execute the NN Fleet development plans he met as he refused to bow to pressure to abandon the plans after his (Soroh) sudden removal from office due to the coup of 1975 that brought General Murtala Muhammed to power. I had a wonderful insight into the rich history of the NN to rely on as a guide. The experiences of the civil war were brought to bear by those who fought the war to execute the impressive warship acquisition programme in the history of NN.

The subsequent visits of the EMGEPRON delegation were to define details of the various proposals and forward them to NHQ. I led the efforts to set up the Directorate of Ship Design and Construction while I was DME at NHQ and this was useful for the ongoing processes. Commodore (later Rear Admiral) E Ijioma was the Director in charge at NHQ and the Chief of Naval Plans had the supervisory responsibility. Brazilian President Inacio Lula's visit to Nigeria, during the administration of Chief Olusegun O Obasanjo, had Vice-Admiral Napoleao on the Delegation, and this added impetus to our efforts. The NHQ was fully involved with our efforts at the NND that produced the specifications for a Town Class Coastal patrol boat which was basically to be the workhorse of NN with a range and endurance of about seven days at sea at economical speed without replenishment.

This marked the birth of the warship commissioned as the NNS ANDONI. The objective of the number of ships to be constructed and commissioned annually was never achieved. The development of the design specifications was a joint effort and a cost-sharing arrangement was agreed to with EMGEPRON that would provide mainly the expertise while the NN provides the bulk of the funding and depending on how many could be exported to West African countries a profit-sharing formula would be agreed between the parties. Some officers expected EMGEPRON to bring money and expertise and also come to Nigeria to build the ships except the first one. This was not realistic but it was in the domain of the NHQ and I focussed on developing NND facilities to meet the standard requirements for warship design and construction and involving Dorman Long staff for computer-assisted design facilities and production of technical drawings.

The job on the NNS ARADU had progressed to the point where I started preparations for harbour and sea trials. The CO was still not taking measures to ensure he got in line with the progress being made as he had his ideas of the progress being made. The CNS on his routine visit to see things for himself had a first-hand impression of the situation and expressed his displeasure by warning the CO that if his attitude did not change, he would be removed. It was not long after that Commodore BA Raji was appointed to replace Commodore PS Adeniyi as CO.

The new CO came with a positive attitude and I gave him the support he needed to keep abreast of developments related to improving the operational state of NNS ARADU, the Flag Ship. The training of the men on board who had not gone to sea for a long time needed attention as the job completion progressed. The discussions on the various stages of trials enabled us to plan to gradually work up the ship. I assured the CO that I would go to sea with him when he was ready and would be his additional MEO.

The first attempt to go for a sea trial with me onboard as agreed was almost aborted as we left the NND pool with the usual tug assistance. The size of the NNS ARADU could be intimidating for a first time outing. The CO wanted to return to berth as one of the main mains could not be engaged when he ordered it. I told him that there would be no turning back and I left the bridge to assist the technical staff sort out the problem. On my return to the bridge, the NNS ARADU was out at sea and had a problem-free first day at sea and returned to harbour.

The pumps and fittings on the main dock gate undergoing repairs were dismantled and taken to relevant workshops for servicing and repairs. The dock gate structural repairs and fitting of new seals were the only major works being done at the site where the gate was on a support structure. The concentration of workers was greatly reduced at the gate location as major works were going on in the workshops.

There were many "intelligence visitors" to the NND including a young officer who had just passed out of the NN Intelligence school and was having his first appointment to the NND where he had no experience of technical procedures. His intelligence report to the NHQ and consequently to the CNS accused me of slowing down the repair works. I got a letter from the Director of Naval Intelligence (DNI) warning me and spelling out the consequences that were all geared towards retiring me. I had Dorman Long workers doing the hull repairs and the quality of work being done was just the same as the high standards achieved on the pressure vessels for the oil industry and which the EMGEPRON technical staff on a visit to the NND assessed as higher than what was achieved on the submarines being constructed in Brazil and which I saw on my visit there.

I rejected contractors who would do a shoddy job. Considering the complicated efforts required to lift the gate out of water for repairs, there could be no compromise on the quality of work especially the welding, surface treatments, and fixing of seals. The NN had become used to awarding contracts to whoever showed up and laid claims to unverified expertise and on many occasions I had to manage the disasters that resulted. I was focused on doing quality jobs so that the dock gate would serve the NN for a long time before the next intervention and it was my lot to ensure adherence to standards no matter the consequences for me. I continued with my usual briefings to the CNS on the progress of work based on the schedules.

On completion of all works including installation of all pumps and equipment serviced and repaired in workshops, I set up a team to inspect the entire dock gate in readiness to float the dock gate and subsequent positioning in the slots to seal up the dock and pump down. There had been an accumulation of silt, mud, and debris compacted on the dock floor for months while the dock gate crises were resolved. The floating crane returned to NND and refloated the dock gate. On positioning the dock gate in the slot, the dock was pumped down to reveal the huge mass of silt, mud, and debris to be cleared.

I assessed the requirements to clear the mess and I knew I did not have the luxury of months that it took to clear the dock in 1990. I determined that I would need to assemble artillery of equipment in an excellent operational state. I carried out a survey in the Lagos area for the availability of extra pumps, lift equipment, evacuation trucks to transport the murk out of the NND, and various lengths of water hoses and protective wear for the workers. I set a target of three weeks to clear the dock. It was in April 2005.

As the work was progressing, I had the usual problem of visitors at the NND to observing and making recommendations to CNS as they wished. The CNS was advised that what I intended to accomplish in three weeks, and which in the past took several months to accomplish, could be done in two weeks. The CNS asked me why I could not get the job done in two weeks. I told him of my plan and the assembly of artillery of equipment I had put together to do the job in three weeks what took several months in the past to do. The CNS again threatened me with retirement if I did not complete the job in two weeks.

I knew I barely had two weeks left to be retired but I was determined that I would be working and be at peak performance to the very last minute because I was serving my country and not any individuals. I abandoned my office and spent long hours at the dockside coordinating the work going on with the artillery of equipment deployed and I was satisfied with the progress and the commitment of the workforce.

It was at this period that the NN Sports week was taking place at Abeokuta and this took many officers off their normal duty posts. I ensured all those that needed to be at Abeokuta from the NND left for the sports week and I readjusted accordingly. I was the only Admiral in the NN that did not show up at Abeokuta and there were sports prize awards that I was announced to come forward and do the presentation to winners only to be declared absent. I was beside the dock engaged in battles clearing mud and mess in the main dock. The conclusion of the sports fiesta coincided with the last weekend I was expected to last on active service in the NN.

As the final ceremony was concluded, the CDS and CNS left Abeokuta in a convoy and headed for Lagos. On getting to Lagos, an officer noticed the convoy and phoned me. The officer informed me that the route and direction taken by the convoy indicated most probably that the CDS and the CNS were heading straight for the NND. The officer advised me to be prepared and not to be caught unawares. I was grateful that in such trying moments I had a friend with compassion. I did not tell any of my staff and did not organise a quarter guard at the gate as I did not have enough men around and there was no time to get them cleaned and organised.

I went to the entrance gate and left instructions to have a lookout towards Bonny Camp and Bar Beach and once the particular convoy was sighted I should be alerted. The CDS and CNS were headed for the NND and on being alerted, I dashed to the main gate on Ahmadu Bello Way and received them there. I apologised for not being able to organise a quarter guard. The CDS and CNS decided to step out of their cars and walk through the NND complex to the docks. As I led them past the NND Medical Centre and workshops, the CDS commented on the clean environment. I was slightly relieved but on my guard.

I took them and their aides to walk across the main dock gate top walkway platform. On sighting the artillery of equipment deployed, the CDS suddenly stopped and marvelled as he asked me how the NND managed to get some of the motorised equipment down on to the main dock floor that was now in the final stages of the cleaning operation. I gave a brief explanation of the operations to get the equipment down. As they left the dockside and were heading for the NNS ARADU, I took permission from the CNS to detach and face my ordeal of works ongoing.

I returned to my duty post surrounded by dirt and equipment dealing with all aspects of the operation. It was when they left the NND establishment that I reflected on the possibility that I could have got the instant retirement treatment promised if there was any observed shortcoming and had the CNS found something to complain about as they walked around. There were still attempts to get me retired despite the impressive progress made within such a short time. I was reliably informed that the CNS had to suspend the idea as a close friend of his warned him that if he removed me from the NND or retire me at that moment the NN would collapse on him and stressed that the NN had no Admiral or senior officer that could take on the variety of jobs and responsibilities I was saddled with and making impressive progress which was not appreciated.

I continued to draw inspiration from the fact that the intention of the President, Commander-in-Chief was to have an effective fighting NN and since 1999 I had been associated with the groundworks to realise his objectives. In my prayers, I remember the great wonderworker, St Anthony of Padua as the gentlest of saints and others who stood fast and faced adversity with humility and service. I then remembered my teenage choice to serve the country and the bells of allegiance ring loud demanding loyalty to the President, Commander-in-Chief to continue doing my best and if retirement comes it will meet me prepared and at peace that it met at my best serving country. It did not matter if all I have been doing was cleaning mud and debris to conclude complex main dock repairs and put it back into operations.

I got the main dock cleaned out and started preparations to dock three ships at the same time because of the pressure from the Western Fleet that the ships were having serious underwater leakages as usual. On successful docking of the ships, I sent a team to inspect them to determine the extent of the hull damages resulting in the underwater leakages. The team could not identify any serious underwater damages. I went on board and on sighting one of the COs, I told him that it appeared they raised a false alarm for docking when there was no problem to warrant it. I told him that they would have a very short stay in the dock and would soon be out of the dock and returned to the Western Fleet to continue their deception and idleness. I informed the CNS of the situation and the plan to execute the routine docking servicing and painting of the underwater hull areas.

I had consistently requested and reminded the authorities of the need to call in the manufacturer's specialist staff to carry out their duty as specified in the maintenance manuals. I told the CO NNS AMBE to ensure his staff stopped any work on the main engines that would involve an erratic adjustment of the engine governors as the contractor's staff (GUS-TEK) were inexperienced and causing damages. I warned that there could be an explosion on board if the governor's problems were not expertly handled. The NNS AMBE watertight compartment design was such that the ship would sink immediately in the event of a propulsion main engine explosion.

It was onboard one of the Mark 9 Corvettes that the bad practice of tampering with the main engine governors was freely encouraged perhaps to prove me wrong as an alarmist against progress. An explosion occurred onboard NNS ENYIMIRI as the main engine governor was being randomly adjusted. A young marine engineering officer, a Sub Lieutenant, was instantly killed by the explosion and many ratings suffered various degrees of severe burns in addition to other injuries. On getting the information that the ship was almost sunk alongside, I got a boat and despatched some of the heavy-duty floats at the NND with a team and took off by road to the naval Base at Apapa to render assistance.

I got on board the ship in danger as the uppermost continuous deck was virtually all below water. I quietly prayed that the ship I was standing on would never go under and memories of the NNS DORINA sinking alongside flashed by. As I made efforts to approach the entrance hatch and ladder steps into the engine room, I saw the carnage caused by the explosion. Several mangled structures partially covered by flooding water being pumped out conveyed to me the enormity of the explosion force. A rating standing nearby informed me that the dead body of the young officer was still trapped below in the flood. I stood still and honoured the dead with a salute and silent prayers for his soul. I then surveyed the damaged structures still not covered by floodwater and heard of the evacuation of many sailors with various injuries to the Naval Hospital at Ojo Naval Barracks.

The grief of the families affected flooded my mind. How would the NN explain to the parents of a young officer just starting his career that reckless practices led to his death? Later, I was told that Rear Admiral LOB Agbaje was approaching the NND when he got the phone call about the explosion and he turned back. The ship was saved, the dead buried while those severely injured would be left with scars for life; there will be no lessons learnt. It would be business as usual. It was sickening.

I was at home with a visitor when I received a phone call from the CNS who was in London with the local contractor chief executive (GUS-TEK). He asked me in a rather harsh tone why I had not repaired the generators for electric power supply to the NND. I informed him of the efforts being made and the priority rating as the NND had other sources but he was insistent to know why I had not engaged the services of the local contractor who had not been able to repair any of the main diesel engines on the NNS AMBE and diesel generator engines on NNS ARADU. Also, my advice to follow best practices was turned down because the shoddy work by the local contractor was prefered. I was asked to stop my explanations and taken to task for why I had not engaged the local contractor who was damaging engines and very expensive spare parts. I had also been reported for not providing the spare parts to repair the overhead crane installed on the NNS AMBE for the new diesel engine installed by the contractor to be removed again for the local contractor's intervention in the NND mechanical workshop. I had been reduced to performing petty errands at the NND for the contractor through the CNS orders. Why did the nation invest so heavily in my development? I was the excuse for the contractor's failures.

I pleaded to no avail for the CNS to listen to me but I was told to prepare, write, and hand in my retirement application before he returned.

I was caught unaware with the speed of the CNS harsh verbal delivery but not his intentions and my visitor, who worked with Chevron guessed rightly that "there is no one that can talk to you like that if not the CNS or someone higher than him."

My visitor wondered why I should be treated in such a manner. My daughter Diana Ahaoiza, a secondary school student then, who was nearby, unknown to me, advised me to give them their job and go and look for another one. This was as soon as the visitor had left. I contacted the Naval Secretary, Rear Admiral AR Adesokan, who told me that should I submit such a letter it would be instantly approved. There is no consideration for institutional demands.

I resorted to taking it one day at a time and I informed my wife that I would be prematurely retired at any moment. I had to think carefully about retirement that was not due and the effect it would have on my family. I have had enough but abruptly leaving was not right considering the appalling situation in the NN that needed a voice and action for the sake of those that looked forward to a bright future as I had as a Sub Lieutenant at the concluding stages of my course at RNEC, UK. The future looked bleak with the lack of unity of command essential for a total focus on the development of the institution.

I had visited the NNS AMBE and was being seen off by the CO when I emphasised the need to remind his crew and especially the technical personnel to ensure the contractor working onboard did not engage in activities that would cause more damages than repairs. The CO asked me why I like putting myself in front of the barrels of guns manned by detractors. I told him that I had attained the rank of a Rear Admiral and he, the CO, still had three steps to get there. I told him to get behind me as I put myself in front of barrels of guns and he would be saved. I had been part of the team that determined the NN Fleet requirements and bought very expensive spare parts including a new MTU propulsion engine when I was at FMC between 1990-1993. I was now witnessing, as the ASND, the waste of such precious engineering masterpieces of an MTU engine and other critical spare parts on the NNS AMBE.

What is military service and all the training about if not to man your guns and face the enemy or those set on destroying the country you bear and owe allegiance to serve? If it is your job to face the barrel of the guns of the enemy, what is extraordinary being in front of the barrels of guns made of the cumulative intrigues of detractors? I was not reckless and would not be deterred. I told the CO that I appreciated his concern but that was what being a Rear Admiral in the NN entailed.

The next sea outing for the NNS ARADU had the CNS onboard and I had to go again. The CO had done a good job on his crew and was adhering to the advice I had been giving him. I was very proud that the CNS had such a pleasant day at sea and as we returned to harbour, the tug master was battling with a very strong ebb tide that made the turn into and through the narrow pool entrance gap a nightmare as the ship was very close to colliding with the concrete jetty wall. It was a close call as the CNS thought that the turn was going to result in a crash against the concrete jetty wall. I moved closer to the CNS and assured him that this was the routine each time the NNS ARADU was caught in strong tides at that location. The CNS was relieved on scaling through and securing alongside. He was pleased with the outing and the performance of the ship as there was no operational defect recorded or reported.

I was informed by the CNS of the invitation for the International Fleet Review in Portsmouth to commemorate 200 years of the RN battle fleet victory of 1805 at the Battle of Trafalgar under the command of Lord Horatio Nelson. The CNS promised to fax the letter of invitation to me to pass on to the CO, NNS ARADU. This implied taking charge of the preparations. On receipt of the letter, I noticed the signature on the letter of invitation was that of Admiral Sir Alan West, the First Sea Lord. I was thrilled having read the account of his ordeal on board the HMS ARDENT at the Battle of Falklands. It was clear to me in 1992 when I read the memoirs of Admiral Sandy Woodward that he was on track to be the First Sea Lord and the transparent RN system for emergence and appointment never failed him over the years.

Admiral Alan West was the CO of HMS ARDENT the Plymouth-based RN frigate that took "one hell of a hammering" from Argentinean Air Force bombings in the Battle of San Carlos waters during the critical phase of amphibious landings in the Falkland War on 21 May 1982. As a Commander aged 32 then, he was the youngest Frigate commander.

The ordeal of his ship was summed up by Admiral Sandy Woodward, the Battle Group Commander in his book "ONE HUNDRED DAYS" thus: "With one-third of his ship's company killed or wounded, and with terrible fires blazing below deck, Alan ordered them to prepare the 4.5-inch gun and face the enemy once more." The loss of his ship, the HMS ARDENT, and the bravery of the young CO and his crew can be appreciated when it is known that they came under "one of the most concentrated hammering ever suffered in the history of RN naval sea-battle from Cape St Vincent to Jutland." I was spurred into action to ensure the NNS ARADU honoured this hero, celebrate Lord Nelson, and have NN participate in the first-ever International Fleet review with The Lord High Admiral, Her Majesty Queen Elizabeth II in attendance. I was excited because of the exposure the NN personnel would have to a very rich history by participating. It was an opportunity for excellent education on the conduct of naval affairs.

What a historic event and what an honour to have Admiral Alan West sign that letter of invitation that I would be acting upon as I was with the RN in Plymouth, during the Falkland War and shared the anxieties of the war and the ordeals of my RNEC Manadon contemporaries in the hostile cold winter waters of the South Atlantic. I was making sure my country's name was recorded in history by the NNS ARADU being present in Portsmouth. This was the first International Fleet Review to be attended by a ship from the NN and it would be in commemoration of a famous naval battle of Trafalgar 200 years ago. This was a rare event.

I had several difficult times with the CNS because of the type of reports he was receiving on the NND from CFMC and the contractor whose company was called GUS-TEK that was almost running a parallel NN engineering department dictating standards of performance that was wasting resources being devoted to the refit of ships in the Fleet. I have had several warnings from the CNS that he was wary of my positions on several issues though I was never proven wrong and the results showed positive trends.

I was at the CNS residence one early morning as he prepared to leave for the airport for Abuja. There was a fiery outburst from the CNS as he stormed past me from the large sitting room of the institutional residence; and as I followed him to his car, he ignored me, entered into his official car, and departed for the airport. The ASND was an Administrative Authority directly responsible to the CNS and my appearances at the institutional residence had become routine. On occasions, we had relaxed discussions and had the normal advice a good boss will give about the forces at play at the next level. What had gone wrong again?

The wife of the CNS witnessed the fury and called me into the sitting room and offered me a seat. I saw the contractor sitting in a corner very relaxed. She tried to calm me down but my voice did not betray any annoyance and she listened to my response as the contractor was also listening. I told her that it would be a shame if, after huge expenditures on the refit of ships and other maintenance tasks, there was nothing to show as achievements. I said that as an Administrative Authority reporting directly to the CNS and an Admiral, I had a responsibility to ensure that he, the CNS, succeeded so that he could confidently act and lead us all as our failures would weaken him and I would not like to be part of his failure but certainly part of his success. The CNS wife had no response and I politely left. The contractor heard me loud and clear in the most polite way I could act.

I had called the CO NNS ARADU to my office the day I got the faxed letter of invitation and gave him a copy. He was elated after I explained the significance of the invitation to him. I told him that the NNS ARADU would require a lot of work and a good voyage plan to make it to Portsmouth. I was emphatic that the NNS ARADU in its present state was not what I would consider operational for the voyage to Portsmouth. I told the CO that the NNS ARADU, NN, and Nigeria must be registered proudly as part of the Trafalgar 200 celebration. This was not an annual event but a rare one in history. I could not explain the complex preparations to him at once. I told him that I would be frequenting the ship thenceforth and we would start immediately by cleaning and clearing all junks and dirt, top to bottom, from the ship to reveal defects.

I engaged several NND teams and dedicated contractors to set to work and it looked like the ship would never make it to Portsmouth by June barely five months away. I also advised the CO to ensure he had good officers and men appointed on board and ensure they had at least two pairs of those uniforms that would be worn frequently. I did daily stroll to the ship and the CO had his lookouts and were always available to receive me on board to inspect the jobs being carried out.

As the preparations gained momentum and the departure date was set, the CO told me as he was escorting me from the ship to my office that the range and scope of activities related to the Fleet Review were complex and confusing. I told him that I was glad he was confused at that stage and I added that it is a good reflection that he was taking the task with professional seriousness. I told him that his simple task was to navigate the NNS ARADU from Lagos to Portsmouth and have his men well dressed with a ship wearing new coats of paints while the RN provided essential harbour boats for movement to and from the berth or mooring. I then added that he should not attempt to impress the masters of sea in their sanctuary. The CO felt relieved and he appreciated that I was telling him to have a simple plan and adhere to its execution. I assured the CO that I would get his ship to an operational state that would guarantee him seven days cruising without operational defect but he must plan the first stop at a port well served by an airport and access to maintenance and logistics facilities. The NN Flagship had not had such a long cruise for a very long time since it sailed from Germany to Lagos in 1981 after delivery by Blohm+Voss shipyard to the NN.

The WEO and MEO of the NNS ARADU were Commander (later Rear Admiral) AL Akintola and Commander (later Commodore) JS Giwa respectively. I gave them instructions on the management of technical personnel and equipment in their charge as I did my daily runs to the ship to prepare the men and material for the International Fleet Review. They were also advised to thoroughly investigate and report any observed defects, at the first port of call and should not be in a hurry to leave. I had given the CO enough background information and had gone to sea with him to enable him to have a mind set to understand and manage situations.

This was to ensure the NNS ARADU had access to maximum support and care. I was, however, worried that the contractor, GUS-TEK, was given the four main generators to service and repair for long and had not impressed me as usual. I received a report of the shoddy jobs being carried out. When they wanted to add the main diesel propulsion engines to their contract awards to sort out a very critical repair, I made sure the contractor did not get it and I told the MEO and WEO to ensure the contractor did not carry out any jobs except the generators given to them long ago. I had the cooperation of the CO, MEO, and WEO to limit the interference of the contractor that should never have been allowed on board.

I was not comfortable with the state of the generators and told the CO, MEO, and WEO to monitor the situation and take precautions. The NNS ARADU set sail on 31 May 2005 and the CNS was around to see off the ship from the NND. The departure ceremony was brief and I stayed in the background to watch the hassle for front seats. I had done my job and the NNS ARADU and crew wore a proud, new look. The NNS ARADU sailed and after seven days had a stopover at Dakar, Senegal. There was no operational defect reported during this stage of the cruise.

There was a reported detection of leakage of water into the lubricating oil sump of one of the two main diesel propulsion engines as the ship was leaving Dakar. The CO decided to return to harbour and the technical staff did a good job of identifying the cause as a cracked cylinder liner. They forwarded the list of spare parts required to repair the leakage. I was cut off from the proceedings and Messrs GUS-TEK took over the management of technical requirements dealing directly with the NHQ and CNS. I was reliably informed of the difficulties in sourcing the spare parts and relying on my knowledge of the NN Technical Stores Depot and the NND stock holdings, those spare parts that were available were identified and packaged for freighting to Dakar.

I had assured the CO, MEO, and the WEO of NNS ARADU that I would do all I could to assist. The ship had had seven days of sailing hitch-free. The journey from Dakar to Portsmouth had problems and the ship's company did a magnificent job of managing them to get to Portsmouth and create the greatest surprise of Trafalgar 200 International Fleet Review.

I was at the NHQ Abuja in June, working on the new warship project as Chairman of a Committee set up to define the final requirements and specifications. I had been working on this with the Brazilian shipyard ENGEPRON and evolved a design called NN WORKHORSE and happy with the progress made so far towards the commencement of execution of the project plans. The sessions had been lively for most of the week we spent and as we concluded the exercise I was informed that a signal had just been released appointing me CFMC and Commodore E Kpokpogri would take over as the ASND. The NHQ had the air of intrigues about a successor to the CNS and I had received calls and advice before I departed from Lagos, that conveyed one warning message-they are fighting hard to replace me as CNS.

The CNS had flown to the UK and after attending the International Fleet Review, he was relieved of his appointment as the CNS but curiously, the officer to take over from him was not announced. It has been the practice that the officer to take over would have been approved and would have been announced at the same time the retirement of the incumbent is announced. The indications were that the President, Commander-in-Chief was not happy with the handling of the situation as such has never happened before. What happened? This situation led to intensive acts of intrigue as what was happening was being openly discussed. I got to know from interactions at the NHQ that I was to take over and should have been announced at the same time the CNS letter of disengagement from service was released.

I was in Abuja and I went to see a principal staff officer in the Presidency as he had inputs into the decision-making process and would know much about the situation. I wanted to know the situation and why there was no announcement of the officer to take over from the outgoing CNS as it had never happened that an incumbent CNS was relieved and his replacement was not announced immediately. This facilitated the waves of open intense intrigues that drew diverse attention. I had learnt from the RN that the First Sea Lord emerges over the years and is known that as the transparent system process takes its course, officers are prepared for higher responsibilities. It is not a last-minute hassle as the tales of intrigues at the NHQ testified. In the past, the progress of similar CNS succession procedures was openly discussed in the NN as I highlighted earlier about the appointment of Vice Admiral Murtala A.H. Nyako that was openly discussed for some years.

A marine engineer officer had impressively emerged after due process and was not someone schooled in sharing or "eating" public money. This was part of the shameless message being spread around among other trivialities such as being a marine engineer he should not be allowed to head a highly technical service where most routine decisions being taken are about engineering. There was also the dominant influence of oil companies involved in bunkering that was supporting a Rear Admiral considered friendly to them. It appeared that the pressure was on to undermine the intention of the President, Commander-in-Chief.

I was determined to meet the principal staff officer in the Presidency for the following reasons. First, the nature of the ongoing discussions was seriously damaging the NN Engineering Branch whose officers undergo the most intensive education and training for several years to serve in the NN and who are routinely under intense pressures due to the nature of the responsibilities they have for the operational state of warships in the NN inventory. They had other important responsibilities for the birth of the warships. Modern warships are intensively an engineering environment. Secondly, I had become the subject of the ongoing intense discussions regarding why an incumbent CNS should be relieved of office and the successor was not announced. The third reason was that it was known that the President, Commander-in-Chief does not retire a CNS without approving the officer to take over immediately. There were wild inventions of excuses regarding why I was not allowed to take over as the CNS that convey wrong impressions about me and were very damaging to the career I have struggled hard to build for service. Lastly, I have restrained from getting involved in the open discussions of what was going on and wanted to take advantage of being in Abuja to pursue the truth and have the rest of my mind on return to Lagos. I had received warning calls on how efforts are being made to undermine the President, Commander-in-Chief.

I needed to be mentally prepared to cope with the abject hatred and other petty acts that resulted in a negative image of me for being an engineer who impressively emerged above others to be the CNS and, as I am at the exit door from active service, my military service record matters most. I felt betrayed and isolated by the NN as officers freely generated their explanations of why I was not allowed to take command as the CNS. This has become my albatross till today.

The principal staff officer at the Presidency was unusually uneasy and told me that "they will not allow an engineer to be CNS" because the feeling was that it was the tradition in the NN. I then informed him that the history of the NN should not be distorted as the first Nigerian CNS, Vice Admiral JEA Wey was a marine engineer officer and was considered the most experienced naval officer to head the NN at the time he was appointed to take over from Commodore AR Kennedy, the last RN officer to head the NN. Vice Admiral Wey was prepared for the office as it is the practice in the RN. I then added that if there were other reasons, they should be made known as there was no documented policy or statutes stipulating that an engineer who had gone through the intensive education, training, and experiences including commanding warships as I had, should be prevented from becoming the CNS. I had a discussion in 2004 with Rear-Admiral Nelson B Soroh, who took over from Admiral Wey as the CNS, on this issue and he confirmed to me that there was no such policy. This, I highlighted to the principal staff officer should he want confirmation to guide the Presidency properly as the President had appointed me.

I had impressively emerged top from a due process and my approved appointment was expected to have been announced. But the principal staff officer asked me to recommend an officer to be appointed as the CNS. I suspected that he was setting a trap for me. I was being asked to find a substitute for me to overturn the decision already made that I am the new CNS, and this could be an act of consequently undermining the intention of the President, Commander-in-Chief. I asked the principal staff officer what the problem of the NN was for which I was being asked to suggest another Rear Admiral for consideration as CNS to solve and eliminate an engineer considered most qualified to be CNS. He was shocked at my question and could not give me an answer. It did appear that it was normal that decisions and approvals of the President, Commander-in-Chief can be overturned and there would be no consequence. I needed no other proof. It has been a very common practice in Nigeria as public servants take pride in undermining the President/Head of State, Commander-in-Chief, and other authorities and they boast about it. This incident is the first one in the AFN and is very unique.

I took my cap ready to leave his office and he pressed me further to suggest a name. I emphatically told him that I did not know how to run down colleagues and he knows me for that as he has never witnessed or heard me blackmailing or talking recklessly about anyone. I explained to him that if those who did not want me to be CNS had defined the problem the NN was facing and the needed solution, then there would be a criterion for comparative analysis of the qualities of available Rear Admirals excluding those tainted by engineering. I summed up by telling him that those carrying out such an exercise could write the names of all the Rear Admirals in the NN excluding engineers and put them in a hat for a lottery draw. As I left, he respectfully saw me off.

How can a decision be made to appoint the headship of a very important arm of the Armed Forces of a very important country when the problem of the establishment is not known? I know that from the intentions of the President, Commander-in-Chief since 1999, he wanted the NN Fleet involved in inshore waters operations and at sea with guns blazing to maintain maritime security for a thriving economy. This is, therefore, the careless, casual, and reckless manner with which the nation-state affairs are conducted by most of those with access to state power to advise the President, Commander-in-Chief. Nigerians are not productive as regards the nation-state development as they easily resort to tribal/ethnic, religious, and other parochial interests such as economic sabotage and petty loose talks to decide important national issues. It is, therefore, the vogue that everyone is qualified for every job as long as it relates to government MDAs where there are public offices to abuse and funds to waste. There may be good ideas about getting jobs done but it is established in Nigeria that government MDAs have a duty to destroy the country. As individuals pursue their good, evil reigns and the resulting corruption is simply wickedness visited on people.

In a properly managed professional military, career planning allows the emergence of qualified officers over the years and there is hardly any change to allow those not qualified. In Nigeria, it is those not fit for office that are supported to rubbish those qualified. This is how material and human resources are wasted in Nigeria and consequently, the country cannot realise its potentials. Those responsible are celebrated all over Nigeria with various recognitions to convey the message that being unproductive, incompetent and an economic saboteur pays handsomely. There is a very serious and endemic SYSTEMIC PROBLEM that

Nigeria must solve as its only problem in the way of its progress; it is PERVERTED MORALITY. It undermines everything from top to bottom very effectively no matter the efforts and resources put in. Public office holders seem to be under instructions and on oath to waste the country. The prevailing situation makes it is almost impossible to think and be productive. It makes Nigeria a wasteland of abandoned projects as human and material assets are routinely wasted.

According to Nicholas Rescher in his book, Objectivity, "Morality is by its very nature geared to safeguarding the interests of others as best as we can manage it in prevailing circumstances. ...For it is morality's object to equip people with a body of norms (rules and values) that make for peaceful and collectively satisfying coexistence by facilitating their living together and interacting in a way that is productive for the realisation of the 'general benefit' of the wider community as a whole." He summarised that in morality's case, one is geared to fostering patterns of action and interaction that promote the best interests of people in general. The dehumanising way slaves were treated and the categorisation of Nigeria's present-day coastline as Slave Coast during the transatlantic slave trade graphically demonstrate how we fail to promote the best interests of people in general. Nigerians are not equipped with a body of rules and values (norms) that make for peaceful and collectively satisfying coexistence. The majority of Nigerians cannot think of the real needs of other people in their actions and deliberations. Poor quality thinking delivers mediocrity as its product that deprives the people of the opportunities for their well-being.

It is not strange in history to note how subordinates undermine leaders. It is part of human nature that must be put under control by having strong state institutions and being equipped with norms to avoid its destructive consequences. President Franklin D Roosevelt during WW2 had to take action to bring his service chiefs under control as they were running their shows against his intentions to the extent that the possibility of a coup was being discussed. The President brought in retired Admiral William D Leahy back to active service to play a role that led to the creation of the office of Chairman Joint Chiefs of Staff for the US military (Source: Commander-in-Chief by Nigel Hamilton).

The problems of the Dark Ages in Europe were solved by the moral rebirth of the people, as articulated by the humanists of the era, to restructure their mindset with a set of norms. This transition to the modern era (Renaissance) released the creative initiatives of the people that led to the start of the first in the series of industrial revolutions that have shaped and is shaping the modern world.

The problem of undermining the President, Commander-in-Chief in Nigeria is very common that no single individual can solve. It is a way of conducting public affairs and explains the failures of the government to meet the needs and aspirations of the people. This is the routine promotion of the worst to rubbish the others. There must be a collective resolve and honesty to respect authority for the unity of command for common good. Nigerians do not know the need to understand allegiance and loyalty in a republic to connect and relate properly with the treasure of a nation-state for their well being. The AFN is dysfunctional and the civil society is disorganised and lacking orientation. Nigerian society consequently is politically immature, without social order and lacking appropriate direction.

The moral foundation is lacking in Nigeria as evident in how Nigerians massively attend religious houses to pray to the good God only to turn around immediately and embrace evil evident in the deprivations of the people that openly manifest. There are inappropriate awareness and character of the elite in leadership positions.

The creative initiative of Nigerians is being stifled and real development cannot take place. There is no moral compass to direct attention to thousands of abandoned projects nationwide and also to determine why the basic infrastructure that the colonial administration left behind in 1960 collapsed. No individual can engineer the required moral rebirth until there is a critical mass of the people that are involved in the journey to control and prevent the open undermining of authority. The nation-state Nigeria is in distress and cries for help. The military leadership has to help the process of rebirth with norms so that allegiance and loyalty reign in AFN to set good examples.

Unfortunately, AFN personnel swear by Almighty God to 'bear true and faithful allegiance to the Commander-in-Chief of the Armed Forces of the Federal Republic of Nigeria....' This is wrong though it is based on the official format of the First Schedule Armed Forces Oath. Nigeria is a Republic with an elected president and representatives. The supreme power is held by the people who mandate those elected to act on their behalf. Nigerians, therefore, should bear true allegiance to faithfully serve their country, causes, constitution, and flag as they decide which symbolises their nation-state. Loyalty is then pledged to an individual elected and mandated as president, commander-in-chief. It is in the system of monarchy that allegiance which is a duty of fidelity is to the monarch (including heirs and successors) that is believed to define the nation-state. Military personnel in Nigeria have to understand this reality so that they are always totally committed to a nation-state's causes and not that of any individual.

After deliberately putting terrible bad causes in place, there would be complaints later that things are not working fine and wayward excuses and explanations easily emerge and all is willfully forgotten regarding the bad causes put in place. In a vital national institution without a strategic plan and quality seasoned planners for development, it is impossible to embark on any programme of action to achieve sustainable results such as credible military capabilities. The chaotic approach to the appointment of the CNS and other service chiefs in Nigeria devalues the high offices as factors related to the development of the institution do not matter and are not considered a priority. I had just concluded a very important committee work at the NHQ early in July 2005 about the future of the NN to commence execution by December 2005. I had been appointed CNS and should be implementing but authority was undermined. I sensed colossal waste as I experienced the intrigues about the appointment of a new CNS as the office remained unoccupied till early August 2005 despite having an appointed CNS: Rear Admiral Isa.

It is very depressing and I wondered why I should aspire to an office where one would be so compromised with little or no time to achieve anything tangible. Some of the Rear Admirals who were considered not fit to be appointed the CNS found political sponsors and senior officers such as Admiral I Ogohi and Vice Admiral SO Afolayan. These are two officers that could have easily contributed to support the President, Commander-in-Chief continue to have the officer that emerged, approved and appointed to take office. They, surprisingly, contributed to undermining the apex national command authority. Their candidates would later call me and I felt their regrets. It is nothing personal. It is the institution being weakened. I have experienced how lonely leadership can be; any President, Commander-in-Chief facing the internal contradictions of Nigeria would suffer terribly the traps of intrigues in isolation. It is impossible to know all that is happening and that is why people are appointed and trusted to help and make the President, Commander-in-Chief succeed. It is why the military establishment emphasises the unity of command that respects the intentions of the President, Commander-in-Chief with the citizens expressing loyalty that is the requirement of allegiance to the country.

On my return to Lagos, the principal staff officer at the Presidency phoned me and was still talking about me suggesting someone for an appointment as the CNS. I almost told him to stop undermining the President, Commander-in-Chief, and acknowledge my appointment as the CNS. It was appropriate to hold back as I assessed that, in the circumstances, he would also be under intense pressure. I had assessed the nature of the petty intrigues going on and was sorely disgusted. I stood my ground that I would not engage in recklessly damaging the reputation of colleagues and he started mentioning names for me to comment on them. I did not take his bait and stuck to my basic principles on this kind of matter. The office of the CNS looked so cheap and worthless if this was how officers were assessed instead of adhering to emergence based on competence as a best practice. I emphasised again that anyone of their choice would be their decision and I would have no part in such a decision as they tried to undermine my appointment and the intentions of the President, Commander-in-Chief for an effective NN. It is not right to take military appointments as a favour done to anyone but for service in the national interest as sworn on oath to God.

It would be normal and in keeping with the known strong character of the President, Commander-in-Chief between 2005-2007 that he would wonder why they were delaying the release of the name of the successor to the outgoing CNS and the argument about my being an engineering specialist would be advanced. I was sure that this would annoy him as an army engineer officer who has had no such restrictions in his very distinguished and inspiring career. It was considered that the problems of the NN, a highly technical service, should be the main consideration for the emergence of a CNS as well as a record of accomplishments. If I was found to be very qualified well above all others that were compared, why should I be punished and the institution denied critical services needed? There were no competitors and the matter of my qualification for appointment as the CNS was settled. Why then announce the disengagement of the incumbent and refuse to announce his successor approved by the President Commander-in-Chief?

The game of petty intrigues lasted for about a month while they tried to find excuses to block my appointment. There were also plots to undermine the intention and authority of the Commander-in-Chief, despite his impressive track record since 1999, to get the military establishment on its feet and as I experienced in the one month tour of military establishments in November 1999 with the members of the National Assembly. This undermining would not be attempted in a professionally-run navy with appropriate orientation because it would delegitimatise whoever emerged from the chaos of intrigues as a replacement for my orderly emergence and appointment. This also indicates that the military institution in Nigeria is sadly comfortable with undermining the very important unity of command and consequently the President, Commander-in-Chief that absolute loyalty must always be pledged by service personnel who bear allegiance to serve the country. It is such undermining that adversely affects troop commitment in battle and the development of military capabilities. There are so much routinely left undone and it appears that there is no one in charge.

I had for long begun to understand that there were forces that could trap any President, Commander-in-Chief mandated by the electorates to be the Chief Executive Officer (CEO) of Nigeria to which all bear allegiance to serve through adherence to absolute loyalty to the CEO. I use the word trap because of the complicated nature of Nigeria's web of vicious internal contradictions that are exploited to undermine the President, Commander-in-Chief who probably only remind those involved about his true feelings and no one would care. This matter became so publicly discussed that as I walked past a group of Lieutenants, one of them exclaimed: 'Sir, we do not see anything wrong with you an engineer becoming our CNS.' That it had gone to this level, I felt bad and very uncomfortable with the intense discussions openly going on with a clear message about what was happening.

There is the institution of the President, Commander-in-Chief which is hybrid (formal and informal mix), and the institution of the Presidency that is a bureaucratic setup with a diversity of staff officers from various sources introducing diverse interests. Both institutions are the two sides of the same coin. The poor mix of the power structure as a result of Nigeria's internal contradictions simply generates the sets of traps of influences that are almost impossible to control. Both institutions suffer infiltrations that tend to undermine the mandate given to the President, Commander-in-Chief by the electorate. The political direction of the country is stuffed with poor thinking skills and consequently easily compromised. It becomes easy for individuals and interest groups to issue ultimatums not based on how to build a Nigeria where all belong but for very parochial reasons that draw the nation-state into a perpetual state of crises and insecurity. This state of affairs undermines state institutions and constituted authority. The mix of formal conducts of state affairs following universal principles with informal ones flowing from cultural and traditional practices is a most undesirable setup for the improper running of the country as it is virtually impossible to be decisive in the national interest.

There were other reasons related to oil bunkering and the superiority complex of seamen most of whom swear that they will never take orders from an engineer officer. At NDA, the best Naval cadets are selected to take on very demanding engineering courses and those who do not measure up are allowed back into the seaman branch. While I briefly had command of the NNS ARADU at sea some years back to solve problems, a Lieutenant Commander who was the Navigation and Direction Officer of the ship left the post he should have manned and disappeared from the enclosed bridge in the emergency because he would not take orders from me. The same officer as a Captain on a ship at NND walked up to me and stated jovially that they, seamen, would tolerate me as the CNS to solve the huge problems of the NN. I never engaged anyone in discussions except the DG SSS I had as a colleague and friend.

I was considered an obstacle to sharing and "eating" money and would wipe out illegal bunkering activities in Nigeria's maritime domain. I wondered what else an officer who bears allegiance and swore an oath to God to serve his country would do. Compromise and connive with economic saboteurs to destroy the country he swore to serve? Destroy the country and its institutions that he swore to sacrifice his life for under a binding covenant? I was expected to lobby and negotiate to be allowed to do all of these wicked acts that are considered as the system's normal. My family ethics and values reinforced by good military ethics and values ensured that the path I would take would always conform to serving the national interest. It is an honour, duty, and country. What a privilege I have to serve; I thought. The conference of high profile office holders that hold this view that I am an obstacle to their corrupt practices wasting Nigeria is very depressing and a reflection of how the power of bad examples directs the conduct of nation-state affairs. I joined to serve my country and it was a teenager's wish undiminished even as I became an Admiral along a path so strewn with formidable challenges from the start that would have derailed me. It was a very lonely course despite efforts to relate and belong.

I quickly got my handing over notes finalised and handed over to Commodore Kpokpogri on 20 June 2005 and prepared to take over command as the CFMC to keep going. I had difficulty getting Rear Admiral LOB Agbaje to hand it over to me and eventually I was informed that I could take over and go through files and documents available. This act was not surprising to me and it was a reflection of the pettiness that had become common in the NN. Perhaps he thought a CNS should not be taking over the office of CFMC. The mess he created was swept away and all around me was a disgraceful display of how serious issues in the conduct of the affairs of the NN were routinely handled. There was also the expectation of many that I would take office at the next moment as the CNS. My devotion was to the job at hand and I started taking steps to implement the decision to move the office to Moloney Street.

On 26 June 2005 as I sat in an office as the CFMC for the first time, I received a call from Captain JS Giwa, the MEO of NNS ARADU, informing me that the NNS ARADU had just secured to a buoy at Portsmouth and the CO asked him to phone me immediately and thank me for all that I had done to get them to Portsmouth. The MEO added his profuse gratitude and emphasised that they stuck to my advice and instructions. I assured him that I was proud of their achievement despite the enormous problems during the passage and wished them well. The CO never called me throughout until the NNS ARADU returned to Lagos. This is one of the petty divisions that has created a false sense of entitlement of privileges by seamen officers in the NN that has no official basis and yet becomes an article of faith in use to ruin the NN. All calls to me were made by two engineers on board. The Commodore as CO, being a seaman officer, should not be talking to a Rear Admiral, perhaps for being an engineer. But he obeyed me in Lagos while I got him, his crew, and ship ready for the celebration in Portsmouth. On receiving the good news, I immediately called my staff to arrange the conference room for a reception to celebrate the NNS ARADU and I gave money from my purse for the purchase of drinks and small chops. I explained to the gathering the historical significance of the arrival of the NNS ARADU at Portsmouth and the exposure it would give to the crew.

The NNS ARADU had a record of many serious problems and had been alongside for most of its life so far. I was embarrassed while at the NDU, Washington DC, 2000/2001 about the poor record of the ship graphically described on a website as basically a nightclub. I had fought hard on two occasions to get the ship back to sea. This was the only pride of the NN as a Flag Ship that could not be managed well because of a very poor attitude to technological innovations; and an indication of lack of preparedness.

This is what Steve Bush wrote on the NNS ARADU in his book, 'Trafalgar 200 International Fleet Review-A Pictorial Record': "Perhaps the biggest, but the most welcome surprise was the arrival in the anchorage of the Nigerian frigate NNS ARADU. Although her intention to participate was announced a long time ahead of the event, many in naval circles doubted that the ship would arrive. A Meko 360 built in Germany, the ship was commissioned in 1982 but has had a very patchy career ever since. In 1987, she suffered two groundings and a collision. Following a lengthy refit she again ran aground in 1994 and by 1995 was assessed as being beyond economic repair. She had rarely ventured to sea in the intervening periods and there had been reports that she was being used for some less than salubrious activities in the interim. In recent years, efforts had been made to restore the ship to a seaworthy state, and her arrival in the Solent late on 26 June was evidence of tremendous efforts put into getting the vessel back to sea-although the vessel was looking "tired" (note the canvas hangar door) the crew were evidently proud of their ship and their participation at the review." This was a testimony of good record-keeping by a developed country about the NN. The efforts in recent years mentioned spanned the periods I spent onboard as MEO and when the Ship was under my command as ASND for refit and readiness for the International Fleet Review.

The NNS ARADU began her delayed return to Nigeria in early July with a portable diesel generator strapped to the middle of the flight deck! The delayed return was mainly because of the poor performance of the generators that I had commented on the shoddy work done by the contractor that did more damage to the NN Fleet than successful repairs for which payments were made.

The same contractor was involved with supplying a generator in the UK to strap in the middle of the flight deck of the NNS ARADU, a mockery in the international arena, with foreign exchange paid. The NND was refused the job of getting the ship's generators ready for the voyage. The CNS was at the Fleet Review with his team and contractor. The four main generators failed and a strap-on-deck generator was put on a helicopter deck in Portsmouth and who cared about the embarrassment being caused by Nigerians in Portsmouth as long as foreign currency was freely released and spent? This priority pursuit of spending money at all costs had debased and destroyed our sense of decency for appropriate professional expression to prevail. Perverted morality reigns. I chose long ago the lonely road to be damned and drew inspiration from acquiring a good knowledge of what I must do based on learning from good examples since my childhood. The NN had the opportunity to do better at 200 years of Trafalgar Fleet Review.

The outgoing CNS returned to Abuja from the UK and yet no announcement of his successor. I received a surprise phone call from Chief Kayode, a close friend of Vice-Admiral SO Afolayan, the out-going CNS. Chief Kayode told me that he was with the outgoing CNS who had been praising my efforts at the NND and that the only achievements he could lay claim to throughout his tenure of four years were what I achieved in about eighteen months as the ASND. He asked me if I wanted to speak with the CNS. I thanked him for the gesture but declined to speak to the out-going CNS using his phone. I appreciated the out-going CNS' kind words. Why would the same person brand me as someone difficult to work with while reports about me in official records said otherwise? The out-going CNS could have supported my appointment as the CNS to consolidate what I had achieved on his behalf. The groundwork for the commencement of warship construction at the NND that I spearheaded was set for realisation. That is what the NND was established to do and a major transformation of the NN was about to begin.

It was common knowledge that after receiving his letter of retirement from the NN and his successor was not announced, seamen Rear Admirals were out to ensure one of them became the CNS to scuttle any chance of my appointment taking over command of the NN. I had earlier stated before the principal staff officer in the Presidency that if a process set up turned up a marine engineer officer and Rear Admiral by the name Anthony Odogba Musa Ajoku Isa, and was being ridiculed, all other Rear Admiral's names could be put in a hat for a draw to produce their kind of CNS unofficially. That surely makes a mockery of the NN. I requested to be allowed to serve Nigeria that all commissioned officers bear allegiance to serve. Anyone appointed by undermining the intention of the President, Commander-in-Chief would eternally remain an illegal CNS. It must be so in the national interest. It is not tolerated that the cherished unity of command that flows from the Commander-in-Chief can be so undermined with crude impunity. A hurried process emerged to manipulate political intrigues for someone to replace Rear Admiral Isa. Individuals become experts to promote their brand of CNS.

There is no room for a marine engineer officer in their NN seamen kingdom. This orientation has been destroying the human and material resources available to the NN and has almost made the engineering branch in the NN extinct. A credible modern navy is all about engineering. There exist in the NN a poor attitude to technological innovations and development of requisite quality personnel in the right quantity essential for the preparedness of a Naval force.

I was pressed with information and enquiries regarding why an in-coming CNS was being prevented from taking over from Vice Admiral SO Afolayan; consequently, the office was not allowed to function for some weeks as the very intense intrigues by interest groups that were not helpful to the President, Commander-in-Chief pressed on for installation of their candidate that cannot qualify to emerge in a competitive official process. The pressure was mounted to find a replacement for a marine engineer officer. This is what I felt it was all about but there were other reasons. This was a clear case of undermining the apex command authority, President, Commander-in-Chief, and military unity of command. It is a destructive routine in Nigeria whose cause(s) must be addressed if the country is to develop credible military capabilities and be respected in the world.

This act of impunity at such a level is a major reason why it is very difficult, and in many cases, impossible in Nigeria for an elected President, Commander-in-Chief to freely exercise the mandate given by the electorates in a general election. The sovereignty of the nation-state is routinely rendered ineffective. The President, Commander-in-Chief certainly had a CNS in mind, approved and appointed, that he was not allowed to have in the office between the time Vice Admiral SO Afolayan vacated office towards the end of June and 02 August 2005. The loyalty of whoever is eventually appointed after such intense political intrigues that were playing out in the open would be divided and can never be total to the President, Commander-in-Chief. The issue of allegiance to the country becomes irrelevant. It is that serious. This is a continuation of the ills of politicisation of the military in Nigeria that military personnel especially the leadership cherish. Those so charged with leadership in the NN want to do what they like with the institution and waste its human and material resources. It is impossible to give the mandatory serious attention to the complex needs of the warships in the Fleet for operational efficiency.

The pathetic situation that Nigeria is in whereby the President, Commander-in-Chief is routinely caught in a web of traps can be appreciated from the way General Stanley Allen McChrystal's unflattering remarks about Vice President Joe Biden and other high profile US Government officials was handled. President Barack Obama decided to retire the General without consulting the military hierarchy in the exercise of his powers as Commander-in-Chief. The Defence Secretary, Mr Robert Gates, and the military hierarchy were doing their best to save the General's career as President Obama recalled him to Washington DC from his duty post in Afghanistan. On knowing that the President had made up his mind to retire the General, the Defence Secretary and the military hierarchy, whose efforts were already in the public domain, had to quickly retrace their steps and fall in line with the

President's decision. There was no counterforce to sabotage or undermine the President, Commander-in-Chief.

General SA McChrystal was one of the finest generals in the US Army and this could have been used to save his career but everyone deferred to the apex national command authority for the common good. This is how a proper military establishment is managed where no one dares to attempt to undermine the intentions of the Commander-in-Chief that are in the national interest.

I was at home reflecting on developments when Captain (later Vice Admiral and CNS) DJ Ezeoba called at my residence. His residence was near mine at Ikoyi, Lagos. He informed me that it was common knowledge that I was facing obstacles regarding the intrigues blocking my taking office as the CNS. He asked me if I would agree to his taking up my issue and get some help. He stated his terms for making it happen, claiming that he had done a similar job before in respect of a Chief of Defence Staff. I had a visit much earlier from Rear Admiral BON Amusu, my former CO onboard the NNS ARADU who was then retired. I appreciated his kind gesture and genuine goodwill as he came to my office to wish me good luck. He noticed I was very pensive and barely talking.

 I knew some of the formidable forces in official circles networked to oil companies working hard on their agenda and also the preference of the oil companies. I had had a visit, many months earlier, before the retirement of the outgoing CNS, from one of my retired course mates from the NDA, Commander Dennis Omessa, who crudely told me that there was a feeling by Rear Admiral GT Adekeye that I was blocking his chances of becoming the CNS. He was then FOC EAST based in Calabar putting together his network. He had an excellent network and connection with the oil industry and coupled with the high profile government officials involved in the oil business, it was easy to understand the dangers ahead for me and when the interests of the Niger Delta militants in the oil industry were taken into consideration, there was a lot of room for sabotage. A senior civilian staff at NND observing events summoned courage and told me that I was in a danger fearing for me and suggested steps I should take for my safety. I thanked him and told him not to worry much as I believed the will God will be done for me. What was going on when there was no official due process regarding the appointment of a new CNS in progress then? It was very disgusting but not strange to me.

I was not committed to the overtures of Captain DJ Ezeoba mainly because of my knowledge of the nature of the hidden forces against my appointment. Captain Ezeoba was surprised that I was not keen on lobbying for my approved appointment. I hate lobbying for appointments for any reason and chiefly for the demotivating effect that would adversely affect my commitment to serve with absolute loyalty and because I do not want to be drawn into the comparative judgement of the performances of my colleagues. It was the duty of the officially constituted authorities to do their duty to the country with honour. The office of the Chief of the Naval Staff has lost its purpose and it will not be allowed to function for a CNS to SERVE the country with absolute loyalty as the influence of parochial interests override that of the nation-state and undermine the institution of the President, Commander-in-Chief with impunity. The CDS and service chiefs in this Nigerian setting would always have divided loyalty and are more inclined towards their sponsors in a network to undermine the authority of the President, Commander-in-Chief. Where then does the Navy Board and other services' Councils derived their authority from when the members undermine the elected apex authority with impunity on the issues under consideration? Bearing allegiance to the country and its causes will not be tolerated.

It is important to draw the attention of Nigerians to the issue of commitment to the causes of the nation-state as the highest priority for proper orientation regarding relating properly to the country. This should be the collective pursuit and direction so that all citizens believe that they have obligations to the nation-state higher causes to which they all must commit to and be responsible for above all others for common good. The President, Commander-in-Chief in the republic would then be constantly reminded to appreciate that all citizens are equal together with him or her before the law. This is essential so that commissioned officers would not doubt where the interest of the mandated apex command authority rest for the proper exercise of the unity of command. This is to eliminate the reign of the biases of an ethnic and religious group in the mindset of the President for example among others. The institution of the President, Commander-in-Chief would then be always respected for the exercise of authority so that all commissioned officers know that the higher causes of the nation-state are to be served at all times. This should be the source of inspiration for the confidence required for national security based on the proper conduct of nation-state affairs where undermining of authority is never tolerated.

The audience I had with the principal staff officer in the Presidency and my experiences working closely with many CNSs over the years was enough to guide me to tread with caution. Also, I had a previous audience with a CNS in line of duty who in a state of disgust showed me a list of high profile public servants involved in illegal bunkering and I wondered if any President/Head of State, Commander-in-Chief in this peculiar Nigerian setting could effectively be in charge of the country. Is any President, Commander-in-Chief allowed to freely function in Nigeria and not be imprisoned or trapped by the Presidency and other parochial interests in networks? There are traps of influences and the legitimate intentions of the Commander-in-Chief are easily substituted by illegitimacy through acts of impunity. It is the reason some service chiefs believe that they wield the ultimate authority and the President, Commander-in-Chief does not matter. Indeed, Nigeria cannot have credible Armed Forces capabilities for the defence and security of the country. The President, Commander-in-Chief of the Armed Forces of the Federal Republic of Nigeria can never feel safe and the country suffers bouts of insecurity.

There was a lot I did not know about those that Captain Ezeoba would contact and I would not engage in a desperate lobby that would involve compromises during my tenure if I took over as the CNS, I thought. I had my doubts about the suggestions of his brand of goodwill and I would be vindicated later as events to get me out of service unfolded in the second half of 2007.

I had consistently deferred to the fact that I had seen and heard enough to tread cautiously. A very informed friend of the NN would later explain to me that it was good I left the centre stage of the vicious NN intrigues and have some well-deserved respite as the Commandant NWC, though not the best for the NN. He was right as there was a lot I looked forward to achieving for the NN in the finest tradition of Wey-Soroh-Adelanwa strategic planning and implementation, which gave me hope as a Sub Lieutenant in 1977 that they were building a formidable Navy to give me a bright career. I was released from an evil enclave set on destroying the NN instead of building to have a bright future for those coming behind and which was put in jeopardy. What a failure of my generation! I would always remember those who looked up to me and my generation to give them hope. What a waste of opportunities!

I came to realise that the era of Wey-Soroh-Adelanwa represented the golden era when strategic planning and execution guided by the lessons of the civil war took the NN to a height whereby the international community took notice and wondered what Nigeria was up to. This background led to the discussions among scholars of strategy for a South Atlantic Security Organisation that would pool the military resources of Nigeria, Brazil, and Argentina as South Africa was still under the apartheid regime and isolated. In fact, in my interaction with Admirals Soroh and Adelanwa, I got to know that the plan was to develop a credible defence industry that would export warships to West African countries. Brazil had similar strategic plans at the same time with the NN to export. Brazil has excelled, taking advantage of similar opportunities Nigeria has wasted and continues to do.

I would later be comforted on reading about the experiences of General DD Eisenhower who after two terms as President of the US applied to Congress that he wished to be addressed as General and not as President as he discovered that the high highest political office in the US did not give him comparative job satisfaction as he had in the military where he had a full expression of professional development and application of his expertise.

The highest office in the NN without the freedom for strategic planning and execution to build, maintain, and train for credible naval capabilities simply devalues that high office. I would continue to be satisfied being allowed to have professional fulfilment as Commandant at the NWC and NDC.

I had a very successful research project at the NDU on "Planning Process and the Future of the Nigerian Navy." I have had a good run at the NND and embarked on a programme to make the NND start serious warship design and construction with a well-negotiated agreement with EMGEPRON of Rio de Janeiro, Brazil. This would also include the development of parts of the NND to be fitted with a synchro lift for the construction of a category of warships that cannot fit into the two twin docks. The NN had some land across the lagoon at Tarkwa Bay which some European entrepreneurs were planning to take up and develop more construction facilities. In respect of the EMGEPRON proposed agreement, Admiral Napoleao was on the delegation of the President of Brazil to Nigeria. I had planned to transform the NND-Tarkwa Bay axis into a major construction hub. Some other proposals were already at advanced stages at MOD.

I was set to get the NN truly transformed, starting by December 2005, to be designing and constructing classes of warships for effective presence in the sub-region. These would take more than four years to put on course for realisation in about ten years of continuous efforts for tangible results. I would not be allowed to be the CNS and follow through for four years to have a solid foundation for others to build upon, in the tradition of Wey-Soroh-Adelanwa, to give hope to future generations for satisfactory careers. The experiences at Manadon, UK, and Intermarine in Italy enabled me to have a practical experience in the art, science, and technology of warship design and construction and having direct access with the design staff of the USA and European Defence Industries involved in the MCMV project that attracted international acclaims.

The Intermarine shipyard had told the NHQ that NNIC staff had collected so much information that made them look up to us, on occasions, to guide them. I had documented faithfully all stage documentation related to design, construction, factory, harbour, and sea trials that formed an impressive library. There were several huge reserves of information brought from Italy which South Korea did not have up to 5% of and built their version of the MCMV with the little information they had. The NN had a team that could have been kept together to design and build warships in Nigeria but preferred to avoid them and continue the embarrassing practice of building abroad warships that can be built in Nigeria. I was greatly prepared professionally. I was driven by a purpose and it was not in my culture to do otherwise. I had gone far with the foundational works and set for realisation. These were well documented in the NN setup. The NN Workhorse project would later be taken abroad for partial execution denying Nigeria the opportunity for their immediate construction in Nigeria. Nigeria has foreign currency to spend.

It has been a very challenging eighteen months for me in command as the ASND. I was satisfied that I succeeded in all tasks I was assigned by the NHQ and more. I had miraculously stepped over the retirement traps set up to catch me. I regretted that despite the huge challenges the NN faced, there was so much deceit and mediocre professional standards freely applied to the most sophisticated collection of warships the NN ever had. They blistered with the latest technologies Nigeria could afford from leading European and USA defence industries that require absolute attention to details of the operation, maintenance, and logistics.

The dream of Vice Admiral JEA Wey, Rear Admiral NB Soroh, and Vice Admiral MA Adelanwa was to have a Navy meeting international standards and building capacities and capabilities for warship design and construction for sustainable development of the NN. The efforts of Vice Admiral MAH Nyako especially when he was CNS, 1990-1992, suffered setbacks as soon as he left office. It was a betrayal as earlier explained.

The President, Commander-in-Chief as of 2005, Chief Olusegun Obasanjo was the military Head of State that inspired the implementation of the most effective strategic plan that equipped the NN and the world paid attention. I was almost driven to tears on occasions as he struggled between 1999-2007 to wake up the generation of the NN officers performing below standards as the impressive acquisitions he inspired were wasting away and he was undermined. I had successfully led NN efforts in Italy for the MCMVs and appreciated the enormous opportunities available and which were taken advantage of to have one of the most successful designs and construction efforts that attracted US attention and change of direction for their OSPREY class Minehunters project. The NN could have carried on with these achievements to develop its base for warship design and construction in Nigeria. I saw as the ASND how the NN was wasting opportunities and resources and was poised to address it as CNS. It was not to be and the NN would later be building new ships else where and in the Gulf region as of 2020.

One early morning, news filtered in that Rear Admiral GT Adekeye had been announced the CNS. It had been a long night of terrible intrigues at the Presidential Villa Abuja and only the actors in the unpleasant decision-making process undermining national interest experienced each other's act. The proceedings had not gone well and it was a pre-emptive announcement. There were sour grapes and appeasement to calm frayed nerves.

I phoned the principal staff officer in the Presidency and he told me that he was also just getting to hear about the announcement on the radio. He was part of the plot to appoint Rear Admiral GT Adekeye and yet he was just hearing of it for the first time on the radio. I had been careful and avoided making comments to anyone. The following day, I was informed from a very unusual source that the President, Commander-in-Chief was considering me for appointment as the Commandant, National War College, Abuja. This was approved by the President following the law establishing the College and I was informed by a signal from the NHQ a few days later and felt very relieved.

I survived the retirement that would have followed for being a CNS that was not allowed and for having the same seniority with Rear Admiral GT Adekeye. I was relieved and grateful to the President, Commander-in-Chief, Chief Olusegun Obasanjo, GCFR, that I was not retired after previous attempts by the NN failed and I focused immediately on the task ahead as Commandant of the apex military educational institution in Nigeria. I was thrilled.

It is very interesting to note that Vice Admiral SO Afolyan and Rear Admiral GT Adekeye are from Kwara State from Local Governments that were close and the Chief of Staff to the President, Commander-in-Chief is also from Kwara State. The wide network coordinated into the Presidency to prevent my taking over Command of the NN was well established. The network of oil companies, high profile public, and civil servants were well entrenched and I can understand the traps of influences at play due to the internal contradictions of Nigeria that will not allow proper functioning of national institutions. When truth and rightness were established to guide my emergence as the CNS, such an entrenched network found petty excuses one of which was that I am an engineer and not suitable to command a service that is all about engineering. This is an example of how Nigeria earns disrespect in the international arena and an explanation as to why the country cannot develop despite the huge resources it is blessed with. This matter of sabotage will continue to hunt and influence action.

Sometime in the last quarter of 2006, a visitor to my institutional residence in Abuja after I took over command as Commandant told me that I should get ready as the President, Commander-in-Chief had directed that I should be called upon to take over as the CNS. My immediate reaction was to tell the visitor that I was not interested as I was happy with the job I was doing at the College. I have always liked staying at a duty post long enough to make an impact and there was already a lot I had at hand at the college.

Within barely one month at the FMC, while my appointment at CNS was being sabotaged, I had successfully achieved the movement of the FMC Headquarters to the former Ministry of Defence and Services Headquarters complex on Moloney Street. The CFMC office was the same office used by CNSs before the final relocation to Abuja and I will be the first to use it since it was vacated. As I settled down in the office waiting for Rear Admiral B Noshiri, my successor as the new CFMC, I reflected on the cruel irony of sitting in an office used by previous CNSs except the outgoing CNS. Had I become the former CNS? I had phoned Rear Admiral Noshiri and we agreed on the time for the handing/taking over ceremony on the day given in the appointment signal. He failed to turn up and I signed off my handing over notes and left the office. I had been on the Board for the promotion of Rear Admirals and had made contributions to make sure Rear Admiral Noshiri made it. It appears he was annoyed with his appointment as Commander FMC.

On the irony of being the first to settle in the old CNS office space after relocation to Abuja, I reflected on the luck of being denied opportunities from my secondary school days when I was not given a scholarship; then the issue of turning down my nomination to go to the UK on passing out from NDA and giving the slot to another cadet; to the removal of my name from the list of officers to be appointed Military Administrators with the NN losing its slot and then, the actions by very powerful interest groups to prevent me from taking over as the CNS. I could look back at these events and say that I was being prepared for a unique battle at the National War College. I had the feeling but did not quite know exactly what was in store for me but I seemed mentally prepared for hard knocks.

I was scheduled to take over command at the National War College, Abuja on 08 August 2005. I was to report to start the handing/taking over procedures on 31 July to enable me to take over command on 08 August. I contacted the outgoing Commandant and informed him that I would be arriving on 31 July to report at the College on 01 August 2005 as notified by a signal from NHQ. He told me that he would be ready to hand over command to me by 08 August. I was invited to attend the handing/taking over ceremony for the new CNS which was delayed as the new CNS had to be decorated as Vice Admiral by the President, Commander-in-Chief, Chief Olusegun Obasanjo. After the ceremony, I proudly accompanied the CNS to his office and felt relieved that my coursemate from the NDA was in charge. Vice Admiral GT Adekeye shared some light-hearted moments with the senior officers who accompanied him to his office. The CNS invited me to come and share the sofa with him. But I told him that I was not comfortable sharing the seat with him as the CNS. He uttered the familiar humming sound he uses to address me and to which I would normally respond "GT." I told the CNS that things had changed and out of respect I could no longer exchange those banters with him.

The CNS thought I was already at the College and on hearing that I was returning to Lagos, he showed me a letter informing him to attend the National War College Governing Board meeting scheduled for the following day 03 August 2005. He asked me if I was attending the Board meeting and I told him I would not be attending. I told him that I had agreed with the outgoing Commandant, Rear Admiral AG Adedeji, to take over command at the College on 08 August 2005. He asked me if I knew what I was doing and I told him that Rear Admiral Adedeji was my friend and I took my leave and headed for the airport. Rear Admiral AG Adedeji had already conducted his own pulling out the ceremony and I looked forward to arriving in Abuja on 07 August 2005.

CHAPTER EIGHTEEN

Transforming National War College to National Defence College

The four days I spent in Lagos while waiting to take over command at the National War College was devoted to preparing for the challenges of the new appointment. I was aware I had to deliver an inauguration lecture and reflected on the mass retirement of Rear Admirals the previous month which was an indication of poor career planning and stunted growth of the NN despite the impressive new warships that were added to the inventory from 1972 to1988.

I decided that the topic of my lecture would be: "Growing the Nigerian Armed Forces Organisation: The Imperative of Strategic Leadership." Strategic leadership is about looking far into the future while catering to the present with deliberate efforts to build and maintain organisational knowledge that must be at the heart of the organisation's strategy for success. It is also about preparing and grooming the next set of capable leaders. This would involve quality leadership that knows how to invest in personnel and prepare them to take over when such quality leadership leaves the scene. It is about building the very best organisation with the very best human resource that can be attracted and retained.

The components of the fighting strength of an armed force have been established to be moral, mental power, physical fitness, and material assets (Sound Military Decision Making, US Naval Publication). The first three are developed in the human element which must be properly developed and applied to the material component. The material component is rendered impotent if the human element is not properly developed as strategic leaders of the highest quality.

I had been given a rare opportunity to transform the apex educational and training institution of the Nigerian Armed Forces and I was set to go and get the job done. I was set to prepare at the College senior officers (military and civilian) for strategic leadership.

I arrived at the local wing of the Nnamdi Azikiwe Airport, Abuja by a morning flight from Lagos. There, I met the Deputy Commandant Major General Nuhu Bamalli who had served as ADC to the former Military President, General Ibrahim B Babangida, and the College

Secretary Air Commodore JO Duke, my coursemate at NDA. I was pleasantly surprised as I was welcomed at the airport tarmac and escorted to the waiting convoy to take us to the Army Headquarters Command Guest House where a chalet was rented for me. I was briefed on what my programme the next day would be. I offered them lunch elsewhere after having some drinks with me.

I phoned Rear Admiral AG Adedeji and informed him of my arrival, thanking him for the arrangements made for my reception and accommodation. I asked him if we could have lunch and he gladly accepted. I used the opportunity to pay a courtesy call on him. I had a very relaxed afternoon with Rear Admiral Adedeji and he briefed me mostly on what would normally not be in the elaborate handing over notes he had prepared for the ceremony the following day.

I was received at the college the following day and went straight to the Commandant's office for the handing/taking over ceremony. The formalities were completed with the handover of the college flag as a mark of change of command. I escorted the former Commandant to his car as he departed from the College. I called the Deputy Commandant and had his briefing which was followed by that of the College Secretary. I went through the handing over notes and familiarised myself with the office setting. I released a signal communicating to the appropriate authorities that I had taken over command at NWC.

I later visited the Honourable Minister of Defence, Chief of Defence Staff, Chief of Staff to the President, Commander-in-Chief, Service Chiefs (Army, Navy and Air Force) DG-SSS, Senate and House of Representative Chairmen of Defence Committees as well as Minister of Federal Capital Territory. I inspected the participants' quarters at Apo opposite the Legislator's quarters and the barracks facilities at Ushafa. The Presidential Fleet also had some of its personnel quartered at the barracks. I took the opportunity of being at the barracks to pay a courtesy call on the Chief of Ushafa and the Local Government Headquarters for the area. I toured the College permanent site land at Jabi District which my predecessor had fenced.

The College has many houses at Gwarinpa Estate and a plot of land on 69 Road which was being encroached upon. I would eventually take steps to drive away the illegal occupants and secure the plot. The plot was later developed as housing quarters for Directing Staff and Guest Lecturers after my tenure.

The Honorable Minister of Defence was Engr Rabiu Musa Kwankwaso, a former Governor of Kano State; the Minister of State was Mr Roland Oritsejafor. I had a most pleasant working relationship with them. The Permanent Secretary at the Ministry of Defence was Dr Haruna Sanusi. The Minister is the Chairman of the College Governing Board while the Permanent Secretary is the Secretary of the Board. I requested a copy of the minutes of the College Board meeting that was held on 03 August 2005 from the Permanent Secretary. The other members of the College Governing Board as at the time I took over command were the Chief of Defence Staff (CDS) General A Ogomudia, Chief of Army Staff (COAS) Lieutenant General Martin Luther Agwai, Chief of the Naval Staff (CNS), Vice Admiral GT Adekeye and Chief of Air Staff (CAS) Air Marshal JD Wuyep and the Commandant of the College.

The Inspector-General of Police Mr Sunday Ehindero is an alumnus of the College. He assured me, during my courtesy call, of his support and requested additional admission slots for his officers. The DG Nigeria Intelligence Agency (DG NIA) was Ambassador Uche Okeke who was Minister Counsellor at the Nigeria Embassy in Rome while I was Federal Government Chief Delegate in Italy. The DG NIA took the opportunity of my courtesy call on him to announce the institution of a prize for the best research paper on Intelligence by the participants in the college. This was an excellent gesture from the DG and I appreciated it.

I had barely three weeks left before the resumption of NWC Course 14. I was very disappointed with the state of disrepair and poor maintenance of the participants' quarters at Apo Quarters and the main administrative building. I called a meeting of the principal staff officers to present my observations on the state of the participants' quarters and the main administrative building. There was very little money available and I was starting, barely able to meet any basic requirements. I stopped any expenditure on the institutional house and the office of Commandant immediately until I received funds from the Federal Government budget allocation.

I had visits from contractors seeking jobs and I discussed the state of participants' quarters and the lack of funds for intervention immediately. I had one offer from a contractor to enter into a contract with the College and carry out the work in phases and wait to be paid when the College had funds. I set up a team from the maintenance department to survey the quarters and estimate the cost in phases. We then negotiated the cost estimate with the contractor and agreed on the phased work and payment. The contractor reported on the poor construction of the houses and said some were beyond economic repairs. I inspected the buildings and saw that some walls were on the verge of falling apart. I would later receive similar reports on the state of houses in Gwarinpa Estate. The poor state of accommodation for participants was very embarrassing. A permanent solution was necessary.

My predecessor's efforts to start construction on the new permanent site was not successful. The last College Governing Board meeting decided not to approve the design and cost estimate of nine billion Naira presented for the commencement of the project at the site already fenced at Jabi.

I made an appointment for a meeting with the CDS and have his views regarding the situation at the College. I arrived at the CDS office and had to wait for a long time. His staff officers passed me by into and out of his office and asked me if the CDS knew I was there. I felt the CDS was not going to see me or were very busy but I still waited until I heard from him one way or the other. Brigadier General M Agu, a Directing Staff at the College phoned me to say that the CDS called him and told him to inform me that he was not ready to see me and that I should leave the Defence Headquarters and return to the College and make another appointment. I appreciated the fact that there must be urgent matters he was addressing as I witnessed the pace of his principal staff officers entering and leaving his office.

Brigadier General Agu is a Nigerian Army Signal specialist officer who was close to the CDS, also a Nigeria Army Signal Officer. On my return to my office, I called the Brigadier General and asked him to make a fresh appointment for me with the CDS. He did and I met with the CDS. I informed him that I came to solicit for his guidance on the conduct of the affairs of the College. The CDS informed me that he was not impressed with the quality of the Research Fellows at the College as he considered their research outputs below standard. I took note of the need to improve them as they constitute the academic backbone of the College.

I had a very encouraging meeting with the COAS, CAS, and CNS. I was assured by the COAS and CAS that priority would be given to the NWC regarding faculty staff appointments and tenure. This encouraged me to raise issues of appointment of officers to and from the College with them and I got their promised priority attention. They never failed me and I ensured I never took their support for granted. The COAS once wanted the Deputy Commandant to follow him on an official visit to Pakistan. He called me and asked me if I could spare him for a few days as he was also the College Director of Studies. I happily released my Deputy as an order from the COAS.

I went to see the COAS on the sudden retirement of Brigadier General M Agu. I informed the COAS that Brigadier General Mike Agu received a letter asking him to apply for voluntary retirement a few days after taking over as the Principal Staff Officer (PSO) Coordination which was an internal appointment I made. I requested for an extension of his active duty service as he would deem proper. The COAS was not aware of the letter of retirement to the Brigadier General.

He held a telephone conference discussion with the Military Secretary in Lagos and one of the General Officers Commanding (GOC) a Division as I listened. It was agreed among them that the retirement letter would be withdrawn and an extension of six months granted. This was perfectly in order and I thanked him profusely. He told me that before the day ends, a signal would be released reappointing the Brigadier General to the College.

When I entered his office, the COAS invited me to share his three-seater with him. When I refused because I was duty-bound to accord him professional respect, he looked at me and told me that I held an appointment of a three-star General which he was also holding. It was as if he was welcoming an equal in rank to his office. He was correct about the rank and it was expected that I would wear the rank as provided in the law establishing the College.

The College establishment law states that the Commandant shall be a three-star General/Admiral/Marshal and I was expected to be so decorated on the assumption of office. As I had always done I placed the interests of the institution above self to avoid controversies and simply noted the repeated promises to implement the simple administrative procedure in obedience to the law. I did not want to draw attention that would create obstacles for me regarding what I wanted to achieve for the College. I would rather be the underdog for now.

I retained Brigadier General Agu as a contract staff when his six months active service extension, which I asked for, ended with the approval of the HMOD. I appointed the Brigadier General as a Director of Information Communication Technology (ICT) at the College with a mandate to develop the ICT facilities to a standard required of the institution. He liaised with the Education Trust Fund for funding. He had a smooth transition into retirement. Based on my priorities, I had bought and issued a laptop to each of the over 120 participants. This was the first time such issues were made at the College and to improve the skills of the participants the Directing Staff and Directors were each issued a lap-top and an online exercise was introduced. It was very essential to enforce at this time the acquisition of computer skills by participants for their strategic leadership education and training.

I was approached to release one of my staff officers to accompany the HMOD for a conference in Europe. Brigadier General Agu fitted the bill and I sent his name to the HMOD who approved it. I told Brigadier General Agu that it was left to him to justify my recommendation to the HMOD to retain him at the College on his retirement. All went well at the conference and it was easy for me to commit to writing my request to have him retained at the College after retirement. I got the HMOD's approval.

I visited the Honourable Minister of Federal Capital Territory, Mallam Nasir El-Rufai along with the Deputy Commandant to get acquainted with the Honourable Minister and also to ask for his support and guidance with the permanent site project as some relevant approvals for the land utilization and drawings would be handled by his ministry. I was well received and I informed the Minister that the project execution would require his approval and attention.

I was politely seen off by the Minister and as I bade him goodbye someone who had been sitting in his office followed me and introduced himself by giving me his complimentary card showing that he worked for El-Rufai and Partners; a quantity surveyor company. I requested him to see me in my office for further discussions as the El-Rufai and Partners was linked to Sheltarch, the consortium leader company owned by a former Minister of FCT Arch Ibrahim Bunu. The El-Rufai and Partner executive kept the appointment and I discussed with him the possibility of reviving the permanent site project. I was told that the project was dead and could no longer be revived and the company was pursuing the payment of over one hundred million Naira for their consultancy services. I repeated my demand for their assistance to revive the project and he repeated his earlier response. I advised him to think over it and feed me back.

Arch Ibrahim Bunu came to see me and emphasized that they were only interested in collecting their money. I had some very important background information on the interests the permanent site project had already attracted. I searched for the architectural drawing produced by the consultants many years ago for the permanent site and got more information regarding the network of the consortium put together and now waiting to collect the money appropriated in the 2005 budget for the College permanent site project. El-Rufai and Partners was the Quantity Surveyor for the group.

In continuation of my courtesy calls, I was granted an audience by the Chief of Staff to the President, Commander-in-Chief of the Armed Forces, Major General Abdullahi Mohammed (Rtd), a calm and very mature father figure. I thanked him for his contributions to my appointment as Commandant and told him that I would be counting on his support, that of the President and the Presidency to see through the programmes of the College. He congratulated me on my appointment and advised me that I should always go through the Ministry of Defence in all matters for which I would require the attention of the President.

I also visited the DG-SSS and solicited his support; he advised me to try and manage the appointment given to me. He knew and participated in the politics that played out in denying me taking up the appointment of the CNS a few weeks earlier. I told him that I was giving the appointment my very best professional attention. I would later relate with the National Assembly through the Chairmen of Senate Committee on Defence and that of the House of Representative Committee on Defence and other Ministries, Departments and Agencies (MDAs). I made approaches to several foreign Embassies and High Commissions for the world tour programme which brought their Ambassadors and High Commissioners to the College for presentation on their countries. I established very good relations with them and in particular the British High Commissioner, Sir Richard Gozney, and the Canadian High Commissioner David Angel. I secured approval to visit all the over thirty countries the College selected for study tours worldwide during my tenure.

I decided on the main focus of my activities during my tenure as a Commandant. I used the inauguration lecture to give my thoughts and ideas regarding preparing selected officers with diverse backgrounds for strategic leadership. I was guided by the College Mission which emphasises preparing selected senior military officers and their civilian equivalent (Director level) from MDAs for strategic leadership in national and international settings. I determined that I would get all necessary approvals and start the permanent site construction based on current and future requirements; define and implement a new curriculum that is focused on higher direction and management of national defence and security; implement the decision to change the name from National War College to National Defence College and ensure a real transformation that would allow innovations; improve on the existing infrastructure at the College to provide the appropriate environment and improve the education standards of the College.

I had the minutes of the College Governing Board meeting of 03 August 2005 to also guide me. In my meetings with the Chairman and members of the College Governing Board, I got to know what influenced the decision not to approve the permanent site project. There was a need for new thinking and approach towards the project. The obstacles ahead had to be carefully avoided to make progress with the College transformation I was set to embark on.

I travelled to Lagos to attend to some matters and the marriage ceremony of the daughter of Mr Andrew Abu in early September 2005. I received information regarding capital project budget processes being hurried through in my absence. I had not been fully briefed on the processes being undertaken. On my return, I asked for details and it was tough getting a brief from the College Secretary. I had to impose some movement restrictions before I was given the details of the mess created. I was shown letters written to the Presidency and the MOD and signed on my behalf following due process procedures. I never approved the letters. The mess would not create a good impression of the College and I immediately ordered the withdrawal of the letters and the cancellation of all the proposed awards that had gone through. I was told that the Presidency and MOD had representatives on the committee that carried out the processes. I insisted on the cancellation of the mess and the withdrawal of the letters. The orders were carried out and this generated a storm of protests from the many beneficiary contractors. This was not a popular decision but it would have created a huge problem of credibility for the College if I had allowed the mess to be processed at the Presidency by BMPIU.

I received many threats and one warned me that I would not last till December 2005 before I would be removed and retired. The exercise was repeated with fewer contractors and the appropriate letters were written to the Presidency and MOD under due process procedures. I was later commended by the relevant representatives on the committee from the Presidency on the decisive steps I took to clean up the mess. I had determined the course I would take and maintain the credibility of the College.

I received a letter from the Economic and Financial Crimes Commission (EFCC) and I thought the new setup under Mr Nuhu Ribadu was getting involved to investigate petitions connected to my order to cancel and repeat the capital projects contract awards. That was far from the contents of the letter. I was invited as a resource person for the workshop for the pioneer staff of EFCC. I would later invite the EFCC Chairman to the College to deliver a lecture. He started the lecture by commending my efforts at the College and considering the bashing I had been receiving many were surprised.

In 2007, I was asked to be the Chairman of the Graduation Lecture at the University of Abuja delivered by Nuhu Ribadu. My initial remarks were very much a good introduction to Ribadu's lecture.

The CNS was having a reception in his hometown, Offa, in Kwara State in early October 2005 and I left Abuja to spend a night at Okene and drive to Offa the following day. On approaching Itakpe, close to Okene, my convoy was stopped. We thought the long line of vehicles was caused by a police checkpoint. Someone was bleeding profusely. I was informed of an armed robbery gang operating out of view due to the topography of the road. On confirming the information, I tried to reach the Inspector General of Police and get assistance but did not succeed. I had no idea how many armed robbers were operating and the weapons they had. I called my escort commander and his men and prepared them to take on the armed robbers. I talked to them about our responsibilities to defend Nigerians wherever they may be. We checked our communication sets and took off to take on the armed robbers. As we climbed up the hill into their full view, we saw two vehicles parked into which the armed robbers started to rush into and took off in opposite directions. I ordered the chase of the vehicle speeding away in our front and as we caught up with them the vehicle veered into a cul de sac. I relayed orders that the armed robbers should not be allowed to disembark and take positions to fire at us. The escort commander, Petty Officer (later Master Warrant Officer) AZ Audu, was swift in opening the doors of the vehicle with his men and pulled all the armed robbers out. They were swiftly wrestled to the ground and disarmed. I was proud of the professionalism of my escorts.

The armed robbers were policemen in uniform and they used a police car. I asked for their Divisional Police Office location and dispatched my security car and an armed escort to take one of the robbers to bring the Divisional Police Officer (DPO) to the scene. The passengers that had formed long queues in both directions started gathering around the police armed robbers and they were about to start a lynching mob action on the robbers when I ordered their dispersal to continue their journey. The DPO arrived with my details and I asked him if the robbers were his men and if the vehicle belonged to his Division. He confirmed that the policemen were his men and the vehicle was marked and painted in police colours. I ordered the names and official numbers of the policemen and their DPO to be taken. I ordered their weapons to be returned to the DPO as they were meant for duties and I warned the DPO to stop the robbery by his men.

At Okene, I was able to get the Inspector General of Police (IGP). I briefed him on the encounter and the actions I had taken. The IGP asked me to forward a report to him when I returned to Abuja. Later that evening, my neighbourhood in Okene came under a heavy Ak-47 attack. It was getting to 2200 hours and I did a muster parade of all my men and all were accounted for. I asked my security officer to take charge of the weapons and take orders from me should the residence be threatened. The firing ceased about midnight perhaps they had exhausted their ammunition and there was no attempt to stop them. The following morning, we set out of town at 0600 hours for Offa and took a different route out of Okene through Ogaminana. My convoy came to a partial roadblock created by felled trees. I noticed bloodstains on the road and stopped. I asked my escorts to take defensive positions and as I was in mufti together with my Flag Lieutenant and one of my security details, we all came out of our cars and mingled with the labour hands to clear the felled trees. As we progressed, policemen started emerging from the bush and I asked them what was happening that resulted in blood spills on the road. They told us that they came under heavy attack from armed robbers that outnumbered them and their men that suffered injury were evacuated and taken to hospital. I suspected that they were carrying out the robberies on early morning travellers and on sighting us, they ran into the bush to hide considering what happened to their colleagues the previous day. They hid their weapons in the bush as they emerged. I asked them to join in the task of clearing the roadblocks and this was quickly accomplished. This incident would be part of my report to IGP.

Back in Abuja, I informed the CDS General A Ogomudia of the encounters and the report IGP asked me to give him. The CDS was very appreciative of the actions I took and asked me to send him a copy of my report to the IGP for a follow up at meetings with the President, Commander-in-Chief.

The policemen were all arrested and brought to Abuja for identification and disciplinary procedures. The CDS wrote a letter of commendation to me for bravery which I dedicated to the men who performed their duties with impressive professionalism. The issue of security personnel being involved in armed robbery operations had been known for a long time but there had been no conclusive proof until I provided some through those encounters. There were no reports of armed robbery operations for many months in the area. The situation deteriorated again the following year-2006.

I had gathered enough information regarding the several failed attempts to start the permanent site project in Abuja since the establishment of the College in 1992. I had been informed by the consulting firm Sheltarch Associates that it would be impossible to get the project started given its history. I approached the HMOD and briefed him on my findings as regards the state of infrastructure at the College and the urgent need to start the permanent site project so that the College would meet its national and international commitments and objectives that informed its establishment. Given the latest College Governing Board decision, he was not committed in his response and I sensed that if I offered something new he might have a rethink and allow due process to get the project restarted.

I set up a Project Team at the College headed by a Nigerian Army architect in the College Maintenance Department. Two civilian architects and a quantity surveyor among others were later added to the committee. Most of the members of the team had followed me on my visits to familiarise myself with the College facilities and their states. I told them that their task was to provide solutions in the form of architectural design drawings to the accommodation problems of the College for implementation as the College's permanent site. The assessment of the design drawings of the Sheltarch showed that the company only covered the requirements for the number of participants at inception and which was now more than four times the number. The staff strength and requirements had grown well beyond the expectations. It was decided that a new design concept would have to be evolved to meet the realities and cater for the future.

I developed a sketch of a solution for the participants' accommodation blocks and asked for their inputs to assess their understanding of the problems and the relevance of the solutions sketched. I ended the session when I was satisfied that they understood what was required and asked them to take the design concept and produce architectural drawings in stages for subsequent meetings. On achieving a satisfactory standard, I asked for a compact copy on A4 size paper to enable me to make very brief presentations to the HMOD. I took the HMOD by surprise when I presented him with the drawings in a compact form and told him that I had not awarded any contract nor involved any consultant as I was relying on the resources freely available at the College. He was impressed and I told him that I would continue with other buildings that would be designed to solve specific problems and cater to the future needs of the College.

The HMOD gave me a very positive reaction to our efforts and told me to keep him updated. I tasked the team following the procedure and design concept I had evolved with the main administrative block and this was very daunting because of the requirements for a National Defence College and not the War College it was. They did a very good job on the administrative block which would have two lecture theatres together with syndicate rooms and offices for administrative and academic staff as well as a helicopter landing pad. I briefed the HMOD with the next set of drawings produced and he reminded me that the budget proposals for the year 2006 were being finalised and that I should speed up the design process and have a cost estimate to guide me in making recommendations to be captured in the budget proposals of the Ministry of Defence for the College.

The Mess Complex facilities and the African Centre for Strategic Research and Studies buildings' designs were the next targets to have a realistic basis for a cost estimate by the Quantity Surveyor. The team was inspired when I told them that the HMOD was in support of our efforts. I managed to recommend one billion Naira to start with for budgetary allocation and it was considered reasonable and I was introduced to the Director of Administration who coordinated the Ministry's budget. I also had to brief the Permanent Secretary and the Director of Joint Services at the MOD.

I had to learn fast as the inter-departmental competition was fierce. I had my proposal dropped to eight hundred million and a few days later as the final proposals were being readied to forward to the Minister of Finance, the College permanent site allocation dropped to two hundred million Naira and I had to locate the Director of Budget whose body language conveyed to me that I would get nothing. I informed the HMOD of the vanishing allocation and the possibility of getting nothing. He smiled at me and I got it. Welcome to the politics of resource allocation.

The Minister of Finance Mrs Ngozi Okonjo-Iweala came to the NWC to deliver a lecture and I briefed her on the permanent site project and the importance of realising the project. She seemed impressed and with the developments at the MOD, I went and saw her in her office and she promised that she would try and get me three billion Nairas if the MOD would push it through to her office and told me that Dr Haruna Sanusi was with her at the Ministry of Finance and I should go to him and inform him of her intention. The MOD did not help matters and I had nothing in the budget proposal. I was devastated; it seemed as if I had come to a dead end.

The HMOD called a meeting in the first quarter of 2006 to discuss aspects of the budget proposals. The sitting arrangement had me seated to the immediate left of the HMOD and I noticed there was no written agenda. The HMOD started the meeting and brought up the impending payment issue pegged at well over a hundred million Naira to Sheltarch. The HMOD turned towards me and informed the meeting that so much was in the process of being paid to a contractor when I had nothing to hold on to in the next budget. I was expected to state that I had nothing in the 2006 budget and, therefore, the available fund should be released to the College to support our efforts so far. Shetarch stopped work years ago and should have no justification asking for payment for consultancy services for a dead project. The look on the faces of the Directors at the meeting was mean and directed at me. The HMOD asked me the same question again and I was silent.The HMOD stated that since the Commandant was not interested in the money, the Consultant should be paid. There was the relief on the faces of those in attendance and the HMOD left the conference room. I followed him out and disappeared from the MOD. I would have nothing in the budget for 2006.

I knew some of the formidable interests sponsoring the payment to Sheltarch Associates. I had told Arch Ibrahim Bunu, the owner of Sheltarch that since his intention was to be paid the amount appropriated in the 2005 budget for the NWC capital project and cut off his ties with the project as he considered it dead and would never be revived, I would not stand in his way. Shetarch was paid and there was no fund to support our efforts.

The President, Commander-in-Chief was invited to the College for an event to address the participants but sent the HMOD to represent him. I wrote to the President, Commander-in-Chief for an audience with the participants of Course 14 at the Presidential Villa. I sent this through the HMOD who forwarded it. I got a reply some weeks later giving me 07 March 2006. The budget was still in the process of being finalised by the Minister of Finance before the President presented it to the National Assembly. I was directed to select my team and forward the list to the Presidency for clearance. I discussed with the HMOD that I would like to go with all the participants, academic staff, and senior civilian staff. I was warned that the President might cancel the visit with such a large delegation. I told the HMOD that I did not want to select a group that would be targeted as my favourites for I knew my real intention for requesting the audience. I sent in the list through the HMOD. The President approved my large delegation.

I had all the permanent site project design drawings reduced to A4 papers and arranged in formats and the cost estimates were on the last pages of the rather bulky document. I crafted a short speech highlighting the good things about the College related to the national needs and aspirations for which it was set up. The international dimension of the College was reflected by the foreign participants in the course. The solution to problems faced by the college was the immediate commencement of the construction of the permanent site. This was the structure of my address.

We drove into the Presidential Villa in a convoy of buses and were taken into the Federal Executive Council chambers. I was given a seat to the left of the President, Commander-in-Chief; the Honourable Minister of State for Defence Mr Roland Oritsejafor sat to the right with the CDS next to him. The CDS called me over to his end and told me that he still did not know why such a huge delegation was in the Presidential Villa and in the Federal Executive Council chambers warning that if there was nothing serious from me, we might be driven out of the Villa knowing that the President did not tolerate nonsense.

I told him and to the hearing of the Minister of State that I was there because of the permanent site project. Though the Minister knew of my struggles for funds, he never got any briefing that we were in the Villa because of the permanent site project. The CDS asked me if I was prepared. I confidently told him that I was prepared and this calmed their nerves. I returned to my seat to arrange my materials for quick delivery for effect. I had a two-page speech and the compiled drawings and cost estimates and a small College gift as protocol allowed.

The President entered the chamber and took his seat after which we were asked to sit. I was called upon after a very brief protocol to address the President. When, in my speech, I got to the issue of the permanent site as the solution to the problems being faced by the College, the President's countenance changed and he did a half swivel on his seat as if he was about to get up and storm out. This episode coincided with my final statement.

I moved towards him as he got up and presented to him the compiled drawings and requested him to accept the small gift from the College community. The President went to his podium with the drawings and started turning over the pages. He smiled and made a light-hearted joke about the round shape of the buildings he was looking at. He asked me how much had been spent so far in contracts awarded and I told him that I had not awarded any contracts but had been relying on the intellectual resources of the staff available to me at the College. He then estimated that about four hundred million Naira would have been spent so far on what was before him had contracts been awarded. He then asked the Minister of State if there was anything in the 2006 budget in the final stages of preparation. The Minister was silent for a few seconds and at that instant, he looked across towards me and I nodded like a lizard prompting him to say that there was something in the budget for the project. The Minister of State obliged.

The President then turned to the audience and stated that it would be a shame if the Federal Government could not support the efforts made so far. He then gave his approval in principle for the project to take off. It was a very close shave for if the Minister had said there was nothing, it would have been a disaster for me. The President ended the proceedings and took the compiled drawings bound for him. I heaved a sigh of relief. We took a group photograph with the President outside the chambers.

I held a brief discussion with the Minister of State after the group photograph and he confirmed that the HMOD would be informed that the President had been told that the College permanent site would have an allocation in the 2006 budget. This was a mission most accomplished beyond my expectation and since I kept my plans to my chest and heart, not many understood the significance of what was achieved. I was however alerted that there were still hurdles ahead. I took note as I kept up the pressure on the Minister of State to make the MOD act on the assurance given to the President that there was allocation in the 2006 budget in respect of the College permanent site project.

At the National Assembly, I had the support of the Chairman of the House of Representatives Committee on Defence, Honourable Wole Oke. He had been introduced to me by the Governor of Osun State, Prince Olagunsoye Oyinlola in my office when the Governor paid me a courtesy call. Honourable Wole Oke was fully aware of the permanent site project and had been morally supportive. The only problem with his support was that he was not trusted and I was warned to keep him away from the project otherwise there would be no allocation from the MOD.

The budgeting process would involve him following the National Assembly procedure. The efforts so far yielded two hundred and fifty million Naira when the 2006 budget was passed into law. This appropriation by the National Assembly gave full legal backing for the commencement of the College permanent site construction project. This was of huge significance for me but a very small amount of money considering the huge cost of the entire project. If this would be the rate of the annual appropriation, it would take well over a century to complete the project.

I called for a meeting of the College Governing Board to get the necessary backing for the project given the earlier decision taken on 03 August 2005 which put a stop to it. The support of the HMOD needed to be officially documented. At the meeting, the politics of the Armed Forces and MOD led to a question on the legality of my actions so far and the prime mover was the representative of the CNS Rear Admiral N Idirisu, a coursemate at the NDA. He was adamant that all that I had achieved were illegal and not even the intervention of the President, Commander-in-Chief could save the situation.

I did not know if he was acting following the directives of the CNS and I wondered what had gone wrong so soon with the NN set up at the NHQ. The Permanent Secretary and Secretary of the Board observed that I had not called a Board meeting since I took over command at the College. I did not contest these submissions. There were several developments taking place at the same time and I had to focus on what advanced the causes favourable to the execution of the project. What I could read from his attitude was that the CNS was not in support of the project. I was utterly disappointed. The Board meeting ended without a clear direction.

I continued to push. I wrote to the HMOD to get approval to commence the procurement process following the Procurement Act under the supervision of the Budget Monitoring and Price Intelligence Unit (BMPIU) in the Presidential Villa headed by a Senior Special Adviser to the President, Professor Ade Wahab. I got the HMOD approval and I contacted the Head of BMPIU for directives and he was very receptive. I ordered an advertisement calling for consultants and construction companies to be placed in selected national newspapers after satisfying the requirements of BMPIU. The response was very good because every known major consulting and construction company in Abuja showed a keen interest in the project.

Arch Ibrahim Bunu of Sheltarch Associates who was now aware of the advertisement in the newspapers visited me and told me that his company was the sole consultant for the project and was responsible for setting up the consortium of contractors to handle the project. I reminded him of his decision to opt-out and that I kept to my line that they could go ahead and collect their money and would thereafter not be associated with the College permanent site project anymore. Sheltarch Associates had received payment, taking all the money that was in the 2005 budget for the permanent site project and left me with nothing. He refused to join me and redesign the project for relevance. I also told him that his previous design work was no longer relevant and I had pooled resources and settled for a new design that had been presented to the President, Commander-in-Chief based on current realities.

He warned me that he would contact BMPIU and take over. I was silent and he left my office. He returned some days later and told me that he would write a petition to EFCC, Independent Corrupt Practices Commission (ICPC), and Code of Conduct Bureau (CCB) as well as copy other agencies and establishments of government. This man had been a Minister of the Federal Republic of Nigeria and at all times I had been giving him all the due respect. I replied that we were in a free country and he was free to do what he liked. This seemed to put him off guard for some seconds before recollecting himself to tell me that he would give me a copy. I thanked him for that consideration and he left.

He wrote his petition and brought a copy to me. I accorded him all due respect and received the copy and I glanced through as he had his cup of tea. I did not comment on the contents and that was it. I never bothered to read the petition seeing the long list of addresses for distribution. The Procurement Act highlights the Federal Government policies on accountability and transparency as well as the procedures to follow. I had no private deal with any of the contractors and I carried on with the tasks at hand. The pressures from various sources started mounting.

The objective of changing the name of the College to National Defence College guided the design of the core buildings at the permanent site. It was pointed out from several discussions during meetings at the DHQ and at the College with Service Chiefs as well as the faculty staff that there was no centre for joint warfare training for the Armed Forces. The need to design two curricula, one for higher management of defence and security and joint warfare came to light; it dawned on the College that it would be necessary to run two faculties, the second one being for Joint Warfare for senior Lieutenant Colonels/Commanders/Wing Commanders that would be battalion commanders and equivalent responsibilities in joint warfare for the other two services. The main administrative block would have two main lecture theatres for the two faculties.

As for the Africa Centre for Strategic Research and Studies (ACSRS), the Economic Community of West African States (ECOWAS) mandated the College for strategic level training for Peace Support Operation personnel. I had a meeting with the President of ECOWAS

Commission His Excellency Ibn Chambas at his office in Abuja and he selected his staff to meet with my project team to determine requirements as former Heads of State would be expected to have PSO meeting at the ACSRS. Also, the Senior Managers course in PSO would be conducted at the College for the UN. I directed the Acting Provost of the ACSRS to lead the efforts and the building design was modified to accommodate the new requirements.

The Mess facilities were designed to have a large hall that would be used for dining and also have the capacity to seat the audience for graduation dinner which were annually held in hotels at a great cost to the College. There would be provisions to accommodate visiting lecturers, swimming pools, and fitness facilities. The buildings including the participant quarters as earlier described were designed to solve specific problems and provide a secure and appropriate environment for the participants and staff of the College to meet the objectives of national and international commitments.

The estimate for the permanent site project from the College Project Team was about N9.0 billion and this estimated cost was included in the presentation to the President, Commander-in- Chief. The commencement of the procurement process enabled the advertisement in newspapers and the consultants and construction contractors were grouped into three categories following laid down guidelines by BMPIU based on the Procurement Act.

The categorisation was submitted to the BMPIU and approved. I was determined to use the Category A list to ensure good standards to meet the requirements. The consultants were asked to do detailed work on the preliminary designs and cost estimates. The total cost of the project shot up to about N34.0 billion and I had a credibility problem on my hand to manage. I needed to take another look at the whole project design and cost and I asked Julius Berger Plc, a leading construction company in Nigeria to give me their expert assessment. I was advised on the technical complexity of the administrative and the ACSRS buildings. The company arrived at a cost that was in the same range as the summation of all individual submissions by the various consultants. I was then confident to commit the new cost estimates in writing in a briefing and it was appropriately distributed. The BMPIU also had the opportunity to take me to the task. I noticed that it was not wise to mention Julius Berger's input as a reference as some people would consider their costs as always on the high side. I backed up my analysis with more details on the requirements developed to solve the problems being identified with relationships to the objectives dictated by the

College mission. I had a good reservoir of information to leverage at various levels of defence. I was able to establish consistency in presentations when occasions demanded.

I had a tough time understanding the new BMPIU changing at will, the directives, and the interpretation of the Procurement Act. Some of the staff of BMPIU were unnecessarily hard and intolerant which led to their use of unpleasant language against us and even some Directors at the MOD that were involved in processing our correspondences with them were not spared. There was the emphasis on the fact that the College had only N250.0 million appropriated and this was simply not worth moving ahead until all money required was appropriated. This is the law but I believed that it was not realistic. What do I do with this "small" money? I had decided to be faithful in small things to be considered worthy of big responsibility regarding management of what was considered a huge amount being expected. I was under pressure to spend the available "small" money on some aspects of various soil tests and preliminaries. I would not go that way and it was considered that I did not want to share the 'small' money.

I would have setbacks and more resistance to the processing of documents related to the permanent site project. At a stage, the file on the project went "missing" at the MOD and after days of being tossed about, a staff member told me in confidence that it was locked up in a particular Director's cabinet and that was his way of making sure I complied with his demands. The College was very low on available funds and I had no choice but to issue a cheque immediately to my Flag Lieutenant to withdraw money from my salary account to secure the release of the file from "detention." I had convinced the MOD to accept the new costing as I told the HMOD and Permanent Secretary that I had valuable assessment input from Julius Berger regarding costs.

The next challenge was to convince the President and the Presidency (BMPIU) to get approval. The BMPIU had other plans for me and I was convinced of their motives. I needed more money to be appropriated and also needed the approval of the President for the release of funds. I was hitting brick walls and getting serious headaches. The other programmes of the College were progressing well and indicating how the year 2006 was being spent. I improved on the budgeting process at the College starting with logging on to the Integrated Personnel Pay and Information System (IPPIS) for transparency which other staff at the College could relate with as it was linked to the Office of the Accountant General of the Federation.

I received a telephone call from the HMOD Engr Rabiu Musa Kwankwaso which was rare as I had access to him and was always given immediate audience whenever I called at his office. His voice was tense. He asked me why I was employing new staff when there was a Federal Government embargo on new employments. He wondered where I would get the money from to pay them with the embargo. He added that the President, Commander-in-Chief was not happy with the development and it appeared he must have been taken to task. He wanted an immediate explanation for going against the Federal Government embargo.

I was very lucky that I was not facing the fury of the President, Commander-in-Chief directly and the urgency in the HMOD voice conveyed the seriousness of the situation. I had set up a committee under-documented established procedures and the employment exercise was approved by the College Governing Board.

I explained to the HMOD that there was a College Governing Board approval for the employment and a committee was set up consisting of agencies outside the military establishment as directed by extant laws and regulations. I further explained that I had the College fully captured in the Integrated Personnel Pay and Information System (IPPIS) in the Accountant General of the Federation's office and linked for personnel management. The issue of where I would get money from had been carefully considered. The Government Budgeting system had given the College an envelope that gives the limit on the fund that would be available in the fiscal year under consideration.

I had taken care of the College budgeting requirements and the IPPIS had been used to capture those that would be employed and this was made known to the Account General of the Federation. In summary, I explained that the financial limit given to the College would not be exceeded and I would not be requesting any extra funding. I had the fund to cater to the new employees and they had been captured based on their known categories and as required.

The telephone conversation ended quickly and I never had any queries again. The Committee concluded its assignment and the list of the successful candidates was submitted to the College Governing Board for approval and those that turned up to take up their appointments assumed duty. The IPPIS helped to get the entire College Budgetting system reorganised and enabled me to focus on more challenges. The College would be commended for being the first MOD department to log on to the IPPIS and this was the saving grace when the Ministry was taken to task regarding budget management.

The first world study tour I would participate in was in May 2006 in selected countries in various regions of the world took my team to Malaysia, the USA, and the UK. The reception I received at the Heathrow Airport on arrival was exciting. As I set foot off the British Airways aircraft that brought my team from Washington DC and was adjusting my hand luggage, I was saluted by a British MOD officer/staff (a retired Marine Lieutenant Colonel) who said to me: "On behalf of Her Majesty's Government, you are welcome to the United Kingdom, Sir."

The officer took my hand luggage and led me to the Nigerian Defence Adviser at the Nigeria High Commission Major General Mohammed Said and the Deputy Defence Attache Captain (later Rear Admiral) Victor Adedipe who were standing at the end of the aircraft disembarkation tunnel. Arrival routines were swiftly and impressively completed.

I had a very successful tour and was hosted to a dinner at Lancaster House, part of the Buckingham Palace complex, by the Vice Chief of Defence Staff General Sir Timothy J. Granville-Chapman. The Nigerian High Commissioner to the UK Dr Christopher Kolade was in attendance and made the day a very grand affair. I had no prior briefing of such an elaborate protocol and must give credit to the British High Commissioner to Nigeria Sir Richard Gozney, the Nigerian High Commissioner to the UK, and the Defence Adviser at the Nigerian High Commission.

I had to respond to the speech of the Vice Chief of Defence Staff. I wrote the speech and submitted it for the inputs of the High Commission and had it returned in good shape. The Vice CDS arrived with one staff car and had with him, in the same car, the College Secretary at Royal College of Defence Studies (RCDS), London, and his Military Assistant. It was that simple.

All went on well at the dinner reception. I had a pleasant evening with the Vice CDS. In my response to his speech, I highlighted the assistance rendered to Nigeria to set up the NWC and also that collaboration with the Royal College of Defence Studies would be pursued to re-establish relations cut off during the military government of General Sani Abacha. The College Secretary at the RCDS told me that the RCDS tie would be sent to the President, Commander-in-Chief, General Olusegun O. Obasanjo, an alumnus of the College. This was collected and delivered to the President in his office.

The visit to the Commander-in-Chief Fleet Headquarters was very emotional for me. It was located at Portsmouth overlooking the Naval

Base. I had a vintage view of the Portsmouth Naval Base that was the home port for the HMS TORQUAY, the training ship I served on in 1978. I was hosted by the Deputy C-in-C Fleet Vice Admiral Tim Clements. As we watched the warships at their berths, the Deputy C-in-C thought of the good old days when the RN had more warships, and the strength of the RN in terms of personnel was impressive. I could observe the modern warships and their array of missiles and fire control radars and told him that the modern weapons carried by the smaller Fleet were more deadly precision weapons than those of the dreadnoughts and their lesser classes blistering with an array of heavy guns that lacked accuracy possessed by the modern warship's weapons we were viewing. I treasure the heavy book on "Britain and the Sea" that he presented to me. I had been with the RN and appreciated that Britannia Ruled the Waves.

The visit to HMS VICTORY, Admiral H Nelson's Flagship at the battle of Trafalgar, which is still the RN Flag Ship was a summation of RN history to the team and there was a lot for the participants to learn. I trailed behind them remembering my days at the Naval Base with my wife then a student living at a hostel nearby. The visit to the UK military establishments and defence industries was a fantastic reminder of the excellent times I had and how they all shaped my career for good.

The visit to Malaysia made a unique impression on the participants. We were received on arrival at the Kuala Lumpur International Airport (KLIA) by the Nigerian High Commission reception team and driven to our hotel in the central area near the famous Twin Towers building. The drive from the airport took about one hour fifteen minutes and I decided to join one of the buses to the hotel and interact with the participants. The visit to the Malaysian military Headquarters showed us the need for a stronger military relationship with Malaysia and in the following years, I supported the moves that led to the establishment of the Nigeria Defence Attache section at the Nigerian High Commission in Malaysia. There was a reception for my team and the study tour syndicate at my in-law's residence in Kuala Lumpur attended by the Nigerian High Commissioner to Malaysia Dr Wahab Dosunmu as well as some staff of the International Medical University where a Nigerian Professor FI Achike was a lecturer. The Professor was close to my second son and daughter who were studying at the University.

I had to share a week between the USA and Malaysia and had to fly through London to meet the study tour teams halfway through their study tour. I was briefed by the Defence Adviser at the transit lounge of Heathrow Airport of the efforts being made to accord transit services to all the visiting NWC teams that passed through London and was informed of a sad incident of an unofficial member of one of the study tour teams being detained by the Immigration and later released but had to be monitored in the USA.

I was very disappointed that the Defence Attache's efforts in establishing such an excellent relationship with the British Border Authority staff at Heathrow would be so undermined. I joined the USA visiting team at the National Defense University and was happy to be back there and was warmly received. I was glad to see Prof James E Toth again and he was most pleased that I had become a Rear Admiral and wished me well. I discussed the need to establish a collaborative effort and possible exchange of lecturers and he offered me valuable advice. I visited the Army War College at Carlisle with the tour team and was able to compare notes with the staff of the College. The Nigerian Ambassador to the USA was Dr George Obiozor with whom I had a very interesting discussion on international relations. I invited him to deliver a lecture on a topic related to our discussion at the NWC, Abuja, which he honoured two months later. I visited an ICAF coursemate Ted Gronda and his wife Tutu from Rivers State with their two young children in Maryland. I joined the family for a short fishing trip and returned to the hotel to get set for the flight to London for the week-long visit to the UK and which I highlighted earlier.

On my arrival at the Nnamdi Azikiwe International Airport, Abuja I was met by the senior officer who was the PSO Coord and who sponsored the lady and instructed a staff officer under him to cover her up thereby causing embarrassment at Heathrow Airport and the follow up by the US Immigration on the same lady in the USA. I was furious with the PSO Coord and avoided his welcome gestures at the airport.

The officer at the head of the delegation claimed that he did not know of anyone on his delegation that was not uniform personnel or of the College staff. He was informed that there was a delay at the immigration desk being caused by someone on his delegation that was not on the official list and he told the authorities that he did not know but the staff officer under him knew.

I set up a Board of Inquiry under the Deputy Commandant and the report failed to establish a prima facie case against the PSO Coord as the lady he sponsored had valid visas which she secured in Abuja as she was processed with the delegation. I could not take any further disciplinary action but the damage had been done to the international image of the College. I decided to take some administrative measures but realised that it would result in his immediate retirement in a manner that could not be justified as procedures would not be followed.

After a presentation session in the College auditorium on the tours, I rounded up the session and I apologised to the members of the team for the embarrassment caused them at Heathrow Airport and I asked the PSO Coord who was responsible for the act to follow my example and apologise. He came to the podium to play a smart game and as he was leaving the podium, I called him back to the podium to apologise properly and respectfully to the participants as I had done and it was properly done. This is important as I considered the participants as future leaders of the Armed Forces of Nigeria that must be taught to learn how to trust and be trusted as well as show respect to those being led. The qualities of a leader must reflect positive character traits. I felt it was no use keeping such a senior officer at the College who did not enjoy my confidence at such a level.

I approached Lieutenant General OA Azazi, the COAS, and explained the situation to him and requested that he should be posted out of the College. He asked me to put it in writing. I read his mood and was not sure of his intention. This was also when I was expecting a Deputy Commandant and Director of Studies to be posted to the College. I had approached the COAS and told him that, according to the requirements at the College, the officer most suitable to be appointed as the Deputy Commandant was Brigadier General A Danbazzau who had been serving as a Principal General Staff Officer to the HMOD. I had proposed that Brigadier General A Audu, the staff at the College, replace Brigadier General Dambazau and I discussed the matter extensively with the HMOD who was convinced that the appointments would advance the careers of both officers and since both of them were from the same state. I approached the COAS and CDS, General ML Agwai on the proposals and discussions I had with the HMOD and the request by the COAS to put it in writing to him since the HMOD had agreed.

The CDS also supported the proposal and the letter to COAS who I had final discussions with and all seemed perfectly in order. I was betrayed by the response to my letter as I was told in writing that NA posts officers under the direction of the COAS and not the Commandant. This was not the understanding and support I had from General ML Agwai and Air Marshal J Wuyep who acted promptly to maintain the ideals of the College. The PSO Coord was appointed as the Deputy Commandant and Director of Studies and supported by bureaucratic sophistry. I went to the CDS, General ML Agwai, and showed him the response of COAS. He advised me to stay calm and not react.

The new appointment of the PSO Coord, I thought, would not be fair to the participants for two reasons. He had not known the participants who were about to pass out and their report would have to be written and, secondly, the incident at Heathrow Airport could influence the action related to compilations of results at such a critical stage. I made sure the outgoing Deputy Commandant delayed taking over at his new post so that he would complete the compilation of results and write the reports of the participants. This was complied with but generated another protest that I refused a posting by the COAS. I was only making sure of the integrity of the process that would determine the future of about 120 senior officers of the Armed Forces and MDAs. I was subjected to all manners of intrigues but succeeded in ensuring that the participants got a fair deal and they did to my satisfaction.

The resumption of the new course had the PSO Coord stepping in as the Deputy Commandant, Director of Studies. I was put in an extremely difficult situation in addition to the problems of the permanent site project. I had to be vigilant regarding the College's ideals regarding creating a level playing field for the participants and made sure I monitored proceedings; it was all part of my responsibilities at the higher level of the management of the Armed Forces of Nigeria. I had bought a logo piece at Arizona Airport in the USA in May 2001 as I got the news that I was being posted as a DS to the NWC. On it is written: "To teach is to touch a life forever." It is very important to make positive impacts on the common good rather than seeking to be good for the wrong reasons.

I received a call early one morning 22 August 2006 from the Presidency informing me that I should report at the President's office for a meeting on the permanent site project and also come with the tie from the RCDS to present to the President. The meeting with the President was scheduled for 0900 hours. I called the officer heading the project team and asked him to go to the College and collect the briefing documents on the project and meet me at the Presidential Villa with two other members of the College Project Team. I arrived at the Presidential Villa and waited for my staff who joined me in the waiting room. I collected the briefing documents and arranged them while refreshing my memory.

I told my staff that we would be meeting with the President as soon as he finished a meeting. I was soon informed he was rounding up. We were taken into the President's conference room where we met him seated. I was asked by the Chief of Staff to sit to the right of the President. The BMPIU team led by Professor Kunle Ade Wahab streamed in and took their seats to the left of the President. The Chief of Staff started by informing the President that the Commandant, NWC, and BMPIU team had been brought before him because they could not agree on how to proceed with the permanent site project and wanted his intervention. The President suddenly turned to his right and asked what I had to say regarding the problem as presented before him.

I thanked the President for the audience and went straight to talk about the procurement process (based on the Procurement Act) that we had been following under the guidance of the BMPIU. I drew attention to the fact that I had to do all the design work and have a total picture of the project to know how to phase the execution and make efficient use of the funds that would be approved and released. I pleaded that I had applied the little knowledge available and the meagre fund appropriated in the budget.

The President turned in the direction of those gathered to his left and asked them what was their problem with the Commandant. Professor Wahab hesitated for a few seconds and gathered himself together and told the President that the College had only two hundred and fifty million Naira in the budget and the Commandant was behaving as if he had all the money available as required by the Procurement Act to proceed with the project.

The President turned towards me and started collecting all the briefing documents including drawings from me. I was preparing for the worst when he arranged all the documents and packed them under his flowing traditional dress and got up stating, as he headed for the exit into his office, that if the College had no sufficient funds it was the responsibility of the Federal Government of Nigeria to provide the funds. The conference room was filled with eerie silence and I observed the sad mood of the staff of the BMPIU led by Prof Wahab. The President had gone against his staff and supported the Commandant for the cause of the College. I stood up as the President left and I waited for the next directive from the Chief of Staff who was already on his feet.

Professor Wahab and his BMPIU team left and the Chief of Staff followed them out. I trailed behind with my team of three including myself. At the lobby, I saw the ADC to the President, Colonel (later Major General) CA Jemitola climbing up the stairs looking towards me.

He advised the Chief of Staff that I should be allowed to give the President a present that had been given to the representative of the President at an event at the College. I was led to the President's office. I also had with me the RCDS tie I was given by the College Secretary to present to the President. I had two other reasons to have the audience with the President in addition to another surprise. I saluted and made the two presentations to him. He was pleased that the RCDS remembered him and I took the opportunity to inform him of the reception given to my team at the historic Lancaster House. The tension of the meeting with the BMPIU was over as the President went into a monologue drawing on his personal experiences and lectured me on the need to tread carefully to get things through because decision making and taking require patience. I got the message. He graciously spent quite a lot of time in his office with me. As I left his office, the Chief of Staff followed me out and told me to go straight to the office of the BMPIU and meet with Professor Wahab.

I was directed to the office of Professor Kunle Ade Wahab at the wing of the Presidential Villa complex. I got a very hostile reception as most of his staff that followed him to the meeting were still smarting from the President's response to their complaints against me. I was visited with a barrage of derogatory remarks. They started by telling me that the President was on my side because of our military background. I was given a thorough dressing down and told that they were professionals of repute and should have the final say. I was told that those of us in the military do not have the brains for academic pursuits. Military personnel were considered not fit for their level of intellectual pursuit and application to professional matters.

At this juncture, I felt I should reply as the interests of the institution I headed far outweighed any other consideration. I told the audience that I was a Chartered Marine Engineer and a Fellow of the Institute of Marine Engineering, Science and Technology, London. The message was that I had a comparative professional standing with them. They mellowed down and Engr Emeka M. Ezeh asked me if I had any relationship with The Nigeria Society of Engineers as he was Vice President. I told him that I was a member of the Nigeria Society of Engineers and also, for three years, was a member of the Public Affairs Board of the Society. He changed his mind and hostile mood and gave me his complimentary card. The other staff with the professor were also silenced and I was advised to consult them as I progressed with the project. I would continue to encounter similar treatment at meetings and in correspondences.

I was invited to the BMPIU office in respect of some architectural drawings that were forwarded for their due diligence. The criticism of the drawing was scathing and at a stage, Sunday Echono (later a Permanent Secretary) handling the related matters at the BMPIU threatened that he would hand over my architect to the EFCC for reasons best known to him. The threat is very common in the Nigerian civil service. As Professor Wahab turned his attention to me, I told them that the responsibility was mine and I should be the one to be handed over to the EFCC. I put forward my arms to be handcuffed if that was the beginning of EFCC procedures.

Professor Wahab looked at me for a few seconds with my hands stretched ready to be handcuffed. He collected his papers and returned to his desk. I then told Sunday Echono that we were open for corrections, additions, and alterations and if there were any other requirements to be met, the College team was ready to consider them and act appropriately. The meeting came to an inconclusive end and as we left, I told them that we had taken note and would improve.

I sent the architects on the project team for training and bought some equipment for them to enhance their productivity and we had ready our general arrangement drawings which were issued to consultants to guide them on the College specifications. I managed to establish simple procedures for handling very complex matters related to the permanent site project. All correspondences from the College would be forwarded to the MOD for their due diligence and thereafter forwarded to the BMPIU. I concentrated my efforts on seeking support for the project and this was the most difficult task as every interested party wanted to be awarded contracts while funds had not been approved. I was walking a very tight rope given the attention the project of this magnitude had attracted.

When we received the approval of the BMPIU for the categories of Consultants and Construction contractors, I decided that I would focus my attention on category A lists. There was a need for a very experienced Project Manager and I got Aim Consultants Limited approved for the project. The Consultants had a very varied experience in Abuja and Nigeria and I felt the permanent site project was in very safe hands to help me navigate the very treacherous paths.

I was informed that the land given to the College at Jabi District was being allocated to Ministers and other prominent Nigerians in government. I wrote a letter to the HMOD for the matter to be taken up with the President, Commander-in-Chief. The response from the President was a directive to the Minister of FCT to consider and attend to the matter. I had a major problem on my hand. It was not long when Aim Consultants informed me that they would no longer be the Project Manager since all the land allocated for the project had been allocated to prominent Nigerians and there was no alternative land allocated for the College permanent site project. I had more information on the moves, piling up pressure on me. How would I take on the might of high government officials including members of the Federal Executive Council?

I decided that I would no longer deal directly with the Minister of FCT and wrote to the CDS, then General ML Agwai, to keep him abreast of developments as the HMOD was the arrowhead of the struggle. The HMOD Engr Rabiu Musa Kwankwaso had resigned from the Federal Executive Council towards the end of 2006 to prepare for elections in 2007 for the governorship of Kano State and was replaced by Ambassador Thomas I Aguiyi-Ironsi, son of the first military Head of State, Major General Thomas Aguiyi Ironsi.

The budget preparations for the next fiscal year 2007 were in full swing by September 2006 and I had not been able to make use of the N250 million in the 2006 budget. I had been under pressure to use the money for other College capital projects and award contracts. This would be a mistake that would derail the permanent site project. I resisted all pressures and had to also contend with internal pressures within the College. The President, Commander-in-Chief had been informed that that amount of money was in the budget for 2006 and was about to lapse. I directed my finance officer to write to the MOD and liaise with the Central Bank of Nigeria and the Accountant General of the Federation that the money would be rolled over into the 2007 budget and I would make efforts for additional allocation. I only succeeded in getting an additional N50 million Naira in the 2007 budget. I was running out of time and my objective of getting the construction started was becoming a mirage. I monitored the budgeting process to ensure I did not lose the money allocated no matter how small.

I was also monitoring developments regarding the allocation of the land on which construction was to start to prominent Nigerians. The sentries I ordered to be posted there were without arms but had a communication set and horsewhips to keep off those who were coming to start the process of taking over a property duly allocated to the

College. I had all the allocation papers secured. As pressure mounted from the allottees, I informed the CDS and the Inspector General of

Police (IGP) that should anyone trespass on the College property, they would be detained and immediately handed over to the police. I had some members of my staff seeking allocation for themselves. I had applied for land in Abuja since 1989 and had not been allocated any plot. The Minister of FCT decided to act on my application and allocated a very small plot at Karshi on the outskirts of Abuja where there was no access road. I was being tempted to ask for a better plot and would have been given part of the College permanent site being distributed at Jabi District.

The College facilitated the appointment of the former Head of State General AA Abubakar GCFR as the Patron of the Africa Chapter of International Association of Peace Keeping Training Centres (IAPTC) through a resolution at the meeting in New Delhi, India. The investiture was at the Kofi Annan Peacekeeping Training Centre at Accra Ghana. I could not attend the ceremony but my representative, the Acting Dean of Africa Centre for Strategic Research and Studies, did a good job highlighting the efforts being made to get the College permanent site project started and this included the facility for the Peace Support Operations training at a strategic level based on ECOWAS mandate and also the recognition given by the UN. The Dean had been following the development of the design with ECOWAS and the College project team. The former Head of State decided to write to the President, Commander-in-Chief in support of the College's efforts as Nigeria was lagging in the development of facilities required for the exercise of the mandate given to the College.

When I received a copy of the letter to the President, I wrote to the HMOD and the CDS notifying them of the action taken by the former Head of State. A few days later, the CDS informed me that he was asked by the President if he was in the picture as regards the letter of support for the College permanent site. I took the opportunity to brief the CDS regarding the implications of the actions being taken by the Minister of FCT and which could derail the permanent site project. I requested the CDS to step in as the HMOD had already written to the President and discussed the matter with him. The CDS made an appointment with the Minister of FCT and I was adequately prepared for the meeting.

At the scheduled meeting was a DHQ Principal Staff Officer and a Branch Chief who was a Major General and I had with me the Head of the College Project Team. The meeting was held in the office of the Minister. The CDS tabled the request of the College after apprising the

Minister of the progress made so far to start construction at the Jabi District site allocated to the College and which was being allocated to individuals. The Minister responded that the Abuja Master Plan he was trying to restore did not accommodate any educational institution in the District and the College being designated a War College, it should not be near the city centre and suggested an outpost isolated from any area that has a concentration of people. The Minister preferred a solution to give us a site as much as we want far away in the bush where we could conduct war studies. The CDS and I were prepared and we gave details of the location of similar Colleges in some selected countries and also informed him that the Federal Government had approved the change of name to National Defence College. The Minister and his staff later accepted that the College permanent site would be located within the city and close to government establishments for ease of access in the conduct of the affairs of the College.

The CDS had a flexible approach so that it would not seem as if we invaded the Minister's office to force his hand as he realised that the College must be within the city. The CDS added that we did not mind any site within the city as long as it was ready to commence development immediately. The Minister decided to set up a joint committee to look at an alternative site within the city and if there was no site available for immediate commencement of construction, the College would be allowed to continue the development of the Jabi District site. I nominated the Head of the College Project Team to be a member of the Joint Committee for the inspection and selection of the site. I followed up with the submission of drawings for approval to commence construction as the committee work was in progress and as agreed during the meeting.

There was no alternative site available for immediate commencement of the construction of the College permanent site and I thought that the Minister would keep to his words. The year was ending and I was focusing on the budget process to ensure the College gets improved funding. The Minister of Federal Capital Territory failed to keep his promise that the College would retain the Jabi District site with infrastructure including the fence built by the College.

CHAPTER NINETEEN

The Battle to Save the College Permanent Site Land

As I returned from work to my residence at Niger Barracks, I was informed by the Director of Administration that heavily armed policemen accompanied by some bulldozers were at the fenced site at Jabi District and had started pulling down the fence. The sentries stationed there were not armed and had been instructed that should they encounter any armed groups they should withdraw and inform the College authority.

I ordered the College Director of Administration (DOA) to open the armoury and arm the duty personnel and move them to meet me at the permanent site at Jabi. The DOA hesitated by asking me for the Rule of Engagement and I reminded him that he distributed copies to all personnel based on my instructions and I had mine. Why would he be asking me for the rule of engagement when I was leading the operation?

I got the CDS online and told him that I had already initiated my response to a developing situation that I had been briefing him about and I was on my way to take charge with my armed troops. I told the CDS that I would also inform the Inspector-General of Police and sensing the urgency of the moment, he told me to leave that to him and proceed accordingly. I appreciated the CDS' understanding of not asking why I did not take permission. What excuse would I have if I could not defend a piece of the Federal Capital Territory allocated to the College under the command of an Admiral? Speed was essential and I was on the move. A civilian Minister having armed men destroying a military property is a reckless provocation that could not be tolerated.

At the site, I saw that about a hundred meters of the fence had been pulled down and the heavily armed policemen and the bulldozers had disappeared. The armed personnel from the College were still on the way and I went around to survey the extent of the damages and see if there were any traces of the Minister's demolition squad. They had all disappeared. They must have been informed of the actions being taken to respond.

When the DOA arrived with the armed personnel from the College, they met me walking around. The DOA had failed to act decisively and I wondered what would have happened if I had met the demolition squad and a shootout ensued. I ordered that henceforth the sentries should be armed and issued with live ammunition. The implications were clear. I felt the Minister was rude to the CDS who led a team to his office to explain to him the situation. This was an extraordinary honour done to the Minister which he failed to appreciate. I sent an officer to the Minister to find out if he authorized the demolition.

I was reliably informed that the Minister denied knowledge of the demolition squad sent to the site. I wrote to the Minister and documented the story so far including the finding of the committee set up to get an alternative site. I informed the Minister that henceforth, the sentries at the site would be armed with live ammunition and he was advised to keep his staff away from the site.

The Minister started spreading his false story that I had given orders to the sentries to shoot him at sight. I was expecting that this would trigger a response from the President, Commander-in-Chief and I kept watch for the next development. There was no incident for some weeks and I relaxed the state of readiness of the sentries. They were to arrest any trespassers and bring them to the College for processing and handing over to IGP. The CDS and IGP were informed of this procedure. I had a draft letter of handing over to IGP ready with the Military Police post.

A former Minister's (Defence) son, went to challenge the sentries showing them a letter of allocation and his intention to take possession of the allocated portion of the plot. He was arrested and brought to the College detention centre and in a matter of minutes the letter to the IGP with the details of the trespasser was signed and he was handed over to the police. He was locked up.

I received a call as I was about closing for the day from the former Minister. He told me that it was his son that had been locked up. I looked again at the copy of the letter I sent to IGP and saw the name of his son whose wedding I attended. I apologised to the former Minister but emphasised that due to the enormous problems being encountered, the procedure was such that his son was handed over immediately to the IGP who had the powers to detain him and that I had nothing to do with the case again.

The College lecture programmes brought many distinguished personalities to interact with the participants ranging from foreign Heads of State, Ministers of the Federal Government of Nigeria, Heads of Departments and Agencies as well as international resource persons. The Commandant was the only military commander that could invite a foreign head of state. This range of resource persons provided me with the opportunity to brief widely on the permanent site project.

I had one such visitor who happened to be very close to the President, Commander-in-Chief unknown to me. He is Chief Jonathan Olopade who was also very well known to the National Security Adviser, Lieutenant General Mohammed Aliyu Gusau (Rtd). I briefed him in my office and told him that I was having problems getting adequate budgetary allocation to make meaningful progress. I had praised the efforts of the President so far in supporting the project. He then told me that to get the attention of the President, he must be in a relaxed state which he rarely had in the pressure cooker of the Presidential Villa. He told me to give him a very crisp summary of the financial requirements as he was scheduled to meet the President at a location that would be very conducive to have his full attention. I gave him the summary which he took away. I got a call from him later instructing me to forward my requirements through the HMOD.

I had to sound out the HMOD as the time was getting close to the end of the second term tenure of the President and the World Study tour was already planned to take me to Belgium, India, and Japan. The HMOD was very swift in telling me to stop such an ambitious proposal that would be rejected. I did not mention to him that I had already got the approval in principle but was only expecting documentation to make it officially binding. I pleaded my case passionately with the HMOD and assured him that the chances of not getting it approved were slim. The HMOD reluctantly asked for my proposal which I presented to him, broken down into four phases totalling about thirty-five billion Naira with the first phase put at about twenty-three billion Naira.

The HMOD was again very apprehensive but I kept up the pressure and would not tell him that the President was waiting for the letter as I wanted the HMOD to be convinced by me that the phasing and the cost estimates had been well thought out. I had to provide overwhelming proof of the thorough work that was put on virtually one page. The first phase on completion would enable the College to start functioning at the site.

In the summary, I stated that going by the appropriations in the 2006 and 2007 budgets, it would take about a century to realise the project. I managed to win the confidence of the HMOD and he read the brief letter and added a paragraph inviting the President to do the foundation laying ceremony by late April 2007 which would be about a month to handing over on 29 May 2007 to the new President. I was very pleased.

The HMOD sent the letter dated 27 March 2007 to the President and by 29 March, the expected response of the President was committed into writing with directives to the Honourable Minister of Finance (HMOF) and HMOD for follow-up action. This was unbelievable. A meeting was fixed for 11 April 2007 with the HMOF and the HMOD after the Federal Executive Council meeting. I sensed that this was a load I could not carry alone. I went to the CDS and briefed him and requested him to lead me to the meeting to be held in the office of the HMOF.

The CDS General ML Agwai took charge and I felt relieved as the news spread that I had hit a jackpot and people wondered how I achieved such a feat. It was as if I had been given all the Defence Budget for my personal use. I had to carefully manage this unprecedented success and breakthrough. The period covered the Presidential election and the transition. I was facing a new wave of rejection and hate for this was a project that my predecessor put forward at nine billion Naira and it was rejected by the College Governing Board and here I was with a Presidential nod for about thirty-five billion Naira.

I noticed that the only genuine supporters I had were the CDS, General ML Agwai, the HMOD, Engr Rabiu Musa Kwankwaso and his successor Ambassador Thomas I Aguiyi- Ironsi, President Olusegun Obasanjo, GCFR and his successor, President Umaru Musa Yar'Adua, GCFR as well as General AA Abubakar, GCFR, former Head of State, Chief Olopade and the National Security Adviser, Lieutenant General Mohammed Aliyu Gusau. At the College Steering Group meeting, I announced the progress made and the President's inspiring support for the funding of the entire project, and instead of jubilation, I noticed a very mournful look on the faces of the generals and senior civilian staff in the room. I took notice and quickly changed the topic. The service chiefs also seemed confused about how I got such an opening to the state treasury.

I was conscious of more tough battles ahead as I still had issues pending with the Minister of FCT, Mallam Nasir el-Rufai. I had to make moves to get the Federal Executive Council to approve the first structure for construction. I had deposited the President's response with BMPIU as well as all the analysis of the contractors' submissions and all I had to do was to request for the first Certificate that would enable the MOD to submit the Federal Executive Council Memorandum. I needed to get a letter of no objection from HMOF and also the CBN was kept in the picture because the three hundred million Naira was readily available to meet the first stage payment after the Federal Executive Council approval and the signing of the contract. I was very lucky to have succeeded in protecting what was considered a small amount that I was expected to spend by awarding wasteful contracts just to share money.

I received a call from the Chief of Army Staff (COAS) Lieutenant General AO Azazi informing me that Stabilini Visinoni Limited had complained that I manipulated the bidding process and relegated the company to the second position to favour another construction giant that emerged first in order of merit. I was satisfied that any of the three contractors that made the order of merit of the first three would be capable of performing to our entire satisfaction. I replied to the COAS that a committee carried out the exercise and the result was forwarded to MOD and from there to BMPIU in the Presidency and I never had the opportunity to alter anything as all the biddings submitted were opened in the presence of all the contractors who signed what they submitted and consequently there was no room to manipulate an open and transparent process.

The COAS sent the Chief Executive of the company to me. I brought out a copy of the report as forwarded for processing and I told him he could look through and identify the evidence of manipulation. He apologised to me that the mistake he found was their fault. The company sent me a letter commending me for the transparent process. It was left to BMPIU to decide which of the three top contenders got the contract.

The first in the order of merit was considered to be overloaded with Federal Government contracts and for some other reasons, Stabilini Visinoni was approved though the committee had recommended the first in order of merit and I had endorsed it. A certificate was issued by BMPIU and I started the process of preparing the Federal Executive Council memorandum. I had at all times took care that the interests of the College permanent site project were not compromised as regards quality execution according to the defined specifications to solve problems.

The preparation of the Federal Executive Council Memorandum and the forwarding of the draft of the amendment of the College Establishment Act for the change of name of the College to National Defence College took centre stage with preparations for the 2007 World Study tour. The Minister of FCT was still thinking of how to deal with the issue of a new site to allocate to the College while I commenced preparation of the site at Jabi District to start construction on getting Federal Executive Council approval.

I was scheduled to visit Belgium, India, and Japan with my team for the tour series. I left instructions for the PSO Coord to forward the draft of the amendments of the College Establishment Act to the National Assembly and seek the assistance of the Chairman House Committee on Defence, Honourable Wole Oke. I was virtually in Abuja while in Belgium as I was being briefed on developments and I had to reach out to HMOD for the relevant correspondences he had to authorize and sign related to the permanent site and the amendment bill. I had to generate some of the follow-up correspondences for the PSO Coord to sign on my behalf and submit after seeking clearance from HMOD.

I was on the verge of cancelling my tour programme when I was advised that it would be negatively interpreted. I was physically in Belgium but mentally hooked to Abuja and was able to make some progress. The visit to the Waterloo battle site where Napoleon was defeated relaxed my mind as we were taken through some of the highlights of the battle. I reflected on a lot of soldiers in battle and related it to what I was going through. It seems at all times the soldier is going through the realities of battle without respite.

I passed through London on my way to Brussels and I was informed that the Permanent Secretary Dr Haruna Sanusi was in Switzerland on a medical trip. I was able to reach out to him through the Defence Adviser and register my sympathy and goodwill. This enabled me to have an idea of the set up at MOD and who to refer to for assistance regarding the issues I was pursuing. The visit to the Belgian military establishments revealed a unique set up regarding the higher management of defence where the emphasis is placed on combat commanders rather than service chiefs.

The participants were able to learn some lessons regarding the management of defence at operational and strategic levels. I was able to spend most of the week in Brussels attending to matters in Abuja and was relieved that appreciable progress was being made on matters being pursued related to the permanent site project. The team left Brussels by train for Paris Charles De Gaulle International Airport to catch a flight to New Delhi. I was fully tuned into the tour programme and I had to split the last week of the study tour between India and Japan to monitor the syndicates visiting the two countries as planned.

The visit to the Taj Mahal at Agra to the North of New Delhi was very interesting. I was impressed with the quality of precise measurements of slabs used in the construction of the monument and the work of the artisans of the era. It is a befitting edifice of love. The investment in education in India was showcased as we visited many establishments dedicated to curriculum development as well as research and development.

The Indian Chief of Army Staff, Gen JJ Singh, visited Nigeria the previous year and delivered a lecture at NWC. We were given presentation by his staff officers at the Indian Army headquarters. The highlight of my visit was to the National Defence College where I had sent a team led by Commodore OS Ibrahim (later Admiral, CNS, and CDS) on an exchange programme I had initiated with the assistance of the India Defence Attache in Abuja, Colonel Dixit. The Commandant, a Vice Admiral, and a Major General were my guests at Abuja in furtherance of this exchange programme which I was also able to initiate with National Defense University Washington DC using the same team led by Commodore OS Ibrahim whom I had appointed as Director of Curriculum Development.

I had the second part of the working week in Tokyo, Japan. I was received at the Ministry of Foreign Affairs and hosted at the National Defence College where there was a joint session with participants of NWC and their Japanese counterparts. The Nigerian Ambassador, Alhaji Adamu Aliyu, accompanied me to the Foreign Affairs Ministry and we had to be in the vicinity of the complex about 30 minutes to the appointed time to ensure we kept precisely to the time given. I departed Tokyo and had a stopover in Kuala Lumpur en route to Abuja and was hosted by the Nigerian High Commissioner to Malaysia.

Back in Abuja, I was briefed by the PSO Coord regarding some surprising developments. The first was that the Minister of FCT within the two weeks I was away had built a tarred road, drainages, borehole, and overhead water tank in addition to the installation of a transformer and the erection of electric poles supplying electric power to a new site at Piwoyi on the airport road. I was informed that I could drive straight to the new site which was not possible two weeks ago and all was ready for the foundation laying ceremony by the President. The following morning I inspected the new site and was impressed that so much could be achieved within two weeks. I was told that a special task force was set up and worked twenty-four hours each day for the two weeks. It was a miracle.

The second development was the alleged demand of Honourable Wole Oke that the sum of about twenty million Naira is paid to the members of the National Assembly through him for the processing of the amendment bill submitted. I had considered Honourable Wole Oke a friend of the College as he was introduced to me by the Governor of Osun State Prince Olagunsoye Oyinlola on the second day of my taking over command at the College in my office and was always welcomed to the College. He was also the Chairman of the House of Representatives

Committee on Defence. I could not imagine him asking for money from my representative.

I invited him to my office and asked him why he was demanding money from my representative. He told me that the good progress being made at the College was my legacy and I should pay for my name to be recorded on the roll of honour. This ended our discussion as I told him I did not want to be remembered for doing my routine duty. He felt slighted and he would henceforth be organising powerful government officials against me. He left my office in a state that told me I was in for a very rough time ahead.

I commended the efforts of the Minister of FCT for the excellent effort in providing essential infrastructure at the new Piwoyi site. The Minister, through his representative at the site, demanded that I should hand over the allocation papers for the site at Jabi District and remove the armed soldiers on guard duties there. I sent a message that as a man under military authority I had to get approval from the CDS and it would take some days. The Minister was not happy with this delay but I had no choice.

I got the CDS who was on his way from Washington DC through London. I briefed him on the impressive provision of infrastructure at the new site and also added that we had a better deal in terms of the size of land being given to the College. I also informed the CDS that I would wait for him to return and give him more details before seeking his approval to hand over the Jabi District plot and take over the Piwoyi District plot. I sent a message to the Minister of FCT explaining to him that steps were being taken to properly do the exchange with appropriate documents.

When the CDS returned to Abuja he gave me the go-ahead to hand over the Jabi District plot. I had been informed that the Minister of FCT was under tremendous pressure from those highly placed government officials to whom he had allocated the Jabi District plots as they were about to leave the office on 29 May 2007. I got an appointment to see the Minister of FCT and give him a present I bought while abroad on hearing of the wonderful efforts he put in to give the College a better deal.

The meeting was very cordial and I assured him that I did not harbour any grudges against him as I have a responsibility for the College and I also recognised he had responsibility for the FCT. We had a good laugh and he asked me if I had a plot of land in FCT. I told him that what he allocated to me in Karshi was in a bush and not worth developing. He asked his staff to find me a better land to allocate to compensate me but it was too late and I took it in good faith. I was expected to ask for plots at Jabi District and that would have compromised me most embarrassingly and killed the project. I followed up the goodwill established with the Minister of FCT and was assured of more plots for the College at the new site to compensate the College for the resources committed at Jabi District. This facilitated plans to have a very secure permanent site that would allow for future developments. I had submitted an estimated cost of the College loss to the Minister for compensation.

The CNS informed me that he would like to show me the new Naval Barrack land in the Lugbe District of Abuja he was able to get from the Minister of FCT. He invited me to go to the site with him. I was worried that this might be interpreted as keeping me informed of NN developments as it was being discussed that he might be leaving office and would most likely hand it over to me. On the day of the visit I was dressed in the normal white working rig; on reaching his residence just nearby, I noticed he was in a blue rig. I took permission from him to return to my residence and change. I requested the CNS to allow us to stop over at the NWC permanent site which was along the same route and he agreed. We shared his official staff car.

We stopped over and I showed him the College permanent site being prepared for the foundation laying ceremony after which we proceeded to the NN new barracks site. We spent some time walking around the NN site which had been fenced and I commended his efforts. At the end of the tour, I escorted the CNS back to his office.

I had the battle of the Federal Executive Council for the first approval to commence the construction of the participant quarters at the Piwoyi permanent site. I had BMPIU approval to commence the construction of the first participants' quarters and commit the three hundred million Naira to it. I felt there was no use waiting for a large lump sum of money to be available before commencing the construction because administrative procedures take time to progress though this was against the Procurement Act. I knew that as soon as money was available there would be intense pressure to commit funds recklessly. I experienced that sort of pressure with the first allocation of two hundred and fifty million Naira which was topped up by fifty million Naira in the 2007 annual budget. I had the unflinching support of the Director of Planning, Research, and Statistics at MOD, Mrs I Onayemi who understood my position and endured many insults from BMPIU. She was the silent hero who felt she was just doing her job. She never failed me no matter how badly I performed.

I worked with the staff of the Director of Joint Services to write the Federal Executive Council Memorandum. We locked up ourselves in his small office at MOD to craft the document. We produced the memorandum after two days of wading through documents to get all the facts required. I then had to link up with the Federal Executive Council (FEC) Secretariat. I was lucky to have a Director there I had known while I was preparing for the project in Italy in 1984. I was able to secure a date on the FEC schedule for submission of the memorandum.

The HMOD had to assess the most suitable time to submit it. I could only pray that the formidable forces against me would not prevail. The HMOD won the day and the President, Commander-in-Chief was in his best element and was on the side of the College and the HMOD. The FEC approved the memorandum and the minutes of the meeting related to the subject were sent to MOD and I got a copy through my contact for a follow-up. The President, Commander-in-Chief, Chief Olusegun O Obasanjo GCFR has been most inspiring and a very important milestone was achieved. The first structure of a new National Defence College was approved for construction. This is history so recorded. It was time for the first contract to be signed and I asked the MOD to sign on behalf of the College to avoid the pressures that would mount from concerned quarters. And by 07 June 2007, the contract was signed. The new President, Alhaji Umaru Musa Yar'Adua, took his oath of office on 29 May 2007 and I had a new set of challenges.

I sent in a brief on the permanent site project through the Permanent Secretary to the new President as soon as the contract was signed. The new Federal Government Ministers were not yet appointed. I also mentioned that the name of the College had been changed to National Defence College; the amendment bill was before the National Assembly. I fixed 27 July 2007 for the foundation laying ceremony. The foundation laying ceremony at the new Piwoyi site would be for National Defence College after which signboards bearing the change of name and car plate numbers would take effect. It was as if the impossible was becoming possible. I gave the preparations the best attention I could muster and made sure the protocol list for the invitation of dignitaries was followed up.

The Diplomatic Corps was given due priority given the interest shown by the G-8 and EU countries for the Peace Support Operations contributions some of them intended to make to the College during the construction of the permanent site. I took the time to especially brief the new CDS and the three service chiefs. The new Federal Executive

Council had just been constituted. The leadership and key members of the National Assembly were also invited.

The CNS was a bit apprehensive of the chances of getting the President to attend and I knew why. The new President was considering a possible change of service chiefs and there were also moves to extend the tenure of the incumbent. I was again being considered and to get the President to attend the College ceremony would be a huge boost for me. This is the way they thought. I had more serious issues with the transformation of a vital national institution. I could not afford to fail.

I had the support of Julius Berger Plc that did a great job of sending a truckload of materials to prepare the site and produced the commemorative plaque for the President to unveil during the ceremony. The last few days were spent on a rehearsal at the site. I had decided that I would not deliver the welcome speech. I deferred to the new CDS though I was the Chief Host. I had briefed him and he agreed to welcome the President to his very first outing since taking office.

I detailed Commodore (later Vice Admiral and CNS) Dele Ezeoba to take charge of the ceremony. I would only escort the President to do the foundation laying ceremony and the unveiling of the plaque with a brief description of the project as the chief host. The CDS would be invited to formally welcome the president to the ceremony in his capacity as the country's most senior military officer. The President after unveiling the plaque would thereafter deliver his speech. I would encounter a series of dramatic intrigues.

The new Minister of Defence was the former Head of Civil Service and later Secretary to the Federal Government, Alhaji Mahmud Yayale Ahmed. The Minister of State for Defence was Mrs Fidelia A Njeze who had just reported for duty the previous day. I had arrived early to start receiving the dignitaries and there was a good turnout of dignitaries and spectators.

I was moving into a position to receive the CDS and the service chiefs together with the Inspector General of Police when I was approached to read a letter from BMPIU signed by the Acting Director-General Engr Emeka N Ezeh. I wondered why this was not taken to my office to be properly documented. As the letter was given some sort of urgency, I read the concluding paragraph and got the message. The BMPIU was accusing me of illegally committing the Federal Government to incur expenditure to the tune of over ten billion Naira. This was calculated to be a serious financial crime that would end any career abruptly. I closed the file and told my Flag Lieutenant to keep it out of view and focus on the ceremony. The CNS representative at my first College board meeting described the project as illegal and now with a new President, there are new combats to brand the project so.

As the new CDS, General OA Azazi, and the entourage of service chiefs and IGP arrived I received them. The CDS casually told me that the President phoned him and wanted to know if he was aware that I was inviting him for an illegal project and he told the President that he did not know about the project. The COAS, CNS, CAS, and the representative of IGP were with the CDS. The Chairman of Stabilini Visinoni was the CDS' friend and he had spoken to me on their behalf and I had briefed him on all the project milestones. How could he tell the President that he knew nothing about the project?

He asked me to ring the Presidential Villa and explain myself. I told him that I could not just pick up the phone and start ringing the President because it would be a breach of protocol. The CDS was the most senior military adviser to the President and I was standing before him. The CDS got the ADC, Lieutenant Colonel (later Brigadier General) Mustapha Onoyiveta, to the President on his mobile phone and asked me to speak with him. The ADC asked me why I was embarrassing the President by asking him to come and be associated with an illegal project? The ADC added that the President was getting ready to come for the ceremony when he was briefed that the project was illegal. The Permanent Secretary was already seated.

I then knew that BMPIU Acting Director-General who signed the letter delivered to me at the site was the point man for the coordination of the sabotage. I told the ADC to the hearing of CDS and the distinguished entourage surrounding me that the project was backed by law as appropriated for in the 2006 and 2007 budgets and I had the approval of MOD to contact BMPIU for the tendering process which led to securing a Due Process certificate from BMPIU to proceed to FEC after securing a letter of no-objection from the Ministry of Finance. On fulfilling all these conditions over eighteen months, the MOD forwarded a memorandum to FEC which was approved after which a contract was signed between the MOD/NWC and the contractor to commit the three hundred million Naira in the budget. In all these, I had not done anything illegal.

The ADC told me that nobody mentioned anything that I had told him to the President, Commander-in-Chief. The impression was that I was alone doing things in isolation. He told me to standby because he was going to brief the President and feed me back. I told the CDS and the distinguished entourage that I was told to hold on and wait for the President to be briefed. We all waited in the full glare of the audience gathered who did not know the high tension intrigue playing out in front of them.

The ADC called me back and told me that the President asked him to confirm from me that what I had narrated was the truth. I told the ADC that I was using the phone of the CDS who was standing by my side and listening to me with the three service chiefs as witnesses. I confirmed to the ADC that I had given the President the facts and that the project was not illegal. The new HMOD and HMOSD arrived and were escorted to take their seats.

Barely twenty minutes after my confirmation that the project was not illegal the President's advanced party arrived and started setting up their equipment. The President arrived shortly. Thank you Alhaji Umaru Musa Yar'Adua Grand Commander of the Federal Republic, President, Commander-in-Chief of the Armed Forces of the Federal Republic of Nigeria for your grand strategic leadership. Thank you, ADC for your fast factual briefs. What a moment. I must be dreaming.

The CDS and the service chiefs were seated. I briefed the Permanent Secretary that the President had been told that the project was illegal and I walked away. I requested HMOD to move closer to the seat of the President the position I was expected to occupy as the Chief Host and decided I would be far away from the President and cool down. The arrival of the President saw many dignitaries on their feet trying to have a handshake with him. I pulled back and allowed the security details to do their job. After the President's security staff had isolated the President from the crowd I was asked to take charge. I requested the CDS and service chiefs to take a position to welcome the president and I stood in line with them to be the last. I saluted and welcomed the President and led him to inspect the Quarter Guard. After inspecting the Quarter Guard I led him to his seat.

As we walked to the President's seat he looked back and discovered that it was only his ADC that was behind us. The President told me that he was told that the project was illegal. I repeated what I told the ADC in a matter of very few seconds that I had that rare privacy with him. I led him to his seat and gave him a copy of the programme. The Master of Ceremony Commodore Ezeoba conducted the ceremony so well that I almost fell asleep sitting next to COAS.

The CDS gave the welcome address and I was invited to give a project brief and invite the President to perform the ceremony. I could hardly speak as I was emotionally drained but composed to satisfy myself that the evil plot had failed. I spoke briefly and invited the President to perform the foundation laying ceremony and unveil the elaborate granite plaque. The President on unveiling the plaque spared some moments to read the words engraved for posterity. This was the very first plaque he would unveil as President, Commander-in-Chief. It was also his first official outing as President, Commander-in-Chief since he took office about eight weeks earlier.

The President gave his speech in which he formally pronounced the change of name to National Defence College. He went on to add that he had been well briefed on the permanent site project which had been well designed and phased for implementation. He declared that he would not like the project implementation to drag on for decades like the Nigerian Defence Academy permanent site project in Kaduna. He promised to complete phase one by 2010. He instructed that a financial flow plan should be submitted to him immediately.

I was completely thrown off guard to receive such a huge commendation and support. The President had embraced a major project of his predecessor and promised accelerated development. This was a victory lap at the very spot it was planned I would be openly disgraced and humiliated out of office. It was evident that the former and new Presidents could see and appreciate the intrigues I was battling and showed statesmanship and exemplary leadership. Immediately after attending to the President as he departed after the ceremony I was surrounded by the CDS and service chiefs who were subdued. I thanked them for their presence and support in their different ways.

The CDS General OA Azazi and CNS Vice Admiral GT Adekeye were my course mates at NDA while the Chief of Army Staff, Lieutenant General L Yusuf was a year our junior. The Chief of Air Staff was Air Marshal F Dike. I gave them all their due respect. I saw them off without providing them refreshments because the College reception team failed me despite the provisions made for them. When the CDS and Service Chiefs demanded the champagne to celebrate I apologised to them for my inability to provide the champagne. Mission accomplished.

The President, Commander-in-Chief has clearly stated his intention and following the principle of unity of command, I cannot fail to understand what to do and what not to do whether I have further contact with him or not. This is why mental maturity and strength are developed in military leaders for sound judgements based on an understanding of guiding principles. The inspiring leadership of Chief Olusegun O Obasanjo to get the project on a sound footing and the impressive support given by General AA Abubakar a former Head of State, Commander-in-Chief constitutes a unique trinity of inspiration that got me going again as I reflected on what has transpired at the ceremony.

It was special and I just had to keep on fighting drawing inspiration from the quality support at the highest level of command since 2006.

The very person first to congratulate me was the Finish Ambassador to Nigeria who was the Chair of the EU Commission. She approached me as soon as the President left the site and gave me a very warm handshake. She was pleased that the President was personally present and told me that this would be used to rally the support of EU countries to support the Peace Support aspects of the project and on which I had briefed the EU Ambassadors in Bamako, Mali, and the G-8 countries Ambassadors in Abuja two years earlier.

Back in my office, I noticed the absence of a celebratory mood after a very successful ceremony. Only one Director at the Ministry of Defence, Mrs Augustina Ediae, Director, Air Force, phoned to congratulate me and stated that I had achieved what was considered an impossible task. I knew that the establishment at MOD was against me and I knew their reasons all along but for the efforts of the Director Planning, Research, and Statistics, Mrs I Onayemi who had just retired after doing so much and enduring insults from BMPIU on my behalf and most importantly the College. She was my hero as she experienced all the intrigues at the MOD and endured them all.

I had to reflect on why the new President, Commander-in-Chief barely seven weeks in office and with the key Presidency Staff that served the immediate past President intact, would be told that the project was illegal even though BMPIU directives were followed. It was the same BMPIU that issued a certificate that facilitated the approval of the FEC under the immediate past President, Commander-in-Chief. The Director-General of BMPIU was on the team that almost derailed the project at a meeting with the immediate past President at the initial stages when I was struggling to get all the necessary approval from various MDAs.

It should trouble any decent human being why the new President, Commander-in-Chief should be lied to and it was documented in a letter that was sent to me. The scale and scope of the sabotage were beyond comprehension. I had to be on guard for the next treacherous move. This move would be from Honourable Wole Oke, Chairman of the House of Representatives Committee on Defence who led a joint National Assemble Defence Committee members to do an oversight function to find fault about two months after the ceremony.

I had no time to waste and in the spirit of the RNEC Manadon motto: "Beat the iron while it is red hot," I called the leader of the Project team who had become the arrowhead of the intrigues and gave him instructions to draw up the financial flow plan covering the period

2007 to 2010 and demanded it should be ready the following day. The following day by late afternoon I scrutinised it and met with the HMOD and the Permanent Secretary and explained the recommended financial flow plan for the three years required to complete phase one. This was then submitted to the President, Commander-in-Chief. I had no further correspondence on this issue which I took to mean acceptance.

I was absorbed with the preparations for the passing out of the participants of Course 15 which was scheduled for the 10 August 2007. At about 0400 hours I got a call from the National Hospital that Rear Admiral IN Katagum had passed away. He had been transferred from Azare to Abuja as he wanted to be near me for the company while receiving treatment at the hospital.

I informed the CNS of the death of the Admiral and was also in touch with Rear Admiral S Saidu (former CNS). I got ready a team and ambulance to convey the late Admiral's body and his family members to Azare for burial that same day. I went to the National Hospital to pay my respect and explain all the transport arrangements I had made and comforted the family members around. I sadly witnessed with profound respect the departure of the late Admiral's body and rushed to my residence to get ready for the graduation ceremony.

I had scheduled the College Governing Board meeting for the week after the graduation before closing for the summer break the following week. I had interviews to conduct for all the participants and had to go through all of their reports to enable me to have my own opinion of each one of them. The main agenda for the Board meeting was the new curricula for the College for Higher Direction of National Defence and Security Studies and Joint Warfare Course as determined by DHQ with inputs from services HQs. The Deputy Commandant had a memorandum to give effect to my promotion which was to have been done following the law establishing the College.

I withdrew the memorandum as very unnecessary and not for Board consideration as it was covered by the law and only needed documentation. It was a promotion earned. I did not want any distraction as I was presenting the case of the two officers retired by the CNS and who were allowed to complete the course on the orders of CDS, then General ML Agwai, but to the displeasure of CNS. The HMOD had confronted me regarding the issue in his office and I told him that since the College Board was going to sit it would be better presented there and a final decision taken. The memorandum presented in the case of the two officers showed that they had completed the course and were recommended to the College Board for the award of certificates and fellowship of the College.

The background to this was that the CNS in March 2007 had got approval to retire prematurely several officers comprising Rear Admirals, Commodores, and Captains. Two participants on Course 15 at the College: Captain GN Alily and Captain HA Efenudu were affected. On receiving the notice of their retirement, I called the CNS who was outside the country and asked for his directives as they were retired on disciplinary grounds without known due process.

The CNS told me to withdraw them immediately from the course and I complied. At a scheduled meeting with the CDS, General ML Agwai that included the service chiefs and the Commandants of tri-services institutions at DHQ, I gave them my written brief. The CNS was represented as he was out of town again. The CDS took notice of the fact that I had two officers short of the strength at the beginning of the course and during the interactive session on my brief, he asked me why I had reported a number that was short by two officers. I told him that they were retired and withdrawn from the course. The CDS asked for the contributions of the senior officers present including his principal staff officers at DHQ. It was established that officers who retired in the past while on course at the College were allowed to complete their courses. It was decided that the officers should be recalled as they had only missed a few days since their withdrawal and had not missed much to affect their performance. The officers were recalled to continue their course.

When the CNS returned to work, I went to brief him and to my surprise, the CNS accused me of reporting him to CDS that he had retired two officers and that I requested for their return to complete the course. He told me that as the CNS, he retired the two officers, and I, as Commandant, returned them to the College to complete their course against his orders. I told him that he should refer to the minutes of the meeting with the CDS and follow the decision. I tried to advise him about joining issues with his subordinates that he should be mentoring or grooming for leadership. He would use the advice I gave against me later. The officers later took their retirement cases to court and won.

On the day of the College Board meeting at which the results would be presented, the sitting arrangement had the CDS and I beside each other. As the CDS and I entered the Boardroom he went straight for his seat label and replaced it with that of the CNS and asked me to sit near him with the COAS between us. I knew then there had been some discussions of impending intrigue.

I succeeded in getting through the memos on the curricula with the CDS asking for deferred action on the one for Joint Warfare pending when the permanent site would be completed by 2010 but was later approved at the follow-up Board sitting a week later. The follow-up actions to implement the change of name of the College to National Defence College including the changes to the College Establishment Act, Decree 21 of 1997 to be sent to the National Assembly were approved.

The last memorandum was on the retired officers who had completed the course. The HMOD on receiving the memorandum and comments from other members of the Board approved the memorandum. The CNS turned to me with rage and threatened me that he would deal with me for allowing the officers to complete the course. He stated again that he retired officers and I allowed them to remain in the College. The COAS tapped me on my lap to keep quiet and not respond.

The HMOD sensing the tension and tirade of the CNS against me called for a lunch break to cool tempers. The COAS reminded me that I should know that though CDS and CNS were my course mates at NDA, I was dealing with very dangerous people and should be very careful. The College was not under the CNS and had its Governing Board and the NN had its Navy Board both Chaired by the HMOD. I do not report to CNS and the appointment of the Commandant is made by the President, Commander-in-Chief. The College by law is commanded by a three-star Admiral just like the NN though I was not yet wearing the rank partly due to my reluctance despite the HMOD prompting as of August 2005. I was then mindful of the intrigues and undermining of authority in the appointment of the CNS and as played out openly between May and August 2005 and I did not want the College transformation to suffer.

I took the HMOD and the Permanent Secretary to my office for their lunch break and the CNS joined them. I had to leave my office to attend to other members of the Board (CDS, COAS, CAS, and HMOSD) in the mess. I was embarrassed that I could be so openly threatened and not a word of caution at least from the Chairman of the Board. The Board reconvened after the lunch break and finished off the business of the day. The CNS would go-ahead to start implementing his threat immediately.

I received two days later a letter dated 27 August 2007 citing a memorandum released in May 2007 on selected courses from NDA that were affected by a decision early May 2007 on changes to our terms and conditions of service regarding the length of service. My course mates at NDA were affected but there was a law that superseded this administrative decision by the Armed Forces Council in respect of my appointment. The CNS was not aware of the existence of this law so far. There was no indication of the commencement date of the three months terminal leave that would end the day before the commencement of the voluntary retirement. The letter failed the test of a normal notification to direct putting in an application for voluntary retirement. This letter of threat did not meet official requirements but it would later be invoked in very unusual and abnormal circumstances as part of the abuse of state powers by public officers. In normal service, the CNS should have been retired immediately for the threat pronounced and being implemented.

I was invited to deliver the lead paper at the Chief of the Naval Staff Annual Conference that took place at Sokoto between 29 October-02 November 2007. The paper was titled "Logistics for Effective Nigerian Navy Operational Capabilities-An Overview." I highlighted the wastages over the decades and the lack of appreciation of the absolute attention to details of the upkeep and operations requirements of modern warships of NN Fleet. The attention I drew to wastages brought to focus on the problems of NNS AMBE and other ships. It was not long after that NNS AMBE suffered a very serious fire incident which was considered normal. I had earlier been committed to a program at the National Institute for Policy and Strategic Studies, Jos as an external examiner for a set of participants that was also scheduled for a day within the week of the CNS conference. I had to take leave of the CNS after the delivery of my paper and headed for Jos.

Some officers came to me since I became Commandant NWC to complain about the treatment the CNS was giving to them that resulted in or tending towards premature termination of their career. The copies of petitions that I received on these matters made me consider offering some advice to CNS but I noticed this would not be tolerated because I started receiving insulting official correspondence from staff officers at NHQ questioning actions I took on NN personnel in a tri-service institution. I was even queried that a committee set up by CDS and which I inherited as Commandant could not ask for the naval officer on the committee to be communicated by the secretary of the committee to attend proceedings. I asked the Director of Administration at the College to attend to such correspondences as appropriate. When I had my seniors from NDA as service chiefs, I was given all the respect the office of the Commandant deserved. I now had my course mates at NDA as CDS and CNS and I was being humiliated by their staff officers.

I kept my distance and they enjoyed indiscriminate removal and deployment of officers to the College that went against the College regulations. I had within two years four Deputy Commandants who were also Directors of Studies and the Directing Staff posting also suffered similar high turnovers. As from August 2007 when I was implementing the name change and introduction of a new curriculum, I was the only member of the academic staff that maintained the continuity required of the Director of Studies. The CNS once called me and asked for the best naval officers I had on the academic staff. I released Commodore GJ Jonah for a temporary appointment and on completion, he was appointed out of the College though he was the Director of Academic Research and Analytical Support. I was not consulted.

The next challenge I had to handle was when the CNS had a quarrel with his Naval Secretary Commodore OS Ibrahim and decided to post him back to the College as a Directing Staff. I pleaded with the CNS to post him to the College and I would give him an appropriate position. The Commodore had been a Directing Staff at the College. I did not want him to be humiliated. I appointed Commodore OS Ibrahim the pioneer Director of the Directorate of Curriculum Development approved by the College Governing Board. It was in this capacity that I sent him as leader of two teams to National Defence College, India, and National Defense University Washington DC on an exchange programme. Commodore OS Ibrahim would later be promoted to Rear Admiral and go on to become CNS and later CDS as a four-star Admiral.

I had over the years come to understand the international best practice that military personnel bear allegiance to serve the nation-state and not individuals and avoided being drawn into the irrational treatment of personnel as if they owe their existence and progress to their commanders who expect pledge of allegiance and loyalty to them. Nigeria is a Republic and not a monarchy. Allegiance is to a country or an entity that possesses sovereignty while loyalty is to the President, Commander-in-Chief because he or she has been mandated by the electorates to exercise authority as the CEO of the nation-state and is expected to always act in the national interest or the credible exercise of unity of command. Loyalty is thereby closely linked and the same with allegiance to the country. The attitude of poor treatment of personnel has become a trademark of some of the service chiefs in the Armed Forces of Nigeria who on occasions exercise authority over personnel in manners that dehumanise them and abuse their human rights.

It is common practice that fellow officers view themselves as competitors. This has led to pettiness, jealousy, envy, and greed. I had also received copies of petitions written by officers complaining about their careers being abruptly terminated as a result of activities related to illegal oil bunkering and which were not given due process of proper investigations and follow up actions. The officers came to give me copies of their petitions to appeal to CNS to allow justice to be done by following established procedures properly. I could do nothing as I sensed that I would not be listened to despite my assumed closeness to CNS. I saw from the information contained in the petitions that very senior military officers both serving and retired as well as highly placed public officers were being accused of illegal bunkering and on being apprehended they cause problems for the officers.

The buildings at the College had suffered many years of defect and deterioration. Its present state did not do justice to the image of the College considering the number of international dignitaries and foreign Heads of States that visit it as resource persons. The appearance and state of the infrastructure needed urgent improvements at the temporary site being used. The budgetary allocation was grossly inadequate and I had to improve on the budget system of the College using the experiences of the permanent site project struggles.

The government had introduced the Integrated Personnel Pay and Information System (IPPIS). It was used to great advantage by the College. I ordered the Finance Department to liaise with the office of the Accountant General of the Federation and Ministry of Finance and ensure that the College was captured in the IPPIS. This enabled me to evolve a budgeting process that ensured reasonable projections with cost estimates for effective planning for resource availability. There were many residential buildings at Gwarinpa Housing Estate that were beyond economic repairs and needed to be pulled down for new buildings. It was established that the main administrative block also needed long-term rehabilitation and the foundation was laid for the subsequent yearly budgetary allocations for the facelifts. The upper floor of the liaison office on Dodan Barracks entrance road in Lagos was to be converted to provide accommodation for officers on duty tour to Lagos to save on hotel bills. The land at Gwarinpa Housing Estate for the construction of DS Quarters was secured; it was almost lost to the industry. I was able to secure the present structures and plan for the future of the College with the permanent site project. I started the major work to provide better infrastructure for the College and made staff officers follow a procedure for making provisions in annual budgets for resource availability.

The College had many international engagements and was also involved with the Challenges Project for the UN which was supported by Sweden and I had to attend a session at the UN Headquarters for the presentation of the final report in early 2006 to the UN Secretary-General, Kofi Anan. The COAS as of 2006 Lieutenant General ML Agwai and I were in New York Headquarters for the presentation. The College was able to conduct the UN Senior Mission Leaders course for Peace Support Operations in March 2007. These drew attention to the need to develop the college.

I led the College delegation that was involved with the conferences for the drafting of the first Peace Support Operations Doctrine for the UN Department of Peacekeeping in Sweden and Accra, Ghana. I was opportune to Chair a session of the follow-up conference at Kofi Annan Peacekeeping Centre at Accra, Ghana, after the meeting in Sweden in September 2006. I was awarded the UN Under-Secretary-General Recognition for outstanding contribution to UN Peacekeeping efforts. The College was awarded the Presidency of the Africa Chapter of International Association of Peacekeeping Training Centre (IAPTC) for 2006/2007 and in this capacity I had to travel to the conference in Santiago, Chile, to canvass the African Chapter's position to host the 2008 Conference in Abuja. I was able to convey the invitation to General ML Agwai to be a resource person at the Santiago conference and was able to convince him to attend.

As the President of the Africa Chapter, I used the opportunity to canvas support for the IAPTC conference in Abuja and had a strong presence with General ML Agwai around. The ECOWAS mandate to three West African countries, Nigeria, Ghana, and Mali to be centres of excellence for Peace Support Operations training at Strategic, Operational and Tactical levels respectively led to the signing at ECOWAS Headquarters of the Memorandum of Understanding for the efforts to take effect. I was at AU Headquarters, Addis Ababa, with the Patron of the Africa Chapter, General AA Abubakar GCFR, former Head of State, for a meeting on the assessment of the training needs of peacekeeping training centres in Africa. The AU PSO Department had Mr Bereng Mtimkuly to administer the proceedings which were rounded off with a well attended cultural evening event.

There were visits by the President of Ghana, John Agyekum Kufuor, and President of Sierra Leone Ahmed Tedjan Kaba to the College to deliver lectures in 2005 and 2006 respectively. The College gained international recognition between 2005 and 2008 and this gave me the impetus to drive the process for the commencement of construction at the permanent site of the college to attract more international opportunities and collaboration to improve standards. I learnt and gained experiences that helped me to cope with the challenges at the college.

Amazingly, a project I started without funding in 2005 and which the consultants had abandoned was now attracting major construction contractors in Nigeria as well as very reputable consultants with very powerful public officers and prominent citizens supporting them. I concentrated my efforts on defining specifications and doing the detailed design of the buildings for the permanent site before I received funds. The staff of MOD never took the project seriously until the College started receiving funds. I had done all the tendering processes and secured the President's directives to source for funding in subsequent budgets from 2008 till completion in 2010.

There were moves to remove me from the College by August 2007 because the President acted against the intentions of those who tried to stop him from turning up for the foundation laying ceremony. The volatile College Governing Board meeting later was a warning to me. In the midst of all these, there was the move to implement my promotion to Vice-Admiral which was earned and also due by law and considered well deserved by the HMOD as of 2005. In a proper military setup, they will never be denied no matter how long.

The PGSO to the HMOD informed me in his office that necessary administrative steps were being taken. I was faced with a situation whereby the law stipulated that I should be a three-star Admiral on appointment as the Commandant but the CNS thought he was doing me a favour by obeying the law for common good in line of duty.

The prevailing situation was what I call the triumph of reckless and casual wishes of individual commanders over institutional procedures. There is the pervasive poor management of personnel and this is terrible cancer that kills initiative in personnel and encourages the rot in the system to continue. It is impossible to concentrate on doing any serious job to grow the institution as individual commanders act with impunity in total disregard of the President, Commander-in-Chief. This creates a queuing system for officers to take turns on what individuals consider as lucrative appointments simply to have access to money to waste and allow all manners of illegalities in matters related to the national economy, defence and security among several others. This is the summary of why there is so much struggle to get appointed and no one cares about performance. There is unfettered access to awesome state powers meant for development just for the sake of abusive use.

The civil service of the Federal Republic of Nigeria has made a lot of contributions to the underdevelopment of Nigeria. I have experienced over the years that most civil servants would easily abuse people they are expected to serve. I would, however, narrate the exceptional intervention of the Secretary to the Government, Chief Ufot Ekaete. I had an appointment with him regarding a cheque returned to me by a Presidential Committee on Implementation of a Federal Government Housing policy. The cheque for the 10% down payment was late to arrive as I had problems raising the amount with my bank. The time given to effect the payment was very short. I was set to lose the family residence in Lagos which was offered to me based on the Government Policy.

I went to the Secretary of the committee to appeal the rejection of my payment. The insults I received from him made me approach the Secretary to the Government. It appeared that there had been several complaints about the abuses. The Secretary to the Government called the abusive Implementation Committee boss and asked him about his abusive attitude towards people. He claimed that the unrealistic time given in the policy document was the reason for his attitude and the rejection of the late 10% down payment.The Secretary to the Government told him that the rejection and his abusive attitude were not acceptable and that it was evident from the many reports he had received that the policy was not working. The Secretary to the Government then told the abusive public officer that if a policy was not working it was his responsibility to write to the President and recommend what would work instead of abusing people. Chief Ufot Ekaete reaffirmed my belief that enough quality personnel are lacking in Nigeria and impunity fills the vacuum.

I had to follow up on the goodwill of the Secretary to the Government with an audience with the Honorable Minister of Works and Housing Chief Olusegun Mimiko. I explained my problem to the Honourable Minister who wondered why an Admiral and the Commandant of theNational Defence College could not raise 10% down payment while officers of the rank of Majors had successfully paid for houses that were far more expensive than mine.

I told him that I did not compete in these matters with anybody. I only look ahead of me and do not look at who is to my right and left and at my back otherwise, I would simply take the public fund meant for the College and pay thereby grounding the operation of the College. I then said that my juniors who had paid for far more expensive houses were an indication that those behind me were doing better and that is what a father wishes for his children. I told the Minister that as a public servant, the time and amount demanded within the short period given for payment was not realistic and it would only encourage public officers to take public money at their disposal and pay the government to own government houses.

The Honourable Minister phoned the Secretary of the Implementation Committee asking him to stay active on my house and allow me to process the bank loan to pay for the house. I appreciated the wisdom of the Secretary to the Government and the Honourable Minister of Works and Housing.

The College academic programme brought in an impressive array of resource persons from the three arms of the Government, including Ministries, Departments, and Agencies, universities, the international community including serving foreign Heads of States. I had been a Directing Staff for two years and four months (August 2001-December 2003) and listened to many interesting and insightful lectures covered by the curriculum. The main message I have been able to get from the series of lectures up to the period of my tenure as the Commandant was that Nigeria lacks the capacity for its development and there was no official policy regarding the capacity building. The issue of corruption has been highlighted over the years but, unfortunately, it appears this is generally an accepted way of conducting government business with the private sector as collaborators. Nigeria is simply throwing money at problems and not solving them. There is so much corruption and it is the main reason people scramble to be in government or hold public offices. The main problem is perverted morality that makes it virtually impossible for a Nigerian to think first of others before self. Nigerians are yet to know how to address this problem for lasting solutions.

The Governor of the Central Bank of Nigeria, Professor Chukwuma Charles Soludo, came to the College to deliver a lecture and commented on the need for individuals to save financial resources. This received an unfavourable response from the audience. The Governor thought that the impressive gathering of senior officers comprised a very rich elite but almost all of the audience had been impoverished by the savage devaluation of the Naira and poor management of the economy

As I rounded off the lecture session, I drew attention to the underlying reasons for the reaction of the audience and cited examples of, how within two decades, the devaluation of the Naira made the officers poor because their pay could no longer meet the basic needs of their families. There was no one in the audience that could buy a new car from their resources. The Governor took note and promised to look into the issue.

A few months later, it was in the news that the suggestion made at the College to bring the exchange rate to double digits was the subject of a letter from the Governor to the President for implementation over some time. This move was politicised and never approved. There were many other contributions from the College on policy matters.

When there was a crisis in the House of Representatives, about Speaker Honourable Patricia Eteh, an external lecturer from one of the universities invited as a resource person at the college, suggested that the military should stage a coup and return to power. I was in the central lecture hall to listen to part of the lecture. I was scheduled for a meeting with the HMOD but on hearing the lecturer's suggestion, delayed my meeting. The lecturer went on to state that the Armed Forces of Nigeria were a default political party in times of leadership crisis which would seem to indicate that civilians were not ready for democratic governance.

In rounding up the lecture, I told the audience that the military had no business staging a coup to get involved again in the political governance of Nigeria. I thanked the external lecturer for his lecture but warned him to avoid inciting the military. I turned to the participants and staff and warned them that the era of coups in Nigeria was gone and whoever attempted a coup would not survive a barracks revolt. I advised that civilians should be allowed to make mistakes and correct themselves in a learning process that would strengthen the democratic process.

Two days later, the House of Representatives resolved the crisis. I would later be the Chairman of a Committee set up by the CDS, General ML Agwai, on the depoliticisation of the Nigerian Armed Forces. This allowed me to appraise the situation and recommend that there was a lot of work to do to keep the Nigerian military personnel from involvement in the political governance of the country.

The last week of November 2007 witnessed the state tours and I decided that the Commandant's team would visit Kaduna State to be near Abuja in case I was recalled for a budget defence at the National Assembly. I knew that the Chairman of the House Committee on Defence was very busy erecting obstacles to sabotage the College Permanent Site project; some of my staff led by the College Permanent Site Project Coordinator were conniving with him.

The GOC, 1 Division of the Nigerian Army, Major General Moses Obi, laid a pleasant ambush for my convoy. He received me on the outskirts of the city as a mark of respect. Major General Obi had been a DS (as a Brigadier General) with me at the College and had been impressed with my programme for the transformation of the College. After the reception, the GOC and his entourage led us into the city and gave us a brief reception at his Headquarters. After inspecting the Quarter Guards, we had refreshments in the office of the GOC along with his principal staff officers. I was impressed with the maintenance works just completed on the building. I highly commended the GOC for the efforts and I felt proud of him. He responded by informing his officers that I had made the point at the College while he was on my staff of the need for higher standards in maintaining infrastructure and the environment at military establishments. I believe a very good message of paying attention to military assets was catching on and I would continue to see improvements all over in the years ahead.

The courtesy call on the Governor of Kaduna State, Alhaji Namadi Sambo, an architect, (later Vice President of Nigeria) took place immediately after the reception by the GOC. He was represented by the Deputy Governor, Patrick Yakowa, who was in his final year at St John's College Kaduna when I was in form one there. He hardly knew me and I was proud to introduce myself to him, drawing his attention to our common experience many years ago. He gave us a great reception and our interactive session with him was educative. I was informed after the audience that my attention was needed immediately in Abuja to face the House of Representative Committee on Defence and the HMOD would be leading the team. I immediately returned to Abuja to prepare for the meeting at the National Assembly.

The HMOSD Mrs FA Njezeh led the team and other relevant heads of the military establishment were also invited. I was told to include the College Permanent Site Project Coordinator in my delegation and bring along all the old drawings of the initial permanent site design done by Sheltarch Associates. The plot was very clear. I knew all along the role being played by the staff from the College I was told to include in my team. I asked him to bring all the old design drawings for the meeting.

The other heads of military establishments made their defence and were quickly released and praised for their good work. I knew I was the target and hell was let loose on me as the Chairman of the Defence Committee, Honourable Wole Oke, accused me of not using my staff well to keep to the simple original designs for the permanent site by Sheltarch. I reminded him that the design was no longer relevant and the new design which had been approved by the President, Commander-in-Chief was already undergoing construction.

The Chairman turned to the College Permanent Site Project Coordinator and related with him as the 'authority' at the College. I almost stormed out of the chambers but for the presence of the HMOSD who gave me a sign to play along. The Chairman got all the answers he wanted from his choice authority and collected the old drawings from him. He asked for the drawings when he came for a visit at the project site with a joint team of the National Assembly claiming they came for an oversight function. I asked the College Project Coordinator to collect a note listing the drawings and documents handed over to the Chairman. There was a plan that as soon as I leave the College, the new design being implemented would be simplified or cancelled so that low-grade contractors could be deployed to the site. I would later see in the College Museum a model donated by the Project Coordinator after I left the College, dated 2006, while I was commandant. The designs being implemented were being destroyed or hidden as the project was brought to a stand still to justify cancelling all I had done or achieved. The money approved was wasted in the attempt to cancel the designs to implement the model in the Museum.

The College community was divided with very few in support. Some wanted the project sabotaged to be allocated plots by the Federal Capital Development Authority at the Jabi District site already fenced by the College and others were annoyed that I was not allowing the sharing of project money allocated as the MOD wanted. Some were not happy that I was succeeding in transforming the National Defence College. There were moves from several quarters that knew that in the next three years (2008-2010) I had in place a plan already being executed successfully and charted the course for the flow of about 23 billion Naira to complete phase one of the permanent site project by 2010. The new President had received the financial flow plan for the entire phase one project. In the Supplementary Budget released by November 2007, the President kept his promise and released one billion Naira for the project to start more structures. I went to the HMOD, Alhaji Mahmud Yayale Ahmed, and briefed him on the supplementary budgetary appropriation and he directed me to project utilization.

I had a meeting with the Project Team and it was decided that the Africa Centre for Strategic Research and Studies, Officers' Mess and Games Facility, and Payment of Consultants as approved by BMPIU and related to the priority jobs be listed and forwarded for Due Process Certification by the BMPIU. The HMOD approved the plan and I sent a letter to the BMPIU through the MOD for the release of relevant certificates. Three Due Process Certificates were released by BMPIU to the College through MOD on 04 December 2007 covering five lots from the total approved covering the phase one structures which had been tendered for and scrutinised by the BMPIU. I proceeded with the staff of MOD to write the three relevant Memoranda for the approval of the Federal Executive Council due to sit on Wednesday 12 December

2007. These were completed and submitted to the Permanent Secretary for his vetting and approval by the HMOD.

I received a visitor from the office of the Permanent Secretary, a European contractor with a message that the Permanent Secretary instructed him to liaise with me and ensure that his company was among those being covered by the Memoranda being prepared for the FEC. I was to replace one of the contractors already certified by the BMPIU with the new company. This was insane and impossible.

He also told me that the MOD staff had since concluded plans to destroy my career and he, a foreigner and a European, would save my career if I could do the impossible and get him on the list for the FEC consideration and approval in the next few days. I asked him if he knew the over one year long procedures the College had gone through to get approvals that led to the BMPIU releasing the certificates for the memos to the FEC. He told me that he was experienced enough and knew the procedure but he was sent on an errand and because of the sympathy he had for me, he was discussing with me to act and satisfy the Permanent Secretary and the staff at the MOD to save my career that I had worked so hard for over three decades from being destroyed. I had calmed down and gathered myself and told him that I was a commissioned officer under the authority and would not complain if those above me who sent him to me could get another set of Due Process Certificates from the BMPIU for me to carry out the exchange as demanded by them. He told me again that he had deep sympathy for me and was only trying to help me.

At this stage, I wished a hell hole could open and consume him instantly out of my sight. How can I wear a commission with my life on the line to serve my country and someone from another country to which I owed no allegiance, come to me to exercise such authority as to save my career? I told him to take my message back and that I would act on a fresh certificate from the BMPIU that favoured him. He told me that he would be back.

The following day a familiar Nigerian contractor came to me with the same message from the office of the HMOD. His utterances were the same with an emphasis on sympathy for me because of the plan to destroy my career and his willingness to save it. I told him what I told the European contractor the previous day and he also promised to come back. Both contractors came back to continue putting pressure on me to do what was impossible. I asked them in their separate meetings with me why, with their experience, they were asking me to do what they knew was impossible. After these encounters, I went to see the HMOD to collect the signed FEC Memoranda and he told me that he had not signed because he had sent them back to the Permanent Secretary.

I went to the Permanent Secretary's office and I was greeted by a very hostile response from one of his staff who accused me of refusing to give contracts to the Permanent Secretary's contractors sent to me. I was seated with the Permanent Secretary as his staff delivered his tirades. The hostile staff had followed me into the office to continue his accusations. I told him that his boss and I have had a great relationship and I was hearing these bad comments for the first time. I asked him to leave me and the Permanent Secretary alone and he was asked to leave. I did not need to ask the Permanent Secretary for the FEC Memoranda because he repeated the same accusations of not honouring his contractors. I told him that I would go to the College and come back to see him.

I came back and gave him good feedback. The Project Coordinator at the College I had been directing the Permanent Secretary's contractors to had briefed me that a particular contractor closest to the Permanent Secretary always got contracts within the College limits and would immediately sell the contract and come back with another contractor's name for another contract. The contractor would then go to the office of the Permanent Secretary and report that he was not attended to and would be given another note. I retrieved a note the Permanent Secretary sent to me regarding another contractor approved by the BMPIU and whose certificate was the subject of one of the three memos before him for the HMOD signature. I showed the Permanent Secretary his handwritten note to me requesting assistance for the contractor and I showed him the certificate highlighting the contractor's name and the memorandum shuttling between him and the HMOD and which had passed the deadline for submission to the FEC Secretariat.

In addition to all these, the Permanent Secretary had been dealing directly with Stabilini Visinoni and I had reports of what was happening and the frustrations encountered. I had told all contractors and consultants at a joint meeting at the beginning of the tendering processes that I had no personal interest and did not expect anything from them because I have never been associated with demanding money or favour from contractors in my career. They were free to satisfy whoever they wanted to satisfy but will execute the relevant aspect of the project to the exact standards and specifications that were my duty to ensure compliance. The Permanent Secretary was speechless as I presented evidence to him; he simply shook my hand and I left him.

The following day, the Permanent Secretary arrived at the College for a ceremony that had the HMOD representing the President, Commander-in-Chief. He was followed by the HMOSD Mrs FA Njeze. The Permanent Secretary was with the representative of the CNS Vice Admiral GT Adekeye when he drew my attention to a comment that the Navy Board had sat and the Memorandum that he was expecting to implement the law regarding my promotion was not seen at the Board meeting. He added, that he did not see any memorandum to retire me either.

I had been warned several times from different sources, of plans at the MOD, to destroy my career and many actors were recruited. Three days, later a letter was hurriedly delivered to me in my office by a very young Lieutenant from the office of the Naval Secretary notifying me of a request for my voluntary retirement. My response was expected by 24 December 2007 and the letter was dated Tuesday 11 December 2007. I was very busy preparing for the end of term procedures which demanded my absolute attention as they related to vetting reports of the performances of the participants.

The young officer was tense as he was hiding the acknowledgement copy of the letter behind his back when he handed me the letter. I opened the letter and glanced through it. I dismissed the young officer and he brought forward the acknowledgement copy for me to sign and stated that the Naval Secretary who sent him wanted me to sign. I told him to tell the Naval Secretary that I had received the letter and would respond. The procedures for handling such letters were rudely abandoned in the haste. On Thursday 13 December 2007, I was about to close for the day at around 1900 hours to attend the end of the year reception planned for the participants when the Deputy Commandant, Major General JOS Oshanupin came to my office and told me that it appeared I did not know that a new Commandant had been appointed to take over from me as of 31 December 2007. I had been informed in the letter notifying me to put in for voluntary retirement that I would retire on 31 December 2007 and start my terminal leave on 01 January 2008. The normal procedure then was to receive the notice for voluntary retirement giving six months notice and start terminal leave three months to the date of retirement. All my course mates from the NDA affected had left the service and the three of us remaining had appointments made by the President, Commander-in-Chief whose intention was known and being adhered to. I had an appointment tenure of three years by law and was in my third year with about seven months left to complete it.

I had been doing the annual end of year reception at my official residence since I became Commandant and had always invited the service chiefs, the HMOSD, and HMOD as well as other senior staff of the MOD. When I got to my residence from the office, I had a quick change from my uniform to civil wear and rushed to have dinner when I was told that the Naval Secretary was in the living room. I asked the Naval Secretary to join me at the dining table which he did but declined an invitation to share the meal with me. I told the Naval Secretary that I had received the letter and wondered why I was not contacted before the letter was written as there was information I would have given for the CNS to be properly advised. All members of the Navy Board and chairman were compromised and involved in the intrigues against me.

I also asked why there was such a rush in sending the letter. There was no response from the Naval Secretary apart from telling me that he was around to represent the CNS at the function. This was the first time the CNS would attempt to show presence even by representation. I finished my meal and as we rose to enter the main sitting room, the Chairman of the Senate Committee on Navy, Senator Chris Anyanwu came in and was being offered a seat. I welcomed her and we all sat down to wait for me to be informed that all was set for the reception. The Senator requested to have an audience with me to discuss the two retired officers who completed the course at the College and had petitioned the Senate long ago. I told the Naval Secretary to proceed to the reception area while I attended to the Senator. On getting to the reception area a few minutes later, I was told that the Naval Secretary walked out of the residence and left.

The Senator remained with me for the reception and was joined by some of the senior staff of the MOD. The mood at the reception was subdued as the news had gone round that a new commandant was appointed some hours ago. The release of the appointment signal was timed to coincide with the reception and I was being asked by many of the guests if I knew about the new appointment. I told them I was aware and had a job to entertain the participants who would be leaving the following day for the Christmas holidays.

I was disappointed that the primary school pupils who had come to sing some Christmas Carols could not be properly looked after by those charged to organise the reception and they had to leave early. I tried to manage the ever-changing moods at the reception. I have for several years watched how the NN celebrated officers retiring from service and how shabbily many were treated. There was nothing strange about what I was experiencing. I was expecting my wife and children to start arriving the following week for Christmas because I intended to spend the holidays quietly in Abuja with my family around. After all, I knew it would be my last Christmas in service.

The College Steering Group meeting the following Monday was used to announce to the College formally that a new Commandant had been appointed and I asked all Heads of Department to start writing my handing over notes. I was conscious of the mood some months back when I announced that the President, Commander-in-Chief had approved funding of phase one of the permanent site project and had much information on the intrigues and the part many of them had been playing regarding the permanent site project.

I concluded the meeting by summarising the critical stage the College transformation was in and prayed that at all times the interests of the institution would be uppermost in their minds and that I should not be the focus of what was happening. I still had much to do to keep matters related to the College on track but what had been accomplished was not reversible and I felt happy that the College was in far better shape on all aspects related to its mission. It can only get better.

After the meeting, I went to see the HMOD with a copy of the appointment signal. As I was entering the HMOD's office, the Permanent Secretary appeared suddenly. I informed the HMOD that a new Commandant had been appointed and I showed him the signal. The Permanent Secretary cut in and said that the appointment of the new Commandant was illegal as the President, Commander-in-Chief makes the appointment and not the CNS as provided by the law. I then stated that going by what the Permanent Secretary has said, I was still the Commandant and they both concurred that it was so. I told them I would return to my duty post and took my leave.

I went to see the CDS and I was told he was at his official residence. I went there and met him preparing to leave for an assignment. I informed him that there was a law guiding the appointment of the Commandant of the College and he was surprised and simply stormed out and left me stranded. I was not surprised as he was monitoring my response to the signal appointing a new Commandant.

I decided to respond to the letter notifying me to put in an application for voluntary retirement and provided information regarding the appointment that is the prerogative of the President, Commander-in-Chief. I politely asked for an extension of time to complete the legal tenure that had about seven months to go. This was unnecessary but the alternative was to state bluntly that the CNS and his staff at the NHQ did not know what they were doing as the matter required the attention and approval of the President. I knew that they had been rushed into taking action to write to me to retire voluntarily and it was always a pride to officers writing on behalf of the CNS to act not as military staff officers but personal errand assistants doing things the way they like to please the boss. Where do they derive authority from when they undermined the President, Commander-in-Chief and disobey laws?

I submitted my letter personally on 24 December 2007 to the Naval Secretary in his office and my attempt to engage him in a discussion was rebuffed. It was impossible to retire a commissioned officer in so short a time and there would be no time for due process to ensure vetting of my records and other matters. The speed was not surprising and not being responded to reflected the vicious plan to damage my career with corrupt procedures and documented lies to deceive. Impunity in a military institution where individuals do what they like to destroy reigns.

The reply to my letter was dated 26 December 2007 and it was delivered to my residence that same day as the Naval Secretary wanted me to know he works on all days especially during the Christmas holidays. The letter confirmed that the Navy Board would not approve my request for an extension of time and stated that it was too late to ask for an extension but the President, Commander-in-Chief had still not been contacted given the procedure that should be followed to act according to the law. The Navy Board had not sat and yet a decision was so authoritatively taken in anticipation. The plan to destroy my career to pave the way for those involved to have access to the money approved for the permanent site project was being implemented. There would be no due process and the normal procedure would not be followed. I recalled some past incidents and was not surprised at the actions being taken against me. The following canter through some past incidence is essential for appreciating the current intrigues.

I was invited to the graduation ceremony of the National Institute for Policy and Strategic Studies (NIPSS) in Jos in November 2005. I arrived, a day earlier and was received by the Director-General of NIPSS in his office where I met Vice-Admiral OM Akhigbe, the former Chief of General Staff with whom I have had very good relations.

The Vice Admiral responded to my greeting by saying that I was the man that should have taken office as the CNS a few months ago but was denied the appointment. I said that they did not want me because I was a marine engineer. We had a very interesting discussion regarding inter-departmental rivalry in the NN. The Director-General observed from my statements that I was a very satisfied marine engineer officer. He got a call that the representative of the Special Guest of Honour, the

President, Commander-in-Chief had arrived and been taken to the guest house. He excused himself to go and receive him. I escorted Vice-Admiral OM Akhigbe to the guest house allocated to him.

The representative of the President was Alhaji Mahmud Yayale Ahmed, then Head of Civil Service of the Federation. The CNS, Vice-Admiral GT Adekeye also attended the graduation ceremony. In his opening statement, Alhaji Mahmud Yayale Ahmed described the CNS as the very best and most qualified to hold the office and added that he was part of the supporters that ensured that he got the job above others. He probably learnt of my conversation with Vice-Admiral Akhigbe. The reality is that he acted in concert with those who undermined the authority of the President to deny the officially appointed CNS his dues. His candidate never emerged in any official due process but through an unofficial route couched in political intrigues. Alhaji Mahmud Yayale Ahmed would later be the HMOD crafting my exit from my duty post again undermining the authority of another President, Commander-in-Chief.

The following year 2006, the CNS planned a Presidential Fleet Review and invited some foreign Navies to participate. The Brazilian Navy was invited but the invitation got to them late as its naval deployment plans for the year had long been carried out. I was contacted by the representative of EMGEPRON in Nigeria to help by contacting Admiral Napoleao with whom I had an excellent relationship to assist. I reached out to Admiral Bonaparte Napoleao Gomes and he made a case to the Brazilian Navy to release a ship to make it under a very tight schedule.

I was informed by the Brazilian Defence Attache in Abuja of the ship's programme and advised that the CO and crew would be happy to receive me onboard. I accepted to visit the ship and made some presentations of gifts to mark the very good gesture of making it to Lagos at very short notice. The visit was very successful and I had a very good interaction with the CO and the crew. The Brazilian Navy would reciprocate this gesture by inviting the NN to send a ship to its international Fleet Review in which the NNS ARADU, NN Flag Ship, took part. The CNS flew to Brazil and had a much better reception than on his previous visit in 2005 and I was proud of the honour accorded him this time around for the Fleet Review with NNS ARADU. When the NNS ARADU returned to Lagos, I visited the ship and congratulated the CO and some of his officers for taking part in the Brazilian International Fleet Review. I had been involved in the Trafalgar 200 Anniversary International Fleet Review in Portsmouth UK and glad of this follow up to Brazil. I was happy that the NN was developing the confidence to attend International Fleet Reviews. These long sea voyages constitute the ultimate naval professional school for sailors as I had experienced. The CNS would give this as a reason to HMOD, Alhaji Mahmud Yayale Ahmed, while he cannot work with me by December 2007 and wants me out and retire in haste. I did not join the military to serve a CNS but the country.

At the Conference of Chiefs of Naval Staff of Navies of African countries held at Hilton Hotel Conference Centre in Abuja, Vice Admiral OM Akhigbe who was to moderate the final session attended by the Commander of US Africa Command, could not make it. I was called upon to step in and preside over the final session. I had been at the two-day conference and had no problem handling the session. The conference ended on a very good note. On occasions, the CNS would call upon me to salvage situations and I always gave my best and never evaded or gave excuses. I did not have reciprocal support and I felt abandoned by the NN at the College expected to fail.

I was invited to have an audience with the Governor of Ogun State Gbenga Daniels at the state liaison office at Asokoro, Abuja, in November 2007. I met the Governor and the Secretary to the Government of the Federal Republic of Nigeria (SGF), Babagana Kingibe. He invited me in respect of the supply and installation of lifts for the permanent site high rise buildings. The company he recommended was reputable and had done many such installations in many buildings nation-wide. I assured the Governor of my support regarding his proposal and he was pleased. The meeting ended on this note and we all rose and walked out to see off the SGF. I could have pleaded with the Governor to ask the SGF to act and ensure the release of my appointment as the CNS/CDS. I resisted the urge because I had been reliably informed that huge amounts of money had been shared and it would take a miracle for them to release my appointment. It has become a common practice to hold on to approvals given by the President, Commander-in-Chief, and undermine such by making demands on those appointed. I had information about the intriguing delays related to my appointment as the CNS/CDS as the year 2007 ended.

I had been reliably informed in 2005 that the oil companies in Nigeria were allegedly behind the incumbent CNS, Vice-Admiral GT Adekeye's appointment as he had served on appointments in the Niger Delta region for some years and was well connected. I am now being asked to respond to political demands mixed with those of oil companies. I was expected to state that I would compromise national security and the economy if I was allowed my approved appointment by the President. I had sworn to an oath to defend my country and would compromise that oath on becoming a CNS. It has always been a duty, honour, and country.

I was told in 2005 as intrigues played out that it was feared that if I was allowed to be the CNS I would wipe off illegal oil bunkering, the Niger Delta militants, and acts of economic sabotage. That is precisely how I would like to be remembered in addition to raising the professional standards of the NN Fleet that have been messed up for decades as the priority among other needs of the NN.

I travelled to Sokoto where the CNS Annual Conference for 2007 took place between 29 October-02 November. I was already committed to the National Institute for Policy and Strategic Studies (NIPSS) as an external examiner and had been scheduled. I had to request the Director-General to change the date for the sitting of the panel so that I could attend the conference as I was later informed to present the lead paper. I had a clash of programmes the previous year and had to send a representative to the NIPSS. I had given Commodore Dele Ezeoba my paper to critique in addition to two other DS at the College and I decided that he would follow me to Sokoto and follow up the syndicate discussions after my departure for the NIPSS.

In Sokoto, Commodore J Egbele, also a DS from the College came to my hotel room to inform me that a decision had been taken that Commodore Ezeoba was not wanted at the conference and should return to Abuja despite being listed as a member of my team. I decided to contact the CNS and insist that Commodore Ezeoba should remain but was advised to let him return to Abuja as there was more to the move. I followed the CNS on a visit to the Sultan of Sokoto which was part of the programme. I tried to engage him in a discussion regarding the directive for a member of my team to be asked to leave Sokoto and return to Abuja but he evaded me and I left for my suite.

After delivering my lead paper, I was told by the moderator of the session not to respond to any questions raised as there was a plan to embarrass me. The moderator took up the lead executioner of the plan, Rear Admiral GJ Jonah, and told him to reserve his questions for the syndicate discussion. This was to avoid confrontation.

At end of the session, I informed the CNS that I would be leaving for the airport to catch a flight to Abuja and then travel by road to Jos. I explained to him the situation at the NIPSS where the examination panel had to postpone sitting and the concerned participants had been on edge.

I would face, a few days later, a humiliating treatment at the ceremonial sunset ceremony in Lagos where the protocol was deliberately not followed as I was treated as if I was absent. I endured it all and took a position with other Admirals for the sunset ceremony led by the CNS. I returned to Abuja to face the intrigues playing out.

There were several unprecedented and deliberate interferences, as everywhere, in the conduct of the College affairs since August 2005 to make me take inappropriate actions that would be taken as excuses to brand me as an undisciplined Admiral and build up cases against me. I received some insulting correspondences from staff officers at the NHQ signed on behalf of the CNS. The CNS came for the graduation ceremony of Course 14 in August 2006. When he sighted my Naval Assistant, Commander S Lassa, the CNS passed a comment that the officer had become a Naval Assistant again. On my appointment as Commandant, I gave the Naval Secretary then Commodore OS Ibrahim my requirements for the appointment of a Naval Assistant to work with me. I was told after a search that he was the one officer who met the requirements and I approved the recommendation subject to the NHQ decision. His professional qualities and performance earned him the appointment.

I wondered why the CNS would come down so low to pass such comments at the College grand ceremony. The following week, the new Naval Secretary Commodore BA Raji, former CO NNS ARADU called me and asked if I requested a change of my Naval Assistant as the CNS had approved the removal of Commander S Lassa and his replacement. How can my Naval Assistant be changed abruptly without informing me and another approved for me without my scrutiny or input?

I told the Naval Secretary that I would discuss it with the CNS. The discussion was a rebuff as I was told that all NN personnel were under the CNS and he could deploy them as he wished. This is one of the misconceptions that most Service Chiefs have and which have been used to destroy the establishment. I did not experience this pettiness with General ML Agwai and Air Marshal J Wuyep as the COAS and CAS respectively. Why should my coursemates at NDA go so low simply because I was appointed to take over as the CNS in 2005 and as the CDS by December 2007 and was happy to be out of the NN doing a job to which I was appointed by the President, Commander-in-Chief at the College?

I have to recollect the above incidents as they would assist in understanding how the minds of the leadership of the Armed Forces in

Nigeria focus on petty issues. There is no serious work going on to yield sustainable credible results. This explains the poor capacity and the lack of capabilities required of a fighting force. There is also the perfected art of undermining the authority of the President, Commander-in-Chief and government just to feel important.

On Christmas Day, I entertained guests and had lunch with my family. We had a group photograph by the Christmas tree in the large sitting room. I had shielded my family from the tension I had been going through although I had been hinting and preparing the mind of my wife for whatever might eventually happen to me. After the family group photograph with the College photographer, I noticed the very relaxed mood of the children and I felt I should inform them that the time had come for me to retire. I appreciated the children's education and the progress they had made. I encouraged them to keep on doing their best and ensure they earned their degrees and help one another and especially the last born. My first three children were in various stages of completing their degree courses. The last born was about completing his secondary school education. I went to the office as usual on 27 December to work on my hand over notes to guide the new Commandant when a final decision was made on the illegal appointment made by the CNS.

On 02 January 2008, I was in the office when Rear Admiral GJ Jonah, without notice, as is the practice, came to the College and my office. I welcomed him to the office and asked him if I could offer him tea or refreshment, a courtesy I always extended to senior officers and guests. His posture turned nasty instantly and he told me that he would not take any refreshments. I asked him if he had seen the CNS as there were administrative issues to resolve. The answer I got was a rude outpouring of his recent actions. He told me that he had been appointed by the CNS and had come to take over. The President, Commander-in-Chief is no more the apex legal authority in their reckoning.

I reminded him that he should have, as a matter of courtesy, called me to tell me he was coming to the College. He went on to accuse me of maintaining high standards of performance and always taking officers to task by asking questions. I advised him to take it easy and be patient as there were serious issues to resolve and I showed him the cover page of the note for handing over I was writing which had his name printed as the in-coming Commandant. He flared up again and told me that he was not speaking his native language to me and that he wanted to take over immediately. He added that he had seen my file at the NHQ and asked me why I was seeking an extension of time to complete the lawful tenure when he had been appointed by CNS to replace me? He became personal and it did not matter to him that his appointment was illegal and had no authority of the President, Commander-in-Chief. At this stage, I asked him to leave the office and the College and return to his office at the NHQ until the issues were resolved.

I called the Deputy Commandant and told him what had happened and the utterances of Rear Admiral GJ Jonah. He wondered how someone junior to him could do that in the office he was hoping to take over. It was then I knew that the College would lose both the Commandant and Deputy Commandant who was also the Director of Studies at the same time. I told the Deputy Commandant that I would no longer tolerate the acts of indiscipline in the office and College grounds and should Rear Admiral GJ Jonah appear at the College, he was free to deal with him.

The information about the conduct of Rear Admiral GJ Jonah got to the Presidency. The Vice President is from the same state as Rear Admiral GJ Jonah and had close family relationships. I could understand his audacity. The Chief of Staff to the President on hearing of the encounter from his sources called the CNS and told him to stay his actions against me. The CNS was annoyed and dropped the phone on the Chief of Staff. It appeared there was no more harmony. I received the information not long after the incident and I was disgusted that such a serious act of indiscipline by CNS would be condoned at the highest level of the Federal Government.

I was getting more information on the depth of the intrigues I was experiencing and more would surface. I got a message that the Chief of Staff wanted to see me find a way out. He termed it a soft landing. This is a familiar terminology used to ask officers who have committed an offence and looking for a way out. I had not committed any offence and I had endured being sabotaged and substituted as the CNS against the intention of the President, Commander-in-Chief. The CNS and Chief of Staff are from the same state and have been close for a long time. I was almost alone. I would continue to rely on reaching the Presidency through the MOD as I have always done despite the odds.

I went to see the HMOD Alhaji Mahmud Yayale Ahmed and the Permanent Secretary Dr Haruna Sanusi. I was asked what I wanted and I told them to follow the procedures, terms, and conditions of service for officers of the Armed Forces and the law and arrive at the correct decision. I was assured that all issues related to the matter would be presented in a memorandum to the President, Commander-in-Chief. This was all I wanted and whatever the President, Commander-in-Chief decided after being properly and correctly advised, I would be assured no one would mess up my career and service records. I went to College and carried on with my work. The second term would start on 07 January.

I decided to travel home to Okene to have some respite as my family had left Abuja so that the children would return to their various schools. I returned to Abuja from Okene on the evening of 06 January 2008 and met heightened security around my residence at Niger Barracks. I noticed very unusual Naval Police patrols on the move and a naval sentry posted at the Niger Barracks main gate. I was warned by some civilian friends that I was in grave danger and needed to move out of the official residence to a safe location. My naval personal staff were being withdrawn and I relied on the Army and Air Force components who had not been removed. When my naval cook was withdrawn and replaced with a new cook, I stopped eating food cooked in the kitchen of the institutional house. I was ready with my emergency survival carton packed with a small cooking stove and other few items set up in my bedroom. I took a small pot and plate to complement my survival pack. I was safe in my bedroom where I started cooking for myself. I needed no steward anymore. I asked the domestic staff to look after the other parts of the residence.

I received a letter from the CDS who comes from the same state as the Vice President and Rear Admiral GJ Jonah that I should hand over to the Deputy Commandant by 11 January 2008 and leave the College to comply with the voluntary retirement notification I had received without consultation with the President, Commander-in-Chief. I noticed that every statement in the letter from the CDS was not backed by valid references and authority. I went to the CDS office and had a meeting with him. I asked him if he knew of the contents of the letter with his signature. He said he was aware. I drew his attention to the inconsistencies and the implications and he became jittery and took the phone to call his Military Assistant to bring a publication or file to him to cross-check. He could not complete the call and he suddenly dropped the phone and picked his cap to leave the office. He eventually went into the toilet and on coming out, he abruptly left his office and I also left for the College.

I continued with the College routines as the students had resumed and were on edge. On the cover page of my handing over notes, I changed the name of the in-coming Commandant to Acting Commandant, Major General JOS Oshanupin as directed by the CDS. I prepared to leave the College also as directed illegally by the CDS. I had to obey orders and complain later as the Navy Board members had isolated the President, Commander-in-Chief. They all knew that their memorandum would not be approved if they recommended retirement and had to isolate him by refusing to send the memorandum. Some senior officers thought I was leaving the College because Major General JOS Oshanupin is from my state. I only knew of his state of origin as I prepared to change names on the handing over notes to comply with the CDS' wish and he made a statement that drew my attention to his state of origin.

I was asked to acknowledge receipt of the CDS illegal letter and have no option other than to leave to avoid disruption of College routines. I decided that I would write a response to the CDS letter and address it to the CNS/NHQ as directed and tell them that I had complied with their order and prayed for compassion in whatever action they might wish to take. I could not apply for voluntary retirement but leave the office at the College and reported to the NHQ to press the case of the memorandum to the President, Commander-in-Chief. I decided to visit the HMOD and the Permanent Secretary to assess their positions before handing over my response to the CDS letter to the NHQ. I had two letters ready to hand over to the HMOD, one for him and the other for the President, Commander-in-Chief. The one for the HMOD was to draw attention again to the law and the need to consult the President, Commander-in-Chief on this matter and the other letter was to the President seeking audience on this matter as due process was not being followed and the intention was also to undermine two well-known intentions of the President, Commander-in-Chief. The HMOD and Permanent Secretary met with me in the HMOD's office.

The meeting started with a presentation of my two letters for consideration. The HMOD on reading my letter to the President got upset and stated that the buck stopped with him as the HMOD and Chairman of the Navy Board. He did not mention his Chairmanship of the College Governing Board which had me and all Service Chiefs and the CDS as members. That would have attracted opposition. In the case of the Navy Board, only the CNS and CDS are members with the Permanent Secretary as the Secretary of all the Boards and Councils under the HMOD.

The Permanent Secretary's contribution was to draw my attention to the information communicated to them by CNS and CDS to the effect that they could not work with me and would not like to have me around in the Armed Forces. No commissioned officer has the commission to serve a Service Chief or CDS to be liked or not as a condition to remain in service as loyalty demands serving the country bearing its allegiance. The Permanent Secretary was at the centre of the intrigues because of the permanent site project money. The HMOD then cut in and blamed me for not discussing my issue with the Permanent Secretary. I told them that I have had no problem working with them and cited examples of the support I had been giving to them. The Permanent Secretary told me that the CNS was not happy that I single-handedly got the Brazilian Navy to honour his invitation to the Lagos International Fleet Review, an honour that was denied him.

I reflected on how problems identified were speedily attended to at the RNEC Manadon UK, National Defense University Washington DC, and in Italy at high levels of the military command, compared with the evasive actions I was experiencing at the Precidency, MOD, DHQ, and the NHQ in Nigeria. How can the nation-state manage its defence and security that require honest and decisive actions at all times following unity of command to inspire troop morale with this dysfunctional state of affairs?

The real reasons were being camouflaged and I knew them. This is how state powers that should be devoted to building and sustaining strong state institutions are wasted as they are used to punish individuals to make them conform to illegal conducts and deceits that are covered up by bureaucratic sophistry with deft declarations of political correctness to be hailed as been correct. They do not allow truth and rightness arrived at to determine issues as such determinants of morality achieved in Nigeria is the beginning of intrigues to offer deceptive advice to higher authorities. Honesty, the foundational principle of all good human beings seek is lacking in the conduct of government and public affairs.

I once again reminded them of the memorandum to the President and I was told the HMOD had the final say and there would no longer be any memorandum. The Permanent Secretary then threatened me by stating that I should be prepared to receive the same harassment being given to the Chairman of EFCC, Nuhu Ribadu, to get him out of office. The harassment also included threats to life which I was already experiencing. It is note worthy that Nuhu Ribadu's car was attacked with gunshots as he escaped an assassination attempt. It is interesting what is tolerated and celebrated in the Armed Forces of Nigeria!

Both the HMOD and the Permanent Secretary were now issuing threats and sealing off my access to the President, Commander-in-Chief. The CDS and CNS had told me that the President, Commander-in-Chief did not matter and their decisions must prevail over the intentions of the President, Commander-in-Chief. The HMOD was also of the same disposition. With this posture by HMOD, CDS, CNS and Permanent

Secretary in tow, whose authority do they exercise at the Navy Board? No officer should be commissioned in a republic to serve any individual but the nation-state and its causes. I was a threat to their ambitions and since the HMOD and Permanent Secretary's interests converged and the Chief of Staff to the President had been silenced, though a crafty accomplice, the Navy Board had decided without due process and sitting. These are actions against the sacred oath taken on commission invoking God. No member of the Navy Board ever mentioned that they were acting on the orders or directives of the President, Commander-in-Chief who they even refused to send a memorandum that they knew was the proper thing to do. There is no command and control of the AFN from the only legal apex authority mandated through a general election.

I returned to the College and put finishing touches on my letter in response to the CDS' letter ordering me to hand over and leave the College. I went to NHQ the following day to seek the CNS final audience. On being informed by his Naval Assistant that I was around, the CNS ordered him to tell me to get out of the NHQ. This, the Naval Assistant was struggling to tell me and I told him not to worry. I heard it all over the communication set.

I gave my letter to my Flag Lieutenant who witnessed the incidents to deliver to the Naval Secretary. I would not be seen at the NHQ again for the next six years when I was called for a meeting to resolve the matter on 07 July 2014. I went to see the HMOD to let him know that I had been politely following their orders and directives and stressed that due processes were not being followed. The HMOD for the first time kept me waiting in his Secretary's office where I met him reading newspapers and he behaved as if he did not know I was around. When he finished reading the newspapers, he opened the door to his office and I followed him in. He offered me a seat beside him and, once again, I appealed to him regarding the unfair treatment I had been given. He only told me that he would look into the matter. This was my final act in his office. I went to the Permanent Secretary and he gave me a hurried goodbye handshake. I returned to the College and concluded plans to hand over by 14 January 2008 to the Deputy Commandant, Major General JOS Oshanupin.

In the evening of the day my letter was sent through my Flag Lieutenant to the Naval Secretary, I met with the CDS at his official residence. I met him attending to guests after which he turned his attention to me. I requested a private audience and we retreated into his study. I told him that it had been embarrassing to me that I could not discuss with the CNS and himself as officers were wondering why three of us (CDS, CNS and Commandant) that were course mates at the NDA should be so openly against each other. The CDS cut me off and asked me who my coursemates were? I went to the matter at hand and told him that I had responded to his letter and would comply although he knew the letter was not proper as the President, Commander-in-Chief had not been consulted as required by law.

He told me that since I had handed over the letter, there was nothing he could do. I noticed a feeling of relief in him and left. When we came out of the study into the main sitting room adjoining the dining room, Mrs Alero Azazi, a quiet pleasant lady I had known for over three decades, drew our attention to the table set for dinner. The CDS took his seat at the head of the table and as I was heading for the exit door, she called me to join the CDS at the table. I was overwhelmed by her stressed look of concern as she beckoned me to the seat she was drawing for me. I remember the moments I had been a guest at their residence in London while I was at the RNEC, Manadon. She then had her very young lovely children keeping the house very lively and I was always assured of a private room to myself. I had enjoyed her cooking and she took care of me and my wife in her very quiet and effective way.

I drew close to the back of the CDS seated and stopped. She pulled out the chair fully urging me to have a seat and have dinner with the CDS. I hesitated as I waited for the CDS to invite me to join him. The CDS sat motionlessly and did not utter a word or even look in my direction. The mood was not welcoming.

I looked at his wife and told her that I would be leaving. She tried her best but the CDS had by his actions and utterance shown both in the study and at the dining table he was not comfortable having me around. I left full of emotion and sympathy for Alero.

I did not doubt that what the COAS, Lieutenant General Luka Yusuf, told me in August 2007 during the very stormy College Governing Board meeting that I should be very careful with the CNS and CDS, that they were very dangerous human beings. Mrs Alero Azazi, by this narrative here, I assure you that I will always treasure your hospitality and goodwill.

I reported for duty for the last time at the College on 14 January 2008. I had debated in my mind whether to address the College community and bid them goodbye but I was reluctant to do it to avoid giving out details about the role of those perpetuating the intrigues against me including those at the College. There was a lot that I could not divulge and especially the one billion Naira released and which triggered my abrupt leaving. There was also the issue of appointments that the President, Commander-in-Chief was expected to make. I also wanted to avoid revealing the intrigues about appointments as the CNS or CDS.

I decided to tell the College community that I was leaving. I told the Deputy Commandant to arrange for me to hand over to him after addressing the College community. The address was short. I went to the office and handed over and departed the National Defence College to the official residence to continue my gradual packing out as I had no one to assist me anymore; this was to my advantage as my new location would be unknown for some time. I was careful not to let out my hideout.

I decided to write directly to the President, Commander-in-Chief of the Armed Forces to inform him that I had left my duty post without his approval and no due process took place. I have always given preference to acting within a chain of command as this is a cardinal demand of the profession of arms. The intention of the compromised Navy Board Chairman and members was to force a voluntary retirement but I had not committed any offence to attract such treatment and I did not apply for voluntary retirement as the NN is a voluntary service. I also highlighted the law establishing the College and how it was set aside. I was still the Commandant because the President's approval was still needed to appoint the Deputy Commandant in an acting capacity. The Acting Commandant could not carry out any documentary signature changes for bank accounts operations and these had to be referred to me for action so that the College administration did not break down.

I had been the last Commandant of National War College and the first Commandant of National Defence College. This sums up a transformation I am very proud of. The leadership at the College after my departure still had much to do to stay the course and it was lacking from my immediate successor who was consumed by his agenda. The project would not be completed by 2010 and funds would be wasted in defiance of the intentions of the President, Commander-in-Chief of the Armed Forces. The Federal Executive Council was bypassed and direct labour became the order of the day as corruption took over. The three BMPIU Due Process certificates issued and the accompanying Federal Executive Council memos prepared were wasted and never processed. The money released was wasted.

The College would never be the same. I had been consistent in achieving my set objectives to my satisfaction. I was confident that I would have done the same for the NN had I been given the chance to serve as the CNS with a reasonable length of tenure for strategic planning and implementation. It is essential to think of the span of Wey-Soroh-Adelanwa years that gave the NN a formidable Fleet. I left on this very positive note, satisfied that I had the opportunity to serve my country with the National Defence College transformation as a worthy legacy within just over two years and five months. This would not have been possible without the critical support of Chief Olusegun O Obasanjo, GCFR, General AA Abubakar GCFR, and Alhaji Umaru Musa Yar'Adua GCFR. General ML Agwai worked hard to convince Mallam Nasir El-Rufai that the military only gives up a territory to gain more to its strategic advantage. I want to thank them but words will fail me. They were only rendering exceptional services in the national interest, each in very unique circumstances. They had led the enormous effort to set up the College on a great path for development.

I would later seek the intervention of the National Assembly through the Senate President to demand solutions following articles of war and established military procedures. I am out of service but not retired. I got to know that news was spread within the NN and the Armed Forces that I was working against the interests of NN and was planning to install a Nigerian Army officer as the Commandant. The CNS had led a campaign of fake news and this bad leadership was simply copied by the Naval Secretary and the others especially Rear Admiral GJ Jonah who went before his church audience to give testimony that he won a victory that was considered impossible over me to become Commandant.

I came to believe that my parents gave me the name Odogba, which is an elephant, for a reason. They saw the future. Time will reveal the truth which has no expiry date. I reflected on my career journey starting with my teenage desire to serve my country to the present and was full of satisfaction. There was nothing more I could do now for the College and the AFN institution. I am grateful for my upbringing and the coveted opportunity to serve the country. I assure those officers of NN who went through the rigours of qualifying as naval engineers that they were the very best even if they are not allowed unofficially to be the CNS.

All naval engineers should be inspired that I have never lobbied for any job and was considered most qualified to be appointed the CNS and CDS in addition to other high profile appointments. They must, therefore, believe that the AFN institution and specifically the NN if properly managed would not tolerate the best to be managed by the worst as such is wasting the resources invested for the defence and security of the country. All Officers must continue to strive to be the very best they can be to serve, create, grow and sustain the very best smart organisations for the development of the country and respect for authority.

The President, Commander-in-Chief of the Armed Forces of Nigeria, the only CEO of the nation-state mandated by the electorate in a general election, had approved and appointed me as CNS after impressively emerging top of the Rear Admirals in NN that were considered. This is my destiny fulfilled as I was officially judged most competent to command the NN. The unofficial actors against my official appointment probably expected me to join them who were bent on disrespecting the decision of the CEO to destroy the country as their condition for me to take up my appointment. This implied pledging loyalty to them. Such acts would be illegal and it is important to note that they were also unofficial actors or forces that were not mandated by the electorates as the CEO of the nation-state in a general election. They stopped the President, Commander-in-Chief from having his CNS. I joined the military to SERVE the country and should never be part of destructive forces to DESTROY it. I am fulfilled in another sense that I kept the faith.

This is the score I present to all naval engineers and that young officer who rushed to greet me at a Mobile Petrol Station near Malu Road Barracks, Apapa, and congratulated me on my report from the NDU, Washington DC and told me that some officers like him had copied my report to keep in their possession as that was the ideal they aspired to. I want to tell all NN officers who went through the cadet route at the NDA that they are all potential CNSs. I assure them that they will be fulfilled if they have the positive mindset to serve the country and focus on excelling at all duty posts bearing true allegiance to Nigeria and expression of absolute loyalty to the President, Commander-in-Chief for the unity of command in the nation-state interest only.

I can state that should I be asked if there is anything I would like to do differently in my career starting from the NDA selection board proceedings, I would say that there is absolutely none. I made my decision while in secondary school and kept it in focus for my fulfilment. The realisation of my teenage dream to be a marine engineer and serve my country is very special and my total and unwavering commitment to serve the country at all times is an act of thanksgiving with gratitude to Nigerian taxpayers for the opportunity to serve. This is the fulfilment of my part of the covenant that comes from voluntary service to the country in the military. Has the Government fulfilled its part?

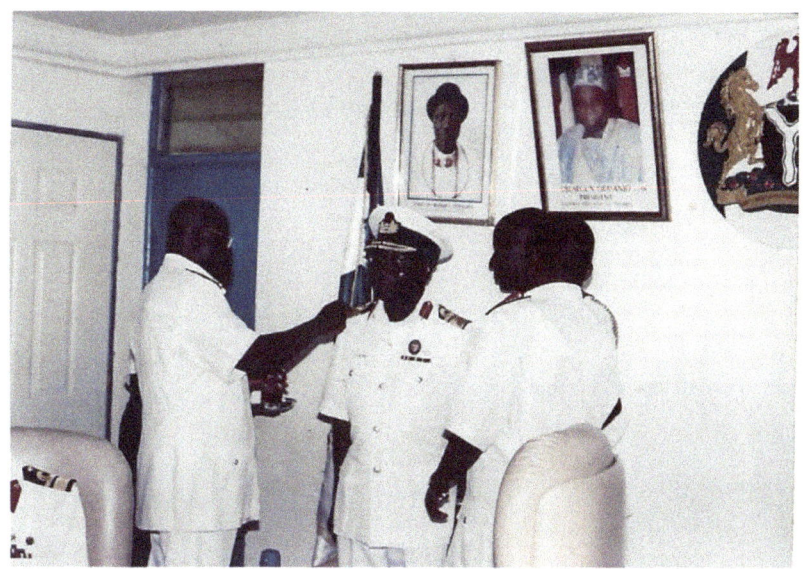

Decorated with the rank of Rear Admiral by the Chief of the Naval Staff, Vice Admiral Samuel Afolayan, January 2004.

Right to left, Rear Admiral Anthony Isa, Chairman Joint Chiefs of Staff of Pakistani Armed Forces, General Mohammed Aziz Khan on a visit to Dockyard, Rear Admiral S Kolawole and Commodore E Kpokpogri.

Rear Admiral Anthony Isa with His Excellency Bola Ahmed Tinubu, Governo of Lagos State with his Deputy His Excellency Femi Pedro during a flood incident in Lagos in June 2004.

Inspection by General Alexander Ogomudia, Chief of Defence Staff, to assess readiness for Exercise "TAKUTE EKPE" May 2004.

Nigerian Naval Dockyard Basin 2004: NNS ARADU F89, Merchant ship awaiting docking and two tua boats MIRA and RIMA in the small twin docks.

Fabrication Plant at Nigerian Naval Dockyard for oil industry pressure vessels 2004.

Navy Day Celebrations June 2004 Events at Naval Dockyard. From left to right, Honorable Minister of Defence, Musa Rabiu Kwankwaso, Chief of the Naval Staff Vice Admiral Samuel Afolayan and Rear Admiral Anthony Isa.

Tour of National War College on taking over command, Left to right, Major General Nuhu Bamali, Deputy Commandant, Rear Admiral Anthony Isa and Air Commodore Orok Duke, College Secretary.

Rear Admiral Anthony Isa with General JJ Singh, Chief of Army Staff of Indian Army on visit to National War College.

Rear Admiral Anthony Isa hosting Ambassador of Finland to Nigeria Her Excellency Anna-Lisa Korhonen

Visit of the Ambassador of Ethiopia to Nigeria, His Excellency Yohannes Genda Gimbi.

Visit of the Ambassador of Japan to Nigeria to deliver a lecture at the College.

High Commisioner of Nigeria to UK His Excellency Dr Christopher Kolade hosting National War College Delegation at the Nigeria High Commission, London, May 2006.

Rear Admiral Anthony Isa presenting the Permanent Site Project Proposals at the heart of the National War College Transformation to President, Commander-in-Chief of the Armed Forces Chief Olusegun O Obasanjo GCFR at the Presidential Villa Federal Executive Council Chamber, March 2006.

Rear Admiral Anthony Isa, fourth from right, President, Commander-in-Chief, Olusegun O Obasanjo, Mr Roland Oritsejafor, Minister of State for Defence, General Alexander Ogomudia in a group photograph with staff and participants of National War College after a successful visit.

Rear Admiral Anthony Isa (right) as President of African Peace Support Trainers Associations at a Conference at Africa Union (AU) Headquarters, Addis Ababa, Ethiopia with the Patron of the Association General AA Abubakar GCFR (left) and Mr Bereng Mtimkuly (middle) of AU Peace Support Operations Department.

Rear Admiral Anthony Isa escorting the President, Commander-in- Chief, Alhaji Umaru Musa Yar'Adua GCFR and responding to the President's remarks about the project legal status.

President performing the Foundation Laying Ceremony for National Defence College at Piwoyi District 27 July 2007. Minister of Defence Alhaji Mahamud Yayale Ahmed, second from the right, looks on.

First from left, Vice Admiral Ganiyu Adekeye, Chief of the Naval Staff; Rear Admiral Anthony Isa, Air Marshall Paul Dike, Chief of Air Staff; General Andrew Azazi, Chief of Defence Staff and Lieutenant General Luka Yusuf, Chief of Army Staff in conference while waiting for the President's arrival for the permanent site ceremony.

Four Blocks of Participants Quarters at the Permanent Site completed and in use.

Court Yard of one of Participant's Quarters.

Directing Staff Quarters construction in final finishing stages.

Headquarters Building of National Defence College u dergoing construction.

Front row, fifth from right, Rear Admiral Anthony Isa, Air Marshal Oladayo Amao Chief of Air Staff, General Lucky Irabor Chief of Defence Staff, Major General Bashir Salihi Magashi Minister of Defence, Rear Admiral Oladele Daji Commandant National Defence College, at the inauguration by the Minister of Defence of the National Defence College 9-storey Directing Staff Quarters at the College Permanent Site, Piwoyi, Abuja on 05 August 2021.

Visit of the President of Republic of Ghana His Excellency John Agyekum Kufuor to National War College November 2005.

Visit of the President of the Republic of Sierra Leone His Excellency Alhaji Dr Ahmad Tejan Kabbah, September 2006. Behind him is the Honourable Minister of Defence of Nigeria, Ambassador Thomas Aguiyi Ironsi.

CHAPTER TWENTY

Out of Service and My Struggle for Justice

Since I was denied my duty post, I have been pressing for fairness and justice because I believe that one officer unjustly treated by the contrived system raises the spectre of unjust treatment for all officers and men in the Armed Forces of Nigerian. I worry that if the impunity to which I have been subjected is not arrested and is allowed to continue to run riot, the armed forces as an institution would be anything but a unified, credible force able to perform its assigned constitutional roles. I struggle for justice in this regard for the correct exercise of awesome state powers being wasted and not used for building strong state institutions for nation-building and which the Nigerian Armed Forces must play a leading role with a moral force based on the foundational principle of honesty that is lacking.

The forces against me are formidable but I am encouraged in my determination to right the wrongs against me and save other officers and men of the armed forces from being victims of impunity, unfairness, and injustice. I am willing to make this sacrifice because, in every society and every institution, sacrifices must be made by the few to save the many. This is not just about me; it is more importantly about making the powers that be or those with access to state powers recognise the dangers inherent in public officers and civil servants refusing to play by the rules because of their interest and, in my case, subverting the President, Commander-in-Chief and making him appear impotent. I have no illusions about the rough struggle ahead but I know, surely, that justice may be delayed but it would eventually not be denied.

I have experienced first hand how helpless the President, Commander-in-Chief of the Armed Forces of the Federal Republic of Nigeria can be as public officers usurp his powers. This is the main reason the Ministries, Departments, and Agencies of Government are the sources and causes of the problems the country suffers. They personalise or wear state powers that should be used to build strong state institutions. There is no order in the conduct of nation-state affairs as individuals have their agenda. Our country is not allowed to function properly because individuals use the instrument of public offices to undermine procedures and laws as they abuse state powers to create weak state institutions so that they can be recognised as more powerful than the state.

They resort to all bureaucratic sophistry and its variants to cover up their misdeeds and create the impression that they act within the law and extant regulations. The people have no confidence in state institutions and public officers because of this trend thereby resulting in insecurity.

The fact remains that by my reply to the CDS letter of 08 January 2008 to comply with their acts of impunity, I opted to be out of service implying being without a duty post but I never resigned my commission or retired voluntarily. There is the oath sworn to Almighty God that is binding; a very important foundational principle. In these circumstances, there can be no voluntary retirement of Rear Admiral Anthony Odogba Musa Ajoku Isa, NN/0317.

My active duty status remains intact until outstanding problems are solved to pave way for an application for voluntary retirement. The military establishment personnel commissioned or enlisted are not civil servants. The military institution, therefore, is unique and different from other professions; although it may take some best practices from many professional disciplines, it does not conform to any. It has a unique status based on warfighting requirements and the obligation of the ultimate sacrifice of life in the line of duty. There is a covenant with the obligation on the part of the state to always treat personnel with fairness without any limitations of time and statutes to inspire their commitment and initiatives to the causes of the country.

The connivance by the members of the Navy Board to undermine the President, Commander-in-Chief, and sabotage the permanent site project to share the money released is a classic testimony of how the country's defence establishment has been systematically destroyed. The compromised Navy Board lost the authority to sit and decide that I should leave my duty post held by the direct exercise of the authority of the President, Commander-in-Chief. They should all have recused themselves from handling matters related to me and handed them over to the Commander-in-Chief under the normal or best practices procedure.

This applies to all commissioned officers and other personnel in similar situations. I recall that during the General Ibrahim Babangida administration, a Captain who had been court-martialled petitioned against his trial and pointed out that the incumbent CNS was biased and would not be fair to him in reviewing the decisions of the court. The

CNS had the case taken away from him and decided by the Commander-in-Chief without the CNS in attendance at the review of the case.

The Acting Commandant had difficulties with the administration of the college because there was no proper handing over of authority that would be recognised by establishments the College conducts official businesses with. I was contacted and I continued to sign cheques for the payment of salaries. I was still in my official residence and directed my Flag Lieutenant to be reporting at the office to monitor situations before he was abruptly posted out a few days later. At a stage, I was being expected to resume duties but a compromised Navy Board decision on 15 January 2008 was linked illogically to my letter asking for compassionate considerations as my application for voluntary retirement. I was phoned by the Honourable Minister of State for Defence and told that they decided to retire me and she expressed regret that they took that decision. She was very distressed at the very compromised proceedings as the members of the Navy Board undermined the authority and intentions of the President, Commander-in-Chief declaring him not relevant, where did they derive legitimacy from to sit on my matter?

The money released for the permanent site project was allegedly shared using bureaucratic sophistry. The MOD, DHQ, and NHQ were all compromised in this terrible act but I became the culprit for not belonging to their system that does not respect the apex authority of the President, Commander-in-Chief in a republic and set in wasting the country.

On 08 February 2008, I wrote a letter to the President, Commander-in-Chief informing him that I was forced to leave my duty post to which I was assigned by him by members of a compromised Navy Board. The President was on a state visit to China within the first week of February 2008 when the officer illegally appointed in December 2007 was allowed by the same group to take over the office of the Commandant, National Defence College. Indeed there was nothing the President could do.

The new Commandant went for a church service a few days later and decided to give testimony that he finally won a fight to take over the office. He publicly mentioned my name before the congregation. I also received a telephone call from a retired Commodore with whom I had a good relationship at the Western Naval Command in 1981 prevailing on me to leave the College so that the new Commandant could take over to enable his relation who was a Commodore have the opportunity for a higher appointment. When I told him that I had left the College and was not in the way of anyone's progress, he was very embarrassed.

I returned the staff cars to the College and asked the Finance Officer to proceed and ensure the new Commandant was given all he wanted and I left the institutional house on 28 February 2008 to a private residence. On the day of my final departure from the institutional residence, I was taken by surprise by the personal staff in the residence who had contributed money and bought a present for me. The most senior among them was asked to come and present it and express their gratitude to me. He told me that they knew the treatment I was being subjected to and understood that I had done nothing wrong. They wished me well.

Just before I reached the gate, an item I forgot was rushed to me by the steward, shouting: "Sir, this is your own. You will need it, sir." It was an item I needed - a container I used for cooked food storage when I travel. At my hideout, Alfa helped me to offload the few personal effects into the house. I thanked him and said goodbye as I was about to shut the door. He could not hold back his tears and told me that he would not leave me to suffer and if they wanted they could retire him that day. I pleaded with him to leave as he was then a sergeant and still had his career ahead of him.

He sat on the bonnet of the car he was to drive away and said that he had never seen military personnel treated this way and he knew that I had done nothing wrong. He asked me: "Sir if you at your rank and our Commandant, are treated this way what is the hope for us?" I continued pleading with him to leave. He requested that I should allow him to come to the house to be checking on me and also that anytime I needed him I should call him. I agreed and thanked him. I did not have a proper farewell from the officers. I only addressed them and bade them goodbye in the main College auditorium.

When I left my official residence, I felt a sudden release from a pressure cooker. Peace of mind suffused me. Friends donated a dining table and chairs and a television set to me to enable me to settle down in my hideout. I had a bed and a cooker in the kitchen. That was very okay as my family was in Lagos and would move to Abuja by November 2008 after our last son graduated from King's College by July. In my isolation, I decided to keep away from military institutions. I was cut off and was not receiving any emoluments.

I was being harassed by several phone calls from strangers. I kept track of important events and the on-going mischief. The President,

Commander-in-Chief was still monitoring the situation. The members of the Navy Board promised to forward a memo to him on my case. He had concluded to appoint me as the CDS. The Navy Board tried to scuttle it by resorting to the setting up of a Board of Inquiry to investigate the Permanent Site project management under me. Already, they had allegedly shared the N1.0 billion released in the supplementary budget through some bogus contracts to stop the permanent site project. But they changed their mind because they were warned that I did nothing wrong in the management of the project; that I followed due process to obtain the Federal Executive Council approval and that a Board of Inquiry would only expose them.

They eventually set up a committee to review the project design and this was merely a cosmetic exercise. They could not alter the designs significantly and the project concepts remained intact. All these were delay tactics to divert the attention of the President, Commander-in-Chief, who was constantly asking them to account for why I left my duty post. The pressure to discontinue the permanent site project despite the national security pressing needs especially for joint warfare capabilities was intense. It appears that there was anger that I started the construction program and later individual services War Colleges were established including universities as from 2015. The urgent need was for joint officers training for joint warfare that the second faculty at NDC would cater for as from 2010. The NDC permanent site project was seriously slowed down and those interested held sway, wasting resources allocated.

I was prevailed upon in June 2008 to have a meeting with the HMOD and find a way out and I agreed. Besides, I got useful information regarding how the HMOD thought that with me at the College, there would be no access to waste the permanent site fund. I had the meeting with the HMOD in his office in June 2008. I went along with a copy of the letter I wrote to the President, Commander-in-Chief dated 08 February 2008. He glanced through it and asked me to leave the letter with his Naval Assistant, a naval officer well known to me.

There was still the consideration for implementing my appointment as CDS. This was a subject of discussion some days later at the MOD from where I got a call from a Director warning me that such an appointment would be blocked because other interested parties had candidates as they thought it was their turn to produce a CDS. The problems and demands of the institution do not matter. This is the political culture in the AFN that has destroyed cohesion in the institution. Unfortunately, military appointments are considered as a favour done to individuals or interest groups. This adversely affects the allegiance/loyalty of personnel regarding commitment to serve.

There would be many parochial reasons and falsehoods to advance to ensure I did not get the job. Such reasons were twisted to favour others. It did not matter that Admiral I Ogohi was appointed the CDS while his senior Lieutenant General V Malu was appointed as the COAS; both of them were of the same rank at the time of their appointments.

Their seniority mix did not matter. The Chief of Air Staff, Air Marshal I Alfa appointed at the same time, was from the same part of Nigeria as Admiral I Ogohi. It also did not matter that Vice Admiral SO Afolayan and Vice Admiral GT Adekeye were from the same state. These would have been used against me if I were to be so favoured.

The three Due Process certificates I got from the BMPIU were never used to date and contracts were awarded to cancel the project using the money I left behind. The project review panel report did not favour such action. The new Commandant went wild, telling whoever listened, and especially the CDS and CNS, that I was sitting on a huge treasure and refused to distribute or share the money. He projected himself as the systems commandant ready to open the College treasury for looting. I would be comprehensively hated for this act against the "system."

The College Permanent Site project would have been stopped had I not got new land and started construction that reached an advanced stage before I left the college. The main signboard along Airport Road that told the world that a major project was on-going was destroyed and the FCDA began working on revoking the allocation of the plots of land.

The College lost more than half the plots I had secured and the situation would have been worse but if I did not continue to appeal to the Chief Executive Officer of Development Management Limited (DML) who was a former Director at the FCDA to help me save the project as more revocation of the plots would kill it. I continued making efforts behind the scenes to keep the project on course. The promise by the President, Commander-in-Chief to complete the project by 2010 weighed heavily on my mind considering the implications for national security.

There were many fronts of conspiracy to sabotage the project and this was what Aims Consultants foresaw and withdrew from taking up the Project Management role. The choice of DML was strategic and I continued to encourage the company to stay on and help to keep the project alive as they were bent on pulling out. I had to work my phones as I stayed out of sight. I had to ensure the permanent site project was not stopped and cancelled, and all the money approved for it was wasted. With access to awesome state powers to perpetuate such waste, it is almost impossible to stop the systemic corruption in action. This is the attraction for high profile appointments.

There were new appointments of the CDS and CNS in August 2008. I monitored the situation as the new set up settled down. General AO Azazi was replaced by Air Marshal Paul Dike and Vice Admiral GT Adekeye was replaced by Vice Admiral II Ibrahim. The reasons for the new appointments were more than one. The President, Commander-in-Chief was very annoyed and upset that the outgoing CDS had to force me to leave my duty post as Commandant against his intention.

I had tried to impress on General Azazi and Vice Admiral Adekeye that going against articles of war to undermine the known intentions of the President, Commander-in-Chief would never be tolerated. There is no President, Commander-in-Chief that would be happy to hear that a service chief rudely dropped a phone on his or her Chief of Staff.

I was not surprised to hear that the removal of the CDS was linked to the actions taken against me. The HMOD and Permanent Secretary that instigated the CDS and CNS to act and get me out of office remained with their staff at their duty post at the MOD to continue the intrigues.

It is over ten years as of 2020 that the project has suffered the delays that the President, Commander-in-Chief warned that he would not want to happen and went on to release the fund for it for completion by 2010. They would never want to hear of me being around their system. There was propaganda machinery in force and succeeding service chiefs (including the CDS and CNS) would continue the deceptions, lies, and hatred because I dared to start the permanent site and was concluded for appointment as the CDS or CNS. How I emerged in 2005, giving no room for manipulations and leading to the President, Commander-in-Chief's approval of my appointment as the CNS, generated intense negative feelings against me. It appeared all those concerned generated their wild stories to satisfy themselves as long as such were against me. I continue to bear the albatross in addition to all the hate and intrigue I have been going through for succeeding at Manadon in the manner I did and more.

There were attempts to get my case across for the attention of the President, Commander-in-Chief. One of such attempts took place on 01 October 2009 when the President, Commander-in-Chief, Alhaji Umaru

Musa Yar'Adua, GCFR, restated that he never authorised my removal from my duty post, at the College, and was sad that each time he requested for a brief, he was given excuses. He was cautioned that there were some of those responsible for my removal from the College still in place in positions of power. Besides, there is corrupt documentation that exists to continue the intrigues.

I was directed to forward my case to the new service chiefs for a memo to be presented to the President. I sent in a letter to the new CNS and copied the new CDS. I then met with the CNS for the first time and gave the CDS a copy of the letter. The CNS Vice Admiral II Ibrahim was shocked to know that I had not even carried out a retirement routine and was receiving no emolument. He reasoned that the matter was beyond the Navy Board and would be discussed with the new HMOD and CDS for a presentation to the President, Commander-in-Chief to decide.

I also met the new CDS Air Chief Marshal Paul Dike who was very uneasy for reasons best known to him. He was never comfortable with me since he was appointed the Chief of Air Staff and while I was at the College as Commandant. My attendance at the celebration of his appointment at his hometown in Delta State also showed that he was not comfortable with me. He evaded me for the two days I was in his hometown and Asaba where he opted out of the golf round pairing me with him in competition to round off his celebration. He never appreciated that I honoured his invitation.

The new HMOD is a lawyer and Senior Advocate of Nigeria and also believes that the matter adversely affecting me was for the President, Commander-in-Chief to decide because the Navy Board, MOD, and the military hierarchy at the NHQ and DHQ had been compromised and could no longer be relied upon. The CNS informed me that the issue was discussed at a Navy Board meeting and the President, Commander-in-Chief was also contacted and was waiting for the memo to make the decision. I was assured that before the end of 2009, the issue would be resolved.

The President, Commander-in-Chief, unfortunately, was evacuated to Saudi Arabia for medical attention towards the end of October 2009. I was assured that as soon as he returned and was able to resume normal duty, my case was high on his agenda to resolve based on the discussion he had with the CNS. But the President died on May 5, 2010.

I was facing many difficulties and this affected my membership of The Institute of Marine Engineering, Science and Technology, London. I defaulted in payment of my subscription for two years and I was removed from the register as a Fellow. I had to write to explain how the movement of the Institute's Headquarters to another location added to my problems and I was graciously allowed to retain my Fellow status, otherwise, I would have been relegated to Member.

I was elected Member on 5 November 1982 with membership number 45538 and Fellow on 22 May 1987 with the same membership number. I was again elected Fellow on 29 September 2010 with a new membership number 8010838. Once again the great Institute made me proud of it. The CNS, Vice Admiral II Ibrahim signed all sections of the election form that also affirmed my duty post as the MOD/DHQ. The CNS directed the Deputy Defence Adviser, London to handle the correspondence related to the processing of my election applications in London. This was a reflection that my active duty status remains intact, awaiting the decision of the President, Commander-in-Chief.

The Vice President, Dr Goodluck Jonathan, who had been acting through the Doctrine of Necessity passed by the National Assembly, took over as the President, Commander-in-Chief of the Armed Forces on May 5, 2010, on the death of the President. The HMOD was relieved of his office along with other Ministers during the transition. The transition period at the MOD without an HMOD allowed Directors to quickly attend to my matter that was awaiting a memo to the President under the previous dispensation and a letter was written to me, signed by two Directors, informing me that a Navy Board had retired me and the matter was closed. How? Their permanent site project fund interests reign supreme.

I never received this correspondence as it was not meant to get to me but was documented. I presented my case in writing to the new HMOD and as I was following up, the Deputy Director handling the matter got to know that I had not received the correspondence and wanted to find out more about the case from me. He pretended to have a solution and I patiently watched him manoeuvre until he told me that the letter signed by the two Directors, as soon as the immediate former HMOD left the Ministry, could not be reversed. I told him that there could be no retirement by the Navy Board as I never applied for voluntary retirement. The government must faithfully fulfil the voluntary service obligation based on the voluntary service covenant.

The Deputy Director told me that I wrote a letter to the CNS indicating that I was ready to voluntarily retire. I asked for the letter and he showed me the letter in which I asked for compassion in whatever they decided to do. I told the Deputy Director that when anyone asks for compassion, it indicates distress that the applicant wants to be taken out of by solving the problems. It was, therefore, mischievous to take that letter indicating distress as an application for voluntary retirement.

The Deputy Director on realising the mess caused exclaimed that he did not want to mess up his career. He added that the new National Security Adviser, General AO Azazi, was waiting for their response. The message was very clear. A new Permanent Secretary from the same state of Bayelsa as General Azazi had taken over at the MOD. I knew the trend and what to expect.

I had earlier explored the possibility of a letter to the National Security Adviser, Lieutenant General Aliyu Mohammed Gusau, who was recently called back to the Office of the NSA immediately after the death of President Umaru Musa Yar'Adua. Lieutenant Colonel LKK Are, former DG SSS, was appointed his assistant. I discussed my matter with the former DG SSS and he agreed that I should write. The former DG SSS, Are, was later appointed as the Acting NSA. On the day I went to deliver my letter at the NSA's office, I met a photo session bidding General Aliyu Mohammed Gusau farewell.

I was in for another deception as nothing was done till the Acting NSA left office. I visited him at home and had some discussions and observed his casual statements that gave clues of his intention. Also, I got the impression that undermining the decisions of the President, Commander-in-Chief was a routine by government officials. General OA Azazi phoned him as we were discussing and he asked me if I wanted to speak to him. I declined.

A few weeks later, General AO Azazi was appointed as the substantive NSA. General Azazi received my letter at the office of the NSA and wrote to the MOD for their response. There was no substantive Minister yet. The havoc being caused to punish me continued. The actions of the Deputy Director that was asked to handle the matter and others including the new Permanent Secretary at MOD were, thereafter, to satisfy General Azazi, hence the Deputy Director's reply to me that he did not want anyone to mess up his career. I explained to them that the person who caused the problem, General OA Azazi, should not be allowed to interfere again as he would cause more havoc. The MOD senior Directors wanted to save their jobs and they freely expressed it.

On 29 November 2010, my wife was leaving home for work when the civilian security detail I employed gave her a letter of threat and live ammunition dropped at the gate and found in the early hours of the morning with a message that I had been a target for some time but they had not been successful and promised to get me in the next forty-eight hours. I had earlier in 2008 dealt with threats to my sister at Okene in which I involved the State Security Services.

I calmed my wife down and she went to work. I went to the office of the Inspector General of Police who asked me to quickly put up a letter to him. This, I did in his office and attached the threat letter and the live ammunition as exhibits. I left the IGP's office assured that appropriate actions would be taken.

On my return home, I phoned the new CNS Vice Admiral OS Ibrahim and informed him of the incident and the need for the NHQ to follow up on the Police investigation. The CNS asked the Director of Naval Intelligence to send a team to my house to investigate my children living with me. They found that none of my children was living with me and duly reported to the CNS.

I phoned the CNS over a month later to find out if there was any progress. The CNS blew up, telling me that all I worked for in my career would be destroyed if I did not back off and accept what had been done to me. This threat and several others are routine in the Armed Forces of Nigeria. They all knew that what was done to me was wrong and the refusal to act and solve the problems was now the accepted culture.

I had to write to the Honourable Minister of Justice and Attorney General of the Federation and the new HMOD for their intervention. In my letter to the new HMOD, I narrated the role played by the NSA as the CDS, in causing the problems and I asked that the same person should not be allowed to continue punishing me.

I also wrote directly to the President, Commander-in-Chief highlighting the problems and the obstacles being put in place against me by the NSA and other interested parties. The efforts to get the President, Commander-in-Chief to act were resisted by the NSA who deployed his network at the MOD and the Presidency.

The NSA and Minister of Justice and Attorney General of the Federation once clashed in the Federal Executive Council chamber over the meddlesomeness of the NSA who was preventing the complementary efforts of the two Ministers to get the President, Commander-in-Chief to attend to and decide the matter. I had also reported in my letter of the threat to my life and the live ammunition deposited at my gate with a deadline of 01 December 2010 to carry out the assassination. It was expected that I would run out of the country into exile if their attempts or pressure were kept up, hence the desperation at my residential gate. I had been warned of Nuhu Ribadu treatment in January 2008 at MOD in the presence of HMOD.

Indeed the CNS, Vice Admiral OS Ibrahim, as of January 2011 must be privy to very classified information to warn me the way he did that all I had worked for would be destroyed should I continue to seek for fair treatment. The series of actions by the NSA and collaborators against me show how an individual and interest groups can single-handedly or in networks hold the Government of the Federal Republic of Nigeria to ransom and render the entire machinery of government impotent. General AO Azazi was more powerful than the President, Commander-in-Chief of the Armed Forces of the Federal Republic of Nigeria. As the CDS, he told me that President Umaru Musa Yar'Adua did not matter because he could do what he liked and there would be no consequences. Alhaji Mahmud Ahmed Yayale and Dr Haruna Sanusi, HMOD and Permanent Secretary respectively felt the same way between July 2007 and August 2008. As they felt the same way, no request from me to meet with the President, Commander-in-Chief would be entertained. President Goodluck E Jonathan could not take any decision that would solve my problems because he could not afford to displease the NSA. This is how Nigeria is being routinely wrecked by easy access to power without control.

I continued to expand my points of contact to push my case through the military hierarchy, the Presidency, and the President. I knew my records as related to the problems were being corrupted with lies, hate, and deceit and I kept on trying to make my case and point out the corruption of procedures. The forces the NSA organised against me were formidable; the extent of mischief being caused was beyond my comprehension. The tenures of office for Vice-Admiral OS Ibrahim and Vice Admiral DJ Ezeoba as CNSs were characterised by attempts to ridicule me, to perhaps, satisfy the NSA. When Vice-Admiral OS Ibrahim moved up as the CDS, Vice-Admiral DJ Ezeoba took over as the CNS.

I was preparing to attend the burial of Rear Admiral GA Shiyanbade, a former Commandant of the NWC, in the UK in May 2013 and urgently needed a visa. I approached the CNS for administrative support as was given to me in 2010. I was handed over to the Naval Provost Marshal as it was his schedule. I assembled all documents listed for me and sent them in a sealed envelope with the visa fee and my active duty Identity Card (IC). The identity card was removed at the NHQ and the money was counted in the presence of Sergeant Alfa and placed in the envelope with other documents I had sent. The letter that was written to General OA Azazi, the NSA, from the MOD which I never knew about, was copied from my file at the NHQ and given to Seargent Alfa to deliver to me without an envelope to seal it. The entire package was sent back to me without my IC. I contacted the CNS and he was deliberately evasive.

I wrote to the acting HMOD who was the substantive Minister of State and informed her of the incident. I told her I had a good photocopy of the IC and would, henceforth, be using it as my active duty identity card. I also requested the return of my IC because an officer whether on active service or retired must always be with an IC. There are procedures for change of ICs for military personnel.

I contacted the Visa section of the UK High Commission and a five-year visa was issued to me within twenty-four hours to meet up with the burial ceremony. I followed their defined protocols. It was a show of shame by the CNS. Admiral OS Ibrahim and Vice-Admiral DJ Ezeoba became the agents for the reversal of the progress made by Vice-Admiral II Ibrahim who was the CNS when President Umaru Musa Yar'Adua was on course to solve the problem. Both of them reversed the progress made by Vice-Admiral II Ibrahim and created new problems for me. They acted with impunity to serve individuals defying articles of war.

In a letter written on 09 January 2012 by the Permanent Secretary, MOD, Mr LN Awute, to the NSA based on the staff work by the CNS and staff at NHQ, it was stressed that I "should not be allowed to determine which correspondence, from constituted authority and lawful authority, to accept and which to reject." Those abusing public offices to punish me were now "constituted authority and lawful authority". There was no mention of how procedures were suddenly evaded repeatedly to arrive at an instant Navy Board decision that retirement had taken place when I had no application for voluntary retirement before the board. They even worked during the holidays and a letter dated 26 December 2007 threatening me with compulsory retirement was delivered to me as I prepared to have lunch on Boxing Day with my family. The letter also contained a decision of a Navy Board expected to sit in the future. The military hierarchy was also confused in their correspondence as there were desperate attempts to evade issues and justify wrong actions. These were in pursuit of carefully planned actions to destroy my career as narrated to me for over a year because of the permanent site project and being considered qualified to be appointed as the CNS and later CDS by the new President, Commander-in-Chief.

I struggled to survive the onslaughts between September 2010 and June 2012 when General Azazi was relieved of his appointment as the NSA. I approached the National Assembly leadership and had a meeting with the Senate President, Senator David Mark in Uyo where he had a meeting with me. This was facilitated by Senator Deen Abatemi-Usman representing Kogi Central Senatorial District. After a series of consultations, the Chairman of the Senate Committee on Defence Distinguished Senator George Thompson Sekibo wrote to the HMOD on 04 June 2014 highlighting the need to solve the problems adversely affecting my life and career to avoid creating bad impressions about the treatment of military personnel.

The HMOD was expected to give feedback on the resolution of the matter and consequently, I had to be patient for due process to take its course. I needed to keep my reminders updated between 2010 and 2014 at the NHQ, DHQ, and the MOD and provide relevant information to counter the corrupted documentation and disinformation against me.

I carefully went through all relevant correspondences and especially the letter to the President, Commander-in-Chief of the Armed Forces dated 31 July 2012 seeking his decision in respect of the developments that adversely affect my career and life. I prayed for the following in the letter following established and known articles of war:

1. 1. Assignment to a duty post as I have a commission for service to the country I bear allegiance to serve. This is important to facilitate effective communication for the resolution of the issues raised and for the respectful exercise of the authority of the Commander-in-Chief as I have not left the service nor carried out any discharge routine.
2. 2. Restoration of those benefits and entitlements hastily, wrongfully, and illegally withheld for normal and dignified treatment as a commissioned active duty officer while issues are attended to. The assignment of duty post sorts out the details of the requirements for essential resolution of the problems caused as I am an officer on leave.
3. 3. Promotion due and contemplated for long up to December 2007 and in line with the law enacted for the conduct of the affairs of the college. This is also supported by the Harmonised Terms and Conditions of Service which stipulates

4. 4.   that promotion due has to be given and not deprived even when under consideration for retirement.

4. 4.   Security provisions given threats to my life and those of the members of my family. I have been living almost under seclusion since leaving the college, necessitating vital commitments that have deprived me of resources invested for sustenance. I rely on the generosity of friends.

5. 5.   Resolution of related administrative issues and putting records right as personal references have caused distortions and deprivation of benefits. It has also made it impossible to attend to other administrative requirements such as sorting out my housing loan defaults detected by the Federal Housing Loan office and which the Naval Headquarters has not resolved because of the possible mix up of my records in the haste to get me out of office.

The above list was based on the official procedures set in motion to solve my problems between September 2009 and September 2010 and rooted in the Armed Forces Covenant to solve my problems and will always be relevant in a voluntary military service to solve similar problems. Such problems would be waiting to be solved and a proper military institution would not leave them unsolved and pronounce them closed. The list is a framework based on established best practices. This was also based on the feedback by Vice Admiral II Ibrahim, then the CNS within the period, as regards presentation to President Umaru Musa Yar'Adua whose intentions were undermined to get me out of my duty post as Commandant. The office of the CNS was handling my administrative matters and he, the CNS, took charge and devolved responsibilities as he considered appropriate. I was treated as an active-duty officer and on leave. My letters mostly had Nigerian Navy Headquarters address and all had signature block as Rear Admiral AAM ISA with NN/0317 my active duty official number. I am out of service but not retired.

The CNS had tried to trace my financial records to sort out the Federal Housing Loan deductions and failed to find any trace. He detailed an officer to go to Lagos and search for the documents at the Central Pay Office but this did not yield the desired results. My financial records were missing and this is an important record I had to scrutinise as a routine and clear outstanding issues. I had been informed of the destruction and distortion of my records and this did not surprise me as I had been warned. Some officers at NHQ at various time since 2010 after the change of CNS claimed that my records are in order but I have not been allowed access to them for scrutiny. The NN institution is not allowed to function as individuals in positions of authority want to have their ways to be served.

My files were being accessed by whoever wanted them to document what they want. I also had a vicious assault on the permanent site project documents aimed at their destruction and some hidden to avoid access. They undermined all intentions of the President, Commander-in-Chief, and caused delays so that the funds I struggled to get approvals for can be embezzled or wasted. I was accused of being in a hurry to complete the project when they were not yet compensated by embezzlement. It is not surprising that Nigeria has many abandoned projects on which huge amounts of money had been released littering the landscape of Nigeria as a testimony to the efficiency of public servants in Nigeria.

I received the sad news of the death of the mother of Fred Stappen, Madam Christine on 28 December 2013. She died at 95 years. Her son's message to me expressed the love she had for me. Fred's father, Mr Fritz Johannes, died on 26 March 1986. I have an excellent relationship with the Stappen family in Germany that endures. Such a relationship has been a very important source of inspiration in my life as I have very fond memories of their goodwill.

I was surprised by 2013 that the flexible terms and conditions regarding the length of military service were unknown to the staff at the NHQ and other service Headquarters. The rigid statement in the civil service rules was being applied in the military thereby depriving the institution of the benefits of the flexibility it is expected to bring for career planning to ensure institutional knowledge is developed and applied for credible military capabilities that take a long time to achieve.

It is completely lost on the AFN that the most important function of military commanders is the perfection of materials and human resources to the point of readiness for commitment to war or operations once they are required. This takes a lot of time, an important factor in the strategic planning process that requires the commitment of quality personnel. The operative word in the Harmonised Terms and Conditions of Service for Officers is "MAY". It stipulates that an officer may serve for a length of time and thereafter there are provisions for extensions after which the President, Commander-in-Chief may decide to retain an officer for as long as he or she may determine. This is to ensure secure tenures for military capabilities management by application of organisational knowledge. The President, Commander-in-Chief in this regard is not supported by the service chiefs who claim sole authority to do what they like with the careers of officers. It becomes impossible to carry out the most important function of military commanders as developed expertise and skills acquired are wasted.

I have noticed in my years of service with developed Armed Forces in Europe and the USA that service chiefs behave in manners that convey that they have no power over personnel as guidelines are defined and career reviews are carried out with periodic interviews with commissioned officers for career planning. The craze in the Armed Forces in Nigeria is about waiting for turns and implementation of civil service rules to abuse state powers to punish and deny dues. I have taken time to address this issue and explain that the Armed Forces is not a civil service and length of service is not rigidly fixed. Besides, there abound examples of how military personnel deprived of their dues are eventually given and how they are treated. In fact, service personnel have a lifelong commitment and in the US Armed Forces, the active and retired/reserved lists are all treated together and this facilitates the recall of officers from retirement to active duty routinely. There are very poor attitudes and ignorance in the setup in Nigeria that would not allow for the proper management of the Armed Forces and consequently its present embarrassing state of impotence.

I put pressure on the HMOD, Lieutenant General Aliyu Mohammed Gusau, for the matter to be presented to the President, Commander-in-Chief of the Armed Forces in 2014. There was reluctance given the spread of opposition against me. I contacted a friend of the HMOD who intervened and I was asked to meet the CNS, Vice-Admiral U Jibrin, for a meeting to resolve the matters. The message was passed to me by the Permanent Secretary Aliyu Isma'ila when I called at his office to find out the outcome of the discussions held with the HMOD. The CNS was expected to call me and inform me but the Permanent Secretary was surprised that I had not been told. I called the CNS and he confirmed that he had been directed to hold a meeting with me and get the issues resolved. The CNS gave me 07 July 2014 for the meeting with his Branch Chiefs and the Naval Secretary in attendance.

The meeting was expected to be short but lasted for a long time. The HMOD graciously phoned in and spoke to me to cooperate and get all issues resolved after speaking with the CNS. I was most grateful for this wonderful gesture and I stood up in the presence of all gathered - as a mark of respect to the HMOD - as I spoke to him on the CNS phone. The CNS had introduced the Branch Chiefs present and the Naval

Secretary and assured me that they attended the meeting to ensure a comprehensive response to resolve my issues.

I was asked to present my case. I started by telling them that I had not retired voluntarily and was receiving neither salary nor pension. I emphasised that I was out of service but not retired or decommissioned as I still had my active duty commission voluntarily sworn on oath with obligation of a covenant.

I then went on to highlight the sequence of events that led to my leaving the college duty post I was assigned by the President, Commander-in-Chief immediately after the supplementary budget was released and we had money to proceed with the permanent site project. I highlighted the details of the haste and how normal procedures were put aside. There was no opportunity to put in an application for voluntary retirement as I was being threatened on all fronts and simply asked for compassion regarding whatever they wanted to do as I left the college according to their wish. I thanked them for allowing me to serve the NN and the AFN. I know that the NN and AFN are used to serve the country. I said to the gathering that our allegiance was to the country as we all joined the armed forces to serve and that the lack of understanding of this very important principle was a major problem in the Armed Forces of Nigeria. It is the duty of the President, Commander-in-Chief to thank all commissioned officers for services rendered to the country and it is to him that military personnel pledge their loyalty to serve the country and it causes not any service chief.

The CNS and the staff of the NN cannot thank any commissioned officer for services to the NN as expressed in a letter to me. There is no such service rendered as the NN is only an instrument of the policy used to serve the country. The CNS and his officers were speechless as if in disbelief. The CNS started to apologise profusely on realising the enormity of the problems and the other officers joined in to apologise for what I had been going through. I had doubts about the sincerity of their apologies and their subsequent actions after the meeting proved me right.

In response to the questions by the CNS regarding what I wanted, I brought out the letter I wrote to the President, Commander-in-Chief dated 31 July 2012 listing the points in subparagraphs 1.1 to 5.5. I went through the points explaining that they were all based on procedures, terms, and conditions of service, and the laws enacted for the conduct of the affairs of the College. The Armed Forces covenant demands fair treatment to personnel and not human right abuses. I cited best practices to support all points made. I then emphasised that I was not asking for any special treatment but for the proper steps to be taken to give me all entitlements and dues earned as a commissioned officer. I then emphasised that once the issues were satisfactorily resolved, a date could then be set for me to put in for voluntary retirement. The expectation is to allow the institution to work and avoid individual biases prevailing.

They were very sensitive to only the issue of promotion and said that the NN had no allowance for the provision. I briefed them that the allowance was for the National Defence College and it was covered by the law. It is also supported by the terms and conditions of service stipulating that promotions due have to be given even as officers undergo retirement procedures. I reminded the audience that the promotion of the CNS on appointment has no backing of the law and does not go through any board before they start wearing the rank.

One of the Branch Chiefs in a desperate move stated that they did what they liked and not what the law and articles of war stipulated and that they even disobeyed court rulings. I had put forward the issues to be resolved following the law and articles of war. The Naval Secretary had no input as I noticed he had come with a position to present with documents and he was the focus of the CNS but remained very quiet.

The CNS then concluded by asking for my copy of the letter to the President, Commander-in-Chief which listed the issues to be resolved as in my letter dated 31 July 2012. I then advised that based on the attempts between 2009-2010 to solve the problems, a memo to the President, Commander-in-Chief seeking his decision and approval to implement was all that was required. The CNS promised to feed me back and the meeting ended with the impression that a framework for resolution would be worked out and the solutions as discussed would be implemented following due process. The CNS respectfully thanked me and escorted me out of his office pleading my availability to contribute to the NN whenever I was called upon.

I had anticipated an early response but none came. On 04 September 2014, I phoned the CNS and he was very hesitant and made statements that seemed to show he was no longer aware of the meeting of 07 July 2014 in his office with his Branch Chiefs and the Naval Secretary. He then told me that I had been sent two letters which I had not seen. I had left my address for delivery of letters by the Naval Courier service but they chose to post the letters using my post office box number which caused a delay.

I went to the post office and collected two letters from the NHQ. The first letter was dated 30 July 2014 and the second one was dated 11 August 2014. The first letter was requesting me to contact the Naval Secretary for undefined follow-up procedures not related to solving the problems while the second letter cancelled the first letter and enclosed a letter dated 16 January 2008 citing a Navy Board meeting of 15 January 2008 that decided to retire me. The day, 15 January 2008, was a holiday for the Armed Forces Remembrance Day celebration and I handed over the college to the Acting Commandant on 14 January 2008, the same day my letter asking for compassion was submitted. This was a record in the speed of convening the meeting of a Navy Board, having the minutes of the meeting ready, and carrying out the administrative procedures at the MOD and then NHQ for a letter conveying decision the following day.

This exceptional speed happens only for destructive purposes in the Armed Forces of Nigeria. The letter dated 16 January 2008 stated that I should sign an acknowledgement section and return to the NHQ to make subsequent procedures legal. I was told on 14 January 2008 by the CNS, Vice Admiral GT Adekeye to get out of the NHQ; that is the same CNS who dropped the phone on the Chief of Staff to the President, Commander-in-Chief and nothing happened. I replied to the CNS who chaired the meeting of 07 July 2014 that I had nothing to do with the letter and explained the inconsistencies that made the letter a document of treason as it undermined the superior authority of the President, Commander-in-Chief. I could not be associated with such acts of undermining authority. In my reply, I gave details of the sequence of events related to the meeting of 07 July 2014 and the expectation that a memo conveying subparagraphs 1.1 to 5.5 would be submitted to the President for consideration and approval.

The CNS and his staff at the NHQ were trying to act in denial of the meeting due to the intervention of interested parties that were against the resolution of my problems. How I emerged and got appointed as CNS in 2005 still annoys them among other petty grudges earlier highlighted. I later heard that I attended the meeting with the CNS on 07 July 2014 and refused to negotiate a monetary settlement as compensation. It has been a practice to clear many cases of abuse of office that abruptly terminated the career of officers with payment of millions of Naira to the affected officers. These officers had either gone through court-martial and/or retired and were receiving pensions. They, thereafter, went to court and won their cases up to the Supreme Court.

I once again reminded the CNS and his staff at the NHQ in my reply to the letters that I had not been part of a voluntary retirement process and still have intact my active duty commission. Also, the haste to get me out of the office to waste the money for the permanent site construction project which was to be completed and put to use by 2010 seriously undermined national security given the deteriorating internal security situation. I never discussed monetary compensation with the CNS and his staff officers. They knew I would not tolerate such a solution. No amount of money will buy honour and compensate for the use of the name of God in the oath sworn on commission for acts of deception.

I was being branded as one looking for special treatment while other officers who took their cases to court and won had collected millions of Naira and did not ask for reinstatement following court orders. This is how the NN institution is destroyed with decisions not in consonance with official policy. The use of lies and deception ensures almost nothing is allowed to function properly. Indeed the NN officers are made to believe that they joined the NN to serve the NN at the expense of the country and pledge loyalty to the CNS instead of the President, Commander-in-Chief. Allegiance to higher causes that define loyalty is meaningless to most of them. The staff officers draw and solicit support from unofficial outside sources such as those officers who had retired and still control them to undermine the President, Commander-in-Chief.

I had to write to the HMOD by December 2014 to thank him for his efforts and report the unfortunate developments to him. I reported that what was discussed at the meeting was being denied and I was being asked to accept a corrupted procedure and documentation I was never a party to. I pointed out that I had not received any emoluments since January 2008.

The HMOD, CDS, and CNS as at the time had a rethink and I was informed, as I went to the NHQ to follow up, that the issues involved were complicated and would require me to appear before them and have a discussion and a better understanding for resolution. I was asked to standby to appear. The beginning of 2015 was electrified with the Presidential campaign and there was also a National Defence Policy Review under the Chairmanship of AVM Mohammed Umaru, the former Military Governor of Kano State. I submitted a memo that the Chairman called me to have further discussions on and took the opportunity to inform me of the position of the CDS on my matter.

I received a subtle warning that I was too old to be asking to be treated under established articles of war. I explained the ethics of the profession that stipulates that all entitlements and dues earned by military personnel must be given and should never be denied. I also explained that the members of the Navy Board as of 2008 were all badly compromised and should have recused themselves having undermined higher authority and no longer possess the authority to decide my issues. The Chairman understood the issues and promised to convey the salient points put across.

The Navy Board met on 23 March 2015. It was the second first Navy Board of the year taking place on my matter. The first took place on 15 January 2008 during the Armed Forces Remembrance Day celebration and holiday for Armed Forces personnel. The recent Navy Board already had a predetermined decision to continue with the decision that undermined the authority of the President, Commander-in-Chief. The CDS and CNS as members of the Navy Board were not allowed to comment. The whole process lasted for just about five minutes and there was no discussion but the announcement of a decision.

I received a letter dated 01 April 2015, the day the result of the Presidential election was announced, informing me of the decision of the Navy Board of 23 March 2015. In the letter, it was said that the Navy Board reviewed all the facts. The meeting lasted for about five minutes and there was no discussion; yet all facts were reviewed. I was denied a fair hearing appearance and no discussion was allowed at the Navy Board. President Goodluck Ebele Jonathan lost the election to Major General Muhammadu Buhari.

I replied to the letter immediately pointing out that the decision of the Navy Board was not implementable. This was after I phoned the CNS to explain to me how to implement the decision and he had no answer. I then told the CNS that I would reply appropriately to convey the fact that the Navy Board took a decision that was not implementable. The reply I got reflected lack of understanding of the referred articles of war. I waited for the President-elect to take office on 29 May 2015 and make a summary of the presentation on the matter. The desperate attempt by the network was to hold on to a retirement that never took place to punish me.

I elaborated on my February 2015 presentations to the National Defence Policy Review Committee and sent them to the President's Transition Committee under cover of a comprehensive letter dated 07 April 2015 in which I highlighted the poor state of the Nigeria Armed Forces and the need to take effective charge starting with definition and implementation of appropriate force structure for credible military capabilities given the grave internal security challenges. I emphasised the need to start building a new Armed Forces as a priority as the set up inherited could not cope with the defence and security challenges. I pointed out that Nigeria had no credible military establishment. The submissions had a common focus of immediately solving the current internal security problems and taking charge starting with how the Commander-in-Chief takes effective charge with a well-defined National Command Authority and force structure with clearly defined responsibilities.

I managed to link up to Lieutenant General A Danbazzau, a former COAS, who had been in charge of the President-Elect's campaign security. I delivered a copy to his office on his instruction. On the 29 May 2015, at his inauguration, the President spoke of the decision to move the Army Headquarters Command to the theatre of operation. The COAS was asked to relocate to the theatre. This surprised me. This was a decision reflecting a lack of understanding of force structure issues for effective command and control. I phoned Lieutenant General A Danbazzau and asked why such a declaration and his evasive response marked the last time he picked up my call. The AFN is not used to strategic planning for force generation and employment issues and the relevant joint capabilities management.

I had emerged as a candidate for appointment as the Minister of Defence and he, Danbazzau, was being considered for appointment as the NSA. The political considerations were not my turf and I was concentrated on getting my problems solved as the President, Commander-in-Chief was going through a prolonged period of seven months permutations to appoint his ministers and this wasted the enormous goodwill that he had on winning the election.

I started a comprehensive compilation of the outstanding issues affecting my life and career in June 2015 to send to the new President, Commander-in-Chief. The compilation was submitted towards the end of September 2015 as names were still being floated for appointment as Minister of Defence. I had much earlier been reliably informed to standby as it was considered that I met the requirements for decisive interventions to get the Armed Forces on a sound footing for the ongoing operations against terrorists and insurgents.

I am not a member of any political party and was denied my Permanent Voter's Card to exercise my voting right as data capture for the temporary voter's card I used for the 2011 election could not be used for the issuance of a valid Permanent Voter's Card. The politicians wanted their party members to be appointed Ministers and at a meeting, it was considered that I was not known politically though professionally sound for the appointment. I was dropped and I did not need any explanation.

Because of the President's agenda on the economy, corruption, and insecurity, I was certain that there would be timely consideration and many observers of the travails I have been going through were also optimistic of a prompt response to my case. I was mistaken, together with others, as I started getting feelers that the vestiges of the vested interests were keeping guard at the Presidency. The familiar documented corruption would be recycled and old file pages were dusted up. I had been requesting to meet with the President, Commander-in-Chief since 2007 when I held an appointment made by law by the President, Commander-in-Chief.

I started experiencing a new round of bureaucratic sophistry indicating no fair access and consideration of the real issues. The compromised bureaucracies would be referred to again. The responses were a rehash of bureaucratic sophistry more pronounced as new entrants of College Permanent Site interests took a post in the Presidency and the MOD would not tolerate exposure of how funds had been wasted so far. The responses from the NHQ evaded the issues and focussed on familiar narratives of political correctness tagged based on the Armed Forces Council administrative decision.

The standard normal practice in all circumstances for voluntary retirement is that a six month's notice for retirement is given and the date for a three months terminal leave is also communicated with the notice so that the retirement procedures are completed on the completion of the terminal leave and the first day of retirement is the day that follows. If any reasons make it impossible to have the six months notification and the three months terminal leave, a discussion is held regarding how to handle matters arising including financial and/or other compensations. The notice to retire, according to the Harmonized Terms and Conditions of Service for the Nigerian Armed Forces Officers, is a routine career procedure. It is when such career procedures are followed that legitimacy is given to actions taken to effect a voluntary retirement.

Retirement is, therefore, only voluntary if correct procedures are followed and outstanding issues and/or problems are resolved so that the fundamental principle of the Armed Forces covenant mandating institutional fairness to personnel is strictly adhered to. In the haste to get me out of my duty post to have access to recklessly spend public funds, all of the above were not adhered to. The reality was that the HMOD, Permanent Secretary, CDS, and CNS teamed up to fight the President, Commander-in-Chief as regards the exercise of powers or authority not delegated to them. Threats were issued to me.

The letter written to me dated 27 August 2007 was a letter of the threat issued immediately after a stormy College Board meeting during which the CNS threatened to deal with me. This threat was a grave offence committed by the CNS that the HMOD knew about and tolerated at the College Board meeting.

The next letter of notification of voluntary retirement dated 11 December 2007 asking me to put in a letter of voluntary retirement by 24 December 2007 to retire by 31 December and commence my terminal leave with effect from 01 January 2008 is simply not in line with normal procedures that accords legitimacy. It was a move to waste funds just released and allow for more corruption. The submissions I made to the President, Commander-in-Chief of the Armed Forces of the Federal Republic of Nigeria gave facts that clearly show that no retirement took place as all procedures for normal actions were not adhered to.

The officers affected by the Armed Forces Council administrative decision had all left except those of us holding appointments made by the President, Commander-in-Chief following extant laws and his known intentions. I was singled out by members of the Navy Board with a convergence of interests undermining the President. This was why the memo by HMOD to the President was not written by December 2007 and forwarded to the President who was waiting to receive it at the time. It was also just to cause me the enormous problems that I have been facing because of their agenda for the funds for the permanent site project.

The Chief of Staff wrote to the CDS on 24 August 2016 stating that there was an allegation of wrongful retirement and a response was required to enable a presentation to the President, Commander-in-Chief. This was the response to the reminder I sent to the President. The CDS replied that I was retired by a Navy Board that met 15 January 2008 having spent more than 35 years and six months on active service. The CDS added that having retired, I could not again be asking for the promotion that I had lawfully earned. The CDS concluded his letter by stating that he did not know what my grievances were or what I wanted from the NN. He failed to find out why the NN is treating me like a persona non grata; an active-duty officer in a voluntary service? The

CDS, General Gabriel Olonishakin, was a principal staff officer to HMOD when General Azazi was NSA and was very knowledgeable about the matter. He had told me then as a Brigadier General that NN was free to do what it likes. This is the general orientation.

The Chief of Staff's response also overlooked all the facts in my submissions relating to the pursuits of the undermining personal interests and destructive motives of the members of the compromised Navy Board and agreed that I was retired and started addressing me as a retired officer in the follow-up correspondence.

I found out that Alhaji Isamaila Isa Funtua, the owner of Bullet Construction Company had bought the entire Permanent Site contract and all contractors cleared by BMPIU were taken off the project except Stablini. I also found out that he is a very close confidant of the President, Commander-in-Chief, and very influential in the Federal Government. The contractors displaced from the Permanent Site took their case to court. I could only hope that the project would not be derailed with someone closed to power involved and Stabilini also on site.

There was no demand to my knowledge by the Chief of Staff since September 2015 for proof of a retired status being enjoyed as was claimed by the CDS despite the evidence at the disposal of the Presidency to the contrary. I studied all correspondences from the NHQ, DHQ, MOD, and the Presidency and wonder how Nigerians survive routine evasion of issues and solutions to problems by public officials.

In a series of my follow-up correspondences that were mainly sent to the President, Commander-in-Chief as reminders, I highlighted the impact of poor attitude and orientation in the military hierarchy that is causing the country serious security problems. In one of such letters dated 09 October 2018, I pointed out that the higher direction of national defence and security was being conducted with a poor attitude to personnel matters as I have experienced.

I wrote: "These constitute serious national security issues that will never inspire troops in all states of readiness and/or engagement in defence of the country. It sadly conveys that troops in harm's way with serious pressing known issues that can be easily resolved will be recklessly abandoned to suffer the onslaught of the enemy so that the sinful luxury of personal interests that undermine national security interests can be celebrated. This is a serious portrayal that Nigeria has no military establishment that can be relied upon for effective national defence. It is openly not being prepared, perfected, and readied for effective national defence... It is very important to note that when these are happening and perpetuated by a military hierarchy that is happily lying and deceitful to the President, Commander-in-Chief as in this matter, there are very grave dangers to the nation-state and the efforts to build and use its institutions for nation-building."

I further pointed out in the same letter that the bad examples on open display by the military hierarchy have many adverse effects on national security interests and I specifically noted: "This is so as these bad examples have become common knowledge that simply issue commands to Nigerian Armed Forces personnel with categorical stringency: Do not be committed to serving the country with dedication as such will be severely punished as an official policy to serve as deterrence to others who dare serve with commitment."

The Chief of Army Staff Lieutenant General Tukur Buratai stated publicly a few months later, after I submitted the letter of 09 October 2018, that the troops fighting insurgents in the North East of Nigeria were not committed. There are reports that many personnel are resigning because they are fed up with the way they are being treated to fight a war. There is a leadership failure that I had long identified. There is a need for urgent actions to redress. It is essential to note that if Nigeria cannot build and maintain a credible Armed Forces institution for the defence and security of the country it is an indication that it has failed comprehensively to develop other institutions essential for the proper running of the country. The Armed Forces must perform the integrative function highly expected of it for national development and be so to be relied upon at all times. These constitute the first determinant as regards if Nigerians can run an effective modern nation-state for the well being of the people; that is, meeting their needs and aspirations in a harmonious setting. Nigeria is not being respected because it failed in these matters. Bearing allegiance and pledging loyalty by military personnel demands mandatory adherence by the country to a covenant to fairly treating those who serve and have served together with their family.

I have elaborated enough on the factors responsible for this sorry state of affairs since I was a junior officer witnessing what leadership preferences were and which have now assumed critical and adverse dimensions for the country. I am inclined to state that there is no clue or willingness on the part of the leadership up and down the chain of command to act appropriately as the situation gets worse. The few who dare are easily subdued to belong to the majority and survive. It is a favour done to be appointed and consequently, serving the country is strange to leadership, public officers, and civil servants. It is a very complex problem for the country that consequently suffers a lack of committed service. How is the nexus between allegiance and loyalty understood in Nigeria?

The problems in the way of understanding started with the way the services came into being and go deep into the founding years of the nation-state. Nigerians who were enlisted to serve in the Armed Forces were told they belonged to a Sovereign Royalty in the UK and never grasped and internalised what it takes to have an Armed Forces focused on their nation-state defence and security before the coup of 15 January 1966 that set off a chain of destructive tendencies. The highest causes of the nation-state have been disconnected from bearing allegiance as it is a pledge to an individual who must be served above all else. Allegiance to nation-state causes is strange. In a very diverse country such as Nigeria, it is very difficult for service personnel to pledge loyalty to someone else outside their ethnic group for example. It becomes easy to be swayed to act against the nation-state by disrespecting and undermining authority as portrayed on 15 January 1966 and there after.

The colonial administrations set up a fighting force made up of an ethnic group to suppress another ethnic group and defend the empire elsewhere. All the ethnic groups later became part of Nigeria in 1914. This background may have attracted some of the officers who joined to think of using the military in Nigeria for imposing their will on others in the country. Allegiance to the nation-state, that is fidelity to a sovereign entity demands that loyalty to the republic be respectfully expressed in conduct through the government or President/Head of State mandated by the electorates for decisive government actions for common good. This nexus is not recognised in the mindsets of most Nigerians as they cannot relate to causes of their nation-state higher than those of individuals and groups in their calculations. Military personnel in Nigeria do not, therefore, have the correct orientation of the ethics of the profession of arms. There is the lack of dedication and commitment to the nation-state to properly serve.

State powers are personalised or worn by politicians, public officers and civil servants and used with impunity so that influential individuals emerge as substitutes for strong state institutions. The state powers are thereby wasted and not allowed to be used to build strong state institutions required for nation-building. As no Nigerian or Nigerian group founded the country, why do all Nigerians who were given equal opportunities to equally belong legally to a country as from 1914 not having the orientation of equality to be inclusive in the conduct of the nation-state affairs?

Armed Forces personnel in Nigeria swear an oath to God to "bear true allegiance faithfully to the President, Commander-in-Chief of the Armed Forces of the Federal Republic of Nigeria…" This idea is copied from the monarchial system of Britain. It should not be in a republic and Nigerians have failed to be true to their Republican status since 1963. In the British monarchial system, the Queen or King, heirs, and successors constitute the symbol of the state to whom all swear an oath of allegiance. The origin is detailed in the Magna Carta (15 June 1215) which is a document guaranteeing British political liberties (Wikipedia). This is a unique setting based on UK history.

A republic is a state. It is a public property in which all citizens are equal as none is above the law. The people in such a state possess the supreme power. The people, therefore, mandate representatives and a president, commander-in-chief to govern them. In such a republic, allegiance is a duty of fidelity freely committed by the citizens to their state with sovereignty which is an entity higher than any individual. Allegiance is loyalty to a cause but an expression of the pledge of loyalty is more person oriented but to the state (WikiDiff.com). The symbols that define such a state reflect the people's belief system based on circumstances. There is a social contract obligation as the people pledge their loyalty to the President, Commander-in-Chief. It is a form of respect for authority conferred. There is also respect for the representatives and constituted authorities. All act in the national interest to earn or give such respect. Loyalty is an assurance of commitment and devotion that the law will be followed by all parties. The CEO of the state takes a lead in the observance of the rule of law to achieve defined national security objectives for the common good.

Allegiance in a republic such as Nigeria should be an obligation of loyalty to the nation-state, flag, and its causes as expressed in the national anthem, swearing to follow the laws of the country. It is an expression of commitment and devotion in the firmest sense of the word. (www.yourdictionary.com).

The "First Schedule Armed Forces Oath" is sworn to God to "bear true and faithful allegiance to the President, Commander-in-Chief of the Armed Forces of the Federal Republic of Nigeria…" It is based on this that the President signs and issues "Parchment of Commission" hinged on trust that the officer is loyal, courageous, and of good conduct and is expected to observe and execute all laws, orders, and instructions from the President, Commander-in-Chief or superior officers. Bearing allegiance to an individual in a republic would not allow military personnel in Nigeria to be committed and devoted to the country and related higher causes. Military involvement in the political governance of Nigeria added to the problems as groups emerge as "boys" with commitment and devotion to individuals. This has a contagion effect in many sectors and vice-chancellors of universities in Nigeria have their "boys" in their administration.

The bearing of allegiance to an individual is the source of confusion in the AFN as personnel are thereby charged to serve an elected individual and not a nation-state that is a republic. The higher causes of the nation-state which all should believe in and commit to in a republic where all are equal and none above the law is not referred to or emphasised. The personnel of the AFN and Nigerians, therefore, easily serve individuals while a republic is proclaimed and documented in the constitution. There is no guide to inspire commitment and devotion to serving the country when individuals are expected to be served. Public officers do what they like with public offices and funds and there is no value guide for essential social and political orders needed for the orderly conduct of nation-state affairs in a republic with diversity. They routinely act with impunity competing to undermine state institutions and authorities. Nation-state causes and belief systems have no ethnicity, religion or interest group biases. They appeal to and inspire all citizens.

The President, Commander-in-Chief of the Armed Forces, the CEO of the nation-state, exists in four traps. The first one is the trap of those who think because they have been very close to the President for a very long time, it is time to reap the fruits of being close and supportive of his struggles over the years. The second group belongs to those who think that they laboured to bring him to political prominence and they must always be around to ensure they influence state affairs for their benefits. They openly flaunt their influences and are celebrated in Nigeria as key drivers of government action.

These two groups struggle to influence and take control of the presidency. Thirdly, the Presidency has established its ways of conducting nation-state affairs and has its brand of bureaucracy controlled by various interest groups networked with the civil service for repeated referrals of matters that slow down governance.

The fourth trap is that of the political party in power whose members take Nigeria as a conquered territory that will be shared as public offices must be occupied by their members only. These four traps render the President and the Presidency almost impotent and public servants and Boards/Councils members set up, do what they like and do not care about building strong state institutions. They allow strong individuals the freedom to do what they like. It is tasking for the President, Commander-in-Chief to have a grasp of the correct assessment of situations.

There is anarchy in a democracy that is supposed to be an open, orderly, and inclusive system for governance. What obtains is a closed and exclusive garrison system for the punishment of the citizens considered not belonging. Public officers take their offices as an allocation to be used to punish with impunity and halt the process of solving problems. Is there anyone really in charge in Nigeria if the CEO of the nation-state is rendered impotent and lied to?

In this state of affairs, powerful freelance individuals that were never elected compete for supremacy and prevent the President from taking required actions because they operate the traps of influence to hold sway. Those who wield real power in Nigeria are not elected by the people, that is, they do not have the mandate of the electorates, and the diffusion of power makes Nigeria a very ungovernable political space. This convoluted power architecture was cultivated mostly by the members of the Armed Forces that got the institutions involved in the prolonged political governance of the country.

Several times, I was reminded that I was not grateful to the NN and the Armed Forces for appointing me as a Commandant. I had to thank the Armed Forces for allowing me to serve it and not the country in my letter asking for compassion in my great distress caused by what was happening to me. Perhaps it is why a commitment to serve the country is punished just as I am experiencing.

It is noteworthy that the Armed Forces that have important responsibilities for integrative functions in the conduct of the nation-state affairs cannot perform such functions. The MOD cannot integrate the three services into an effective force and the military establishment in Nigeria has been at the forefront of very divisive tendencies that the country is suffering. There are constant calls for the Armed forces to cooperate amongst themselves without emphasis on joint warfare operations and training as planned for execution at the NDC on completion of the permanent site slated for 2010 and since delayed. Why the shift of emphasis from joint warfare to building military Universities and individual service war colleges despite the deteriorating national security situation and the poor joint effort in operations?

It becomes clear to me why a President, Commander-in-Chief can be easily prevented from having a CNS he appointed and wanted. It is even more disturbing that his successor tried to implement the same appointment but was sabotaged. I sympathise with anyone elected President, Commander-in-Chief of the Armed Forces of the Federal Republic of Nigeria in the prevailing circumstances where almost every public servant and military officers want to exercise the powers of the President, Commander-in-Chief. In addition, internal contradictions enable powerful individuals and groups to exercise undue influence beyond control.

In 2013 and 2017, I was invited to the National Defense University, Washington DC US by the Chairman of the Joint Chiefs of Staff for Quadrennial National Security Seminars. In 2013, I was processed officially as an active-duty officer through official circles. In 2017, I was invited and a letter of invitation and request to the CDS by the Chairman Joint Chiefs of Staff for sponsorship was duly forwarded and I was copied. I applied to the CDS for the sponsorship and he forwarded it to CNS who refused to act and I had to eventually borrow money from my bank as I made several trips to the NHQ but was denied approval.

On my return from the US, I rendered a report to the CDS on issues that affect the security of Nigeria. The bank informed me of the due date to pay back the loan and I contacted the CDS and he kindly refunded the exact amount of the loan. I reflected on how sadly Nigerians most often fail to take responsibility for their country regarding its security and wellbeing of its citizens.

I was also engaged by Friedrich Ebert Stiftung, Nigeria Office, for a series of Nigerian Universities interactive sessions with postgraduate students in conjunction with the Society for International Relations Awareness. I was impressed with the programme objectives and the target group. It was an opportunity to reshape thinking about the image of Nigeria. I kept myself mentally busy between 2017- 2019 with the sessions at the University of Lagos, University of Ibadan, Obafemi Awolowo University Ife, University of Nigeria Nsukka, University of Abuja, University of Benin, Afe Babalola University Ado-Ekiti, Elizade University Ilara Mokin, and Uthman Dan Fodio University Sokoto. I was also within the same period invited to chair examination panels at National Institute for Policy and Strategic Studies (NIPSS), Jos for three years.

These activities kept me busy and I had very interesting interactions with professors from several universities in Nigeria that served on the panels as external examiners. I had a series of Research Projects from the participants at the course at NIPSS covering diverse issues by senior staff of Ministries, Departments, and Agencies of Governments including the defence and security sector. Some non-governmental organisations had participants in the programme too. I had good pannel sessions with the internal and external examiners from NIPSS and various universities in Nigeria and other agencies. The interactions with the participants were very educative as regards the diversities of interests and their strategic focus.

I have always tried to review the actions I take in response to the developments I experience. This enables me to put myself on the spot and ask if I am fair to others and if there was any need to continue the courses of action embarked upon. I also reflected on how I was viewed on my return from the RNEC Manadon. I realised since then that competence, achievements and knowledge creation and use are not tolerated and the subsequent warnings to me to be careful confirmed this. This trend has been my lot since my days at the NDA. I tried to improve my knowledge of how well-established Armed Forces around the world are managed at all levels up to the level of the Commander-in-Chief. I have learnt much earlier how order and discipline constitute the mortar that holds together a military force in action and a lot depends on military leadership with the fortitude to stay the course.

I constantly remember that a military Commander's task as defined by experts is the perfection of the assets at his disposal to a point of readiness for war or operations. I had been taught at the RNEC that I was being educated and trained to be first and foremost a complete naval officer with a community of knowledge, and secondly, a marine engineer officer with responsibilities to inspire personnel in combat. I have reflected on this upbringing in all my career assignments. I did not betray those principles. I strived to justify returns on huge investments made in my education and training. These are the realities I have to take into consideration as I struggle to have my military records perfect and effect my voluntary retirement with fairness that is a demand of Armed Forces Covenant.

Admiral John Sandy Woodward and his staff (in the South Atlantic in 1982) and the home staff (in the UK) for the hundred days that they were separated by 8,000 miles, never differed in the decisions they took during the Falkland war. The publications and procedures were simply followed as a team that had trained together. There were order and discipline up to and down the hierarchy and chain of command as the unity of command was respected.

Take the case of a Japanese Second Lieutenant Hiroo Onoda during the Second World War who escaped into the jungle of the Philippines and conducted guerrilla warfare for almost thirty years. The decision of the Japanese High Command to engage the Phillippine High Command to amicably provide honourable surrender and the heroic return of Onoda to Japan highlights the principle that no one will be left behind or abandoned by the military institution. Onoda's initiatives were respected by the Japanese High Command and this helps to explain why Japanese troops would be committed to serving that country.

Benjamin Oliver Davies Jr, a West Point graduate, retired as a Lieutenant General in 1970. He had suffered a denial of dues being an African-American. In retirement, he was honoured on 09 December 1998. Davies became a General of the highest order with the US military when he was awarded his fourth general's star.

It is also noteworthy that about 263 generals senior to General DD Eisenhower still served the US during the Second World War after he was appointed the Allied Supreme Commander. That is, many that were his senior served under him in Europe. This is about the development and application of expertise. The above examples (from the Mantle of Command by Nigel Hamilton; One Hundred Days, by Admiral John Sandy Woodward and Wikipedia) show the responsible management of personnel.

In Nigeria, there is the reckless and casual treatment of personnel that wastes national assets. Threats and abusive languages are frequently used against military personnel in Nigeria by superiors and it does not matter that such acts should immediately terminate the carrier of such superior officers in leadership positions. The power of good examples has been my guide from childhood and I continue to learn from icons of such examples.

President Barack H Obama in a ceremony in the White House on 15 September 2014 honoured several service personnel that participated in several wars over decades and who were denied their dues. Those who were present in the White House for the award of their dues were in their ceremonial uniform to be honoured by their Commander-in-Chief. The lesson Nigerians must learn from this ceremony is that honours, dues and entitlements denied when earned will always be given when facts come to light. There are no time limits, laws or statutes allowed to stand in the way of justice. This is the military best practice for solving such problems.

After he assumed office on 29 May 2015, I made a very comprehensive presentation to the President, Commander-in-Chief Muhammadu Buhari and many observers believed that based on his pronouncements, the matter would be speedily resolved and used as a good example regarding the direction of his administration. It was not to be and I would be subjected to more inconsistencies and asked to come to terms with the fact that I have been retired without legal procedures.

The Vice President, Professor Yemi Osinbajo intervened and established that I was wrongly treated and needed fair access and just treatment. His intervention met a brick wall and no response. It will always hurt me deeply that the Vice Prsident was so treated. The Chief of Staff to the President, Abba Kyari, was in charge and several appeals to him through personal contact by Her Excellency Dame Pauline Tallen (later Federal Minister of Women Affairs) and reminders written to the President, Commander-in-Chief were treated to evade all the issues by adopting autocratic methods and bureaucratic sophistry of MOD, DHQ and NHQ.

In late January 2020, my son Adaeiza was preparing to return to college. As I worked on writing this book into a late hour of the night I surprisingly heard some soothing notes from the piano which had not been played for some time. It was being played by my son. I paused and remembered Vice Admiral PS Koshoni who inspired its purchase. Barely two days later, I received the news of the passing away of the Admiral. He was born on 17 April; I got married on 17 April. I attended his funeral in Lagos in February 2020. I met Rear Admiral O Olumide who was an octogenarian. This was the last time I saw of him as he passed away five months later. I fondly appreciate their immense contribution to my career development. A new Chief of Staff in the person of Professor Ibrahim Agboola Gambari was appointed in April 2020 as the former Chief of Staff died in March due to a corona virus disease infection. I submitted a brief to the new Chief of Staff.

On 20 April 2020, I wrote a letter to the CNS requesting necessary steps to be defined towards the resolution of related outstanding issues to enable my disengagement from the active service list. I emphasized the need for fair treatment and access that would enable procedures that are legally binding as only such would facilitate voluntary disengagement from the active service list. Also, attention was drawn to the developments at the National Defence College and the MOD that created very abnormal situations having adverse effects that are known and documented.

The CNS approved a meeting with selected principal staff officers at the NHQ. The meeting took place on 20 July 2020 with a plea that I should cooperate and have a closure. There was no mention of the steps to take which was expected to be the agenda for the meeting. In my response, I told the team that I am a victim without powers and have been suffering the actions of those holding public offices. I briefed them on how the problems were deliberately caused and the reasons for the haste by all the members of the Navy Board. I had some supporting documents as evidence which they copied and I was asked for the way forward. I advised them to make an honest and objective presentation to the President, Commander-in-Chief narrating the incidents as presented and also take into consideration the years that have elapsed with documentation in official circles in the national and international arena stating that I am still on the active service list. Such a presentation is also the only route for the resolution of outstanding issues. There were related developments at the Presidency between 2005-2007 regarding my appointment as the CNS and the later approval for me to take over as the CDS towards the end of 2007 when the fund was released to progress with the intentions of the President, Commander-in-Chief for the College permanent site project. Furthermore, there have been streams of correspondence with the President, Commander-in-Chief. The team appeared to agree on how to handle these developments and the meeting ended.

A week after the meeting, I contacted the NHQ to find out if a memo had been prepared for the attention of the CNS. This resulted in a message to me by electronic mail (smartphone) conveying that the Naval Secretary forwarded to the leader of the NHQ team a letter from the DHQ. The letter was citing a communication with the Chief of Staff in the Presidency between 2016-2017, conveying that I have been retired and the matter is closed. Consequently, I was informed, that the NHQ has no basis to communicate with me. This also implies that the meeting I had had no official standing. Why did it take place?

I was more surprised when I read in the same electronic mail that there would be no memo or written report to the CNS as the matter is closed as directed by the letter from the CDS. I requested the return of the documents I submitted supporting my submissions at the meeting of 20 July 2020 as I was informed that the NHQ would not use the new information available to make an honest and objective presentation to the President, Commander-in-Chief. I had assumed that Presidency could not make a presentation to the President, Commander-in-Chief as the reply to the letter from the Chief of Staff from the NHQ through the DHQ evaded the issues and dwelt on being bureaucratically correct to support the hasty actions of the compromised members of the Navy Board as at January 2008. The issues evaded are now before the NHQ supported by documents not possessed before the meeting of 20 July 2020 and there is an attempt to steer clear of the issues again. They do not want the correct facts to get to the President, Commander-in-Chief and I am expected to continue to suffer their deliberate acts of inflicting punishment they happily take as normal. They state that it is my turn to be punished. For what offence?

I wrote a letter dated 03 August 2020 to the CNS, who refused to grant me audience since 2015 (he retired in January 2021) and explained the proceedings of the meeting of 20 July 2020. I highlighted the conclusion of the meeting that a memo would have to be written to the President, Commander-in-Chief to have the only opportunity for resolution of the outstanding issues itemised and discussed at the meeting with new facts supported by documents. I emphasised the need to make an honest and objective presentation to the President, Commander-in-Chief as it is now evident again that the NHQ, DHQ, and MOD have not addressed the relevant issues so far in their presentation to the Presidency.

I reminded the CNS, in the letter, of the oath sworn to before the almighty God, as all commissioned officers did, to be true to the President, Commander-in-Chief. These are summed up in the exercise of the unity of command that seeks direction from the President, Commander-in-Chief to guide actions. It is noteworthy that President Umaru Musa Yar'Adua as of early October 2009, expressed his frustration as these same evasive tactics were deployed to prevent his decisions to solve the problems caused me. Honesty is about truth and justice and a critical requirement for committed service to the country; that is, the good results we seek in military problem solving which the conduct of war is all about, flow from honesty.

The following week, I contacted the NHQ for an update on the progress being made and I was informed by the Principal General Staff Officer to the CNS that the officers (Admirals and a Commodore) who attended the meeting with me on 20 July 2020 were at a loss regarding how to handle my submissions with the new facts presented and supported by documents. Besides, I was informed that the NHQ now realises the complexity of the problems created and how to go about the resolution of the outstanding issues. It was admitted that they were having great difficulties regarding what to do. I was not surprised by their admission that the problem is unique in NN history as it has never happened in the NN and I add in the Nigerian Armed Forces. I emphasised again to them at the NHQ that it should be conveyed to the CNS that the only opportunity for solutions is the objective presentation of the truth to the President, Commander-in-Chief for due process to take its course for resolution of the outstanding issues. This has been deliberately evaded for long, not minding the consequences that I have been suffering together with members of my family and the bad examples that have adverse impacts on Armed Forces personnel. How then can military personnel serve Nigeria with a commitment to this type of orientation and attitude at these levels of leadership?

As I was pursuing the efforts at the NHQ, I sent a reminder letter to the President, Commander-in-Chief, and also to the Vice President. Both letters were dated 27 May 2020 and submitted the same day. I once again highlighted the fact that the matters adversely affecting my life and career be taken from the military hierarchy and the MOD for the relevant due process of best practices for presentation to the President, Commander-in-Chief to secure his decisions for implementation.

It is sad to note that Nigeria is being deliberately prevented from sustainable development by public officers and, consequently, there has been no focus and continuity to develop quality manpower to drive relevant processes. There is no commitment to serve Nigeria and most public officers turn government establishments into breeding grounds for problems that the society suffer instead of being problem solvers. This is the tragedy of Nigeria as one observes the frantic efforts made by politicians, public, and civil servants to be useful to themselves only as they routinely convey that they are serving the country that they are destroying.

Though Nigerians have acquired much knowledge from all corners of the earth and excelled, the inability to render quality services in the national interest shows that they probably do not understand the knowledge acquired despite the impressive show of certificates. Nigeria cannot gainfully participate in the only major industry of modern times; that is, knowledge. It is why the large population would continue to suffer amid an abundance of resources. Allegiance is to self and loyalty is demanded autocratically from those near to self. The only major problem Nigeria has to solve now is perverted morality so that the needs and aspirations of others in society feature prominently in our thinking, deliberations, and actions. That is when honour, duty, and country dominate thinking and direct Nigerians to focus on the common good for their collective well-being. There has to be an understanding of requirements, obligations and responsibilities by the individual for a committed and beneficial relationship with the nation-state.

There is no expertise readily available for the effective management of a modern nation-state called Nigeria. Individuals behave as if the knowledge acquired is for their benefit only. This posture is not reflective of an educated person. The emphasis has been mostly on self so that as members of small interest groups they get recognised to be appointed to public offices as compensation or allocation for whatever. There can be no serious undertaking for nation-building that results from outputs of credible statecraft. Those so exposed to public offices hardly understand why they hold public offices and resort to all manners of intrigues to sustain themselves. There are no structures for grooming personnel for public offices and consequently, they hardly know how to serve the people as everyone feels they are qualified for any job as long as it is a government job funded by public money.

The case of the Armed Forces of Nigeria is most pathetic as its personnel are disorientated with a poor attitude from the officers' corps that is expected to provide leadership with a balance of education, training and good personal qualities. The poor management of the institution is a clear indication out there in the open in the international arena that Nigeria cannot have a credible military. Why bother using the appellation of a nation-state while in this state of being that the country cannot conduct an effective and respectable foreign policy? Military strategy has bearing on Foreign policy. The AFN has been an embarrassment in conduct.

Nigeria suffers perverted morality that results in poor statecraft that is used to routinely sew failures which public officers expect to yield successes as they do not appreciate the implications of their shortcomings and the complexities of statecraft that demand very high standards of performances to achieve results for common good. Nigerians do not bother to know their obligations, the level of commitment required to bearing true allegiance to the nation-state and why loyalty is pledged. Consequently, the country is not being served and problems needing immediate solutions are allowed to pile up and selectively solved based on favourable biases of those in positions of authority. The resulting isolation of those not favoured breeds insecurity and bad governance. It is an acutely lonely road to travel to serve such a country with commitment.

I have not been paid any form of emolument for about thirteen years (as of 2021) and all other entitlements have been denied by successive leadership at the NHQ, DHQ, MOD and the Presidency. The insecurity being suffered by Nigeria will take some years more ahead before the light of hope appears in a very dark tunnel that is getting darker because the leadership of the AFN and governments are very comfortable with a very corrupt operating system. The waste of awesome state powers that should be directed towards building strong state institutions that would provide opportunities for nation-building demands a cry for justice as I also demand. Justice to the state is the foundation for the justice I seek.

I was advised many times to take my matter to court as the military hierarchy for long was not willing to solve my problems. I gave very careful consideration to this option but I was always convinced that it was not appropriate for me to do so.

I reflected, as I concluded this chapter, on what would I have done better in my career if given a second chance, I always came to the same point that there was nothing I would do differently. It is not that I am perfect and did everything well. I always challenge myself daily to do my best knowing that my best was not good enough to meet the complex needs of the organisation where I had my duty post. I did not have control over the circumstances that set limits on what I could achieve daily but I had control to make sure that such limitations do not prevent me from addressing my failures the next day and keep on trying to achieve more despite the odds. I, therefore, valued and encouraged team efforts.

The internal contradictions that drive the political direction of the country have created an institution of the President, Commander-in-Chief that cannot function properly under the principles guiding the conduct of the affairs of a modern nation-state. The principles informed the 1648 Treaty of Westphalia and the most important of the principles being sovereignty. Sovereignty is about decisive actions in the nation-state interest. There is a culture of abusing power meant for the public good. And when public servants engage in routine abuse of state powers, it is impossible to have strong state institutions whose outputs the citizens should rely on to build a nation. The leadership at all levels in Nigeria cannot be relied upon to act decisively in the national interest.

I have encountered variants of intrigues and my study of the incidents reveals that the greatest problem is how to overcome individual factors that have created mindsets without the guide of morality as realised during the Renaissance period. I sum it up again as perverted morality. It is accepted to undermine authority and abuse state powers as everyone wants to be the boss exercising authority. There is no consideration of public good but small individual pursuits to satisfy self at the expense of the majority. Lies and deception become services delivered at all levels of government. At best, achievements are mediocre as it is impossible to embark on complex undertakings to meet larger public needs. The creative energy and initiative of individuals cannot be released. It is why Nigeria cannot earn the respect of the world; a truth Nelson Rolihlahla Mandela has stated. Nigerians have to restructure their mindsets with the tool of morality for Nigeria to develop and meet the expectation of the large population. The AFN that should be at the forefront of developments has become a problem for the nation-state.

It is the poor state of the AFN institution that makes me feel that opportunities were being lost for its growth for long due to the experiences of the factors that played out as I was not allowed to take up my appointments as the CNS and CDS as approved. The institution is disoriented as manifest in a lack of understanding of allegiance to the country and loyalty related to respect for the authority of the President, Commander-in-Chief. There is no respect for authority in Nigeria. There is almost no honesty and attempts to be decent are lacking as it is a routine to be held and accepted for capacity to sabotage efforts and destroy whatever project government approved to allow sharing of money. Those so involved can claim that all their actions are correct citing adherence to policies, laws and procedures with claims of their infallibility. There exist a cult of evil, that is their system, one must belong in public service to survive.

It is against this background of formidable obstacles that I feel very much fulfilled with what I could achieve as I served my country. The legacies of the RNEC Manadon achievements, National Defence College transformation and permanent site construction still ongoing with many completed structures put into use, the MCMVs project in Europe and the NN transformation among others give me the unique satisfaction of being very much fulfilled beyond my expectations. I just wanted, as a teenager, to be a marine engineer and serve my country in the military. I was directed by the shining lights of allegiance and loyalty to thunder my way through the tunnel of bundles of obstacles serving my country to my entire satisfaction with the unique inspiring support of two sitting Presidents and a former Head of State. The three of them had a continuity of succession in the office between 1999-2007. It is that special!

Epilogue

I felt a sense of relief after writing this book as I was able to get over my reluctance to write. I came to understand better why I had been put under pressure by many people to write and document my career experiences. Apart from the initial reflections that led me to determine what the title of the book would be, I did not know how it would run and end. It was as if I was putting pieces of a very big jigsaw puzzle together that I had no clue of what it would look like. At times it was a journey of discovery and I simply allowed facts at my disposal to guide me and relive my experiences.

I came to terms with the fact that suffering and sacrifice with humiliation were reality checks on my life's journey. I became more appreciative of the rare critical supports I had as I faced the challenges that came my way. At a stage, I asked myself that if had known that there were such formidable obstacles on my career path would I have gone ahead to take them on? I never knew nor had time to reflect on the dangers ahead as I simply felt I had a duty to keep on trying to serve. At times I paused to reflect on the magnitude and complex web of the intrigues that I had to encounter in the line of duty. I wondered about the absence of support from most public officers for nation-state causes and felt as if I was in foreign enemy territory but the events have etched themselves in my mind as precious memories of what happened in Nigeria with Nigerians aided by several sources at my disposal.

I realised in my career journey that to know the truth and be trusted I had to experience suffering from humiliation and make sacrifices as such enable understanding and give meaning to realities of life. At a stage, my decisions to get a difficult task done were qualified and called 'stupid' for holding on to universal principles to solve related problems. I took this as part of the qualifications to get things done and enduring it worked well beyond my expectations. My life experiences were realised through relationships with people of differing opinions and motives, and these coupled with the various environments I interacted with constituted the engine-room for the events that happened. I have done a narrative of the events and I have the rare opportunity of some impressions about the outcome of the effort, that is, this book. I present the impressions expressed to the readers of this book to share what I may not have grasped as I experienced events and as I was writing. They are eminently the right people with rich experiences and in addition my bosses who know far better than me. I thank them immensely for aptly summing up from their various valuable perspectives what this book is about.

I will continue to do my duty to the country as the messages they have conveyed indicate more daunting challenges ahead. I am most humbled by their observations that this book is a contribution to works in progress for a better country and its survival.

From a serving Governor of a State and Chairman, Nigeria Governors' Forum:

As a historian, and indeed a scholar of security, I find this book by Rear Admiral Anthony Isa very illuminating as it illustrates very succinctly the travails of a young, committed and ambitious Nigerian in his interesting naval career journey.

The memoir is presented as a first-person narrative of the Rear Admiral's experiences, struggles and responses to systemic challenges. From a humble beginning, Rear Admiral Isa started with a very deliberate vision of a career as a marine engineer in the service of his country.

Rear Admiral Isa achieved distinction at several important junctures in his career. It is on record that he won a top prize for his research work on emerging material technology at the Royal Naval Engineering College in the United Kingdom and led a Nigerian Naval team which achieved a feat with the emerging technology for the design and construction of very sophisticated warships in Europe which eventually attracted the attention of the United States Navy. This was not all.

Rear Admiral Isa also gave insight into the impressive transformation he undertook at the National Defence College where he started the permanent site project to provide a conducive environment for Nigerian Armed Forces Officers.

Many scholars and professionals in intelligence, security, and war studies including my humble self, have attempted to review the Nigerian military architecture and actions over the last decade but none of our submissions will replace the invaluable insights from this memoir by this exceptional military officer.

It is important to mention that there were several instances in the book where the Rear Admiral suffered humiliation for being a young marine engineer officer of distinction. However, these setbacks merely helped in strengthening this author in a manner that better prepared him for more rigorous leadership challenges.

Drawing from interesting insights in his book: Allegiance and Loyalty in Service – My Life in the Nigerian Navy, I make bold to describe Rear Admiral Anthony Isa as an intelligent and disciplined professional with enormous capacity to unbundle complex issues. His book is a study in the conduct of our nation-state affairs and especially about building and maintaining our national military establishments that over time have proved to need urgent attention and reengineering for our survival.

He has served at operational and strategic levels in appointments such as commanding officer of warships and Commandant of the National War College which he transformed to the National Defence College. Rear Admiral Isa's known attributes are driven by his deep and sincere allegiance and loyalty to Nigeria.

He was assigned specific difficult duty posts due to his exemplary leadership skills of being at his best to always serve his country. Rear Admiral Isa experienced both suffering and sacrifice while still maintaining remarkable composure in the finest traditions of military service.

This book has opened my eyes to several coded attributes of the Nigerian Navy and should open your eyes too. I consider this memoir a national treasure that should be sought after by all inquisitive minds in search of truth, change and national prosperity. It is a leadership guide for future generation of officers and governments and could help guide our efforts to make right the wrongs of today.

Dr. John Kayode Fayemi
Governor of Ekiti State & Chairman,
Nigeria Governors' Forum

From a Former Nigerian Chief of Defence Staff:

The importance of this book is far-reaching and it is not just about the personal story of the author, Rear Admiral Isa. His courageous and tough perseverance that characterised his experience in the Nigerian Navy should be an inspiration to generations aspiring to leadership in very challenging circumstances and obstacles. It touched on his reliance on known universal principles at all times throughout his career when faced with formidable challenges. The title of this book is of immense significance in Nigeria and he has offered his perspective on allegiance and loyalty that demand absolute respect for authority and unity of command under the Commander-in-Chief in a republic, and the leadership qualities required to inspire fortitude. He has emphasised the need for order in the conduct of military affairs in Nigeria. These reflect ultimate military deep thinking essential for success in battles.

There are significant issues that make this book a must-read. Rear Admiral Isa has seriously addressed the urgency required for professional rebuilding and maintenance of the Nigerian military and its establishment for the credible growth of our democracy as an open inclusive system and survival of Nigeria. This is a red alert for the solution to the problem of force structure because of the many wasted opportunities that have led to a dysfunctional military establishment that makes it virtually impossible to develop military capabilities for credible defence and security of the homeland. The craving by personnel for what is considered favourable appointment and attending courses for the pursuit of a comfortable career are fall out of politicization that has seriously eroded professionalism. There is the neglect of the commander's primary responsibility for preparing assets for the hour of reckoning, to account for returns on investment when duty calls which also bring about suffering and sacrifice for the defence and security of our citizens.

This book has lucidly elaborated on the need for equity and trust that are much required from the political and military leadership for credibility at the high direction of national defence and security. To enable the people have the confidence that military capabilities are managed in the national interest for their well-being. The narrative in this book highlights the linkages that can inspire or mar the essential total commitment of service personnel to the country's causes at all times stressing that the vital interests of Nigeria demand a guarantee of a secure homeland where Nigerians would be treated fairly and justly by law-abiding leadership respecting their rights. How Rear Admiral Anthony Isa managed the challenges he experienced in service should serve as a guide about how to greatly reduce the intrusion of politics into purely military affairs that have hobbled the progress of the Armed Forces of Nigeria.

This book is recommended to all military personnel especially those that function at operational and strategic levels, strategic leaders in public and private sectors, students of management, political and social sciences and the general public.

General Martin Luther Agwai CFR NAM
Former Nigerian Chief of Defence Staff

From a Former Flag Officer Commanding, Nigerian Naval Training Command:

This is an endorsement of an autobiography I readily got absorbed to write. I was very much involved with the upbringing of Admiral Anthony Isa from my vantage position while he was a naval cadet. As a staff officer at the Naval Headquarters in the personnel and training department, I observed his brilliant academic pursuit and commitment to duty until I retired from service in December 1992. The title of this book, *Allegiance and Loyalty in Service: My Life in the Nigerian Navy* is a most appropriate testimony that depicts the officer's true character. It is so as some of his contemporaries call him 'Obedient Servant 'while others prefer to call him the 'gentle' man of the service, due to his gentle disposition most of the time.

His brilliant achievements began at the Nigerian Defence Academy (NDA) where he graduated in 1973 and won awards for being the Best Naval Cadet and for being first in Combined Services Subjects. At the Royal Naval Engineering College, Manadon, UK, where he was reluctantly accepted as a result of his academic background being NDA, he obtained in July 1977 a BSc degree in Mechanical Engineering and had the distinction of winning a coveted prize for the best interdisciplinary research project. This was followed immediately by Marine Engineering Specialisation Course and later by an MSc degree in Advanced Marine Engineering in 1983 from the same College. He capped his outstanding academic achievements at the National Defense University, Washington DC in 2001 with MSc in National Security and Resource Strategy and won the President's Strategic Vision award, the highest award given by the University for research and writing and the Distinguished Graduate award for being among the top-performing students.

On Admiral Isa's return from his studies and appointment on a project in Italy, he was at various times involved with the efforts to uplift the NN from coastal and ceremonial duties to meet the challenges brought to the fore by the Nigerian civil war as new and sophisticated warships were procured. The development of the NN logistics system for operational efficiency of NN Fleet and the commissioning of the NN Dockyard and its expansion were opportunities that Admiral Isa took advantage of to contribute to developments in shore and afloat appointments. He served as General Manager Production at the NN Dockyard and later returned to command the establishment as Admiral Superintendent before he was appointed as Commandant, National War

College which he successfully transformed to National Defence College and got Presidential approval for the commencement of the construction of the permanent site. At the stage of improved fund release for the project, there ensued a struggle among power blocks for control and this led to his abrupt and unceremonial removal from the College by a letter from Naval Headquarters. To date the status of his exit from service is unknown.

Admiral Isa's decision to write this book is a profound statement about the education of the younger generation to inspire and guide them properly to always be at their best to serve the country and manage better the challenges they will encounter. It is important to note that what happened to the officer is enough to discourage anyone from committed and loyal service. Despite Anthony's distinguished services and outstanding academic excellence, how he was swept out of office is not encouraging, but the officer has shown exemplary courage to put what happened in a perspective to enable lessons to be learnt for a better future so that those who serve the country would embrace hard work driven by loyalty and allegiance. Admiral Anthony Isa is a good example for the younger generations to emulate. It is in that regard that I congratulate Admiral Anthony Isa for this wonderful disposition, commitment and loyalty to serve the country. I endorse this book to be read by all those who have the opportunity to do so in order to build a greater and more stable Nigeria.

Rear Admiral Hamzat M. Sanni
Former Flag Officer Commanding,
Nigerian Naval Training Command

From a Nigerian Journalist, Editor and Author:

Rear Admiral Anthony Isa was one of the most brilliant officers in the Nigerian Navy. His academic laurels and professional competence are in full display in this important memoir, **Allegiance and Loyalty in Service: My Life in the Nigerian Navy.** From his first day in the Nigerian Defence Academy to his unceremonial departure as Commandant of the National Defence College, some 35 years later, Admiral Isa never wavered in his sense of duty and his loyalty to the nation. The importance of this book goes far beyond his personal story. His courageous and brutal expose of the mediocrity and the intrusion of politics that have effectively hobbled the Nigerian Navy by denying brilliant and competent officers the right to lead the service aright underscores its importance. What he has written about the ugly face of the Nigerian Navy is replicated in the Nigerian Armed Forces. Politics has damaged the services. Admiral Isa's principled stand did not endear him to the system, his superiors and the politicians-and he suffered abject humiliation for it. This book is not his revenge. His objective, consistent with his principle, is not to wash the dirty uniforms in the public but to tell it as it is and hope that the powers that be would wake up to, and take on, the urgent task of ending the rot in the Armed Forces, enthrone merit and reward qualifications and proven competence.

Dan Agbese
Author of *Ibrahim Babangida: The Military, Politics and Power in Nigeria.*

I believe that the Nigeria idea is being articulated for a definition to rally all Nigerians to do their duty to the country. The matters related to the causes of the country should always serve as the moral compass in our relations as citizens to the country to ensure its survival. I hope this would inspire others to write and document their experiences in the line of duty to the country. All Nigerians should demand truth, justice and equity so that they are always treated fairly. It is the way of giving an account of our stewardship in a manner that respects our humanity and as servants of the people. Dr John Kayode Fayemi has stated that this book is a 'national treasure'. In his capacity as the Governor of Ekiti State and Chairman, Nigeria Governors' Forum he expresses his love for this country in a very profound manner by his statement. He has challenged all Nigerians with his quality of thinking to do the same in the conduct of Nigeria's affairs.

Index

About The Author

Rear Admiral Anthony Isa started his naval career at the Nigerian Defence Academy, Kaduna and served in the Nigerian Navy. He had all of his engineering education and training at the Royal Naval Engineering College, Manadon, Plymouth, United Kingdom ending with the Advanced Marine Engineering Course (Dagger). Later in his career, he attended Eisenhower School for National Security and Resource Strategy at the National Defense University, Washington DC, USA and received the highest award given by the University. He held several appointments at various levels of command and served as Federal Government of Nigeria Delegate on a project in Europe for some years. He was the Commandant of National War College and on transformation, Commandant of National Defence College in Abuja, Nigeria. He is married with children and grand children.

Lightning Source UK Ltd.
Milton Keynes UK
UKHW020741090223
416624UK00005B/514/J